POPULAR MUSIC

GARLAND REFERENCE LIBRARY
OF THE HUMANITIES
(VOL. 642)

POPULAR MUSIC
A Reference Guide

Roman Iwaschkin

Garland Publishing, Inc. • New York & London
1986

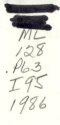

ML
128
.P63
I95
1986

Library of Congress Cataloging-in-Publication Data

Iwaschkin, Roman, 1948–
Popular music.

(Garland reference library of the humanities ;
vol. 642)
Includes index.
1. Music, Popular (Songs, etc.)—Bibliography.
I. Title. II. Series: Garland reference library of
the humanities ; v. 642.
ML128.P63I95 1986   016.78′042   85-45140
ISBN 0-8240-8680-5

Printed on acid-free, 250-year-life paper
Manufactured in the United States of America

For Catherine
- who showed me the way.

CONTENTS

PART TWO: BIOGRAPHY

INTRODUCTION

Popular music in its various forms is undoubtedly -- along with
the motion picture -- America's most successful and influential
cultural product. It dominates and maintains the recording
industry and radio, both at home and abroad; and millions
throughout the world are entertained by it around the clock.

Yet, so surrounded are we today by it, that it is all too easy
for us to forget just how recent a development this musical genre
is.   There have, of course, always been favorite songs and
performers; but these were nearly always of a disparate and
regional nature.   It was not until the middle of the last
Century, when Stephen Foster's melodies swept the Nation in an
unprecedented fashion, that the concept of popular music as an
independent commercial and cultural entity began to crystallize.

Even so, the genre remained predominantly regional until the early
part of our Century.   Its transition to a national and international force can be seen as the direct result of three near-
simultaneous developments: the exodus and dispersal of New
Orleans' jazz musicians after the 1917 closure of the City's
Storyville red-light district; the maturation of sound recording;
and the advent of radio broadcasting.   The combination of
what the concert world saw as untutored musicians looking for new
work with these young industries hungry for fresh musical material
set the scene for popular music's characteristic synthesis of the
artistic and the commercial that was to set it apart from other
musical activity and give it its unique flavor.

During our Century it has taken many forms.   Distinct styles
have emerged from the common musical pool, and have in turn been
reabsorbed to fuel fresh creations.   Writers and researchers in
the popular music field have generally tended to deal with its
components as if they were separate entities, influenced to a
greater or lesser degree by each other, but nevertheless individual musical forms in themselves.   The present writer would
contend that this approach, understandable as it may be, is
seriously misguided, and a barrier to the understanding of the
distinctive nature of popular music and its general cultural
influence.   Only when considered as a whole can the development
of the genre through the continuous interaction of its constituent
elements be fully comprehended.

With the growth of scholarly interest in popular music, both in

itself and as part of our general cultural framework, the need for
a comprehensive guide to its literature has long been apparent.
The present work is an attempt to record the material that has been
produced across the entire popular music field.   The aim has
been to provide the serious researcher with a systematically
arranged vade mecum, not only as a guide to the literature, but
also as a contribution towards the understanding of the topic
itself.

It is predominantly confined to works published in the English
language in the United States and Britain, although the international nature of popular music has required the inclusion of
significant works published in other countries and languages.
All known editions have been cited.   Coverage is essentially
from the beginnings of the genre to 1984; however, for continuity
a number of 1985 titles are also included.   The compiler has
attempted to inspect every item personally; where this has
not been possible sufficient bibliographical and other information
has been provided for an assessment of the material to be made.

The general structure employed will be apparent from the Table of
Contents.   For the convenience of the reader, categories of
literature have been cited in the same order throughout the work:

   Reference Materials

   Annuals and Yearbooks

   General Guides and Overviews

   Criticism

   Essay Collections

   Illustration Collections

   Miscellanea

   General Histories
       Comprehensive Works
       Periods and Styles

   Regional Histories

   Venues

   Sociological Aspects

My grateful thanks go to the Librarians and staff of Berkshire
County Library, especially at Slough and Shinfield Park, Reading;
the University of London; and the British Library for the
assistance received in the compilation of this Guide.   I am
particularly indebted to my wife, Catherine, for her invaluable
help, encouragement, and forbearance during the creation of the
present work.

Roman Iwaschkin
Fleet, Hampshire
August 1985

ABBREVIATIONS

comp.	compiler
Conn.	Connecticut
D.C.	District of Columbia
ed.	edition
(ed.)	editor
p.	pages
Pr.	Press
rev.	revised

Popular Music

PART ONE: THE MUSIC

A. POPULAR MUSIC GENERALLY

1. REFERENCE MATERIALS

(a) Bibliographies

1. Booth, Mark W. <u>American Popular Music: a Reference Guide</u>.
   Westport, Conn.: Greenwood Pr., 1983. 212p., bibliogs.,
   indexes. (American Popular Culture)
   Essay format. Coverage to 1981; includes approximately
   1,100 books and periodicals.

2. Cooper, B. Lee. <u>A Popular Music Handbook: a Resource for
   Teachers, Librarians, and Media Specialists</u>. Littleton,
   Colorado: Libraries Unlimited, 1984.   p., discogs.
   Covers 1950 to date. Includes teaching units for popular
   music studies.

* Denisoff, R. Serge. <u>American Protest Songs of War and Peace:
   a Selected Bibliography and Discography</u>.
   * Cited below as item 4106.

3. Hanel, Ed. <u>The Essential Guide to Rock Books</u>. London: Omnibus
   Pr., 1983.   p., illus.
   Selective; annotated. Arranged in literature categories.

4. Haywood, Charles. <u>Bibliography of North American Folklore and
   Folksong</u>. New York: Greenberg, 1951. <u>2nd. rev. ed.</u>: New York:
   Dover, 1961. <u>2 vols.</u>, 1,292p., discogs., index.
   Based on his Phd. thesis, same title, Columbia University,
   1951. Includes books, song collections, and periodical
   articles. Covers regional, ethnic, Black music, occupational,
   Indian tribes, and other material. Some annotations. Second
   edition not updated.

5. Hoffman, Frank. <u>The Literature of Rock, 1954-78</u>. Metuchen,
   New Jersey; London: Scarecrow Pr., 1981. 337p., illus.
   Includes books and periodical articles. Covers the United
   States and Britain. Annotated.

6. Horn, David. <u>The Literature of American Music: a Fully
   Annotated Catalogue of the Books and Song Collections in
   Exeter University Library</u>. Exeter, Devon: The American Arts
   Documentation Centre in association with the University Library,
   1972. 170p., index.
   Covers folk, sacred, classical, popular and jazz. Listings
   restricted to items held by the Centre. Preliminary to, and
   superseded by item 7.

Bibliographies (cont.)

7. Horn, David. <u>The Literature of American Music in Books and</u>
    <u>Folk Music Collections</u>. Metuchen, New Jersey; London: Scare-
    crow Pr., 1977. 556p., index.
         Classified; annotated. Restricted to American musical
    developments; international coverage of literature. Supplants
    item 6.

8. Inge, M. Thomas (ed.). <u>Handbook of American Popular Culture</u>.
    Westport, Conn.: Greenwood Pr., 1979-81. <u>3 vols</u>., 1,385p.,
    indexes.
         Collection of bibliographical essays by specialist
    authors on fifty subject areas. Short histories of each
    topic, with selective critical bibliographies. Includes
    popular music, stage entertainment, jazz, the record industry,
    and related subjects.

9. Jackson, Richard. <u>United States Music: Sources of Bibliog-</u>
    <u>raphy and Collective Biography</u>. Brooklyn, New York:
    Institute for Studies in American Music, 1973. 80p., index.
         Lists and describes ninety books: reference, historical,
    regional, and genres (folk, Black music, blues, ragtime,
    jazz, pop, sacred, opera, women in music, and Twentieth-
    Century music.)

10. Kendrick, Terry A. <u>Rock Music</u>. London: Library Association,
    Public Libraries Group, 1981. 27p., index. (Readers' Guides,
    37)
         Selective, annotated checklist of currently-available
    material.

 * Mecklenburg, Carl Gregor, <u>Herzog zu</u>. <u>1971/72/73 Supplement</u>
    <u>of International Jazz Bibliography, and Selective Bibliography</u>
    <u>of Some Jazz Background Literature, and Bibliography of Two</u>
    <u>Subjects Previously Excluded</u>.
         * Cited below as item 635.

11. Noyce, John Leonard, and Alison Skinner. <u>Rock Music Index</u>.
    Brighton, East Sussex: Noyce, 1977. 15p., bibliog.
         British rock periodicals.

12. Taylor, Paul. <u>Popular Music Since 1955: a Critical Guide to</u>
    <u>the Literature</u>. Westport, Conn.: Greenwood Pr.; London:
    Mansell, 1985. 533p., index.
         Narrative form. Descriptive, critical guide to monographs,
    periodicals, and trade literature.

                              (b) Indexes

13. <u>Popular Music Periodicals Index</u>. Edited by Dean and Nancy
    Tudor. Metuchen, New Jersey; London: Scarecrow Pr. annual,
    1974- .
         Indexes articles in popular music periodicals.

(c) Encyclopedias and Dictionaries

14. **Fan Club Directory**. Birmingham, England: Y.B.A. Music.
    Qly., 1983-

* Gammond, Peter, and Peter Clayton. **Dictionary of Popular Music**.
    * Cited below as item 1383.

* ————. **A Guide to Popular Music**.
    * Cited below as item 1383.

* Gillett, Charlie, and Simon Frith. **Rock File**.
    * Cited below as item 4275.

15. Jasper, Tony. **The Seventies: a Book of Records**. London: Fut-
    ura, 1980. 416p.
    Facts and figures on rock music of the decade; articles; and
    charts.

16. Kinkle, Roger D. (ed.). **The Complete Encyclopedia of Popular
    Music and Jazz, 1900-1950**. New Rochelle, New York: Arlington
    House, 1974. 4 vols., 2644p., illus., bibliog., discogs., ind-
    exes.
    Volume 1: Chronological listing of Broadway musicals and
    popular songs since 1909. Also includes motion picture musicals,
    and representative recordings. **Volume 2**: Biographical dictionary
    of artists, with selective discographies. **Volume 3**: Continues
    Volume 2. **Volume 4**: Appendices (awards, bibliographies, indexes.)

(d) Almanacs

17. Brickell, Sean, and Rich Rothschild. **The Pages of Rock History**.
    Norfolk, Virginia: Donning, 1983.   p., illus.
    Datebook January-December of dates and anniversaries.

18. Formento, Dan. **Rock Chronicle: Today in Rock History**. New
    York: Delilah; London: Sidgwick and Jackson, 1982. 367p., illus.
    Datebook.

19. Hendler, Herb. **Year by Year in the Rock Era: Events and Con-
    ditions Shaping the Rock Generations That Reshaped America**.
    Westport, Conn.: Greenwood Pr., 1983. 350p., bibliog.
    Sourcebook covering 1954-81.

20. Marchbank, Pearce, and Miles (comps.). **The Illustrated Rock
    Almanac**. New York; London: Paddington Pr., 1977. 191p., illus.
    Datebook. Includes non-rock events.

* Nugent, Stephen, and Charlie Gillett. **Rock Almanac**.
    * Cited below as item 4283.

Almanacs (cont.)

21. Rolling Stone. <u>The Rolling Stone Rock Almanac: the Chronicles of Rock and Roll.</u> By The Editors of <u>Rolling Stone.</u> Foreword by Peter Wolf. New York: Macmillan, 1983; London: Macmillan (U.K.), 1984. 386p., illus., index. (A Rolling Stone Press Book) Datebook, 1954 to date. Includes record charts.

2. ANNUALS AND YEARBOOKS

22. <u>Contemporary Music Almanac.</u> Edited by Ronald Zalkind. New York: Schirmer; London: Collier-Macmillan, 1980. 947p., illus. Survey of rock and jazz developments for the year. Only one edition published (1980-81).

23. Disc. <u>Disc Christmas Annual, 1959-60.</u> London: Charles Buchan's Publications, 1959. 63p., illus. Current performers and popular music developments.

24. Go. <u>Go Pop Annual.</u> Prepared by the Editorial Staff of <u>Go</u> Magazine in New York, Los Angeles, and London. New York: Pyramid Publications, 1968.   p., illus. Only issue.

25. Groove. <u>Groove Annual.</u> London: Harry Darton. annual, 1971-? Emphasis on teen pop. Current performers; events.

26. Hot Press. <u>The Hot Press Yearbook.</u> Dublin: Steady Rolling Publishing, 1980. 79p., illus. Rock survey. Only issue.

27. Music Scene. <u>Music Scene Annual.</u> London: I.P.C. Magazines, 1973.   p., illus. Only issue.

28. Music Star. <u>Music Star Annual.</u> London: I.P.C. Magazines. annual, 1973-76. Rock.

29. Musician, Player and Listener. <u>The Year in Rock, 1981-82.</u> New York: Delilah, 1981. 272p., illus., discog., bibliog. Survey of year. Includes features and charts. Only issue.

30. New Musical Express. <u>New Musical Express Annual.</u> London: I.P.C. Magazines. annual, 1955-73. Current popular music scene. 1974 edition (published 1973) has title <u>Hot Rock Guide.</u>

31. No. 1. <u>The No. 1 Picture Book.</u>   London: I.P.C. Magazines. annual, 1984- Features reprinted from <u>No. 1</u> rock and pop magazine. Cover title: <u>The No. 1 Book.</u>

32. Pelham Pop Annual. London, Pelham, 1970. 120p., illus.
    Only issue.

33. Pop Weekly. Pop Weekly Annual. Manchester: Pop Weekly.
    annual, 1963-66.
    Continued 1966-? as Pop Ten/Teenbeat Annual.

34. Radio Luxembourg. The Official Radio Luxembourg Book of Record
    Stars. London: Souvenir Pr. in association with World Distrib-
    utors. annual, 1962-66.
    Continued as Fab 208 Annual. London: I.P.C. Magazines.
    annual, 1968-

35. Radio Telefis Eirann. Radio Two Annual. Dublin: R.T.E.
    annual, 1980-
    Rock and pop survey.

36. Rock and Roll Yearbook, 1957. New York: Filosa Publications,
    1956; Bolton, Lancashire: Dalrow Publications, 1957. 100p., illus.
    Only issue.

37. Rock On. Rock On Annual. London: I.P.C. Magazines, 1979. 78p.,
    illus. (A Fleetway Annual)
    Cover date: 1980. Only issue.

38. The Rock Yearbook. London: Virgin Books; New York: Grove Pr./
    Delilah (1980); St. Martin's Pr. (1981-). annual, 1980-
    Detailed survey of year. Covers rock, jazz, and black pop-
    ular music. Includes charts (United States and Britain); bib-
    liographies; and discographies.

39. RPM: Review of Popular Music. Exeter, Devon: The International
    Association for the Study of Popular Music. annual, 1981-
    Title changed to Popular Music, 1982; published London: Camb-
    ridge University Press, 1982- . Collection of scholarly and
    critical articles, with each volume centered on a specific theme.

40. Summer Pop. London: New English Library, 1973. 32p., illus.
    Features on current scene. Only issue.

41. Supersonic. Supersonic Annual, 1978. London: I.P.C. Magazines,
    1977. 78p., illus. (A Fleetway Annual)
    Teen pop emphasis. Only issue.

42. Top of the Pops Annual. Manchester: World Distributors. annual,
    197?-
    Survey of current scene; linked with British TV program, Top
    of the Pops.

43. Top Pop Scene. London: Purnell. annual, 1972-78.

44. Top Pop Stars. London: Purnell. annual, 1964-70.

45. Top Twenty. London: New English Library, 1963; London: Mayflower,
    1964; London: Purnell, 1965-67. annual, 1963-67.

46. Valentine. <u>Valentine Pop Special</u>. London: Amalgamated Pr.
    (later I.P.C. Magazines). annual, 1959-70.
        Title varies

47-48. Omitted.

49. The Year in Music. London: D.H. Jewell. annual, 1977-78.
        Includes lists of record companies, fan clubs, etc. Covers
    rock and pop.

50. Zig Zag. <u>Zig Zag Year Book, 1981</u>. London: Zig Zag, 1981.   p.
        Listings of record companies, producers, studios, etc.; also
    features, chiefly on business and technical aspects.

3. GENERAL GUIDES AND OVERVIEWS

51. Bill, J. Brent. <u>Rock and Roll</u>. Old Tappan, New Jersey: Revell,
    1984. 160p.

52. Busnar, Gene. <u>It's Rock 'n' Roll</u>. New York: J. Messner, 1979.
    256p., illus.

53. Bygrave, Mike. <u>Rock</u>. Art director: Linda Nash; special con-
    sultant: Paul Murray. London: Hamish Hamilton, 1977; New York:
    Franklin Watts, 1979. 61p., illus., index.
        Aimed at young readers, but useful for adults. Comprehensive
    account of all aspects of contemporary popular music and its
    production.

54. Cash, Tony (ed.). <u>Anatomy of Pop</u>. London: British Broadcast-
    ing Corporation, 1970. 132p., illus., index.
        Collection of articles. Accompanies British TV program, same
    title, 1971. Includes brief bibliography.

55. Dachs, David. <u>Anything Goes: the World of Popular Music</u>.
    Indianapolis: Bobbs-Merrill, 1964. 328p., illus., index.
        Emphasis on business aspects, and their influence on pop and
    jazz.

56. Dufour, Barry. <u>The World of Pop and Rock</u>. Special consultant:
    Dave Laing. London: Macdonald Educational, 1977. 61p., illus.,
    bibliog., index.
        Aimed at young readers.

57. Hall, Douglas Kent, and Sue C. Clark. <u>Rock: a World as Bold as
    Love</u>. Photographed and edited by Douglas Kent Hall from inter-
    views by Sue C. Clark. New York: Cowles, 1970. 192p., illus.,
    index.
        Thematic compilation of interview excerpts from interviews
    conducted in 1969.

58. Jasper, Tony. <u>Probe on Pop</u>. London: S.C.M. Pr., 1970. 32p.,
    illus. (Probe, 6)
        Survey from religious and moral viewpoint.

59. ———. Understanding Pop. London: S.C.M. Pr., 1972. 192p.,
     illus., bibliog.
          Expansion of item 58. Broad survey, aimed at readers with
     little or no knowledge of the subject. Includes glossary.

60. Lane, Peter. What Rock is All About. New York: J. Messner,
     1979. 256p., illus., bibliog., index.

61. Mabey, Richard. Behind the Scenes. Harmondsworth, Middlesex:
     Penguin, 1968. 65p., illus. (Penguin Education: Connexions sr.)
          For British secondary school students as part of a social
     sciences course.

62. ———. The Pop Process. London: Hutchinson Educational, 1969.
     190p., bibliog.
          Aimed at teachers in British secondary schools.

63. Moore, Thurston (ed.). The Pop Scrapbook. Assistant editor:
     Leslie Norman. Cincinnati: Artist Publications, 1953. 48p.,
     illus.

64. Myra, Harold, and Dean Merrill. Rock, Bach, and Superschlock:
     a Christian Book About a Beautiful Thing Called Music. Phila-
     delphia; New York: A.J. Holman, 1972. 123p., illus., bibliog.

65. Nye, Russell. The Unembarrassed Muse: the Popular Arts in
     America. New York: Dial Pr., 1970. 497p., bibliog.
          Considers musical theater, jazz, country, rhythm and blues,
     and rock in their cultural context.

66. Petrie, Gavin (ed.). Pop Today. London: Hamlyn, 1974. 128p.,
     illus. (A Disc Special)

67. ———. Rock Life. London; New York: Hamlyn, 1974. 128p.,
     illus. (A Melody Maker Special)

68. Pike, Jeff. Rock World. London: Marshall Cavendish, 1979.
     61p., illus., index.
          Aimed at adolescents.

69. Playboy. Playboy's Music Scene. Chicago: Playboy Pr., 1972.
     189p., illus.
          Rock survey.

70. Powell, Peter. Peter Powell's Book of Pop. Illustrated by
     Dave Bowyer. London: Armada, 1980. 123p., illus., discogs.
          By British disk jockey.

71. Robinette, Richard W. American Popular Music. Chula Vista,
     California: A Mul Dur Publishers, 1975. 135p., illus., bibliog.
          Outline study syllabus.

72. Rock Times. London: D.C. Thompson, 1981. 67p., illus.
          Magazine-format survey of current scene.

73. Rublowsky, John. Popular Music. New York: Basic Books, 1967.
    164p., illus. (Culture and Discovery Books)
       Follows the manufacture of a hit tune from recording session
    to exploitation internationally.

74. Wilson, Earl. The Show Business Nobody Knows. Chicago: Cowles;
    London: W.H. Allen, 1972. 428p., illus., index.
       Gossip and anecdotes about major entertainers, including
    popular music figures.

                            4. CRITICISM

                          (a) General Works

75. Bangs, Lester. Rock Gomarrah. In collaboration with Michael
    Ochs. New York: Delilah, 1983. 192p., illus.

 * Battcock, Gregory (ed.). Breaking the Sound Barrier: a Crit-
    ical Anthology of the New Music.
          * Cited below as item 285.

76. Durant, Alan. Conditions of Music. London: Macmillan, 1984.
        p. (Language, Discourse, Society)
       Argues that sounds become music in specific conditions of
    performance, audience and address. Structuralist approach to
    musicology through case studies contrasting the madrigal and
    rock. No consideration of the influences of folk, Tin Pan
    Alley, or black music on rock.

77. Herman, Gary. Rock 'n' Roll Babylon. London: Plexus; New York:
    Perigee, 1982. 192p., illus.
       Exposition of the destructive pressures of rock stardom.

78. Meltzer, Richard. The Aesthetics of Rock. New York: Something
    Else Pr., 1970. 346p., illus., bibliog. notes.
       Highly subjective philosophic analysis. Almost incomprehen-
    sible.

79. ———. Gulcher: Post-Rock Cultural Pluralism in America,
    (1649-1980). San Francisco: Straight Arrow Books, 1972. 147p.
       Essays.

80. Peters, Dan. Why Knock Rock? Minneapolis: Bethany House, 1984.
    160p.

81. Raker, Muck (pseud. of John Tobler). Rock Bottom: the Book of
    Pop Atrocities. London; New York: Proteus, 1981. 143p., illus.
       Bad taste in rock chronicled. Includes flexidisk, The Deal,
    by Pat Campbell.

82. Tyler, Tony. I Hate Rock and Roll: an Illustrated Diatribe.
    London: Vermilion Books, 1984. 127p., illus.
       Denunciation of rock music and business, by ex-journalist.

(b) Language

83. Hibbert, Tom. <u>Delilah's International Dictionary of Rock Terms</u>.
New York: Delilah, 1983. 176p., illus.
Over one thousand cliches explained, with sources where possible, and examples. British edition published as <u>Rockspeak:
the Dictionary of Rock Terms</u>. London: Omnibus Pr., 1983.

84. Shaw, Arnold. <u>The Lingo of Tin-Pan Alley</u>. New York: Broadcast Music, 1950. 22p.
Dictionary of terms used by musicians, radio program direct-
ors, and the recording business.

(c) Popular Music and Other Art Forms

85. Bane, Michael. <u>White Boy Singin' the Blues: the Black Roots
of White Rock</u>. London; New York: Penguin, 1982. 269p., index.
Exposition of influences and interplay.

86. Bluestein, Gene. <u>The Voice of the Folk: Folklore and American
Literary Theory</u>. Amherst: University of Massachusetts Pr.,
1972. 170p., bibliog., index.
Examines attitudes of American writers to folk culture, and
their belief in its high cultural value. Covers use of jazz,
blues, and rock as literary themes.

*   Collins, John. <u>African Pop Roots</u>.
* Cited below as item 617.

*   Lydon, Michael. <u>Boogie Lightning</u>.
* Cited below as item 587.

87. Melly, George. <u>Revolt Into Style: the Pop Arts in Britain</u>.
London: Allen Lane; Garden City, New York: Doubleday, 1971.
(Anchor Books). 245p.
Popular music and other popular culture, and their interact-
ion, during the 1960s.

88. Middleton, Richard. <u>Pop Music and the Blues: a Study of the
Relationship and its Significance</u>. London: Gollancz, 1972.
271p., bibliog., index.
Exposition of what popular music has done with its sources
in the blues. Includes chapter discographies. Based on auth-
or's Dissertation, York University, 1969-70.

89. Miller, William Robert. <u>The World of Pop Music and Jazz</u>.
St. Louis: Concordia Publishing House, 1965. 112p., bibliog.,
discog. (The Christian Encounters sr.)

90. Redd, Lawrence N. <u>Rock is Rhythm and Blues: the Impact of the
Mass Media</u>. East Lansing, Michigan: Michigan State University
Pr., 1974. 167p., illus., bibliog. refs.

Popular Music and Other Art Forms (cont.)

91. Roberts, John Storm. <u>The Latin Tinge: the Impact of Latin</u>
    <u>American Music on the United States</u>. New York; London: Oxford
    University Pr., 1979. 246p., illus., bibliog., discog.

5. ESSAY COLLECTIONS

92. Christgau, Robert. <u>Any Old Way You Choose It: Rock and Other</u>
    <u>Pop Music, 1967-1973</u>. Baltimore: Penguin, 1973. 330p., index.
    Critical essays previously published in periodicals.

93. Creem. <u>The Rock Revolution</u>. Edited by Richard Robinson and
    the Editors of <u>Creem</u> Magazine. New York: Popular Library,
    1976. 219p., illus., index.
    Reprinted articles from <u>Creem</u>.

94. Duncan, Robert. <u>The Noise: Notes From a Rock 'n' Roll Era</u>.
    New York: Ticknor and Fields, 1984. 288p., illus.

95. Eisen, Jonathan (ed.). <u>The Age of Rock: Sounds of the Americ-</u>
    <u>an Cultural Revolution--a Reader</u>. New York: Random House, 1969.
    388p., illus., index.
    Anthology of thirty articles, mostly previously published.

96. ————. <u>The Age of Rock, 2: Sights and Sounds of the American</u>
    <u>Cultural Revolution</u>. New York: Random House, 1970. 339p., illus
    Forty-two articles reprinted.

97. ————. <u>Twenty Minute Fandangos and Forever Changes</u>. New York:
    Random House, 1971; London: Wildwood House, 1973. 270p., illus.

98. Elmlark, Walli, and Timothy Beckley. <u>Rock Raps of the 70s</u>.
    New York: Vantage Pr., 1971. Reprinted: New York: Drake, 1972.
    165p.

  * Giddins, Gary. <u>Riding on a Blue Note: Jazz and American Pop</u>.
     * Cited below as item 753.

99. Goldman, Albert. <u>Freakshow: the Rocksoulbluesjazzsickjewblack-</u>
    <u>humorpoppsych Gig and Other Scenes from the Counter-Culture</u>.
    New York: Atheneum, 1971. 387p.

100. Goldstein, Richard. <u>Goldstein's Greatest Hits: a Book Mostly</u>
     <u>About Rock 'n' Roll</u>. Englewood Cliffs, New Jersey; London:
     Prentice-Hall, 1970. 228p., index.
     Articles previously published in periodicals, 1966-69.

101. Hill, Deborah. <u>Cuts From a San Francisco Rock Journal</u>. San
     Francisco: And Books, 1981. 400p., illus.

102. International Conference on Popular Music Research. <u>Popular</u>
     <u>Music Perspectives: Papers from the First International Conf-</u>

erence on Popular Music Research, Amsterdam, June 1981. Edited by David Horn and Philip Tagg. Göteborg; Exeter, Devon:
International Association for the Study of Popular Music, 1982.
250p.
    One paper is in French.

103. Jewell, Derek. The Popular Voice: a Musical Record of the 60s
and 70s. London: Deutsch, 1980; London: Spere, 1981. 256p.,
illus., index.
    Pieces previously published in London's Sunday Times.

104. Landau, Jon. It's Too Late to Stop Now: a Rock and Roll Journal. San Francisco: Straight Arrow Books; New York: Simon and
Schuster, 1972. 227p., illus., discog.
    Reviews and other pieces originally published 1967-72.

105. Marcus, Greil. Mystery Train: Images of America in Rock 'n'
Roll Music. New York: Dutton, 1975 (reprinted 1982); London:
Omnibus Pr., 1977. 289p., discog., index.
    Blues and rock essays: Harmonica Frank; Robert Johnson; The
Band; Sly Stone; Randy Newman; Elvis Presley; and their place
in American music and culture.

106. ——— (ed.). Rock and Roll Will Stand. Boston: Beacon Pr.,
1969. 182p., discogs.
    Twenty-one pieces by seven West Coast writers.

  * Nanry, Charles (ed.). American Music: From Storyville to
Woodstock.
    * Cited below as item 386.

107. New Musical Express. Greatest Hits: the Very Best of N.M.E.
London: I.P.C. Magazines, 1974. 95p., illus.

108. Norman, Philip. The Road Goes On Forever: Portraits From a
Journey Through Contemporary Music. London: Elm Tree Books,
1982. 206p., illus.; New York: Simon and Schuster, 1982. 224p.,
illus. (A Fireside Book); London: Corgi, 1984. 269p., illus.
    Essays and profiles. Originally published in London's Times
and Sunday Times.

109. Palmer, Tony. Born Under a Bad Sign. Illustrated by Ralph
Steadman. London: Kimber, 1970. 192p., illus., bibliog.
    Reprints of Observer articles, and reworkings of television
scripts.

110. Rolling Stone. The Rolling Stone Rock 'n' Roll Reader. Ed. by
Ben Fong-Torres. New York; London: Bantam, 1974. 783p.
    Approximately 130 news items and features, 1967-72.

111. ———. What's That Sound? The Contemporary Music Scene from
the Pages of Rolling Stone. Ed. by Ben Fong-Torres. Garden
City, New York: Doubleday, 1976. 426p. (Anchor Books) (A Rolling Stone Pr. Book)

112. Sander, Ellen. Trips: Rock Life in the Sixties. New York:
      Scribner's, 1973. 272p., illus.

113. Schafer, William J. Rock Music: Where it's Been, What it Means,
      Where it's Going. Minneapolis: Augsburg Publishing House, 1972.
      128p., illus., bibliog., discog.

114. Seldes, Gilbert V. The Seven Lively Arts. New York: Harper,
      1924. 398p., illus. 2nd ed. New York: Sagamore Pr., 1957.
      326p.
           Attempt to garner critical acceptance of pop songs, ragtime,
      jazz, and musical theater.

115. Sinclair, John. Guitar Army: Street Writings/Prison Writings.
      Designed by Gary Grimshaw. New York: Douglas Book Corporation,
      1972. 366p., illus.
           Radical invective, dealing with the role of rock music as
      a weapon in the "Cultural Revolution."

  *   ————, and Robert Levin. Music and Politics.
        * Cited below as item 769.

116. Variety. The Spice of Variety. Ed. by Abel Green. New York:
      Henry Holt, 1952. 277p.

117. Williams, Paul. Outlaw Blues: a Book of Rock Music. New York:
      Dutton, 1969; New York: Pocket Books, 1970. 191p., illus.,
      bibliog., discog.
           Articles first published in Crawdaddy, 1966-68.

                        6. ILLUSTRATION COLLECTIONS

118. Belsito, Peter, Bob Davis, and Marian Kester. Streetart. San
      Francisco: Last Gasp, 1981.   p., illus.
           Collection of punk posters from San Francisco.

119. Benyon, Tony. The Lone Groover's Little Read Book. London:
      Eel Pie Publishing, 1981. 96p., illus.
           Compilation of The Lone Groover strip cartoon series from
      the New Musical Express.

120. Betrock, Alan (ed.). Rock 'n' Roll Movie Posters, 1956-68.
      New York: Shake Books, 1979.   p., illus.
           Large-format reproductions in color.

121. Bourgeon, J.P. (illustrator). Starlettes. New York: Delilah,
      1984. 80p., illus.

122. Brown. Charles. The Art of Rock and Roll. Englewood Cliffs,
      New Jersey; London: Prentice-Hall, 1983. 208p., illus.

123. Burns, Mal (comp.). Visions of Rock. Introduction by Nicolas
      Locke. London; New York: Proteus, 1981. 64p., illus.
           Illustrations and paintings of rock stars.

124. Carvainis, Maria, and Roger Lax. The Moustache Book. New
     York: Quick Fox, 1978.

125. Chesher, Debbie (ed.). Starart. Dewington, Alberta: Starart
     Productions, 1979.   p., illus.
         Limited edition of 300 copies. Collection of paintings
     and other artwork by Joni Mitchell, John Mayall, Cat Stevens,
     Klaus Voorman, Ron Wood, and Commander Cody.

126. Davies, Llewlyn "Chalkie". Pointed Portraits: Photographs by
     Chalkie Davies. London: Eel Pie Publishing, 1981. 110p., illus.
         Rock artists, photographed 1977-81.

127. Ellis, Robert. The Pictorial Album of Rock. Foreword by Phil
     Collins. London: Salamander, 1981. 224p., illus., index.

128. Farren, Mick (ed.). Get On Down: a Decade of Rock and Roll
     Posters. London: Studio Vista, 1976. 96p., illus.

129. The Great Poster Trip. Palo Alto, California: Communication
     Arts, 1968.   p., illus.
         Collection of 204 San Francisco rock posters by Wilson, Mouse,
     Kelly, Griffin, Moscoso, and other artists; advertising Fillmore
     and Avalon Ballroom performances, 1966-67.

130. Hammond, Harry, and Gered Mankowitz. Hit Parade: a Thirty-Five
     Year Perspective of the Pop Performer. New York: Harper and
     Row, 1983; London: Plexus, 1984. 160p., illus.
         Photographs by Hammond (1950s-1960s) and Mankowitz (1963-
     date).

131. Hammond, Harry. Pop People: Photographs. London: Sidgwick and
     Jackson, 1984. 160p., illus., index.
         Largely from the 1950s.

132. Heavy Metal in Japan:HM Photobook. London: Omnibus Pr., 1983.
     128p., illus.
         Performance photographs, taken in Japan.

133. Hirsch, Abby (ed.). The Photography of Rock. Indianapolis:
     Bobbs-Merrill, 1972; London: Aidan Ellis, 1973. 238p., illus.

134. Johnston, Tom. Sex 'n' Dogs...Pop With its Pants Off. London:
     Hook Books, 1981.   p., illus.
         Satirical cartoons, first published in London's Standard.

135. Kelly, Alton, and Stanley Mouse. Mouse and Kelly. Limpsfield,
     East Sussex: Paper Tiger, 1980.   p., illus.
         Collection of their posters and other artwork.

136. Leibowitz, Annie. Photographs. New York: Pantheon Books, 1983;
     London: Thames and Hudson, 1984. 144p., illus.

137. Lowry, Ray. It's Only Rock 'n' Roll: Comic Strips and Cartoons.
     Manchester: New Manchester Review, 1980. (Reprinted London:
     Pluto Pr., 1981.) 93p., illus.

* McCartney, Linda. <u>Linda's Pictures</u>.
      * Cited below as item 1957.

* ————. <u>Photographs</u>.
      * Cited below as item 1958.

138. Marks, J., and Linda Eastman (later Linda McCartney). <u>Rock
     and Other Four-Letter Words: Music of the Electric Generation</u>.
     New York: Bantam, 1968. 256p., illus.
          Conglomeration of illustrations, prose, and graphics.
     Review in <u>Rolling Stone</u>, 1 March 1969, claims that many of
     the photographs credited to Eastman are in fact not hers.

* Ochs, Michael. <u>Rock Archives: a Photographic Journey Through
     the First Three Decades of Rock and Roll</u>.
          * Cited below as item 244.

139. Oxtoby, David, and David Sandison. <u>Oxtoby's Rockers</u>. Oxford:
     Phaidon; New York: Dutton, 1978. 80p., illus.
          Paintings by Oxtoby; text by Sandison. Most of them were
     destroyed in an accident shortly after publication.

140. Peellaert, Guy, and Nik Cohn. <u>Rock Dreams</u>. London: Pan;
     New York: Popular Library, 1974; New York: Knopf, 1982.
     146p., illus.
          Paintings by Peellaert, based on rock songs and singers.
     Originally published in France, 1973.

141. Rowlands, John. <u>Spotlight Heroes: Two Decades of Rock and
     Roll Superstars as Seen Through the Camera of John Rowlands</u>.
     New York: McGraw-Hill, 1981. 160p., illus.

142. Seef, Norman. <u>Hot Shots</u>. New York: Flash Books; London:
     Book Sales, 1976. 95p., illus.
          Photographs of rock performers.

143. <u>Sex and Drugs and Rock 'n' Roll</u>. Introduction by Miles.
     San Francisco: Gallo, 1984. unpaged, illus.
          Compromising photographs of rock stars.

144. Yates, Paula. <u>Rock Stars in Their Underpants</u>. Introductions
     by Peter Cook and Paul Gambaccini. London: Virgin Books,
     1980. 86p., illus.

7. MISCELLANEA

(a) General

145. Bangs, Lester, and Michael Ochs. <u>Rock Secrets</u>. New York:
     Delilah, 1982. 192p., illus.

146. Edwards, Joseph. <u>Top Tens and Trivia of Rock and Roll, and
     Rhythm and Blues</u>. St. Louis: Blueberry Hill Publishing, 1974.
     632p., discogs.

147. Environmental Communications. <u>Musical Houses: Homes and Sec-ret Retreats of Music Stars</u>. Philadelphia: Running Pr., 1980. p., illus.

148. Frampton, Mary. <u>Mary Frampton's Book of Rock Recipes</u>. Garden City, New York: Doubleday, 1980. p.

149. Green, Jonathon (comp.). <u>The Book of Rock Quotes</u>. London; New York: Omnibus Pr., 1977. 120p., illus. <u>Rev. ed</u>. London: Omnibus Pr., 1978. 126p., illus. <u>Updated ed</u>. London: Omnibus Pr.; New York: Delilah, 1982. 128p., illus.
    Over two thousand quotations from rock personalities.

150. Jakubowski, Maxim (comp.). <u>The Wit and Wisdom of Rock and Roll</u>. London: Unwin Paperbacks, 1983. 172p.
    Quotations from rock figures.

151. Lazell, Barry, and Daffyd Rees. <u>The Illustrated Book of Rock Records: a Book of Lists</u>. London: Virgin Books; New York: Delilah, 1982. 192p., illus.

    ————. <u>The Illustrated Book of Rock Records, Volume 2</u>. London: Virgin Books; New York: Delilah, 1983. 192p., illus.

152. Leach, Robert. <u>How the Planets Rule the Superstars</u>. London: Everest, 1975. 173p., illus.
    Astrology.

153. Marsh, Dave, and Kevin Stein. <u>The Book of Rock Lists</u>. New York: Dell; London: Sidgwick and Jackson, 1981. 642p., illus., bibliog., discog. (A <u>Rolling Stone</u> Pr. Book)

154. Stallings, Penny. <u>Rock 'n' Roll Confidential</u>. London: Vermilion, 1985. 256p., illus.
    Gossip and scandal.

155. Tobler, John, and Alan Jones. <u>The Rock Lists Album</u>. London: Plexus, 1982. 159p., illus.

156. Worth, Fred L. <u>Thirty Years of Rock and Roll Trivia</u>. New York: Warner Books, 1980. 288p., illus.

(b) Quizzes

157. Allan, John. <u>The Rock Trivia Quizbook</u>. New York: Drake, 1976. 182p., illus.

158. Dachs, David. <u>The Pop-Rock Question and Answer Book</u>. New York: Scholastic Book Services, 1977. p., illus.

159. Dellar, Fred. <u>Rock and Pop Crosswords</u>. London: Zomba Books, 1983. 128p., illus.
    Includes flexidisk of musical clues.

Quizzes (cont.)

160. Eldin, Peter. "Top of the Pops" Quiz. London: Armada, 1980.
     128p., illus.
         Linked with British television show, Top of the Pops.

161. Feigenbaum, Joshua, and David Schulps. Rock Quiz. New York:
     Perigee, 1983. 160p., illus.

162. Goodgold, Edwin, and Dan Carlinsky. Rock 'n' Roll Trivia.
     With More Than Four Hundred Questions and Answers, and an
     Eight-Page Photoquiz on the Music You Grew Up To. New York:
     Popular Library, 1970. 127p., illus.

163. Grant, Michael. The Blandford Book of Rock and Pop Cross-
     words. Poole, Dorset: Blandford Pr., 1984. 128p.

164. Hale, Tony. Quiz Kid. London: British Broadcasting Corpor-
     ation, 1977. 125p., illus.
         Based on British television show, same title.

165. Jasper, Tony. Rock Mastermind: the Ultimate Pop and Rock
     Music Quizbook. Poole, Dorset: Blandford Pr., 1983. 176p.,
     index.

166. ———. Simply Pop. London: Queen Anne Pr., 1975. 80p.,
     illus.

167. Kinn, Maurice (ed.). The Armada Pop Quiz Book. Crosswords
     by Derek Johnson. London: Armada, 1975. 124p., illus.

168. Lazell, Barry, and Daffydd Rees. The Illustrated Pop Quiz.
     London; New York: Proteus.
     Vol. 1: 1983. 64p., illus.
     Vol. 2: 1984. 64p., illus.

169. Lehner, Jack. The Ivy League Rock and Roll Quiz Book. New
     York: Delilah, 1983. 144p., illus.

170. Marsh, Dave. Rocktopion: Unlikely Questions and Their
     Surprising Answers. Chicago: Contemporary Books, 1984.
     224p., illus.

171. Read, Mike. Mike Read's Rock and Pop Quiz Book. London: Elm
     Tree Books/Sphere, 1981. 91p., illus.

172. Rees, Daffydd, and Luke Crampton. The Great Rock and Roll
     Trivia Quiz Book. London: Virgin Books, 1983.   p., illus.

173. Rice, Jo, Tim Rice, Paul Gambaccini, and Mike Read. The
     Guinness Hits Challenge. Enfield, Middlesex: Guinness
     Superlatives, 1984.   p., illus.

174. Rider, David. Johnnie Walker's "Pop the Question." London:
     Everest, 1975. 137p., illus.
         Based on disk-jockey Walker's British radio program.

175. Rockola Rock Trivia Quizbook. Toronto, Ontario: Rockola, 1979.
      120p.

176. Schaffner, Nicholas, and Elizabeth Schaffner. 505 Rock and
      Roll Questions Your Friends Can't Answer. New York: Walker,
      1981. 160p. (Columbus Books)

177. Sinclair, Jill, and Frances Whitaker. Pop Quiz, from the B.B.C.
      Television Programme. London: British Broadcasting Corporation,
      1982. 64p., illus.

178. Tobler. John. and Cathy McKnight. Pop Quest: So You Think You
      Know All About Rock 'n' Pop. London: Independent Television
      Books/Arrow, 1978. 125p., illus. (Look-In Books)
         Based on British television series, Pop Quest.

179. Uslan, Michael, and Bruce Solomon. The Rock 'n' Roll Trivia
      Quiz Book. New York: Simon and Schuster, 1978. 127p., illus.
      (A Fireside Book)

                     8. GENERAL HISTORIES

                     A. Comprehensive Works

180. Barnes, Edwin Ninyon Chaloner. American Music: from Plymouth
      Rock to Tin Pan Alley. Washington, D.C.: Music Education Pub-
      lications, 1936. 22p.

181. Boeckman, Charles. And the Beat Goes On: a Survey of Pop Music
      in America. Washington, D.C.: R.B. Luce, 1972. 224p., illus.

182. Booth, John Bennion (ed.). Seventy Years of Song. London:
      Hutchinson, 1943. 80p., illus.

183. Denis, Paul. Singer Super Sound. With Michael Denis and
      Christopher Denis. New York: Benjamin, 1969. 128p., illus.
      (A Rutledge Book)

184. Eberly, Phillip K. Music in the Air: America's Changing Taste
      in Popular Music, 1920-1980. Philadelphia: Hastings, 1982.
      448p., illus. (Communications Arts Books)

185. Ewen, David. All the Years of American Popular Music. Engle-
      wood Cliffs, New Jersey; London: Prentice-Hall, 1977. 850p.,
      illus., index.

186. ————. The History of Popular Music. New York: Barnes and
      Noble; London: Constable, 1961. 229p., bibliog. (Everyday
      Handbooks)

187. ————. The Life and Death of Tin Pan Alley: the Golden Age
      of American Popular Music. New York: Funk and Wagnalls, 1964.
      380p., bibliog.

Comprehensive Works (cont.)

188. Ewen, David. Panorama of American Popular Music: the Story of
     Our National Ballads and Folksongs; the Songs of Tin Pan Alley,
     Broadway, and Hollywood; New Orleans Jazz, Swing, and Symphon-
     ic Jazz. Englewwod Cliffs, New Jersey: Prentice-Hall; London:
     Bailey Brothers and Swinfen, 1957. 365p., index.

189. Farmer, Paul. Pop. London: Longman, 1979. 24p., illus.
     (Longman's Music Topics)
          For British secondary school students.

          ———. The Story of Pop. Harlow, Essex: Longman, 1982. 24p.,
     illus. (Longman's Music Topics)
          Revised and rewritten.

190. Finck, Herman. My Melodious Memories. London: Hutchinson,
     1937. 304p., illus.

191. Goldberg, Isaac. Tin Pan Alley: a Chronicle of the American
     Popular Music Racket. Introduction by George Gershwin. New
     York: John Day, 1930. 341p., illus., index.

          ———. Tin Pan Alley: a Chronicle of American Popular Music.
     Introduction by George Gershwin. With a Supplement From Sweet
     and Swing to Rock 'n' Roll by Edward Jablonski. New York:
     Ungar, 1961. 371p., illus., index.

192. Green, Abel, and Joe Laurie, Jr. Show Biz: from Vaude to Video.
     New York: Holt, 1951. Reprinted: Port Washington, New York:
     Kennikat Pr., 1972. 2 vols., 613p.

193. Hamm, Charles E. Yesterdays: Popular Song in America. New
     York; London: Norton, 1979 (reissued 1983). 553p., illus.,
     bibliog., index.

194. Kinscella, Hazel Gertrude. History Sings: Backgrounds of
     American Music. Lincoln, Nebraska; New York: University Pub-
     lication Company, 1940. 528p., illus., bibliogs. 2nd ed.:
     Lincoln, Nebraska: University Publication Company, 1948. 560p.,
     illus., bibliogs.
          Text for schools.

195. Lee, Edward. Music of the People: a Study of Popular Music in
     Great Britain. London: Barrie and Jenkins, 1970. 274p., illus.,
     bibliog., index.
          Written in 1967. Survey from before medieval period to 1967.

196. Martin, Deac (pseud. of Claude Trimble Martin). Deac Martin's
     Book of Musical Americana. Englewood Cliffs, New Jersey; London:
     Prentice-Hall, 1970. 243p., illus.

197. Melody Maker. Fifty Years of Music. London: Melody Maker,
     1976. 56p., illus. (A Melody Maker Special)
          Published to celebrate Melody Maker's fiftieth anniversary.

198. Middleton, Richard. From Liszt to Music Hall. Prepared for
the (Open University) Course Team. Milton Keynes, Buckinghamshire: Open University Pr., 1978. 68p., illus., bibliog. (An
Arts Foundation Course: Arts and Society in an Age of Indust-
rialisation)
     Study text.

199. Morris, Berenice Robinson. American Popular Music: the Beginning Years. New York: Franklin Watts, 1970. 63p., illus.
     Aimed at younger readers.

200. ———. American Popular Music: the Growing Years, 1800-1900.
New York: Franklin Watts, 1972. 87p., illus.

201. ———. American Popular Music: the Twentieth Century. New
York: Franklin Watts, 1974. 86p., illus., bibliog.

202. Myrus, Donald. Ballads, Blues, and the Big Beat. New York:
Macmillan; London: Collier-Macmillan, 1966. 136p., illus.,
discog., index.

  * Nanry, Charles (ed.). American Music: from Storyville to Woodstock.
        * Cited below as item 386.

203. Nettel, Reginald. Seven Centuries of Popular Song: a Social
History of Urban Ditties. London: Phoenix House, 1956. 248p.,
illus., bibliog., index.

204. Palmer, Tony. All You Need is Love: the Story of Popular Music.
London: Weidenfeld and Nicolson/Chappell; New York: Grossman,
1976; London: Futura; New York: Penguin, 1977. 323p., illus.,
index.
     Based on British television series. Grossman edition is
printed in sepia.

  * Radio One. The Story of Pop.
        * Cited below as item 208.

205. Robinette, Richard. Historical Perspectives in Popular Music:
a Historical Outline. Duboque, Iowa: Kendall-Hunt, 1980. 162p.,
illus., bibliog.
     Text for music appreciation course

206. Shepherd, John. Tin Pan Alley. London: Routledge and Kegan
Paul, 1982. 154p., illus., bibliog., discog., index. (Routledge Popular Music)

207. Spaeth, Sigmund Gottfried. A History of Popular Music in
America. New York: Random House, 1948; New York: Theatre Arts
Books, 1950; London: Phoenix House, 1960. 729p., bibliog., index.
     Appendix lists songs, 1770-1948, by year of publication.

208. The Radio One Story of Pop: the First Encyclopedia of Pop.
London: Phoebus, 1973-74.
     Issued in twenty-six weekly parts. Reissued 1975 in forty
weekly parts. Published in book form as item 209.

Comprehensive Works (cont.)

209. The Story of Pop. London: Octopus, 1974; London: Phoebus,
      1976. 253p., illus., index.
         Adaption of item 208.

210. Whitcomb, Ian. After the Ball. London: Allen Lane;
      Harmondsworth, Middlesex: Penguin, 1972. 312p., index.

         ————. After the Ball: Pop Music From Rag to Rock. New
      York: Simon and Schuster, 1973; Baltimore: Penguin, 1974.
      312p., index.
         By one-time rock singer. Personal memoir coupled with
      anecdotal history of Twentieth-Century popular music trends.

211. ————. Tin Pan Alley: a Pictorial History (1919-1939). With
      Complete Words and Music of Forty Songs. New York: Paddington
      Pr.; London: Wildwood House, 1975. 253p., illus., bibliog.,
      discog.

                        B. PERIODS AND STYLES

                        (a) 1800-1920's

                        (1) General

212. Brooks, Henry Mason (comp.). Olden-Time Music: a Compilation
      From Newspapers and Books. Boston: Ticknor, 1888. 283p.

213. Burton, Jack. In Memoriam: Oldtime Show Biz, With Headstones
      For the Minstrels, the Grand Op'ry House, the Road Show, the
      One-Night Stand, the Big Top, Burlesque, and Vaudeville; and
      a Few Tears For the Great White Way That Used-To-Be. New
      York: Vantage Pr., 1965. 102p.

214. Disher, Maurice Willson. Victorian Song: From Dive to
      Drawing Room. London: Phoenix House, 1955. 256p., illus.,
      index.

   * MacInnes, Colin. Sweet Saturday Night.
         * Cited below as item 1011.

215. Mander, Raymond, and Joe Mitchenson (comps.). Victorian and
      Edwardian Entertainment From Old Photographs. London:
      Batsford, 1978. 120p., illus.

216. Pearsall, Ronald. Edwardian Popular Music. Newton Abbot,
      Devon: David and Charles; Detroit: Gale, 1973; Rutherford,
      New Jersey: Fairleigh Dickinson, 1975. 207p., illus.,
      bibliog., index.

217. ————. Victorian Popular Music. Newton Abbot, Devon: David
      and Charles; Detroit: Gale, 1973. 240p., illus., bibliog.,
      index.

218. Taws, Nicholas. <u>A Music for the Millions: Antebellum Demo-
      cratic Attitudes and the Birth of American Popular Music</u>.
      New York: Pendragon, 1984. 160p., illus. (The Sociology of
      Music, 3)

                        (2) **Barbershop**

219. Cook, Will. <u>Melodies for Millions: a Twenty-Five Year History</u>.
      Kerosha, Wisconsin: Society for the Preservation and Encourage-
      ment of Barber Shop Quartet Singing in America, 1965. 122p.,
      illus.
         History of the Society.

220. Kennedy, R. Emmet. <u>Mellows: a Chronicle of Unknown Singers</u>.
      New York: A. and C. Boni, 1925. 183p.

221. ————. <u>More Mellows</u>. New York: Dodd, Mead, 1931. 178p.

222. Spaeth, Sigmund Gottfried. (ed.). <u>Barber Shop Ballads: a Book
      of Close Harmony</u>. Illustrated by Ellison Hower. Foreword by
      Ring Lardner. New York: Simon and Schuster, 1925. 61p., illus.
         Songs and musical examples interspersed in text. Includes
      two double-sided 78 r.p.m. records.

223. ————. <u>Barber Shop Ballads and How to Sing Them</u>. Foreword
      by Ring Lardner. New York: Prentice-Hall, 1940. 125p., illus.
         Completely rewritten version of item 222; retaining only
      the foreword and some illustrations.

                     (b) Dance Band Era

      Histories of this Period are cited below as items 841-861.

                     (c) World War II

224. Huggett, Frank E. <u>Goodnight Sweetheart: Songs and Memories of</u>
      the Second World War. London: W.H. Allen, 1979. 192p., illus.,
      bibliog.

                     (d) Rock and Pop

                     (1) General

225. Belz, Carl. <u>The Story of Rock</u>. New York: Oxford University
      Pr., 1969; London: Oxford University Pr., 1971. 256p., illus.,
      discog., index. <u>2nd ed</u>. London; New York: Oxford University
      Pr.; New York: Harper and Row, 1972. 286p., bibliog., discog.,
      index.

226. Berry, Peter E. "...<u>And the Hits Just Keep on Comin'</u>."
      Syracuse, New York: Syracuse University Pr., 1977. 278p.,
      illus., bibliog. refs., discog.
         By disk-jockey "The Flying Dutchman."

Rock and Pop (cont.)

227. Bill, J. Brent. Rock and Roll. Old Tappan, New Jersey: Revell,
      1984. 160p. (Power Books)
          From Christian viewpoint.

228. Brown, Charles. The Rock and Roll Story. Englewood Cliffs,
      New Jersey; London: Prentice-Hall, 1984. 128p., illus.

229. Chambers, Iain. Urban Rhythms. London: Macmillan, 1984.
      272p., illus. (Communications and Culture)

  *   Clark, Dick. Dick Clark's The First Twenty-Five Years of Rock
      and Roll.
          * Cited below as item 245.

230. Cohn, Nik. Pop from the Beginning. London: Weidenfeld and
      and Nicholson, 1969. 238p., illus., index.

          ————. Rock from the Beginning. New York: Stein and Day,
      1969. 256p., illus., index.

          ————. Awopbopaloobop Alopbamboom: Pop from the Beginning.
      London: Paladin, 1970. 244p., illus., index.
          Expansion of Pop from the Beginning.

231. Flans, Robyn. Music Mania. Creskill, New Jersey: Sharon Pub-
      lications; London: Starbooks, 1983. 96p., illus.
          Developments since The Beatles.

232. Flattery, Paul. The Illustrated History of Pop. Edited by
      Andrew Bailey. Designed by John McConnell. London: Wise
      Publications/Music Sales, 1973; New York: Drake (as The Illus-
      trated History of British Pop), 1975. 128p., illus., discog.
      (A Music Sales Magazine Special)

233. Gabree, John. The World of Rock. Greenwich, Conn.: Fawcett
      Publications, 1968. 176p., illus., discog. (A Gold Medal Book)

234. Gillett, Charlie. The Sound of the City: the Rise of Rock and
      Roll. New York: Outerbridge and Dienstfrey, 1970; New York:
      Dell, 1972. 375p., bibliog., discog., index. London: Souvenir
      Pr.; London: Sphere, 1971. 387p., bibliog., discog., index.
      Rev. ed. London: Souvenir Pr.; New York: Pantheon; New York:
      Dell, 1983. 515p., bibliog., index.

  *   Grossman, Lloyd. A Social History of Rock Music.
          * Cited below as item 368.

235. History of Rock. London: Orbis, 1982-84.
          Issued in weekly parts, with index. Includes flexidisks.
      Accompanied by record album releases of musical examples.

236. Hodenfield, Chris. Rock '70. New York: Pyramid Books, 1970.
      140p., illus.

237. Hopkins, Jerry. The Rock Story. New York: New American Lib-
     rary, 1970. 222p., illus., bibliog., discog.

238. Horst, Brian van der. Rock Music. New York: Franklin Watts,
     1973. 90p., illus.
     Aimed at younger readers.

239. Jahn, Mike. Rock: from Elvis Presley to the Rolling Stones.
     New York: Quadrangle/New York Times Book Company, 1973. 326p.,
     illus., discog., index.

240. Katz, Frederic M. Rock: the History, Criticism, and Discog-
     raphy of Rock-and-Roll. New York: William Morrow, 1968.   p.,
     illus., discog.

241. Kent, Jeff. The Rise and Fall of Rock. Stoke-on-Trent, Staff-
     ordshire: Witan, 1983. 484p., illus., discog., index.

242. Laing, Dave. The Sound of Our Time. London: Sheed and Ward,
     1969; New York: Quadrangle, 1970. 198p., bibliog.
     History from philosophical viewpoint.

243. London, Herbert I. Closing the Circle: a Cultural History of
     the Rock Revolution. Chicago: Nelson-Hall, 1984. 184p.

244. Ochs, Michael. Rock Archives: a Photographic Journey Through
     the First Three Decades of Rock and Roll. Edited by Jim
     Fitzgerald. Garden City, New York: Doubleday, 1984. 416p.,
     illus. (A Dolphin Book)

245. Olsen, Michael, and Bruce Solomon. Dick Clark's The First
     Twenty-Five Years of Rock and Roll. New York: Dell, 1981.
     512p., illus.

246. Pascall, Jeremy. The Illustrated History of Rock Music. London;
     New York: Hamlyn, 1978. 222p., illus., bibliog., index. New
     enlarged ed. London; New York: Hamlyn, 1984. 236p., illus.,
     bibliog., index.

247. Peck, Ira (ed.). The New Sound / Yes! Preface by Murray the K.
     New York: Four Winds Pr., 1966. 133p., illus.
     Historical essays reprinted from Time magazine.

248. Pollock, Bruce. When Rock Was Young: a Nostalgic Review of the
     Top Forty Era. New York: Holt, Rinehart and Winston, 1981.
     224p., illus.

249. Rogers, Dave. Rock 'n' Roll. London: Routledge, Kegan and Paul,
     1982. 160p. (Routledge Popular Music)

250. Rolling Stone. The Rolling Stone Illustrated History of Rock
     and Roll. Edited by Jim Miller. New York: Random House; London:
     Big O Publishing, 1976. 382p., illus., index. (A Rolling Stone
     Press Book). Rev ed. The Rolling Stone Illustrated History of
     Rock and Roll, 1950-1980. New York: Random House, 1980; London:
     Picador, 1981. 474p., illus., index. (A Rolling Stone Pr. Book)
     Second edition is almost completely rewritten.

Rock and Pop (cont.)

251. Saporita, Jay. Pourin' It All Out. Secaucus, New Jersey:
     Citadel Pr., 1960. 224p., illus.

252. Shaw, Arnold. The Rock Revolution. New York: Collier Books;
     London: Collier-Macmillan, 1969; New York: Paperback Library,
     1971. 215p., illus., discogs., index.

253. Soul, Pop, Rock, Stars, Superstars. London: Octopus, 1974.
     255p., illus.
        Adapted from item 208.

254. Stambler, Irwin. The Guitar Years: Pop Music from Country
     and Western to Hard Rock. Garden City, New York: Doubleday,
     1970. 137p., illus.

255. Tobler, John, and Pete Frame. Rock 'n' Roll: the First
     Twenty-Five Years. New York: Bookthrift, 1981. 256p., illus.

256. Whitcomb, Ian. Whole Lotta Shakin': a Rock 'n' Roll Scrapbook.
     London: Arrow/E.M.I. Music, 1982. 200p., illus.
        History through press cuttings.

257. Yorke, Ritchie. The History of Rock 'n' Roll. Prepared in
     association with CHUM. Toronto: Methuen; London: Eyre Methuen,
     1976; New York: Methuen, 1977. 174p., illus.
        Written for Canadian radio station.

                          (2) 1950s

                          (a) General

258. Baker, Chuck. The Rockin' Fifties: a Rock and Roll Scrapbook.
     A Fast Encounter With the Generation That Spawned Rock and
     Roll and Student Unrest, Howdy Doody and Revolution, Elvis
     Presley, and Flights in Space! Woodland Hills, California:
     Avanco, 1973. 175p., illus., discog.

259. Bird, Brian (pseud. of Archibald Brian Bird). Skiffle! The
     Story of Folk-Song With a Jazz Beat. Foreword by Lonnie
     Donegan. London: Hale, 1958. 125p., illus., bibliog., index.

260. Busnar, Gene. It's Rock 'n' Roll: a Musical History of the
     Fabulous Fifties. New York: J. Messner, 1979. 256p., illus.,
     index. (Wanderer Books)

261. Rogers, Dave. Rock 'n' Roll. London; Boston: Routledge and
     Kegan Paul, 1982. 148p., illus., bibliog., discog., index.
     (Routledge Popular Music)

262. Shaw, Arnold. The Rockin' Fifties. New York: Hawthorn Books,
     1974. 200p., illus.

(b) Doowop

263. Engel, Edward. White and Still All Right. Scarsdale, New York:
Rock Culture Books, 1978.   p., illus., discogs.
      History of white doowop groups on the East Coast.

264. Groia, Philip. They All Sang on the Corner: New York City's
Rhythm and Blues Vocal Groups of the 1950s. Setauket, New
York: Edmond Publishing, 1973 (rev. ed. 1974). 147p., illus.,
discogs., index.

————. They All Sang on the Corner: a Second Look at New
York City's Rhythm and Blues Vocal Groups. West Hempstead,
New York: Phillie Dee Enterprises, 1983. 192p., illus.,
discogs., index.

(3) 1960s

(a) General

265. Bronson, Harold. Rock Explosion: the British Invasion in Photos,
1962-1967. Los Angeles: Rhino Books, 1984.   p., illus.

266. Charlesworth, Chris. Rock Heritage: the Sixties. London; New
York: Proteus, 1984. 160p., illus.

267. Harry, Bill, and Miles. Mersey Beat: the Beginning of the
Beatles. New York; London: Omnibus Pr., 1978. 96p., illus.
      Replica pages from Liverpool's Mersey Beat magazine, formerly
edited by Bill Harry.

268. Jasper, Tony. Fab! The Sounds of the Sixties. Poole, Dorset:
Blandford Pr., 1984. 288p., illus.

 * Leigh, Spencer. Let's Go Down The Cavern.
      * Cited below as item 324.

269. May, Chris, and Tim Phillips. British Beat. London: Socion
Books, 1974. 104p., illus., index.
      Details of British scene; covers over one thousand groups,
1962-67.

270. Pichaske, David. A Generation in Motion: Popular Music and
Culture in the Sixties. New York: Schirmer, 1979. 248p.,
illus., discog., index.

271. Pollock, Bruce. When the Music Mattered: Rock in the 1960s.
New York: Holt, Rinehart and Winston, 1984.   p., illus.

272. Schaffner, Nicholas. The British Invasion. New York; London:
McGraw-Hill, 1982. 316p., illus., bibliog., index.
      History of British rock acts successful in the United States,
1964 to date.

273. Trow, Michael Arthur. The Pulse of '64: the Mersey Beat. New
York: Vantage Pr., 1979. 36p., illus.

(b) Commercial Folk

274. De Turk, David A., and A. Poulin (eds.). The American Folk
      Scene: Dimensions of the Folk Song Revival. New York: Dell,
      1967. 334p., illus., bibliog. (A Laurel Original)
           Collection of thirty-two essays.

275. Dunson, Josh. Freedom in the Air: Song Movements of the Sixties.
      New York: International Publishers, 1965. (Little New World
      Paperbacks, 7). Reprinted: Westport, Conn.: Greenwood Pr.,
      1980. 127p., bibliog., discog.
           Topical song movement, up to 1964.

276. Gahr, David, and Robert Shelton. The Face of Folk Music.
      Secaucus, New Jersey: Citadel Pr., 1968. 372p., illus.
           Text by Shelton; photographs by Gahr. Performers and
      writers of the Folk Revival, mid-1960s.

277. Laing, Dave, Karl Dallas, Robin Denselow, and Robert Shelton.
      The Electric Muse: the Story of Folk into Rock. London: Eyre
      Methuen, 1975. 182p., illus., index.
           Essays on the historical relationship.

278. Rodnitzky, Jerome L. Minstrels of the Dawn: the Folk-Protest
      Singer as a Cultural Hero. Chicago: Nelson-Hall, 1976. 192p.,
      illus., bibliog., index.

279. Vassal, Jacques. Electric Children: Roots and Branches of
      Modern Folkrock. Translated and adapted by Paul Barnett.
      New York: Taplinger, 1976. 270p., illus., bibliog., index.
           Originally published in France.

280. Von Schmidt, Eric, and Jim Rooney. Baby, Let Me Follow You
      Down: the Illustrated Story of the Cambridge Folk Years.
      Garden City, New York: Doubleday, 1979. 317p., illus. (Anchor
      Books)
           Informal history, by participant.

(4) 1970s to Date

(a) General

281. Downing, David. Future Rock. St. Albans, Hertfordshire:
      Panther, 1976. 172p., discog.

282. Turning On: Rock in the Late Sixties. Foreword by Mike Read.
      London: Orbis, 1984. 240p., illus.
           Includes chronologies of key developments for each year,
      1966-70.

283. Van der Kiste, John. Roxeventies: Popular Music in Britain,
      1970-79. Torpoint, Cornwall: Kawabata, 1982. 41p., illus.

(b) New Wave

284. Anscombe, Isabelle, and Dike Blair. <u>Punk.</u> Photographs by
Roberta Bayley. New York: Urizen Books, 1978. 128p., illus.

285. Battcock, Gregory (ed.). <u>Breaking the Sound Barrier: a Critical Anthology of the New Music.</u> New York: Dutton, 1981.
288p., illus.

286. Birch, Ian, and Pearce Marchbank. <u>The Book With No Name.</u>
Introduction by Richard Strange. London: Omnibus Pr., 1982.
72p., illus.
   History of the "New Romantics" rock movement.

287. Boston, Virginia. <u>Shock Wave.</u> London: Plexus, 1978. 128p.,
illus.

288. Burchill, Julie, and Tony Parsons. <u>"The Boy Looked at Johnny:"
the Obituary of Rock and Roll.</u> London: Pluto Pr., 1978. 96p.
   Strident critical history of British punk rock movement.

289. Coon, Caroline. <u>1988: the New Wave Punk Rock Explosion.</u>
London: Star Books, 1977; New York: Hawthorn Books, 1978;
London: Omnibus Pr., 1982. 128p., illus.
   Largely reprints of her articles on new wave music from
London's <u>New Musical Express.</u>

290. Davis, Julie (ed.). <u>Punk.</u> London: Millington, 1977. 128p.,
illus.

291. Hennessey, Val. <u>In the Gutter.</u> London: Quartet, 1978. 95p.,
illus. (Quartet Diversions)
   Chiefly illustrated.

292. Noble, Peter. <u>Future Pop: Music for the Eighties.</u> New York:
Delilah, 1983. 160p., illus.

293. Palmer, Myles. <u>The New Wave Explosion: How Punk Became New
Wave, Became the Eighties.</u> London; New York: Proteus, 1982.
128p., illus.

294. Sniffin' Glue. <u>The Bible.</u> London: Michael Dempsey for Big O
Publishing, 1978. 80p., illus.
   Reprint of all ten issues of London's new wave fanzine
<u>Sniffin' Glue</u> (1976-77). Entire contents written by Mark Perry.

295. Tobler, John. <u>Punk Rock: a Complete Guide to British and American New Wave.</u> London: Phoebus, 1977.   p., illus.

(c) Salsa

296. Gordon, Raoul (ed.). <u>Salsa.</u> New York: Gordon Pr., 1976.   p.,
illus.

Rock and Pop (cont.)

(d) Sacred Pop

297. Baker, Paul (pseud. of T. Edmondson). Why Should the Devil
      Have All the Good Music? Jesus Music — Where it Began, Where
      it Is, and Where it Is Going. Prelude by Pat Boone. Foreword
      by Larry Norman. Waco, Texas: Word Books, 1979. 235p., illus.,
      bibliog.

298. Burt, Jesse Clifton, and Duane Allen. The History of Gospel
      Music. Foreword by Dottie Rambo. Nashville: K and S Pr.,
      1971. 205p.
          History of Twentieth-Century Southern white gospel. Includ-
      es biographical directory giving tabulated information on
      approximately two hundred artists.

299. Ellinwood, Leonard Webster. The History of American Church
      Music. New York: Morehouse-Gorham, 1953. 274p., bibliog.
          Includes biographical appendix.

300. Solid Rock: the Christian and Contemporary Music. Glasgow:
      Pickering and Inglis in conjunction with British Youth for
      Christ, 1980. 49p., illus.
          Contemporary white gospel and gospel rock music.

9. REGIONAL HISTORIES

(1) North America and Britain

(a) Canada

301. Yorke, Ritchie. Axes, Chops, and Hot Licks: the Canadian Rock
      Music Scene. Edmonton, Alberta: Hurtig, 1971. 224p., illus.,
      discog.

(b) Hawaii

302. Kanahele, George S. (ed.). Hawaiian Music and Musicians: an
      Illustrated History. Honolulu: University Pr. of Hawaii, 1979.
          p., illus., bibliog.

303. Todaro, Tony. The Golden Years of Hawaiian Entertainment,
      1874-1974. Honolulu: T. Todaro Publishing Company, 1974.
      496p., illus., discog.

(c) Memphis

304. Palmer, Robert. A Tale of Two Cities: Memphis Rock, New Orleans
      Roll. Brooklyn, New York: Institute for Studies in American
      Music, 1979. 38p., illus. (I.S.A.M. Monographs, 12)

(d) New Haven

305. Lepri, Paul. The New Haven Sound, 1946-1976. New Haven, Conn.:
      The Author, 1979. 160p., illus., discog.

(e) New Orleans

* Palmer, Robert. <u>A Tale of Two Cities: Memphis Rock, New Orleans Roll</u>.
     * Cited above as item 304.

(f) Oklahoma

306. Savage, William W., <u>Jr</u>. <u>Singing Cowboys and All That Jazz: a Short History of Popular Music in Oklahoma</u>. Tulsa: University of Oklahoma Pr., 1983. 200p., illus.

(g) San Francisco

307. Burt, Rob, and Patsy North. <u>West Coast Story</u>. London: Hamlyn/ Phoebus, 1977. 96p., illus.
     Adapted from item 208.

308. Doukas, James N. <u>Electric Tibet</u>. San Marcos, California: Dominion Pr., 1969.   p., illus.

* Hill, Deborah. <u>Cuts From a San Francisco Rock Journal</u>.
     * Cited above as item 101.

309. ———. <u>The San Francisco Rock Experience</u>. San Francisco: Anthelion Pr., 1979.   p., illus.

(h) Texas

310. Reid, Jan. <u>The Improbable Rise of Redneck Rock</u>. Photographs by Melinda Wickman. Austin, Texas: Heidelberg Publishers, 1974. Reprinted: New York: Da Capo Pr., 1977. 342p., illus.
     Texas rock, and progressive country.

311. Willoughby, Larry. <u>Texas Rhythm, Texas Rhyme</u>. Edited by Barbara Rodriguez. Austin, Texas: Texas Monthly Pr., 1984. 208p., illus.

(i) Wales

312. Jarman, Geraint. <u>Gwreiddiau Canu Roc Cymraeg</u>. Penygroes, Gwynedd: Cyhoeddwyd Gyda Chydweithrediad B.B.C. Radio Cymru gan Gyhoeddiadau Mei, 1981. 58p., illus.
     History of Welsh rock music. Linked with British Broadcasting Corporation's Radio Wales program series.

(2) Other Countries

(a) Australia

313. Oram, Jim. <u>The Business of Pop</u>. London; Sydney, New South Wales: Horwitz Publications, 1966. 130p., illus.
     History of Australian trends to 1965.

314. Taylor, Ken. <u>Rock Generation: the Inside Exclusive</u>. Melbourne, Victoria: Sun Books, 1970. 149p., illus.
     By Australian record company executive.

(b) Austria

315. Hanslick, Edward. Vienna's Golden Years of Music, 1850-1900.
      Translated and edited by Henry Pleasants. New York: Simon
      and Schuster, 1950. 341p., illus.
          Collection of historical essays.

(c) Soviet Union

316. Gambino, Thomas. Nyet: an American Rock Musician Encounters
      the Soviet Union. Englewood Cliffs, New Jersey; London:
      Prentice-Hall, 1976. 183p.

10. VENUES

(1) Buskers

317. Campbell, Patricia J. Passing the Hat: Street Performance in
      America. New York: Delacorte Pr., 1981. 288p.

318. Cohen, David, and Ben Greenwood. The Buskers: a History of
      Street Entertainment. Newton Abbot, Devon: David and Charles,
      1981. 208p., illus., bibliog., index.

319. Crowhurst-Lennard, Suzanne H., and Henry L. Lennard. Public
      Life in Urban Places. Southampton, New York: Gondolier, 1984.
      80p.
          Street musicians.

(2) Clubs

(a) General Works

320. Morris, Gina. Happy Doin' What We're Doin': the Pub Rock Years,
      1972-1975. San Francisco: Nightbird Pr., 1984. 65p., illus.

321. Weil, Susanne, and Barry Singer. Steppin' Out: a Guide to Live
      Music in New York. New York: East Woods Pr., 1980.   p., index
          Popular music venues.

322. Wootton, Richard, and Charlie McKissack. Honky Tonkin': a
      Guide to Music U.S.A. London: The Authors, 1977. 27p. illus.

      Wootton, Richard. ———. 2nd ed. London: The Author, 1978.
      179p., illus.
          Includes accommodation guide. Updated by Honky Tonkin'
      Newsletter, 1978-79.

      ———. Honky Tonkin': a Travel Guide to American Music.
      London: Travelaid Publishing; New York: East Woods Pr., 1980.
      192p., illus.

(b) Individual Clubs

(1) Cavern

323. Barrow, Tony (comp.). On the Scene at The Cavern. Introduct-
      ions by Ray McFall and Bob Wooler. Morecambe, Lancashire:
      Tony Barrow International, 1984.   p., illus.
         Reprint of pamphlet published privately by The Cavern in
      1964, then under the pseudonymn "Alistair Griffin."

324. Leigh, Spencer. Let's Go Down The Cavern: the Story of
      Liverpool's Merseybeat. With charts by Pete Frame. London:
      Vermilion, 1984. 215p., illus., discog.
         The Club and artists who appeared there. Includes genea-
      logical charts of Merseybeat groups.

(2) Rendezvous

325. Roebuck, Julian B., and Wolfgang Frese. The Rendezvous: a
      Case Study of an After-Hours Club. New York: Free Pr., London:
      Collier-Macmillan, 1976. 278p.

(3) Village Vanguard

326. Gordon, Max. Live at the Village Vanguard. New York: St.
      Martin's Pr., 1980. Reprinted: New York: Da Capo Pr., 1982.
      146p.

(3) Concerts

327. Farren, Mick, and George Snow. Rock 'n' Roll Circus: the
      Illustrated Rock Concert. London: Pierrot Publishing; New
      York: A and W Publishers, 1978. 117p., illus.
         Performance photographs.

328. Gold, Mick. Rock on the Road. London: Futura, 1976. 160p.,
      illus.
         Photographs by the author.

329. Gorman, Clem. Back Stage Rock: Behind the Scenes With the
      Bands. London: Pan, 1978. 205p., illus.

330. Greater London Council. Code of Practice for Pop Concerts:
      a Guide to Safety, Health, and Welfare at One-Day Events.
      London: Greater London Council, 1976. 34p., illus. 2nd ed.:
      London: Greater London Council, 1978.   p., illus.

331. Lewis, Laurie. The Concerts. Limpsfield, East Sussex: Paper
      Tiger; New York: A and W Publishers, 1979. 119p., illus. (A
      Dragon's World Book)
         Collection of performance photographs.

332. Pertwee, John. By Royal Command. Newton Abbot, Devon: David
      and Charles, 1981. 175p., illus., index.
         History of the Royal Command Performances.

Concerts (cont.)

333. Stein, Howard. <u>Promoting Rock Concerts: a Practical Guide</u>.
      With Ronald Zalkind. New York: Schirmer, 1979.   p.

                        (4) Festivals

334. Allen, Rod. <u>Isle of Wight, 1970: the Last Great Festival</u>.
      <u>A Picture Record</u>. London: Clipper Pr., 1970. 60p., illus.

335. Clarke, Michael. <u>The Politics of Pop Festivals</u>. London:
      Junction Books, 1982. 203p., illus., bibliog. notes, index.

336. Eisen, Jonathan (ed.). <u>Altamont: Death of Innocence in the</u>
      <u>Woodstock Nation</u>. New York: Avon, 1970. 272p., illus.
      (A <u>Fusion</u> Book)

337. Great Britain. Advisory Committee on Pop Festivals. <u>Pop</u>
      <u>Festivals: Report and Code of Practice</u>. London: Her Majesty's
      Stationery Office, 1973. 147p., illus., bibliog., index.
          Chairman of Committee: Dennis Stevenson.

338. ————. Working Group on Pop Festivals. <u>Free Festivals:</u>
      <u>First Report of the Working Group on Pop Festivals</u>. London:
      Her Majesty's Stationery Office, 1976. 38p.

339. Hopkins, Jerry, Baron Wolman, and Jim Marshall. <u>Festival!</u>
      <u>The Book of American Music Celebrations</u>. New York: Macmillan;
      London: Collier-Macmillan, 1970. 191p., illus.
          Documents twelve rock, folk, jazz, and country festivals,
      1967-69.

340. National Association of Youth Clubs. Politics Working Party.
      <u>Night Assembly</u>? London: National Association of Youth Clubs,
      1972. 11p., illus.
          Consideration of abortive British legislation aimed at
      increasing official control over rock festivals.

341. Sandford, Jeremy, and Ron Reid. <u>Tomorrow's People</u>. London:
      Jerome Publishing, 1974. 128p., illus.
          Festivals and their audiences.

342. Santelli, Robert. <u>Aquarius Rising: the Rock Festival Years</u>.
      New York: Dell, 1981. 292p., illus., bibliog., index.
      (Delta Books)
          Describes major American festivals.

343. Spitz, Robert Stephen. <u>Barefoot in Babylon: the Creation of</u>
      <u>the Woodstock Music Festival, 1969</u>. New York: Viking Pr.,
      1979. 513p., illus., index.

344. Young, Jean, and Michael Scott Lang. <u>Woodstock Remembered</u>.
      New York: Ballantine, 1979. 128p., illus.
          By the organizers of the Festival.

(5) Motion Pictures, Television and Video

345. Blacknell, Steve. <u>The Story of "Top of the Pops.</u>" Wellingborough, Northamptonshire: Stephens, 1984. 160p., illus.
       History of long-running British pop music television series.

346. Bowles, Jerry G. <u>A Thousand Sundays: the Story of the Ed
   Sullivan Show</u>. New York: Putnam, 1980. 213p., illus., index.

347. Burt, Rob. <u>Rockerama: Twenty-Five Years of Teen Screen Idols</u>.
   Poole, Dorset: Blandford Pr.; New York: Delilah, 1983. 208p.,
   illus., bibliog., index.

348. ————. <u>The Tube</u>. Bristol: Purnell, 1983. 63p., illus.
       History of British television rock show, <u>The Tube</u>.

349. Dellar, Fred. <u>The New Musical Express Guide to Rock Cinema</u>.
   Foreword by Monty Smith. London: Hamlyn, 1981. 191p., illus.
       Covers motion pictures featuring rock music, 1950-80. Arr-
   anged alphabetically by titles.

350. Jenkinson, Philip, and Alan Warner. <u>Celluloid Rock: Twenty
   Years of Movie Rock</u>. London: Lorrimer, 1974. 135p., illus.,
   filmog., index.
       Critical history.

351. Lovitt, Chip. <u>Video Rock Superstars</u>. New York: Donald I. Fine,
   1984. 96p., illus.

352. Rawkins, Sue. <u>Video Rock</u>. New York: Morrow; London: Hamlyn,
   1984. 64p., illus.
       Descriptions of significant promotional videos.

353. Reed, Bill, and David Ehrenstein. <u>Rock on Film</u>. London: Virgin
   Books; New York: Delilah, 1981. 296p., illus.
       Gives details, casts, songs, and credits for 483 productions.

354. Shore, Michael (comp.). <u>The Rolling Stone Book of Rock Video:
   the Definitive Look at Music on Film, From Elvis Presley and
   Before to Michael Jackson and Beyond</u>. New York: Morrow, 1984.
   184p., illus. (A <u>Rolling Stone</u> Pr. Book)

(6) Juke Boxes

355. Krivine, John. <u>Juke Box Saturday Night</u>. London: New English
   Library, 1977. 160p., illus., index.
       History of juke boxes.

356. Lynch, Vincent, and Bill Henkin. <u>Jukeboxes: the Golden Age</u>.
   Photographs by Kazuhiro Tsuruta. Preface by David Rubinson.
   Berkley, California: Lancaster-Miller; London: Thames and Hud-
   son, 1981. 110p., illus.
       History from point of view of design.

11. SOCIOLOGICAL ASPECTS

357. Braun, D. Duane. Toward a Theory of Popular Culture: the
      Sociology and History of American Music and Dance, 1920-1968.
      Ann Arbor, Michigan: Ann Arbor Publishers, 1969. 195p.,
      bibliog. notes.
          Account of trends, and analyses of their causes.

358. Denisoff, R. Serge. Sing a Song of Social Significance.
      Bowling Green, Ohio: Bowling Green University Popular Pr.,
      1972. 229p., illus., bibliog., index.
          Based on articles previously published 1966-70. Analysis
      of protest song movements from 1940s to 1970s; and the social
      effects of rock music.

359. ————, and Richard A. Peterson (eds.). The Sounds of Social
      Change: Studies in Popular Culture. Chicago: Rand McNally,
      1972. 332p., bibliogs., index.
          Collection of articles analyzing use of popular music as
      protest; and in other social movements, including Nazism,
      the International Workers of the World, and Black Power.

360. Doney, Malcolm. Summer in the City: Rock Music and a Way of
      Life. Berkhamstead, Hertfordshire: Lion Publishing, 1978.
      133p., illus. (An Aslam Lion Book)
          Questions, from a Christian viewpoint, the promises of new
      lifestyles offered by rock music. Doubts their validity.

361. Farren, Mick, and Edward Barker. Watch Out, Kids. London:
      Open Gate Books, 1972. 126p., illus.
          Exposition of rock music's part in contemporary youth
      movements. Written from a radical viewpoint.

362. Fletcher, Peter. Roll Over, Rock: a Study of Music in Con-
      temporary Culture. London: Stainer and Bell, 1981. 175p.,
      index.

363. Frith, Simon. The Sociology of Rock. London: Constable; New
      York: Pantheon, 1978. 255p., bibliog., index.
          Study of rock and its audience; and the interaction betwwen
      the industry and consumers. Superseded by item 364.

364. ————. Sound Effects: Youth, Leisure, and the Politics of
      Rock'n' Roll. London: Constable; New York: Pantheon, 1983.
      294p., bibliog., index. (Communication and Society)
          Totally revised version of item 363.

365. Fuller, John G. Are the Kids All Right? The Rock Generation
      and its Hidden Death Wish. New York: Times Books, 1981. 262p.
          Contends that rock stars have a death wish, and pass on
      their self-destructive urges to their audiences.

366. Garlock, Frank. The Big Beat: a Rock Blast. Greenville, South
      Carolina: Bob Jones University Pr., 1971. 54p., bibliog.
          Anti-rock tract, from Christian moral viewpoint.

367. Garner, Peter. Pop Goes the Gospel. Gerrards Cross, Bucking-
      hamshire: W.E.C. Youth, 1978. 12p. (Camp Talk, 10)
          Pop music seen from a Christian viewpoint.

368. Grossman, Lloyd. A Social History of Rock Music: From the
      Greasers to Glitter Rock. New York: David McKay, 1976.   p.,
      illus.

369. Hall, Stuart, and Paddy Whannel. The Popular Arts. London:
      Hutchinson Educational, 1964; New York: Pantheon, 1965. 480p.,
      illus., bibliog., discog.
          Analysis and history of popular music, and its commercial
      and cultural role in Britain, 1950s-1960s. Aimed at British
      educationalists.

370. Harker, David. One For the Money: Politics and Popular Song.
      London: Hutchinson, 1980. 301p., illus., bibliog., index.

371. Hebdige, Dick. Subculture: the Meaning of Style. London:
      Methuen, 1979. 195p., illus., bibliog., index.
          British youth movements related to changing musical tastes.

372. Hibbard, Don, and Carol Kaleialoha. The Role of Rock: a Guide
      to the Social and Political Consequences of Rock Music. Engle-
      wood Cliffs, New Jersey; London: Prentice-Hall, 1983. 216p.

373. Hoffman, Abbie. Woodstock Nation: a Talk-Rock Album. New York:
      Random House; New York: Vintage Books, 1969. 153p., illus.
          Radical political speculations based on concept of the
      "Woodstock Nation."

374. Jasper, Tony. Sound Seventies. Great Yarmouth, Norfolk: Gall-
      iard, 1972. 60p., illus.
          Uses popular songs as study examples for the Christian life.

375. ————. Today's Sound: a New Approach to Christian Education
      and Studies in Modern Living. Great Yarmouth, Norfolk: Gall-
      iard, 1970. 65p., illus.
          Christian themes illustrated by popular songs.

376. Kanter, Kenneth A. The Jews on Tin Pan Alley: the Jewish
      Contribution to American Popular Music, 1870-1940. Hoboken,
      New Jersey: Ktav, 1981. 226p., illus.

377. Kent, Greta. A View from the Bandstand. London: Sheba Fem-
      inist Publishers, 1983. 48p.
          The role of women in popular music, as seen by female
      musicians.

378. Larson, Bob. Hindus, Hippies, and Rock and Roll. McCook,
      Nebraska: The Author, 1969.   p.
          Anti-rock tract, from a Christian moral viewpoint.

379. ————. Rock. Farmington Hills, Michigan: William Tyndale
      College Pr., 1980.   p.
          Anti-rock tract.

380.   ———. Rock and Roll: the Devil's Diversion. McCook, Neb-
        raska: The Author, 1970. 176p., illus., bibliog. notes.
        Anti-rock tract, from Christian moral viewpoint.

381.   ———. Rock and the Church. Carol Stream, Illinois: Creation
        House, 1971. 90p., bibliog. refs.
        Christian anti-rock argument.

382.   Laurie, Peter. Teenage Revolution. London: Blond, 1965.
        156p., bibliog.
        Sociological study of youth culture. Includes consideration
        of musical tastes and attitudes.

383.   Lawhead, Steve. Rock Reconsidered: a Christian Looks at
        Contemporary Music. Grove, Illinois: Inter-Varsity Pr., 1981.
        156p.

384.   McGregor, Craig. Up Against the Wall, America. Sydney, New
        South Wales; London: Angus and Robertson, 1973. 72p., illus.
        Collection of essays on the theme of social unrest in the
        United States. Large emphasis on popular music trends as a
        reflection of current events.

385.   Millar, Gavin. Pop! (Pop: Hit or Miss?). Bromley, Kent:
        Axle Publications, 1963. 12p. (Axle Spokes, 3)
        Christian/moral consideration of British popular music.

386.   Nanry, Charles (ed.). American Music: from Storyville to
        Woodstock. Foreword by Irving Louis Horowitz. New Brunswick,
        New Jersey: Transaction Books, 1972. 290p., bibliog. refs.
        (Culture and Society)
        Collection of conference papers on jazz and rock; seen as
        reflecting changes in American life and society.

387.   Noebel, David A. The Marxist Minstrels: a Handbook on Commun-
        ist Subversion of Music. Tulsa, Oklahoma: American Christian
        College Pr., 1974. 346p., bibliog. refs.
        Contends that popular music is part of a Communist subversion
        attempt, directed from Moscow.

388.   ———. Rhythm, Riots, and Revolution: an Analysis of the
        Communist Use of Music: the Communist Master Music Plan.
        Tulsa, Oklahoma: Christian Crusade Publications, 1966. 352p.,
        bibliog. refs.

389.   Orman, John. The Politics of Rock Music. Chicago: Nelson-Hall,
        1984. 224p., illus.

390.   Savary, Louis M. The Kingdom of Downtown: Finding Teenagers
        in their Music. Ramsey, New Jersey: Paulist/Newman Pr., 1967.
        138p., illus.

391.   ——— (ed.). Popular Song and Youth Today. New York: Assoc-
        iation Pr., 1971. 160p., illus. (Youth World)
        Exploration of the relationship of popular songs to everyday
        life.

392. Stewart, Tony (ed.). Cool Cats: Twenty-Five Years of Rock 'n'
      Roll Style. London: Eel Pie, 1981; New York: Delilah, 1982.
      161p., illus.
          Collection of essays on music, dance, fashion and style.
      Includes pieces by Ian Dury and Paul Weller.

393. Taylor, Rogan P. The Death and Resurrection Show: from Shaman
      to Superstar. London: Blond, 1985. 224p., illus., bibliog.,
      index.
          The evolution of show business from Shamanistic origins.
      Contends that every device employed by entertainers has its
      origin in magical practice; that "showbiz magic is real magic."
      The Christian Church's opposition to popular entertainment has
      been based on this realization.

B. FOLK MUSIC

1. REFERENCE MATERIALS

(a) Bibliographies

394. Clark, Keith (comp.). <u>Folk Song and Dance: a List of Books</u>. London: National Book League/ English Folk Dance and Song Society, 1972. 48p., illus.

395. Denver Folklore Center. <u>The Denver Folklore Center Catalog and Almanac of Folk Music</u>. Edited by Harry M. Tuft. Denver: Denver Folklore Center, 1965.   p., illus., discog.
     Only issue of planned annual. Listings of Black and White folk music materials. Includes listings of early jazz records.

   * Haywood, Charles. <u>Bibliography of North American Folklore and Folksong</u>.
     * Cited above as item 4.

396. Henry, Mellinger Edward. <u>A Bibliography for the Study of American Folksongs, with many Titles of Folk-Songs (and Titles That Have to Do with Folk-Songs) from Other Lands</u>. London: Mitre Pr., 1936. 142p.
     Checklist of approximately three thousand books, articles from periodicals, and parts of books. Includes popular music items. In one alphabetical sequence, by author or title. Superseded by item 4.

   * Lawless, Ray McKinley. <u>Folksingers and Folksongs in America</u>.
     * Cited below as item 1465.

397. Lomax, Alan, and Sidney Robertson. <u>American Folk Song and Folk Lore: a Regional Bibliography</u>. New York: Progressive Education Association, 1942. 59p.
     Lists approximately four hundred items, in thirteen sections. Brief annotations. Includes Black and White Spirituals; also occupational folk music items.

398. Nettl, Bruno. <u>Reference Materials in Ethnomusicology: a Bibliographical Essay</u>. Detroit: Information Service, 1961. 46p. (Studies in Music Bibliography, 1). <u>2nd ed</u>. Detroit: Information Coordinators, 1967. 40p. (Studies in Music Bibliography, 1)
     Describes and evaluates 129 books and periodical articles. Deals with folk music as a branch of ethnomusicology.

399. O'Brien, John. <u>Bibliography, Resource Material, and Background Notes on Folk Song, Music and Dance</u>. New York: New School for Social Research, 1934. 22p.

Bibliographies (cont.)

400. Sandberg, Larry, and Dick Weissman. The Folk Music Sourcebook.
      New York: Knopf, 1976. 260p., discogs., filmogs.
           Lists books, periodical articles, instrumental primers,
      records and films. Also gives addresses of publishers and
      distributors.

                (b) Encyclopedias and Dictionaries

   * Baggelaar, Kristin, and David Milton. Folk Music: More Than
      a Song.
           * Cited below as item 1464.

   * ————. The Folk Music Encyclopaedia.
           * Cited below as item 1464.

   * Lawless, Ray McKinley. Folksingers and Folksongs in America.
           * Cited below as item 1465.

   * Stambler, Irwin, and Grelun Landon. Encyclopedia of Folk,
      Country, and Western Music.
           * Cited below as item 1466.

                    2. ANNUALS AND YEARBOOKS

401. Folk Directory. London: English Folk Dance and Song Society.
      annual, 1966-
           Listings of performers, events, publications, and services.

                  3. GENERAL GUIDES AND OVERVIEWS

402. Bookbinder, David. What Folk Music is All About. Photographs
      by the author. New York: J. Messner, 1979.   p., bibliog.,
      index.

403. Howes, Frank. Folk Music of Britain--and Beyond. London:
      Methuen, 1969. 307p.

404. Jones, Max (ed.). Folk: a Review of People's Music: Part One.
      London: Jazz Music Books, 1945. 32p.
           No further parts issued.

405. Lloyd, Albert Lancaster. The Singing Englishman: an Introduct-
      ion to Folksong. London: Workers' Music Association, 1944.
      70p. (Keynote Series, 4)

406. Lomax, Alan. Folk Song Style and Culture. With contributions
      by the Cantometrics Staff, and with the editorial assistance
      of Edwin E. Erikson. Washington, D.C.: American Association
      for the Advancement of Science, 1968. 363p., illus.

407. Nettl, Bruno. Folk and Traditional Music of the Western
      Continents. Englewood Cliffs, New Jersey; London: Prentice-
      Hall, 1965. 213p., illus., bibliogs., discogs., index.

      ————. ————. With chapters on Latin America by Gérard
      Béhagne. 2nd ed. Englewood Cliffs, New Jersey; London:
      Prentice-Hall, 1973. 258p., illus., bibliogs., discogs., index.

408. ————. An Introduction to Folk Music in the United States.
      Detroit: Wayne State University Pr., 1960. 122p., index.
      Rev. ed.: Detroit: Wayne State University Pr., 1962. 126p.,
      index. 3rd ed.: Folk Music in the United States: an intro-
      duction. Revised and expanded by Helen Myers. Detroit: Wayne
      State University Pr., 1976. 187p., bibliog., index.

409. Williams, Peter. Bluff Your Way in Folk and Jazz. London:
      Wolfe, 1969. 64p. (The Bluffer's Guides)
         Humorous introduction to the key elements.

410. Woods, Fred. The Observer's Book of Folk Song in Britain.
      London: Warne, 1980. 192p., illus., bibliog., index. (The
      Observer's Pocket Series)

                    4. ESSAY COLLECTIONS

411. Dowdey, Landon Gerald (ed.). Journey to Freedom: a Case Book
      With Music. Chicago: Swallow Pr., 1969. 106p., illus., bibliog.
         Anthology of poems, prose extracts, and songs. Grouped
      thematically to illustrate the quest to find freedom from any
      form of tyranny. For reading aloud in groups. Appendix of
      tunes.

                    5. GENERAL HISTORIES

412. Ames, Russell. The Story of American Folk Song. Edited under
      the supervision of Thomas K. Scherman. New York: Grosset and
      Dunlap, 1960. 276p. (The Listener's Music Library)

413. Berger, Melvin. The Story of Folk Music. New York: S.G.
      Phillips, 1976. 127p., illus., bibliog., indexes.
         American folk music.

414. Brand, Oscar. The Ballad Mongers: the Rise of Modern Folk Song.
      New York: Funk and Wagnalls, 1962 (reprinted 1967); Westport,
      Conn.: Greenwood Pr., 1979. 240p., bibliog., index.
         History of the urban folksong movement; by folksong performer.

415. Grafman, Howard, and B.T. Manning. Folk Music, U.S.A. Robert
      Amft, art director. Articles by Pete Seeger, Win Stracke.
      Secaucus, New Jersey: Citadel Pr., 1962. 144p., illus.

416. Harker, David. Fakesong: the Manufacture of British folksong,
      1700 to the Present Day. Milton Keynes, Buckinghamshire: Open
      University Pr., 1985. 224p., illus., index. (British Popular
      Music in the Nineteenth and Twentieth Centuries)
         Study text.

*   Lee, Ed. <u>Folksong and Music Hall</u>.
      * Cited below as item 1009.

417. Lloyd, Albert Lancaster. <u>Folk Song in England</u>. London:
     Lawrence and Wishart in association with the Workers' Music
     Association, 1967. 433p., bibliog., index.; London: Panther
     for the Workers' Music Association, 1969. 445p., bibliog.,
     index.
       The standard history.

418. Munro, Ailie. <u>The Folk Music Revival in Scotland; including
     The Folk Revival in Gaelic Song, by Morag MacLeod</u>. London:
     Kahn and Averill, 1984. 359p., illus., bibliog., index.
       General history, plus the modern revival of interest.

419. Nettel, Reginald. <u>Sing a Song of England: a Social History
     of Traditional Song</u>. London: Phoenix House, 1954. 286p., illus.

420. Van der Horst, Brian. <u>Folk Music in America</u>. New York: Frank-
     lin Watts, 1972. 79p., illus., bibliog. (A First Book)
       History aimed at younger readers.

421. Woods, Fred. <u>The Folk Revival: the Rediscovery of a National
     Music</u>. Poole, Dorset: Blandford Pr., 1979. 133p., illus.,
     index.
       Developments in Britain.

6. SOCIOLOGICAL ASPECTS

422. Denisoff, R. Serge. <u>Great Day Coming: Folk Music and the
     American Left</u>. Urbana, Illinois: University of Illionois Pr.,
     1971. 220p., illus., bibliog., discog., index. (Music in
     American Life)
       Analysis of twentieth-century use of folk music as vehicle
    for political ideology. Traces the development of a political
    fad into a mass-medium commodity.

C. COUNTRY MUSIC

1. REFERENCE MATERIALS

(a) General Works

423. Brown, Toni, and Joe Flint. The D.J.'s Almanac of Country Music. Provo, Utah: Liberty Pr., 1983. 394p.

424. Wootton, Richard. The Illustrated Country Almanac. London: Virgin Books, 1982.   p., illus.

(b) Encyclopedias and Dictionaries

* Brown, Len, and Gary Friedrich. The Encyclopedia of Country and Western Music.
    * Cited below as item 1468.

* Dellar, Fred, and Roy Thompson. The Illustrated Encyclopedia of Country Music.
    * Cited below as item 1472.

* Gentry, Linnell (ed.). A History and Encyclopedia of Country, Western, and Gospel Music.
    * Cited below as item 1476.

* Sakol, Jeannie. The Wonderful World of Country Music.
    * Cited below as item 1490.

* Shestack, Melvin. The Country Music Encyclopedia.
    * Cited below as item 1491.

* Stambler, Irwin, and Grelun Landon. Encyclopedia of Folk, Country, and Western Music.
    * Cited below as item 1466.

2. ANNUALS AND YEARBOOKS

425. Billboard. The World of Country Music. New York, later Los Angeles: Billboard Publications. annual, 1963–
    Emphasis on business aspects.

426. British Country Music Association. Yearbook. Newton Abbot, Devon: British Country Music Association. annual, 1977–

427. The Original Country Music Who's Who. Edited by Thurston Moore. Denver: Cardinal Enterprises, 1960. unpaged, illus.

   The Country Music Who's Who. Edited by Thurston Moore. Denver: Heather Publications, 1964–65. New York: Record World, 1970.
    Emphasis on business aspects. Includes general features.

Annuals and Yearbooks (cont.)

428. <u>Country Music World and Yearbook</u>. Fairfax, Virginia: Country
     Music World and Yearbook, 1964. unpaged, illus.
          Masthead title: <u>The Country Music Yearbook of Artists</u>.
     Only issue.

429. <u>Country Music Booking Guide</u>. Cincinnati: A.B.C. Leisure
     Magazines. Amusement Business Division. annual, 197?-

430. <u>Countrywide Annual Yearbook</u>. Fairfax, Virginia: Country
     Publishing. annual, 1973-

431. "<u>Opry</u>" Yearbook. Chatham, Kent: Country Music Enterprises,
     1969. 60p., illus.
          Only issue.

3. GENERAL GUIDES AND OVERVIEWS

432. Chalker, Bryan. <u>Country Music</u>. With additional material by
     others. London: Phoebus, 1976. 95p., illus.

433. Cornfield, Robert. <u>Just Country: Country People, Stories,
     Music</u>. With Marshall Fallwell, Jr. New York: McGraw-Hill,
     1976. 176p., illus., bibliog., index.

434. Dellar, Fred, and Richard Wootton. <u>The Best of Country Music</u>.
     London: Octopus, 1980. 96p., illus., index.

435. Gaillard, Frye. <u>Watermelon Wine: the Spirit of Country Music</u>.
     New York: St. Martin's Pr., 1977.   p.

436. Mason, Michael (ed.). <u>The Country Music Book</u>. New York:
     Scribner's, 1983. 384p., illus.

437. Randall, Paul. <u>Country Music: Facts, Fallacies, and Folklore,
     Volume 1</u>. College Grove, Tennessee: Union and Confederacy,
     1982. 76p., illus.
          No second volume.

438. Worth, Fred L. <u>The Country and Western Book</u>. New York: Drake,
     1977. 94p., illus.

4. ESSAY COLLECTIONS

439. Edwards, John. <u>The Published Works of the Late John Edwards</u>.
     Kingswinford, Staffordshire: Society for the Preservation and
     Promotion of Traditional Country Music, 1973. 75p., discogs.
          Originally published as special issue of New Zealand's
     <u>Country and Western Spotlight</u>, 1962. Ariticles originally
     written for that journal.

440. Hemphill, Paul. <u>The Nashville Sound: Bright Lights and Country</u>
     <u>Music</u>. New York: Simon and Schuster, 1970. 289p., index.
          Surveys of the Nashville scene; and conversations with per-
     formers and other country music figures.

441. Tosches, Nick. <u>Country: the Biggest Music in America</u>. New
     York: Stein and Day, 1977; London: Plexus, 1983. 257p.,
     illus., bibliog., index.

442. Western Folklore. <u>Commercially Disseminated Folk Music:</u>
     <u>Sources and Resources: a Symposium</u>. (<u>Western Folklore</u>, vol.
     XXX, no. 3: July, 1971.) Reprinted: Los Angeles: John
     Edwards Memorial Foundation, 1971. 75p., bibliog., discog.
          Collection of papers on the work of the John Edwards Mem-
     orial Foundation in research into early country music.

                         5. MISCELLANEA

443. Country Music Association. <u>Behind the Record of the Country</u>
     <u>Music Association</u>. Nashville: Country Music Association, 196?
          p.
          Promotional brochure.

444. Dellar, Fred, and Richard Wootton. <u>The Country Music Book of</u>
     <u>Lists</u>. London: Thames and Hudson, 1984. 175p., illus.

445. Hume, Martha. <u>You're So Cold I'm Turning Blue: Martha Hume's</u>
     <u>Guide to the Greatest in Country Music</u>. New York: Viking Pr.;
     London: Penguin, 1982. 202p., illus., bibliog.
          Listings and features.

446. Humphreys, Don, and Barbara Humphreys. <u>The Country Music</u>
     <u>Quiz Book</u>. Garden City, New York: Doubleday, 1978.   p.
     (Dolphin Books)

                     6. GENERAL HISTORIES

                  (a) Comprehensive Works

447. Carr, Patrick (ed.). <u>The Illustrated History of Country Music</u>.
     By the Editors of <u>Country Music</u> Magazine. Garden City, New
     York: Doubleday, 1979. 359p., illus.

  * Gentry, Linnell (ed.). <u>A History and Encyclopedia of Country,</u>
     <u>Western, and Gospel Music</u>.
          * Cited below as item 1476.

448. Green, Douglas B. <u>Country Roots: the Origins of Country Music</u>.
     Foreword by Merle Travis. New York: Hawthorn Books, 1976.
     238p., illus., discog., index.
          Includes chronology in appendix. Author is Oral Historian,
     Country Music Hall of Fame, Nashville.

Comprehensive Works (cont.)

449. Grissim, John. <u>Country Music: White Man's Blues.</u> New York:
     Paperback Library, 1970. 299p., illus.

450. Malone, Bill C. <u>Country Music U.S.A.: a Fifty-Year History.</u>
     Austin, London: University of Texas Pr. for the American
     Folklore Society, 1968. 422p., illus., bibliog., discog.
        The standard history. Based on the author's PhD. dissert-
     ation <u>A History of Commercial Country Music in the United
     States,</u> 1920-1964, University of Texas, 1965.

451. <u>Pictorial History of Country Music.</u> Denver: Heather Enter-
     prises, 1969-70. 3 vols.,   p., illus.
        Material originally published in item 427.

452. Pouliot, Les. <u>John Thayer and Don Bruce Together Present The
     History of Country Music: a 36-Hour Radio Documentary.</u> Written
     by Les Pouliot, assisted by Hugh Cherry. Produced by Don Bruce.
     Memphis: J. Thayer and D. Bruce Together, 1970. 915p.
        Scripts.

453. Price, Steven D. <u>Take Me Home: the Rise of Country and West-
     ern Music.</u> New York: Praeger, 1974. 184p., illus., bibliog.,
     discog., index.
        Includes appendix of brief biographical sketches of leading
     performers.

454. Shelton, Robert. <u>The Country Music Story: a Picture History
     of Country and Western Music.</u> Photographs by Burt Goldblatt.
     Indianapolis: Bobbs-Merrill, 1966; New Rochelle, New York:
     Arlington House, 1971. 256p., illus., discog., index.

455. Stambler, Irwin, and Grelun Landon. <u>Golden Guitars: the Story</u>
     of Country Music. New York: Four Winds Pr., 1971. 186p.,
     illus., bibliog. refs.

456. Walthall, "Daddy" Bob. <u>The History of Country Music.</u> Houston:
     Walthall Publishing Company, 1978. unpaged, illus.

457. Wilson, D.K. <u>Country-Western Music and the Urban Hillbilly.</u>
     Los Angeles: John Edwards Memorial Foundation, 1970. 22p.,
     bibliog., discog. notes. (J.E.M.F. Reprint, no. 16)
        Reprinted from the <u>Journal of American Folklore</u>, April/June,
     1970. Traces country music development from rural folk tradit-
     ion to commercial big business.

458. Wolfe, Charles K. <u>Tennessee Strings: the Story of Country Music
     in Tennessee.</u> Knoxville, Tennessee: University of Tennessee Pr.
     1977. 118p., illus., bibliog., index.

(b) Periods and Styles

(1) Bluegrass

459. Artis, Bob. Bluegrass: From the Lonesome Wail of a Mountain
Love Song to the Hammering Drive of the Scruggs-Style Banjo:
the Story of an American Musical Tradition. New York: Hawthorn
Books, 1975. 182p., illus., bibliog., discog., index.

460. Beckman, Tom. The Bluegrass Companion. Edited by Jean Donohue.
Cincinnati: T. Beckman and Associates, 1982. 126p., illus.

461. Cantwell, Robert. Bluegrass Breakdown: the Making of the Old
Southern Sound. Urbana, Illinois: University of Illinois Pr.,
1984.   p., illus., bibliog., discog., index. (Music in
American Life)

462. Hill, Fred. Grassroots: an Illustrated History of Bluegrass
and Mountain Music. Rutland, Vermont: Academy Books, 1980.
132p., illus.

463. Marshall, Howard Wright. "Keep on the Sunny Side of Life:"
Pattern and Religious Expression in Bluegrass Gospel Music.
Los Angeles: John Edwards Memorial Foundation, 1974. 43p.,
bibliog. notes. (J.E.M.F. Reprint, no. 31)
      Reprinted from the New York Folklore Quarterly, March 1974.
Includes select concordance of Biblical references.

464. Price, Steven D. Old as the Hills: the Story of Bluegrass
Music. New York: Viking Pr., 1975. 110p., illus., discog.

465. Rosenberg, Neil V. From Sound to Style: the Emergence of
Bluegrass. Los Angeles: John Edwards Memorial Foundation,
1967. 8p., bibliog. notes. (J.E.M.F. Reprint, no 11)
      Reprinted from the Journal of American Folklore, vol. 80,
no. 316. Sees Bluegrass as a distinct type of commercial music.

(2) Cowboy

466. Allen, Jules Verne. Cowboy Lore. San Antonio, Texas: Naylor,
1933 (reprinted 1950 and 1971). 165p., illus.
      By early performer in the field. Background information on
cowboy culture; plus complete texts of thirty-seven songs sung
by the author during his musical career.

467. Wright, Zelma H. The Big Bend Country: Song Voices of the
Southwest. Beaumont, Texas: The Author, 1975. 32p., illus.

(3) Modern

468. Corbin, Everett J. Storm Over Nashville: a Case Against
      "Modern" Country Music. Nashville: Ashlar Pr., 1980. 202p.

  *   Reid, Jan. The Improbable Rise of Redneck Rock.
        * Cited above as item 310.

7. VENUES

(a) Festivals

469. Ahrens, Pat J. Union Grove: the First Fifty Years. Columbia,
      South Carolina: The Author, 1975. 243p., illus., bibliog.
        History of the Old Time Fiddlers' Convention, held at Union
      Grove, North Carolina.

(b) Grand Ole Opry

470. Hay, George D. A Story of The Grand Ole Opry. Nashville:
      The Author, 1953. 62p., illus.
        History of the radio program by its founder.

471. Hurst, Jack. Nashville's Grand Ole Opry. New York: Abrams,
      1975. 404p., illus., index.

472. McDaniel, William R., and Harold Seligman. The Grand Ole Opry.
      New York: Greenberg, 1952. 69p., illus.

473. Tassin, Myron. Fifty Years at The Grand Ole Opry. Gretna,
      Louisiana: Pelican Publishing, 1975. 112p., illus.

474. Wolfe, Charles K. The Grand Ole Opry: the Early Years, 1925-35.
      London: Old Time Music, 1975. 128p., illus., bibliog., discogs.
      (Old Time Music Booklets, 2)
        Includes facsimile reproductions of contemporary newspaper
      reports.

(c) Louisiana Hayride

475. KWKH. KWKH's Louisiana Hayride. Shreveport, Louisiana: Radio
      Station KWKH, 195?   p., illus.
        Souvenir booklet detailing the history of the program.

8. SOCIOLOGICAL ASPECTS

476. Davis, Paul. New Life in Country Music. Foreword by Cliff
      Richard; introduction by George Hamilton IV. Illustrated by
      Richard Deverell. Worthing, West Sussex: Walker, 1976. 111p.,
      illus.
        American country singers who have become born-again
      Christians are examined.

D. CAJUN MUSIC

477. Ancelot, Barry J. The Makers of Cajun Music: Musiciens Adiens et Réoles. Austin; London: University of Texas Pr., 1984. 160p., illus.

478. Daigle, Pierre V. Tears, Love, and Laughter: the Story of the Acadians. Church Point, Louisiana: Acadian Publishing Enterprise, 1972. 135p., illus.
    Background information; plus profiles of Cajun performers. Includes tunes and texts of six traditional Cajun songs.

479. Leadbitter, Mike. French Cajun Music. Bexhill-on-Sea, Essex: Blues Unlimited, 1968. 15p., illus. (Collectors' Classics, 12)
    Brief history. Includes record company information; also listing of records available at time of writing.

E. BLACK MUSIC

1. GENERAL WORKS

(1) REFERENCE MATERIALS

(a) Bibliographies

480. The Black List: the Concise Reference Guide to Publications,
and Broadcasting Media of Black America, Africa, and the
Caribbean. New York: Panther House, 1970. 289p.

481. Borneman, Ernest. American Negro Music. London: The Author,
1940. 215p.

482. Brignano, Russell C. Black Americans in Autobiography: an
Annotated Bibliography of Autobiographies and Autobiographical
Books Written Since the Civil War. Durham, North Carolina:
Duke University Pr., 1974. 118p., indexes.
     Lists many items on music and dance. Appendix of pre-1865
items recently reprinted. Annotations give brief biographical
information, and United States library locations.

483. Colvig, Richard (comp.). Black Music: a Checklist of Books.
Oakland, California: Oakland Public Library, 1969. 20p.

484. De Lerma, Dominique-René. Bibliography of Black Music.
Westport, Conn.: Greenwood Pr., 1981- . (The Greenwood
Encyclopedia of Black Music)
vol. 1: Reference Materials. 1981. 124p.
vol. 2: Afro-American Idioms. 1981. 220p.
vol. 3: Geographical Studies. 1982. 284p.
vol. 4: Theory, Education, and Related Studies. 1984. 254p.

485. ———. The Black-American Musical Heritage: a Preliminary
and Selective Bibliography. Kent, Ohio: Kent State University,
School of Library Science for the Midwest Chapter of the Music
Library Association, 1969. 45p. (Explorations in Music
Librarianship, 3)
     Lists seven hundred items. Supersede by item 484.

486. ———, David Baker, and Austin B. Caswell. Black Music Now:
a Source Book on Twentieth Century Black-American Music.
Kent, Ohio: Kent State University Pr., 1974.   p.
     Superseded by item 484.

487. De Lerma, Dominique-René. The Negro and Music: a Bibliography
and Discography. Bloomington, Indiana: The Author, 1968. 49p.
     Bibliographical contents superseded by item 484.

Bibliographies (cont)

488. Howard University. Library. <u>Dictionary Catalog of the</u>
     <u>Arthur B. Spingarn Collection of Negro Authors</u>. Boston:
     G.K. Hall, 1970. 2 vols.,   p.
         The Collection holds a large amount of concert and popular
     music written by Black composers; also literature on Black
     music.

489. Johnson, James P. <u>Bibliographical Guide to the Study of</u>
     <u>Afro-American Music</u>. Washington, D.C.: Howard University
     Library, 1973. 24p. (Consciousness, 4. Bibliographical Series,
     1, 1)

490. Lawrenz, Marguerite Martha. <u>Bibliography and Index of Negro</u>
     <u>Music</u>. Detroit: Board of Education of the City of Detroit,
     1968. 52p.
         For educators.

491. McCabe, Jane A. <u>Black Entertainers and the Entertainment</u>
     <u>Industry; and, Black American Athletes, Compiled by Robert S.</u>
     <u>Wood and Wilmer H. Baatz</u>. Bloomington, Indiana: Indiana
     University Libraries, 1969. 23p. (Black American Bibliography)

492. New York Public Library. Schomburg Collection of Negro Lit-
     erature and History. <u>Dictionary Catalog</u>. Boston: G.K. Hall,
     1962. 9 vols.,   p. <u>First Supplement</u>. Boston: G.K. Hall,
     1967.   p. <u>Second Supplement</u>. Boston: G.K. Hall, 1972.   p.
         The Collection includes music, and musical literature.

493. Porter, Dorothy B. <u>The Negro in the United States: a Selected</u>
     <u>Bibliography</u>. Washington, D.C.: Library of Congress, 1970.
     313p.
         Arranged by topics. Includes musical items.

494. San Diego State College. Library. <u>Afro-American Bibliography</u>:
     <u>a List of the Books, Documents, and Periodicals on Black-Amer-</u>
     <u>ican Culture Located in San Diego State College Library</u>. Com-
     piled by Andrew Szabo. San Diego: San Diego State College
     Library, 1970.   p.

495. Skowronski, JoAnn. <u>Black Music in America: a Bibliography</u>.
     Metuchen, New Jersey; London: Scarecrow Pr., 1981. 723p., index.
         Coverage to 1969.

496. Standifer, James A., and Barbara Reeder. <u>Source Book of</u>
     <u>African and Afro-American Materials for Music Educators</u>.
     Washington, D.C.: Contemporary Music Project, Music Educators
     National Conference, 1972. 147p., bibliogs., discogs.
         Includes books, periodicals, dissertations, and records.

497. University of Utah. Marriott Library. <u>Black Bibliography</u>.
     Salt Lake City: University of Utah, 1974. 825p., index.
     (Bibliographic Series, vol. 2)
         Confined to the holdings of the Marriott Library, post-1954.

498. Williams, Ora. <u>American Black Women in the Arts and Social
     Sciences: a Bibliographical Survey.</u> Metuchen, New Jersey;
     London: Scarecrow Pr., 1973. 141p., illus., discog.
          Confined to material "edited or created by American Black
     women" (introduction); coverage consequently incomplete.

499. Work, Monroe Nathan. <u>A Bibliography of the Negro in Africa
     and America.</u> New York: H.W. Wilson, 1928. Reprinted: New
     York: Argosy-Antiquarian Limited, 1965. 698p., index.
          Includes many musical items. Some annotations.

                    (b) Encyclopedias and Dictionaries

  * <u>Illustrated Encyclopedia of Black Music.</u>
          * Cited below as item 1501.

                    (2) GENERAL SURVEYS AND OVERVIEWS

500. Dennison, Tim. <u>The American Negro and His Amazing Music.</u>
     New York: Vantage Pr., 1963. 76p.

501. Goines, Leonard, and Ellsworth Janifer. <u>The Black Musical
     Experience.</u> New York: Harper and Row, 1974.   p.

502. Handy, D. Antoinette. <u>Black Music.</u> Ettrick, Virginia: B.M.
     and M., 1974.   p.

                              (3) CRITICISM

503. Roberts, John Storm. <u>Black Music of Two Worlds.</u> New York:
     Praeger, 1972; London: Allen Lane, 1973; New York: Morrow,
     1974. 286p., illus., bibliog., discog., index.
          Examination of the relationship between Black musical forms
     in Africa and the Americas; and the distinctive regional blends
     produced by the interchange.

504. Sidran, Ben. <u>Black Talk: How the Music of Black America
     Created a Radical Alternative to the Values of Western Literary
     Tradition.</u> New York: Holt, Rinehart and Winston, 1971. 201p.

                         (4) ESSAY COLLECTIONS

505. Chametzky, Jules, and Sidney Kaplan (eds.). <u>Black and White
     in American Culture: an Anthology from "The Massachusetts
     Review."</u> Amherst: University of Massachusetts Pr., 1969.
     478p., illus.
          Includes essays on spirituals, early jazz, and the blues.
     Material originally published 1959-69.

506. Cunard, Nancy (ed.). Negro Anthology, Made by Nancy Cunard,
      1931-1933. London: Nancy Cunard at Wishart and Company, 1934.
      Reprinted: Westport, Conn.: Negro Universities Pr., 1969.
      854p., illus.

      Negro: an Anthology. Edited and abridged. With an Introduct-
      ion by Hugh Ford. New York: Ungar, 1970; London: Quartet,
      1981. 464p., illus.
      Collection on the theme of improvement of Blacks as a race.
      Music section covers jazz, dance, theater, motion pictures,
      and Black music in the Americas and Africa. Abridged edition
      contains 100 pieces; full edition has 250.

507. De Lerma, Dominique-René(ed.). Black Music in our Culture:
      Curricular Ideas on the Subjects, Materials, and Problems.
      Kent, Ohio: Kent State University Pr., 1970. 263p., bibliogs.,
      discogs., index.
      Material from seminar Black Music in College and University
      Curricula (Indiana University, 18-21 June, 1969.) Papers
      concerned with the development of formal Black Music studies.

508. ———. Reflections on Afro-American Music. Kent, Ohio: Kent
      State University Pr., 1973. 271p., bibliog., index.
      Proceedings of the Second and Third Seminars held by The
      Black Music Center, 1971 and 1972. Papers on Black Art and
      vernacular music.

509. Dundes, Alan (ed.). Mother Wit From the Laughing Barrel:
      Readings in the Interpretation of Afro-American Folklore.
      Englewood Cliffs, New Jersey; London: Prentice-Hall, 1973. 673p.
      Includes articles on jazz and blues.

510. Jackson, Bruce (ed.). The Negro and His Folk-Lore in
      Nineteenth Century Periodicals. Austin:University Pr., 1967.
      374p., bibliog., indexes.
      Includes musical items. Chronological arrangement, 1838-
      1900.

511. Katz, Bernard (ed.). The Social Implications of Early Negro
      Music in the United States. With Over 150 of the Songs, Many
      of Them With Their Music. New York: Arno Pr., 1969. 146p.,
      illus., bibliog., index.
      Reprinted articles.

512. Locke, Alain LeRoy (ed.). The New Negro: an Interpretation.
      Book decoration and portraits by Winold Reiss. New York: A.
      and C. Boni, 1925. Reprinted: New York: Arno Pr./New York
      Times, 1968 (The American Negro: His History and Literature)
      452p., illus., bibliog.
      Includes pieces on musical topics.

513. Patterson, Lindsay (ed.). The Negro in Music and Art. New
      York: Publishers Company, 1967. 2nd ed.: New York: Publishers
      Company, 1969. 304p., illus., bibliog., index. (International
      Library of Negro Life and History, 3)
      Anthology of book excerpts and periodical articles. Many
      musical items.

514. Southern, Eileen (ed.). Readings in Black American Music.
      New York: Norton, 1971. 302p., index.
          Documents Black music history, 1623-1969. Accompanies
      item 525.

                    (5) GENERAL HISTORIES

515. Brooks, Tilford. America's Black Musical Heritage. Engle-
      wood Cliffs, New Jersey; London: Prentice-Hall, 1984. 336p.,
      illus., bibliog., discog., index.

516. Clark, Francis A. The Black Music Master: a Fascinating, but
      Truthful Setting Forth of Facts, Giving Indisputable Evidence
      That the Primitive Black Peoples Were the First Natural
      Musicians! Who, in Unconscious Obedience to Great Natural
      Laws Within Them, Did Crudely and Awkwardly, but None the
      Less Certainly, Give to the World the Earliest Practical
      Demonstration of Making Music! Philadelphia: The Author,
      1923. 32p., illus.

517. Cuney-Hare, Maud. Negro Musicians and Their Music.
      Washington, D.C.: Associated Publishers, 1936 (Reprinted:
      New York: Da Capo Pr., 1974). 439p., illus., bibliog., index.
          Black music in Africa and the United States. Includes
      biographies of contemporary "Torch Bearers."

518. Hughes, Langston, and Milton Meltzer. Black Magic: a Pictorial
      History of the Negro in American Entertainment. Englewood
      Cliffs, New Jersey; London: Prentice-Hall, 1967. 375p.,
      illus., index.

519. Isaacs, Edith J.R. The Negro in the American Theater. New
      York: Theatre Arts, 1947 (Reprinted: College Park, Maryland:
      McGrath, 1968). 143p., illus.
          Stress on spoken drama, but includes coverage of music
      and dance.

  *   Jackson, Bruce (ed.). The Negro and His Folk-Lore in
      Nineteenth Century Periodicals.
          * Cited above as item 510.

  *   Kebede, Ashenafi. The Roots of Black Music: the Vocal,
      Instrumental, and Dance Heritage of Africa and Black America.
          * Cited below as item 618.

520. Locke, Alain LeRoy. The Negro and His Music. Washington,
      D.C.: The Associates in Negro Folk Education, 1936. (Bronze
      Booklets, 2). Reprinted: Port Washington, New York: Kennikat
      Pr., 1968. 142p., bibliogs. Reprinted (as The Negro and His
      Music; and, Negro Art: Past and Present): New York: Arno Pr.,
      1969. 142p.; 122p., bibliogs. (The American Negro: His
      History and Literature, 2)

521. Nelson, Rose K., and Dorothy L. Cole. <u>The Negro's Contribut-
      ion to Music in America</u>. New York: Service Bureau for Inter-
      cultural Education, 1941. 23p.
          For use in schools.

522. Reagon, Bernice. <u>A History of the Afro-American Through His
      Songs</u>. New York: New York Educational Department, Albany.
      Division of Humanities and Arts, 1969.   p.
          Accompanied by audio tape. For school use.

523. Roach, Hildred. <u>Black American Music: Past and Present</u>.
      Boston: Crescendo, 1973. <u>Rev. ed.</u>: Boston: Crescendo, 1976.
      199p., illus., bibliog., discog., index.

524. Rublowsky, John. <u>Black Music in America</u>. New York: Basic
      Books, 1971. 150p., illus., bibliog., index (Culture and
      Discovery)
          Aimed at schools.

525. Southern, Eileen. <u>The Music of Black Americans: a History</u>.
      New York: Norton, 1971. 552p., illus., bibliog., index.
      <u>2nd ed.</u>: New York; London: Norton, 1983. 602p., illus.,
      bibliog., index.
          Accompanied by item 514.

526. Tallmadge, William H. <u>Afro-American Music</u>. Washington, D.C.:
      Music Educators National Conference, 1957. <u>Rev. ed.</u>: Buffalo,
      New York: College Bookstore, State University College, 1969.
      16p., bibliog.

527. Trotter, James M. <u>Music and Some Highly Musical People:
      Containing Brief Chapters on, I: a Description of Music;
      II, the Music of Nature; III, a Glance at the History of Music;
      IV, the Power, Beauty, and Uses of Music. Following Which Are
      Given Sketches of the Lives of Remarkable Musicians of the
      Colored Race. With Portraits, and an Appendix Containing
      Copies of Music Composed by Colored Men</u>. Boston: Lee and
      Shepherd; New York: C.T. Dillingham, 1878. Reprinted: New
      York: Johnson, 1968; Chicago: Afro-American Pr., 1969. 505p.,
      illus.
          The first serious history.

                         (6) SOCIOLOGICAL ASPECTS

   * Katz, Bernard (ed.). <u>The Social Implications of Early Negro
      Music in the United States</u>.
          * Cited above as item 511.

528. Walton, Ortiz. <u>Music: Black, White, and Blue: a Sociological
      Survey of the Use and Misuse of Afro-American Music</u>. New
      York: Morrow, 1972 (Reprinted 1980). 180p., bibliog. refs.,
      index.
          Polemical view of the cultural exploitation of Black
      musicians working in a business dominated by other cultures.

2. SACRED MUSIC

(1) REFERENCE MATERIALS

(a) General Works

529. Billboard. <u>The World of Religious Music</u>. New York: Billboard
Publications. annual, 1967- .
Emphasis on business aspects.

530. <u>Gospel Music</u>. Nashville: Gospel Music Association. annual,
197?- .
Trade contact directory.

531. <u>Gospel Music Booking Guide</u>. Cincinnati: A.B.C. Leisure
Magazines, Amusement Business Division. annual, 197?- .

(b) Bibliographies

* Hefele, Bernhard. <u>Jazz-Bibliography</u>.
  * Cited below as item 631.

532. Jackson, Irene V. <u>Afro-American Religious Music: a Bibliog-
raphy and a Catalogue of Gospel Music</u>. Westport, Conn.:
Greenwood Pr., 1979. 211p., illus., indexes.
No annotations.

(c) Encyclopedias and Dictionaries

* Gentry, Linnell (ed.). <u>A History and Encyclopedia of Country,
Western, and Gospel Music</u>.
  * Cited below as item 1476.

(2) CRITICISM

* Ricks, George Robinson. <u>Some Aspects of the Religious Music
of the United States Negro: an Ethnomusicological Study With
Special Emphasis on the Gospel Tradition</u>.
  * Cited below as item 4210.

(3) GENERAL HISTORIES

533. Blackwell, Lois S. <u>The Wings of the Dove: the Story of Gospel
Music in America</u>. Introduction by Brock Speer. Norfolk,
Virginia: Donning, 1978.   p., bibliog., index.

534. Broughton, Viv. <u>Black Gospel: an Illustrated History of the
Gospel Sound</u>. Poole, Dorset: Blandford Pr., 1985. 160p.,
illus., index.

535. Ferlita, Ernest. _Gospel Journey_. Minneapolis: Winston Pr.,
      1983. 128p., illus.

  *   Gentry, Linnell (ed.). _A History and Encyclopedia of Country,_
      Western, and Gospel Music.
          * Cited below as item 1476.

536. Heilbut, Tony. _The Gospel Sound: Good News and Bad Times._
      New York: Simon and Schuster, 1971. 350p., illus., discog.,
      index; Garden City, New York: Anchor Pr., 1975. 364p., illus.,
      discog., index.
          Critical history based on interviews with performers.

537. Walker, Wyatt T. _Somebody's Calling My Name_. Valley Forge,
      Pennsylvania: Judson Pr., 1979.   p., bibliog. refs., index.

538. Warrick, Mancel, Joan R. Hillsman, and Anthony Manno. _The_
      Progress of Gospel Music: from Spirituals to Contemporary
      Gospel. New York: Vantage Pr., 1977. 99p., illus., bibliog.,
      indexes.

                  (4) SOCIOLOGICAL ASPECTS

539. Riedel, Johannes. _Soul Music Black and White: the Influence_
      of Black Music on the Churches. Minneapolis: Augsburg, 1975.
      159p., bibliog., discog.
          Analysis of "soul" elements shared by all forms of Black
      music; its influence on Black and White church music, and on
      popular music generally.

                        3. RAGTIME

                  (1) REFERENCE MATERIALS

  *   Hefele, Bernhard. _Jazz-Bibliography_.
          * Cited below as item 631.

                  (2) GENERAL SURVEYS AND OVERVIEWS

540. Farmer, Paul. _Ragtime and Blues_. London: Longman, 1979.
      24p., illus. (Longman Music Topics)
          For school use.

541. Morath, Max. _A Guide to Ragtime_. New York: Hollis Music,
      1963. 128p.

542. Waldo, Terry. _This is Ragtime_. Foreword by Eubie Blake.
      New York: Hawthorn Books, 1976. 244p., illus., discog., index.

(3) CRITICISM

543. Schafer, William J., and Johannes Riedel. The Art of Ragtime:
     Form and Meaning of an Original Black American Art. With
     assistance from Michael Polad and Richard Thompson. Baton
     Rouge: Louisiana State University Pr., 1973; New York: Da
     Capo Pr., 1977. 249p., illus., bibliog., index.
     Includes transcriptions of original rags.

(4) GENERAL HISTORIES

544. Berlin, Edward A. Ragtime: a Musical and Cultural History.
     Berkeley; New York; London: University of California Pr.,
     1980. 248p., illus., bibliog., index.
     Includes Location Index for Piano Rags in Selected Anthol-
     ogies.

545. Blesh, Rudi, and Harriet Janis. They All Played Ragtime: the
     True Story of an American Music. New York: Knopf, 1950;
     London: Sidgwick and Jackson, 1958. 338p., illus., bibliog.,
     discog., index. Rev. ed.: New York: Grove Pr., 1959. 345p.,
     illus., bibliog., discog., index. Revised and With New Addit-
     ional Material, Including Scores to Thirteen Never Before
     Published Ragtime Compositions: New York: Oak Publications,
     1966. 347p., illus., bibliog., discog., index. 4th ed.:
     New York: Oak Publications; London: Music Sales, 1971. 347p.,
     illus., bibliog., discog., index.
     The standard history. Includes listings of cylinder
     records and player piano rolls.

546. Jasen, David A., and Trebor Jay Tichenor. Rags and Ragtime:
     a Musical History. New York: Seabury Pr., 1978.   p., index.
     (A Continuum Book)
     Includes structural analyses of compositions; and listing
     of three thousand rags.

4. BLUES

(1) REFERENCE MATERIALS

(a) General Works

547. Blues Friends Worldwide. Address Listing. Gouda, Holland:
     Blues Friends Worldwide, 1972. 23p.

548. German Blues Circle. German Blues Guide. Frankfurt/Main,
     West Germany: German Blues Circle, 1976. 20p. 2nd ed.: 1977.
     104p. 3rd ed.: 1979/80. 107p.

Reference Materials (cont.)

(b) Bibliographies and Indexes

* Hefele, Bernhard. <u>Jazz-Bibliography</u>.
  * Cited below as item 631.

549. Hickerson, Joe. <u>A Bibliography of the Blues</u>. Washington, D.C.:
     Library of Congress, Archive of Folk Song, n.d. 16p.

* Steenson, Martin. <u>Blues Unlimited, 1-50: an Index</u>.
  * Cited below as item 4791.

(2) GENERAL GUIDES AND OVERVIEWS

550. Blues Project. <u>The Sound: the Blues Project</u>. Photography by
     Gerald Jacobson. New York: McGraw-Hill, 1968. 160p., illus.
     (A Young Pioneer Book)
     Accompanies Elektra record, <u>The Blues Project</u>.

551. Cook, Bruce. <u>Listen to the Blues</u>. New York: Scribner's, 1973;
     London: Robson Books, 1975. 263p., illus., index.

552. Leiser, Willie. <u>I'm a Road Runner, Baby</u>. Bexhill-on-Sea,
     Essex: Blues Unlimited, 1969. 38p., illus.
     Account of Swiss blues fan's tour of the United States in
     search of blues artists.

(3) CRITICISM

(a) General Works

553. Evans, David. <u>Big Road Blues: Tradition and Creativity in the
     Folk Blues</u>. Berkeley; New York; London: University of Californ-
     ia Pr., 1981. 379p., illus., bibliog., index.

554. Garon, Paul. <u>Blues and the Poetic Spirit</u>. Edited by Tony Russ-
     ell. Preface by Franklin Rosemont. London: Eddison Pr., 1975;
     New York: Da Capo Pr., 1978. (Roots of Jazz). 178p., illus.,
     bibliog., index.

555. Lehmann, Theo. <u>Blues and Trouble</u>. Foreword by Martin Luther
     King, <u>Jr</u>. Berlin: Henschel Verlag, 1966. 190p., illus., discog.
     In German. Includes appendix of blues lyrics in English.

556. Murray, Albert. <u>Stomping the Blues</u>. New York: McGraw-Hill,
     1976; London: Quartet, 1978. 264p., illus., index.
     Urban, professional, dance-based blues forms. Argues that
     urban blues is not a folk culture, but a self-conscious form
     of fine art, chosen by its practitioners, and studied.

557. Oliver, Paul. <u>Screening the Blues: Aspects of the Blues
Tradition</u>. London: Cassell, 1968; New York: Oak Publications
(as <u>Aspects of the Blues Tradition</u>), 1970. 294p., bibliog.,
index.
      Survey of the effects of recording on the nature of the
blues, its themes, and its development.

558. ————. <u>Songsters and Saints: Vocal Traditions on Race Records</u>.
London: Cambridge University Pr., 1984. 336p., illus., discog.,
index.
      Accompanied by record, same title, Matchbox Bluesmaster
Series, MSEX 2001/2002.

559. Roxin, Charles. <u>Aspects of the Blues</u>. Fairport, New York:
Space Age Printers, 1973. 16p.

                    (b) Blues and Other Art Forms

560. Baker, Houston A., <u>Jr</u>. <u>Blues, Ideology, and Afro-American
Literature: a Vernacular Theory</u>. Chicago; London: University
of Chicago Pr., 1984. 288p., illus.

 *   Bane, Michael. <u>White Boy Singin' the Blues: the Black Roots
of White Rock</u>.
         * Cited above as item 85.

 *   Cone, James H. <u>The Spirituals and the Blues: an Interpretation</u>.
         * Cited below as item 4200.

561. Ellison, Mary. <u>Extensions of the Blues</u>. London: John Calder,
1981.   p.
      Effects of blues on jazz, pop, poetry, dance, drama, motion
pictures, and other American art forms.

 *   Farmer, Paul. <u>Ragtime and Blues</u>.
         * Cited above as item 540.

 *   Middleton, Richard. <u>Pop Music and the Blues: a Study of the
Relationship and its Significance</u>.
         * Cited above as item 88.

562. Russell, Tony. <u>Blacks, Whites, and Blues</u>. London: Studio Vista;
New York: Stein and Day, 1970. 112p., illus., bibliog., discog.,
index. (Blues Series)
      Interaction of Black and White music, and different approach-
es to a common repertoire.

 *   Vulliamy, Graham. <u>Jazz and Blues</u>.
         * Cited below as item 730.

(4) ESSAY COLLECTIONS

563. Leadbitter, Mike (ed.). <u>Nothing But the Blues</u>. London:
      Hanover Books, 1971. 261p., illus.
          Articles reprinted from the first fifty issues of <u>Blues
      Unlimited</u>.

564. Oliver, Paul. <u>Blues Off the Record: Thirty Years of Blues
      Commentary</u>. London: Baton Pr., 1984. 296p., illus.
          Reprints of his articles and sleeve notes.

(5) GENERAL HISTORIES

(a) Comprehensive Works

565. Charters, Samuel Barclay. <u>The Roots of the Blues: an African
      Search</u>. London: Marion Boyars, 1981; New York: Putnam's, 1982.
      151p., illus.
          Author's travels in West Africa in search of blues sources.

566. Feather, Leonard Geoffrey. <u>A History of the Blues</u>. New York:
      Hansen, 1972. 200p., illus.

567. Groom, Bob. <u>The Blues Revival</u>. London: Studio Vista; New
      York: Stein and Day, 1971; Hatboro, Pennsylvania: Legacy
      Books, 1983. (The Paul Oliver Blues Series). 112p., illus.,
      bibliog., discog.
          Growth of White interest in blues, particularly in the 1960s.

568. Lang, Iain. <u>The Background of the Blues</u>. London: Workers'
      Music Association, 1943. 55p., discog. (Keynote Series, 2)
          Based on an article first published in <u>The Saturday Book</u>,
      1941. Superseded by item 569.

569. ————. <u>Jazz in Perspective: the Background of the Blues</u>.
      London; New York: Hutchinson, 1947; New York: Da Capo Pr., 1976.
      (Roots of Jazz). 148p., illus., discog., index.
          Expansion of item 568.

570. Oakley, Giles. <u>The Devil's Music: a History of the Blues</u>.
      London: British Broadcasting Corporation, 1976; New York:
      Taplinger, 1977; New York: Harcourt, Brace, Jovanovich, 1978.
      (A Harvest/H.B.J. Book). 287p., illus., bibliog., index.
      <u>Rev. ed.</u>: London: British Broadcasting Corporation, 1983. 287p.,
      illus., bibliog., discog., index.
          Based on British television series. Accompanied by double
      LP record of material especially recorded for the program (Red
      Lightnin', 1981.)

571. Oliver, Paul. <u>The Story of the Blues</u>. London: Cassell, 1968;
      London: Barrie and Rockliff; Philadelphia: Chilton; Harmonds-
      worth, Middlesex: Penguin, 1969 (reprinted 1972). 176p., illus.,
      bibliog., discog., index.

572. Palmer, Robert. _Deep Blues_. New York: Viking Pr., 1981;
      London: Macmillan London, 1982. 310p., illus., bibliog., index.

573. Pearson, Barry Lee. _Sounds So Good to Me: the Bluesman's Story_.
      Philadelphia: University of Pennsylvania Pr., 1984. 208p.

                    (b) Periods and Styles

                    (1) Country Blues

574. Charters, Samuel Barclay. _The Country Blues_. New York: Rine-
      hart, 1959; Reprinted: New York: Da Capo Pr., 1975. (Roots of
      Jazz). 288p., illus. London: Michael Joseph, 1961. 203p.,
      illus.
          Da Capo Pr. edition has new introduction by the author;
      Michael Joseph edition has extra appendix.

575. Oster, Harry. _Living Country Blues_. Hatboro, Pennsylvania:
      Folklore Associates; Detroit: Gale, 1969; New York: Minerva Pr.,
      1975. 464p., illus., bibliog., discog., index.
          Includes words of 230 songs, recorded in Louisiana, 1955-61.

576. Titon, Jeff T. _Early Downhome Blues: a Musical and Cultural
      Analysis_. Urbana: University of Illinois Pr., 1977. 296p.,
      illus., bibliog., index. (Music in American Life)
          Includes record in pocket.

                            Memphis

577. _Beale Street, U.S.A.: Where the Blues Began_. Bexhill-on-Sea,
      Essex: Blues Unlimited, 1969; Hatboro, Pennsylvania: Legacy
      Books, 1983. (The Paul Oliver Blues Series). 12p., illus.,
      bibliog.
          Originally issued by the City of Memphis Housing Authority.
      Describes Beale Street at the turn of the Century.

578. Lee, George W. _Beale Street: Where the Blues Began_. Foreword
      by W.C. Handy. New York: R.O. Ballou, 1934; College Park,
      Maryland: McGrath, 1965. 296p., illus.

579. Olsson, Bengt. _Memphis Blues and Jug Bands_. London: Studio
      Vista; New York: Stein and Day, 1970; Hatboro, Pennsylvania:
      Legacy Books, 1983. (The Paul Oliver Blues Series). 112p.,
      illus., bibliog., discog.
          Includes appendix of Brunswick records made in Memphis,
      1929-30; also texts of blues songs recorded by Memphis bluesmen.

Country Blues (cont.)

Mississippi

580. Ferris, William R. <u>Blues From the Delta</u>. London: Studio
     Vista, 1970; New York: Stein and Day, 1971; Garden City, New
     York: Doubleday, 1978 (Anchor Books); New York: Da Capo Pr.,
     1983 (Roots of Jazz). 111p., illus., bibliog., discog.

581. Leadbitter, Mike. <u>Delta Country Blues</u>. Bexhill-on-Sea, Essex:
     Blues Unlimited, 1968. 47p., illus.
       Post-1945 developments and performers. Includes account of
     beginnings of <u>Sun</u> record company.

Piedmont

582. Bastin, Bruce. <u>Crying for the Carolines</u>. London: Studio Vista,
     1971; Hatboro, Pennsylvania: Legacy Books, 1983. (The Paul
     Oliver Blues Series). 112p., illus., bibliog., discog., index.
       North and South Carolina, northern Georgia, and parts of
     Virginia.

Savannah

583. Oliver, Paul. <u>Savannah Syncopators: African Retentions in the
     Blues</u>. London: Studio Vista; New York: Stein and Day, 1970.
     112p., illus., bibliog. notes., discog., index. (Blues Series)
       Argues that the music of the West African rain forests has
     few shared characteristics with blues, despite widespread
     assumptions to that effect.

(2) Urban Blues

584. Keil, Charles. <u>Urban Blues</u>. Chicago; London: University of
     Chicago Pr., 1966. 231p., illus., bibliog. notes, index.
       Contemporary Chicago blues. Includes examination of Bobby
     Bland stage show as example of typical performance in the idiom.

585. Rowe, Mike. <u>Chicago Breakdown</u>. London: Eddison Pr., 1973;
     New York: Drake Publishers, 1975; New York: Da Capo Pr. (as
     <u>Chicago Blues: the City and the Music</u>), 1981. 226p., illus.,
     bibliog., discog., index.
       Includes listing of Chicago Rhythm and Blues hits, 1945-59.

5. RHYTHM AND BLUES

(1) GENERAL GUIDES AND OVERVIEWS

586. Moore, Thurston (ed.). **Rhythm and Blues Scrapbook.** Cincinnati:
Artist Publications, 1952. unpaged, illus.

(2) CRITICISM

587. Lydon, Michael. **Boogie Lightning.** Photographs by Ellen Mandel.
New York: Dial Pr., 1974; New York: Da Capo Pr., 1980. 229p.,
illus., bibliog. refs.
Collection of essays on the relation of rock to rhythm and
blues, its source. Da Capo Pr. edition has foreword by B.B.
King.

* Redd, Lawrence N. **Rock is Rhythm and Blues.**
* Cited above as item 90.

(3) GENERAL HISTORIES

588. Berry, Jason. **Up From the Cradle of Jazz: New Orleans Rhythm
and Blues, and Beyond.** Baton Rouge: Louisiana State University
Pr., 1984. 392p., illus.

589. Broven, John. **Walking to New Orleans: the Story of New Orleans
Rhythm and Blues.** Bexhill-on-Sea, Esse : Blues Unlimited,
1974. **2nd ed.:** Bexhill-on-Sea, Essex: Flyright Records; Gretna,
Louisiana: Pelican Publishing, 1977. 249p., illus., bibliog.,
discog., index.
Includes appendix listing personnel of major New Orleans
bands; hits by New Orleans singers, 1946-72.

590. McCutcheon, Lynn Ellis. **Rhythm and Blues: an Experience and
Adventure in its Origin and Development.** Arlington, Virginia:
Beatty, 1971. 305p., illus., discogs.

591. McGowan, James A. **Hear Today! Here to Stay! A Personal History
of Rhythm and Blues.** Clearwater, Florida: Sixth House Pr.,
1983. 196p., illus.

6. SOUL

(1) GENERAL GUIDES AND OVERVIEWS

592. Billboard. <u>The World of Soul</u>. New York: Billboard Publicat-
      ions, 1968.   p., illus.
         Emphasis on business aspects.

593. Hoare, Ian, Clive Anderson, Tony Cummings, and Simon Frith. <u>The</u>
      <u>Soul Book</u>. Edited by Simon Frith. London: Eyre Methuen, 1975;
      New York: Dell, 1976 (Delta Books). 206p., illus., index.
         Collection of essays.

594. Larkin, Rochelle. <u>Soul Music! The Sound, the Stars, the Story</u>.
      New York: Lancer Books, 1970. 192p., illus.

(2) GENERAL HISTORIES

595. Garland, Phyl. <u>The Sound of Soul: the Story of Black Music</u>.
      Chicago: Henry Regnery, 1969; New York: Simon and Schuster,
      1971. 256p., illus., bibliog. notes, discog., index.
         Soul elements traced through the history of Black music forms.

596. Haralambos, Michael. <u>Right On: From Blues to Soul in Black</u>
      <u>America</u>. London: Eddison Pr., 1974; New York: Drake Publishers,
      1975; New York: Da Capo Pr., 1979 (Roots of Jazz). 187p., illus.,
      illus., bibliog., discog., index.
         Examines the transition in popularity from blues to soul.
      Based on author's dissertation <u>Soul Music and the Blues: Their</u>
      <u>Meaning and Relevance in Northern United States Black Ghettoes</u>,
      University of Minnesota, 197?

597. Hirshey, Gerri. <u>Nowhere to Run: the Story of Soul Music</u>. New
      York: Times Books; London: Macmillan London, 1984. 384p., illus.

598. Shaw, Arnold. <u>The World of Soul: Black America's Contribution</u>
      <u>to the Pop Music Scene</u>. New York: Cowles, 1970; New York:
      Coronet Communications, 1971. 306p., illus., discog., index.
         Includes discussion of White imitators.

Philly Soul

599. Cummings, Tony. <u>The Sound of Philadelphia</u>. London: Eyre
      Methuen, 1975. 157p., illus., index.

7. RAP AND HIP HOP

* Hager, Steven. Hip Hop: the Illustrated History of Break Dancing, Rap Music, and Graffiti.
    * Cited below as item 1254.

600. Toop, David. The Rap Attack: African Jive to New York Hip Hop. London: Pluto Pr., 1984. 160p., illus., discog.

8. CARIBBEAN MUSIC

(1) GENERAL GUIDES AND OVERVIEWS

601. Burnett, Michael. Jamaican Music. London: Oxford University Pr., 1982. 48p., illus., bibliog., discog. (Oxford Topics in Music)

602. Sealey, John. Music in the Caribbean. With Krister Malm. Introduction by The Mighty Chalkdust (Hollis Liverpool.) London: Hodder and Stoughton, 1982. 44p., illus., bibliog.
    For use in schools.

(2) PERIODS AND STYLES

(a) Calypso

603. Elder, Jacob D. From Congo Drum to Steel Band: a Socio-Historical Account of the Emergence and Evolution of the Trinidad Steel Orchestra. St. Augustine, Trinidad: University of the West Indies, 1969. 21p.

(b) Reggae

604. Bergman, Billy. Reggae and Latin Pop: Hot Sauces. With Andy Schwartz, Rob Baker, and Tony Sabournin. Poole, Dorset: Blandford Pr., 1985. 144p., illus., index. (Planet Rock, 1)

605. Clarke, Sebastian. Jah Music: the Evolution of the Popular Jamaican Song. London: Heinemann Educational, 1980. 216p., illus., bibliog. notes, discog., index.
    Appendix profiles major figures.

606. Corley, Steve. Reggae! Soul Music of Jamaica. Oklahoma City: Tune the World Music, 1980.   p., illus.

607. Davis, Stephen, and Peter Simon. Reggae International. London: Thames and Hudson; New York: Knopf, 1983. 192p., illus.

608. Farmer, Paul. Steelbands and Reggae. Harlow, Essex: Longman, 1981. 24p., illus. (Longman Music Topics)
     For school use.

609. Johnson, Howard, and Jim Pines. Reggae: Deep Roots Music. London: Proteus in association with Channel Four Television, 1982. 127p., illus.
     Accompanies British television series.

610. Kallyndyr, Royston, and Henderson Dalrymple. Reggae: a Peoples' Music. London: Carib-Arawak Publications, 1973. 38p.

(3) SOCIOLOGICAL ASPECTS

611. Barrett, Leonard Emanuel. The Rastafarians: the Dreadlocks of Jamaica. Kingston, Jamaica; London: Heinemann, 1977. 257p., illus., bibliog., index.
     Includes discussion of reggae.

612. Davis, Stephen, and Peter Simon. Reggae Bloodlines: in Search of the Music and Culture of Jamaica. Garden City, New York: Anchor Pr., 1977; London: Heinemann Educational, 1979. 216p., illus., bibliog., discog.
     Text by Davis; photographs by Simon. Includes interviews with reggae artists.

613. Hebdige, Dick. Reggae, Rastas, and Rudies. Birmingham, England: University of Birmingham, 1974.   p. (C.C.S. Occasional Paper, 24)

614. Plummer, John. Movement of Jah People. Birmingham, England: Press Gang, 1979.   p.
     Rastafarian movement in Britain, particularly in the City of Birmingham. Includes discussion of reggae.

615. Thomas , Michael, and Adrian Boot. Jamaica: Babylon on a Thin Wire. New York: Schocken Books, 1977. 96p., illus.
     Text by Thomas; photographs by Boot. Includes discussion of Jamaican music forms. Continued by item 616.

616. ————. Jah Revenge. London: Eel Pie, 1983.   p., illus.
     Continues item 615.

9. AFRICAN POP

617. Collins, John. African Pop Roots. Slough, Berkshire: Foulsham, 120p., illus.
     Influence of African popular music on other popular music is included.

618. Kebede, Ashenafi. The Roots of Black Music: the Vocal, Instrumental, and Dance Heritage of Africa and Black America. Englewood Cliffs, New Jersey; London: Prentice-Hall, 1982. 162p., illus., index.

619. Nketia, J.H. Kwabena. The Music of Africa. New York: Norton,
      1974; London: Gollancz, 1975. 278p., illus., bibliog., discog.,
      index.
          Emphasis on traditional music forms; some discussion of
      African pop.

F. JAZZ

1. REFERENCE MATERIALS

(a) General Works

620. Bookings: Who and Where Worldwide. Vienna: Jazz Forum, 1976. 50p. (Jazzman's Reference Book, 2)

621. Dorfman, Mel, and Reeva Gibley. International Jazz Contact Directory. Cambridge, Massachusetts: Mel Dorfman Jazz Enterprises, 1973. 25p.

622. Jazz-Kompendium International. Berlin: Gerhard Kowalski Verlag. annual, 1980- .
      Jazz contacts world-wide.

623. Markewich, Reese. Jazz Publicity: Bibliography of Names and Addresses of International Jazz Critics and Magazines. Riverdale, New York: The Author, 1973. 24p.

      ————. Jazz Publicity II: Newly Revised and Expanded Bibliography of Names and Addresses of International Jazz Critics and Magazines. New York: The Author, 1974. 25p.
      Address list -- not a bibliography.

624. Recordings and Bookings Worldwide. New York: International Jazz Federation. annual, 1979- . (Jazzman's Reference Book, 3)

(b) Bibliographies

625. Asman, James, and Bill Kinnell. Jazz Writings. Chilwell, Nottinghamshire: Jazz Appreciation Society, 1945. 26p.

626. Barazetta, Giuseppe, and Liborio Pusateri. Bibliografia. Milan: The Authors, 1968. 19p.

627. Chaumier, Jacques. La Littérature du Jazz: Essai de Bibliographie. Le Mans: The Author, 1963. 39p.
      In French. 232 items; brief annotations.

628. Clark, Chris. Jazz. London: Library Association, Public Libraries Group, 1982. 50p., index. (Readers' Guides, 39)
      Annotated; includes only titles in print. Supersedes item 630.

   * Cooper, David E. International Bibliography of Discographies: Classical Music, and Jazz and Blues.
       * Cited below as item 4321.

Bibliographies (cont.)

629. Edwards, Marvin J. A Guide to the Literature of Jazz. (place
      unknown): Aleatory Pr., 1964. 10p.

  *   Elings, Arie. Bibliographie van de Nederlands Jazz.
          * Cited below as item 926.

630. Haselgrove, J.R., and Donald Kennington. Readers' Guide to
      Books on Jazz. London: Library Association, County Libraries
      Section, 1960. 16p. (Readers' Guides, New Series, 55)
      2nd. ed.: London: Library Association, County Libraries Group,
      1965. 16p., discog. (Readers' Guides, New Series, 83)
          Classified arrangement; limited to in-print material. Super-
      seded by item 628.

  *   Haywood, Charles. Bibliography of North American Folklore and
      Folksong.
          * Cited above as item 4.

631. Hefele, Bernhard. Jazz-Bibliography/Jazz Bibliographie: Inter-
      national Literature on Jazz, Blues, Spirituals, Gospel, and
      Ragtime Music. With a Selected List of Works on the Social
      and Cultural Background. From the Beginning to the Present.
      Munich; New York; London; Paris: K.G. Saur, 1981. 368p.,
      index.
          Lists 6,600 books and periodical articles. Some brief
      annotations. Particularly strong on German material.

632. Howard Tilton Memorial Library. Catalog of the William Ransom
      Jazz Archive. Boston: G.K. Hall, 1984. 900p.

633. Kennington, Donald. The Literature of Jazz: a Critical Guide.
      London: Library Association, 1970; Chicago: American Library
      Association, 1971. 142p., indexes.

      ————, and Danny Read. The Literature of Jazz: a Critical
      Guide. 2nd. ed.: London: Library Association Publishing;
      Chicago: American Library Association, 1981. 236p., index.
          Narrative format. Includes books, pamphlets, dissertations,
      theses, periodicals, and motion pictures. Many errors in both
      editions.

634. Meadows, Eddie S. Jazz Reference and Research Materials: a
      Bibliography. New York: Garland Publishing, 1980. 312p.,
      indexes. (Critical Studies on Black Life and Culture, 22.
      Garland Reference Library of the Humanities, 251)
          Selectively annotated. Includes books, periodical material,
      and dissertations; early 1960s to 1978.

635. Mecklenburg, Carl Gregor, Herzog zu. International Jazz Bib-
      liography: Jazz Books from 1919 to 1968. Strasbourg: Heitz,
      1969. 193p., indexes. (Collection d'Etudes Musicologiques, 49)
          Includes blues, ragtime, jazz, and jazz-influenced music.
      Excludes poetry, fiction, primers, and certain ephemeral mat-
      erial. 1,562 items listed. Eleven indexes.

————. 1970 Supplement to International Jazz Bibliography; and, International Drum and Percussion Bibliography. Graz, Austria: Universal Edition, 1971. 59p.; 43p. (Studies in Jazz Research, 3)
     Lists 429 items published 1968-70. Drum and percussion section lists 358 items. No indexes.

————. 1971/72/73 Supplement to International Jazz Bibliography; and, Selective Bibliography of Some Jazz Background Literature; and, Bibliography of Two Subjects Previously Excluded. Graz, Austria: Universal Edition, 1973. 246p. (Studies in Jazz Research, 6)
     Lists 1,302 items published 1971-73. New subjects are dissertations, and "Beat, Rock, Pop." Material partly supplied by others; listed even if incomplete or contradictory.

636. Merriam, Alan P., and Robert J. Benford. A Bibliography of Jazz. Philadelphia: American Folklore Society, 1954; New York: Kraus Reprint, 1970; New York: Da Capo Pr., 1970 (Roots of Jazz). 145p., indexes.
     Lists 3,437 books and periodical items. No annotations: elaborate coding scheme used to describe material.

 *   Moon, Pete. A Bibliography of Jazz Discographies Published Since 1960.
     * Cited below as item 4322.

637. Reisner, Robert George. The Literature of Jazz: a Preliminary Bibliography. Introduction by Marshall W. Stearns. New York: New York Public Library, 1954. 53p.
     Checklist of books, periodicals, and periodical articles.

————. The Literature of Jazz: a Selective Bibliography. 2nd. ed., rev. and enlarged. New York: New York Public Library, 1959. 63p.
     World-wide coverage. Approximately 1,575 entries, selectively annotated.

638. Ruecker, Norbert. Jazz Index: Bibliographie unselbständiger Jazzliteratur/Bibliography of Jazz Literature in Periodicals. Frankfurt/Main, West Germany: The Author. quarterly (later bi-monthly), 1977- .
     Indexes approximately fifty jazz periodicals by keywords. Prefaces in German and English.

639. Staffordshire County Library. Jazz: a Selection of Books. Stafford: Staffordshire County Library, 1963. 9p. (Books for Young Adults, 2)
     Annotated. Lists approximately sixty items, including tutors.

640. Voigt, John, and Randall Kane. Jazz Music in Print. Winthrop, Massachusetts: Flat Nine Music, 1975. 66p. 2nd. ed.: Boston: Hornpipe Music Publishing, 1978. unpaged.

Bibliographies (cont.)

641. Wiedemann, Erik. Boger om Jazz. Copenhagen: Nationalmuseet,
      Nationaldiskotet Handbiblioteket, 1962. 13p.
          In Danish.

                  (c) Encyclopedias and Dictionaries

  *   Case, Brian, and Stan Britt. The Illustrated Encyclopedia
      of Jazz.
          * Cited below as item 1537.

  *   Feather, Leonard Geoffrey. The Encyclopedia of Jazz.
          * Cited below as item 1550.

  *   Hayes, Milehan, Ray Scribner, and Peter Magee. The Encyclo-
      pedia of Australian Jazz.
          * Cited below as item 1570.

  *   Heerkens, Adriaan. Jazz Picture Encyclopedia.
          * Cited below as item 1571.

  *   Kinkle, Roger D. (ed.). The Complete Encyclopedia of
      Popular Music and Jazz, 1900-1950.
          * Cited above as item 16.

642. Longstreet, Stephen, and Alfons Michael Dauer. Knaurs
      Jazzlexikon. Munich; Zurich: Knaur, 1957. (2nd. ed.: 1959;
      3rd. ed.: 1961; 4th. ed.: 1963.) 324p., illus.
          In German. Brief entries by specific topics. Illustrated
      with paintings by Longstreet.

  *   Panassié, Hugues, and Madelaine Gautier. Dictionary of Jazz.
          * Cited below as item 1589.

  *   ———. Guide to Jazz.
          * Cited below as item 1589.

                  2. ANNUALS AND YEARBOOKS

643. American Jazz Annual. New York: Hemisphere Pr., 1956. 98p.,
      illus.
          Only issue.

644. Annual Review of Jazz Studies. Edited by Michael Morgenstern
      and Charles Nanry. New York: Transaction Books. annual,
      1982- .

645. Blackstone, Orin (ed.). The Jazzfinder '49. Containing
      Permanent Reference Material. New Orleans: The Author,
      1949. 152p., illus., bibliog., discog.
          Only issue.

646.   Dance Music Annual. London: J. Dilworth, 1951.   111p., illus.
        Only issue. Covers big bands, jazz, and popular dancing.

647.   Down Beat. Down Beat Music Annual (later Down Beat Music
        Handbook.). Chicago: Maher Publications. annual, 1956- .

648.   ————. Down Beat's Yearbook of Swing. Edited by Paul Eduard
        Miller. Introduction by Fletcher Henderson. Chicago: Down
        Beat Publishing Company, 1939. Reprinted: Westport, Conn.:
        Greenwood Pr., 1978. 183p., illus., bibliog., discog.

649.   ————. Miller's Yearbook of Popular Music. Edited by Paul
        Eduard Miller. Chicago: P.E.M. Publications, 1943. 195p.,
        illus., bibliog., discog.
        Covers big bands and jazz.

650.   Esquire. Esquire's Jazz Book. Edited by Paul Eduard Miller.
        Introduction by Arnold Gingrich. New York: Smith and Durrell,
        1944 (Reprinted: New York: Da Capo Pr., 1978); New York: A.S.
        Barnes, 1944. 230p., illus., discog.

        ————. Esquire's 1945 Jazz Book. Edited by Paul Eduard
        Miller. Introduction by Arnold Gingrich. New York: A.S. Barnes,
        1945 (Reprinted: New York: Da Capo Pr., 1979). 256p., illus.,
        discog. New York: Editions for the Armed Forces, 1945. 352p.,
        discog.

        ————. Esquire's 1946 Jazz Book. Edited by Paul Eduard
        Miller. Introduction by Arnold Gingrich. New York: A.S. Barnes,
        1946 (Reprinted: New York: Da Capo Pr., 1979). 202p., illus.,
        discog. Folio size ed.: New York: A.S. Barnes, 1946. 90p.,
        illus., discog.

        ————. Esquire's 1947 Jazz Book. Edited by Ernest Anderson.
        New York: Smith and Durrell, 1947; New York: A.S. Barnes, 1947.
        96p., illus., discog.
        All volumes consist of material reprinted from Esquire.

651.   ————. Esquire's Jazzbook. Edited by Paul Eduard Miller, and,
        for England, by Ralph Venables. From the Esquire Jazz Books,
        1944-1946. London: Peter Davies, 1947. 184p., illus.
        Selection of material from item 650.

652.   Jazzforschung/Jazz Research. Edited by Friedrich Körner and
        Dieter Glawischnig. Vienna; Graz, Austria: Universal Edition.
        irreg., 1969- .
        Cosponsored by the International Society for Jazz Research,
        and the Hochschule für Musik und Darstellende Kunst. Chiefly
        in German, with English summaries; some English material.

653.   Jazz-Hot. L'Annuaire du Jazz. Paris: Jazz-Hot. annual, 1950-
        53.

654.   Jazzways: a Yearbook of Hot Music. Edited by George S. Rosen-
        thal and Frank Zachery, in collaboration with Frederic Ramsey,
        Jr., and Rudi Blesh. Cincinnati: Jazzways, 1946; New York:
        Greenberg, 1947; London: Musicians' Pr., 1947. 120p., illus.,
        discog.

655. Johnson, Frank, and Ron Wills (eds.). <u>Jam: an Annual of Swing</u>
      <u>Music</u>. Sydney, New South Wales: Tempo Publishing Company,
      1938. 48p., illus.
           Only issue.

656. McCarthy, Albert John (ed.). <u>The P.L. Yearbook of Jazz, 1946</u>.
      London: Nicholson and Watson, 1947. 188p., illus. (Editions
      Poetry)
           P.L. = Poetry London.

           ————. <u>The P.L. Jazzbook, 1947</u>. London: Nicholson and Watson,
      1948. 172p., illus.

           ————. <u>The Jazzbook, 1955</u>. London: Cassell, 1955. 173p.,
      illus.

657. Metronome. <u>The Metronome Yearbook</u>. New York: <u>Metronome</u>.
      annual, 1950-59.
           Edited, 1950-55, by Barry Ulanov and George Thomas Simon;
      1956-59, by Bill Coss. Material reprinted from <u>Metronome</u>.

   * Noble, Peter (ed.). <u>The Yearbook of Jazz, 1946: an Illustrated</u>
      <u>"Who's Who" of Jazz Personalities</u>.
           * Cited below as item 1588.

                     3. GENERAL GUIDES AND OVERVIEWS

658. Asman, James, and Bill Kinnell (eds.). <u>American Jazz</u>.   Chilwell,
      Nottinghamshire: Jazz Appreciation Society, 1945-6.
      <u>No. 1</u>: 1945. 22p.
      <u>No. 2</u>: 1946. 22p.

659. ————. <u>Jazz</u>. Chilwell, Nottinghamshire: Jazz Appreciation
      Society, 1944. 20p.

660. ————. <u>Jazz To-day</u>. Chilwell, Nottinghamshire: Jazz Apprec-
      iation Society, 1945. 24p.

661. Blesh, Rudi. <u>America's Contribution to Jazz</u>. Bombay: United
      States Information Service, 1949. 7p.

662. Chilton, John. <u>Teach Yourself Jazz</u>. Foreword by George Melly.
      Sevenoaks, Kent: Teach Yourself Books, 1979; New York: David
      McKay, 1979. 186p. (Teach Yourself Books)
           Total revision of item 686.

663. Collier, Graham. <u>Inside Jazz</u>. London: Quartet; New York: Four
      Winds Pr., 1973. 144p., illus.
           Introductory text by British jazzman.

664. D.J.L. (pseud.). <u>Introducing Jazz: Talks to a Catholic Youth</u>
      <u>Club</u>. Toronto; London: St. Paul Publications, 1959. 100p.

665. Dale, Rodney. _The World of Jazz_. Oxford: Phaidon, 1980; New
     York: Bookthrift, 1982. 192p., illus.
        Includes biographical appendix of jazz musicians.

666. Delaunay, Charles. _De la Vie et du Jazz_. Paris: Jazz-Hot,
     1939. 95p. Rev. ed.: Lausanne, Switzerland: Editions de l'
     Echiquier, 1946. 70p.

667. Enefer, Douglas Stallard. _Daily Dispatch Jazz Book_. Manchest-
     er, England: _Daily Dispatch_, 1954. 95p., illus.

668. Feather, Leonard Geoffrey. _The Book of Jazz: a Guide to the
     Entire Field_. New York: Horizon Pr., 1957; London: Barker,
     1959; New York: Meridian Books, 1960. 280p., bibliog. notes,
     discog., index. Revised and updated edition: _The Book of Jazz
     From Then Till Now: a Guide to the Entire Field_. New York:
     Horizon Pr., 1965. 280p., bibliog. notes, discog., index.
        Introductory text utilizing a "series of instrument-by-
     instrument histories."

669. Fox, Charles. _Jazz in Perspective_. London: British Broadcast-
     ing Corporation, 1969. 88p., illus., bibliog., discog.
        Based on British radio series.

670. ————, and Valerie Wilmer. _The Jazz Scene_. Special photog-
     raphy by Valerie Wilmer. London; New York: Hamlyn, 1972.
     127p., illus., bibliog., index.
        Chiefly illustrated.

671. Gammond, Peter, and Peter Clayton. _Know about Jazz_. Illustr-
     ated by Rosalind Hayte and Charles Pickard. London; Glasgow:
     Blackie; Toronto: Ryerson Pr., 1964. 62p., illus., discogs.
        Amalgam of text, photographs, drawings and paintings.
     Includes brief biographical sketches of key figures.

672. Gee, John, and Michael Wadsley. _Intro: the Younger Generation_.
     Tring, Hertfordshire: Society for Jazz Appreciation in the
     Younger Generation, 1944. 24p.

673. Gee, John (ed.). _That's a Plenty_. Hemel Hempstead, Hertford-
     shire: Society for Jazz Appreciation in the Younger Generation,
     1945. 32p., illus.

674. Gillenson, Lewis N. (ed.). _Esquire's World of Jazz_. Comment-
     ary by James Poling. New York: Esquire, 1962 (Reprinted 1963);
     London: Bowker, 1963. 224p., illus., discog., index. Revised,
     updated ed.: New York: Crowell, 1975. 228p., illus., discog.,
     index.
        Illustrated with paintings. Discography by John Lessner.
     Material first published in _Esquire_.

675. Goldberg, Isaac. _Jazz Music: What It Is, and How to Understand
     It_. Girard, Kansas: Haldeman-Julius, 1927. 64p.

676. Harris, Rex. Enjoying Jazz. London: Phoenix House; New York:
     Roy Publishers, 1960. 160p., illus., bibliog. (Excursions)
     Rev. ed.: London: Phoenix House, 1963. 157p., illus., bibliog.
     (Excursions)
          Aimed at younger readers.

677. Heaton, Peter. Jazz. London: Burke; Toronto: Ambassador Pr.,
     1964. 92p., illus. (Music in Our Lives)

678. Hentoff, Nat. Jazz Is. New York: Random House, 1976; London:
     W.H. Allen, 1978; New York: Avon Books, 1978; New York: Lime-
     light Editions, 1984. 288p., illus., bibliog., index.

679. Hodeir, André. Introduction à la Musique de Jazz. Paris:
     Larousse, 1948. 128p. (Formes, Ecoles et Oeuvres musicales)
          In French.

680. ———. Jazz: its Evolution and Essence. Translated by David
     Noakes. New York: Grove Pr., 1956; London: Secker and Warburg,
     1956; New York: Da Capo Pr., 1975 (Roots of Jazz); New York:
     Grove Pr., 1979 (Evergreen Edition). 295p., discog., index.
          Translation, with a new section on contemporary developments
     of Hommes et problèmes du jazz: suivi da La religion du jazz.
     Paris: Portulan, 1954. Emphasis on contemporary developments;
     assumes that modern masterpieces are superior to older ones.

681. ———. Le Jazz, cet inconnu. Preface by Charles Delaunay.
     Paris: Editions France-Empire, 1945. 220p. (Collections
     Harmoniques)
          In French.

682. Howe, Martin. Blue Jazz: Advanced Record of Jazz and its
     Present Day Acceptance. Bristol: Perpetua Pr., 1934; Bristol:
     White and White, 1936. 34p.

683. Jacobs, Gordon. A Study of Jazz. Wednesbury, Staffordshire:
     The Author, 1944. 8p.

684. Lee, Edward. Jazz: an Introduction. London: Kahn and Averill;
     Dallas: Crescendo Books, 1972. 188p., bibliog., discog., index.

685. Levey, Joseph. The Jazz Experience: a Guide to Appreciation.
     Englewood Cliffs, New Jersey; London: Prentice-Hall, 1983.
     158p., illus.

686. Lindsay, Martin. Teach Yourself Jazz. London: English Univ-
     ersities Pr., 1958. 150p., bibliog. (Teach Yourself Books)
          Many errors; little grasp of the subject. Completely
     rewritten for the Teach Yourself series by John Chilton. See
     item 662, above.

687. McCalla, James. Jazz: a Listener's Guide. Englewood Cliffs,
     New Jersey; London: Prentice-Hall, 1982. 152p., illus., bibliog
     index.

688. Mendl, Robert William Sigismund. The Appeal of Jazz. London:
      Philip Allen, 1927. 186p., illus.
          Confuses jazz with current popular music trends. Attempts
      to place jazz into the mainstream of European "serious" music.
      Author unaware of the work of Black jazzmen.

689. Michaelis, Adrian, and Cecile Creed. An Outline of Aframerican
      Jazz. San Francisco: Standard Oil Company of California, 1945.
      18p.

690. Myrus, Donald. I Like Jazz: a First Book About Jazz for
      Swinging People. New York: Macmillan; London: Collier-Macmill-
      an, 1964. 118p., illus., discog.

691. Nelson, Stanley Rupert. All About Jazz. Foreword by Jack
      Hylton. London: Heath, Cranton, 1934. 190p., illus.
          Emphasis on contemporary British scene.

692. Osgood, Henry Osborne. So This is Jazz. Boston: Little, Brown,
      1926; New York: Da Capo Pr., 1978 (Roots of Jazz). 258p., illus.,
      index.
          Emphasis on commercial aspects, and white concert jazz. No
      consideration of Black jazz artists.

693. Ostransky, Leroy. Understanding Jazz. Englewood Cliffs, New
      Jersey; London: Prentice-Hall, 1977. 352p., illus., bibliog.,
      index. (A Spectrum Book)

694. Panassié, Hugues. La Bataille du jazz. Paris: Albin Michel,
      1965. 220p. (Collection Aujourd'hui)
          In French.

695. ———. Jazz Panorama. Paris: Deux Rives, 1950. 283p., discog.
          In French.

696. Pearce, Cedric. Trumpet in the Night: a Background to the
      Enjoyment of Jazz Music. Melbourne, Victoria: William H.
      Miller, 1945. 22p.

697. Postgate, John. A Plain Man's Guide to Jazz. London: Hanover
      Books, 1973. 145p., bibliog., index.
          Includes glossary of jazz terms.

698. Price, Ray. Introduction to Jazz. Melbourne, Victoria: The
      Australian, 1971. 13p., illus.

699. Rivelli, Pauline. Jazz Conversation. New York: Jazz Pr., 1963.
      48p.

700. Sales, Grover. Jazz: America's Classical Music. Englewood
      Cliffs, New Jersey; London: Prentice-Hall, 1984. 240p., illus.

701. Shapiro, Nat. This Music Called Jazz. New York: Jazztone Soc-
      iety, 1955. 12p.

702. Simon, George Thomas. <u>The Feeling of Jazz</u>. Drawings by Tracy
      Sugarman. New York: Simon and Schuster, 1961. 95p., illus.

703. Ulanov, Barry. <u>A Handbook of Jazz</u>. Foreword by Kingsley Amis.
      New York: Viking Pr., 1957 (Reprinted: Westport, Conn.: Green-
      wood Pr., 1975); New York: Macmillan, 1957. 248p., discog.,
      index. London: Hutchinson, 1958. 204p., discog., index.
          Includes biographical appendix.

  *   White, Mark. <u>The Observer's Book of Jazz</u>.
          * Cited below as item 1609.

704. **Williams, Martin T. <u>Where's the Melody? A Listener's Intro-
      duction to Jazz</u>.** New York: Pantheon Books, 1966 (Reprinted:
      New York: Da Capo Pr., 1983); New York: Minerva Pr., 1967.
      <u>Rev. ed.</u>: New York: Pantheon Books, 1969. 205p., bibliog.,
      discogs., index.
          Collection of introductory essays.

  *   Williams, Peter. <u>Bluff Your Way in Folk and Jazz</u>.
          * Cited above as item 409.

                              4. CRITICISM

                          (a) General Works

705. Berendt, Joachim Ernest. <u>Der Jazz: eine zeitkritische Studie</u>.
      Stuttgart: Deutsche Verlagsanstalt, 1950. 96p. (Der Deutschen-
      spiegel: Schriften zur Erkenntnis und Erneuerung, 39)
          In German.

706. Borneman, Ernest. <u>A Critic Looks at Jazz</u>. London: Jazz Music
      Books, 1946. 53p., bibliog. notes.
          First published serially in <u>The Record Changer</u> as <u>An Anthro-
      pologist Looks at Jazz</u>. Attempts to set critical standards.

707. Coeuroy, André, and André Schaeffner. <u>Le Jazz</u>. Paris: C. Ave-
      line, 1926 (Reprinted: Sharon Hill, Pennsylvania: Sharon Hill,
      1983). 150p. (La Musique moderne, 2)
          The first book-length critique.

708. Ostransky, Leroy. <u>The Anatomy of Jazz</u>. Seattle: University of
      Washington Pr., 1960; Westport, Conn.: Greenwood Pr., 1973.
      362p., bibliog., index.

709. Panassié, Hugues. <u>Hot Jazz: the Guide to Swing Music</u>. Trans-
      lated by Lyle and Eleanor **Dowling from** <u>Le Jazz hot</u>. Especially
      revised by the author for the English edition. New York: Wit-
      mark, 1936 (Reprinted: Westport, Conn.: Greenwood Pr., 1970);
      London: Cassell, 1936. 363p., discog.
          Originally published Paris, 1934, by Corrêa, with an intro-
      duction by Louis Armstrong. Written without hearing many key
      figures; consequent errors corrected in item 710.

710.   ———. *The Real Jazz*. Translated from the French by Anne
        Sorells Williams. Adapted for American publication by Charles
        Edward Smith. New York: Smith and Durrell; Toronto: McLeod,
        1942; New York: Crown, 1950; Norwood, Pennsylvania: Telegraph
        Books, 1981. 326p., discog. 2nd revised and enlarged ed.:
        New York: A.S. Barnes; London: Thomas Yoseloff, 1960; West-
        port, Conn.: Greenwood Pr., 1973. 284p., discog.
            Translated from manuscript badly damaged in wartime transit.
        Thesis is that most white jazz musicians are inferior to Black
        artists; and that modern movements are not jazz. Reprinted
        in French as *La véritable musique de jazz*, Paris: Laffont,
        1946; revised and enlarged ed., 1952. Condensed French version
        published as *La Musique de jazz et le swing*, Paris: Corrêa,
        1945.

711.   Pleasants, Henry. *Death of a Music? The Decline of the*
        European Tradition and the Rise of Jazz. London: Gollancz,
        1961. 192p., bibliog.
            Argues that modern serious composers have become divorced
        from the audience; contrasts this with the position in jazz.

712.   ———. *Serious Music -- and All That Jazz! An Adventure in*
        Music Criticism. New York: Simon and Schuster; London: Goll-
        ancz, 1969. 256p., index.
            Expansion of the argument of item 711, as applied to modern
        jazz. Sees the same division between it and popular music.

713.   Rock, John. *Africa Sings, and, The Psychology of Jazz*.
        Colombo, Ceylon: General Pr., 1946. 16p.

714.   Sargeant, Winthrop. *Jazz: Hot and Hybrid*. New York: Arrow
        Editions, 1938. 234p., illus., bibliog., index. *New and*
        enlarged ed.: New York: Dutton, 1946. 287p., illus., bibliog.,
        index. (3rd. ed., as *Jazz: a History*) New York: McGraw-Hill,
        1964; Reprinted (as *Jazz: Hot and Hybrid*): New York: Da Capo
        Pr., 1975. 302p., illus., bibliog., index.
            Attempt at scientific musicological analysis. Jazz treated
        as a distinct idiom.

(b) Language

715.   Allen, Harold Byron, Hensley C. Woodbridge, and Norman D.
        Hinton. *Minor Dialect Areas of the Upper Midwest, (by) H.B.*
        Allen; A Tentative Bibliography of Kentucky Speech, (by) Hens-
        ley C. Woodbridge; The Language of Jazz Musicians, (by) Norman
        D. Hinton. University, Alabama: University of Alabama Pr. for
        The American Dialect Society, 1958. 48p., illus. (Publications
        of The American Dialect Society, 30)

716.   Burley, Dan. *Dan Burley's Handbook of Jive*. New York: Jive
        Potentials, n.d. 127p., illus.
            Dictionary of terms associated with bebop. Includes liter-
        ary parodies employing "hip" language.

717. Burley, Dan. <u>Dan Burley's Original Handbook of Harlem Jive.</u>
      New York: The Author, 1944. 158p., illus.
          The idiom of Harlem Blacks, "transmitted and transfused,
      extracted and distilled, absorbed and reflected" (Foreword.)

718. Calloway, Cab. <u>Cab Calloway's Cat-alogue.</u> New York: Mills
      Artists, 1938. 8p.
          Definitions of Harlem jive terms, the majority directly
      related to swing.

          ————. <u>The New Cab Calloway's Cat-ologue.</u> Revised 1939 ed-
      ition. New York: Mills Artists, 1938. 8p.

          ————. <u>The New Cab Calloway's Hepsters' Dictionary: the
      Language of Jive.</u> New York: The Author, 1944. 15p.
          Included as appendix to item

719. Filmer, Vic. <u>Jive and Swing Dictionary.</u> Penzance, Cornwall:
      The Author, 1947. 20p.

720. Gold, Robert S. <u>Jazz Lexicon: an A-Z Dictionary of Jazz Terms
      in the Vivid Idiom of America's Most Successful Non-Conformist
      Minority.</u> New York: Knopf; Toronto: Random House, 1964. 363p.,
      bibliog.
          Terms defined, and traced to earliest recorded use. Based
      on his PhD. dissertation <u>A Jazz Lexicon,</u> New York University,
      1962.

          ————. <u>Jazz Talk: a Dictionary of the Colorful Language that
      has Emerged from America's Own Music.</u> Indianapolis: Bobbs-
      Merrill, 1975; New York: Da Capo Pr., 1982. (Roots of Jazz).
      329p., bibliog.
          Revised and updated.

721. Gonzales, Babs. <u>Be-Bop Dictionary, and History of its Famous
      Stars.</u> New York: Arlain Publishing Company, 1947. 14p., illus.

722. ————, and Paul Weston. <u>Boptionary: What is Bop?</u> Hollywood,
      California: Capitol Records, 1949. 8p.
          Glossary of terms.

723. Henderson, Stephen. <u>Understanding the New Black Poetry: Black
      Speech and Black Music as Poetic References.</u> New York: Morrow,
      1973. 394p. (An Institute of the Black World Book)

724. Horne, Elliot. <u>The Hiptionary.</u> New York: Simon and Schuster,
      1963. 78p.
          Dictionary.

725. Rusch, Robert D. <u>Jazz Talk.</u> Secaucus, New Jersey: Lyle Stuart,
      1984. 192p., illus.

726. Shelly, Low. <u>Hepcats' Jive Talk Dictionary.</u> Derby, Conn.:
      T.W.O. Charles, 1945. 50p.

727. Tamony, Peter. <u>Jazz: the Word, and its Extension to Music: a
      Reprise.</u> San Francisco: The Author, 1968. 20p.

(c) Jazz and Other Art Forms

728. Grossman, William Leonard, and Jack Farrell. **Jazz and Western Culture.** New York: New York University Pr., 1956.   p.

* Miller, William Robert. The World of Pop Music and Jazz.
     * Cited above as item 89.

729. Schafer, William John. **Brass Bands and New Orleans Jazz.** With assistance from Richard B. Allen. Baton Rouge: Louisiana State University Pr., 1977. 134p., illus., bibliog., discog., index.

730. Vulliamy, Graham. **Jazz and Blues.** London; Boston: Routledge and Kegan Paul, 1982. 156p., illus., bibliog., discog., index. (Routledge Popular Music)
     For use in schools.

5. ESSAY COLLECTIONS

731. Balliet, Whitney. **Dinosaurs in the Morning: Forty-One Pieces on Jazz.** Philadelphia: Lippincott (Reprinted: Westport, Conn.: Greenwood Pr., 1970); Toronto: McClelland, 1962. 224p. Harmondsworth, Middlesex: Penguin, 1963. 202p. London: Phoenix House, 1964. 224p.
     Material first published in the New Yorker, 1957-62.

732. ———. **Ecstasy at the Onion: Thirty-One Pieces on Jazz.** Indianapolis: Bobbs-Merrill, 1971; Westport, Conn.: Greenwood Pr., 1982. 284p., index.
     From the New Yorker, 1967-71.

733. ———. **New York Notes: a Journal of Jazz, 1972-1975.** Boston: Houghton Mifflin, 1976; New York: Da Capo Pr., 1977. 250p.
     From the New Yorker.

734. ———. **Night Creature: a Journal of Jazz, 1975-80.** New York; London: Oxford University Pr., 1981. 294p., illus.
     From the New Yorker.

735. ———. **The Sound of Surprise: Forty-Six Pieces on Jazz.** New York: Dutton, 1959 (Reprinted: New York: Da Capo Pr., 1978); Toronto: Smithers, 1960. 237p., index. London: Kimber, 1960. 254p., index. Harmondsworth, Middlesex: Penguin, 1963. 202p., discog., index.
     From the New Yorker, 1954-59.

736. ———. **Such Sweet Thunder: Forty-Nine Pieces on Jazz.** Indianapolis: Bobbs-Merrill, 1966; London: Macdonald, 1968. 366p., index.
     From the New Yorker, 1962-66.

737. Berendt, Joachim Ernst. Ein Fenster aus Jazz: Essays, Port-
     raits, Reflexionen. Frankfurt/Main: Fischer, 1977. Revised
     and enlarged ed.: Frankfurt/Main: Fischer Taschenbuch Verlag,
     1978. 431p.
       In German.

738. ————. Variationen über Jazz: Aufsätze. Munich: Nymphenburg-
     er Verlagsbuchhandlung, 1956. 2nd. ed., 1959; 3rd. ed., 1963.
     227p., illus., discog.
       In German.

739. Brown, Sandy. The McJazz Manuscripts: a Collection of the
     Writings of Sandy Brown. Compiled and introduced by David
     Binns. London: Faber, 1979. 168p., illus., discog., index.
       By British jazz clarinettist; compiled after his death at
     age 46.

740. Cerulli, Dom, Burt Korall, and Mort Nasatir (eds.). The Jazz
     Word. New York: Ballantine, 1960. 240p., illus. London:
     Dobson, 1962. 192p.
       Anthology of essays from periodicals, liner notes, press
     releases, etc.

741. Condon, Eddie, and Hank O'Neal. The Eddie Condon Scrapbook
     of Jazz. New York: St. Martin's Pr.; New York: Galahad Books,
     1973; London: Hale, 1974. 288p., illus.
       Mixture of text and illustrations, with memoir of his own
     career by Condon.

742. Condon, Eddie, and Richard Gehmann (eds.). Eddie Condon's
     Treasury of Jazz. New York: Dial Pr. (Reprinted: Westport,
     Conn.: Greenwood Pr., 1975); Toronto: Longmans, 1956. 488p.
     London: Peter Davies, 1957. 510p.
       Material by various writers, 1946-55. Includes short stories
     on jazz themes.

743. Dance, Stanley, James Asman, and Bill Kinnell. Jazz Notebook.
     Newark, Nottinghamshire: Jazz Appreciation Society, 1945. 24p.

744. Davis, Nathan. Writings in Jazz. Duboque, Iowa: Gorsuch
     Scarisbrick, 1984. 185p.

745. Delaunay, Charles, and Robert Goffin (eds.). Jazz '47. Intro-
     duction by Pierre Seghers. Paris: Société Intercontinental du
     Livre, 1947. 76p., illus.
       Illustrated with drawings and paintings.

746. De Toledano, Ralph (ed.). The Frontiers of Jazz. New York:
     Oliver Durrell, 1947. 2nd. ed.: New York: Frederick Ungar,
     1962. 178p., bibliog. notes, index.
       Material previously published in periodicals, 1926-47.

747. Dexter, Dave, Jr. Jazz Cavalcade: the Inside Story of Jazz.
     With a foreword by Orson Welles. New York: Criterion Music,
     1946; New York: Da Capo Pr., 1977 (Roots of Jazz). 258p.,
     illus., bibliog., index.

748. Ellison, Ralph. <u>Shadow and Act</u>. New York: Random House, 1964
(Reprinted: London: Secker and Warburg, 1967). 317p. New York:
New American Library, 1966. 302p.
Essays, a third on jazz and blues, from literary periodic-
als, 1955-64.

749. Feather, Leonard. <u>The Passion for Jazz</u>. New York: Dell, 1978.
(Delta Books); New York: Horizon Pr., 1980.   p., illus.

750. ———, and Jack Tracy. <u>Laughter From the Hip: the Lighter
Side of Jazz</u>. Drawings by A. Birnbaum. New York: Horizon
Pr., 1963. <u>With a New Introduction by Leonard Feather</u>: New
York: Da Capo Pr., 1979. 175p., illus.
Satires and other humorous pieces.

751. Frankenstein, Alfred V. <u>Syncopating Saxophones</u>. New York:
R.O. Ballou, 1925. 103p., illus.

752. Gammond, Peter (ed.). <u>The Decca Book of Jazz</u>. Foreword by
Milton "Mezz" Mezzrow. London: Muller; Toronto: Saunders,
1958. 432p., illus., discog., index.
By chiefly British contributors.

753. Giddins, Gary. <u>Riding on a Blue Note: Jazz and American Pop</u>.
New York; London: Oxford University Pr., 1981. 313p., discog.,
index.

754. Gleason, Ralph J. <u>Celebrating the Duke, and Louis, Bessie,
Billie, Bird, Carmen, Miles, Dizzy, and Other Heroes</u>. Boston:
Little, Brown, 1975. (An <u>Atlantic Monthly</u> Pr. Book). New York:
Dell, 1976. 280p., illus., index.
Essays, liner notes, interviews, and articles.

755. ——— (ed.). <u>Jam Session: an Anthology of Jazz</u>. New York:
Putnam; Toronto: Longmans; London: Peter Davies, 1958. 319p.,
illus., bibliog., discog.
Includes items by musicians.

756. Green, Benny. <u>Drums in My Ears</u>. London: Davis-Poynter; New
York: Horizon Pr., 1973. 188p.
Periodical articles, 1958-70.

757. Harrison, Max. <u>A Jazz Retrospect</u>. Newton Abbott, Devon: David
and Charles; Dallas, Texas: Crescendo Publishing, 1976. 223p.,
bibliog. refs., index.
Material previously published in periodicals.

   * Hentoff, Nat, and Albert John McCarthy (eds.). <u>Jazz: New
Perspectives on the History of Jazz</u>.
      * Cited below as item 810.

758. Hodeir, André. <u>Toward Jazz</u>. Translated by Noel Burch. New
York: Grove Pr., 1962; New York: Da Capo Pr., 1976 (Roots of
Jazz). 224p., illus., bibliog. refs., index.
Material previously published in periodicals, 1953-59.
Includes discussion of his critical theories.

759. Hodeir, André. The Worlds of Jazz. Translated by Noel Burch.
      New York: Grove Pr., 1972. 279p. (Evergreen Books)
           Some items previously published in periodicals. Rejects
      jazz developments after Charlie Parker. Originally published
      as Les Mondes du jazz, Paris: Union Générale d'Edition, 1970
      (2nd. ed.: 1972).

760. James, Burnett. Essays on Jazz. London: Sidgwick and Jackson,
      1961; New York: Da Capo Pr., 1985 (Roots of Jazz). 205p.
      Material originally published in Jazz Monthly.

761. Jones, Le Roi. Blues People: Negro Music in White America.
      New York: Morrow; Toronto: McLeod, 1963; London: MacGibbon
      and Kee; New York: Apollo Editions, 1965; Westport, Conn.:
      Greenwood Pr., 1980. 244p., bibliog. notes, index.
           Polemical essays surveying the developments in jazz and
      blues in the United States, related to Black cultural and
      social advancement.

762. ————. Black Music. New York: Morrow, 1967 (Reprinted: West-
      port, Conn.: Greenwood Pr., 1980); New York: Apollo Editions,
      1968; London: MacGibbon and Kee, 1969. 223p., illus., discog.
           Articles and reviews, first published 1959-67. Jazz in the
      context of Black life in the United States.

763. Jones, Max, and Albert John McCarthy. Jazz Review: a Miscell-
      any. London: Jazz Music Books, 1945. 23p., discog.

764. McCarthy, Albert John, and Max Jones (eds.). Jazz Folio.
      London: Jazz Music Books, 1944. 24p.

765. ———— (eds.). Jazz Miscellany. London: Jazz Music Books,
      1944. 28p.

766. Miller, William H. Jazz Impressions. Melbourne, Victoria:
      The Author, 1945. 8p.

767. ————. Reprints and Reflections. Melbourne, Victoria: The
      Author, 1946. 8p.

  *   Nanry, Charles (ed.). American Music: from Storyville to
      Woodstock.
           * Cited above as item 386.

768. Schwerké, Irving. Kings Jazz and David (Jazz et David, rois):
      Twenty-Seven Studies on Music and Modern Musicians, of Which
      the Studies on Jazz and American Composers are in French and
      English; the Others in English. Paris: Privately Printed for
      the Author by Les Presses Modernes, 1927. 259p.

           ————. Views and Interviews: a Reprint of Twenty-Seven Stud-
      ies on Music and Musicians. Paris: Les Orphelins, 1936. 213p.

  *   Simon, George Thomas. Simon Says: the Sights and Sounds of the
      Swing Era.
           * Cited below as item 859.

769. Sinclair, John, and Robert Levin. Music and Politics. New
      York: World Publishing Company, 1971. 133p., illus. (Jazz
      and Pop Books)
          Record reviews and articles, previously published in Jazz
      and Pop, 1965-71. Chiefly jazz; some consideration of rock.
      Written from radical viewpoint. Sinclair was manager of
      polemical rock group, MC-5.

770. Traill, Sinclair (ed.). Concerning Jazz. London: Faber,
      1957. 180p., illus., discog. (Popular Books)
          Mainly British contributions.

771. ————, and Gerald Lascelles (eds.). Just Jazz. London:
      Peter Davies, 1957. 226p. and 218p., illus., discog.
          Features, plus complete British discography of 1956 jazz
      releases. Discography paged separately.

          ———— (eds.). Just Jazz, 2. London: Peter Davies, 1958.
      193p. and 253p., illus., discog.

          ———— (eds.). Just Jazz, 3. London: Landsborough Publicat-
      ions; London: Four Square Books, 1959. 347p., illus., discog.

          ———— (eds.). Just Jazz, 4. London: Souvenir Pr., 1960.
      128p. and 159p., illus., discog.

772. Turner, Frederick. Remembering Song: Encounters With the New
      Orleans Jazz Tradition. New York: Viking Pr., 1982. 144p.,
      illus.

773. Ulanov, Barry, and George Thomas Simon (eds.). Jazz 1950.
      New York: Metronome, 1950. 104p.
          Assessments of the state of jazz, as of 1950.

774. Vian, Boris. Chroniques de jazz. Edited and introduced by
      Lucien Malson. Paris: La Jeune Parque, 1967; Paris: Union
      Générale d'Editions, 1971. 288p.
          Material first published in Jazz-Hot and Combat.

   * Williams, Martin T. Where's the Melody? A Listener's Intro-
      duction to Jazz.
          * Cited above as item 704.

   * Williamson, Ken (ed.). This is Jazz.
          * Cited below as item 1616.

                    6. ILLUSTRATION COLLECTIONS

775. Berendt, Joachim Ernst (comp.). Jazz-Optisch. Munich: Nymph-
      enburger Verlagshandlung, 1954. 72p., illus. 2nd. ed.:
      Zurich: Sansouci, 1956. 3rd. ed.: 1958; 4th. ed.: 1959. 75p.,
      illus.
          Photographs.

776. Bock, Richard, William Claxton, and Nesuhi Ertegun. _Jazz West Coast: a Portfolio of Photographs_. Hollywood, California: Linear Productions, 1955. 88p.
    Portraits of current performers.

777. Brask, Ole. _Jazz People: Photographs by Ole Brask_. Text by Dan Morgenstern. Foreword by Dizzy Gillespie. Introduction by James Jones. New York: Abrams, 1977. 300p., illus.

778. Delaunay, Charles. _Hot Iconography (Portraits)_. Paris: _Hot-Jazz_, 1939. 16p., illus.
    Photographs.

779. Friedman, Carol, and Gary Giddins. _A Moment's Notice: Photographs of American Jazz Musicians_. New York: Schirmer Books, 1983; London: Collier-Macmillan, 1984. 141p., illus.
    Text by Giddins.

780. Goldblatt, Burt. _Burt Goldblatt's Jazz Gallery_. New York: Newbold Publishing, 1982. 200p., illus.
    Photographs.

781. Gottlieb, William P. _The Golden Age of Jazz: On Location Portraits in Words and Pictures of More Than Two Hundred Outstanding Musicians From the Late 30's Through the 40's_. New York: Simon and Schuster; London: Quartet, 1979; New York: Da Capo Pr., 1985. 160p., illus., index.
    Author was reporter/photographer covering the jazz scene.

782. Hirschfeld, Albert. _Harlem as Seen by Hirschfeld_. Text by William Saroyan. New York: Hyperion Pr., 1941. 30p., illus.
    Includes coverage of jazz scene.

783. Matisse, Henri. _Jazz_. Munich: Piper, 1957. 51p., illus.
    Paintings and illustrations. "Printed for the Members of The Museum of Modern Art, New York."

784. National Portrait Gallery, Washington, D.C. "A Glimmer of Their Own Beauty": Black Sounds of the Twenties. Washington, D.C.: National Portrait Gallery, 1971. 32p., illus., bibliog.
    Exhibition catalog.

785. Oliver, John (ed.). _Jazz Classic: an Album of Personalities From the World of Jazz_. London: Tolgate Pr., 1962. 96p., illus. (A _Top Numbers_ Special)
    Photographs.

786. Ramsey, Frederic. _Where the Music Started: a Photographic Essay_. New Brunswick: Rutgers University, Institute of Jazz Studies, 1970. 34p., illus.
    Exhibition catalog. Photographs taken 1951-60. Pictures people of the Deep South, and their music.

787. Redfern, David. _David Redfern's Jazz Album_. Introduction by Buddy Rich. London: Eel Pie, 1980. 160p., illus., index.
    Photographs.

* Rockmore, Noel, Larry Borenstein, and Bill Russell. <u>Preserv-</u>
  <u>ation Hall Portraits: Paintings by Noel Rockmore</u>.
  * Cited below as item 896.

* Rose, Al, and Edmond Souchon. <u>New Orleans Jazz: a Family</u>
  <u>Album</u>.
  * Cited below as item 898.

788. Stock, Dennis, and Nat Hentoff. <u>Jazz Street</u>. Photographs by
  Dennis Stock. Introduction and commentary by Nat Hentoff.
  Garden City, New York: Doubleday; London: Deutsch, 1960. 193p.,
  illus.

789. Wilmer, Valerie. <u>The Face of Black Music</u>. Introduction by
  Archie Shepp. New York: Da Capo Pr., 1976. 118p., illus.
  Photographs.

7. MISCELLANEA

790. Baker, David, and Jeanne Baker (comps.). <u>Jazz Quiz Book</u>.
  Edited by Lisa Baker. Bloomington, Indiana: T.I.S., 1984.
  72p.

791.1 Lyttelton, Humphrey. <u>Humphrey Lyttelton's Jazz and Big Band</u>
  <u>Quiz</u>. London: Batsford, 1979. 95p., illus.

791.2 Williamson, Ken. <u>Jazz Quiz, 1</u>. Durham, England: Panda Publications, 1945. 24p., illus.

  ————. <u>Jazz Quiz, 2</u>. Durham, England: Panda Publications,
  1946. 28p., illus.

8. GENERAL HISTORIES

(a) Comprehensive Works

792. Berendt, Joachim Ernst. <u>Jazz: a Photo History</u>. Translated by
  William Odom. New York: New York: Schirmer Books; London:
  Deutsch, 1979. 355p., illus., discog., index.
  Originally published in German: Frankfurt/Main: Wolfgang
  Krüger Verlag, 1978, as <u>Photo-Story des Jazz</u>.

793. ————. <u>Das Jazzbuch: Entwicklung und Bedeutung der Jazzmusik</u>.
  Frankfurt/Main: Fischer, 1953. 240p., illus., discog., index.

  ————. <u>Das neue Jazzbuch: Entwicklung und Bedeutung der</u>
  <u>Jazzmusik</u>. Frankfurt/Main: Fischer, 1959. 318p., illus.,
  discog., index.

  ————. <u>The New Jazz Book: a History and Guide</u>. Translated
  from the German by Dan Morgenstern. New York: Hill and Wang,
  1962; London: Peter Owen, 1964. 314p., illus., discog., index.
  <u>2nd. ed.</u>: New York: Hill and Wang, 1964; <u>rev. ed.</u>: New York:
  Hill and Wang, 1970. 314p., illus., discog., index.

Comprehensive Works (cont.)

Berendt, Joachim Ernst. Das Jazzbuch: von New Orleans bis
Free Jazz: Entwicklung, Musiker, Elemente, Ensembles und Definition der Jazzmusik. Frankfurt/Main: Fischer, 1968. 334p.,
di cog., index.

————. The Jazz Book: From New Orleans to Rock and Free Jazz.
Translated by Dan Morgenstern, and Helmut and Barbara Bredig-
keit. New York: Lawrence Hill, 1973. 459p., discog., index.
Rev. ed.: New York: Lawrence Hill, 1975; London: Hart-Davis,
MacGibbon; London: Paladin, 1976. 459p., discog., index.

————. Das Jazzbuch: von Rag bis Rock: Entwicklung, Elemente,
Definition des Jazz, Musiker, Sänger, Combos, Big Bands, Electric Jazz, Jazz-Rock der siebziger Jahre. Mit ausführlicher
Discographie. Frankfurt/Main: Fischer, 1973. 426p., illus.,
discog., index.

————. Das Jazzbuch: von Rag bis Rock: Entwicklung, Elemente,
Musiker, Sänger, Combos, Big Bands. Neue illustrierte Ausgabe
mit erweiterte Discographie. Frankfurt/Main: Wolfgang Krüger
Verlag, 1976. 419p., illus., discog., index.

————. Das grosse Jazzbuch. Frankfurt/Main: Wolfgang Krüger
Verlag, 1981. 480p., illus., discog., index.

————. The Jazz Book: From Ragtime to Fusion, and Beyond.
With a New American Discography. Translated by Dan Morgenstern
and Helmut and Barbara Bredigkeit. Westport, Conn.: Lawrence
Hill, 1982. 436p., discog., index.

————. The Jazz Book: From New Orleans to Jazz Rock, and
Beyond. Translated by Helmut and Barbara Bredigkeit, with
Dan Morgenstern. London: Granada, 1983; London: Paladin, 1984.
530p., discog., index.
Discography (of British releases) by Brian Priestley.

794.   ———— (ed.). Die Story des Jazz: vom New Orleans zum Rock
Jazz. Mit Beiträgen von Werner Burkhardt, Reimer von Essen,
Leonard Feather, Ekkehard Jost, Karl Lippegans, Manfred Miller
und Dan Morgenstern. Stuttgart: Deutsche Verlagsanstalt, 1975.
209p., illus., bibliog., discog., index. Reinbek bei Hamburg:
Rowohlt, 1978. 285p., illus., bibliog., discog., index. (Rororo
Sachbuch, 7120)

————— (ed.). The Story of Jazz: From New Orleans to Rock.
Englewood Cliffs, New Jersey: Prentice-Hall; London: Barrie
and Jenkins, 1978. 192p., illus., bibliog., discog., index.

795.   Blesh, Rudi. This is Jazz: a Series of Lectures Given at the
San Francisco Museum of Art. San Francisco: The Author, 1943;
Los Angeles: Arts and Architecture, 1944; London: Jazz Music
Books, 1945. 36p., bibliog. notes, discog.
The development of New Orleans jazz outlined. Author con-
siders other styles to be inferior.

796. ————. <u>Shining Trumpets: a History of Jazz</u>. New York: Knopf;
      Toronto: Ryerson, 1946; London: Cassell, 1949. 365p., illus.,
      discog., index. <u>2nd. revised and enlarged ed.</u>: New York: Knopf
      (Reprinted: New York: Da Capo Pr., 1975); Toronto: McClelland;
      London: Cassell, 1958. 410p., illus., discog., index.
         Includes appendix of musical transcriptions. Extends the
      argument of New Orleans superiority originally presented in
      item 795.

797. Boeckman, Charles. <u>Cool, Hot, and Blue: a History of Jazz for</u>
      <u>Young People</u>. Washington, D.C.: R.B. Luce, 1968; New York:
      Washington Square Pr., 1970. 157p., illus., bibliog.

798. Coeuroy, André. <u>Histoire generale du jazz: strette, hot, swing</u>.
      Paris: Editions Denoël, 1942. 256p., discog.

799. Collier, James Lincoln. <u>The Making of Jazz: a Comprehensive</u>
      <u>History</u>. Boston: Houghton Mifflin; London: Macmillan, 1978;
      New York: Dell, 1979 (A Delta Special); London: Macmillan,
      1981 (Papermac Series). 543p., illus., bibliog., discog.,
      index.

800. Condon, Eddie. <u>We Called it Music: a Generation of Jazz</u>.
      Narration by Thomas Sugrue. New York: Holt, 1947 (Reprinted:
      Westport, Conn.: Greenwood Pr., 1970). 341p., illus., discog.,
      index. London: Peter Davies, 1948. 287p., illus., discog.,
      index. <u>Newly revised ed.: With Complete Discography by Dave</u>
      <u>Carey</u>. London: Transworld Publishers, 1962. 224p., illus.,
      discog., index. (Corgi Books)
         Autobiography of Condon, interspersed with history by Sugrue.
      Original discography by John Swingel.

801. Dauer, Alfons M. <u>Der Jazz: seine Ursprünge, und seine Entwick-</u>
      <u>lung</u>. Kassel: Erich Röth, 1958. 284p., illus., discog. (Das
      Gesicht der Völker)
         Includes musical transcriptions. Concentrates on the dev-
      elopment of the musical elements of jazz. In German.

802. Dexter, Dave. <u>The Jazz Story: from the '90s to the '60s</u>.
      Foreword by Woody Herman. Englewood Cliffs, New Jersey; London:
      Prentice- 11, 1964. 176p., illus., bibliog., discog.

803. Driggs, Frank, and Harris Lewing. <u>Black Beauty, White Heat: a</u>
      <u>Pictorial History of Classic Jazz, 1920-1950</u>. New York: Morrow,
      1982. 360p., illus.

804. Ehrich, Lillian. <u>What Jazz is All About: Illustrated With a</u>
      <u>Portrait Gallery of Jazz Greats</u>. New York: J. Messner, 1962;
      London: Gollancz, 1963. 181p., illus., bibliog., index. <u>Rev.</u>
      <u>ed.</u>: New York: J. Messner, 1975. 255p., illus., bibliog., index.
         History aimed at younger readers.

805. Finkelstein, Sidney. <u>Jazz: a People's Music</u>. Secaucus, New
      Jersey: Citadel Pr.; Toronto: McLeod, 1948; New York: Da Capo
      Pr., 1975 (Roots of Jazz). 278p., illus., discogs., index.
         Written from Marxist viewpoint.

806. Francis, André. Jazz. Translated and revised by Martin T.
     Williams. New York: Grove Pr. (Evergreen Books); Toronto:
     McClelland; London: Calder, 1960; New York: Da Capo Pr., 1976.
     (Roots of Jazz). 189p., illus., bibliog., discog.
          Originally published as Jazz, Paris: Editions du Seuil, 1958.

807. Goffin, Robert. Aux frontières du jazz. Preface by Pierre
     MacOrlan. Paris: Editions du Sagittaire, 1932. 256p., illus.
     (Les Documentaires)
          In French. The first distinction between hot jazz and
     commercial forms.

808. ———. Jazz: from the Congo to the Metropolitan. Translated
     by Walter Schaap and Leonard Feather. Introduction by Arnold
     Gingrich. Garden City, New York: Doubleday, Doran, 1944 (Re-
     printed: New York: Da Capo Pr., 1975). 254p., bibliog. New
     York: Editions for the Armed Forces, 1943. 384p.

     ———. Jazz: from Congo to Swing. London: Musicians Pr., 1946.
     273p., illus., bibliog.

     ———. Nouvelle histoire du Jazz: du Congo au Bebop. Intro-
     duction by Carlos de Radzitzky. Brussels: L'Ecran du Monde;
     Paris: Les Deux Sirènes, 1948. 334p.
          Revision; in French.

809. Harris, Rex. Jazz: an Account of its Origin and Growth. From
     the Early Drum Rhythms to the Highly Developed Music of the
     Present Day. Harmondsworth, Middlesex; Baltimore: Penguin,
     1952. 224p., illus., bibliog., discogs., index. (Pelican Books)
     2nd. ed.: 1953. 256p., illus., bibliog., discogs., index.
     3rd. ed.: 1954. 256p., illus., bibliog., discogs., index.
     4th. ed.: 1956. 272p., illus., bibliog., discog., index.
     5th. ed.: 1957. 272p., illus., bibliog., discog., index.

     ———. The Story of Jazz. With an afterword and discography
     by Sheldon Meyer. New York: Grosset and Dunlap, 1955 (Reprint-
     ed: Westport, Conn.: Greenwood Pr., 1980). 280p., discog.
     2nd. ed.: New York: Grosset and Dunlap, 1960. 280p., discog.
     (The Listener's Music Library)

810. Hentoff, Nat, and Albert John McCarthy (eds.). Jazz: New
     Perspectives on the History of Jazz by Twelve of the World's
     Foremost Jazz Critics and Scholars. New York: Rinehart, 1959
     (Reprinted: New York: Da Capo Pr., 1975); London: Cassell, 1960.
     387p., illus., bibliog., discog., index. London: Quartet, 1977.
     342p., illus.
          Specially-commissioned historical essays.

811. Hobson, Wilder. American Jazz Music. New York: Norton, 1939
     (Reprinted: New York: Da Capo Pr., 1976); London: Dent, 1940.
     230p., illus., discog., index. Rev. ed.: London: Dent, 1941.
     227p., illus., dicog., index.

812. Jones, Max (ed.). Jazz Photo Album: a History of Jazz in Pict-
     ures. London: British Yearbooks, 1947. 96p., illus.

813. Kaufman, Frederick, and John P. Guckin. The African Roots of
     Jazz. With advice from Cyril O. Earl. Sherman Oaks, Calif-
     ornia: Alfred Publishing, 1979. 148p., illus., bibliog.,
     index.
         Includes two records of musical examples.

814. Keepnews, Orrin, and Bill Grauer, Jr. (comps.). A Pictorial
     History of Jazz: People and Places, from New Orleans to Modern
     Jazz. Text and captions by Orrin Keepnews. New York: Crown,
     1955; London: Hale, 1956; London: Spring Books, 1959. 282p.,
     illus., index. New ed., revised by Orrin Keepnews: New York:
     Crown, 1966; London: Spring Books; London: Hamlyn, 1968. 297p.,
     illus., index.
         Chiefly illustrated.

815. Megill, Donald D., and Richard Demory. Introduction to Jazz
     History. Englewood Cliffs, New Jersey; London: Prentice-Hall,
     1984. 200p., illus.

816. Morgenstern, Dan. The Jazz Story: an Outline History of Jazz.
     New York: New York Jazz Museum, 1973.   p., bibliog., discog.

  * Nanry, Charles (ed.). American Music: from Storyville to
     Woodstock.
         * Cited above as item 386.

817. Newman, Charles. White Jazz. Garden City, New York: Doubleday,
     1984. 216p., illus.

818. Niemoeller, Adolph Frederick. The Story of Jazz: an Account
     of the Origin and Development of Hot Music. Girard, Kansas:
     Haldeman-Julius, 1946. 32p.

819. Noble, Peter. Transatlantic Jazz: a Short History of American
     Jazz, and a Study of its Leading Exponents and Personalities.
     Including a Guide to Classical Jazz Records, and a Complete
     Bibliography. London: Citizen Pr., 1945. 96p., bibliog.,
     discog.

820. Paul, Eliot. That Crazy American Music. Indianapolis: Bobbs-
     Merrill, 1957 (Reprinted: Port Washington, New York: Kennikat
     Pr., 1970). 317p., bibliog. Toronto: Saunders, 1957; (as That
     Crazy American Music: the Story of North American Jazz) London:
     Muller, 1957. 280p.

821. Polillo, Arrigo. Jazz: a Guide to the History and Development
     of Jazz and Jazz Musicians. Translated from the Italian by
     Peter Muccini. English edition edited by Neil Ardley. London;
     New York: Hamlyn, 1969. 160p., illus., bibliog., index. (A
     Little Guide in Colour)
         Originally published as Conoscere il jazz, Milan: Mondadori,
     1967.

822. Shapiro, Nat, and Nat Hentoff (eds.). Hear Me Talkin' to Ya:
     the Story of Jazz by the Men Who Made It. New York: Rinehart,
     1955 (Reprinted: New York: Dover, 1966). 432p., indexes.
     London: Peter Davies, 1955. 383p. Harmondsworth, Middlesex:
     Penguin, 1982. 414p.

823. Stearns, Marshall W. The Story of Jazz. New York; London:
     Oxford University Pr., 1956; London: Sidgwick and Jackson, 1957.
     367p., illus., bibliog., index.
     Bibliography compiled by Robert George Reisner.

     ————. The Story of Jazz: With an Extended Bibliography, and
     a Syllabus of Fifteen Lectures on the History of Jazz. London:
     Muller; New York: New American Library, 1958. (A Mentor Book).
     272p., illus., bibliog., index.

     ————. The Story of Jazz: New Edition. New York; London:
     Oxford University Pr., 1970. 384p., illus., bibliog., index.

824. Tirro, Frank. Jazz: a History. New York: Norton, 1977; London:
     Dent, 1979. 457p., illus., bibliog., discog., index.

825. Travis, Dempsey J. (comp.). An Autobiography of Black Jazz.
     Washington, D.C.: Urban Research Institute, 1983. 460p., illus.
     Reminiscences by members of the jazz community.

826. Ulanov, Barry. A History of Jazz in America. New York: Viking
     Pr., 1952 (Reprinted: New York: Da Capo Pr., 1972); London:
     Hutchinson, 1958. 382p., index.

827. Werner, Otto. The Origins and Development of Jazz. Duboque,
     Iowa: Kendall-Hunt, 1984. 160p.

828. Wilson, John Stuart. Jazz: Where It Came From, Where It's At.
     Washington, D.C.: United States Information Agency, 1970. 76p.,
     illus.
     For overseas distribution only.

829. Woodward, Woody. Jazz Americana: the Story of Jazz, and, All-
     Time Jazz Greats, From Basin Street to Carnegie Hall. Los
     Angeles: Trend Books, 1956. 128p., illus., discog.

                         (b) Periods and Styles

                           (i) General Works

830. Gridley, Mark C. Jazz Styles. Englewood Cliffs, New Jersey;
     London: Prentice-Hall, 1978. 421p., illus., bibliog., discog.,
     index.
     Chronological survey and comparison; based on educational
     courses taught by the author. Both bibliography and discography
     are annotated.

831. Mecklenburg, Carl Gregor, Herzog zu. Stilformen des Jazz: vom
     Ragtime zum Chicago-Stil. With a discography by Manfred Scheff-
     ner. Vienna: Universal Edition, 1973. 196p., discog. (Reihe
     Jazz. Ergänzungen, 1)

832. Taylor, Billy. Jazz Piano: a Jazz History. Duboque, Iowa:
     William C. Brown, 1982. 264p., illus.
     Piano styles chronicled and examined.

(ii) Early Jazz

833. Grossman, William Leonard, and Jack W. Farrell. The Heart of Jazz. Line drawings by Lamartine Le Goullon. New York: New York University Pr., 1956 (Reprinted: New York: Da Capo Pr., 1976); London: Vision Pr., 1958. 315p., illus., bibliog. notes, index.
   Concentrates on New Orleans traditional jazz style, as performed by White revivalists in California. Calls for "amateur maintenance of the tradition."

834. Longstreet, Stephen. The Real Jazz, Old and New. Baton Rouge: Louisiana State University Pr., 1956; Westport, Conn.: Negro Universities Pr., 1966; Westport, Conn.: Greenwood Pr., 1969. 202p., illus.
   Personal account of traditional jazz. Illustrated by the author.

835. Lyttelton, Humphrey. The Best of Jazz: Basin Street to Harlem: Jazz Masters and Masterpieces, 1917-30. London: Robson Books, 1978; Dallas: Crescendo Books, 1979. 214p., illus., discog., index. London: Penguin, 1980. 239p., illus., discog., index.

836. Matthew, Brian. Trad Mad. London: World Distributors, in association with Souvenir Pr., 1962. 128p., illus. (Consul Books)
   Account of the British traditional jazz boom, late 1950s to early 1960s.

837. Middleton, Richard. The Rise of Jazz. Prepared for the (Open University) Course Team. Milton Keynes, Buckinghamshire: Open University Pr., 1979. 76p., illus., bibliog. (Arts: A Third-Level Course: The Rise of Modernism in Music, 1890-1935. Units 25-27)
   For use as part of a study course.

838. Panassié, Hugues. Cinq mois à New York (Octobre 1938-Février 1939): Souvenirs. Paris: Corrêa, 1947. 164p.

839. ———. Douze années de jazz (1927-1938): Souvenirs. Paris: Corrêa. 1946. 281p., illus.

840. Schuller, Gunther. Early Jazz: its Roots and Musical Development. New York; London: Oxford University Pr., 1968. 401p., bibliog. notes, discog., index.
   To beginnings of big band era.

(iii) Swing and Dance Band Era

Allen, Stuart S. The Stars of Swing: Swing Who's Who, America and Britain.
   * Cited below as item 1527.

Swing and Dance Band Era (cont.)

841. Arundel, Paul. This Swing Business: a Survey of British Dance
      Music Today. London: Arthur Unwin, 1947. 24p., illus.

842. Bookson, Martin (ed.). Jive Times. London: Tottenham Rhythm
      Club, 1943.   p.
      Essays on swing.

843. Colin, Sid. And the Bands Played On. Foreword by George
      Chisholm. London: Elm Tree Books, 1977. 139p., illus.,
      bibliog., discog.
          British dance bands, 1919-55. Author played with the bands
      of Ambrose, Jack Jackson, and others. Accompanied by double
      long-play record, And the Bands Played On (Decca DDV 5001/2),
      featuring the bands described.

844. Cons, Carl, and George Von Physter. Destiny: a Study of Swing
      Musicians. Chicago: Down Beat Publishing Company, 1938. 20p.,
      illus.

  *   Dance, Stanley (ed.). Jazz Era: the Forties.
          * Cited below as item 1544.

  *   ———. The World of Swing.
          * Cited below as item 1545.

845. Fernett, Gene. Swing Out: Great Negro Dance Bands. Midland,
      Michigan: Pendell Publishing, 1970. 176p., illus., index.

846. ———. A Thousand Golden Horns: the Exciting Age of America's
      Greatest Dance Bands. Midland, Michigan: Pendell Publishing,
      1966. 171p., illus.

  *   Gottlieb, William P. The Golden Age of Jazz: On Location
      Portraits in Words and Pictures of More Than Two Hundred
      Outstanding Musicians, from the Late 30's Through the 40's.
          * Cited above as item 781.

847. Graves, Charles (pseud. of Charles Patrick Ranke). One Hundred
      Facts on Swing Music. London: Naldrett Pr., 1948. 32p.
      (Smatterbooks, 4)

848. Jackson, Arthur. The World of Big Bands: the Sweet and Swing-
      ing Years. Foreword by Edmund Anderson. New York: Arco Pub-
      lishing; Newton Abbot, Devon; Vancouver: David and Charles,
      1977. 130p., illus., bibliog., index.

849. Jackson, Edgar, and Leonard Hibbs. Encyclopaedia of Swing.
      London: Decca Record Company, 1941. 83p. New ed.: London:
      Decca Record Company, 1942. 94p.

850. Leslie, Peter. Big Bands of the Thirties. London: New English
      Library, 1971.   p., illus.

851.   Lyttelton, Humphrey. The Best of Jazz, II: Enter the Giants.
       London: Robson Books; Dallas: Crescendo Books, 1981. 239p.,
       illus., bibliog., discog., index.
       Jazz developments in the Thirties. Continues item 835.

852.   McCarthy, Albert John. Big Band Jazz. London: Barrie and
       Jenkins; New York: Putnam, 1974; New York: Berkley Publishing,
       1977; London: Peerage, 1983. 360p., illus., bibliog., discog.,
       index.

853.   ————. The Dance Band Era: the Dancing Decades, from Ragtime
       to Swing, 1910-1950. London: Studio Vista; Philadelphia:
       Chilton, 1971; London: Spring Books, 1974. 176p., illus.,
       bibliog., discog., index.

854.   Pearsall, Ronald. Popular Music of the Twenties. Newton
       Abbot, Devon: David and Charles; Totowa, New Jersey: Rowman
       and Littlefield; Detroit: Gale, 1976. 176p., illus., bibliog.,
       index.
       General trends, particularly the rise of jazz to mass pop-
       ularity. Emphasis on British scene.

855.   Rosenkrantz, Timme. Swing Photo Album. Copenhagen, Denmark:
       The Author, 1939. 37p., illus.

       ————. Swing Photo Album, 1939: a Revised Reissue of Photo-
       graphs Based on Timme Rosenkrantz's Swing Photo Album, 1939.
       Incorporating a Section of Photographs From Other Rosenkrantz
       Publications, including "Jazzrevy and Swing Music." Lowestoft,
       Suffolk: Scorpion Pr./Dobell's Record Shop, 1964. 44p., illus.
       Chiefly illustrated.

856.   Rowe, John. Swing Souvenir. London: Findon Publications,
       1946.   p.

857.   Rust, Brian Arthur Lovell. The Dance Bands. London: Ian
       Allen; New Rochelle, New York: Arlington House, 1974. 160p.,
       illus., index.

858.   Simon, George Thomas. The Big Bands. Foreword by Frank
       Sinatra. New York: Macmillan; London: Collier-Macmillan,
       1967. 537p., illus., discog., index. Rev. ed.: New York:
       Macmillan; London: Collier-Macmillan, 1971. 584p., illus.,
       discog., index. 3rd. ed.: New York: Macmillan; London: Collier-
       Macmillan, 1974. 596p., illus., discog., index. 4th. ed.:
       New York: Schirmer Books; London: Collier-Macmillan, 1981.
       614p., illus., discog., index.
       The standard swing history.

859.   ————. Simon Says: the Sights and Sounds of the Swing Era,
       1935-1955. New Rochelle, New York: Arlington House, 1971.
       491p., illus., index.
       Selected articles by Simon from Metronome, 1935-55. Includ-
       es appendix listing Metronome band reviews, 1935-46.

Swing and Dance Band Era (cont.)

860. Thornes, Vernon M. (ed.). Swing Music Art. Dewsbury, York-
      shire: The Author, 1943. 24p.
           Essay collection.

  *   Treadwell, Bill. The Big Book of Swing.
           * Cited below as item 1603.

  *   Walker, Leo. The Big Band Almanac.
           * Cited below as item 1607.

861. ————. The Wonderful Era of the Great Dance Bands. Berkley,
      California: Howell-North Books, 1964; Garden City, New York:
      Doubleday, 1972. (A Windfall Book). 315p., illus.

  *   White, Mark. The Observer's Book of Big Bands.
           * Cited below as item 1608.

                        (iv) Modern Jazz

862. Backus, Rob. Fire Music: a Political History of Jazz. New
      York: Vanguard Books, 1976. 164p., illus., bibliog. refs.
           Emphasis on Black avant-garde jazzmen and their work.
      Argues that Black music forms developed in tandem with the
      advancement of Black society generally.

863. Budds, Michael J. Jazz in the Sixties: the Expansion of
      Musical Resources and Techniques. Iowa City: University of
      Iowa Pr., 1978. 141p., bibliog., index.

864. Carles, Philippe, and Jean-Louis Comolli. Free Jazz/Black
      Power. Paris: Editions Champ Libre, 1971. 435p.
           In French.

865. Feather, Leonard Geoffrey. Inside Be-Bop. New York: J.J.
      Robbins, 1949. Reprinted (as Inside Jazz): New York: J.J.
      Robbins, 1949; New York: Da Capo Pr., 1977 (Roots of Jazz).
      103p., illus., discog.
           Concentrates on technical aspects.

866. ————. Jazz: an Exciting Story of Today's Jazz. Design and
      illustrations by Harry Garo. Los Angeles: Petersen, 1958
      (Trend Books); New York: Panda Books, 1959. 80p., illus.

867. Griffin, Nard. To Be Or Not to Bop. New York: Leo B. Workman,
      1948. 24p.
           Bebop and its exponents briefly examined.

868. Jost, Ekkehard. Free Jazz. Graz, Austria; Vienna: Universal
      Edition, 1974; New York: Da Capo Pr., 1981 (Roots of Jazz).
      215p., illus., bibliog., discog.

869. Kofsky, Frank. Black Nationalism and the Revolution in Music.
      New York: Pathfinder Pr., 1970. 280p., illus., bibliog. notes.,
      discog. (A Merit Book)
          Connects Black aspirations and avant-garde Black jazz.

870. Litweiler, John. The Freedom Principle: Jazz After 1958.
      New York: Morrow, 1984. 338p., illus.

871. McRae, Barry. The Jazz Cataclysm. London: Dent; South Bruns-
      wick, New Jersey: A.S. Barnes, 1967; New York: Da Capo Pr.,
      1984 (Roots of Jazz). 184p., discog., index.
          From 1950's "cool" to 1960's free-form styles.

872. Maggs, Jean Malvina. Jazz For Contemporary People. Ilfra-
      combe, Devon: Stockwell, 1961. 62p.
          Developments 1945-60.

873. Mecklenburg, Carl Gregor, Herzog zu. Stilformen des modernen
      Jazz: vom Swing zum Free Jazz. With a discography by Manfred
      Scheffner. Baden-Baden, West Germany: Koerner, 1979. 291p.,
      discog. (Collection d'Etudes musicologiques/Sammlung Musik-
      wissenschaftlicher Abhandlungen, 63)

874. Morgan, Alun, and Raymond Horricks. Modern Jazz: a Survey of
      Developments Since 1939. Foreword by Don Rendell. London:
      Gollancz, 1956; Westport, Conn.: Greenwood Pr., 1977. 240p.,
      discog., index.

875. Oakes, Philip. At the Jazz-Band Ball: a Memory of the 1950's.
      London: Deutsch, 1983. 251p.
          Third volume of his autobiography; tells how he began to
      appreciate modern jazz.

876. Tamony, Peter. Funky. San Francisco: The Author, 1968. 10p.
      (Americanisms: Content and Continuum, 20)

877. Tsoukalas, Nicholas. Modern Jazz Technique; Movements.
      Detroit: The Author, 1962. 3p.

878. Wilmer, Valerie. As Serious as Your Life: the Story of the
      New Jazz. London: Alison and Busby; London: Quartet, 1977.
      296p., illus., bibliog., index.
          Exposition of new Black consciousness as expressed in avant-
      garde Black jazz. Photographs by the author. Includes append-
      ix of biographical information on over 150 musicians associated
      with new jazz.

879. Wilson, John Steuart. Jazz: the Transition Years, 1940-1960.
      New York: Appleton-Century-Crofts; New York: Irvington, 1966.
      185p., illus., bibliog., discog., index.

                           (v) Jazz-Rock

   * Coryell, Julie, and Laura Friedman. Jazz-Rock Fusion: the
      People -- the Music.
          * Cited below as item 1542.

9. REGIONAL HISTORIES

A. UNITED STATES

(a) General Works

880. Ostransky, Leroy. Jazz City: the Impact of Our Cities on the
      Development of Jazz. Englewood Cliffs, New Jersey; London:
      Prentice-Hall, 1978. 274p., bibliog., discog., index. (A
      Spectrum Book)

(b) Individual Cities and States

(i) Chicago

881. Ramsey, Frederic, Jr. Chicago Documentary: Portrait of a Jazz
      Era. London: Jazz Sociological Society, 1944. 36p.
          Script of a dramatised radio documentary.

882. Venables, Ralph G.V., and Stewart Williams. Jazz in Chicago.
      Cardiff, Wales: The Authors, 1946. 24p. (Jazz Information
      Booklets)

(ii) Indiana

883. Schiedt, Duncan P. The Jazz State of Indiana. Pittsboro,
      Indiana: The Author, 1977. 256p., illus., index.
          Emphasis on the Twenties and Thirties.

(iii) Kansas City

884. Russell, Ross. Jazz Style in Kansas City and the Southwest.
      Berkeley, California; London: University of California Pr.,
      1971 (Reissued: 1973; 1982). 292p., illus., bibliog., discog.,
      index.
          Developments in often-overlooked jazz center.

(iv) New Orleans

885. Allen, Richard B. New Orleans Life and New Orleans Jazz:
      Smithsonian Institution 1968 Festival of American Folk Life.
      Washington, D.C.: Smithsonian Institution, 1968.   p., illus.
          Exhibition catalog.

886. Asbury, Herbert. The French Quarter: an Informal History of
      the New Orleans Underworld. New York: Knopf, 1936; Garden City,
      New York: Garden City Pr., 1938. 462p., illus. London: Jarrolds
      1937. 348p.

887. Buerkle, Jack V., and Danny Barker. Bourbon Street Black: the
     New Orleans Black Jazzman. New York; London: Oxford University
     Pr., 1973. 244p., illus., bibliog. notes, index.
        Study of the lives of fifty-one local traditional-style
     jazz musicians.

  * Charters, Samuel Barclay. Jazz: New Orleans, 1885-1967: an
     Index to the Negro Musicians of New Orleans.
        * Cited below as item 1538.

888. Colyer, Ken. New Orleans and Back. Delph, Yorkshire: Brooks
     and Pratt for The Author, 1968. 40p.
        British jazz musician's account of his visit to New Orleans
     in search of jazz during the 1950's.

889. Evans, Oliver. New Orleans. New York: Macmillan, 1959. 195p.,
     illus.
        Includes description of the City's jazz life.

890. French Quarter Interviews. New Orleans: Vagabond Pr., 1969.
     96p., illus.
        Interviews with contemporary figures; including Danny Baker,
     Curator of the City's Jazz Museum.

891. Goffin, Robert. La Nouvelle-Orléans: Capitale du jazz. New
     York: Editions de la Maison Française, 1946. 269p.

892. Kmen, Henry A. Music in New Orleans: the Formative Years,
     1791-1841. Baton Rouge: Louisiana State University Pr., 1967.
     314p., illus.
        History of White New Orleans music. Argues that jazz devel-
     oped in the City as a result of racially discriminatory laws.

893. Longstreet, Stephen. Sportin' House: a History of the New
     Orleans Sinners and the Birth of Jazz. Los Angeles: Sherbourne
     Pr., 1965. 293p., illus.
        Romantic account of life in the City (especially in Story-
     ville) during the early jazz era. Illustrated with the author's
     paintings and drawings.

894. Martinez, Raymond J. (comp.). Portraits of New Orleans Jazz:
     Its People and Places; Miscellaneous Notes. New Orleans: Hope
     Publishers; Gretna, Louisiana: Pelican Publishing, 1971. 63p.,
     illus., bibliog.
        Pieces on jazz development in New Orleans. Illustrated from
     the collections of the New Orleans Jazz Museum.

895. New Orleans Jazz Club. The New Orleans Jazz Museum: Fifth
     Anniversary Celebration. New Orleans: New Orleans Jazz Club,
     1966.   p.

896. Rockmore, Noel, Larry Borenstein, and Bill Russell. Preservat-
     ion Hall Portraits: Paintings by Noel Rockmore. Baton Rouge:
     Louisiana State University Pr., 1968. unpaged, illus.
        Black-and-white reproductions of Rockmore's paintings, with
     brief biographical sketches of the subjects by Borenstein and
     Russell.

New Orleans (cont.)

897.   Rose, Al. <u>Storyville, New Orleans. Being an Authentic</u>
       <u>Illustrated Account of the Notorious Red-Light District.</u>
       Montgomery, Alabama: University of Alabama Pr., 1974. 225p.,
       illus.
            Local history. Includes coverage of jazz.

898.   ———, and Edmond Souchon. <u>New Orleans Jazz: a Family Album.</u>
       Baton Rouge: Louisiana State University Pr., 1967. 304p.,
       illus., index. <u>Rev. ed.</u>: Baton Rouge: Louisiana State Univ-
       ersity Pr., 1978. 338p., illus., index. <u>3rd. rev. and enlar-</u>
       <u>ged ed.</u>: Baton Rouge: Louisiana State University Pr.; Gretna,
       Louisiana: Pelican Publishing, 1984. 416p., illus., index.
            Includes coverage of brass bands; also brief biographical
       sketches of over one thousand musicians.

   *   Stagg, Tom. <u>New Orleans: the Revival.</u>
            Cited below as item 4449.

899.   Williams, Stewart, and Brian Arthur Lovell Rust. <u>Jazz in</u>
       <u>New Orleans</u>. Cardiff, Wales: Jazz Information Publications,
       1946. 28p.

                          (v) New York

                       (a) General Works

900.   Charters, Samuel Barclay, and Leonard Kunstadt. <u>Jazz: a</u>
       <u>History of the New York Scene</u>. Garden City, New York: Double-
       day, 1962; New York: Da Capo Pr., 1981 (Roots of Jazz). 382p.,
       illus., bibliog., discog., index.
            Researched by Kunstadt; written by Charters. Developments
       from turn of Century to late 1950's. Includes material from
       contemporary sources.

901.   Johnson, James Weldon. <u>Black Manhattan</u>. New York: Knopf,
       1930 (Reissued: 1940); New York: Atheneum; New York: Arno Pr./
       New York Times, 1968. 284p., illus., index.
            Includes coverage of jazz and popular music. Author
       (brother of composer J. Rosamond Johnson) was lyricist, and
       prominent local figure.

902.   Shaw, Arnold. <u>The Street That Never Slept: New York's Fabled</u>
       <u>52nd. Street</u>. New York: Coward, McCann, and Geoghegan, 1971;
       New York (as <u>52nd. Street: the Street of Jazz</u>): Da Capo Pr.,
       1977. 378p., illus., index.
            Account of New York's night-life center. Emphasis on its
       jazz clubs, 1930's and 1940's. Long interviews with key
       personalities, interwoven with histories of significant
       venues.

(b) Harlem

903. Clarke, John Hendrik (ed.). <u>Harlem, U.S.A.: the Story of a City Within a City</u>. Berlin: Seven Seas Books, 1964. 361p., illus., bibliog. notes. <u>Rev. ed.</u>: New York: Collier Books, 1971. 388p., illus., bibliog. notes.
     Includes account of the Harlem jazz scene, by William R. Dixon.

   * Hirschfeld, Al. <u>Harlem as Seen by Hirschfeld</u>.
       * Cited above as item 782.

904. Huggins, Nathan Irving. <u>Harlem Renaissance</u>. New York; London: Oxford University Pr., 1971. 343p., illus., index.
     Includes musical coverage.

905. Schoener, Allon (ed.). <u>Harlem On My Mind: the Cultural Capital of Black America, 1900-1968</u>. New York: Random House, 1968. 255p., illus.
     Based on exhibition, Metropolitan Museum of Art, 1968. Compilation of contemporary newspaper items, and photographs. Includes musical (particularly jazz) coverage.

906. Thurman, Wallace. <u>Negro Life in New York's Harlem</u>. Girard, Kansas: Haldeman-Julius, n.d.   64p.
     Includes jazz coverage.

(vi) San Francisco

907. Stoddard, Tom. <u>Jazz on the Barbary Coast</u>. Chigwell, Essex: Storyville Publications, 1982. 192p., illus., bibliog., index.

B. OTHER COUNTRIES

(1) EUROPE

(a) General Works

908. Goddard, Chris. <u>Jazz Away From Home</u>. New York; London: Paddington Pr., 1979; New York: Da Capo Pr., 1985 (Roots of Jazz). 319p., illus., index.
     Account of American-born jazz musicians, singers, and dancers who worked chiefly in Europe. World War One onwards.

Europe (cont.)

(b) Individual Countries

(i) Austria

909. Kraner, Dietrich Heinz, and Klaus Schulz. <u>Jazz in Austria:</u>
<u>Historische Entwicklung und Diskographie des Jazz in Oester-</u>
<u>reich.</u> Graz, Austria; Vienna: Universal Edition, 1972. 95p.,
illus., discog. (Beiträge zur Jazzforschung, 2)
     Discography of Austrian jazz. Historical outline in German
(with English summary); rest of text in English.

(ii) Belgium

910. Pernet, Robert. <u>Jazz in Little Belgium: Historique (1881-1966)</u>;
<u>Discographie (1894-1966)</u>. Brussels: Editions Sigma, 1967.
520p., bibliog., discog.
     Discography of jazz records by, or with, Belgian musicians.
Includes brief historical outline. Text alternates between
French and English. Bibliography cites approximately ninety
books; also periodicals.

(iii) Britain

911. Boulton, David. <u>Jazz in Britain.</u> Foreword by Chris Barber.
London: W.H. Allen; Toronto: Smithers, 1958. 206p., illus.,
discog.

912. Brunton, Louis D. (ed.). <u>Jazz at the Town Hall.</u> Birmingham,
England: The Author, 1948. 48p., illus.

913. Carr, Ian. <u>Music Outside: Contemporary Jazz in Britain.</u> London: Latimer New Dimensions, 1973. 179p., illus., bibliog.,
discog., index.

914. Cotterrell, Roger (ed.). <u>Jazz Now: the Jazz Centre Society</u>
<u>Guide.</u> Preface by Spike Milligan. London: Quartet/Jazz Centre
Society, 1976. 216p., illus., bibliog., filmog., index.
     Outline of the current state of the British jazz scene.
Includes directory of British jazz musicians.

915. Godbolt, Jim. <u>A History of Jazz in Britain, 1919-50.</u> London:
Quartet, 1984. 306p., illus., bibliog., discog., index.

916. Kinnell, Bill (ed.). <u>Midland Rhythm News.</u> Chilwell, Nottinghamshire: The Author, 1943. 12p.

917. Walker, Edward S. <u>Don't Jazz: It's Music; or, Some Notes on</u>
<u>Popular Syncopated Music in England During the Twentieth Cent-</u>
<u>ury.</u> Walsall, Staffordshire: The Author, 1978. 100p., illus.
     The development of British jazz chronicled.

(iv) Denmark

918. Nielsen, Mogens Holmegaard, and Magister Johannes Noergaard.
      Dansk Jazz-Album. Aarhus, Denmark: Etala Musikforlag, n.d.
      80p., illus.
          In Danish.

(v) Finland

919. Granholm, Ake (ed.). Finnish Jazz: History, Musicians, Disco-
      graphy. Helsinki: Foundation for the Promotion of Finnish
      Music, 1974. 39p., discog.
          Includes brief biographies of Finnish jazz musicians.

(vi) Germany

920. Drechsler, Karlheinz. Fascination Jazz: Jazz in der D.D.R.
      Photographs by Sigurd Rosenhaim. Berlin: V.E.B. Lied der
      Zeit, 1974. 124p., illus.
          In German. Account of jazz developments in East Germany.

921. Jazz Kompendium Deutschland. Berlin: Gerhard Kowalski Verlag.
      annual, 1982- .
          Features on the year's developments; plus addresses of
      agents, clubs, artists, record companies, and other organizat-
      ions.

922. Lange, Horst Heinz. Die Geschichte des Jazz in Deutschland:
      die Entwicklung von 1910 bis 1960, mit Diskographie. Lübecke,
      West Germany: Uhle und Kleimann, 1960. 172p., illus., discog.

923. ————. Jazz in Deutschland: die deutsche Jazz-Chronik, 1900-
      1960. Berlin: Colloquium Verlag, 1966. 210p., illus., bibliog.

924. Noglik, Bert, and Heinz-Jürgen Lindner. Jazz im Gespräch.
      Berlin: Verlag Neue Musik, 1978. 184p.
          Jazz in East Germany.

925. Rudorf, Reginald. Jazz in der Zone. Cologne; Berlin: Kiepen-
      heuer und Witsch, 1964. 133p.
          Jazz in East Germany.

(vii) Holland

926. Elings, Arie. Bibliographie van de Nederlands Jazz. Nijmegen,
      Holland: Stichting Algemene Openbare Bibliotheek, 1966. 22p.,
      indexes.
          In Dutch. Bibliography of jazz in Holland. Classified
      arrangement; lists 157 items.

Holland (cont.)

927. Jazz und Geimproviseerde Muziek in Nederland. Utrecht; Ant-
      werp: Uitgverijttet Spectrum, 1978. 199p.

                        (viii) Italy

928. Mazzoletti, Adriano (et al.). Quaranti anni di jazz in Italia.
      Milan: Dischi Ricordi, 1964. 32p.

                        (ix) Norway

929. Angell, Olav, Jan Erik Vold, and Einar Okland. Jazz i Norge.
      Oslo: Gyldendal Norsk Forlag, 1975. 250p., illus.

                        (x) Switzerland

930. Hippenmeyer, Jean-Roland. Le Jazz en Suisse, 1930-1970.
      Yverdon, Switzerland: Editions de la Thièle, 1971. 245p.,
      illus.

                        (2) EASTERN BLOC

931. Batasev, Alexei N. Sovietsky Jazz. Moscow: Muzika, 1972.
      175p., illus.
           In Russian. History and survey of Soviet jazz.

932. Bergl, Milos. Českolovenský Jazz, 1920-1960. Prague: Supra-
      phon, 1965. 22p.
           Jazz in Czechoslovakia.

933. Doruzka, Lubomir, and Ivan Polednák. Českolovenský Jazz:
      minulosta a pritomnost. Prague: Supraphon, 1967. 312p.
           History, and contemporary jazz developments in Czechoslov-
      akia.

   * Gonda, Janos. Who's Who in Hungarian Jazz.
           * Cited below as item 1560.

   * Mazur, Mladen M. A Hundred Names of Yugoslav Jazz: a Short
      Who is Who in Hungarian Jazz.
           * Cited below as item 1581.

934. Starr, S. Frederick. Red and Hot: the Fate of Jazz in the
      Soviet Union, 1917-1980. New York; London: Oxford University
      Pr., 1983. 368p., index.

(3) NON-EUROPEAN COUNTRIES

* Hayes, Milehan, Ray Scribner, and Peter Magee. <u>The Encyclopedia of Australian Jazz.</u>
      * Cited below as item 1570.

935. Uenoda, Setsuo. <u>Japan and Jazz: Sketches and Essays on Japan-
     ese City Life.</u> Tokyo: Taiheiyosha Pr., 1930. 184p., illus.

* Williams, Mike. <u>The Australian Jazz Explosion</u>.
      * Cited below as item 1615.

10. VENUES

(a) Clubs

(i) General Works

936. Asman, James (comp.). <u>The N.F.J.O. Blue Book: Jazz Club Guide
     (Including a History of the N.F.J.O., 1948-1952)</u>. London:
     National Federation of Jazz Organizations, Central Office,
     1953. 100p., illus.

937. Durante, Jimmy, and Jack Kofoed. <u>Night Clubs</u>. New York: Knopf,
     1931. 246p., illus.

938. Glico, Jack. <u>Madness After Midnight</u>. London: Paul Elek, 1952.
     145p., illus. <u>Rev. ed.</u>: London: Paul Elek, 1960. 160p., illus.
         By night club bandleader.

939. Sylvester, Robert. <u>No Cover Charge: a Backward Look at the
     Night Clubs of New York</u>. New York: Dial Pr., 1956. 301p.
     London: Peter Davies, 1957. 218p.

940.1 Walker, Stanley. <u>The Night Club Era</u>. Introduction by Alva
     Johnston. New York: Blue Ribbon Books, 1933. 327p., index.

(ii) Individual Clubs

Birdland

940.2 <u>The Birdland Story</u>. New York: Birdland, 1953. 40p., illus.

Cotton Club

941. Haskins, James. <u>The Cotton Club</u>. New York: Random House, 1977;
     London: Robson Books, 1985. 172p., illus.

Individual Clubs (cont.)

Ronnie Scott's

942. Green, Benny. <u>Jazz Decade, London: Ten Years at Ronnie Scott's</u>.
      Designed and edited by John D'Amicis. Photographs by Frederick
      Warren. London: Kings Road Publishing, 1969. 36p., illus.,
      discog.

943. Grime, Kitty. <u>Jazz at Ronnie Scott's</u>. Photography by Valerie
      Wilmer. London: Hale, 1979. 192p., illus., index.
         Personal recollections, and interviews with performers.

944. Scott, Ronnie. <u>Some of My Best Friends Are Blues</u>. With Mike
      Hennessey. Cartoons by Mel Calman. 125p., illus.
         Reminiscences by owner of the Club.

Stork Club

945. Allen, Mearle L. <u>Welcome to the Stork Club</u>. San Diego: A.S.
      Barnes; London: Tantivity Pr., 1980. 294p., illus.

(b) Festivals

946. Agostinelli, Anthony J. (ed.). <u>The Newport Jazz Festival, Rhode
      Island, 1954-1971: a Bibliography, Discography, and Filmography</u>.
      Providence, Rhode Island: The Author, 1977. 64p.

947. Goldblatt, Burt. <u>The Newport Jazz Festival: the Illustrated
      History</u>. New York: Dial Pr., 1977. 287p., illus., discogs.
         Photography by the author. Coverage 1954-76. Includes
      discography and program for each Festival.

948. Lyons, Jimmy, and Ira Kamin. <u>Dizzy, Duke, the Count, and Me:
      the Story of the Monterey Jazz Festival</u>. San Francisco: Cal-
      ifornia Living Books, 1978. 184p., illus.

949. Playboy. <u>The Playboy Jazz Festival Yearbook</u>. Chicago: <u>Playboy</u>
      Jazz Festivals, 1959. 66p., illus.
         Only issue.

(c) Motion Pictures

950. Gautier, Henri. <u>Jazz au cinéma</u>. Lyon, France: S.E.R.D.O.C.,
      1960. 36p. (Société d'Etudes, de Recherches, et des Document-
      ations Cinématographiques. Premier Plan, 1)

951. Hippenmeyer, Jean-Roland. <u>Jazz sur films, ou, Cinquante-cinq
      années de rapports jazz-cinéma, vus à travers plus de 800 films
      tournés entre 1917 et 1972: filmographie critique</u>. Yverdon,
      Switzerland: Editions de la Thièle, 1973. 125p.

952. Meeker, David. Jazz in the Movies: a Tentative Index to the
      Work of Jazz Musicians for the Cinema. London: British Film
      Institute, 1972. 89p., illus., index.
          Annotated listing of 709 items, shorts and features.

          ————. Jazz in the Movies: a Guide to Jazz Musicians, 1917-
      1977. London: Talisman Books, 1977. 287p., illus., index.

          ————. Jazz in the Movies. London: Talisman Books, 1981;
      New York: Da Capo Pr., 1982 (Roots of Jazz). 336p., illus.,
      index.
          Annotated listing of 3,724 items.

953. Whannel, Paddy. Jazz on Film: a Select List of Films on Jazz.
      London: British Film Institute, 1966. 9p.
          Annotated listing of sixty-one items on release at the time
      of writing.

                        11. SOCIOLOGICAL ASPECTS

  *   Buerkle, Jack V. Bourbon Street Black: the New Orleans Black
      Jazzman.
          * Cited above as item 887.

954. Enefer, Douglas Stallard. Jazz in Black and White. London:
      Alliance Pr., 1945. 63p.

955. Hentoff, Nat. The Jazz Life. New York: Dial Pr., 1961 (Re-
      printed: New York: Da Capo Pr., 1975); London: Peter Davies;
      New York: Apollo Editions, 1962. 255p. London: Hamish Hamilton;
      London: Panther, 1964. 221p.
          Based on discussions with musicians. Da Capo Pr. edition
      has new introduction by the author.

956. Leonard, Neil. Jazz and the White Americans: the Acceptance of
      a New Art Form. Chicago; London: University of Chicago Pr.,
      1962. 2nd. ed.: Chicago; London: University of Chicago Pr.,
      1970. 215p., illus., bibliog., index.
          Examines the transition from hostility to general acceptance.
      Based on the author's dissertation, The Acceptance of Jazz by
      Whites in the United States, 1918-1942, PhD, Harvard University,
      1960.

957. Morris, Ronald L. Wait Until Dark: Jazz and the Underworld,
      1880-1940. Bowling Green, Ohio: Bowling Green University
      Popular Pr., 1980. 231p., illus., bibliog., index.
          Examination of the involvement of organized crime.

  *   Nanry, Charles (ed.). American Music: from Storyville to
      Woodstock.
          * Cited above as item 386.

958. Newton, Francis (pseud. of Eric J. Hobsbawm). The Jazz Scene.
      London: MacGibbon and Kee, 1959; New York: Monthly Review Pr.,
      1960 (Reprinted: New York: Da Capo Pr., 1975. Roots of Jazz).
      303p., illus., bibliog., index. Harmondsworth, Middlesex:
      Penguin, 1961. 295p., bibliog.

959. Routley, Erik. Is Jazz Music Christian? London: Epworth Pr.,
      1964. 12p.

  *   Sidran, Ben. Black Talk: How the Music of Black America
      Created a Radical Alternative to the Values of Western Literary
      Tradition.
          * Cited above as item 504.

G. STAGE AND SCREEN

1. MINSTRELSY

(1) REFERENCE MATERIALS

960. Hare, Walter Ben. The Minstrel Encyclopedia. Boston: Walter
     H. Baker, 1921. 222p., illus.

961. Sampson, Henry T. Blacks in Blackface: a Source Book on Early
     Black Musical Shows. Metuchen, New Jersey; London: Scarecrow
     Pr., 1980. 552p., illus., index.

(2) GENERAL GUIDES AND OVERVIEWS

962. Day, Charles H. Fun in Black; or, Sketches of Minstrel Life.
     With The Origin of Minstrelsy, by Colonel T. Allston Brown.
     New York: De Witt, 1874. 85p.

963. Greenwood, Isaac John. The Circus: Its Origins and Growth
     Prior to 1835. With a Sketch of Negro Minstrelsy. New York:
     W. Abbatt, 1909. 135p.
     Limited to one hundred copies.

964. Jennings, J.J. Theatrical and Circus Life; or, Secrets of the
     Stage, Green Room, and Saw-Dust Arena. St. Louis; Chicago:
     Sun Publishing Company/Laird and Lee, 1892. 608p.
     Includes discussion of minstrelsy.

965. Newcomb, Bobby. A Guide to the Minstrel Stage. New York: C.H.
     Day, 188? 8p.

966. Powell, Herbert Preston. The World's Best Book of Minstrelsy.
     Illustrated by Charles Clark. Philadelphia: Penn Publishing
     Company, 1926. 319p., illus.

(3) CRITICISM

967. Rourke, Constance. American Humor: a Study of the National
     Character. New York: Harcourt, Brace, 1931. 324p., bibliog.
     Garden City, New York: Doubleday, 1953. 253p., bibliog.
     Includes discussion of Blackface humor, and comedy styles in
     minstrel shows.

(4) GENERAL HISTORIES

968. Duncan, Edmondstoune. The Story of Minstrelsy. Detroit:
     Singing Tree Pr., 1968. 336p., illus.

969. Toll, Robert Charles. Blacking Up: the Minstrel Show in Nine-
     teenth Century America. New York; London: Oxford University
     Pr., 1974 (Reissued 1977). 310p., illus., bibliog., index.
     Includes chronological list of Black minstrel troupes.
     Based on the author's dissertation, Blackface Minstrelsy in
     Nineteenth-Century America (University of California at Berkeley,
     1972.)

970. Uttley, Francis L., and Robert Charles Toll (eds.). Old Slack's
     Reminiscences; and, Pocket History of the Colored Profession.
     Bowling Green, Ohio: Bowling Green University Popular Pr., 1973.
     150p.

971. Wittke, Carl. Tambo and Bones: a History of the American
     Minstrel Stage. Durham, North Carolina: Duke University Pr.,
     1930; Westport, Conn.: Greenwood Pr., 1969. 269p., bibliog.,
     index.
     Includes analysis of minstrel show technique.

(5) REGIONAL HISTORIES

972. Revett, Marion S. A Minstrel Town. New York: Pageant Pr.,
     1955. 335p., illus., bibliog.
     Entertainment, including minstrelsy, in Toledo, Ohio; from
     the 1840's to the turn of the Century.

973. Reynolds, Harry. Minstrel Memories: the Story of Burnt Cork
     Minstrelsy in Great Britain from 1836 to 1927. London: Alston
     Rivers, 1928. 255p., illus.

(6) PRODUCTIONS

(a) Staging Guides

974. Branen, Jeffrey T., and Frederick G. Johnson. How to Stage a
     Minstrel Show: a Manual for the Amateur Burnt Cork Director.
     Illustrated by Harlan Tarbell. Chicago: T.S. Denison, 1921.
     65p., illus.

975. Carlton, Albert. The Business End of a Minstrel Show. New
     York: Witmark, 1907. 41p.

976. Courtright, William. The Complete Minstrel Guide: Containing
     Gags, Jokes, Parodies, Speeches, Farces, and Full Directions
     for a Complete Minstrel Show. Chicago: Dramatic Publishing
     Company, 1901. 137p.

977. Dumont, Frank. The Witmark Amateur Minstrel Guide and Burnt
     Cork Encyclopedia. Chicago: Witmark, 1899. 168p., illus.
     Rev. ed.: New York: Witmark, 1905. 149p., illus.

978. Haverly, Jack. Negro Minstrels: a Complete Guide to Negro
     Minstrelsy. Containing Recitations. Chicago: F.J. Drake,
     1902; Upper Saddle River, New Jersey: Literature House; New
     York: Gregg, 1969. 129p.
         Guidance for amateurs, by a successful minstrel manager.

979. James, Edward. The Amateur Negro Minstrel's Guide. New York:
     The Author/Dick and Fitzgerald, 1880. 23p.

980. Newcomb, Bobby. "Tambo:" His Jokes and Funny Sayings. With
     Which is Incorporated Hints to the Amateur Minstrel. New York:
     De Witt, 1882. 60p.

981. Rossiter, Harold. How to Put On a Minstrel Show. Contains
     Complete Practical Instructions on How to Handle Amateur and
     Professional Talent; also Complete Opening Overture; Good
     Selection of End Men's Jokes and Gags; Instructions How to
     Make Up; List of Suitable Songs; etc. Chicago: Harold Rossiter
     Music Company/M. Stein; Milwaukee: C.N. Casper, 1921. 63p.

982. Walker, Kent. Staging the Amateur Minstrel Show. Boston:
     Walter H. Baker, 1931. 96p., illus.

                          (b) Typical Shows

983. Engle, Gary D. (ed.). This Grotesque Essence: Plays From the
     American Minstrel Stage. Baton Rouge: Louisiana State Univ-
     ersity Pr., 1978. 200p.

984. Paskman, Dailey, and Sigmund Gottfried Spaeth. "Gentlemen, Be
     Seated!" A Parade of the Old-Time Minstrels. Profusely Illus-
     trated From Old Prints and Photographs; and With Complete Music
     For Voice and Piano. Foreword by Daniel Frohman. Garden City,
     New York: Doubleday, 1928. 247p., illus., indexes. Rev. ed.:
     New York: C.N. Potter, 1976. 283p., illus., index.
         Concocted example of a minstrel show, as typically performed.
     Includes background information.

                          2. MUSIC HALL

                    (1) REFERENCE MATERIALS

985. Senelick, Laurence (et al.). The British Music Hall, 1840-
     1923: a Bibliography and Guide to Sources. With a Supplement
     on European Music-Hall. Hamden, Conn.: Shoe String Pr., 1981.
     357p. (Archon Books)

(2) ANNUALS AND YEARBOOKS

986. Variety Theatre Annual, 1906-7. London: J.P. Monckton, 1906.
      p., illus.
      Only issue.

(3) GENERAL GUIDES AND OVERVIEWS

(a) Britain

987. Alltree, George W. Footlight Memories: Recollections of Music
      Hall and Stage Life. London: Sampson Low, 1932. 242p., illus.

988. Burke, Thomas. Nights in Town: a London Autobiography. London:
      Allen and Unwin, 1915. 410p., illus.
      Includes accounts of music hall entertainments.

989. Calthrop, Dion Clayton. Music Hall Nights. London: John Lane,
      1925. 147p., illus.

990. Croxton, Arthur. Crowded Nights--and Days: an Unconventional
      Pageant. London: Sampson Low, Marston, 1934. 398p., illus.
      Autobiography; includes descriptions of music halls.

991. Disher, Maurice Willson. Fairs, Circuses, and Music Halls.
      London: Collins, 1942. 47p., illus. (Britain in Pictures)

992. ———. Winkles and Champagne: Comedies and Tragedies of the
      Music Hall. London: Batsford, 1938 (Reprinted: Bath: Chivers,
      1974); New York: (as Music Hall Parade) Scribner's, 1938. 147p.,
      illus.

993. Fitzgerald, Percy Hetherington. Music-Hall Land: an Account of
      That Strange Country. London: Ward and Downey, 1890. 90p.,
      illus.

994. Music Hall Memories (The Masterpieces of Variety). London:
      Amalgamated Pr., 1935-6.   p., illus.
      Published in twenty parts.

995. One of the Old Brigade (pseud.). London in the Sixties (With
      a Few Digressions). London: Everett, 1914. 268p., illus.
      Account of entertainment in London, including music hall.

(b) France

996. Bizet, René. L'Epoque du music-hall. Paris: Editions du
      Capitole, 1927. 188p. (Les Pamphlets du Capitole)
      Limited edition of one thousand copies. Dialogs on French
      music hall; plus sketches of six leading artists.

997. Fréjaville, Gustave. Au music-hall. Paris: Editions du
      Monde Nouveau, 1923. 305p., illus.
           Limited edition of 430 copies.

998. Léon-Martin, Louis. Le Music-Hall et ses figures. Paris:
      Editions de France, 1928. 250p.

999. Verne, Maurice. Aux usines du plaisir: la vie secrète du
      music-hall. Paris: Editions des Portiques, 1929. 276p.

1000. ————. Les Amuseurs de Paris. Paris: Editions de France,
      1932. 302p. (Le Livre d'aujourd'hui)

(4) CRITICISM

1001. Marinetti, Filippo Tommaso. Le Music-Hall: manifeste futur-
      iste. Publié par le "Daily Mail", 21 Novembre, 1913. Milan:
      The Author, 1913. 43p.

1002. Ritchie, James Ewing. The Night Haunts of London; or, Studies
      in Black and Grey. London: Tinsley Brothers, 1880. 295p.
           Anti-music hall tract. Attempts to establish the harmful
      nature of the genre and its venues.

(5) GENERAL HISTORIES

1003. Beaver, Patrick. The Spice of Life. London: Elm Tree Books,
      1979. 208p., illus.
           Music hall and other Victorian popular entertainments.

1004. Burke, Thomas. English Night-Life: From Norman Curfew to
      Present Black-Out. London: Batsford, 1941. 150p., illus.,
      index.
           Includes discussion of music hall.

1005. Cheshire, David Frederick. Music Hall in Britain. Newton
      Abbot, Devon: David and Charles; Rutherford, New Jersey: Fair-
      leigh Dickinson University Pr., 1974. 112p., illus., bibliog.
      (Illustrated Sources in History)

1006. Haddon, Archibald. The Story of the Music Hall: from Cave of
      Harmony to Cabaret. London: Cecil Palmer, 1924. 20p., illus.
      Expanded ed.: London: Fleetway Pr., 1935. 203p., illus.

1007. Hudd, Roy (comp.). Music Hall. London: Eyre Methuen, 1976.
      128p., illus. (Picturefile Series)
           Covers 1850 to World War One. Chiefly illustrated.

1008. Jacques-Charles (pseud. of Jacques Charles). Cent ans de Music-
      Hall: histoire générale du music-hall, de ses origines à nos
      jours, en Grande-Bretagne, en France, et aux U.S.A. Preface by
      Guy des Cars. Geneva; Paris: Jeheber, 1935. 318p., illus.

General Histories (cont.)

1009. Lee, Edward. <u>Folksong and Music Hall</u>. London: Routledge and
       Keegan Paul, 1982. 148p., illus., bibliog., discog., index.
       (Routledge Popular Music)
           Emphasis on music hall.

1010. Leslie, Peter. <u>A Hard Act To Follow: a Music Hall Review</u>.
       Introduction by Pearl Bailey. New York; London: Paddington
       Pr., 1978. 256p., illus., bibliog., index.

1011. MacInnes, Colin. <u>Sweet Saturday Night</u>. London: MacGibbon
       and Kee, 1967. 160p., index. London: Panther, 1969. 189p.,
       index.
           Popular song and music hall in Britain, 1840 to 1920.

1012. MacQueen-Pope, Walter James. <u>The Melodies Linger On: the
       Story of Music Hall</u>. London: W.H. Allen, 1950. 459p., illus.

1013. Mander, Raymond, and Joe Mitchenson. <u>British Music Hall: a
       Story in Pictures</u>. Foreword by John Betjeman. London: Studio
       Vista, 1965; New York: London House, 1966. 208p., illus.,
       discog., indexes. <u>Rev. ed.</u>: London: Gentry Books, 1974.
       243p., illus., discog., indexes.
           Chiefly illustrated.

1014. Rose, Clarkson. <u>Red Plush and Greasepaint: a Memory of the
       Music-Hall, and Life and Times From the Nineties to the Six-
       ties</u>. Foreword by John Betjeman. Introduction by Val Parnell.
       London: Museum Pr., 1964. 152p., illus., index.

1015. Scott, Harold. <u>The Early Doors: Origins of the Music Hall</u>.
       London: Nicholson and Watson, 1946; Wakefield, Yorkshire: E.P.
       Publishing, 1977. 259p., illus., bibliog., index.

1016. Short, Ernest, and Arthur Compton-Rickett. <u>Ring Up the
       Curtain: Being a Pageant of English Entertainment Covering
       Half a Century</u>. London: Herbert Jenkins, 1938; Freeport, New
       York: Books For Libraries Pr., 1970 (Select Bibliographies
       Reprint Series). 319p., illus.
           History of London music hall; also cabarets and vaudeville.

1017. Stuart, Charles Douglas, and A.J. Park (eds.). <u>The Variety
       Stage: a History of the Music Halls</u>. London: T. Fisher Unwin,
       1895. 255p.

1018. Titterton, William Richard. <u>From Theatre to Music Hall</u>. Lon-
       don: Stephen Swift, 1912. 242p.

1019. Variety Artistes' Federation. <u>The Golden Jubilee Book of Show
       Business, 1906-1956: a Literary Panorama of the Theatrical
       Scene Marking the Fifty Years Existence of the V.A.F.</u> Edited
       by George Le Roy. London: Variety Artistes' Federation, 1956.
       40p.

(6) REGIONAL HISTORIES

(a) Britain

1020. Barker, Kathleen. <u>Early Music Hall in Bristol</u>. Bristol:
Historical Association, Bristol Branch, 1979. 20p., illus.
(Local History Pamphlets, 44)
Developments up to 1900.

1021. Mellor, Geoffrey James. <u>The Northern Music Hall: a Century
of Popular Entertainment</u>. Introduction by Ken Dodd. Foreword by George Wood. Necastle-upon-Tyne: F. Graham, 1970.
224p., illus.

1022. O'Rourke, Eva (comp.). <u>Lambeth and Music Hall: a Treasury of
Music Hall Memorabilia; Including Articles, Biographies, Photo-
graphs, Engravings, and Reproductions of Original Material</u>.
London: London Borough of Lambeth, Directorate of Amenity
Services, 1977. unpaged, illus., bibliog.
Portfolio format; consists of twenty-two items in folder.

(b) France

1023. L'Académie du Cirque et du Music-Hall. <u>Histoire du music-hall</u>.
Illustrated by Sergé. Paris: Editions de Paris, 1954. 232p.,
illus.
By various authors.

1024. Bost, Pierre. <u>Le Cirque et le music-hall</u>. Illustrated by
G. Annenkov. Paris: Au Sans Pareil, 1931. 253p., illus.

1025. Damase, Jacques. <u>Les Folies du Music-Hall: a History of the
Paris Music-Hall from 1914 to the Present Day</u>. Translated by
Tony White. Foreword by Noël Coward. London: Blond, 1962;
London; New York: Spring Books, 1970. 191p., illus., bibliog.
Chiefly illustrated. Originally published as <u>Les Folies
du music-hall: histoire du music-hall à Paris, de 1914 à nos
jours</u>, Paris: Editions "Spectacles", 1960; with a preface by
Bruno Coquatrix.

1026. Georgius (<u>pseud. of</u> Charles Lejay). <u>Du Café-concert au
théâtre-chantant</u>. Paris: M. Labbé, 1928. 30p., illus.

1027. Jacques-Charles (<u>pseud. of</u> Jacques Charles). <u>Caf' Conc'</u>.
Paris: Flammarion, 1966. 219p., illus. ("1900" veçu)
Account of Paris scene.

   * ———. <u>Le Journal d'une figurante: roman de moeurs du music-
hall</u>.
      * Cited below as item 4716.

1028. Mariel, Pierre, and Jean Trocher. <u>Paris Cancan</u>. Translated
by Stephanie and Richard Sutton. Edited by Alain de Moinerie.
London: Skilton, 1961. 112p., illus.

Regional Histories: France (cont.)

1029. Mariel, Pierre. __Paris Revue__. Photographs by Daniel Frasnay.
       Translation by Peter Munk. London: Neville Spearman, 1961.
       102p., illus.

1030. Roubaud, Louis. __Music-Hall__. Illustrated by Bécan. Paris:
       L. Querelle, 1929. 193p., illus.

(7) PRODUCTIONS

(a) Staging

1031. Kilgarriff, Michael. __It Gives Me Great Pleasure: the Complete__
       __Vade Mecum for the Old Time Music Hall Chairman. Including__
       __Production Guide and Nearly Six Hundred Patter Entries.__
       London; New York: Samuel French, 1972. 104p.

(b) Typical Skits

1032. Anstey, F. (__pseud. of__ Thomas Anstey Guthrie). __Mr Punch's__
       __Model Music-Hall Songs and Dramas: Collected, Improved, and__
       __Re-arranged from "Punch."__ Illustrations by E.T. Reed. Lon-
       don: Bradbury Agnew, 1892. 172p.

1033. ―――――. __The Young Reciter and Model Music-Hall Songs and__
       __Dramas. New and revised edition.__ Introduction by C.L. Graves.
       London: Methuen, 1931. 305p.
          Reworking of item 1032.

3. VAUDEVILLE TO CABARET

(1) GENERAL GUIDES AND OVERVIEWS

1034. Keegan, Marcia. __We Can Still Hear Them Clapping__. New York:
       Avon, 1975. 158p., illus. (A Flare Book)
          Vaudeville in the United States.

1035. Samuels, Charles, and Louise Samuels. __Once Upon a Stage: the__
       __Merry World of Vaudeville__. New York: Dodd, Mead, 1974. 278p.,
       illus., index.

1036. Smith, Bill. __Two a Day: the World of Vaudeville__. New York:
       Macmillan, 1976.   p., index.

1037. Stein, Charles W. (ed.). __American Vaudeville as Seen By Its__
       __Contemporaries__. New York: Knopf, 1984.   p., illus.
          Journal and other pieces, edited with commentary.

(2) CRITICISM

1038. Allen, Robert C. <u>Vaudeville and Film</u>. Edited by Garth S.
       Jowett. New York: Ayer, 1980.   p., illus. (Dissertations
       on Film)

1039. McClean, Albert F., <u>Jr</u>. <u>American Vaudeville as Ritual</u>.
       Lexington, Kentucky: University of Kentucky Pr., 1965.   250p.,
       illus., bibliog., index.
           Sees vaudeville as a manifestation of the social and
       psychic forces involved in American history.

(3) GENERAL HISTORIES

1040. DiMeglio, John E. <u>Vaudeville, U.S.A.</u> Bowling Green, Ohio:
       Bowling Green University Popular Pr., 1973. 259p., illus.,
       bibliog., index.

1041. Gilbert, Douglas. <u>American Vaudeville: Its Life and Times</u>.
       New York: Whittlesey House, 1940; New York: Dover, 1963;
       Magnolia, Pennsylvania: Peter Smith, 1983. 428p., illus.,
       index.
           Covers 1881 to 1930. Includes listing of acts. Emphasis
       on theatrical aspects, but includes discussion of music.

1042. Laurie, Joe (<u>pseud. of</u> Joseph Laurie, <u>Jr</u>.). <u>Vaudeville: from
       the Honky-Tonks to the Palace</u>. New York: Holt, 1953; Port
       Washington, New York: Kennikat Pr., 1972. 561p., index.
           Covers 1900 to 1930's. Includes discussion of individual
       promoters and impresarios. By former vaudeville star.

1043. Short, Ernest Henry. <u>Fifty Years of Vaudeville</u>. London:
       Eyre and Spottiswoode, 1946; Westport, Conn.: Greenwood Pr.,
       1978. 271p., illus.

1044. Slide, Anthony. <u>The Vaudevillians</u>. New York: Arlington House,
       1981. 192p., illus.

1045. Sobel, Bernard. <u>A Pictorial History of Vaudeville</u>. Foreword
       by George Jessel. Secaucus, New Jersey: Citadel Pr., 1961.
       224p., illus.

(4) REGIONAL HISTORIES

1046. Elliott, Eugene Clinton. <u>A History of Variety-Vaudeville in
       Seattle</u>. Seattle: University of Washington Pr., 1944. 83p.,
       illus., index.
           History, 1852-1914, in this major vaudeville center.

Regional Histories (cont.)

1047. Foster, William Trufant. Vaudeville and Motion Picture
       Shows: a Study of Theater in Portland, Oregon. Portland,
       Oregon: Reed College, 1914. 63p.
            History of local developments, and assessment of the
       effects of vaudeville on young people.

(5) MEDICINE SHOWS

1048. McNamara, Brooks. Step Right Up: an Illustrated History of
       the American Medicine Show. Garden City, New York: Doubleday,
       1976. 233p., illus., bibliog., index.

1049. Webber, Malcolm. The Medicine Show. Illustrated by L.P.
       Harting. Caldwell, Indiana: Caxton Printers, 1941. 265p.,
       illus.

(6) BURLESQUE

1050. Adams, William D. A Book of Burlesque. Norwood, Pennsylvania:
       Norwood Editions, 1980. 220p.

1051. Clinton-Baddeley, Victor. The Burlesque Tradition in the
       English Theatre After 1660. London: Methuen, 1952; New York:
       Benjamin Blom, 1971; New York: Barnes and Noble, 1973. 152p.,
       illus., bibliog.

1052. Corio, Ann. This Was Burlesque. With Joseph DiMona. New
       York: Madison Square Pr., 1968. 197p., illus.

1053. Sobel, Bernard. Burleycue: an Underground History of Burlesque
       Days. New York: Farrar and Rinehart, 1931; New York: B. Frank-
       lin, 1975. 284p., illus.

1054. ———. A Pictorial History of Burlesque. New York: Putnam,
       1956. 194p., illus.

1055. Zeidman, Irving. The American Burlesque Show. New York:
       Hawthorn Books, 1967. 271p., illus., bibliog., index.

(7) CABARET

1056. Appignanesi, Lisa. The Cabaret. New York: Macmillan; London:
       Studio Vista, 1975; New York: Universe Books, 1976. 192p.,
       illus., bibliog., index.

       ———. Cabaret: the First Hundred Years. London: Methuen,
       1984. 192p., illus., bibliog., index.

4. MUSICALS AND REVUE

(1) REFERENCE MATERIALS

(a) Bibliographies

1057. Hatch, James Vernon. <u>The Black Image on the American Stage:
a Bibliography of Plays and Musicals, 1770-1970</u>. New York:
Drama Book Specialists, 1971. 162p., indexes.
Chronologically arranged listing of over two thousand
stage shows. Minstrel shows excluded. All material included
is by or about Blacks. Includes unproduced material, and
that in transcript only; gives library locations.

1058. Salem, James Morris. <u>A Guide to Critical Reviews. Part 2:
The Musical from Rodgers-and-Hart to Lerner-and-Loewe.</u>
Metuchen, New Jersey: Scarecrow Pr., 1967. 353p., indexes.
Chronological arrangement, by seasons. Covers Broadway
musicals from 1920 onwards. Gives show details, plus list-
ings of reviews.

1059. Stratman, Carl Joseph. <u>American Theatrical Periodicals,
1798-1967: a Bibliographical Guide.</u> Durham, North Carolina:
Duke University Pr., 1970. 133p.

1060. Wilmeth, Don B. <u>The American Stage to World War One: a Guide
to Information Sources.</u> Detroit: Gale Research, 1978. 269p.,
index. (Performing Arts Information Guide Series, 4)
Includes books and periodical articles.

(b) Indexes

1061. Drone, Jeanette Marie. <u>Index to Opera, Operetta, and Musical
Comedy Synopses in Collections and Periodicals.</u> Metuchen,
New Jersey; London: Scarecrow Pr., 1978. 171p., bibliog.

(c) Encyclopedias and Dictionaries

(i) Comprehensive Works

* Burton, Jack. <u>The Blue Book of Broadway Musicals and Hollywood.</u>
* Cited below as item 4120.

(ii) Stage

* ———. <u>The Blue Book of Broadway Musicals.</u>
* Cited below as item 4118.

Encyclopedias and Dictionaries: Stage (cont.)

1062. Drinkrow, John. The Vintage Musical Comedy Book. Illustrated From the Raymond Mander and Joe Mitchenson Theatre Collection. Reading, Berkshire: Osprey Publishing, 1974. 146p., illus., discog.
    Plots.

1063. ———. The Vintage Operetta Book. Illustrated From the Raymond Mander and Joe Mitchenson Theatre Collection. Reading, Berkshire: Osprey Publishing, 1972; (as The Operetta Book) New York: Drake, 1973. 124p., illus., discog.
    Plots of fifty works, including musical comedies.

1064. Ewen, David. The Book of European Light Opera. New York: Holt, Rinehart and Winston, 1962; Westport, Conn.: Greenwood Pr., 1977. 297p., illus., discog., index.
    Plots, production histories, show information, and critical evaluations of 167 works by eighty-one composers.

1065. ———. The Complete Book of the American Musical Theater: a Guide to More Than Three Hundred Productions of the American Musical Theater, From "The Black Crook" (1866) to the Present. With Plot, Production History, Stars, Songs, Composers, Librettists, and Lyricists. New York: Holt, 1958; Rev. ed.: New York: Holt, 1959. 447p., illus.

    ———. New Complete Book of the American Musical Theater. New York: Holt, Rinehart and Winston, 1970. 800p., illus.

1066. Green, Stanley. Encyclopaedia of the Musical Theatre. New York: Dodd, Mead, 1976; New York: Da Capo Pr., 1980. 488p., bibliog., discog.

    ———. Encyclopedia of the Musical. London: Cassell; New York: Macmillan, 1977. 488p., bibliog., discog.

1067. Jackson, Arthur. The Book of Musicals: from Show Boat to A Chorus Line. New York: Crown; London: Mitchell Beazley, 1977. 208p., illus., bibliog., discog., filmog., index.

    ———. The Book of Musicals: from Showboat to Evita. Foreword by Clive Barnes. New York: Crown; London: Mitchell Beazley, 1979. 208p., illus., bibliog., discog., filmog., index.

1068. Laufe, Abe. Anatomy of a Hit: Long-Run Plays On Broadway, from 1900 to the Present Day. Introduction by Jack Gaier. New York: Hawthorn Books, 1966. 350p., illus.
    Includes musical comedies.

1069. ———. Broadway's Greatest Musicals. New York: Funk and Wagnalls, 1969. 465p., bibliog., index. Illus. ed.: New York: Funk and Wagnalls, 1970. 481p., illus., bibliog., index. New ed.: New York: Funk and Wagnalls, 1973. 502p., illus., bibliog., index. Rev. ed.: New York: Funk and Wagnalls, 1977; Newton Abbott, Devon: David and Charles, 1978. 544p., illus., bibliog., index.

1070. Lubbock, Mark. <u>The Complete Book of Light Opera</u>. <u>With an</u>
       <u>American Section by David Ewen</u>. New York: Appleton-Century-
       Crofts, 1962. 953p., illus., index.
           Details of eighty-five operettas and musical comedies by
       thirty-three composers, 1850 to date. Includes appendix of
       London productions of American musicals.

1071. McSpadden, Joseph Walker. <u>Light Opera and Musical Comedy</u>.
       New York: Crowell, 1936. 362p.
           Plot summaries. Incorporated into item 1072.

1072. ────. <u>Operas and Musical Comedies</u>. New York: Crowell,
       1946. 607p. <u>Enlarged ed.</u>: New York: Crowell, 1951. 637p.
           Plot summaries. Incorporates the author's <u>Opera Synopses</u>
       and item 1071.

                        (iii) Motion Pictures

   *   Burton, Jack. <u>The Blue Book of Hollywood Musicals</u>.
           * Cited below as item 4119.

1073. Consumer Guide. <u>The Best, Worst, and Most Unusual Hollywood</u>
       <u>Musicals</u>. Compiled by the Editors of <u>Consumer Guide</u>. New
       York: New American Library; Windsor, Berkshire: Fountain Pr.,
       1983. 160p., illus.
           Includes ratings for over 170 musicals.

1074. Fordin, Hugh. <u>The World of Entertainment! Hollywood's Great-</u>
       <u>est Musicals</u>. Garden City, New York: Doubleday, 1975; New
       York: Avon Books, 1976. 566p., illus., filmog.
           Emphasis on movies by producer and lyricist Arthur Freed.
       Includes coverage of the subsequent careers of his proteges.

1075. Green, Stanley. <u>Encyclopaedia of the Musical Film</u>. New York;
       London: Oxford University Pr., 1981. 344p., bibliog., discog.

1076. Hirschhorn, Clive. <u>The Hollywood Musical</u>. London: Octopus,
       1981. 456p., illus., indexes.

1077. Limbacher, James L. <u>Keeping Score: Film Music, 1972-1979</u>.
       Metuchen, New Jersey; London: Scarecrow Pr., 1981. 510p.,
       bibliog., discog.
           Includes listings of award winners.

1078. Taylor, John Russell, and Arthur Jackson. <u>The Hollywood Mus-</u>
       <u>ical</u>. New York: McGraw-Hill; London: Secker and Warburg, 1971.
       278p., illus., filmog., indexes.

   *   Vallance, Tom. <u>The American Musical</u>.
           * Cited below as item 1639.

(2) GENERAL GUIDES AND OVERVIEWS

1079. Agate, James. Immoment Toys: a Survey of Light Entertainment on the London Stage, 1920-1943. London: Cape, 1945; New York: Benjamin Blom, 1969. 264p.
    Coverage includes music hall, revue, and musical comedy.

1080. Tomkinson, Constance. Les Girls. London: Michael Joseph, 1956. 245p., illus.
    Revue and showgirls.

(3) CRITICISM

1081. Altman, Richard. Genre: the Musical. London: Routledge and Keegan Paul in association with the British Film Institute, 1981. 228p., illus., bibliog., indexes (British Film Institute Readers in Film Studies)

1082. Aros, Andrew A. Broadway and Hollywood Too. Diamond Bar, California: Applause Publications, 1980. 60p.

1083. Delamater, Jerome. Dance in the Hollywood Musical. Edited by Diane Kirkpatrick. Ann Arbor, Michigan: U.M.I. Research Pr., 1981. 324p. (Studies in Cinema, 4)

1084. Nathan, George Jean. The Theatre, the Drama, the Girls. New York: Knopf, 1921. 361p.

(4) ESSAY COLLECTIONS

1085. Atkinson, Brooks. Broadway Scrapbook. Illustrated by Hirschfeld. New York: Theatre Arts, 1947; Westport, Conn.: Greenwood Pr., 1970. 312p., illus.
    Material first published in New York's Sunday Times. Includes essays on musicals.

1086. Guernsey, Otis L., Jr. (ed.). Playwrightts, Lyricists, and Composers on the Theater: the Inside Story of a Decade of Theater, in Articles and Comments by Its Authors. Selected From Their Own Publication, "The Dramatists Guild Quarterly." Illustrated by Tom Funk. New York: Dodd, Mead, 1974. 435p., illus.
    Material originally published 1964-74. Includes discussion of theater lyrics.

1087. Kreuger, Miles (ed.). The Movie Musical From Vitaphone to Forty-Second Street, as Reported in a Great Fan Magazine. New York: Dover; London: Constable, 1975. 367p., illus., index.
    Reprinted articles from Photoplay, 1926-1933; with comments.

1088. Limbacher, James Louis (ed.). <u>Film Music: From Violins to</u>
       <u>Video</u>. Metuchen, New Jersey; London: Scarecrow Pr., 1974.
       836p., bibliog., discog., index.
           Chiefly concerned with background music. Reprints of
       articles by various authors.

1089. Loney, Glenn (ed.). <u>Musical Theatre in America: Papers and</u>
       <u>Proceedings of the Conference on the Musical Theatre in</u>
       <u>America</u>. Westport, Conn.: Greenwood Pr., 1984. 441p.,
       illus., bibliog. (Contributions in Drama and Theatre
       Studies, 8)
           Conference held April, 1981. Sponsored jointly by the
       American Society for Theater Research, the Sonneck Society,
       and the Theater Library Association.

                        (5) MISCELLANEA

1090. Appelbaum, Stanley. <u>The Hollywood Musical: a Picture Quiz</u>
       <u>Book</u>. New York: Dover; London: Constable, 1974. 132p.,
       illus., index.

1091. Green, Stanley. <u>The Broadway Musical: a Picture Quiz Book</u>.
       New York: Dover; London: Constable, 1977. 126p., illus.,
       indexes.

                     (6) GENERAL HISTORIES

                   (a) Comprehensive Works

1092. Druxman, Michael B. <u>The Musical: From Broadway to Hollywood</u>.
       South Brunswick, New Jersey: A.S. Barnes; London: Yoseloff,
       1980. 202p., illus., bibliog., index.
           Critical history of movie musicals based on stage works.

                          (b) Stage

1093. Baral, Robert. <u>Revue: a Nostalgic Reprise of the Great</u>
       <u>Broadway Period</u>. Introduction by Abel Green. New York:
       Fleet, 1962. 288p., illus. <u>Rev. ed.</u>: New York: Fleet, 1970.
       296p., illus.
           Includes listing of show casts and credits for over 180
       productions, 1903-45.

1094. Bordman, Gerald. <u>American Musical Comedy: From "Adonis" to</u>
       <u>"Dreamgirls."</u> New York; London: Oxford University Pr., 1982.
       244p., illus., index.

1095. ————. <u>American Musical Theatre: a Chronicle</u>. New York;
       London: Oxford University Pr., 1978. 749p., index.
           Year-by-year account of significant productions.

General Histories (cont.)

1096. Bordman, Gerald. American Operetta: from "H.M.S. Pinafore"
       to "Sweeney Todd." New York; London: Oxford University Pr.,
       1981. 206p., illus., index.

1097. Churchill, Allen. The Great White Way: a Re-Creation of
       Broadway's Golden Era of Theatrical Entertainment. New York:
       Dutton, 1962. 310p., illus., bibliog., index.
           Broadway theater, 1900-1919. Includes coverage of vaude-
       ville, and revue.

1098. Engel, Lehman. The American Musical Theater: a Consideration.
       New York: Columbia Broadcasting System, 1967. 236p., illus.,
       bibliog., discog., index. (A C.B.S. Legacy Collection Book)
       Rev. ed.: New York: Macmillan, 1975. 266p., illus., bibliog.,
       discog., index.

1099. Ewen, David. The Story of America's Musical Theater. Phila-
       delphia: Chilton, 1961. 268p., index. Rev. ed.: Philadel-
       phia: Chilton, 1968. 278p., index.

1100. Gottfried, Martin. Broadway Musicals. New York: Abrams,
       1979. 352p., illus., index.

1101. Green, Stanley. Ring Bells! Sing Songs! Broadway Musicals
       of the 1930's. Introduction by Brooks Atkinson. New Rochelle,
       New York: Arlington House, 1971. 385p., illus., bibliog.,
       discog., index.

           ————. Broadway Musicals of the Thirties. New York: Da
       Capo Pr., 1982. 383p., illus., bibliog., discog., index.

1102.   ————. The World of Musical Comedy: the Story of the Amer-
       ican Musical Stage, as Told Through the Careers of Its Fore-
       most Composers and Lyricists. Foreword by Deems Taylor. New
       York: Ziff-Davis, 1960; New York: A.S. Barnes; London: Yosel-
       off, 1962. 393p., illus., discog., index. New York: Grosset
       and Dunlap, 1962. 397p., illus., discog., index. Rev. and
       enlarged ed.: South Brunswick, New Jersey: A.S. Barnes; Lon-
       don: Yoseloff, 1968. 541p., illus., discog., index. 3rd. ed.:
       South Brunswick, New Jersey: A.S. Barnes; London: Yoseloff,
       1974. 556p., illus., discog., index. 4th. ed.: San Diego,
       California: A.S. Barnes, 1980; New York: Da Capo Pr., 1984.
       494p., illus., discog., index.

1103. Hoyt, Harlowe Randall. Town Hall Tonight. Englewood Cliffs,
       New Jersey: Prentice-Hall, 1955. 292p., illus.

1104. Kislan, Richard. The Musical: a Look at the American Musical
       Theater. Englewood Cliffs, New Jersey; London: Prentice-Hall,
       1980. 262p., illus., index. (A Spectrum Book)

1105. Leavitt, Michael Bennett. Fifty Years in Theatrical Manage-
       ment, 1859-1909. New York: Broadway Publishers, 1912. 735p.,
       illus., index.

1106. Mackinlay, Malcolm Sterling. The Origin and Development of
       Light Opera. London: Hutchinson, 1927; New York: Benjamin
       Blom, 1971. 293p., illus., bibliog.

1107. MacQueen-Pope, Walter James. Nights of Gladness. London:
       Hutchinson, 1956; Philadelphia: Richard West, 1980. 268p.,
       illus., index.
          History of the British musical stage.

1108. ————. Shirtfronts and Sables: a Story of the Days When
       Money Could Be Spent. London: Hale, 1953. 320p., illus.,
       index.
          London theatrical history, mid-1800's to 1950. Includes
       detailed discussion of musical theater.

1109. Mander, Raymond, and Joe Mitchenson. Musical Comedy: a Story
       in Pictures. Foreword by Noël Coward. London: Peter Davies,
       1969; New York: Taplinger, 1970. 176p., illus., index.
          Chiefly illustrated. Covers London productions, 1894-1968.

1110. ————. Revue: a Story in Pictures. Foreword by Noël Coward.
       London: Peter Davies; New York: Taplinger, 1971. 168p.,
       illus., index.
          Chiefly illustrated. Chronicle of London productions.

1111. Mates, Julian. The American Musical Stage Before 1800. New
       Brunswick, New Jersey: Rutgers University Pr., 1962. 331p.,
       illus., bibliog., index.
          Contends that modern musical comedy has its roots in the
       late Eighteenth Century lyric stage. Based on the author's
       thesis The American Musical Stage Before 1800, PhD., Columbia
       University, 1959.

1112. Monette, Paul. Musical Comedy. Los Angeles: Illuminati, 1983.
       p., illus.

1113. Mordden, Ethan. Better Foot Forward: the History of American
       Musical Theater. New York: Grossman Publishers, 1976. 369p.,
       illus., bibliog., index.

1114. ————. Broadway Babies: the People Who Made the American
       Musical. New York; London: Oxford University Pr., 1983.
       244p., index.
          Arranged by topics; details the contributions of key fig-
       ures to these.

1115. Parker, Derek, and Julia Parker. The Story and the Song: a
       Survey of English Musical Plays, 1916-78. London: Chappell/
       Elm Tree Books, 1979. 184p., illus., bibliog., index.

1116. Parks, Melvin. Musicals of the 1930's. New York: Museum of
       the City of New York, 1966.   p., illus.
          Exhibition catalog.

1117. Root, Deane L. American Popular Stage Music, 1860-1880. Ann
       Arbor, Michigan: U.M.I. Research Pr., 1981. 268p. (Studies in
       Musicology, 44)

General Histories (cont.)

1118.   Smith, Cecil Minchener. Musical Comedy in America: from "The
        Black Crook" through "South Pacific." New York: Theatre Arts,
        1950. 374p., illus., index.
            Emphasis on Broadway productions.

        E.N.S.A. (Entertainments National Services Association)

1119.   Dean, Basil. The Theatre at War. London: Harrap, 1956.
        573p., illus.
            History of E.N.S.A. (British World War II troop entertain-
        ment organization; which included popular music in its
        repertoire.)

1120.   Hickford, Jessie. Flags For Curtains; or, Recollections of
        a War-Time Concert Party. Chelmsford, Essex: Essex County
        Library, 1983. 72p., illus.
            Memoir of E.N.S.A. troupe's activities.

                        (c) Motion Pictures

1121.   Aylesworth, Thomas G. History of Movie Musicals. Greenwich,
        Conn.: Bison Books; London: Hamlyn, 1984. 256p., illus.,
        filmog., index.

1122.   Bergan, Ronald. Glamorous Musicals: Fifty Years of Hollywood's
        Ultimate Fantasy. Foreword by Ginger Rogers. London: Octo-
        pus, 1984. 160p., illus., index.

1123.   Feuer, Jane. The Hollywood Musical. Bloomington: Indiana
        University Pr.; London: Macmillan, 1982. 131p., illus.

1124.   Kobal, John. Gotta Sing, Gotta Dance: a Pictorial History of
        Movie Musicals. London; New York: Hamlyn, 1970. Rev. ed.:
        London, New York: Hamlyn, 1983. 320p., illus., bibliog.,
        index.
            Chiefly illustrated; emphasis on cinematic aspects.

1125.   McVay, J. Douglas. The Musical Film. New York: A.S. Barnes;
        London: Zwemmer, 1967. 175p., illus., bibliog.

1126.   Mordden, Ethan. The Hollywood Musical. New York: St. Martin's
        Pr.; Newton Abbott, Devon: David and Charles, 1981. 261p.,
        illus., discog., index.

1127.   Sennett, Ted. Hollywood Musicals. New York: Abrams, 1981.
        384p., illus., bibliog., filmog., index.

1128.   Springer, John Shipman. All Talking! All Singing! All Dancing!
        A Pictorial History of the Movie Musical. Introduction by
        Gene Kelly. Secaucus, New Jersey: Citadel Pr., 1966. 256p.,
        illus.

1129. Thomas, Lawrence B. The M.G.M. Years. Introduction by
       Sidney Skolsky. Commentary on sound-track recording by Jesse
       Kaye. Illustrated by Bob Harmon. Designed by Harry W. Foss.
       New York: Columbia House, 1972. 138p., illus., bibliog.
           History of Metro-Goldwyn-Mayer musical productions.

1130. Woll, Allen L. The Hollywood Musical Goes to War. Chicago:
       Nelson-Hall, 1983. 208p., illus.
           World War II productions.

                        (7) PRODUCTIONS

                          (a) Staging

1131. Eddins, Martha (et al.). There's More to Musicals Than Music.
       Carol Stream, Illinois: Somerset Pr., 1980. 72p., illus.

1132. Engel, Lehman. The Making of a Musical. New York: Macmillan;
       London: Collier-Macmillan, 1977. 157p., index.

1133. ———. Planning and Producing the Musical Show. New York:
       Crown, 1957. 159p., illus. Rev. ed.: New York: Crown, 1966.
       148p., illus., bibliog.
           Guidance for amateurs.

1134. Fuller, John Grant (ed.). Baker's Roaring Twenties Scrapbook:
       a Gay, Naughty, Wild, and Mad Collection of Material To Prov-
       ide Any Group With a Full Evening Revue of the Roaring Twenties.
       Boston: Baker's Plays, 1960. 58p.

1135. Laughlin, Haller, and Randy Wheeler. Producing the Musical:
       a Guide for School, College, and Community Theatre. Westport,
       Conn.: Greenwood Pr., 1984. 160p., illus., bibliog., index.
           Aimed at directors and producers without formal theatrical
       training.

1136. Powers, Bill. Behind the Scenes of a Broadway Musical. New
       York: Crown, 1982. 96p., illus.

1137. Settle, Ronald. Music in the Theatre. London: Herbert Jenk-
       ins, 1957. 96p. (Practical Stage Handbooks Series)

1138. Spencer, Peter Augustus. Let's Do a Musical. London: Studio
       Vista; Chester Springs, Pennsylvania: Dufour Editions, 1968.
       128p., illus., bibliog., index.
           Guide for amateurs.

1139. ———. Musicals: the Guide to Amateur Production. Line
       illustrations by George Prescott. London: John Murray, 1983.
       184p., illus., bibliog., index.
           Item 1138 revised and rewritten.

1140. Tumbusch, Tom. Complete Production Guide to Modern Musical
       Theater. New York: Richards Rosen Pr., 1969. 187p., illus.
       (The Theater Student Series)

Productions (cont.)

1141. Tumbusch, Tom. Guide to Broadway Musical Theater. Additional
       research and compilation by Marty Tumbusch. Foreword by
       Richard Rodgers. New York: Richards Rosen Pr., 1972. 224p.,
       illus., index. (The Theater Student Series)
           Selection guide for prospective producers. Gives outlines
       of 114 Broadway musicals; with details of sets, lighting,
       special effects, etc.

                        (b) Individual Productions

An American in Paris

1142. Knox, Donald. The Magic Factory: How M.G.M. Made "An American
       in Paris." New York: Praeger, 1973. 217p., illus.
           Twenty-five people involved in the movie production detail
       its story.

Annie

1143. Charnin, Martin. Annie: a Theater Memoir. New York: Dutton,
       1977. unpaged, illus.

The Best Little Whorehouse in Texas

1144. King, Larry L. The Whorehouse Papers. New York: Viking Pr.,
       1982. 312p., illus.

The Black Crook

1145. Whitton, Joseph. "The Naked Truth!" An Inside History of
       "The Black Crook." Philadelphia: H.W. Shaw, 1897. 32p.
           By the manager of Niblo's Garden theater, venue of show.

Can't Stop the Music

1146. Woodward, Bronte, and Alan Carr. Can't Stop the Music.
       Designed by Thomas Nozkowski. Los Angeles: Pinnacle Books,
       1980. 143p., illus. (A Newmarket Book Project)
           Photostory of the movie (produced by Carr) starring the
       Village People group.

The Catch Colt

1147.   O'Hara, Mary (pseud.). A Musical in the Making. Chevy Chase,
        Maryland: Markane Publishing Company, 1966. 260p.
            Account of the production of the author's musical play.

Cats

1148.   Lloyd Webber, Andrew. Cats: the Book of the Musical. London:
        Faber and Faber/The Really Useful Company, 1981. 112p.,
        illus.
            Account and production description of the show based on
        T.S. Eliot's poetry collection Old Possum's Book of Practical
        Cats.

Chu-Chin-Chow

1149.   Simpson, Harold. Chu-Chin-Chow: the Story of the Play by
        Oscar Asche. Retold by Harold Simpson. London: Mills and
        Boon, 1916. 76p., illus.

Evita

1150.   Lloyd Webber, Andrew, and Tim Rice. Evita: the Legend of
        Eva Peron. London: Elm Tree Books; New York: Drama Book
        Specialists, 1978; New York: Avon, 1979. 123p., illus.,
        bibliog.
            Includes complete lyrics; musical assessment; and biog-
        raphy of Eva Peron.

Fame

1151.   Fleischer, Leonore. Fame: a Novel. Based on the Alan Parker
        film. Screenplay by Christopher Gore. London: Sphere, 1980.
        255p.

1152.   The Kids From Fame. Edited by Gerry Fallon. Photographs by
        Sven Arnstein. London: I.P.C. Magazines, 1983. 32p., illus.
            Tie-in with stage appearances in Britain by the cast of
        the Fame television series.

1153.   The Official Fame Magazine. London. monthly, Nov. 1982- .
            Linked to the Fame television series.

Individual Productions (cont.)

Fiddler on the Roof

1154.   Altman, Richard. <u>The Making of a Musical: Fiddler on the</u>
        <u>Roof</u>. With Mervyn Kaufman. New York: Crown, 1971. 214p.,
        illus.

Forty-Second Street

1155.   Fumento, Rocco (ed.). <u>Forty-Second Street</u>. Introduction by
        Rocco Fumento. Madison; London: University of Wisconsin Pr.
        for the Wisconsin Center for Film and Theater Research, 1980.
        196p., illus., bibliog. (Wisconsin/Warner Brothers Screenplay
        Series)
            Edited transcript of the screenplay by Rian James and
        James Seymour.

Frankie and Johnny

1156.   Huston, John. <u>Frankie and Johnny</u>. New York: A. and C. Boni,
        1930. 160p., illus.
            Details the stage adaption of the song.

Gigi

1157.   Colette, Sidonie Gabrielle. <u>Gigi, et autres nouvelles</u>.
        Lausanne: La Guilde de Livre, 1944. 217p., illus.

        ————. <u>Gigi: roman</u>. Paris: J. Ferenczi et Fils, 1945. 182p.

        ————. <u>Gigi</u>. Paris: Hachette, 1945. 251p. (Le Livre de
        Poche)
            Includes other stories.

        ————. <u>Gigi</u>. Illustrated by Jacques Cura. Paris: Editions
        Ferenczi, 1952. 123p., illus. (Le Livre moderne illustre)

        ————. <u>Gigi; Julie de Carneilham; Chance Acquaintances</u>.
        New York: Farrar, Straus and Young, 1952. 315p., illus.

        ————. <u>Gigi; and, The Cat</u>. London: Secker and Warburg,
        1953. 193p. (Uniform Edition, 5). Harmondsworth, Middlesex:
        Penguin, 1958. 157p., illus.
            <u>Gigi</u> translated by Roger Senhouse; <u>The Cat</u> translated by
        Antonia White.

        ————. <u>Gigi, and Selected Writings</u>. Foreword by Elaine
        Marks. New York: New American Library, 1963. 256p., bibliog.
        (A Signet Classic)

The Gold Diggers of 1933

1158. Hope, Arthur (ed.). The Gold Diggers of 1933. Introduction
       by Arthur Hope. Madison: University of Wisconsin Pr. for the
       Wisconsin Center for Film and Theater Research, 1980.   190p.,
       illus. (Wisconsin/Warner Brothers Screenplay Series)
           Edited transcript of the screenplay by James Seymour,
       David Boehm, and Ben Markson; from the stage play by Avery
       Hopwood.

Grease

1159. Kelly, Joe. The Grease Guide to Coolness. Edited by Armand
       Eisen. Kansas City: Ariel Books, 1978. 80p., illus.
           Humor; tie-in with the movie.

1160. Sollars, Michael. The Grease Album. Edited by Armand Eisen.
       Kansas City: Ariel Books; Cheltenham, Gloucestershire: Phin
       Publishing, 1978. 80p., illus.
           The Story of the movie.

Grease Two

1161. Rotsler, William. Grease Two: a Novel. Based on the screen-
       play by Ken Finkleman. London: Sphere, 1982. 152p., illus.

The Great Rock'n'Roll Swindle

  *   Moorcock, Michael. The Great Rock'n'Roll Swindle.
         * Cited below as item 3534.

The Great Ziegfeld

  *   Santon, Frederick. M.G.M.'s Ziegfeld Trilogy.
         * Cited below as item 3789.

Hair

1162. Davis, Lorrie. Letting Down My Hair: Two Years With the Love-
       Rock Tribe, From Dawning to Downing of Aquarius. New York:
       Arthur Fields, 1973. 279p., illus. London: Paul Elek, 1974.
       280p., illus.
           Cast member's story, from auditioning for the initial
       production on Broadway, to her leaving in disillusionment.

Individual Productions (cont.)

The Harder They Come

1163. Thelwell, Michael. The Harder They Come. New York: Grove
      Pr.; London: Pluto Pr., 1980. 399p.

The Jazz Singer

1164. Carringer, Robert L. (ed.). The Jazz Singer. Introduction
      by Robert L. Carringer. Madison; London: University of
      Wisconsin Pr. for the Wisconsin Center for Film and Theater
      Research, 1979. 188p., illus. (Wisconsin/Warner Brothers
      Screenplay Series)
          Edited transcript of the screenplay by Alfred A. Cohn;
      from the stage play by Samson Raphaelson. Includes the
      original short story, The Day of Atonement by Raphaelson,
      source of the subsequent productions, first published in
      Everybody's magazine, January, 1922.

1165. Woodley, Richard. The Jazz Singer. Based on the screenplay
      by Herbert Baker. Adaption by Stephen H. Foreman. Based
      on the play by Samson Raphaelson. New York: Bantam; London:
      Corgi, 1980. 192p.
          Novelization of the 1980 remake, starring Neil Diamond.

Jesus Christ Superstar

1166. Braun, Michael. Jesus Christ Superstar: the Authorized
      Version. With Richard Eckford and Peter Stimpson. London:
      Pan, 1972. 188p., illus.
          Story of the productions.

1167. Coleman, John A. Jesus Christ: Superstar, or Savior and Lord?
      Watford, Hertfordshire: The Author, 1972. 33p.
          Critical examination of the productions, from a Christian
      viewpoint. Originally published in Australia by the author,
      1971.

1168. Forristal, Desmond. Superstar, or Son of God? Dublin:
      Veritas/Talbot Pr., 1973. 22p., illus.
          Critical study of the productions, from a Christian view-
      point.

1169. James, David. Jesus Christ Superstar: Photographs. Kings
      Langley, Hertfordshire: Fountain Pr., 1973. unpaged, illus.
          Photographs from the movie production.

1170. Nassour, Ellis, and Richard Broderick. Rock Opera: the Creat-
      ion of "Jesus Christ Superstar", from Record Album to Broadway
      Show and Motion Picture. New York: Hawthorn Books, 1973.
      248p., illus.

Joseph and the Amazing Technicolor Dreamcoat

1171. Rice, Tim, and Andrew Lloyd Webber. <u>Joseph and the Amazing</u>
       <u>Technicolor Dreamcoat</u>. Pictures by Quentin Blake. London:
       Pavilion Books, 1982. 48p., illus.
          The story of the production in verse and pictures. Aimed
       at children.

The Music Machine

1172. Stoddart, Bill. <u>The Music Machine</u>. London: Sphere, 1979.
       150p., illus.
          Novelization of the motion picture.

My Fair Lady

1173. Beaton, Cecil. <u>Cecil Beaton's Fair Lady</u>. London: Weidenfeld
       and Nicolson; New York: Holt, Rinehart and Winston, 1964.
       128p., illus.
          Diary, 1962-3, of his work on the costume design and set
       creation for the motion picture.

Nashville

1174. Tewkesbury, Joan. <u>Nashville: an Original Screenplay</u>. New
       York; London: Bantam, 1976. 255p., illus.
          Cover title: <u>Robert Altman's "Nashville</u>." Novelization of
       the motion picture.

New York, New York

1175. Rauch, Earl Mac. <u>New York, New York</u>. New York: Simon and
       Schuster; London: Coronet, 1977. 173p.
          Novelization of the movie.

No, No, Nanette

1176. Dunn, Don. <u>The Making of "No, No, Nanette</u>." Secaucus, New
       Jersey: Citadel Pr., 1972. 335p., illus. New York: Dell,
       1973. 349p., illus.
          Account of the original 1925 production; also the 1971
       revival.

Individual Productions (cont.)

The Pajama Game

1177. Bissell, Richard Pike. Seven and One-Half Cents. Boston:
       Atlantic Monthly Pr., 1954. 245p.

       ————. A Gross of Pyjamas. London: Secker and Warburg,
       1954. 224p.

       ————. The Pajama Game. Harmondsworth, Middlesex: Penguin,
       1955. 191p.
            Basis of the musical.

Pal Joey

1178. O'Hara, John. Pal Joey. New York: Random House, 1952. 224p.
       London: Cresset Pr., 1952; London: Panther, 1960. 125p.
            Collection of short stories, originally published in the
       New Yorker. Basis of the musical productions.

Pennies From Heaven

1179. Potter, Dennis. Pennies From Heaven. London: Quartet, 1981.
       196p.
            Novelization of the author's screenplay for the British
       television series; subsequently filmed.

Porgy and Bess

1180. Capote, Truman. The Muses Are Heard: an Account of the Porgy
       and Bess Visit to Leningrad. New York: Random House, 1956;
       London: Heinemann, 1957. 182p.
            Chronicle of American cast's performance of the show in
       Leningrad.

1181. Heyward, Du Bose. Porgy. New York: Doubleday, Doran, 1925;
       London: Hodder, 1926. 196p. New illustrated ed.: London:
       Cape, 1953. 127p., illus.
            Novel; basis of the musical.

The Quaker Girl

1182. Simpson, Harold. The Quaker Girl: the Novel of the Play.
       Book by James T. Tanner. London: Mills and Boon, 1910. 255p.

The Rocky Horror Show

1183.   Henkin, William A. The Rocky Horror Picture Show Book. New
        York: Hawthorn Books, 1979. 220p., illus.
           Book of the movie of the stage show.

The Rose

1184.   Fleischer, Leonore. The Rose: a Novel. Based on the orig-
        inal screenplay by Bo Goldman, Michael Cimino, and William
        Kerby. New York: Warner Books, 1979. 254p. London: Barker;
        London: Futura, 1979. 247p
           Novelization of the movie based on the life of Janis
        Joplin; starring Bette Midler.

1185.   Watson, Diana Masters. The Rose. New York: Warner Books;
        London: Star Books, 1979.   p., illus.
           Book of the movie. Illustrated with stills; linked by
        storyline. Not to be confused with item 1184.

Saturday Night Fever/Staying Alive

1186.   Gilmour, H.B. Saturday Night Fever: a Novelization. Based
        on a screenplay by Norman Wexler. From a story by Nik Cohn.
        New York; London: Bantam, 1977. 182p., illus.

1187.   Fleischer, Leonore. Staying Alive: a Novel. From the screen-
        play by Sylvester Stallone and Norman Wexler. Based on
        characters created by Nik Cohn. London: Sphere, 1983. 181p.
           Novelization of the sequel to Saturday Night Fever.

Showboat

1188.   Kreuger, Miles. Show Boat: the Story of a Classic American
        Musical. New York; London: Oxford University Pr., 1978.
        253p., illus., bibliog., discog., index.
           Critical history of the various productions. Chronicles
        the development of the show through its differing versions.

Some Like It Hot

1189.   Wilder, Billy, and I.A.L. Diamond. Some Like It Hot: a Screen-
        play. New York: New American Library, 1959. 144p. (Signet
        Books)
           Filmed, starring Marilyn Monroe.

Individual Productions (cont.)

That'll Be the Day/Stardust

1190. Connolly, Ray. That'll Be the Day. London: Fontana, 1973.
       127p.
            Novelization.

1191. ————. Stardust. London: Fontana, 1974. 157p.
            Novelization of the sequel to That'll Be the Day.

The Threepenny Opera

1192. Tolksdorf, Cäcilie. John Gays "Beggar's Opera" und Bert
       Brechts "Dreigroschenoper." Rheinberg, Germany: Sattler and
       Koss, 1934. 80p., bibliog.
            In German. Based on the author's dissertation, Bonn
       University. Examination of Brecht's work, and comparison
       with its source.

A Tree Grows in Brooklyn

1193. Smith, Betty Wehner. A Tree in the Yard: a Novel. London:
       Heinemann, 1944. 368p.

            ————. A Tree Grows in Brooklyn. Drawings by Richard
       Bergere. New York: Harper and Row, 1947. 420p. London:
       Heinemann, 1947. 368p. Harmondsworth, Middlesex: Penguin,
       1951. 411p. London: Landsborough Publications, 1958. 352p.
       (Four Square Books).
            Source of the Broadway musical; adapted from the novel by
       Arthur Schwartz.

The Unsinkable Molly Brown

1194. Hine, Al. The Unsinkable Molly Brown: a Novel. Based upon
       the stage play. Music and lyrics by Meredith Wollson. Book
       by Richard Morris. Screenplay by Helen Deutsch. Greenwich,
       Conn.: Fawcett Publications, 1964. 143p. (Gold Medal Books)

Yankee Doodle Dandy

1195. McGilligan, Patrick (ed.). Yankee Doodle Dandy. Introduction
       by Patrick McGilligan. Madison; London: University of Wiscon-
       sin Pr. for the Wisconsin Center for Film and Theater Research,
       1981. 239p., illus. (Wisconsin/Warner Brothers Screenplay Ser-
       ies)
            Edited transcript of the screenplay by Robert Buckner and

Edmund Joseph; with additional material by Julius and Philip
Epstein. The original story was by Robert Buckner.

The Ziegfeld Follies

* Santon, Frederick. <u>M.G.M.'s Ziegfeld Trilogy</u>.
  * Cited below as item 3789.

The Ziegfeld Girl

* Santon, Frederick. <u>M.G.M.'s Ziegfeld Trilogy</u>.
  * Cited below as item 3789.

5. VENUES

(a) Comprehensive Works

1196. Elkin, Robert. <u>The Old Concert Rooms of London</u>. London:
      Edward Arnold; New York: St. Martin's Pr., 1955. 167p., illus.
      Music halls and other venues.

1197. Gamble, George, and George Frederick Scotson-Clark. <u>The Halls</u>.
      Pictured by G.F. Scotson-Clark. Introduction by George Gamble.
      London: T. Fisher Unwin, 1899. 72p., illus.
      London music halls. Pictures by Scotson-Clark; text by
      Gamble.

1198. Graham, Philip. <u>Showboats: the History of an American Inst-
      itution</u>. Austin: University of Texas Pr., 1951 (reissued:
      1970). 224p., illus., bibliog., index.
      Detailed account, 1831-1937. Includes chronological list-
      ing of major showboats.

1199. Howard, Diana. <u>London Theatres and Music Halls, 1850-1950</u>.
      London: Library Association, 1970. 291p., bibliog.
      Alphabetically arranged profiles of London theaters, music
      halls, and pleasure gardens. Includes directory of theater
      collections in London.

1200. MacQueen-Pope, Walter James. <u>An Indiscreet Guide to Theatre-
      land</u>. London: Muse Arts, 1947. 135p., index.
      Histories of London theaters, including music halls and
      variety/revue venues.

1201. Mander, Raymond, and Joe Mitchenson. <u>The Lost Theatres of
      London</u>. London: Hart-Davis, 1968. 576p., illus., index.
      Histories of London venues, including music halls and
      variety/revue theaters, that have vanished. Includes many
      illustrations of the buildings; also performance depictions,
      etc.

Comprehensive Works (cont.)

1202. Mander, Raymond, and Joe Mitchenson. The Theatres of London.
       Illustrated by Timothy Birdsall. London: Hart-Davis, 1961.
       292p., illus. Revised and enlarged ed.: London: New English
       Library, 1975. 344p., illus.
           Histories of London venues, including music halls and
       variety/revue theaters.

                        (b) Individual Theaters

Alhambra

1203. Disher, Maurice Willson. The Personality of The Alhambra;
       and, The History of Odeon, by Sir Michael W.S. Bruce.
       Birmingham, England: Odeon Theatres, 1937. 31p.
           History of London's Alhambra theater; also the story of
       the Odeon Theatre Company.

Apollo

1204. Fox, Ted. Showtime at The Apollo. New York: Holt, Rinehart
       and Winston, 1983. 221p., illus.
           History of the theater.

1205. Schiffman, Jack. Uptown: the Story of Harlem's Apollo Theatre.
       New York: Cowles Book Company, 1971. 210p., illus., index.
           Anecdotal history, by son of its founder.

1206. Walker, Jessie. The Apollo Theater Story. New York: Apollo
       Operations, 1966.   p., illus.

Carnegie Hall

1207. Cron, Theodore O., and Burt Goldblatt. Portrait of Carnegie
       Hall: a Portrait in Pictures and Words of America's Greatest
       Stage, and the Artists Who Performed There. New York: Mac-
       millan; London: Collier-Macmillan, 1966. 217p., illus.

1208. Peyser, Ethel. The House that Music Built: Carnegie Hall.
       New York: McBride, 1936. 371p., illus., bibliog., index.
           Includes discussion of the physical aspects of the theater.

1209. Schickel, Richard. The World of Carnegie Hall. New York: J.
       Messner, 1960; Westport, Conn.: Greenwood Pr., 1973. 438p.,
       illus.

Coliseum

1210. Barker, Felix. <u>The House that Stoll Built</u>. London: Muller, 1957. 256p., illus.
    History of London's <u>Coliseum</u> theater. It started life as a music hall.

Daly's

1211. Forbes-Winslow, D., and Robert L. Hadfield. <u>Daly's: the Biography of a Theatre</u>. London: W.H. Allen, 1944. 220p., illus.
    Part One by Hadfield; Part Two by Forbes-Winslow.

Dan Lowery's "Star of Erin" Music Hall

1212. Watters, Eugene, and Matthew Murtagh. <u>Infinite Variety: Dan Lowery's Music Hall, 1879-1897</u>. Dublin: Gill and Macmillan, 1975. 176p., illus., index.

Drury Lane Theatre

1213. MacQueen-Pope, Walter James. <u>Pillars of Drury Lane</u>. London: Hutchinson, 1955. 267p., illus.

Folies Bergère

1214. Castle, Charles. <u>The Folies Bergère</u>. London: Methuen, 1982. 319p., illus., bibliog., index.

1215. Derval, Paul. <u>The Folies Bergère</u>. Translated by Lucienne Hill. Preface by Maurice Chevalier. London: Methuen; New York: Dutton, 1955. 219p., illus.
    Originally published as <u>Folies-Bergère: souvenirs de leur Directeur</u>, Paris: Editions de Paris, 1954.

Gaiety

1216. Hollingshead, John. <u>The Gaiety Chronicle</u>. London: Constable, 1898. 493p.

1217. ———. <u>"Good Old Gaiety:" an Historiette and Remembrance</u>. London: Gaiety Theatre Company, 1903. 79p., illus.

Individual Theaters (cont.)

Gaiety (cont.)

1218.   Hyman, Alan. <u>The Gaiety Years</u>. London: Cassell, 1975.
        230p., illus., bibliog., index.

1219.   Jupp, James. <u>The Gaiety Stage Door: Thirty Years' Reminiscen-
        ces of the Theatre</u>. London: Cape, 1923. 352p., illus.

1220.   MacQueen-Pope, Walter James. <u>Gaiety: Theatre of Enchantment</u>.
        London: W.H. Allen, 1949. 498p., illus., index.
            Includes listing of productions staged there.

1221.   Naylor, Stanley. <u>The Gaiety and George Grossmith: Random
        Reflections on the Serious Business of Enjoyment</u>. London:
        Stanley Paul, 1913. 263p., illus.

Haymarket

1222.   MacQueen-Pope, Walter James. <u>The Haymarket: Theatre of
        Perfection</u>. London: W.H. Allen, 1948. 394p., illus.

Lyric

1223.   Playfair, Nigel. <u>The Story of the Lyric Theatre, Hammersmith</u>.
        London: Chatto and Windus, 1925. 235p., illus.

Palace

1224.   Spitzer, Marian. <u>The Palace</u>. Introduction by Brooks Atkinson.
        New York: Atheneum, 1969. 267p., illus.

Palladium

1225.   Bevan, Ian. <u>Top of the Bill: the Story of the London Pallad-
        ium</u>. London: Muller, 1952. 245p., illus.

1226.   Pilton, Patrick. <u>Every Night at the London Palladium</u>. London:
        Robson Books, 1976. 175p., illus.
            Anecdotal history.

Player's

1227.   Anderson, Jean (ed.). <u>Late Joys at the Player's Theatre</u>.
        London: T.V. Boardman, 1943. 119p., illus.

Radio City Music Hall

1228. Francisco, Charles. The Radio City Music Hall Book: an
       Affectionate History of the World's Greatest Theater. New
       York: Dutton, 1979.   p., illus.

St. James's

1229. MacQueen-Pope, Walter James. St. James's: Theatre of Dist-
       inction. London: W.H. Allen, 1958. 256p., illus.

Theatre Royal

1230. ————. The Theatre Royal, Drury Lane. London: W.H. Allen,
       1945. 350p., illus.
            Was the venue for Ivor Novello's first large-scale musical
       show, Glamorous Night, 1935.

Windmill

1231. Van Damm, Sheila. We Never Closed: the Windmill Story.
       London: Hale, 1967. 191p., illus.
            Story of the revue theater, by one of the owners.

1232. Van Damm, Vivian. Tonight, and Every Night. London: Stanley
       Paul, 1952. 206p., illus.
            History, by husband of Sheila Van Damm.

6. DANCE

(1) REFERENCE MATERIAL

(a) General Works

1233. American Dance Directory. New York: Association of American
       Dance Companies. biennial, 197?- .
           Lists dance companies.

1234. Country Dance and Song. New York: Country Dance and Song
       Society of America. annual, 1968- .
           Contact directory.

1235. Dance Directory: Programs of Professional Preparation in
       American Colleges and Universities. Reston, Virginia:
       American Alliance for Health, Physical Education, Recreation,
       and Dance. annual, 1971- .

1236. Dance Magazine Annual. New York: Danad. annual, 19??- .
           Contact directory; also features.

1237. Dance World. New York: Dance World. annual, 1980- .
           Lists dance companies.

1238. People's Folk Dance Directory. Austin: John C. Steele.
       biennial, 198?- .
           International coverage. Lists folk dance groups, educators,
       publications, suppliers, organizations, etc.

1239. Reynolds, Nancy (ed.). Dance Catalog. New York: Harmony
       Books, 1979. 260p., illus.
           Directory of dance equipment and suppliers.

(b) Bibliographies and Indexes

1240. Belknap, S. Yancey (comp.). Guide to Dance Periodicals: an
       Analytical Index of Articles. Gainesville, Florida: Univer-
       sity Presses of Florida, 1949-58. 7 vols.   p.
           Covers from 1931-56.

1241. Long, Elizabeth Baker, and Mary McKee (comps.). A Bibliog-
       raphy of Music for the Dance. Austin: The Authors, 1936. 47p.
           Classified arrangement. Includes notations of recorded
       music. Includes jazz dance.

1242. Magriel, Paul David. A Bibliography of Dancing: a List of
       Books and Articles on the Dance, and Related Subjects. New
       York: H.W. Wilson, 1936; New York: Benjamin Blom, 1966. 229p.,
       indexes.

       ————. Fourth Cumulated Supplement, 1936-40. New York: H.W.
       Wilson, 1941. 104p.
           Five thousand classified, annotated entries in main work.
       All types of dance included. Gives library locations.

Bibliographies and Indexes (cont.)

1243. Petermann, Kurt. Tanzbibliographie: Verzeichnis der in
deutscher Sprache veröffnetlichen Schriften und Aufsätze
zum Bühnen-, Gesellschafts-, Kinder-, Volks-, und Turniertanz,
sowie zur Tanzwissenschaft, Tanzmusik, und zum Jazz. Munich;
New York: Saur for the Akademie der Künste, Tanzarchiv der
Deutsche Demokratische Republik, Leipzig, 1978. 2 vols.,
1982p.

(2) HISTORIES

(a) General Works

1244. Buckman, Peter. Let's Dance: Social, Ballroom, and Folk
Dancing. Picture research by Enid Moore. London; New York:
Paddington Pr., 1978; Harmondsworth, Middlesex; New York:
Penguin, 1979. 288p., illus., bibliog., index.
Includes tempo table; also chronological currency chart.

1245. Dannett, Sylvia G.L., and Frank Rachel. Down Memory Lane:
Arthur Murray's Picture Story of Social Dancing. New York:
Greenberg, 1954. 191p., illus.

1246. De Mille, Agnes. America Dances: a Personal Chronicle in
Words and Pictures. New York: Macmillan; London: Collier-
Macmillan, 1980. 222p., illus., bibliog., index. (A Helene
Obolensky Enterprises, Inc., Book). New York: Limelight Edit-
ions, 1984. 261p., illus., bibliog., index.
History of dancing in the United States.

1247. Emery, Lynne Fauley. Black Dance in the United States, from
1619 to 1970. Palo Alto, California: National Pr. Books,
1972. 370p., illus., bibliog., index.
Emphasis on social function of popular black dance. Includes dance in minstrelsy, revue, musical comedy; also black
concert dance.

1248. Hallewell, Kit. Blackpool, My Blackpool: One Man's Chronicle
of the Blackpool Dance Festival Over the Years 1931-1978.
Birmingham, England: The Author, 1979. 233p., illus.
Account of Britain's leading ballroom dancing championship.

1249. Kendall, Elizabeth. Where She Danced. New York: Knopf, 1979.
p., illus.
History of social dancing, from its origins to early modern
dance. Includes dance in vaudeville, revue, etc.

1250. McDonagh, Don. Dance Fever. New York: Random House, 1979.
p., illus., index.
History of social and other dancing in the United States.

1251. Nevell, Richard. A Time to Dance. New York: St. Martin's Pr.,
1980.   p., illus., bibliog.
History of American country and square dancing.

Histories (cont.)

(b) Jazz Dance

1252. Giordano, Gus (ed.). <u>Anthology of American Jazz Dance</u>.
       Evanston, Illinois: Orion Publishing House, 1975. 418p.
          Includes historical material.

1253. Stearns, Marshall, and Jean Stearns. <u>Jazz Dance: the Story
       of American Vernacular Dance</u>. New York: Macmillan; London:
       Collier-Macmillan, 1968. 464p., illus., bibliog., index.
          Chronicles the relationship between Afro-American dances
       and American stage dance, from minstrelsy through Broadway.
       Includes listing of motion pictures featuring jazz dancing,
       by Ernest Smith.

(c) Breakdance/Hip-Hop

1254. Hager, Steven. <u>Hip-Hop: the Illustrated History of Break
       Dancing, Rap Music, and Graffiti</u>. New York: St. Martin's Pr.,
       1984. 128p., illus.

(3) VENUES

(a) General Works

1255. Jacob, Ellen, and C. Jonas. <u>Dance in New York</u>. New York:
       Quick Fox, 1980.   p., illus.

1256. Levey, Paula. <u>Dancing in London</u>. London: New English Lib-
       rary, 1981. 161p.

(b) Discotheques

(i) General Works

1257. Abrams, Nalami, and Brian Sheratt. <u>Disco Chic: All the Styles,
       Steps, and Places to Go</u>. New York: Crown, 1979.   p., illus.

1258. Blackford, Andy. <u>Disco Dancing Tonight: Clubs, Dances, Fash-
       ion, Music</u>. London: Octopus, 1979. 80p., illus., index.

1259. Brown, Chris. <u>The Family Album</u>. Woking, Surrey: Hitman,
       1980. 96p., illus.
          Examination of British discotheque scene, including its
       audiences.

1260. Deats, Randy. <u>Dancing Disco</u>. In Collaboration with Laurie
       Devine. New York: Morrow, 1979. 192p., illus. (Quill)
          Based on American television series, same title.

*   Ellis, Ron. <u>Diary of a Discotheque: a Selection of Poems</u>,
    <u>1970-78</u>.
      * Cited below as item 4743.

1261. Goldman, Albert Harry. <u>Disco</u>. New York: Hawthorn Books,
      1978. 174p., illus.
      Discotheques and their dance styles, 1960's and 1970's.

1262. Mad. <u>Mad Disco</u>. Edited by Albert B. Feldstein. New York:
      E.C. Publications, 1980. 32p., illus.
      Includes record. Parody of discotheque scene; from the
      publishers of <u>Mad</u> magazine.

1263. Miezitis, Vita. <u>Night Dancin'</u> Photographs by Bill Bern-
      stein. New York: Ballantine, 1980. 219p., illus.
      Examination of the American discotheque scene, and its
      audiences.

(ii) Administration

1264. Community Council for Somerset. <u>Discos: Guidelines for</u>
      <u>Success</u>. Taunton, Somerset: Community Council for Somerset,
      1983.   p.
      Practical guide.

1265. Emenheiser, Daniel A. <u>Professional Discotheque Management</u>.
      Boston: C.B.I. Publications, 1980. 284p.

1266. Greater London Council. <u>Disco Rules, OK</u>? London: Greater
      London Council, 1979. 12p., illus.
      Recommendations for running trouble-free discotheques;
      aimed at venues licensed by the Council for dancing.

1267. Mann, Willie. <u>The Disk Jockey's Good Dance Guide</u>. New York:
      Exposition Pr., 1984. 64p.

1268. Radcliffe, Joe. <u>This Business of Disco</u>. New York: Billboard
      Publications, 1980. 192p.

1269. Shannon, Doug. <u>Off the Record: Everything Related to Playing</u>
      <u>Recorded Dance Music in the Entertainment Business</u>. Edited
      by Richard W. Kutnick. Cleveland: Pacesetter Publishing
      House, 1982. 403p.
      Includes business aspects of radio disk-jockey work.

1270. Swindells, Adrienne P. <u>Running a Disco</u>. Illustrated by
      Colin Stone. St. Albans, Hertfordshire: Hart-Davis Educat-
      ional, 1977. 48p., illus. (Scanners Series)
      Practical guide; intended for use in schools and colleges.

(c) Motion Pictures

* Delamater, Jerome. <u>Dance in the Hollywood Musical</u>.
   * Cited above as item 1083.

1271. Parker, David L., and Esther Siegel. <u>Guide to Dance in Film:</u>
<u>a Catalog of U.S. Productions Including Dance Sequences.</u>
<u>With Names of Dancers, Choreographers, Directors, and Other</u>
<u>Details</u>. Detroit: Gale Research, 1978. 220p., indexes.
(Performing Arts Information Guide Series, 3)

(4) SOCIOLOGICAL ASPECTS

1272. Cressey, Paul G. <u>The Taxi-Dance Hall: a Sociological Study</u>
<u>in Commercialized Recreation and City Life</u>. Chicago: Univ-
ersity of Chicago Pr., 1932; Westport, Conn.: Greenwood Pr.,
1969. 300p. Reprinted: <u>With an Introductory Essay Added</u>.
Montclair, New Jersey: Patterson Smith, 1969; New York: A.M.S.
Pr., 1972.   p. (Criminology, Law Enforcement, and Social
Problems Series, 76)

1273. Leaf, Earl. <u>Isles of Rhythm</u>. Foreword by Katherine Dunham.
New York: A.S. Barnes, 1948. 211p., illus.
   West Indian dances, customs, and traditions.

(5) DANCE INSTRUCTION

(a) General Works

1274. Dubsky, Dora. <u>Sing and Dance</u>. Hialeah, Florida: Columbia
Pictures, 1977.   p., illus.

1275. Moore, Debbie. <u>The Pineapple Dance Book: an Insider's Guide</u>
<u>to All That's Best in Dance and Exercise Today</u>. Text by
Gay Search and David Roper. London: Pavilion Books, 1983;
New York: Delilah, 1984. 160p., illus.
   By the founder of London's Pineapple Studio. Survey of
current jazz dance; also practical guide to dancercise.

1276. Wayburn, Ned (<u>pseud. of</u> Edward Claudius Wayburn). <u>The Art of</u>
<u>Stage Dancing: the Story of a Beautiful and Profitable Pro-</u>
<u>fession: a Manual of Stage-Craft</u>. New York: Wayburn Studios
of Stage Dancing, 1925. 382p., illus.
   By Broadway director and choreographer, involved with the
Ziegfeld Follies and other long-running shows.

(b) Ballroom

1277. Bonomo, Joe. <u>Improve Your Dancing: a Pictorial Self-Instruct-</u>
<u>ion Course</u>. Brooklyn, New York: The Author, 1938. 32p., illus.

1278.   Castle, Vernon, and Irene Castle. Modern Dancing. Intro-
        duction by Elisabeth Marbury. New York; London: Harper,
        1914. 175p., illus.
             Influential instruction manual. The authors posed for
        the illustrations.

1279.   Engel, Lyle Kenyon. The Fred Astaire Dance Book: the Fred
        Astaire Dance Studio Method. With the assistance of John
        Monte. Illustrated by Josh Pryce. London: Souvenir Pr.,
        1962. 2nd. ed.: New York: Simon and Schuster, 1978; London:
        Pelham, 1979. 184p., illus.

1280.   Francis and Day's New and Original Ball-Room Dances: Contain-
        ing Full Descriptions of All Their Latest Prize Dances.
        London: Francis, Day and Hunter, 1908. 32p.

1281.   Javna, John, and Crispin Peirce. How to Jitterbug: Learn
        Twenty-Five Great Dance Moves, From the Cement Mixer to the
        Sweetheart, From the Butterfly to the Pretzel! New York:
        St. Martin's Pr., 1984. 96p., illus.

   *   Kilbride, Ann T., and A. Algoso. The Complete Book on Disco
        and Ballroom Dancing.
             * Cited below as item 1311.

1282.   Lustgarten, Karen. The Complete Guide to Touch Dancing.
        Photography by Bernie Lustgarten. Chart illustrations by
        Robert Makohin and David Gentry. New York: Warner Books,
        1979.   p., illus.

1283.   Silvester, Victor. The Art of the Ballroom. London: Herbert
        Jenkins, 1936. 263p., illus.

1284.   ————. The Complete Old Time Dancer. With Walter Whitman.
        London: Herbert Jenkins, 1967. 254p., illus.

1285.   ————. Dancing for the Millions: a Concise Guide to Modern
        Ballroom Dancing. London: Odhams Pr., 1949. 128p., illus.

1286.   ————. Modern Ballroom Dancing. London: Herbert Jenkins,
        1927. 249p., illus.

        ————. Modern Ballroom Dancing: History and Practice.
        London: Barrie and Jenkins, 1974; London: Stanley Paul, 1982.
        249p., illus.

1287.   ————. Modern Dancer's Handbook. London: Herbert Jenkins,
        1954. 177p., illus.

1288.   ————. Old Time Dancing. London: Herbert Jenkins, 1949.
        189p., illus.

1289.   ————. More Old Time Dances. London: Herbert Jenkins,
        1951. 124p., illus.

1290. Silvester, Victor. <u>Old Time and Sequence Dancing</u>. <u>Revised</u>
       <u>and combined ed</u>. London: Barrie and Jenkins, 1980. 179p.,
       illus.
            Combines items 1288 and 1291.

1291. ————. <u>Sequence Dancing</u>. London: Herbert Jenkins, 1950.
       191p., illus.

1292. ————. <u>The Theory and Technique of Ballroom Dancing</u>.
       London: Herbert Jenkins, 1932. 159p., illus. <u>2nd. ed</u>.:
       1933. 153p. <u>Rev. ed</u>.: 1936. 181p.

       ————. <u>The Theory and Practice of Ballroom Dancing</u>. Lon-
       don: Herbert Jenkins, 1948. 344p.

1293. ————. <u>This is Jive</u>. London: Danceland Publications, 1944.
       64p., illus.

1294. ————. <u>Victor Silvester's Album</u>. London: Centaur Pr.,
       1955. 150p., illus.
            Articles on ballroom dancing; by various authors.

1295. ————. <u>Victor Silvester's Magic Way to Ballroom Dancing</u>.
       London: Danceland Publications, 1947. 35p., illus.

1296. Stephenson, Richard Montgomery, and Joseph Iaccarion. <u>The</u>
       <u>Complete Book of Ballroom Dancing</u>. Garden City, New York:
       Doubleday, 1980.   p., illus., bibliog., index.

1297. <u>Swing Steps: the Complete Guide to Swing Dancing</u>. New York:
       Louellen Publishing Company, 1937. 65p., illus.

1298. Van Zant, Mayphine. <u>Teach Yourself Ballroom Dancing</u>. Illus-
       trated by Jeanne Radysh. Dance step diagrams by John L. Van
       Zant. New York: D. McKay, 1979. 268p., illus.

1299. Villacorta, Aurora S. <u>Charleston, Anyone</u>? Danville, Illin-
       ois: Interstate Printers and Publishers, 1978. 43p., illus.,
       bibliog.

(c) Belly Dancing

1300. Buonaventura, Wendy. <u>Belly Dancing: the Serpent and the</u>
       <u>Sphinx</u>. London: Virago, 1983. 167p., illus., bibliog.
            History; and practical guide.

1301. Hobin, Tina. <u>Belly Dancing for Health and Relaxation</u>. Lon-
       don: Duckworth, 1982. 96p., illus.

(d) Country and Square Dancing

1302. Hall, J.T. <u>Dance! A Complete Guide to Social, Folk, and</u>
       <u>Square Dancing</u>. New York: Ayer, 1980.   p., illus.

1303.   Kennedy, Douglas, and Helen Kennedy. The Country Dance Book.
        Hatboro, Pennsylvania: Legacy Books, 1979.   p., illus.

1304.   Leisner, Tony. The Official Guide to Country Dance Steps.
        Chicago: Domus Books, 1980. 96p., illus., index.

1305.   Livingston, Peter (ed.). The Complete Book of Country Swing
        and Western Dance... and a Bit About Cowboys. New York:
        Doubleday, 1981.   p., illus. (Dolphin Books)

1306.   Murphy, Edward. Western Dancing. Great Neck, New York: Todd
        and Honeywell, 1983. 64p., illus.

1307.   Piute Pete (pseud.). Piute Pete's Down-Home Square Dance
        Book. New York: Grosset and Dunlap, 1977. 96p., illus.

                          (e) Disco

                     (i) General Works

1308.   American Alliance for Health, Physical Education, Recreation
        and Dance. The Art of Disco Dancing. Reston, Virginia:
        American Alliance for Health, Physical Education, Recreation
        and Dance, 1980. 176p., illus.

1309.   Brown, Alex, and Raymond Draper. The A to Z of Disco and
        Fever Dancing. New Rochelle, New York: Sportshelf, 1979.
            p., illus.

1310.   Cherry, Joetta, and Gwynne Tomlan. Disco Dancing. Photo-
        graphs by Mort Engel. New York: Grosset and Dunlap, 1979.
        96p., illus. (Elephant Books)
            Aimed at younger readers. Includes brief history of disco
        dancing.

   *   Deats, Randy. Dancing Disco.
            * Cited above as item 1260.

1311.   Kilbride, Ann T., and A. Algoso. The Complete Book on Disco
        and Ballroom Dancing. Los Alamitos, California: Hwong Pub-
        lishing, 1979. 280p., illus., bibliog.

1312.   Kollmar, Kerry. Roller Disco Dancing. With photographs by
        Melody Mason. New York: Sterling Publishing, 1979. 84p.,
        illus., index.

1313.   Lauren, Jena. Disco. Photography, production, and design by
        Paul S. Hodara. Los Angeles: Price, Stern and Sloan, 1979.
        63p., illus., index.

1314.   Lovisone, Carter. The Disco Hustle. New York: Sterling Pub-
        lishing; London: Ward Lock, 1979. 96p., illus., index.
            How to do the dance.

Disco (cont.)

1315. Lustgarten, Karen. The Complete Guide to Disco Dancing.
       Photography by Bernie Lustgarten. Chart illustrations by
       Robert Makohin and David Gentry. New York: Warner Books,
       1978. 127p., illus.

1316. Marzano, Dale A. Roller Disco. London; New York: Hamlyn,
       1979. 96p., illus.

1317. Morton, Pamela. The Basics of Disco Dancing. Boston: Amer-
       ican Pr., 1982. 56p., illus.

1318. Muir, Donna. How to Dance. London; New York: Omnibus Pr.,
       1982. 128p., illus.
          Disco dancing.

(ii) Breakdance

1319. Alford, Lucy. Break Dancing. Photography by Clare Muller.
       London; New York: Hamlyn, 1984. 60p., illus.

1320. Bryne, Richard. The Complete Art of Breaking. Edited by
       Mike Lee. Burbank, California: Ohara Publications, 1984.
       128p., illus.

1321. Carter, Eneida, and Miriam Mikalal. Break Dance: the Free
       and Easy Way! Philadelphia: Carter's Free and Easy Public-
       ations, 1984. 32p., illus.
          Instruction; aimed at younger readers.

1322. Holman, Michael. Break Dancing and the New York City Break-
       ers. New York: Freundlich Books, 1984. 272p., illus.

1323. Marlow, Curtis. Break Dancing. New York: Sharon Publications,
       1984. 96p., illus. (Star Books)

1324. Mister Fresh and The Supreme Rockers (pseud.). Breakdancing.
       New York: Avon, 1984. 128p., illus.

1325. Nadell, Bonnie, and John Small. Breakdance: Electric Boogie,
       Egyptian, Moonwalk...Do It! Philadelphia: Running Pr.; Lon-
       don: Futura, 1984. 64p., illus.
          Includes glossary of breakdance terms.

1326. Watkins, William H., and Eric N. Franklin. Breakdance! New
       York: Contemporary Books; Bromley, Kent: Columbus Books, 1984.
       115p., illus.

1327. Yonina (pseud.). Street Dance. London: Zomba Books, 1984.
       96p., illus.
          Breakdance, body popping, etc.

(f) Jazz Dance

1328. Audy, Robert. <u>Jazz Dancing: How to Teach Yourself</u>. Photography by Neil Selkirk. New York: Random House, 1978. 128p., illus.

1329. Becker, Sven, and Larie Winn. <u>Modern Jazz, New York</u>. Edited by Ray Cook. Poughkeepsie, New York: Ray Cook, 1982. 56p., illus.

1330. Beckman, Monica. <u>Jazz Gymnastics at Home and in School</u>. Illustrated by Greta Törnos. London: Lutterworth Pr., 1971. 118p., illus.

1331. Cayou, Dolores K. <u>Modern Jazz Dance</u>. Palo Alto, California: Mayfield Publishing, 1971. 148p., illus.

1332. Cook, Ray (ed.). <u>Jazz Dance Collection: Alvin Ailey, Paul Draper, Peter Gennaro, Billie Mahoney</u>. New York: Dance Notation Bureau, 1965. 17p., illus.
       Dances choreographed by the contributors.

1333. Czompo, Ann I. <u>Recreational Jazz Dance</u>. Homer, New York: A.C. Publications, 1979. 93p., illus., bibliog.

1334. Dow, Allen. <u>The Official Guide to Jazz Dancing</u>. With Mike Michaelson. Northbrook, Illinois: Domus Books, 1980.   p., illus., index.

1335. Fischer-Munsterman, Uta. <u>Jazz Dance and Jazz Gymnastics, Including Disco Dancing</u>. Introduction, edited, and adapted by Liz Williamson. New York: Sterling Publishing; London: Ward Lock, 1978. 120p., illus., index.
       Originally published as <u>Von der Jazzgymnastik zum Jazztanz</u>, Celle, West Germany: Pohl Verlag, 1975. Translated by Dale S. Cunningham.

1336. ———. <u>Jazz Dance, Including Aerobics</u>. Introduction, edited and adapted by Liz Williamson. New York: Sterling Publishing; London: Ward Lock, 1983. 120p., illus., index.
       Revision of item 1335.

1337. Giordano, Gus. <u>American Jazz Dance: Official Syllabus, and Dictionary of Terms</u>. New York: National Council of Dance Teacher Organizations, 1966. 46p.

1338. Goodman-Kraines, Linda, and Esther Kan. <u>Jump Into Jazz: a Primer for the Beginning Jazz Dance Student</u>. Palo Alto, California: Mayfield Publishing, 1983. 115p., illus.

1339. Koebner, Franz Wolfgang. <u>Jazz und Shimmy: Brevier der neusten Tänze</u>. Berlin: Eysler, 1921. 122p., illus.
       In German. Guide to then-current jazz dances.

Jazz Dance (cont.)

1340. Lane, Christy. <u>All That Jazz, and More: the Complete Book of
       Jazz Dancing</u>. El Cerrito, California: Leisure Pr., 1983.   p.,
       illus.

1341. Missett, Judi S., and Dona Meilach. <u>Jazzercise</u>. New York:
       Bantam, 1978.   p., illus.

1342. Sutton, Valerie. <u>Dance Writing: Shorthand for Modern Jazz
       Dance</u>. Newport Beach, California: Movement Shorthand Soc-
       iety, 1982.   p., illus.
          Choreography notation explained.

1343. Traguth, Fred. <u>Modern Jazz Dance</u>. Englewood Cliffs, New
       Jersey; London: Prentice-Hall, 1983. 220p., illus.

1344. Wydro, Luigi, and Kenneth Wydro. <u>The Luigi Jazz Dance Tech-
       nique</u>. New York: Doubleday, 1981. 224p., illus. (Dolphin
       Books)

                              (g) Tap

1345. Draper, Paul. <u>On Tap Dancing</u>. Edited by Fran Avallone. New
       York: Marcel Dekker, 1978.   p. (The Dance Program, 8)

1346. O'Gara, Sheila. <u>Tap It</u>. Music by Elizabeth Baker Long. New
       York: A.S. Barnes, 1937. 88p., illus.

PART TWO: BIOGRAPHY

A. COLLECTIVE BIOGRAPHIES

(A) POPULAR

(i) General

1347. <u>Alphabeat: Who's Who in Pop</u>. London: Century Twenty-One
Publishing, 1969. 126p., illus.
Profiles of current performers.

* Baker, Glenn A., and Stuart Coupe. <u>The New Music</u>.
* Cited below as item 1418.

1348. Bane, Michael. <u>Who's Who in Rock</u>. Researcher: Kenny Kertock.
New York: Facts on File; Oxford: Clio Pr., 1981. 259p., illus.
Approximately 1,200 entries. Brief biographies of major
and minor artists and groups; also entries for record companies and industry figures. No discographies.

1349. Barlow, Andrew. <u>Beat On</u>. Leicester: Golden Eagle, 1982.
192p.
Covers groups and solo artists.

1350. Barnes, Ken. <u>Sinatra and the Great Song Stylists</u>. With
contributions from Stan Britt, Arthur Jackson, Fred Dellar,
and Chris Ellis. London: Ian Allan, 1972. 192p., illus.,
index.
Profiles of popular singers, from Al Jolson to Andy Williams.

1351. Betrock, Alan. <u>Girl Groups: the Story of a Sound</u>. New York:
The Author, 1978; New York: Delilah; London: Omnibus Pr.,
1983. p., illus., discogs.
Includes essays on the genre by Gene Sculatti and Ken
Barnes.

1352. Bianco, David. <u>Who's New Wave in Music, 1976-1980: a Catalog
and Directory</u>. Grosse Point Farms, Michigan: Lunchroom Pr.,
1983. 300p.

1353. Birch, Ian, and Pearce Marchbank. <u>The Book With No Name</u>.
London: Omnibus Pr., 1982. p., illus.
Artists of Britain's "New Romantics" movement, 1982.

1354. Brown, Len, and Gary Friedrich (eds.). <u>Encyclopedia of Rock
and Roll</u>. New York: Tower Publications, 1970. 217p., illus.,
discogs.
Profiles of major and minor artists.

1355. Burlingame, Burl, and Robert Kamohalu Kasher. <u>Da Kine Sound:
Conversations With the People Who Create Hawaiian Music</u>.
Kailua, Hawaii: Press Pacifica, 1978. p., index.

General (cont.)

1356. Busnar, Gene. <u>The Superstars of Rock: Their Lives and Their</u>
       <u>Music</u>. New York: J. Messner, 1980. 224p., illus., bibliog.
              Elvis Presley, The Beatles, The Rolling Stones, The Bee
       Gees, Eric Clapton, Jimi Hendrix, Janis Joplin, Donna Summer,
       Stevie Wonder, and Elton John profiled.

1357. Celebrity Parade. <u>Celebrity Parade Presents Twenty-Five</u>
       <u>Years of Rock 'n' Roll</u>. Foreword by Nick Tosches. New York:
       Lorelei Publishing, 1979.   p., illus.

1358. Charlesworth, Chris. <u>A-Z of Rock Guitarists</u>. London; New
       York: Proteus, 1982. 128p., illus., discogs., index.
              Over two hundred brief profiles.

1359. Claghorn, Charles Eugene. <u>Biographical Dictionary of Amer-</u>
       <u>ican Music</u>. West Nyack: Parker, 1973. 491p., discogs.
              Details of over 5,200 individuals and groups. Covers
       concert music, opera, sacred music, musicals, jazz, ragtime,
       folk, country, popular song, rock, and soul; from the Seven-
       teenth Century to date. One alphabetical sequence.

1360. Clews, Frank. <u>The Golden Disc</u>. London: Brown, Watson, 1963.
       155p., illus. (Digit Books)
              Profiles of performers who were awarded gold disks.

1361. ————. <u>Teenage Idols</u>. London: Brown, Watson, 1963.   159p.,
       illus. (Digit Books)
              Current popular performers.

1362. Colman, Stuart. <u>They Kept On Rockin': the Giants of Rock 'n'</u>
       <u>Roll</u>. Poole, Dorset: Blandford Pr., 1982. 160p., illus.,
       index.
              Profiles of major figures from the 1950's who are still
       musically active. Includes Jerry Lee Lewis, Chuck Berry,
       Fats Domino, Little Richard, Bo Diddley, and others.

1363. Connolly, Ray. <u>Stardust Memories: Talking About My Generation</u>.
       London: Pavilion Books, 1983. 240p., illus.
              Collection of fifty profiles, previously published in the
       British press. Includes postscripts to each piece.

   *   Coupe, Stuart, and Glenn A. Baker. <u>The New Rock 'n' Roll</u>.
              * Cited below as item 1418.

1364. Cross, Colin (comp.). <u>Encyclopedia of British Beat Groups</u>
       <u>and Solo Artists of the Sixties</u>. With Paul Kendall and Mick
       Farren. London: Omnibus Pr.; New York: Quick Fox, 1980. 96p.,
       illus., index.

1365. Dachs, David. <u>Encyclopedia of Pop/Rock</u>. New York: Scholastic
       Book Services, 1972.   p., illus.

1366. ————. <u>One Hundred Pop-Rock Stars</u>. New York: Scholastic
       Book Services, 1981. 320p., illus.

1367. ————. Rock's Biggest Ten. New York: Scholastic Book
       Services, 1979.   p., illus.

1368. Dallas, Karl. Singers of an Empty Day: Last Sacraments for
       the Superstars. Illustrated by Gloria Dallas. London:
       Kahn and Averill, 1971. 208p., illus., index.
           Studies of Frank Sinatra, The Rolling Stones, Elvis
       Presley, John Lennon, The Beatles, Bob Dylan, Brian Jones,
       Jimi Hendrix, and Janis Joplin. Contends that stars are
       "divine victims" whose lives must be sacrificed; their
       choice being between obscurity or an inevitably premature
       death.

    * Dalton, David, and Lenny Kaye. Rock One Hundred.
           * Cited below as item 1432.

1369. Dellar, Fred. Where Did You Go To, My Lovely? The Lost
       Sounds and Stars of the Sixties. London: Star Books, 1983.
       221p., illus.
           Profiles of fifty past performers, and their lives after
       leaving the popular music business.

1370. Elson, Howard. Early Rockers. London; New York: Proteus,
       1982. 127p., illus.
           Profiles of thirteen artists prominent in 1950's rock.

1371. ————, and John Brunton. Whatever Happened To...? The
       Great Rock and Pop Nostalgia Book. Introduction by Gene
       Pitney. London; New York: Proteus, 1981. 159p., illus.
       (Proteus Rocks)
           Brief profiles of over two hundred artists from the 1950's
       to the 1970's; and what became of them.

1372. Emerson, Lucy. The Gold Record. New York: Fountain Pr.,
       1978.   p., illus.
           Profiles of rock musicians.

1373. Engel, Lyle Kenyon. Rock 'n' Roll Stars. London: L. Miller
       and Son, 1956. 64p., illus.
           Current artists profiled.

1374. Ewen, David. Men of Popular Music. Chicago: Ziff-Davis,
       1944 (Reprinted: Freeport, New York: Books For Libraries Pr.,
       1972. Essay Index Reprint Series). 213p., illus., bibliog.,
       discog. New York: Editions for the Armed Services, 1944.
       192p. 2nd. ed.: New York: Prentice-Hall, 1949. 213p., illus.,
       discog.
           Profiles of King Oliver, Irving Berlin, Louis Armstrong,
       W.C. Handy, Meade Lux Lewis, Duke Ellington, Paul Whiteman,
       Ferde Grofé, George Gershwin, Jerome Kern, Richard Rodgers,
       Lorenz Hart, Cole Porter, Benny Goodman, and Raymond Scott.

1375. Fawcett, Anthony. California Rock/California Sound. Laguna
       Beach, California: R. Reed, 1978.   p., illus.
           Interviews with Californian artists.

General (cont.)

1376.   Flip. Flip's Groovy Guide to the Groops! By the editors of
        of Flip Magazine. New York: New American Library, 1968.
        238p., illus. (A Signet Book)
        Details of one hundred contemporary rock groups.

1377.   ———. Flip's Groovy Guide to the Guys! By the editors of
        Flip Magazine. New York: New American Library, 1969. 237p.,
        illus. (A Signet Book)
        Covers chiefly solo artists.

1378.   Fox-Sheinwold, Patricia. Too Young To Die. New York: Bell
        Publishing, 1979 (rev. ed. 1981). 380p., illus.
        Profiles of thirty stars who died prematurely. Includes
        George Gershwin, Hank Williams, Buddy Holly, Billie Holiday,
        Sam Cooke, Brian Epstein, Judy Garland, Brian Jones, Jimi
        Hendrix, Janis Joplin, Duane Allman, Jim Croce, Bobby Darin,
        Cass Elliot, Florence Ballard, Elvis Presley, and John Lennon.

1379.   Frame, Pete. Rock Family Trees. London: Omnibus Pr.; New
        York: Quick Fox, 1980. 34p., illus. (32 fold-out charts)
        Genealogical charts showing the links between personnel
        of rock groups. Originally published serially in Zig-Zag
        magazine.

        ———. Rock Family Trees, Volume 2. London: Omnibus Pr.,
        1983. 34p., illus. (fold-out charts)

        ———. Rock Family Trees. London: Omnibus Pr., 1984. 68p.,
        illus. (fold-out charts)
        Combination of volumes one and two.

1380.   Fredericks, Vic (ed.). Who's Who in Rock 'n' Roll: Facts,
        Fotos, and Fan Gossip About the Performers in the World of
        Rock 'n' Roll. New York: Frederick Fell, 1958. 96p., illus.

1381.   Freedland, Michael. So Let's Hear the Applause: the Story of
        the Jewish Entertainer. Illustrated by Topol. London: Val-
        entine Mitchell, 1984. 262p., illus.
        Collection of interviews and profiles. Includes Al Jolson,
        Sophie Tucker, Eddie Cantor, Irving Berlin, Fanny Brice,
        Danny Kaye, Sammy Cahn, Barbra Streisand, Larry Adler, Frankie
        Vaughan, Bud Flanagan, Bob Dylan, Topol, and others.

1382.   Gambaccini, Paul. Masters of Rock. London: British Broad-
        casting Corporation, 1982. 223p., illus.
        Profiles of twenty-five major artists. Based on the
        author's 1982 British radio series, same title.

1383.   Gammond, Peter, and Peter Clayton. A Guide to Popular Music.
        London: Phoenix House, 1961; New York (as Dictionary of Pop-
        ular Music): Philosophical Library, 1961 (Reprinted: New York:
        Scholarly Pr., 1961). 274p., illus., bibliogs.
        Covers Eighteenth Century to date; chiefly Britain and the
        United States. Emphasis on composers of light music, operetta,

musical theater, and popular song. Limited jazz coverage;
singers and lyricists excluded. Has appendix chronologically
listing stage and screen musical productions, 1725-1960.

1384. Gardner, Graham. <u>Then and Now</u>. Shepperton, Middlesex: The
Author, 1982. 60p., illus., discogs.
Interviews and profiles of British rock artists of the
1950's and early 1960's. Includes Marty Wilde, Kenny Lynch,
Michael Cox, Ricky Vallance, Jerry Lardan, Alvin Stardust,
Jess Conrad, Joe Brown, John Leyton, Craig Douglas, and Heinz.

1385. Gray, Andy (ed.). <u>Great Pop Stars</u>. London; New York: Hamlyn,
1973. 160p., illus.
Covers 1955 to date.

1386. ———. <u>My Top Pop Book</u>. London: Hamlyn, 1974. 47p., illus.
Profiles of current performers; aimed at younger readers.

1387. Gregg, Hubert. <u>Thanks for the Memory: a Personal Spotlight
on Special People in Entertainment</u>. London: Gollancz, 1983.
223p., illus.
Personal reminiscences and profiles of Busby Berkeley,
Cole Porter, Maurice Chevalier, Fats Waller, Fred Astaire,
Lorenz Hart, Noël Coward, Gertrude Lawrence, Judy Garland,
Carroll Gibbons, Al Jolson, Ivor Novello, Jack Buchanan, and
others. Based on author's long-running British radio series,
same title.

1388. Gritter, Headley. <u>Rock and Roll Asylum</u>. New York: Delilah,
1984. 320p., illus.
Performer profiles.

1389. Guitar Player. <u>Guitar Notables: Brief Interviews from
Guitar Player Magazine's "Pros Reply" Column</u>. Saratoga,
California: <u>Guitar Player</u> Productions, 1975. 63p., illus.
Biographical and technical information from Chet Atkins,
Paul Simon, Grant Green, and others.

1390. ———. <u>Rock Guitarists, Volume 1</u>. Saratoga, California:
<u>Guitar Player</u> Productions, 1977. 176p., illus.
Interviews first published in <u>Guitar Player</u>. Includes
Duane Allman, Eric Clapton, Jerry Garcia, Pete Townshend,
Steve Stills, Jeff Beck, Carlos Santana, Jimi Hendrix, Chuck
Berry, Steve Howe, Terry Kath, and others.

1391. ———. <u>Rock Guitarists, Volume 2</u>. Saratoga, California:
<u>Guitar Player</u> Books, 1978. 215p., illus.
Includes Jimmy Page, Bonnie Rait, Robbie Robertson, John
McLaughlin, Jimi Hendrix, Frank Zappa, Jim Messina, Todd
Rundgren, Ted Nugent, and others.

   *   Guralnick, Peter. <u>Feel Like Going Home: Portraits in Blues
and Rock 'n' Roll</u>.
       * Cited below as item 1518.

General (cont.)

1392. Guralnick, Peter. <u>Lost Highways: Journeys and Arrivals of</u>
       <u>American Musicians</u>. Boston: David R. Godine, 1979. 363p.,
       illus., discog., bibliog., index.
           Profiles of contemporary country, blues, and rockabilly
       artists. Based on the author's articles for the musical
       press.

1393. Halfin, Ross, and Pete Makowski. <u>The Power Age</u>. London:
       Eel Pie; New York (as <u>Heavy Metal</u>): Delilah, 1982. 128p.,
       illus.
           Biographies of Heavy Metal rock groups.

1394. Harrigan, Brian, and Malcolm Dome. <u>Encyclopaedia Metallica:</u>
       <u>the Bible of Heavy Metal</u>. London: Bobcat Books, 1981. 93p.,
       illus., discogs.
           Biographies of Heavy Metal rock groups, 1966 to date.

1395. ————. <u>Heavy Metal A-Z: the Definitive Encyclopedia of</u>
       <u>Heavy Metal, From AC/DC Through Led Zeppelin to ZZ Top</u>.
       London: Bobcat Books, 1981. 128p., illus., discogs.

1396. Hayes, Chris. <u>Stairway to the Stars</u>. London: Promise Pr.,
       1947. 38p., illus.
           Jazz and pop profiles.

1397. Hedges, Dan. <u>British Rock Guitarists</u>. Saratoga, California:
       <u>Guitar Player</u> Books, 1978.   p., illus.
           Features on twelve influential rock guitarists. Includes
       transcriptions of their solos; plus analyses of their styles.

1398. Helander, Brock. <u>The Rock Who's Who: a Biographical Diction-</u>
       <u>ary and Critical Discography. Including Rhythm-and-Blues</u>,
       <u>Soul, Rockabilly, Folk, Country, Easy Listening, Punk, and</u>
       <u>New Wave</u>. New York: Schirmer Books; London: Collier-Macmill-
       an, 1982. 686p., illus., index.
           Alphabetical arrangement.

1399. Herring, Peter. <u>Rock Giants</u>. Greenwich, Conn.: Bison Books;
       London: W.H. Smith, 1984. 224p., illus., index.
           British edition for sale only in W.H. Smith bookstores.

1400. <u>The Illustrated Encyclopedia of Rock</u>. Edited by Nick Logan
       and Bob Woffinden. London: New English Library; New York:
       Harmony Books, 1977. 256p., illus., discogs., index.
           Approximately 650 entries profiling major and minor art-
       ists. Discographies for most entries. Based on item

       <u>The Illustrated "New Musical Express" Encyclopedia of Rock</u>.
       Edited by Nick Logan and Bob Woffinden. London: Hamlyn, 1977.
       256p., illus., discogs., index. (A Salamander Book)
           No change in contents for this edition.

       <u>The Illustrated Encyclopedia of Rock</u>. Edited by Nick Logan
       and Bob Woffinden. <u>1978 edition</u>. London: Salamander Books;

New York: Harmony Books, 1978. 256p., illus., discogs., index.
Contents amended; structure of work unchanged.

————. Rev. ed.: London: Salamander Books; New York: Harmony Books, 1982. 288p., illus., discogs., index.
Bulk of contents identical to 1978 edition. Developments of late 1970's and early 1980's covered in addendum; additional material by Mike Clifford, Chris Trengrave, Chris Gill, John Futrell, Debbie Kirby, and Alan Walsh. The original editors demanded that their names be removed from the front cover; references to the New Musical Express also deleted. Entire work superseded by item 1401.

1401. The Illustrated Rock Handbook. Consultant: Mike Clifford. Authors: Pete Frame, John Tobler, Ed Hanel, Roger St. Pierre, Chris Trengrove, John Beecher, Clive Richardson, Gary Cooper, Marsha Hanlon, and Linda Sandall. London: Salamander Books, 1983; New York (as The Delilah Rock and Roll Handbook): Delilah, 1984. 272p., illus., discogs., index.
Based on item 1400. Similar structure; contents entirely reworked and augmented.

1402. Jackson, Jack. Jack Jackson's Record Round-Up. Edited by Don Nicholl. London: Max Parrish, 1955. 128p., illus.
Features on current popular artists; by early British disk-jockey.

1403. Jacobs, David. Pick of the Pop Stars. Nottingham, England: Palmer, 1962. 112p., illus.
Profiles of current performers; by British disk-jockey.

1404. James, Sally. Sally James's Almost Legendary Pop Interviews. London: Eel Pie, 1981. 96p., illus.
Interviews with current artists; conducted by presenter of British television program.

1405. Jasper, Tony, Derek Oliver, Steve Hammond, and David Reynolds. The International Encyclopedia of Hard Rock and Heavy Metal. London: Sidgwick and Jackson, 1983. 400p., discogs.
Alphabetically arranged profiles of "all known Heavy Metal bands." Includes discographies for each entry.

1406. Joynson, Vernon. The Acid Trip: a Complete Guide to Psychedelic Music. Birmingham, England: Babylon Books, 1984.   p., illus., discogs.
Biographical dictionary to performers in the genre, from its 1960's origins to the 1980's British revival.

1407. Katz, Susan. Superwomen of Rock. New York: Tempo Books, 1978. 134p., illus., discogs.
Profiles of Debbie Boone, Rita Coolidge, Olivia Newton-John, Linda Ronstadt, Stevie Nicks, and Carly Simon.

1408. Keen, Alan. The Stars of Rock 'n' Roll. London: The Author, 1966. Book 1: 48p., illus. Book 2: 16p., illus.
Profiles and illustrations of current artists.

General (cont.)

* Kinkle, Roger D. The Complete Encyclopedia of Popular Music and Jazz, 1900-1950.
  * Cited above as item 16.

1409. Lahr, John. Automatic Vaudeville: Essays on Star Turns. London: Heinemann, 1984. 241p., index.
       Profiles of popular music performers.

1410. Laing, Dave, and Phil Hardy (eds.). Encyclopedia of Rock. St. Albans, Hertfordshire: Panther, 1976.
       Vol. 1: The Age of Rock 'n' Roll. 352p., index.
       Vol. 2: From Liverpool to San Francisco. 398p., index.
       Vol. 3: The Sounds of the Seventies. 320p., index.
       Biographical entries, alphabetically arranged within each volume.

       ———. Encyclopedia of Rock: Volumes One to Three in One Volume. London: Aquarius, 1977. 288p.

1411. Leigh, Spencer. Stars in My Eyes: Personal Interviews With Top Music Stars. Foreword by David Hamilton. Liverpool: Raven Books, 1980. 160p., illus.
       Twenty-three current acts interviewed by British disk-jockey. Includes Charles Aznavour, Marc Bolan, Cliff Richard, Sammy Davis, Jr., Dr. Hook, and others.

1412. Lydon, Michael. Rock Folk: Portraits From the Rock 'n' Roll Pantheon. New York: Dial Pr., 1971; New York: Dell, 1973 (Delta Books). 200p., illus.
       Interviews and profiles of Chuck Berry, Carl Perkins, B.B. King, Smokey Robinson, Janis Joplin, The Grateful Dead, and The Rolling Stones. Originally published in periodicals, 1968-71.

1413. McColm, Bruce, and Doug Payne. Where Have They Gone? Rock 'n' Roll Stars. New York: Tempo Books, 1979. 254p., illus.
       Profiles of early stars, and what became of them after leaving the popular music business.

1414. Martyn, Lee. Masters of Metal. London: Zomba Books, 1984. 128p., illus., discogs. (Rock Masters Series)
       Profiles of fifty leading Heavy Metal bands.

1415. May, Chris. Rock 'n' Roll. London: Socion Books, 1974. p., illus., discogs.
       Brief biographies of forty acts from the 1950's.

1416. Miles (pseud. of Barry Miles). The Two-Tone Book For Rude Boys. London: Omnibus Pr., 1981. 80p., illus., discogs.
       Profiles of artists of the briefly flourishing British rock genre. Includes The Specials, The Selecter, Madness, The Beat, The Body Snatchers, The Swinging Cats, and others.

1417. Nash, Peter. <u>Women in Rock</u>. London: Mirror Books, 1983.
       48p., illus.
           Brief profiles of current female artists.

1418. <u>The New Music</u>. Compiled by Glenn A. Baker and Stuart Coupe.
       Wimbledon, Surrey: Ring Publishing, 1980. 128p., illus.
           Biographical dictionary of new-wave rock acts.

       <u>The New Rock 'n' Roll: the A-Z of Rock in the Eighties</u>. Com-
       piled by Stuart Coupe and Glenn A. Baker. London: Omnibus
       Pr.; New York: St. Martin's Pr., 1984. 192p., illus., index.
           Updated revision of <u>The New Music</u>. Includes approximately
       four hundred acts.

1419. New Musical Express. <u>The "New Musical Express" Book of Rock</u>.
       Edited by Nick Logan. Updated by Rob Finnis. London: Star
       Books, 1975. 429p., illus.
           "Parts of this book have already appeared in separate iss-
       ues of <u>The New Musical Express</u>"-- p. 1. The fore-runner of
       item 1400, this work was originally issued in 1974 in the
       form of special supplements to the periodical; themselves
       based on material previously published.

1420. Nichols, Beverley. <u>Are They the Same At Home? Being a Series
       of Bouquets Diffidently Distributed</u>. London: Cape, 1927.
       351p. <u>With an introductory essay by the author</u>: New York:
       Doubleday, 1927. 302p. London: Cape, 1927. 351p. Reissued:
       London: Cape, 1933. 256p.
           Profiles originally published in <u>The Sketch</u>. Includes
       Andre Charlot, C.B. Cochran, Noël Coward, George Gershwin,
       John McCormack, Florence Mills, Marie Tempest, Georges
       Carpentier; and others from non-musical fields.

1421. Nite, Norm N. <u>Rock On: the Illustrated Encyclopedia of Rock
       'n' Roll: the Solid Gold Years</u>. Special introduction by Dick
       Clark. New York: Crowell, 1974; New York: Popular Library,
       1977. 676p., illus., discogs., index. <u>Updated ed.</u>: New York:
       Harper and Row; Toronto: Fitzhenry and Whiteside, 1982. 722p.,
       illus., discogs., index.
           Over one thousand brief biographies of artists who reached
       the Top 100 record charts, 1950 to mid-1960's. Coverage
       includes country and rhythm-and-blues acts.

1422. ———. <u>Rock On: the Illustrated Encyclopedia of Rock 'n'
       Roll: the Modern Years</u>. Special introduction by Wolfman
       Jack. New York: Crowell; New York: Popular Library, 1977;
       New York (as <u>Rock On: the Illustrated Encyclopedia of Rock 'n'
       Roll: the Modern Years, 1964 to the Present</u>): Harper and Row,
       1982. 736p., illus., discogs., index.

       ———. <u>Rock On: the Illustrated Encyclopedia of Rock 'n'
       Roll: the Years of Change, 1964-1978</u>. With Ralph M. Newman.
       Special introduction by Wolfman Jack. New York; London: Har-
       per and Row, 1984. 749p., illus., discogs., index.

General (cont.)

1423. O Magazine. Those Incredible Boys. New York: Sharon Public-
       ations, 1984. 192p., illus.
           Profiles of new-wave rock artists.

1424. Obrecht, James (ed.). Masters of Heavy Metal. New York:
       Morrow, 1984. 194p., illus.

1425. Orloff, Katherine. Rock 'n' Roll Woman. Los Angeles: Nash
       Publishing, 1974. 199p., illus.
           Interviews with female artists working in a male-dominated
       field. Includes Nicole Barclay, Toni Brown, Terry Garthwaite,
       Rita Coolidge, Claudia Linnear, Maria Muldaur, Bonnie Rait,
       Linda Ronstadt, Carly Simon, Grace Slick, Alice Stuart, and
       Wendy Waldman.

1426. Pavletich, Aida. Rock-a-Bye, Baby. Garden City, New York:
       Doubleday, 1980. 281p., index.
           History of women in rock, soul, folk, big bands, and
       country music; told through profiles of key figures.

1427. Payne, Jack. Jack Payne Presents Stars of Melody. London:
       Thomas Publishing, 1956. 94p., illus.
           Profiles of current popular performers; by ex-bandleader.

1428. Pleasants, Henry. The Great American Popular Singers. New
       York: Simon and Schuster; London: Gollancz, 1974. 384p.,
       illus., index.
           Profiles of innovative singers. Includes Al Jolson, Bessie
       Smith, Ethel Waters, Louis Armstrong, Jimmie Rodgers, Bing
       Crosby, Mildred Bailey, Billie Holiday, Ella Fitzgerald, Frank
       Sinatra, Mahalia Jackson, Nat "King" Cole, Hank Williams, Ray
       Charles, Elvis Presley, Judy Garland, Johnny Cash, B.B. King,
       Aretha Franklin, Ethel Merman, Peggy Lee, and Barbra Streis-
       and. No discographies.

1429. Rau, Rutherford. Stars Off the Record. London: Eldon Pr.,
       1955. 93p., illus.
           Brief profiles of popular singers.

1430. Rivelli, Pauline, and Robert Levin (eds.). The Rock Giants.
       New York: World Publishing, 1970; New York (as The Giants of
       Rock Music): Da Capo Pr., 1981. 125p., illus.
           Interviews first published in Jazz and Pop. Includes
       Frank Zappa, Randy Newman, Eric Clapton, Creedence Clearwater
       Revival, and Canned Heat. Also pieces on The Jefferson Air-
       plane, Gary Burton, and general items.

1431. Rock 'n' Roll Personality Parade. London: Weekly Film News,
       1957. 33p., illus.

1432. Rock One Hundred. Edited by David Dalton and Lenny Kaye. New
       York: Grosset and Dunlap, 1977. 280p., illus., index.
           Rock musicians profiled; features one hundred "all-stars
       from rock and roll's Hall of Fame."

1433. Rockwell, Don (ed.). Radio Personalities, 1936. New York: Press Bureau, 1935. 268p., illus.
Current popular music performers are included.

1434. Rolling Stone. The Rolling Stone Encyclopedia of Rock and Roll. Edited by Jon Pareles and Patricia Romanowski. New York: Summit Books; London: Michael Joseph, 1983. 615p., illus., discogs. (A Rolling Stone Pr. Book)
Biographies of rock artists.

1435. ————. The Rolling Stone Interviews. Compiled by the Editors of Rolling Stone. New York: Straight Arrow/Paperback Library, 1971. 465p., illus.
Contents first published in Rolling Stone. Includes Mike Bloomfield, Frank Zappa, Booker T. Jones, Chuck Berry, Jim Morrison, Phil Spector, Bob Dylan, Robbie Robertson, John Fogerty, Little Richard, David Crosby, Grace Slick and Paul Kantner, Mick Jagger, John Lennon, Pete Townshend, Eric Clapton, and Ravi Shankar.

————. The Rolling Stone Interviews, Volume Two. Edited and introduction by Ben Fong-Torres. New York: Warner Books, 1973. 430p., illus.
Includes Bob Dylan, B.B. King, Roger McGuinn, Leon Russell, Stephen Stills, Country Joe McDonald, Johnny Otis, Joe Smith, Marvin Gaye, Paul Simon, and others.

————. The Rolling Stone Interviews, 1967-80: Talking With the Legends of Rock and Roll. Edited by Peter Herbst. Introduction by Ben Fong-Torres. New York: St. Martin's Pr.; London: Barker, 1981. 426p., illus. (A Rolling Stone Pr. Book)
Contents of the two-volume edition, with additions.

1436. Roxon, Lillian. Rock Encyclopedia. New York: Grosset and Dunlap, 1969 (reissued: 1971). 611p., discogs.

————. Lillian Roxon's Rock Encyclopedia. Revised edition, compiled by Ed Naha. New York: Grosset and Dunlap, 1978; London: Angus and Robertson, 1980. 565p., bibliog., discogs.
Brief biographical entries for groups and individuals. Includes appendix of chart listings.

1437. Russell, Wayne. Foot Soldiers and Kings. Brandon, Manitoba: The Author, 1980. 25p., illus.
Chiefly photographs of obscure 1950's rock and roll acts; some biographical information.

1438. Sarlin, Bob. Turn It Up! (I Can't Hear the Words): the Best of the New Singer/Songwriters. New York: Simon and Schuster, 1974. 222p., illus. London: Coronet, 1975. 239p., illus.

1439. Shapiro, Harry. A-Z of Rock Drummers. London; New York: Proteus, 1982. 126p., illus., discogs., index.
Over two hundred brief profiles.

General (cont.)

1440. Shaw, Arnold. <u>A Dictionary of American Pop-Rock</u>. New York:
       Schirmer Books; London: Collier-Macmillan, 1982. 440p.,
       index.
           Biographical dictionary.

1441. Simon, George Thomas. <u>The Best of the Music Makers</u>. New York:
       Doubleday, 1979.   p.

1442. Sinclair, Marianne. <u>Those Who Died Young</u>. London: Plexus,
       1979. 192p., illus.
           Profiles of prematurely deceased stars. Includes Buddy
       Holly, Elvis Presley, Eddie Cochran, Jim Reeves, Gene Vincent,
       Sam Cooke, Otis Redding, Brian Jones, Jimi Hendrix, Janis
       Joplin, Jim Morrison, Duane Allman, Cass Elliot, Paul Kossoff,
       Gram Parsons, Marc Bolan, Keith Moon; and others from non-
       musical fields.

1443. Somma, Robert. <u>No One Waved Good-Bye: a Casualty Report on
       Rock and Roll</u>. Designed by Ronn Campisi. New York: Outer-
       bridge and Dienstfrey, 1971; London: Charisma Books, 1973.
       125p., illus. (A <u>Fusion</u> Book)
           Profiles by Somma and others, some previously published in
       periodicals. Includes Brian Jones, Jimi Hendrix, Brian Epstein
       and Janis Joplin.

1444. Stambler, Irwin. <u>Encyclopedia of Popular Music</u>. Special
       material by Vern Bushman, and others. New York: St. Martin's
       Pr., 1965. 360p., illus., bibliog.
           Biographical dictionary. Emphasis on 1925-65. Includes
       over 380 entries.

1445. ————. <u>Encyclopedia of Pop, Rock, and Soul</u>. New York: St.
       Martin's Pr.; London: St. James Pr., 1975. 610p., illus.,
       bibliog.
           Includes approximately five hundred individuals and groups;
       also entries by topics. Also has essays by Stambler, Johnny
       Otis, and Michael Ochs on the development of popular music.

1446. Steward, Sue, and Sheryl Garratt. <u>Signed, Sealed, and Deliv-
       ered: True Life Stories of Women in Pop</u>. London: Pluto Pr.,
       1984.   p., illus.
           Includes performers, journalists, and others in the field.
       Written from a feminist, political viewpoint.

1447. Stewart, Ed. <u>Ed "Stewpot" Stewart's Book of Pop</u>. London: Pan
       1973. 108p., illus. (A Picolo Book)
           Aimed at younger readers. Profiles of current acts.

1448. <u>Superstars of the Seventies</u>. London: Octopus, 1976. 92p.,
       illus.
           Profiles of rock acts. Adapted from item 208.

1449. Thomson, Liz (ed.). <u>New Women in Rock</u>. New York: Delilah; Lon-
       don: Omnibus Pr., 1982. 96p., illus., discogs.
           Includes sixty recent artists.

1450. Tiger Beat. Superstars. Compiled by the Editors of Tiger
       Beat. New York: Tiger Beat, 1972. 143p., illus.
          Aimed at younger readers. Currently popular artists
       profiled.

1451. Tobler, John. A-Z of Rock Singers. London; New York: Prot-
       eus, 1984. 128p., illus., discogs., index.
          Includes over 250 singers.

1452. ———. Guitar Heroes. London: Marshall Cavendish; New York:
       St. Martin's Pr., 1978. 89p., illus., discog.
          Descriptions of the styles of thirty-two (chiefly rock)
       guitarists; with biographical information.

1453. ———, and Stuart Grundy. The Guitar Greats. London: Brit-
       ish Broadcasting Corporation; New York: St. Martin's Pr.,
       1983. 191p., illus., discogs., index.
          Profiles of B.B. King, Scotty Moore, James Burton, Hank B.
       Marvin, Eric Clapton, Jeff Beck, Pete Townshend, Jimmy Page,
       Ry Cooder, Ritchie Blackmore, Steve Miller, Carlos Santana,
       Joe Walsh, and Brian May. Based on British radio series.

1454. Tosches, Nick. Unsung Heroes of Rock 'n' Roll. New York:
       Scribner's, 1984. 240p., illus.
          Profiles of minor artists.

1455. Tracy, Sheila (comp.). Who's Who in Popular Music: the Brit-
       ish Music Scene. Kingswood, Surrey: World's Work, 1984.
       169p., illus.
          Emphasis on lives, rather than musical activity.

1456. Variety. Variety Obits: an Index to Obituaries in "Variety",
       1905-1978. Compiled by Jeb H. Perry. Metuchen, New Jersey;
       London: Scarecrow Pr., 1980. 309p.

1457. ———. Variety Who's Who in Show Business. Edited by Mike
       Kaplan. New York: Garland Publishing, 1983. 330p.

1458. Weinberg, Max, and Robert Santelli. The Big Beat: Conversat-
       ions With Rock's Great Drummers. Chicago: Contemporary Books,
       1984. 250p., illus.

1459. White, Timothy. Rock Stars. New York: Stewart, Tabori and
       Chang; Bromley, Kent: Columbus Books, 1984. 288p., illus.,
       index.
          Forty major artists profiled.

1460. Who's Who in Show Biz. London: Purnell.
       1964 ed.: 1963. 61p., illus.
       1965 ed.: 1964. 61p., illus.
          Popular music and television personalities.

1461. Wood, Graham. An A-Z of Rock and Roll. London: Studio Vista,
       1971. 128p., illus., discog., filmog.
          Biographical dictionary. Early stars, up to beginnings of
       the Merseybeat era.

General (cont.)

1462. York, William. <u>Who's Who in Rock: an A-Z of Groups, Perform-</u>
<u>ers, Producers, Session Men, Engineers.</u> Seattle: Atomic Pr.;
London: Omnibus Pr., 1979. 237p., discogs. <u>2nd. ed.</u>: Seattle:
Atomic Pr., 1980.   p., discogs. <u>Rev. ed.</u>: New York: Scribner's; London: Barker, 1982. 624p., discogs.
       Brief biographical and career details of approximately
twelve thousand performers and others.

                         (ii) Sacred Popular

  * Baxter, Clarice Howard, and Videt Polk. <u>Gospel Songwriters</u>
    <u>Biography</u>.
         * Cited below as item 1643.

  * Burt, Jesse Clifton, and Duane Allen. <u>The History of Gospel</u>
    <u>Music</u>.
         * Cited above as item 298.

  * Hicks, Darryl. <u>God Comes To Nashville: Spotlights on Music</u>
    <u>City Personalities</u>.
         * Cited below as item 1480.

1463. Knippers, Ottis J. <u>Who's Who Among Southern Singers and</u>
<u>Composers</u>. Lawrenceburgh, Tennessee: James D. Vaughan, 1937.
168p., illus., indexes.
       Biographical dictionary; lists 145 white gospel singers
and composers. Includes portraits for most entries.

                           (B) FOLK

1464. Baggelaar, Kristin, and Donald Milton. <u>Folk Music: More Than</u>
<u>a Song</u>. New York: Crowell, 1976. 419p., illus., discogs.

       —————. <u>The Folk Music Encyclopaedia</u>. New York; London:
Omnibus Pr., 1977. 419p., illus., discogs.
       Biographies of American folk music artists; emphasis on
early 1960's folk music revival.

1465. Lawless, Ray McKinley. <u>Folksingers and Folksongs in America:</u>
<u>a Handbook of Biography, Bibliography, and Discography</u>.
Illustrated from paintings by Thomas Hart Benton and others,
and from designs in Steuben glass. New York: Duell, Sloan,
and Pearce, 1960. 662p., illus., bibliog., discog. <u>New rev.</u>
<u>ed.</u> (with special supplement): New York: Duell, Sloan, and
Pearce, 1965; Westport, Conn.: Greenwood Pr., 1981. 750p.,
illus., bibliog., discog.
       Approximately 225 profiles of performers; also bibliography
of song collections and checklist of song sources. Discography
lists long-playing records only. Supplement covers 1960-65.

1466. Stambler, Irwin, and Grelun Landon. <u>Encyclopedia of Folk,</u>
       <u>Country, and Western Music</u>. New York: St. Martin's Pr.,
       1969; London: St. James Pr., 1975. 396p., illus., bibliog.,
       discog.
            Biographical dictionary, with general features included.
       Approximately five hundred entries.

                            (C) COUNTRY

1467. Bane, Michael. <u>The Outlaws: Revolution in Country Music</u>.
       New York: <u>Country Music</u> Magazine Pr., 1978.   p., illus.
            Modern country musicians profiled. Includes Waylon Jenn-
       ings, Willie Nelson, Tompall Glaser, etc.

1468. Brown, Len, and Gary Friedrich. <u>The Encyclopedia of Country</u>
       <u>and Western Music</u>. New York: Tower Publications, 1971.
       191p., illus.
            Biographical dictionary.

1469. Busnar, Gene. <u>The Superstars of Country Music</u>. New York:
       J. Messner, 1984.   p., illus.

1470. Byworth, Tony. <u>Giants of Country Music</u>. Greenwich, Conn.:
       Bison Books; London: Hamlyn, 1984. 224p., illus., index.

1471. David, Andrew. <u>Country Music Stars: People at the Top of the</u>
       <u>Charts</u>. Edited by Ray Levin. Chicago: Domus Books, 1980.
       96p., illus., discogs., index.

1472. Dellar, Fred, and Roy Thompson. <u>The Illustrated Encyclopedia</u>
       <u>of Country Music</u>. Special consultant: Douglas B. Green.
       Foreword by Roy Acuff. New York: Harmony Books; London:
       Salamander Books, 1977. 256p., illus., discogs., index.
            Biographical dictionary; over 450 entries.

1473. Delmore, Alton. <u>Truth is Stranger Than Publicity</u>. Edited by
       Charles K. Wolfe. Nashville: Country Music Foundation, 1977.
       188p., illus.

1474. Dew, Joan. <u>Singers and Sweethearts: the Women of Country</u>
       <u>Music</u>. Garden City, New York: Doubleday, 1977. 151p.,
       illus. (Dolphin Books) (A <u>Country Music</u> Magazine Pr. Book)

1475. Farah, Cynthia, and Marina Nickerson. <u>Country Music: a Look</u>
       <u>at the Men Who've Made It</u>. El Paso, Texas: C.M. Publications,
       1981. 88p., illus.

1476. Gentry, Linnell (ed.). <u>A History and Encyclopedia of Country</u>,
       <u>Western, and Gospel Music</u>. Nashville: McQuiddy Pr., 1961 (Re-
       printed: St. Clair Shores, Michigan: Scholarly Pr., 1972).
       380p. <u>2nd. ed.</u>: Nashville: Clairmont, 1969. 598p.
            <u>Part One</u>: Articles, previously published in periodicals,
       from 1908 onwards. <u>Part Two</u>: Biographies of over six hundred
       artists.

1477. Gray, Andy. Great Country Music Stars. London; New York:
       Hamlyn, 1975. 176p., illus., bibliog., index.

1478. Hagan, Chet. Country Music Legends in the Hall of Fame.
       Nashville: Nelson, 1982. 256p., illus.

1479. Hefley, James. How Sweet the Sound. Wheaton, Illinois:
       Tyndale, 1981.   p., illus.

1480. Hicks, Darryl. God Comes To Nashville: Spotlights on Music
       City Personalities. Harrison, Arkansas: New Leaf Pr., 1979.
       160p., illus.
          Nashville gospel/country musicians profiled.

1481. Hollaran, Carolyn Rada. Meet the Stars of Country Music.
       Nashville: Aurora Publishers, 1977. unpaged, illus.
          Forty-two profiles.

1482. ————. Your Favorite Country Music Stars. New York: Pop-
       ular Library, 1975. 283p., illus.

1483. Kash, Murray. Murray Kash's Book of Country: an A-Z of All
       That's Best in Country Music. Foreword by George Hamilton IV.
       London: Star Books, 1981. 509p., discogs.
          Biographical dictionary.

1484. Kingsbury, Kenn (ed.). Kingsbury's Who's Who in Country and
       Western Music. Culver City, California: Black Stallion
       Country Pr., 1981. 320p., illus.

1485. Kosser, Michael. Those Bold and Beautiful Country Girls.
       New York: Delilah, 1979.   p., illus.

1486. Lord, Bobby. Hit the Glory Road! Nashville: Broadman Pr.,
       1969. 143p., illus.
          Christian country musicians profiled.

1487. McCabe, Peter, and Rae Rubenstein. Honkytonk Heroes: a Photo
       Album of Country Music. New York: Harper and Row, 1975.   p.,
       illus.
          Text by McCabe; photographs by Rubenstein.

1488. Malone, Bill C., and Judith McCulloh (eds.). The Stars of
       Country Music: Uncle Dave Macon to Johnny Rodriguez. Urbana:
       University of Illinois Pr.; New York: Avon, 1975. 532p.,
       illus., bibliog., discog., index. (Music in American Life)

1489. Moore, Thurston (ed.). Scrapbook of Hillbilly and Western
       Stars. Special section starring sacred singers edited by
       Thurston Moore. Assistant editor: Leslie Norman. Drawings
       by M. Smith. Cincinnati: Artist Publications, 1953. unpaged,
       illus.

   *   The Original Country Music Who's Who.
          * Cited above as item 427.

1490. Sakol, Jeannie. The Wonderful World of Country Music. New
       York: Grosset and Dunlap, 1979; London: Blandford Pr., 1980.
       240p., illus., index.
            Biographical dictionary. Includes general information
       also.

1491. Shestack, Melvin. The Country Music Encyclopedia. New York:
       Crowell, 1974. 410p., illus., discogs. London: Omnibus Pr.,
       1977. 378p., illus., discog.
            Biographical dictionary. Includes general material also.

1492. Tribe, Ivan M., and John W. Morris. Molly O'Day, Lynn Davis,
       and the Cumberland Mountain Folks: a Bio-Discography. Los
       Angeles: John Edwards Memorial Foundation, 1975.   p.
       (Special Series, 7)
            Early country artists.

1493. Zanderbergen, George. Nashville Music: Loretta Lynn, Mac
       Davis, Charley Pride. Mankato, Minnesota: Crestwood House,
       1976.   p., illus.

                        (D) BLACK MUSIC

                    (i) Comprehensive Works

1494. Adams, Russell L. Great Negroes, Past and Present. Edited
       by David P. Ross. Illustrated by Eugene Winslow. Chicago:
       Afro-Am Publishing, 1963; Chicago: Southern, 1969. 182p.,
       illus., bibliog.
            Profiles of Black individuals. Music section includes
       James A. Bland, Harry T. Burleigh, R. Nathaniel Dett, W.C.
       Handy, William Grant Still, William L. Dawson, Paul Robeson,
       Roland Hayes, Dean Dixon, Louis Armstrong, Duke Ellington,
       Marian Anderson, and Bert Williams.

1495. Baker, David N., Linda M. Belt, and Herman C. Hudson (eds.).
       The Black Composer Speaks: a Project of the Afro-American
       Arts Institute, Indiana University. Metuchen, New Jersey;
       London: Scarecrow Pr., 1978. 506p.
            Mainly concert music. Includes chapters by Herbie Hancock
       and Archie Shepp.

1496. Dobrin, Arnold. Voices of Joy, Voices of Freedom: Ethel
       Waters, Sammy Davis, Jr., Marian Anderson, Paul Robeson, Lena
       Horne. New York: Coward, McCann, and Geoghegan, 1972. 127p.,
       illus., bibliog.

1497. Embree, Edwin R. Thirteen Against the Odds. New York: Viking
       Pr., 1946. 261p., illus.
            Includes Marian Anderson, Paul Robeson, and William Grant
       Still.

1498. Handy, D. Antoinette. Black Women in American Bands and
       Orchestras. Metuchen, New Jersey; London: Scarecrow Pr.,
       1981. 319p., illus., bibliog., index.

* Handy, William Christopher. <u>Negro Authors and Composers of the United States.</u>
   * Cited below as item 1652.

1499. ———. <u>Unsung Americans Sung.</u> New York: Handy Brothers Music Company, 1944. 236p., illus.
   Black profiles. Includes musicians.

1500. Hughes, Langston. <u>Famous Negro Music Makers.</u> New York: Dodd, Mead, 1955. 179p., illus., index. (Famous Biographies for Young People)
   Aimed at younger readers. Profiles from the gospel, jazz, opera, and concert fields.

1501. <u>Illustrated Encyclopedia of Black Music.</u> Consultant: Mike Clifford. Authors: John Futrell, Chris Gill, Roger St. Pierre, Clive Richardson, Chris Trengrove, Bob Fisher, Bill Sheehy, and Lindsay Wesker. London: Salamander Books; New York: Harmony, 1982. 224p., illus., discogs., index.
   In chronological sections. Profiles of soul, reggae, rhythm-and-blues, blues, disco, and jazz-funk artists.

1502. Jones, Hettie. <u>Big Star Fallin', Mama: Five Women in Black Music.</u> New York: Viking Pr., 1974. 150p., illus., discog.
   Ma Rainey, Bessie Smith, Mahalia Jackson, Billie Holiday, and Aretha Franklin.

1503. Lovingood, Penman. <u>Famous Modern Negro Musicians.</u> Brooklyn, New York: Press Forum, 1921. 68p., illus.
   Nineteen brief profiles, chiefly from the concert field.

1504. Pascall, Jeremy, and Rob Burt (comps.). <u>The Stars and Superstars of Black Music.</u> London: Phoebus, 1977. 128p., illus.
   Profiles of Black popular music artists. Based on item 208.

1505. Petrie, Gavin (ed.). <u>Black Music.</u> London; New York: Hamlyn, 1974. 128p., illus.
   Profiles of leading Black popular music artists.

1506. Richardson, Ben. <u>Great American Negroes.</u> New York: Press Bureau, 1935. 268p., illus.
   Includes popular entertainers.

1507. Rollins, Charlemae. <u>Famous Negro Entertainers of Stage, Screen, and TV.</u> New York: Dodd, Mead, 1967. 122p., illus.
   Includes Duke Ellington, Louis Armstrong, and Fats Waller.

1508. Southern, Eileen. <u>Biographical Dictionary of Afro-American and African Musicians.</u> Westport, Conn.: Greenwood Pr., 1982. 478p., bibliog., index. (Greenwood Encyclopedia of Black Music)
   Over 1,500 entries for composers, performers, educators, and others; 1640-1950.

* Trotter, James M. <u>Music and Some Highly Musical People.</u>
   * Cited above as item 527.

(ii) Sacred

1509. Anderson, Robert, and Gail North. Gospel Music Encyclopedia.
       Introduction by Don Butler. New York: Sterling Publishing,
       1979. 320p., illus., discogs., index.
       Biographical dictionary.

*   Gentry, Linnell (ed.). A History and Encyclopedia of Country,
       Western, and Gospel Music.
       * Cited above as item 1474.

1510. Hall, J.H. Biography of Gospel Song and Hymn Writers. New
       York: Revell, 1914; New York: A.M.S. Pr., 1971. 419p., illus.
       Seventy-six profiles from the Nineteenth Century.

1511. Odum, Adrue Armstrong. The Hall of Fame of Contemporary
       Contributors to Gospel Music. Washington, D.C.: The Author,
       1947.   p.

(iii) Blues

1512. Arnaudon, Jean-Claude. Dictionnaire du blues. Paris:
       Filipachi, 1977. 296p.
       In French. Approximately four hundred brief profiles.

1513. Bogaert, Karel. Blues Lexicon: Blues, Cajun, Boogie-Woogie,
       Gospel. Antwerp, Belgium: Standaard Uitgeverij, 1972. 480p.,
       illus., bibliog., discogs., index.
       In Flemish. English introductory chapter by John Godrich.
       Biographical dictionary.

1514. Burton, Thomas G. (ed.). Tom Ashley; Bukka White; Tennessee
       Traditional Singers. Knoxville, Tennessee: University of
       Tennessee Pr., 1980.   p., bibliog., discog., index.
       Studies of Tom Ashley, Sam McGee, and Bukka White.

1515. Charters, Samuel Barclay. The Bluesmen: the Story and the
       Music of the Men Who Made the Blues. New York: Oak Publicat-
       ions, 1967. 223p., illus., discog., index.
       Includes Charley Patton, Bukka White, Son House, Skip
       James, Robert Johnson, Blind Lemon Jefferson, Henry Thomas,
       Texas Alexander, and others.

       ————. (The Bluesmen, vol. 2). Sweet as the Showers of
       Rain: the Story and the Music of the Men Who Made the Blues.
       New York: Oak Publications, 1977. 178p., illus., discog.,
       index.
       Regional bluesmen; prior to World War II.

1516. ————. The Legacy of the Blues: a Glimpse Into the Art and
       the Lives of Twelve Great Bluesmen: an Informal Study. London:
       Calder and Boyars, 1975; New York: Da Capo Pr., 1977 (Roots of
       Jazz). 192p., illus., bibliog., discog.

1517. Guitar Player. **Blues Guitarists: From the Pages of "Guitar Player" Magazine.** Saratoga, California: Guitar Player Productions, 1975. 72p., illus., index.
       Interviews and profiles; material previously published.

1518. Guralnick, Peter. **Feel Like Going Home: Portraits in Blues and Rock and Roll.** New York: Outerbridge and Dienstfrey, 1971 (A Fusion Book); London: Omnibus Pr., 1978. 256p., illus., bibliog., discog.
       Muddy Waters, Johnny Shines, Skip James, Robert Pete Williams, Howlin' Wolf, Sam Phillips, Jerry Lee Lewis, Charlie Rich; also general piece on Chess Record company.

1519. Harris, Sheldon. **Blues Who's Who: a Biographical Dictionary of Blues Singers.** New Rochelle, New York: Arlington House, 1979; New York: Da Capo Pr., 1981. 775p., illus., bibliog., filmog., indexes.
       Detailed, critical profiles of 571 artists, 1900-77.

1520. Mitchell, George. **Blow My Blues Away.** Baton Rouge: Louisiana State University Pr., 1971; New York: Da Capo Pr., 1983 (Roots of Jazz). 208p., illus.
       Interviews with Mississippi Delta bluesmen.

1521. Napier, Simon A. (ed.). **Back Woods Blues: Selected Reprints from "Blues Unlimited" Magazine, and Elsewhere.** Bexhill-on-Sea, Sussex: Blues Unlimited, 1968. 55p., illus.
       Profiles of bluesmen.

1522. Neff, Robert, and Anthony Connor (eds.). **The Blues.** Boston: David R. Godine, 1975; London: Latimer New Dimensions, 1976. 141p., illus., index.
       Autobiographical comments by fifty-five blues artists.

1523. Surge, Frank. **Singers of the Blues: Brief Biographies of Seventeen Singers and Musicians Who Helped Develop the Blues Style, and Became Legendary Performers During Their Lifetime.** Minneapolis: Lerner Publications, 1969. 63p., illus. (A Pull Ahead Book)
       Aimed at younger readers. Seventeen profiles.

1524. Welding, Peter. **Bluesmen.** New York: Macmillan, 1971; London: Collier-Macmillan, 1972. p., illus.

(iv) Rhythm and Blues

1525. Shaw, Arnold. **Honkers and Shouters: the Golden Years of Rhythm and Blues.** New York: Macmillan, 1977; London: Collier-Macmillan, 1978. 555p., illus., bibliog., discog., index.
       Twenty-five artists interviewed.

(v) Soul

* Stambler, Irwin. <u>Encyclopedia of Pop, Rock, and Soul</u>.
  * Cited above as item 1445.

1526. Wieder, J., and L. Mattern (comps.). <u>Right On's One Hundred</u>
<u>Super-Soul Stars</u>. New York: New American Library, 1972.   p.,
illus.
      From material previously published in <u>Right On</u>! magazine.

(E) JAZZ

1527. Allen, Stuart S. <u>Stars of Swing: Swing Who's Who, America</u>
<u>and Britain; Articles On Swing; and Record Index</u>. London:
British Yearbooks, 1947. 100p., illus., discog.

1528. Alström, Ove. <u>Portrait of My Pals</u>. Stockholm: Nordisk
Rotogravyr, 1965. 40p.

1529. Balliett, Whitney. <u>Alec Wilder and His Friends</u>. Boston:
Houghton Mifflin, 1974; New York: Da Capo Pr., 1983 (Roots of
Jazz). 205p.
      Includes profiles of Marian McPartland, Bobby Hackett,
Ruby Braff, and others.

1530. ———. <u>American Singers</u>. New York; London: Oxford University Pr., 1979.   p., index.
      Profiles of jazz singers.

1531. ———. <u>Jelly Roll, Jabbo, and Fats: Nineteen Portraits in</u>
<u>Jazz</u>. New York; London: Oxford University Pr., 1983. 197p.,
index.

1532. Baton (<u>pseud</u>.). <u>Famous British Bandleaders</u>. London: Danceland Publications, 1947. 64p., illus.

1533. Berg, Ivan, and Ian Yeomans. <u>Trad: an A to Z of the British</u>
<u>Traditional Jazz Scene</u>. Additional material by Nick Brittan.
Foreword by Bill Carey. London: Foulsham, 1962. 80p., illus.
      Personalities of the 1947-62 British traditional jazz re-
vival profiled.

1534. Blesh, Rudi. <u>Combo, U.S.A.: Eight Lives in Jazz</u>. Philadel-
phia: Chilton; New York: Hayden Books, 1971; New York: Da
Capo Pr., 1979. 240p., illus., bibliog., discog., index.
      Louis Armstrong, Sidney Bechet, Jack Teagarden, Lester
Young, Billie Holiday, Gene Krupa, Charlie Christian, Eubie
Blake.

1535. Britt, Stan. <u>The Jazz Guitarists</u>. Poole, Dorset: Blandford
Pr., 1984. 128p., illus., discogs.
      Includes musical transcriptions.

1536. Bruccoli, Matthew J., C.E. Clark, <u>Jr.</u>, and Richard Layman
       (eds.). <u>Conversations With Jazz Musicians</u>. Detroit: Gale
       Research, 1977. 300p., illus. (Conversations, 7)
           Eleven interviews.

1537. Case, Brian, and Stan Britt. <u>The Illustrated Encyclopedia</u>
       <u>of Jazz</u>. Edited by Trisha Palmer. London: New English
       Library; New York: Harmony, 1978 (<u>rev. ed.</u>: 1979). 224p.,
       illus., discogs., index.
           Biographical dictionary.

1538. Charters, Samuel Barclay. <u>Jazz: New Orleans, 1885-1957: an</u>
       <u>Index to the Negro Musicians of New Orleans</u>. Belleville,
       New Jersey: Walter C. Allen, 1958; London: <u>Jazz Journal</u>, 1959.
       168p., illus., discog., index.

           ————. <u>Jazz: New Orleans, 1885-1963: an Index to the Negro</u>
       <u>Musicians of New Orleans</u>. New York: Oak Publications, 1963;
       New York: Da Capo Pr., 1983 (Roots of Jazz). 173p., illus.,
       discog., index.
           Brief biographies of over two hundred artists who were
       part of the New Orleans jazz scene.

1539. Chilton, John. <u>Who's Who of Jazz: Storyville to Swingstreet</u>.
       London: The Bloomsbury Book Shop, 1970. 447p., illus.
       Philadelphia: Chilton, 1972; New York: Da Capo Pr., 1985
       (Roots of Jazz). 419p., illus.
           Biographical dictionary. Includes over one thousand U.S.
       artists born before 1920.

1540. Claghorn, Charles Eugene. <u>Biographical Dictionary of Jazz</u>.
       Englewood Cliffs, New Jersey; London: Prentice-Hall, 1983.
       377p., index.

1541. Collier, James Lincoln. <u>The Great Jazz Artists</u>. Illustrated
       by Robert Andrew Parker. New York: Four Winds Pr., 1977.
           p., illus., bibliog., discog., index.
           Aimed at younger readers. Includes Jelly Roll Morton,
       Louis Armstrong, Billie Holiday, Charlie Parker, and others.

1542. Coryell, Julie, and Laura Friedman. <u>Jazz-Rock Fusion: the</u>
       <u>People--the Music</u>. Preface by Ramsey Lewis. New York:
       Delacorte Pr.; New York: Dell; London: Marion Boyars, 1978.
       297p., illus., bibliog., discog.
           Profiles and interviews. Includes over sixty popular
       jazz-rock artists.

1543. Dahl, Linda. <u>Stormy Weather: the Music and Lives of a Century</u>
       <u>of Jazzwomen</u>. New York: Pantheon; London: Quartet, 1984.
       371p., illus., bibliog., discog., index.

1544. Dance, Stanley (ed.). <u>Jazz Era: the Forties</u>. London: Mac-
       Gibbon and Kee, 1961 (Reprinted: New York: Da Capo Pr., 1983);
       Chester Springs, Pennsylvania: Dufour, 1962. 253p., discogs.
           Includes biographical information on approximately two
       hundred acts.

1545. ————. The World of Swing. New York: Scribner's, 1974;
New York: Da Capo Pr., 1979. 436p., illus., discog., index.
    Interviews (first published in periodicals, 1962-71) with
forty artists.

1546. Down Beat. Bouquets To the Living. Chicago: Down Beat
Publishing Company, 1956. 32p., illus.

1547. Driggs, Frank. Women in Jazz. Brooklyn, New York: Stash
Records, 1977.   p.
    Profiles; covers 1920 to date.

1548. Evensmo, Jan. Jazz Solography Series. Hosle, Norway: The
Author, 1976.

    Vol. 1: The Tenor Saxophone of Leon "Chu" Berry.

    Vol. 2: The Tenor Saxophones of Henry Bridges, Robert Carroll,
             Herschel Evans, and Johnny Russell.

    Vol. 3: The Tenor Saxophone of Coleman Hawkins, 1929-1942.

    Vol. 4: The Guitars of Charlie Christian, Robert Normann,
             and Oscar Aleman.

    Vol. 5: The Tenor Saxophone and Clarinet of Lester Young,
             1936-1942.

    Vol. 6: The Tenor Saxophone of Ben Webster, 1931-1942.

    Vol. 7: The Tenor Saxophones of Cecil Scott, Elmer Williams,
             and Dick Wilson.

    Vol. 8: The Trumpet of Henry "Red" Allen, 1929-1942.

    Vol. 9: The Trumpets of Bill Coleman, 1929-1945; and, Frankie
             Newton.

    Vol. 10: The Trumpet of Roy Eldridge, 1933-1943.

    Vol. 11: The Alto Saxophone and Other Instruments of Benny
             Carter, 1927-1942.

    Each volume contains biographical information, critical
assessment of work, and complete discography, including radio
broadcast material.

1549. ————. The Tenor Saxophonists of the Period 1930-1942.
Oslo, Norway: The Author, 1969. 150p., discogs.
    Bio-discographies of Leon "Chu" Berry, Herschel Evans,
Coleman Hawkins, Ben Webster, and Lester Young. Compiled
from item 1548 research, but published earlier.

1550. Feather, Leonard Geoffrey. The Encyclopedia of Jazz. Foreword by Duke Ellington. New York: Horizon Pr., 1955; London:
Arthur Barker; Toronto: Smithers, 1956. 360p., illus.,
bibliog., discog., index.
    Biographical dictionary. Profiles of over two thousand
musicians; also general material.

1551. ————. The Encyclopedia Yearbook of Jazz. Foreword by Benny
Goodman. New York: Horizon Pr., 1956; London: Arthur Barker;

Toronto: Smithers, 1957. 190p., illus., bibliog., discog.,
index.
   Updates and continues item 1550.

1552. ───. The New Yearbook of Jazz. Introduction by John
Hammond. New York: Horizon Pr., 1958; London: Arthur Barker;
Toronto: Smithers, 1959. 187p., illus., bibliog., discog.,
index.
   Updates and continues items 1550 and 1551. Contents
incorporated into item 1553.

1553. ───. The New Edition of the Encyclopedia of Jazz:
Completely Revised, Enlarged, and Brought Up to Date.
Appreciations by Duke Ellington, Benny Goodman, and John
Hammond. New York: Horizon Pr.; Toronto: Smithers, 1960;
London: Arthur Barker, 1961. 527p., illus., bibliog.,
discog., index.

───. The New Encyclopedia of Jazz. New York: Bonanza
Books, 1960. 527p., illus., bibliog., discog., index.

───. The New Edition of the Encyclopedia of Jazz. 2nd.
ed.: New York: Horizon Pr., 1968. 527p., illus., bibliog.,
discog., index.
   Supersedes items 1550, 1551, and 1552.

1554. ───. The Encyclopedia of Jazz in the Sixties. Foreword
by John Lewis. New York: Horizon Pr.; New York: Bonanza
Books, 1966; London: Quartet, 1978. 312p., illus., bibliog.,
discog., index.
   Approximately 1,100 biographies.

1555. ───, and Ira Gitler. The Encyclopedia of Jazz in the
Seventies. Introduction by Quincy Jones. New York: Horizon
Pr.; New York: Bonanza Books, 1976; London: Quartet, 1978.
394p., illus., bibliog., discogs., filmog., index.
   Approximately 1,400 biographies.

1556. ───. From Satchmo to Miles. New York: Stein and Day,
1972; London: Quartet, 1974. 258p., illus.
   Profiles of Louis Armstrong, Duke Ellington, Billie
Holiday, Ella Fitzgerald, Count Basie, Lester Young, Charlie
Parker, Dizzy Gillespie, Norman Granz, Oscar Peterson, Ray
Charles, Don Ellis, and Miles Davis. Material previously
published, 1951-72.

1557. ───. The Pleasures of Jazz: Leading Performers on Their
Lives, Their Music, Their Contemporaries. Introduction by
Benny Carter. New York: Horizon Pr., 1976; New York: Dell,
1977. 200p., illus.

1558. Gitler, Ira. Jazz Masters of the Forties. New York: Mac-
millan, 1966; London: Collier-Macmillan, 1967; New York:
Collier Books, 1974; New York: Da Capo Pr., 1982 (Roots of
Jazz). 290p., illus., bibliog., dicogs., index. (Jazz
Masters)
   Critical biographies of bebop-era jazz musicians.

1559. Goldberg, Joe. Jazz Masters of the Fifties. New York:
       Macmillan; London: Collier-Macmillan, 1965; New York: Da
       Capo Pr., 1980 (Roots of Jazz). 246p., illus., bibliog.,
       discogs., index. (Jazz Masters)
            Critical profiles of Gerry Mulligan, Theolonius Monk, Art
       Blakey, Miles Davis, Sonny Rollins, The Modern Jazz Quartet,
       Charles Mingus, Paul Desmond, Ray Charles, John Coltrane,
       Cecil Taylor, and Ornette Coleman.

1560. Gonda, Janos. Who's Who in Hungarian Jazz. Budapest: Inter-
       Konzert, 1974.   p., illus.
            In English. Profiles of thirty-nine Hungarian jazzmen.

1561. Gourse, Leslie. Louis's Children: American Jazz Singers.
       New York: Morrow, 1984. 368p., illus.

1562. Graham, Alberta Powell. Great Bands of America. New York:
       Thomas Nelson, 1951. 185p., illus.
            Profiles of swing and dance bands.

1563. ————. Strike Up the Band! Band Leaders of Today. New York:
       Thomas Nelson, 1949. 160p., illus.
            Profiles of swing and dance band leaders.

1564. Graham, Vic. Band Parade. London: Roy Croft/Fanfare Public-
       ations, 1947.   p., illus.
            Profiles of swing and dance bands.

1565. Green, Benny. The Reluctant Art: Five Studies in the Growth
       of Jazz. London: MacGibbon and Kee, 1962. 191p.
            Critical profiles of Bix Beiderbecke, Benny Goodman, Lester
       Young, Billie Holiday, and Charlie Parker.

       ————. The Reluctant Art: the Growth of Jazz. New York:
       Horizon Pr., 1963; Plainview, New York: Books for Libraries
       Pr., 1975 (Essay Index Reprint Series); New York: Da Capo Pr.,
       1976 (Roots of Jazz). 191p.

1566. Green, Stanley (ed.). Kings of Jazz. Revised by Stanley
       Green. South Brunswick, New Jersey: A.S. Barnes; London:
       Yoseloff, 1978. 367p., illus., bibliogs., discogs.
            Contents originally published as the monograph series,
       Kings of Jazz.

1567. Grime, Kitty. Jazz Voices. London: Quartet, 1984. 184p.,
       illus.

1568. Guitar Player. Jazz Guitarists: Collected Interviews from
       "Guitar Player" Magazine. Introduction by Leonard Feather.
       Saratoga, California: Guitar Player Productions, 1975. 119p.,
       illus., index.

1569. Hadlock, Richard. Jazz Masters of the Twenties. New York:
       Macmillan, 1965; London: Collier-Macmillan, 1966. 255p.,
       illus., bibliog., discogs. (Jazz Masters)
            Profiles of jazzmen active in the 1920's, with critical
       assessments.

1570. Hayes, Milehan, Ray Scribner, and Peter Magee. The Encyclop-
       edia of Australian Jazz. Eight Mile Plains, Queensland,
       Australia: The Authors, 1977. 112p., illus., discogs.
          Biographical dictionary.

1571. Heerkens, Adriaan. Jazz Picture Encyclopedia. Alkmaar,
       Holland: Arti, 1954; London: Anglo-French Literary Services,
       1956. 64p., illus.
          Biographical dictionary. Text in Dutch, English, French,
       and German.

1572. Hodes, Art, and Chadwick Hansen (eds.). Selections From the
       Gutter: Jazz Portraits From "The Jazz Record." Berkeley;
       London: University of California Pr., 1977. 233p., illus.
          Autobiographical articles by blues artists and jazzmen,
       first published in the Gutter column of The Jazz Record.

1573. Horricks, Raymond (ed.). These Jazzmen of Our Time. Photo-
       graphs by Herman Leonard. London: Gollancz; Toronto: Double-
       day, 1959. 236p., illus., index.
          Profiles of sixteen contemporary jazz musicians.

1574. James, Michael. Ten Modern Jazzmen: an Appraisal of the
       Recorded Work of Ten Modern Jazzmen. Foreword by Albert J.
       McCarthy. London: Cassell, 1960. 145p., illus.
          Charlie Parker, Dizzy Gillespie, Bud Powell, Miles Davis,
       Stan Getz, Theolonius Monk, Gerry Mulligan, John Lewis, Lee
       Konitz, and Wardell Gray.

   *   Kinkle, Roger D. The Complete Encyclopedia of Popular Music
       and Jazz, 1900-1950.
          * Cited above as item 16.

1575. Kinnell, Bill (ed.). Jazz Orchestras. Chilwell, Nottingham-
       shire: The Author, 1946. 20p.
          Profiles of leading jazz and dance bands.

1576. Lyons, Len. The Great Jazz Pianists: Speaking of Their Lives
       and Music. New York: Morrow, 1983. 224p., illus. Santa
       Barbara, California: Quill, 1983. 426p., illus.

1577. McCarthy, Albert John, and Max Jones (eds.). Piano Jazz.
       London: Jazz Music Books, 1945.
          No. 1: 28p.
          No. 2: 28p.
          Brief biographies of jazz pianists.

1578. McKee, Margaret. Beale, Black and Blue: Life and Music on
       Black America's Main Street. With Fred Chisenhall. Baton
       Rouge; London: Louisiana State University Pr., 1981. 265p.,
       illus., bibliog., index.

1579. Malson, Lucien. Les Maîtres du jazz. Paris: Presses Univers-
       itaires de France, 1952 (2nd. ed.: 1955; 3rd. ed.: 1958; 4th.
       ed.: 1962; 5th. ed.: 1966; 6th. ed.: 1972). 128p. (Que sais-
       je?)
          Content varies; text length identical. Sixth edition has

critical profiles (in French) of King Oliver, Louis Armstrong, Sidney Bechet, Duke Ellington, Lester Young, Charlie Parker, Theolonius Monk, Miles Davis, and John Coltrane.

1580. Martin, Jose Reyes. <u>Heroes of the Jazz Age</u>. New York: The Author, 1936. 212p.

1581. Mazur, Mladen M. <u>A Hundred Names of Yugoslav Jazz: a Short Who Is Who in Yugoslav Jazz</u>. Zagreb, Yugoslavia: The Author, 1969.   p.

1582. Mellor, Richard. <u>Spotlights of Fame</u>. Auburndale, Massachusetts: The Author, 1953. 68p.
         Brief profiles of leading jazzmen.

1583. Miller, Mark. <u>Jazz in Canada: Fourteen Lives</u>. Toronto; London: University of Toronto Pr., 1982. 245p., illus., index.

1584. Miller, William H. (ed.). <u>Three Brass: Floyd O'Brien, Maxie Kaminsky, Shorty Sherock</u>. Melbourne, Victoria: The Author, 1945. 8p.

1585. Morgenstern, Dan. <u>Jazz People</u>. Englewood Cliffs, New Jersey; London: Prentice-Hall, 1978.   p., illus.

1586. <u>Music Makers: a "Yale" Album of Your Favorite Band Leaders</u>. London: Yale Music, n.d. 40p., illus.
         Dance and swing personalities briefly profiled.

1587. Noble, Peter. <u>Kings of Rhythm: a Review of Dance-Music, and British Dance-Band Personalities</u>. London: Dunlop Publications, 1944. 87p., illus.

1588. ———— (ed.). <u>Yearbook of Jazz, 1946: an Illustrated "Who's Who" of Jazz Personalities</u>. Egham, Surrey: Citizen Pr., 1946. 99p., illus.
         Only issue.

1589. Panassié, Hugues, and Madelaine Gautier. <u>Guide to Jazz</u>. Translated by Desmond Flower. Edited by A.A. Gurwitsch. Introduction by Louis Armstrong. Boston: Houghton Mifflin, 1956 (Reprinted: Westport, Conn.: Greenwood Pr., 1973). 312p., illus., discog. London (as <u>Dictionary of Jazz</u>): Cassell, 1956. 288p., illus., discog.
         Translation and adaption of their <u>Dictionnaire du jazz</u>, originally published: Paris: Laffont, 1954. Brief profiles of "true jazzmen only." Be-bop and other modern exponents excluded.

1590. Panassié, Hugues. <u>Les Rois du jazz: notes biographiques et critiques sur les principaux musiciens de jazz</u>. Geneva: C. Grasset, 1944. <u>2 vols</u>. 252p. <u>Rev. ed.</u>: Geneva: C. Grasset, 1945. 229p.

1591. Placksin, Sally. <u>American Women in Jazz: 1900 to the Present:</u>
       <u>Their Words, Lives, and Music</u>. New York: Wideview, 1982.   p.,
       illus.

1592. Ramsey, Frederic, <u>Jr</u>., and Charles Edward Smith (eds.).
       <u>Jazzmen</u>. New York: Harcourt, Brace, 1939 (Reprinted: St.
       Clair Shores, Michigan: Scholarly Pr., 1972); New York:
       Editions for the Armed Services, 1942; London: Sidgwick and
       Jackson, 1957; New York; London: Harcourt, Brace, Jovanovich,
       1977. 360p., illus., bibliog. refs., indexes.
            Profiles and analyses by nine critics. Editions for the
       Armed Services edition has 320p., and lacks illustrations.

1593. Reisner, Robert George. <u>The Jazz Titans. Including "The</u>
       <u>Parlance of Hip." With Short Biographical Sketches, and</u>
       <u>Brief Discographies</u>. Drawings by Harrison Cruse. Garden
       City, New York: Doubleday, 1960; New York: Da Capo Pr., 1977
       (Roots of Jazz). 168p., illus., bibliog., discogs.
            Thirty-three profiles.

1594. Rivelli, Pauline, and Robert Levin (eds.). <u>The Black Giants</u>.
       New York; Cleveland: World Publishing Company, 1970. 126p.,
       illus. (<u>Jazz and Pop</u> Book Series)
            Interviews, previously published in <u>Jazz and Pop</u>, with
       avant-garde jazzmen. Includes John Coltrane, Pharaoh Sanders,
       Elvin Jones, Sunny Murray, Oliver Nelson, Ornette Coleman,
       Archie Shepp, Alice Coltrane, and others.

       ————. <u>Giants of Black Music</u>. New introduction by Nat
       Hentoff. Afterword by Robert Levin. New York: Da Capo Pr.,
       1979. 128p., illus.

   *   Rose, Al, and Edmond Souchon. <u>New Orleans Jazz: a Family</u>
       <u>Album</u>.
           * Cited above as item 898.

1595. Rosenkrantz, Timme. <u>Jazz Profiles</u>. Copenhagen, Denmark: J.
       A. Hansen Forlag, 1945. 32p., illus.

1596. Sallis, James (ed.). <u>Jazz Guitars: an Anthology</u>. New York:
       Morrow, 1984. 256p. (Quill Paperbacks)
            Profiles of jazz guitarists.

1597. Shapiro, Nat, and Nat Hentoff (eds.). <u>The Jazz Makers</u>. New
       York: Rinehart, 1957 (Reprinted: New York: Da Capo Pr., 1979);
       London: Peter Davies; New York: Grove Pr., 1958. 368p.,
       illus., bibliog. notes, index.
            Twenty-one critical profiles.

   *   Simon, George Thomas. <u>The Big Bands</u>.
           * Cited above as item 858.

1598. Spellmann, A.B. <u>Four Lives in the Bebop Business</u>. New York:
       Pantheon Books, 1966; London: MacGibbon and Kee, 1967; New
       York (as Black Music: Four Lives): Schocken Books, 1970.
       241p., index.
            Cecil Taylor, Ornette Coleman, Jackie McLean, Herbie Nichols.

1599. Stewart, Rex. <u>Jazz Masters of the Thirties</u>. New York: Mac-
       millan; London: Collier-Macmillan, 1972; New York: Collier,
       1973; New York: Da Capo Pr., 1980 (Roots of Jazz). 223p.,
       illus., bibliogs., discogs. (Jazz Masters)
           Critical profiles. Author was contemporary jazz musician;
       had personal knowledge of his subjects.

1600. Summerfield, Maurice J. <u>The Jazz Guitar: Its Evolution and
       Its Players</u>. Gateshead, Tyne and Wear: Ashley Mark Publish-
       ing, 1978. 238p., illus., bibliogs., discogs. <u>Rev. ed.</u>:
       Gateshead, Tyne and Wear: Ashley Mark Publishing, 1980.
       238p., illus., bibliogs., discogs.
           Brief profiles of 116 players. Also general material.

1601. Taylor, Arthur. <u>Notes and Tones: Musician-to-Musician Inter-
       views</u>. New York: Putnam's, 1982 (Perigee Books); London:
       Quartet, 1983. 320p., illus.

1602. Terkel, Studs. <u>Giants of Jazz</u>. Sketches by Robert Galster.
       New York: Crowell, 1957. 215p., illus., discog. <u>Rev. ed.</u>:
       New York: Crowell, 1975. 210p., illus.
           Aimed at younger readers.

1603. Treadwell, Bill. <u>The Big Book of Swing</u>. New York: Cambridge
       House, 1946; Cedar Knolls, New Jersey: Wehman Brothers, 1972.
       130p., illus.
           Profiles of Harry James, Benny Goodman, The Dorseys, Glenn
       Miller, Gene Krupa, Artie Shaw, Woody Herman, Les Brown,
       Charlie Barnet, Stan Kenton, Tex Beneke, Louis Armstrong, and
       Count Basie.

1604. Ullman, Michael. <u>Jazz Lives: Portraits in Words and Pictures</u>.
       Washington, D.C.: <u>New Republic</u> Books, 1980; New York: Quick
       Fox, 1981. 244p., illus., discog. New York: Putnam's, 1982.
       256p., illus., discog. (Perigee Books)

1605. Unterbrink, Mary. <u>Jazz Women at the Keyboard</u>. Jefferson,
       North Carolina; London: McFarland, 1983. 184p., illus.,
       bibliog., index.
           Profiles.

1606. Vedey, Julien (<u>pseud. of</u> Julien L. Robinson). <u>Band Leaders</u>.
       London: Rockliff, 1950. 202p., illus.
           Profiles of swing and dance band personalities.

1607. Walker, Leo. <u>The Big Band Almanac</u>. Pasadena, California:
       Ward Ritchie Pr., 1978. 466p., illus., index.
           Biographical dictionary. Includes over one thousand big
       bands, 1930's to 1950's.

1608. White, Mark. <u>The Observer's Book of Big Bands</u>. London: Warne,
       1978. 192p., illus., discog., **index**. (Observer's Pocket
       Series)
           Biographical dictionary.

1609. White, Mark. _The Observer's Book of Jazz_. London: Warne,
       1978. 192p., illus., bibliog., discog., index. (Observer's
       Pocket Series)
          Biographical dictionary.

1610. Williams, Martin T. (ed.). _The Art of Jazz: Essays on the_
       Nature and Development of Jazz. New York: Oxford University
       Pr., 1959; London: Cassell; New York: Grove Pr., 1960; New
       York (as _The Art of Jazz: Ragtime to Bebop_): Da Capo Pr.,
       1980. 248p., illus., discogs.
          Twenty-one profiles, originally published in periodicals
       and as liner notes.

1611. ─────. _Jazz Masters in Transition, 1957-69_. New York:
       Macmillan; London: Collier-Macmillan, 1970; New York: Da Capo
       Pr., 1982 (Roots of Jazz). 288p., illus. (Jazz Masters)
          Eighty-seven profiles, reviews and interviews. Contents
       originally published in periodicals.

1612. ─────. _Jazz Masters of New Orleans_. New York: Macmillan;
       London: Collier-Macmillan, 1967; New York: Da Capo Pr.,
       1978 (Roots of Jazz). 287p., illus., bibliogs., discogs.,
       index. (Jazz Masters)
          Profiles of Buddy Bolden, Jelly Roll Morton, King Oliver,
       Sidney Bechet, Louis Armstrong, Zutty Singleton, Kid Ory,
       Bunk Johnson, Red Allen, The Original Dixieland Jazz Band,
       The New Orleans Rhythm Kings, and others.

1613. ─────. _Jazz Panorama: From the Pages of "The Jazz Review."_
       New York: Crowell-Collier, 1962; New York: Crowell, 1964;
       New York: Da Capo Pr., 1979 (Roots of Jazz). 318p., illus.
          Thirty-nine profiles, previously published in _The Jazz_
       Review.

1614. ─────. _The Jazz Tradition_. New York; London: Oxford Univ-
       ersity Pr., 1970. 232p., discog. New York; Toronto: New
       American Library, 1971. 191p., discog. _New and rev. ed._:
       New York; London: Oxford University Pr., 1983. 287p.,
       discog., index.
          Profiles, previously published in periodicals.

1615. Williams, Mike. _The Australian Jazz Explosion_. Photographs
       by Jane March. London: Angus and Robertson, 1981. 171p., ·
       illus., index.
          Interviews with thirty-two Australian jazz musicians.

1616. Williamson, Ken (ed.). _This Is Jazz_. London: Newnes, 1960.
       256p., illus.
          Critical profiles of Count Basie, Jack Teagarden, Miles
       Davis, Big Bill Broonzy, Duke Ellington, Ella Fitzgerald,
       Billie Holiday, Sarah Vaughan, and Jelly Roll Morton.

   *   Wilmer, Valerie. _As Serious As Your Life: the Story of the_
       New Jazz.
              * Cited above as item 878.

1617. ————. Jazz People. With photographs by the author.
London: Allison and Busby; Indianapolis: Bobbs-Merrill,
1971. 167p., illus., index. 2nd. ed.: London: Allison and
Busby, 1971; London: Quartet, 1977. 167p., illus., index.
    Interviews with fourteen avant-garde Black jazzmen; with
commentary.

(F) STAGE AND SCREEN

(i) Minstrelsy

1618. Fletcher, Tom. Negro Minstrels. New York: Burdge, 1954.
        p., illus.

1619. Rice, Edward Le Roy. Monarchs of Minstrelsy: From "Daddy"
       Rice to Date. New York: Kenny Publishing Company, 1911.
       376p., illus., index.
           Biographical dictionary. Includes approximately one
       thousand minstrel performers.

(ii) Music Hall

1620. Bingham, Madeleine. Earls and Girls: Dramas in High Society.
       London: Hamish Hamilton, 1980. 178p., illus., bibliog.,
       index.
           The stories of Victorian showgirls who married into Society.

1621. Bullar, Guy R., and Len Evans. "The Performer" Who's Who in
       Variety: a Biographical Record of the Variety Stage. London:
       The Performer, 1950. 337p., illus.
           Includes music hall artists.

1622. Busby, Roy. British Music Hall: an Illustrated Who's Who
       From 1850 to the Present Day. London; Salem, New Hampshire:
       Paul Elek, 1976. 191p., illus.
           Includes approximately five hundred performers.

1623. Felstead, Sidney Theodore. The Stars Who Made the Halls: a
       Hundred Years of English Humour, Harmony, and Hilarity.
       London: T. Werner Laurie, 1946. 192p., illus.
           First-hand profiles.

1624. Fergusson, Louis. Old Time Music Hall Comedians. Leicester,
       England: C.H. Gee, 1949. 63p.
           Profiles. Includes singing comics.

1625. Gammond, Peter (comp.). Your Own, Your Very Own! A Music
       Hall Scrapbook. London: Ian Allan, 1971. 96p., illus.,
       discog.
           Includes list of one hundred "great music-hall songs."
       Also has reproductions of playbills and song covers.

1626. Jacques-Charles (pseud. of Jacques Charles). De Gaby Deslys
       à Mistinguett. Paris: Gallimard, 1932. 249p.
       Profiles of French music hall stars. In French.

1627. Le Roy, George. Music Hall Stars of the Nineties. London:
       British Technical and General Pr., 1952. 70p., illus.,
       bibliog.

1628. Leslie, Petrea. What Sort of Girls Were They? Illustrated
       by Robin Ray. London: Pan, 1962. 156p., illus.
       Biographical sketches of chorus girls.

1629. Nerman, Einar. Darlings of the Gods, in Music Hall, Revue,
       and Musical Comedy: As Seen by Nerman. London: Alston
       Rivers, 1930. 80p., illus.
       Caricatures, first published in The Tatler.

1630. Newton, Henry Chance. Idols of the 'Halls: Being My Music
       Hall Memories. London: Heath, Cranton, 1928. 256p., illus.
       First-hand profiles of music hall artists.

1631. Trumble, Alfred. Footlight Favourites: a Collection of
       Popular American and European Actresses in the Various Roles
       in which They Have Become Famous. With Biographical Sketches,
       Compiled by a Well-Known Author and Journalist Expressly for
       This Work. New York: National Police Gazette Office, (?1880).
       56p., illus. Revised and enlarged ed.: New York: National
       Police Gazette Office, 1881. 63p., illus.
       Music hall and other stage stars profiled.

1632. Variety Stars. London: Variety Publishing Company, 1895.
       40p.
       Autobiographical pieces by music hall artists.

(iii) Musicals

(a) Stage

1633. Appelbaum, Stanley, and James Camner (eds.). Stars of the
       American Musical Theater in Historic Photographs: 361 Port-
       raits From the 1860's to 1950. New York: Dover; London:
       Constable, 1981; Magnolia, Pennsylvania: Peter Smith, 1983.
       176p., illus., index.
       Chiefly illustrated.

1634. Brown, Thomas Allston. History of the American Stage: Cont-
       aining Biographical Sketches of Nearly Every Member of the
       Profession That Has Appeared On the American Stage From 1733
       To 1870. New York: Dick and Fitzgerald, 1870. 421p.
       Includes artists from the musical field.

1635. Marks, Edward Bennett. They All Had Glamour: From the Swed-
       ish Nightingale to the Naked Lady. New York: J. Messner,
       1944; Westport, Conn.: Greenwood Pr., 1972. 448p., illus.,

index.
Covers 1866 to end of the Nineteenth Century. Chapters on G.L. Fox, Lola Montez, and Adah Isaacs Menken; plus brief biographical sketches of other performers.

1636. Strang, Lewis Clinton. Celebrated Comedians of Light Opera and Musical Comedy in America. Boston: The Author, 1901; New York: Benjamin Blom, 1972. 293p., illus., index.
Brief profiles of twenty-three artists. Includes singing comics.

1637. Wearing, J.P. American and British Theatrical Biography: a Directory. Metuchen, New Jersey; London: Scarecrow Pr., 1979. 1007p.

(b) Motion Pictures

1638. Rothel, David. The Singing Cowboys. South Brunswick, New Jersey: A.S. Barnes; London: Yoseloff, 1978. 272p., illus., bibliog., index.

1639. Vallance, Tom. The American Musical. New York: A.S. Barnes; London: Zwemmer, 1970. 192p., illus., index. (Screen Series)
Biographical dictionary. Entries for 509 performers, and others.

(iv) Dance

1640. Cohen-Stratyner, Barbara Naomi. Biographical Dictionary of Dance. New York: Schirmer Books; London: Collier-Macmillan, 1982. 970p., bibliogs.
Brief profiles of over 2,900 performers, and others.

(G) SONGWRITERS AND COMPOSERS

1641. American Society of Composers, Authors, and Publishers. List of Members of the American Society of Composers, Authors, and Publishers, and Affiliated Societies. New York: A.S.C.A.P. annual, 1932- .

1642. ———. The A.S.C.A.P. Biographical Dictionary of Composers, Authors, and Publishers. Edited by Daniel I. McNamara. New York: Crowell, 1948. 483p. 2nd. ed.: New York: Crowell, 1952. 636p. 3rd. ed.: Compiled and edited by The Lynn Farnol Group. New York: A.S.C.A.P., 1966. 845p. 4th. ed.: Compiled by the Jacques Cattell Press. Tempe, Arizona: Jacques Cattell Pr.; New York; London: Bowker, 1980. 589p., index.
Approximately 8,200 entries.

1643. Baxter, Clarice Howard, and Videt Polk (comps.). Gospel
       Songwriters Biography. Dallas: Stamps-Baxter Music and
       Print Company, 1971. 306p., illus., index.
           Profiles of 102 white gospel composers. Emphasis on their
       lives, rather than their works.

1644. Brahms, Caryl, and Ned Sherrin. Song By Song: the Lives and
       Work of Fourteen Great Lyric Writers. Bolton, Lancashire:
       Ross Anderson Publications, 1984. 282p., illus., bibliog.,
       indexes.
           Irving Berlin, Cole Porter, Ira Gershwin, Lorenz Hart,
       Oscar Hammerstein II, Dorothy Fields, Howard Dietz, E.Y.
       Harburg, Noël Coward, Johnny Mercer, Frank Loesser, Alan J.
       Lerner, Sheldon Harnick, and Stephen Sondheim.

1645. Craig, Warren. The Great Songwriters of Hollywood. South
       Brunswick, New Jersey: A.S. Barnes; London: Tantivity Pr.,
       1980. 287p., illus., indexes.

1646. ———. Sweet and Lowdown: America's Popular Song Writers.
       Foreword by Milton Ager. Metuchen, New Jersey; London:
       Scarecrow Pr., 1978. 645p., bibliog., index.
           Biographical dictionary. Covers 1880 to 1977.

1647. Engel, Lehman (comp.). Their Words Are Music: the Great
       Theater Lyricists and Their Lyrics. New York: Crown, 1975.
       p.
           Includes texts of musical comedy songs.

1648. Ewen, David. Great Men of American Popular Song: the Story
       of the American Popular Song Told Through the Lives, Careers,
       Achievements, and Personalities of its Foremost Composers and
       Lyricists: From William Billings of the Revolutionary War to
       the "Folk-Rock" of Bob Dylan. Englewood Cliffs, New Jersey;
       London: Prentice-Hall, 1970. 387p., index.
           Profiles of leading composers and teams. Emphasis on
       Twentieth-Century figures.

       ———. Great Men of American Popular Song: the History of
       the American Popular Song Told Through the Lives, Careers,
       Achievements, and Personalities of its Foremost Composers
       and Lyricists: From William Billings of the Revolutionary
       War Through Bob Dylan, Johnny Cash, Burt Bacharach. Rev. and
       enlarged ed. Englewood Cliffs, New Jersey; London: Prentice-
       Hall, 1972. 404p., index.

1649. ———. Popular American Composers From Revolutionary Times
       to the Present: a Biographical and Critical Guide. New York:
       H.W. Wilson, 1962. 217p., illus., bibliogs., index.
           Biographical dictionary. Includes 130 leading composers.

       ———. ———. First Supplement. New York: H.W. Wilson,
       1972. 121p., illus., bibliogs., index.
           Extends coverage through rock, pop, country, and theater
       music fields.

1650. Finck, Henry Theophilus. Songs and Songwriters. New York:
      Scribner's, 1900. 254p., illus. (Music Lover's Library)
      2nd. ed.: 1902; 3rd. ed.: 1909; 4th. ed.: 1911; 5th. ed.:
      1912 (reissued: 1914; 1923); 6th. ed.: 1928.
      Profiles. All editions have same pagination.

1651. Graham, Neil, and Esther Graham (eds.). What Are Their
      Memorable Songs? New York: Vantage Pr., 1984.   p.
      Profiles of popular songwriters, and record of their works.

   * Hall, J. H. Biography of Gospel Song and Hymn Writers.
      * Cited above as item 1510.

1652. Handy, William Christopher. Negro Authors and Composers of
      the United States. New York: Handy Brothers Music Company,
      1938; New York: A.M.S. Pr., 1976. 24p., bibliog. refs.

1653. Hughes, Gervase. Composers of Operetta. London: Macmillan;
      New York: St. Martin's Pr., 1962; Westport, Conn.: Greenwood
      Pr., 1974. 283p., illus., bibliog.

   * Knippers, Ottis J. Who's Who Among Southern Singers and
      Composers.
      * Cited above as item 1463.

1654. Lawrence, Ruth (ed.). Songwriters and Poets of America.
      New York: Haven Pr., 1945. 574p.
      Profiles.

1655. Society of European Stage Authors and Composers. The
      S.E.S.A.C. Music Guide. New York: S.E.S.A.C., 1943. 63p.,
      discog.
      Biographical dictionary and contact guide.

1656. Staveacre, Tony. The Songwriters. London: British Broadcast-
      ing Corporation, 1980. 191p., illus.
      Leslie Stuart, Lionel Monckton, Ray Noble, Ivor Novello,
      Lionel Bart, Lennon and McCartney, Tim Rice and Andrew Lloyd
      Webber. Based on British television series.

1657. White, Mark. You Must Remember This: Popular Songwriters,
      1900-1980. Foreword by David Jacobs. London: Warne, 1983.
      304p., bibliog., indexes.
      Biographical dictionary.

1658. Wilder, Alec. American Popular Song: the Great Innovators,
      1900-1950. Edited and introduction by James T. Maher. New
      York; London: Oxford University Pr., 1972 (reissued: 1975).
      536p., indexes.
      Profiles of popular songwriters, 1890's to middle of
      Twentieth Century. Emphasis of text is on musical style,
      rather than lyrics. Includes Jerome Kern, Irving Berlin,
      George Gershwin, Richard Rodgers, Cole Porter, Harold Arlen,
      Vincent Youmans, Arthur Schwartz, Burton Lane, Hugh Martin,
      Vernon Duke, and others.

(H) MUSIC INDUSTRY FIGURES

*   American Society of Composers, Authors, and Publishers. List
      of Members of the American Society of Composers, Authors,
      and Publishers.
            * Cited above as item 1641.

*   ———. The A.S.C.A.P. Biographical Dictionary of Composers,
      Authors, and Publishers.
            * Cited above as item 1642.

1659. Muirhead, Bert. The Record Producers' File: a Directory of
      Rock Album Producers, 1962-1984. Poole, Dorset: Blandford
      Pr., 1984. 288p., index.
            Producers and their creations. Includes appendix of chart
      successes.

1660. Oakley, Nik, and Dave Gotz (eds.). The Music Spinners:
      Britain's Radio DJs. London: M.R.P. Books, 1976. 127p.,
      illus.
            Biographical dictionary of disk jockeys.

1661. Tobler, John, and Stuart Grundy. The Record Producers. Lon-
      don: British Broadcasting Corporation, 1982; New York: St.
      Martin's Pr., 1983. 248p., illus., discogs., index.
            Thirteen profiles. Based on British radio series.

B. INDIVIDUAL BIOGRAPHIES

INDIVIDUAL BIOGRAPHIES

ABBA

1662. Abba. Abba By Abba. Compiled by Christen Berg. Stafford, England: Pemberton Publishing, 1980.   p., illus.

1663. ————. Abba In Their Own Words. Compiled by Rosemary York. London; New York: Omnibus Pr., 1982. 128p., illus. From press and television interviews.

1664. Abba Annual. Knutsford, Cheshire: Pemberton Publishing. 1981: 1980. 45p., illus., discog. 1982: 1981. 42p., illus., discog. Aimed at younger readers. Collection of features.

1665. Edgington, Harry, and Peter Himmelstrand. Abba. London: Everest, 1977.   p., illus. New and rev. ed.: London: Magnum Books, 1978. 181p., illus.

1666. Lindvall, Mariane. Abba: the Ultimate Pop Group. Edmonton, Alberta: Hurtig; London: Pop Universal/Souvenir Pr., 1977. 96p., illus.

1667. Tobler, John. Abba For the Record. London: Omnibus Pr., 1980.   p., illus., discog. Bio-discography.

Periodicals

1668. Abba Collectors' Magazine. 32 Redcar Lane, Redcar, Cleveland, England. monthly, August 1984- .

1669. Abba Magazine. Knutsford, Cheshire. monthly, December 1977-October 1983.

ABBOTT, GEORGE

1670. Abbott, George. Mister Abbott. New York: Random House, 1963. 279p. Autobiography of Broadway playwright, producer, and director of musical comedies.

AC/DC

1671.   AC/DC . London: Omnibus Pr., 1984. 96p., illus. (H.M.
        Photobooks)
             Collection of performance photographs.

1672.   Bunton, Richard. AC/DC: "Hell Ain't No Bad Place To Be!"
        London: Omnibus Pr., 1982. 96p., illus., discog. (Savoy
        Editions)

1673.   Dome, Malcolm. AC/DC. London; New York: Proteus, 1982.
        96p., illus., discog.

ACUFF, ROY

1674.   Dunkleberger, A.C. King of Country Music: the Life Story of
        Roy Acuff. Nashville: Williams, 1971. 137p., illus.
             Based on author's interviews with Acuff.

1675.   Schlappi, Elizabeth. Roy Acuff: the Smoky Mountain Boy.
        Gretna, Louisiana: Pelican Publishing, 1977.   p., illus.,
        bibliog., index.

1676.   ―――― (comp.). Roy Acuff and His Smoky Mountain Boys
        Discography. Cheswold, Delaware: Disc Collector Publicat-
        ions, 1966.   p., illus. (Country Research Series). Rev.
        and enlarged ed.: Chswold, Delaware: Disc Collector Public-
        ations, 1966. 36p., illus. (Country Research Series)

ADAM AND THE ANTS

1677.   Adam and the Ants: Antwarriors. Manchester, England: Baby-
        lon Books, 1981. unpaged, illus.
             Biography of Adam Ant (pseud. of Stuart Goddard).

1678.   Maw, James. The Official Adam Ant Story. London: Futura,
        1981. 160p., illus., discog.

1679.   Vermorel, Fred, and Judy Vermorel. Adam and the Ants.
        London: Omnibus Pr., 1981. 47p., illus., discog.

1680.   Welch, Chris. Adam and the Ants. London: Star Books, 1981.
        128p., illus., discog.

                          Lyric Collections

1681.   Adam and the Ants. "Kings": the Official Adam and the Ants
        Song Book. Text by Stephen Lavers. London: Mirror Books,
        1981. 44p., illus.

1682. ————. Prince Charming: Official Song Book. London:
        Mirror Books, 1982. 37p., illus.

ADDERLEY, CANNONBALL

1683. Jepsen, Jorgen Grunnet. Discography of Cannonball Adderley
        (and) John Coltrane. Biographical notes by Knud H. Ditlev-
        sen. Brande, Denmark: Debut Records, 1961. 32p.

ADLER, LARRY

1684. Adler, Larry. It Ain't Necessarily So. London: Collins,
        1984. 254p., illus., index.
        Autobiography.

ALBAM, MANNY

1685. Hentoff, Nat. Manny Albam. New York: Broadcast Music,
        1960. 16p., discog.

ALEMAN, OSCAR

  *   Evensmo, Jan. The Guitars of Charlie Christian, Robert
        Normann, and Oscar Aleman.
            * Cited above as item 1548.

ALLEN, DAEVID

1686. Allen, Daevid. If Words Were Birds. London: Outposts
        Publications, 1964. 24p.
        Poems by former member of Soft Machine and Gong groups.

ALLEN, HENRY "RED"

  *   Evensmo, Jan. The Trumpet of Henry "Red" Allen.
            * Cited above as item 1548.

ALLEN, STEVE (pseud. of Stephen Valentine Allen)

1687. Allen, Steve. Mark It and Strike It: an Autobiography. New
        York: Holt, Rinehart, and Winston, 1960. 432p., illus.

ALLMAN BROTHERS

1688. Nolan, Tom. The Allman Brothers Band. New York: Sire Books,
       1977.   p., illus.

AMRAN, DAVID

1689. Amran, David. Vibrations: the Adventures and Musical Times
       of D.A. New York: Macmillan, 1968; Westport, Conn.: Green-
       wood Pr., 1980. 470p.
          Jazz memoir.

ANDERSON, JOHN MURRAY

1690. Anderson, John Murray. Out Without My Rubbers: Memoirs.
       As told to, and written by, Hugh Abercrombie Anderson. New
       York: Library Publishers, 1954. 253p., illus.
          Broadway director and lyricist remembers. Title refers
       to musical comedy libretto, written by the author.

ANDERSON, LAURIE

1691. Anderson, Laurie. United States. London: Cape, 1984. 232p.
          Book of her six-hour solo show, same title.

ANDERSON, MARIAN

1692. Anderson, Marian. My Lord, What a Morning: an Autobiography.
       New York: Viking Pr., 1956. 312p., illus. London: Cresset
       Pr., 1957. 240p., illus. New York: Avon Books, 1964. 222p.,
       illus.

                        Reference Materials

1693. Simms, Janet L. (comp.). Marian Anderson: an Annotated
       Bibliography and Discography. Westport, Conn.: Greenwood Pr.,
       1981. 243p., illus., index.

                           Biographies

1694. Albus, Harry James. Deep River Girl: the Life of Marian
       Anderson in Story Form. Grand Rapids, Michigan: Eerdman,
       1949. 85p.
          Novelized form.

1695. Newman, Shirlee Petkin. <u>Marian Anderson: Lady From</u>
       <u>Philadelphia</u>. Philadelphia: Westminster Pr., 1965. 175p.,
       illus., bibliog.

1696. Stevenson, James. <u>Marian Anderson: Singing To the World</u>.
       Chicago: Encyclopaedia Britannica Pr., 1963. 189p., illus.
       (Britannica Bookshelf: Great Lives)

1697. Vehanen, Kosti. <u>Marian Anderson: a Portrait</u>. With the
       collaboration of George J. Barnett. New York; London:
       McGraw-Hill, 1941; Westport, Conn.: Greenwood Pr., 1970.
       270p., illus.
            By her Swedish accompanist. Personal memoir of her tours
       in Europe, South America, and the United States, 1931-41.

ANDERSON, MOIRA

1698. Anderson, Moira. <u>Moira Anderson's Scotland</u>. With Netta
       Martin. Guildford, Surrey: Lutterworth Pr., 1981. 160p.,
       illus.
            Illustrated guided tour linked to her Scottish popular
       song repertoire, interwoven with comment and memoir.

ANDREWS, JULIE

1699. Cottrell, John. <u>Julie Andrews: the Story of a Star</u>. London:
       Arthur Barker, 1969. 222p., illus.

       ————. <u>Julie Andrews</u>. London: Mayflower, 1969. 206p.,
       illus.

1700. Windeler, Robert. <u>Julie Andrews: a Biography</u>. New York:
       Putnam; London: W.H. Allen, 1970. 253p., illus., index.

       ————. <u>Julie Andrews</u>. London: Comet, 1984. 223p., illus.,
       discog., filmog., index.
            Revised and updated. Includes listing of her Broadway
       appearances.

ANIKULAPO-KUTI, FELA

1701. Moore, Carlos. <u>Fela, Fela: This Bitch of a Life</u>. London:
       Allison and Busby, 1982. 287p., illus., discog.
            Biography of the Nigerian Afro-beat star and political
       activist.

ARLEN, HAROLD

1702. Jablonski, Edward. Harold Arlen: Happy With the Blues.
       Garden City, New York: Doubleday, 1961. 286p., illus.,
       discog.
           Includes complete listing of his compositions, with det-
       ails of shows and credits.

ARMSTRONG, LOUIS

1703. Armstrong, Louis. Louis Armstrong, a Self Portrait: the
       Interview by Richard Meryman. New York: Eakins Pr., 1971.
       59p., illus.
           Emphasis on his life, rather than his work. Originally
       published (in part), Life, 15 April, 1966.

1704. ————. Satchmo: My Life in New Orleans. New York: Prentice-
       Hall, 1954. 240p., illus. London: Peter Davies, 1955.
       215p., illus. New York: New American Library, 1955 (Reissued:
       1961). 191p., illus. (Signet Books)
           His early career, to his arrival in Chicago to join King
       Oliver, 1922.

1705. ————. Swing That Music. Introduction by Rudy Vallée.
       Music section edited by Horace Gerlach. With special examp-
       les of swing music contributed by Benny Goodman , Tommy
       Dorsey, Joe Venuti, Bud Freeman, Red Norvo, and Louis Arm-
       strong. London; New York: Longmans, Green, 1937. 144p.,
       illus., discog.
           Covers the first thirty-six years of his life. Music
       section has analysis of his playing style; also ten sheet
       music examples of individual improvisations on the original
       song Swing That Music (by Armstrong and Gerlach) by the
       musicians.

1706. Collier, James Lincoln. Louis Armstrong: a Biography. New
       York: Oxford University Pr., 1983; London: Joseph, 1984.
       383p., illus., discog., index.

1707. Goffin, Robert. Horn of Plenty: the Story of Louis Armstrong.
       Translated by James F. Bezou. New York: Allen, Towne, and
       Heath; Toronto: McLeod, 1947; Westport, Conn.: Greenwood Pr.,
       1978. 304p., illus.
           Originally published as Louis Armstrong: le roi du jazz,
       Paris: P. Seghers, 1947.

1708. Jones, Max, and John Chilton. Salute to Satchmo. London:
       I.P.C., 1970. 155p., illus., bibliog., discog., filmog.,
       index. (A Melody Maker Publication)
           Includes a contribution by Leonard Feather.

       ————. Louis: the Louis Armstrong Story, 1900-1971. London:
       Studio Vista; Boston: Little, Brown, 1971. 256p., illus.,

bibliog., discog., filmog., index. London: Mayflower, 1975.
302p., illus., bibliog., discog., filmog., index.

1709. McCarthy, Albert John. Louis Armstrong. London: Cassell;
New York: A.S. Barnes, 1961. 87p., illus., discog. (Kings
of Jazz, 5)
Incorporated into item 1566.

1710. Panassié, Hugues. Louis Armstrong: l'homme, le style,
l'oeuvre. With a complete discography by Charles Delaunay.
Paris: Editions du Belvédère, 1947. 107p., illus., discog.
(Les Maîtres du jazz, 1). Rev. ed.: Paris: Nouvelles
Editions Latines, 1969. 224p., illus., discog.

————. Louis Armstrong. Photograph collection by Jack
Bradley. New York: Scribner's, 1971; New York: Da Capo Pr.,
1979. 148p., illus., discog.

Discographies

1711. Jepsen, Jorgen Grunnet. Discography of Louis Armstrong.
Biographical notes by Knud H. Ditlevsen. Brande, Denmark:
Debut Records, 1959-60.
Vol. 1: 1923-1932. 37p.
Vol. 2: 1932-1946. 20p.
Vol. 3: 1947-1960. 25p.

————. ————. 2nd. rev. ed.: Rugsted Vyst, Denmark:
Knudsen, 1973. 102p.
Text in English.

1712. Siemens Company. Louis "Satchmo" Armstrong: Jazz. Brussels:
Siemens Company, 1964. 9p.
Listing of releases by the Company.

ARNAZ, DESI

1713. Arnaz, Desi. A Book By Desi Arnaz. New York: Morrow, 1976.
322p., illus. New York: Warner Books, 1977. 382p., illus.
Autobiography.

ARNOLD, EDDY

1714. Arnold, Eddy. It's a Long Way From Chester County. Old
Tappan, New Jersey: Hewitt House, 1969. 154p., illus.
Autobiography.

ARROWS

1715.   Harry, Bill. Arrows: the Official Story. London: Everest,
        1976. 141p., illus.
            British rock group, popular on television, mid-1970's.

ASCHE, OSCAR

1716.   Asche, Oscar. Oscar Asche: His Life, By Himself. London:
        Hurst and Blackett, 1929. 256p.
            Autobiography of actor, singer, librettist, director, and
        producer.

ASMUSSEN, SVEND

1717.   Henius, Bent. Svend Asmussen. Copenhagen: Erichsen, 1962.
        80p., discog.
            Bio-discography of Scandinavian jazzman.

ASPEL, MICHAEL

1718.   Aspel, Michael. Polly Wants a Zebra: the Memoirs of Michael
        Aspel. London: Weidenfeld and Nicolson, 1974; London: Fut-
        ura, 1975. 207p., illus., index.
            British disk-jockey.

ASTAIRE, FRED, AND GINGER ROGERS

1719.   Astaire, Fred. Steps in Time. New York: Harper, 1959;
        London: Heinemann, 1960; New York: Da Capo Pr., 1979 (Series
        in Dance). 338p., illus., index.
            Autobiography. Includes listing of his appearances, 1917
        to 1959.

1720.   Carrick, Peter. A Tribute To Fred Astaire. London: Hale,
        1984. 188p., illus., filmog., index.

1721.   Croce, Arlene. The Fred Astaire and Ginger Rogers Book.
        New York: Outerbridge and Lazard; London: W.H. Allen; New
        York: Galahad Books, 1972; New York: Vintage, 1978. 191p.,
        illus.
            Detailed account of their screen career.

   *   Engel, Lyle Kenyon (ed.). The Fred Astaire Dance Book.
            * Cited above as item 1279.

1722.   Freedland, Michael. Fred Astaire. London: W.H. Allen, 1976.
        277p., illus., index. New York: Grosset and Dunlap, 1977.

183p., illus., index. <u>Rev. ed.</u>: London: Comet, 1984. 188p.,
illus.

1723. Green, Benny. <u>Fred Astaire</u>. London; New York: Hamlyn, 1979.
(Reissued 1984). 176p., illus., bibliog., discog., filmog.,
index.

1724. Green, Stanley, and Burt Goldblatt. <u>Starring Fred Astaire</u>.
New York: Dodd, Mead, 1973; London: W.H. Allen, 1974; Garden
City, New York: Doubleday, 1977 (A Windfall Book). 501p.,
illus., discog., index.

1725. Satchell, Tim. <u>Astaire</u>. London: Pavilion Books, 1984.
256p., illus.

1726. Thomas, Bob. <u>Astaire: the Man; the Dancer</u>. With comments
by Fred Astaire. London: Weidenfeld and Nicolson, 1985.
340p., illus., bibliog., index.
    Includes listing of appearances.

Ginger Rogers

1727. Dickens, Homer. <u>The Films of Ginger Rogers</u>. Secaucus, New
Jersey: Citadel Pr., 1975.   p., illus., filmog.
    Critical study.

1728. Richards, Dick. <u>Ginger: Salute To a Star</u>. Brighton, Sussex:
Clifton Books, 1969. 192p., illus., index.
    Includes chronological appendix giving details of her
motion pictures.

ATKINS, CHET

1729. Atkins, Chet. <u>Country Gentleman</u>. With Bill Neely. Chicago:
Regnery, 1974. 226p., illus.
    Autobiography.

1730. O'Donnell, Red. <u>Chet Atkins</u>. Nashville: Athena Music, 1967.
46p., illus.

AUSTIN, BILL JOE

1731. Austin, Bill Joe. <u>The Beat Goes On And On And On</u>. Erwin,
North Carolina: Carolina Arts and Publishing House, 1976.
170p., illus.
    Autobiography of jazz clarinetist.

AUTRY, GENE

*   Autry, Gene. The Art of Writing Songs, and How To Play a
     Guitar.
      * Cited below as item 3822.

1732. Autry, Gene. Back In the Saddle Again. With Mickey Hersko-
      witz. Garden City, New York: Doubleday, 1978. 252p., illus.,
      discog., filmog., index.
        Autobiography.

AYLER, ALBERT

1733. Rissi, Mathias. Albert Ayler: Discography. Adliswil, West
      Germany: The Author, 1977. 9p.

AZNAVOUR, CHARLES

1734. Aznavour, Charles. Aznavour By Aznavour: an Autobiography.
      Translated by Ghilaine Boulanger. Chicago: Cowles Book
      Company, 1972. 283p., illus.

1735. ———. Yesterday, When I Was Young. London: W.H. Allen,
      1979. 202p., illus., index.

BACALL, LAUREN

1736. Bacall, Lauren. Lauren Bacall: By Myself. New York: Knopf,
      1978. 377p., illus. London: Cape, 1978. 384p., illus.
      Sevenoaks, Kent: Hodder, 1980. 512p., illus. New York:
      Ballantine, 1980. 506p., illus.
        Autobiography. Author starred in Applause, Broadway 1970,
      London 1972.

BADDELEY, HERMIONE

1737. Baddeley, Hermione. The Unsinkable Hermione Baddeley. Lon-
      don: Collins, 1984. 240p., illus., index.
        Autobiography.

BAEZ, JOAN

1738. Baez, Joan. Daybreak. New York: Dial Pr., 1968. 159p.
      New York: Avon Books, 1969. 191p. London: MacGibbon and Kee,
      1970. 164p. London: Panther, 1971. 141p.
        Memoir, poetical interludes, and philosophical reflections.

1739. Swan, Peter. Joan Baez: a Bio-Disco-Bibliography. Being a
       Selected Guide to Material in Print, on Record, on Cassette,
       and on Film. With a Biographical Introduction. Brighton,
       East Sussex: Noyce, 1977. 23p., index.

1740. Swanekamp, Joan. Diamonds and Rust: a Bibliography and
       Discography of Joan Baez. Ann Arbor, Michigan: Pierian Pr.,
       1983. 88p., illus.
          Annotated.

BAILEY, PEARL

1741. Bailey, Pearl. The Raw Pearl. New York: Harcourt, Brace,
       and World, 1968. 206p., illus. New York: Pocket Books,
       1969. 189p., illus. New York: Harcourt, Brace, Jovanovich,
       1971. 206p., illus.
          Autobiography.

1742. ————. Talking To Myself. New York: Harcourt, Brace,
       Jovanovich, 1971. 233p.
          More autobiography.

BAKER, JOSEPHINE

1743. Baker, Josephine. Les Memoires de Josephine Baker. Edited
       and adapted by Marcel Sauvage. Illustrated by Paul Colin.
       Paris: Kra, 1927. 186p., illus. Paris: Corrêa, 1949.
       348p., illus.

1744. ————. Une Vie de toutes les couleurs: souvenirs. Edited
       by André Rivollet. Grenoble: B. Arthaud, 1926 (Reissued:
       1935). 116p., illus. (Collection Arc-en-ciel)
          Memoirs.

1745. ————, and Jo Bouillon. Josephine. New York: Harper and
       Row, 1977; London: W.H. Allen, 1978. 302p., illus.
          Autobiography, interspersed with narrative by her husband.

1746. ————, and Marcel Sauvage. Voyages et aventures de Joseph-
       ine Baker. Preface by Fernand Divoire. Paris: M. Seheur,
       1931. 149p., illus.
          Memoir in conversation form.

1747. Haney, Lynn. Naked at the Feast: the Biography of Josephine
       Baker. London: Robson Books; New York: Dodd, Mead, 1981.
       338p., illus., index.

1748. La Camara, Félix, Comte de. Mon sang dans tes veines: roman
       d'après une idée de Joséphine Baker. Illustrated by G. de
       Pogédaieff. Paris: Les Editions Isis, 1931.   p., illus.

BARBER, CHRIS

1749. Rust, Brian Arthur Lovell. Chris Barber: a Biography,
       Appreciation, Record Survey, and Discography. London:
       National Jazz Federation, 1958. 20p.

BARNET, CHARLIE

1750. Barnet, Charlie, and Stanley Dance. Those Swinging Years:
       the Autobiography of Charlie Barnet. Baton Rouge: Louisiana
       State University Pr., 1984. 288p., illus.

1751. Edwards, Ernie, George Hall, and Bill Korst (eds.). Charlie
       Barnet and His Orchestra: Discography. Whittier, California:
       Jazz Discographies Unlimited, 1965. 36p. Rev. ed.: 1967.
       40p.

1752. Garrod, Charles. Charlie Barnet and His Orchestra. Larel,
       Maryland: Jazz Discographies Unlimited, 1970.   p. Spots-
       wood, New Jersey: Joyce, 1973.   p.
          Discography.

BARNUM, PHINEAS TAYLOR see LIND, JENNY

BARRON KNIGHTS

1753. Barron Knights, The. A Change of Lyric. London: E.M.I.
       Music Publishing, 1979. 52p., illus.
          Texts of their popular song parodies.

BASIE, COUNT

1754. Dance, Stanley. The World of Count Basie. New York: Srib-
       ner's; London: Sidgwick and Jackson, 1980. 399p., illus.,
       bibliog., discog., index.

1755. Horricks, Raymond. Count Basie and His Orchestra: Its Music
       and Musicians. Discography by Alun Morgan. London: Gollancz;
       Secaucus, New Jersey: Citadel Pr., 1957; Westport, Conn.:
       Negro Universities Pr.; Westport, Conn.: Greenwood Pr., 1971.
       320p., illus., discog.
          Includes profiles of twenty-two band members; and forty-
       page discography.

1756. Morgan, Alun. Count Basie. Tunbridge Wells, Kent: Spell-
       mount; New York: Hippocrene Books, 1984. 94p., illus.,
       bibliog., discog. (Jazz Masters)

Discographies

1757. Jepsen, Jorgen Grunnet. <u>Discography of Count Basie</u>. Bio-
       graphical notes by Knud H. Ditlevsen. Brande, Denmark:
       Debut Records, 1959. 32p. <u>2nd. ed.</u>: 1960. 43p.

       ————— (ed.). <u>A Discography of Count Basie</u>. Copenhagen:
       Knudsen, 1969.   p.
       <u>Vol. 1: 1929-1950</u>. By Bo Scherman and Carl A. Haellstrom.
       <u>Vol. 2: 1951-1968</u>. By Jorgen Grunnet Jepsen.

BAY CITY ROLLERS

1758. Allen, Ellis. <u>The Bay City Rollers</u>. St. Albans, Hertford-
       shire: Panther, 1975. 157p., illus.

1759. Ballard, Alan, and Bess Coleman. <u>Rollers in America: Ex-
       clusive Souvenir of the Rollers' Trip to America</u>. London:
       Queen Anne Pr., 1975. 50p., illus.
          Chiefly photographs by Ballard. Text by Coleman.

1760. Golumb, David. <u>Bay City Rollers Picture Scrapbook</u>. All
       words by Tony Jasper. London: Queen Anne Pr., 1975. 96p.,
       illus.
          Chiefly photographs by Golumb.

1761. Paton, Tam. <u>The Bay City Rollers</u>. With Michael Wale.
       London: Everest; New York: Berkley Publishing, 1975. 154p.,
       illus.
          By their manager.

Periodicals

1762. <u>The Official Bay City Rollers Magazine</u>. London. monthly,
       December 1974 - June 1978.

BEACH BOYS

1763. Barnes, Ken. <u>The Beach Boys: a Biography in Words and
       Pictures</u>. Edited by Greg Shaw. New York: Sire Books, 1976.
       56p., illus., discog.

1764. Golden, Bruce. <u>The Beach Boys: Southern California Pastoral</u>.
       San Bernadino, California: Borgo Pr., 1976. 59p., illus.,
       discog. (The Woodstock Series, 1)

1765. Leaf, David. <u>The Beach Boys, and the California Myth</u>. New
       York: Grosset and Dunlap; New York: Today Pr., 1978. 192p.,
       illus.

Beach Boys (cont.)

1766.   Preiss, Byron. <u>The Beach Boys: the Authorized Biography</u>.
        New York: Ballantine, 1979. 160p., illus., discog. <u>Rev.</u>
        <u>ed.</u>: New York: St. Martin's Pr., 1983. 112p., illus., discog.

1767.   Ribowsky, Mark, and Bill Feinberg. <u>The Beach Boys</u>. New
        York: Simon and Schuster, 1985. 240p., illus., discog.

1768.   Tobler, John. <u>The Beach Boys</u>. London; New York: Hamlyn/
        Phoebus, 1978. 96p., illus., discog.

                         Discographies

1769.   Elliott, Brad. <u>Surf's Up! The Beach Boys on Record, 1961-</u>
        <u>1981</u>. Ann Arbor, Michigan: Pierian Pr., 1981. 512p., illus.,
        bibliog., indexes. (Rock and Roll Reference Series, 6)
        Includes unreleased and promotional material.

                          Periodicals

1770.   <u>Add Some Music</u>. Box 10405, Elmwood, Conn. 06110. irreg.,
        1979- .

1771.   <u>Beach Boys Stomp</u>. Edited by Mike Grant and Roy Goodge.
        Wealdstone, Middlesex. irreg., later bi-monthly, June 1977- .

1772.   <u>Pet Sounds</u>. Edited by David Leaf. 1546 South Saltaire, Los
        Angeles, California 90025. irreg., 1977- .

BEAT

1773.   Halasa, Malu. <u>The Beat: Twist and Crawl</u>. London: Eel Pie,
        1981. 120p., illus., discog.

BEATLES

                      (i) Bibliographies

1774.   Eva, Lesley. <u>The Beatles: a Twentieth Anniversary Booklist</u>.
        London: Barnet Library Services, 1984. 8p., illus., discog.
            Library booklist. Publishers' details omitted.

1775.   Harry, Bill. <u>Paperback Writers: the History of the Beatles</u>
        <u>in Print</u>. London: Virgin Books, 1984. 192p., illus., index.
            Covers the group collectively, and as individuals. Includ-
        es books and periodicals.

(ii) Autobiographical Material

1776. Beatles, The. The Beatles By Royal Command: Their Own Story
of the Most Fabulous Night of Their Career. London: Daily
Mirror, 1963. 29p., illus.
Account of their 1963 Command Performance at London's
Palladium theater.

1777. ———. Beatles In Their Own Words. Compiled by Miles.
Edited by Pearce Marchbank. Designed by Perry Neville.
London; New York: Omnibus Pr., 1978; London: W.H. Allen,
1982. 128p., illus.
Compiled from press and other interviews.

(iii) Biographies

1778. Bacon, David, and Norman Maslov. The Beatles' England:
There Are Places I'll Remember. San Francisco: 910 Productions; Bromley, Kent: Columbus Books, 1982. 141p., illus.,
bibliog.
Tourist guide to places associated with the group's early
career and personal lives.

1779. Baker, Glenn A. The Beatles Down Under. Glebe, Australia:
Wild and Woolley, 1981. p., illus., discog.
Account of their 1964 tour of Australia and New Zealand.
Includes newspaper reproductions, and interviews with
participants.

1780. Barrow, Tony. Meet The Beatles: an Informal Date in Words
and Personal Album Pictures. Introduced by themselves.
Written and compiled by Tony Barrow. Manchester, England:
World Distributors, 1963. p., illus. (Star Special, 12)
By their press officer.

1781. ———. P.S. We Love You. London: Mirror Books, 1982. 48p.,
illus.
Concentrates on 1962-3.

1782. Omitted.

1783. Bedford, Carol. Waiting For The Beatles: an Apple Scruff's
Story. Poole, Dorset: Blandford Pr., 1984. 296p., illus.,
index.
Account of her life as one of the fans continually gath-
ered at the entrance to Apple Corps' offices; and her relationship with the group, particularly with George Harrison.

1784. Blake, John. All You Needed Was Love: The Beatles After The
Beatles. London: Hamlyn; New York: Putnam's, 1981 (Perigee
Books). 227p., illus.
The lives and careers of the group's members following
its disbandment.

Biographies (cont.)

1785. Boyfriend. The Beatles in Paris. London: Boyfriend, 1964.
       p., illus. (Boyfriend Extra)

1786. ———. The Beatles in Sweden. London: Boyfriend, 1963.
       p., illus. (Boyfriend Extra)

1787. Braun, Michael. Love Me, Do: The Beatles' Progress. Har-
       mondsworth, Middlesex: Penguin, 1964 (Reissued: 1977).
       143p., illus.
            Account of their first tour of the United States, 1964.

1788. Brown, Peter, and Steven Gaines. The Love You Make: an
       Insider's Story of The Beatles. London: Macmillan, 1983;
       London: Pan, 1984. 401p., illus., index.
            Brown was an executive with both N.E.M.S. and Apple.

1789. Burt, Robert (ed.). The Beatles: the Fabulous Story of
       John, Paul, George, and Ringo. London: Octopus; London (as
       The Beatles Story): Phoebus, 1975. 82p., illus., discog.
            Adapted from item 208.

1790. Catone, Marc A. (ed.). As I Write This Letter: an American
       Generation Remembers The Beatles. Ann Arbor, Michigan:
       Pierian Pr., 1982. 256p., illus. (Rock and Roll Remembran-
       ces, 1)
            Letters and drawings from fans, plus memoirs of Beatle-
       mania period.

1791. Cosham, Ralph. The Beatles at Carnegie Hall. London:
       Panther, 1964.   p., illus. (Panther Pictorial)
            Concentrates on their 1964 performances as the first
       rock act to appear at the venue.

1792. Datebook. All About The Beatles. New York: Datebook, 1964.
       p., illus. (A Datebook Special)

1793. Davies, Hunter. The Beatles: the Authorized Biography.
       London: Heinemann, 1968. 374p., illus., discog. New York:
       McGraw-Hill, 1968. 357p., illus., discog. Harmondsworth,
       Middlesex: Penguin, 1968. 374p., illus., discog. New York:
       Dell, 1968. 405p., illus., discog. Rev. ed.: London: May-
       flower, 1978. 400p., illus., discog. New York: McGraw-Hill,
       1978. 381p., illus., discog.
            Revised edition also has different illustrations.

1794. Davis, Edward E. (ed.). The Beatles Book. New York: Cowles
       Book Company, 1968. 224p., discogs.
            Collection of fourteen essays, for and against the group.

1795. De Blasio, Edward. All About The Beatles. New York:
       McFadden-Bartell, 1964. 96p., illus. (McFadden Books)

1796. DiLello, Richard. The Longest Cocktail Party. Chicago:
       Playboy Pr., 1972; London: Charisma Books, 1973. 325p.,

illus., discog. Ann Arbor, Michigan: Pierian Pr., 1984.
p., illus., discog., index.
Insider's account of Apple Corps, and the reasons for its failure. Pierian Pr. edition also has new introduction.

1797. Doney, Malcolm. Lennon and McCartney. Tunbridge Wells, Kent: Midas Books, 1981; London; New York: Omnibus Pr., 1983. 128p., illus., discog.
Their careers, together and separate.

1798. Epstein, Brian. A Cellarful of Noise. London: Souvenir Pr.; Adelaide, South Australia: Rigby; New York: Doubleday; New York: Pyramid Books, 1964. 132p., illus. London: New English Library, 1965. 132p., illus. (Four Square Books) New ed.: London: New English Library, 1981. 119p. Ann Arbor, Michigan: Pierian Pr., 1984. 168p., illus., index. (Rock and Roll Remembrances, 4)
Memoirs (ghostwritten by Beatles' public relations manager, Derek Taylor) of their manager. Includes accounts of other acts managed by Epstein. Pierian Pr. edition has new introduction.

1799. Evans, Mike. Nothing To Get Hung About. Liverpool: City of Liverpool Public Relations Office, 1975. p., illus.
Short account of the group's association with the City.

1800. ————, and Ron Jones. In the Footsteps of The Beatles. Liverpool: Tourism Development Office, Merseyside County Council, 1981. p., illus.
Touring guide to places in the City associated with the group's early career, and their lives.

1801. Fabulous. The Best of The Beatles From "Fabulous." London: I.P.C. Magazines, 1964. unpaged, illus.
Material previously published in Fabulous.

1802. ————. "Fabulous" Goes All Beatles. London: I.P.C. Magazines, 1964. unpaged, illus.
Features and illustrations aimed at adolescents.

1803. Fast, Julius. The Beatles: the Real Story. New York: Putnam's; New York: Berkley Publishing, 1968. 252p., illus.

1804. Freeman, Robert. The Beatles in America: Their Own Exclusive Story and Pictures. Photographs by the Beatles' special photographer, Robert Freeman. London: Daily Mirror, 1964. 32p., illus.
Chiefly illustrated. Account of their 1964 tour.

1805. ————. Beatles Limited. Designed and photographed by Robert Freeman. London: Newnes, 1964. 26p., illus.
Large-format photograph collection.

1806. ————. Yesterday: Photographs of The Beatles. Foreword by Paul McCartney. London: Weidenfeld and Nicolson, 1983. 96p., illus.

Biographies (cont.)

1807. Friede, Goldie, Robin Titone, and Sue Weiner. The Beatles,
       A to Z. New York: Methuen, 1980; London: Eyre-Methuen, 1981.
       248p., illus., discog.
           Biographical information in encyclopedia format. Over
       three thousand entries on all aspects of their careers as a
       group, and separately.

1808. Friedman, Rick (comp.). The Beatles: Words Without Music.
       Introduction by Joe O'Brien. New York: Grosset and Dunlap,
       1968. 80p., illus.
           Question-and-answer format. Quotations about and by the
       group.

1809. Hamblett, Charles. Here Are The Beatles. London: New English
       Library, 1964. 127p., illus. (Four Square Books)
           Collection of illustrations. Includes comment from the
       group, and others.

1810. Harry, Bill. The Beatles' Who's Who. London: Aurum Pr.,
       1982.   p., illus.
           Brief profiles of individuals associated with the group.
       Arranged in chronological, not alphabetical, order. No index.

1811. Hoffman, Dezo. The Beatles Conquer America: the Photographic
       Record of Their First American Tour. Edited by Roxane Street-
       er. London: Virgin Books, 1984. 160p., illus.
           Contains previously unpublished illustrations.

1812. ———. With The Beatles: the Historic Photographs of Dezo
       Hoffman. Edited and designed by Pearce Marchbank. London:
       Omnibus Pr., 1982; New York: Delilah, 1983. 126p., illus.
           Covers 1962-64.

1813. Humphery-Smith, Cecil Raymond, Michael G. Heenan, and Jenifer
       Mount. Up The Beatles' Family Tree. Illustrated by John
       Bainbridge. Northgate, Cambridgeshire: Achievements Limited,
       1966. 12p., illus.
           Genealogical study.

1814. Kahn, Stephen (ed.). The Beatles. New York: Beatle Publish-
       ing, 1964. 65p., illus.

1815. Larkin, Rochelle. The Beatles: Yesterday, Today, Tomorrow.
       New York: Scholastic Book Services, 1974. 108p., illus.

1816. Leach, Samuel R. The Beatles On Broadway. Manchester,
       England: World Distributors, 1964. 32p., illus.
           Account of their first United States tour, 1964.

1817. ———. Follow the Merseybeat Road. Liverpool: Eden Public-
       ations, 1984. 32p., illus.
           Memoir of their early career and lives. Includes guide to
       locations in Liverpool associated with the group.

1818.   Leaf, Earl (ed.). The Original Beatles Book: Delicious
        Insanity, Where Will It End? Los Angeles: Petersen Publish-
        ing, 1964. unpaged, illus. (A Petersen Specialty Publication)

1819.   McCabe, Peter, and Robert D. Schonfeld. Apple To the Core:
        the Unmaking of The Beatles. New York: Pocket Books, 1972.
        200p., illus. London: Martin, Brian, and O'Keeffe, 1972;
        London: Sphere, 1973. 209p.
           Account of the rise and fall of Apple Corps. Emphasis on
        financial aspects.

1820.   Maugham, Patrick. The Beatles. Photographs by Dezo Hoffman.
        London: Pyx Publications; New York: Lancer, 1964. 30p., illus.

1821.   Mellers, Wilfrid. Twilight of the Gods: The Beatles in
        Retrospect. London: Faber and Faber; New York: Viking Pr.,
        1974; New York: Schirmer Books, 1975. 215p., discog., index.
           Musicological study.

1822.   Noebel, David A. The Beatles: a Study in Drugs, Sex, and
        Revolution. Tulsa, Oklahoma: Christian Crusade Publications,
        1969. 64p., bibliog. refs.
           Contends that the group are part of a Communist-inspired
        revolutionary plot.

1823.   ———. Communism, Hypnotism, and The Beatles: an Analysis
        of the Communist Use of Music: the Communist Master Music
        Plan. Tulsa, Oklahoma: Christian Crusade Publications, 1965.
        16p., bibliog. refs. Rev. ed.: 1965. 26p., bibliog. refs.
           Contends that the group use Pavlovian techniques to prepare
        American adolescents for a Communist takeover. Text has 168
        footnotes.

1824.   Norman, Philip. Shout: the True Story of The Beatles. Lon-
        don: Elm Tree; New York: Simon and Schuster, 1981. 400p.,
        illus. London: Corgi, 1982. 426p., illus.
           Definitive biography, to December, 1980. Emphasis on
        period up to 1970 disbandment.

1825.   Parkinson, Norman. The Beatles Book. Words by Maureen Cleave.
        London: Hutchinson, 1964. 32p., illus.
           Photograph collection.

1826.   Podell, Jack J. (ed.). The Beatles Are Here. New York:
        McFadden-Bartell, 1964. 72p., illus.

1827.   Ranson, Arthur, and Angus P. Allan. The Beatles: Their Story
        in Pictures. London: I.T.V. Books, 1982. 49p., illus. (A
        T.V. Times/Look-In Special)
           Drawings by Ranson; text by Allan. Aimed at adolescents.

1828.   Romeo. Beatle-Opaedia. London: Romeo, 1964. 48p., illus.
           Part-work, published as supplement to Romeo. Biographical
        information aimed at adolescents.

Biographies (cont.)

1829. Ross, Carol (ed.). <u>The Beatles Are Back</u>. New York: McFadden-
       Bartell, 1964.   p., illus.

1830. Scaduto, Anthony. <u>The Beatles</u>. New York: New American
       Library, 1968. 157p., illus. (Signet Books)

1831. Schaffner, Nicholas. <u>The Beatles Forever</u>. Harrisburg, Penn-
       sylvania: Stackpole Company, 1977; New York; London: McGraw-
       Hill, 1978. 224p., illus., bibliog., discog., index.
       The group collectively, and as individuals.

1832. ————. <u>The Boys From Liverpool</u>. London; New York: Methuen,
       1980.   p., illus., bibliog., index.
       Aimed at younger readers.

1833. Schaumburg, Ron. <u>Growing Up With The Beatles: an Illustrated
       Tribute</u>. New York: Pyramid Publications, 1976; New York;
       London: Harcourt, Brace, Jovanovich, 1978 (A Harvest/H.B.J.
       Book). 192p., illus.
       Chronology of the group, linked with the author's youth as
       a Beatle fan in Kansas City.

1834. Schultheiss, Thomas (comp.). <u>A Day in the Life: The Beatles
       Day-by-Day, 1960-1970</u>. Ann Arbor, Michigan: Pierian Pr.,
       1980 (Rock and Roll Reference Series, 3); London: Omnibus Pr.,
       1982. 354p., index. New York: Quick Fox, 1983. 336p., illus.
       Chronology.

1835. Shepherd, Billy (<u>pseud. of</u> Peter Jones). <u>The True Story of
       The Beatles</u>. Illustrated by Bob Gibson. London: Beat Pub-
       lications; New York: Bantam, 1964. 224p., illus.

1836. Shipper, Mark. <u>Paperback Writer: a New History of The Beatles</u>.
       Los Angeles: Marship Publications, 1977; New York: Grosset
       and Dunlap; London: New English Library, 1978. 254p., illus.
       Parody of their career.

1837. Spence, Helen. <u>The Beatles Forever</u>. New York: McGraw-Hill,
       1982; Guildford, Surrey: Colour Library Books, 1984. unpaged,
       illus.
       Covers to 1967.

1838. Stokes, Geoffrey. <u>The Beatles</u>. Introduction by Leonard
       Bernstein. Art direction by Bea Feitler. New York: Times
       Books, 1980; London: W.H. Allen/Omnibus Pr., 1981. 246p.,
       illus. (A <u>Rolling Stone</u> Pr. Book)
       Includes two separate dust jackets by Andy Warhol.

1839. Sutton, Margaret. <u>We Love You, Beatles</u>. Illustrated by the
       author. Garden City, New York: Doubleday, 1971. 48p., illus.
       Picture-book biography, aimed at younger readers.

1840. Swenson, John. <u>Yesterday Seems So Far Away</u>. New York: Zebra
       Books, 1977.   p., illus.

1841. Taylor, Derek. <u>As Time Goes By: Living in the Sixties With
       John Lennon, Paul McCartney, George Harrison, Ringo Starr,
       Brian Epstein, Allen Klein, Mae West, Brian Wilson, The
       Byrds, Danny Kaye, The Beach Boys, One Wife, and Six Children
       in London, Los Angeles, New York City, and On the Road</u>.
       London: Davis-Poynter, 1973. 159p., illus., index. San
       Francisco: Straight Arrow Books, 1973. 223p., illus. London:
       Abacus, 1974. 182p., illus., index. Ann Arbor, Michigan:
       Pierian Pr., 1984. 159p., illus., index. (Rock and Roll
       Remembrances, 3)
            Memoir and reflections by the group's public relations
       officer. Pierian Pr. edition has new introduction.

1842. ————. <u>Fifty Years Adrift</u>. Edited and introduction by
       George Harrison. Guildford, Surrey: Genesis Publications,
       1984.   p., illus.
            Memoir. Includes reproductions of letters and other
       memorabila of his involvement with The Beatles. Limited
       edition of two thousand copies.

1843. Tobler, John. <u>The Beatles</u>. London: Deans International
       Publishing, 1984. 192p., illus., bibliog., discog., index.
            For sale only in Britain's W.H. Smith bookstores.

1844. Van Fulpen, Har. <u>The Beatles: an Illustrated Diary</u>. London:
       Plexus, 1984. 192p., illus.
            Chronology. Originally published in Holland as <u>Beatles
       Dagboek</u>.

1845. Williams, Allan. <u>The Man Who Gave The Beatles Away</u>. As told
       to William Marshall. London: Elm Tree Books/Hamish Hamilton;
       New York: Macmillan, 1975; Sevenoaks, Kent: Coronet, 1976;
       New York: Ballantine, 1977. 236p., illus.
            Memoir of the group's early career, by their first manager.

1846. Woffinden, Bob. <u>The Beatles Apart</u>. London; New York: Proteus,
       1981. 145p., illus., bibliog., discog.
            Their lives and careers since the group's disbandment.

                        (iv) Lyric Collections

1847. Beatles, The. <u>The Beatles' Illustrated Lyrics</u>. Edited by
       Alan Aldridge. London: Macdonald; New York: Delacorte Pr.;
       New York: Dell, 1969. Reissued: New York: Delacorte Pr.,
       1979; New York: Dell, 1980; London: Macdonald/Futura, 1980.
       156p., illus., index.
            Lyrics illustrated with artwork by numerous artists,
       photographers, and illustrators.

       ————. <u>The Beatles' Illustrated Lyrics, Number Two</u>. Edited
       by Alan Aldridge. London: B.P.C. Publishing; New York: Dela-
       corte Pr.; New York: Dell, 1971. Reissued: New York: Dela-

Lyric Collections (cont.)

corte Pr., 1979; London: Macdonald/Futura; New York: Dell, 1980. 127p., illus., index.

1848. ———. The Beatles' Lyrics. London: Futura, 1975. 208p., illus.
       Text identical with item 1847; most of the original illustrations dropped.

1849. ———. The Beatles' Lyrics Complete. London: Futura, 1974. 186p.
       Text identical with item 1848, but without illustrations.

1850. ———. The Beatles' Lyrics Illustrated. Introduction by Richard Brautigan. New York: Dell, 1975. 208p., illus., index.
       Text identical with item 1847, but with different illustrations (black-and-white photographs of the group); cover design of original edition retained.

1851. ———. The Beatles' Years: the Story of the Most Famous Group in Modern Times, Told Through Seventy of Their Greatest Songs. Edited by Ray Connolly. London: Collier-Macmillan; New York: Macmillan, 1972. 132p., illus.
       Lyric collection.

1852. ———. Complete Works. Amsterdam: Thomas Rap, 1968. 176p., illus.
       Lyric collection.

1853. ———. Golden Beatles. London: Northern Songs, 1966. unpaged, illus.
       Texts of fifty of their hits.

1854. Campbell, Colin, and Allan Murphy. Things We Said Today: the Complete Lyrics, and a Concordance to the Beatles' Songs, 1960-1970. Ann Arbor, Michigan: Pierian Pr., 1982. 430p., illus. (Rock and Roll Reference Series, 4)
       Lyrics of 189 songs recorded by the group. Concordance by keywords. Includes word frequency lists, and reproductions of handwritten original texts.

1855. Cowan, Philip. Behind The Beatles' Songs: the Book That Sets the Record Straight. London: Polytantric Pr., 1978; London: Landesman Publishing, 1979. 63p., illus., discog.
       Explanation, through quotations from group members, of the original intentions and meanings of key songs.

(v) Discographies

1856. Carr, Roy, and Tony Tyler. The Beatles: an Illustrated Record. London: New English Library; New York: Harmony Books,

1975. 128p., illus. New ed.: London: Triune Books, 1978.
128p., illus. New expanded ed.: London: New English Library; New York: Harmony Books, 1978. 136p., illus.
Bio-discography. New expanded edition reissued 1981,
with update to include Lennon's death.

1857. Castleman, Harry, and Walter J. Podrazik. All Together, Now:
the First Complete Beatles Discography, 1961-1975. Ann
Arbor, Michigan: Pierian Pr., 1976; New York: Ballantine,
1980. 385p., illus., filmog., indexes. (Rock and Roll
Reference Series, 1)
Chronological arrangement. Includes all legitimate
releases, and variants, with chart movements. Supplemented
by item 1858.

1858. ————. The Beatles Again. Ann Arbor, Michigan: Pierian
Pr., 1978. 280p., illus., index. (Rock and Roll Reference
Series)
Continues and supplements item 1857. Index covers both
volumes in one sequence. Also includes complete touring
schedule of the group. Continued by item 1859.

1859. ————. The End of The Beatles? Ann Arbor, Michigan:
Pierian Pr., 1984.   p., illus., filmog., indexes. (Rock
and Roll Reference Series)
Continues item 1858. Covers latter years of the group,
also individual releases in Britain and the United States.
Indexes cover all volumes in one sequence for each index.

1860. Fenick, Barbara. Collecting The Beatles: an Introduction
and Price Guide to Fab Four Collectables, Records, and
Memorabilia. Ann Arbor, Michigan: Pierian Pr., 1982.   p.,
illus. (Rock and Roll Reference Series, 7)
Includes appendix listing approximately one hundred
merchandising licenses granted 1963-64.

1861. Grasso, Rosario. The Beatles in Italy, 1963-1980. Catania,
Italy: Edizioni Dafni, 1981. 320p., illus.
Text in English and Italian. Complete listing of Italian
releases, including variants. Covers group and individual
performances.

1862. Guzek, Arno. Beatles Discography. Copenhagen: The Author,
1976. 72p.

1863. Hansen, Jeppe. Beatles-Diskografi, 1961-1972. Slagelse,
Denmark: Slagelse Centralbibliotek, 1973. 33p. (Musiknyt
fra Slagelse Centralbibliotek)
Text in Danish.

1864. Howlett, Kevin. The Beatles at the Beeb: the Story of Their
Radio Career, 1962-65. London: British Broadcasting Corporation, 1982; Ann Arbor, Michigan: Pierian Pr., 1984. 128p.,
illus., bibliog., discog., index.
Based on British radio program, 1982, produced by the
author. Details of sessions. Includes listing of programs.
Pierian Pr. edition has new introduction.

Discographies (cont.)

1865. Leppert, Neville. The Beatles A to Z. Liverpool: The
       Author, 1976.   p.
            Lists and reviews all tracks released by the group.

1866. Reinhart, Charles. You Can't Do That! Beatles Bootlegs and
       Novelty Records, 1963-1980. Ann Arbor, Michigan: Pierian
       Pr., 1981. 450p., illus., indexes. (Rock and Roll Reference
       Series, 5)
            Includes over nine hundred bootleg and counterfeit records,
       also over four hundred novelty items.

1867. Russell, Jeff. The Beatles Album File and Complete Discog-
       raphy. Poole, Dorset: Blandford Pr., 1982. 223p., illus.,
       index.
            Includes variant releases.

   *   Stannard, Neville, and John Tobler. The Complete Beatles
       Record Guide.
            * Cited below as items 1868 and 1869. (Combined in slip-
       case with no textual amendment.)

1868. ———. The Long and Winding Road: a History of The Beatles
       on Record. By Neville Stannard; edited by John Tobler.
       London: Virgin Books, 1982. 239p., illus., bibliog. Rev.
       ed.: London: Virgin Books, 1983. 256p., illus., bibliog.
            Annotated.

1869. ———. Working Class Heroes: the History of The Beatles'
       Solo Recordings. London: Virgin Books, 1983. 240p., illus.,
       bibliog., index.
            Includes releases by Yoko Ono, also listings of group
       members' involvement with recordings by other artists.

1870. Wallgren, Mark. The Beatles on Record. New York: Simon and
       Schuster, 1982. 336p., illus., index. (A Fireside Book)
            Emphasis on United States releases. Includes chart
       listings for the United States, Britain, and West Germany.

                        (vi) Motion Pictures

1871. Harry, Bill (comp.). Beatlemania: an Illustrated Filmography.
       London: Virgin Books, 1984. 224p., illus.
            Catalog of every motion picture, television, promotional
       clip, and video appearance as a group and as individuals.
       Gives star ratings; also casts and credits.

Individual Productions

Get Back

1872. Cott, Jonathan, and David Dalton. The Beatles Get Back.
London: Apple Publishing, 1970. unpaged, illus.
Originally issued, in Britain only, with their album Get
Back; later available separately. Contains lyrics and
dialog from the production; with comment from the authors,
and photographs by Ethan Russell.

A Hard Day's Night

1873. Beatles, The. The Beatles, Starring in "A Hard Day's Night."
Manchester, England: World Distributors, 1964. 34p., illus.
Official United Artists souvenir. Account of the making
of the motion picture, and the composition of the soundtrack
music.

1874. Burke, John. A Hard Day's Night. London: Pan, 1964. 121p.,
illus. New York (as A Hard Day's Night: a Novel): Dell,
1964. 156p., illus.

1875. DiFranco, J. Philip (ed.). The Beatles in Richard Lester's
"A Hard Day's Night" -- a Director's Notebook. Introduction
by Andrew Sarris. New York: Chelsea House, 1977; New York:
Penguin, 1978.   p., illus.
The complete shooting script, including out-takes. Also
includes interview with Lester, and over 1,100 black-and-
white photographs to form a complete pictorial record of the
production.

1876. Fabulous. Fab Goes Filming With The Beatles. London: I.P.C.
Magazines, 1964.   p., illus.
Stories from the Hard Day's Night set.

1877. Pop Pics. The Beatles' Film. London: Newnes, 1964. 47p.,
illus.
Account of the production.

1878. Sixteen. The Beatles' Movie. New York: Sixteen Magazine,
1964. 47p., illus.

Help!

1879. Beatles, The. The Beatles in "Help!" Novelization by Al
Hine. London: Mayflower; New York: Random House; New York:
Dell, 1965. 158p., illus.
Adaption of Marc Behur's script for the production. Illus-
trated with stills. Random House edition includes lyrics.

Motion Pictures (cont.)

Sergeant Pepper's Lonely Hearts Club Band

1880. Stigwood, Robert, and Dee Anthony. The Official "Sergeant
       Pepper's Lonely Hearts Club Band" Scrapbook: the Making of
       a Hit Movie Musical. New York: Pocket Books, 1978. 80p.,
       illus. (A Wallaby Book)
          Storyline of the production based on The Beatles' album
       of the same title was created by H. Edwards and Robert
       Stigwood.

Up Against It

1881. Orton, Joe. Up Against It: a Screenplay For The Beatles.
       Introduction by John Lahr. London: Eyre Methuen, 1979.
       70p.
          Script for planned, but abandoned, third motion picture
       to star the group. Theme is surreal, futuristic war between
       the sexes.

Yellow Submarine

1882. Beatles, The. The Beatles in "Yellow Submarine" Starring
       Sergeant Pepper's Lonely Hearts Club Band. Produced by Al
       Brodax. Written by Lee Mintoff. London: New English Lib-
       rary, 1968. 128p., illus.
          Novelization of screenplay by Lee Minoff, Al Brodax, Jack
       Mendelsohn, and Erich Segal. Based on the Beatles' song,
       same title.

1883. Wilk, Max. Yellow Submarine: This Voyage Chartered by Max
       Wilk. New York: New American Library (Signet Books); London:
       New English Library, 1968. 128p., illus.

                         (vii) Miscellanea

1884. Adler, Bill (comp.). Dear Beatles. Illustrated by Ernest
       Marquez. New York: Grosset and Dunlap; New York: Wonder
       Books, 1966. unpaged, illus. (Laugh Books)
          Extracts from letters sent by American fans to the group.

1885. ————. Love Letters to the Beatles. Illustrated by Osborn.
       London: Blond; New York: Putnam's, 1964; New York: Simon and
       Schuster, 1965. 91p., illus.
          Facsimiles of fan letters.

1886. Blessing, Adam. Out of the Mouths of The Beatles. New York:
       Dell, 1964. 64p., illus.
           Collection of Beatles photographs, with humorous captions
       referring to current United States politics.

1887. Evans, Mike. The Art of The Beatles. London: Blond for
       Merseyside County Council, 1984. 144p., illus., index.
           Adaption of catalog of an exhibition of artwork, held at
       the Walker Gallery, Liverpool, 1984.

1888. Goodgold, Edwin, and Dan Carlinsky. The Compleat Beatles
       Quiz Book. New York: Warner Books, 1975. 128p., illus.

1889. Harry, Bill (comp.). The Book of Beatle Lists. Poole,
       Dorset: Blandford Pr.; Poole, Dorset: Javelin Books, 1985.
       224p., illus.

1890. House, Jack. The Beatles Quiz Book. London: Collins, 1964.
       32p., illus.

1891. Saroyan, Aram. The Beatles. Cambridge, Massachusetts: Barn
       Dream Pr., 1971. 4p.
           By minimalist poet. Entire text: "John-Paul-George-Ringo."

                        (viii) Periodicals

1892. Apple Scruff Monthly Magazine. London. monthly, 1970-? (early
       1970's)
           Coverage of The Beatles, also Apple Scruffs' activities.

1893. Beatlefan. Box 33515, Decatur, Georgia 30033. bi-monthly,
       1981- .

1894. The Beatles Book. Edited by Johnny Dean. London. monthly,
       August 1965-December 1969. Reprinted (No. 1-40): London.
       monthly, May 1976-August 1979; Reprinted (No. 41-46)
       (as supplement to Record Collector): London. monthly, Septem-
       ber 1979-February 1980. Reprinted (No. 47-77): London. monthly,
       March 1980-September 1982.
           Detailed coverage of the group's activities until near the
       disbandment. Reprint consists of the original text (including
       covers), with new text in surrounding matter.

1895. ———. Edited by Johnny Dean. London: Diamond Publishing
       Group. monthly, October 1982- . (No. 78- .)
           Continues item 1894. New text.

1896. Beatles Playback. Amsterdam. monthly, 1975-?

1897. Beatles/Stones Newsletter and Collectors' Guide. New York.
       monthly, 1980-?
           Listings of recordings available for sale by collectors.

Periodicals (cont.)

1898. Strawberry Fields Forever. 310 Franklin Street, Box 117,
       Boston, Massachusetts 02110. irreg., 1978- .

1899. Tomorrow Never Knows. 86 Shoebury Road, Thorpe Bay, Essex.
       irreg., 1983- .

1900. The Write Thing. Edited by Barbara Fenick. 3310 Roosevelt
       Ct., Minneapolis, Minnesota 55418. quarterly, 1974- .
            International circulation. Features, rare records, books,
       collectors' items, and sales listings.

                        Individual Group Members

Best, Pete

1901. Best, Pete, and Patrick Doncaster. Beatle! The Pete Best
       Story. London: Plexus; New York: Dell, 1984. 192p., illus.
            Best left the group in 1964, immediately prior to their
       success.

Harrison, George

1902. Harrison, George. I, Me, Mine. Guildford, Surrey: Genesis
       Publications, 1978; New York: Simon and Schuster, 1981;
       London: W.H. Allen, 1982. 402p., illus., index.
            Memoir (taped conversations with Derek Taylor), plus
       original drafts of songs with explanations. Genesis Public-
       ations edition limited to one thousand signed copies.

1903. Michaels, Ross. George Harrison: Yesterday and Today. New
       York; London: Flash Books, 1977. 96p., illus., discog.

Lennon, John, and Yoko Ono

1904. Lennon, John. John Lennon: For the Record. (Interviewed) by
       Peter McCabe and Robert D. Schonfeld. New York: Bantam, 1984.
       100p., illus.

1905. ————. John Lennon In His Own Words. Compiled by Miles.
       Designed by Pearce Marchbank. London; New York: Omnibus Pr.,
       1980. 128p., illus.
            Compiled from press and other interviews.

1906. ————. Lennon Remembers: the "Rolling Stone" Interviews by
       Jann Wenner. San Francisco: Straight Arrow Books; New York:
       Popular Library; London: Talmy Franklin, 1971; Harmondsworth,
       Middlesex: Penguin, 1973 (Reissued: 1980). 189p., illus.
            Conducted December, 1970; originally published in Rolling

Stone, December 1970 - January 1971.

1907. ————, and Yoko Ono. <u>The Lennon Tapes: John Lennon and
Yoko Ono in Conversation With Andy Peebles, 6 December, 1980</u>.
London: British Broadcasting Corporation, 1981. 95p.
    Interview with British disk-jockey, conducted two days
before Lennon's death.

1908. ————. <u>The "Playboy" Interviews With John Lennon and Yoko
Ono</u>. Conducted by David Sheff. Edited by G. Barry Golson.
Chicago: <u>Playboy</u> Pr.; New York: Berkley Publishing, 1982.
256p., illus. London: New English Library, 1982. 193p.,
illus.
    Conducted 1980. One-third of text originally published
in <u>Playboy</u>.

1909. Ono, Yoko (comp.). <u>John Lennon: Summer of 1980</u>. With eight
photographers. London: Chatto and Windus, 1984. 111p.,
illus.
    Photographic record of their activities while recording
their album <u>Double Fantasy</u>, shortly before Lennon's death.
Includes album lyrics.

                    Literary and Artistic Works

1910. Lennon, John. <u>Bag One: a Suite of Lithographs</u>. New York:
Lee Nordness Galleries, 1970. 14p., illus.
    Accompanies exhibition, 1970. Limited edition of three
hundred copies. Fourteen of Lennon's lithographs reproduced,
in folder.

1911. ————. <u>John Lennon In His Own Write</u>. London: Cape; New
York: Simon and Schuster, 1964; London: Penguin, 1980. 78p.,
illus.

1912. ————. <u>The Lennon Play</u>. With Adrienne Kennedy and Victor
Spinetti. London: Cape; New York: Simon and Schuster, 1968.
35p., illus.
    Stage adaption of item 1911.

1913. ————. <u>A Spaniard In the Works</u>. London: Cape; New York:
Simon and Schuster, 1965; London: Penguin, 1980. 95p., illus.

1914. ————. <u>The Penguin John Lennon</u>. Harmondsworth, Middlesex:
Penguin, 1966. 157p., illus.
    Combination of items 1911 and 1913.

1915. ————. <u>John Lennon In His Own Write; and, A Spaniard In the
Works</u>. London: Cape; Wellingborough, Northamptonshire:
Panache, 1981. 157p., illus.
    Combination of items 1911 and 1913.

1916. Ono, Yoko. <u>Grapefruit: a Book of Instructions</u>. Introduction
by John Lennon. London: Peter Owen, 1970. 279p., illus.
    One-line avant-garde poems.

Lennon, John, and Yoko Ono (cont.)

Literary and Artistic Works (cont.)

1917. Sauceda, James. The Literary Lennon. Ann Arbor, Michigan:
       Pierian Pr., 1984.   p., illus. (Rock and Roll Reference
       Series, 9)
          Criticism of Lennon's literary works.

Biographies

1918. Burt, Robert (comp.). John Lennon: a Man Who Cared. The
       Fabulous Story of John Lennon and The Beatles. Ridgefield,
       Conn.: Paradise Pr.; Secaucus, New Jersey: Castle Books,
       1980. 82p., illus.

1919. Carpozi, George, Jr. John Lennon: Death of a Dream. New
       York: Woodhill Pr., 1981.   p., illus.

1920. Coleman, Ray. John Winston Lennon: the Definitive Biography,
       1940-1966. London: Sidgwick and Jackson, 1984. 350p.,
       illus., discog., index.
          Includes appendix of lyrics, 1962-66.

1921. ————. John Ono Lennon: Volume Two, 1967-1980. London:
       Sidgwick and Jackson, 1984. 334p., illus., discog., index.
          Includes appendix of lyrics, 1967-80.

1922. ————. John Lennon. London: Futura, 1985.   p., illus.,
       discog., index.
          Combination of items 1920 and 1921.

1923. Connolly, Ray. John Lennon, 1940-1980: a Biography. London:
       Fontana, 1981. 192p., illus., discog., index.

1924. Corbin, Carole Lynn. John Lennon. New York; London: Franklin
       Watts, 1982 (Reissued: 1984). 86p., illus., bibliog., index.
          Aimed at younger readers.

1925. Doncaster, Patrick. Tribute to John Lennon: His Life, His
       Loves, His Work, and His Death. London: Mirror Books, 1981.
       32p., illus.
          Newspaper format.

1926. Fawcett, Anthony. John Lennon: One Day At a Time. A Personal
       Biography of the Seventies. New York: Grove Pr., 1976;
       London: New English Library, 1977. 192p., illus., bibliog.,
       discog.
          Biography, by his personal advisor. Includes chronology.

       ————. John Lennon, 1940-1980: One Day At a Time. New York:
       Grove Pr.; London: New English Library, 1980. 192p., illus.,
       bibliog., discog.
          Updated reprint; includes events to his death.

1927. Garbarini, Vic, and Brian Cullman. Strawberry Fields
       Forever: John Lennon Remembered. With Barbara Graustack.
       Special introduction by Dave Marsh. New York; London:
       Bantam, 1980. 179p., illus. (A Delilah Book)
           Includes full transcript of Newsweek interview, 1980, in
       which Lennon broke his five-year silence. Also has detailed
       chronology. Text reportedly written in six days.

1928. Green, John. Dakota Days. New York: St. Martin's Pr.,
       1983; London: Comet, 1984. 244p., illus.
           By Lennon's astrologer. Account of Lennon's retirement,
       1975-80.

1929. Harry, Bill. The Book of Lennon. London: Aurum Pr., 1984.
       224p., illus.
           Dictionary. Over seven hundred entries.

1930. Lennon, Cynthia. A Twist of Lennon. London: Star Books,
       1978. 173p., illus.
           By Lennon's first wife.

1931. Liverpool Echo. A Tribute to John Lennon. Liverpool:
       Liverpool Echo, 1980. 48p., illus.

1932. Melody Maker. John Lennon: a "Melody Maker" Tribute.
       London: I.P.C. Specialist and Professional Pr., 1980.   p.,
       illus., bibliog., discog.

1933. Pang, May, and Henry Edwards. Loving John: the Untold Story.
       New York: Warner Books; London: Corgi, 1983. 336p., illus.
           Account of her love-affair with Lennon.

1934. Rolling Stone. The Ballad of John and Yoko. Edited by
       Jonathan Cott and Christine Doudna. Art direction by Bea
       Feitler. Garden City, New York: Doubleday; London: Michael
       Joseph, 1982. 317p., illus., index. (A Rolling Stone Pr.
       Book)
           Material previously published in Rolling Stone.

1935. Ryan, David Stuart. John Lennon's Secret. London: Kozmik
       Press Centre, 1982. 251p., illus., index.
           Biography; no secrets.

1936. Shotton, Pete, and Nicholas Schaffner. John Lennon: In My
       Life. Sevenoaks, Kent: Coronet, 1984. 208p., illus., index.
           Biography, by personal friend.

1937. Sunday Times. John Lennon: the Life and Legend. London:
       Sunday Times, 1980. 63p., illus., discog.

1938. Swenson, John. The John Lennon Story. New York: Nordon
       Publications, 1981.   p., illus.

1939. Tremlett, George. The John Lennon Story. London: Futura,
       1975.   p., illus., discog.

Lennon, John (cont.)

Biographies (cont.)

1940. Tyler, Tony. John Lennon: Working Class Hero. The Life and
Death of a Legend, 1940-1980. London: I.P.C. Magazines,
1980. 37p., illus.

1941. Wiener, Jon. Come Together: John Lennon In His Time. New
York: Random House, 1984; London: Faber and Faber, 1985.
380p., illus., bibliog., index.

1942. Wootton, Richard. John Lennon: an Illustrated Biography.
London: Hodder and Stoughton, 1984. 128p., illus. (Twentieth
Century People)
Aimed at younger readers.

1943. Young, Paul. The Lennon Factor. New York: Stein and Day,
1972. unpaged.
Free-verse presentation.

McCartney, Paul

1944. McCartney, Paul. Give My Regards To Broad Street. London:
M.P.L. Communications/Pavilion Books, 1984. 128p., illus.,
discog.
Accompanies McCartney's motion picture, same title.
Account of the production. Includes song lyrics.

1945. ———. Paul McCartney: Composer/Artist. London: Pavilion
Books, 1981. 272p., illus.
Collection of his songs, drawings, and poems.

1946. ———. Paul McCartney In His Own Words. Compiled by Paul
Gambaccini. Designed by Pearce Marchbank. New York: Flash
Books; London: Omnibus Pr., 1976; New York: Delilah, 1983.
112p., illus.
Interview format memoir.

Biographies

1947. Gelly, David. The Facts About a Pop Group: Featuring Wings.
Photographed by Homer Sykes. Introduction by Paul McCartney.
London: G. Whizzard/Andre Deutsch, 1976; New York: Harmony
Books, 1977. 55p., illus. (A Fact Book)
Case study of the group's operation.

1948. Hipgnosis. Hands Across the Water: Wings Tour, U.S.A. Book
design by Hipgnosis. Photographs by Aubrey Powell. Graphics
and illustrations by George Hardie. Edited by Storm Thorgerson and Peter Christopherson. Limpsfield, East Sussex: Paper
Tiger; Los Angeles: Reed Books, 1978. 156p., illus.

1949. Jasper, Tony. <u>Paul McCartney and Wings</u>. London: Octopus,
       1977. 93p., illus., discog.

1950. McCartney, Mike. <u>Thank You Very Much: Mike McCartney's
       Family Album</u>. London: Arthur Barker, 1981. 192p., illus.
            Memoir of the McCartney family, by Paul McCartney's
       younger brother, himself a successful performer with The
       Scaffold group. Includes over 140 photographs by the
       author.

1951. Mendelsohn, John. <u>Paul McCartney: a Biography in Words and
       Pictures</u>. New York: Sire Books, 1977.   p., Illus.

1952. Ocean, Humphrey. <u>The Ocean View</u>. London: M.P.L., 1983.
       p., illus.
            Belated account of 1976 Wings tour of the United States;
       reproduces the author's diaries and drawings.

1953. Pascall, Jeremy. <u>Paul McCartney and Wings</u>. Edited by Pam-
       ela Harvey. London: Phoebus; Secaucus, New Jersey: Chart-
       well Books, 1977. 96p., illus.

1954. Schwartz, Francie. <u>Body Count</u>. San Francisco: Straight
       Arrow Books, 1972; New York: Pyramid Publications, 1974.
       116p.
            Female Casanova tells of her conquests, particularly
       Paul McCartney.

1955. Tremlett, George. <u>The Paul McCartney Story</u>. London: Futura;
       New York: Popular Library, 1974; London: White Lion, 1976.
       192p., illus., discog.

1956. Welch, Chris. <u>McCartney: the Definitive Biography</u>. London;
       New York: Proteus, 1983. 160p., illus., discog.

                         Linda McCartney

1957. McCartney, Linda. <u>Linda's Pictures: a Collection of Photo-
       graphs</u>. Reviewed by Paul McCartney. New York: Knopf;
       London: Cape, 1976; New York: Ballantine, 1977; London:
       Futura, 1978; London: Pavilion Books, 1982. 155p., illus.
            Photographs of Paul McCartney, and other subjects.

1958. ————. <u>Photographs</u>. London: Pavilion Books, 1982. 133p.,
       illus.
            Black-and-white photographs. Some material originally
       published in item 1957.

   *   Marks, J., and Linda Eastman. <u>Rock and Other Four-Letter
       Words</u>.
            * Cited above as item 138.

McCartney, Paul (cont.)

Periodicals

1959. Club Sandwich. Edited by Paul McCartney. London. irreg.,
       February/March 1977- .
           Informal journal of the Wings "Fun Club."

BEATON, CECIL

   * Beaton, Cecil. Cecil Beaton's Fair Lady.
         * Cited above as item 1173.

1960. Spencer, Charles. Cecil Beaton: Stage and Film Designs.
       New York: St. Martin's Pr.; London: Academy Editions, 1975.
       115p., illus., bibliog.

BECHET, SIDNEY

1961. Bechet, Sidney. Treat It Gentle: an Autobiography. New
       York: Hill and Wang, 1960. 240p., illus., discog., index.
       London: Cassell, 1960. 245p., illus., discog., index.
       London: Transworld Publishers, 1964. 255p., discog. With a
       new preface by Rudi Blesh. New York: Da Capo Pr., 1975
       (Reissued: 1978). 240p., illus., discog., index. (Roots of
       Jazz)
           Includes detailed discography, compiled by David Mylne.

1962. Delaunay, Charles. Histoire de Sidney Bechet. Paris: Vogue,
       1959. 12p.

1963. Mouly, Raymond. Sidney Bechet, nôtre ami. Paris: La Table
       Ronde, 1959. 126p., discog.
           Includes complete discography, compiled by Pierre Lafargue.

Discographies

1964. Jepsen, Jorgen Grunnet. Sidney Bechet: Discography. Lübbecke,
       West Germany: Uhle und Kleimann, 1962. 38p.

1965. Mauerer, Hans J. A Discography of Sidney Bechet. Copenhagen:
       Knudsen, 1969. 2 vols., 83p., indexes.
           Chronological arrangement.

BEE GEES

1966.   Gibb, Barry, Robin Gibb, and Maurice Gibb. Bee Gees: the
        Authorized Biography. As told to David Leaf. New York:
        Delilah; London: Octopus, 1979. 160p., illus., discog.
        Autobiography.

                        Biographies

1967.   Davis, Saul. The Bee Gees Biography. London: Chappell,
        1979. p., illus.

1968.   English, David. The Legend: the Illustrated Story of The
        Bee Gees. London: Quartet, 1984. 144p., illus.

1969.   Munshower, Suzanne. The Bee Gees. New York: Quick Fox,
        1978.   p., illus., discog.

1970.   Pryce, Larry. The Bee Gees. London: Panther, 1979; New
        York: Chelsea House, 1981. 144p., illus.

1971.   Stevens, Kim. The Bee Gees. New York: Quick Fox; London:
        Book Sales, 1978; New York: Jove Publications, 1979. 92p.,
        illus., discog.

1972.   Tatham, Dick. The Incredible Bee Gees. London: Futura,
        1979. 144p., illus., discog.

BEEFHEART, CAPTAIN (pseud. of Don Van Vliet)

1973.   The Life and Times of Captain Beefheart. Manchester, Eng-
        land: Babylon Books, 1980. unpaged, illus., discog.
        Collection of biographical pieces.

BEIDERBECKE, BIX

1974.   Baker, Dorothy Dodds. Young Man With a Horn. Boston:
        Houghton Mifflin, 1938. 243p. London: Gollancz, 1938. 286p.
        New York: Readers' Club, 1943. 243p. New York: Editions for
        the Armed Services, 1943. 224p. New York: Dial Pr., 1944.
           p. New York: Penguin, 1945. 184p. Cleveland: World
        Publishing Company, 1946.   p. New York: New American
        Library, 195?   p. London: Transworld Publishers, 1962.
        158p. (Corgi Books). London: Omnibus Pr., 1978. 128p.
        Novelized biography. Filmed, 1950, as Young Man of Music.

1975.   Berton, Ralph. Remembering Bix: a Memoir of the Jazz Age.
        New York: Harper and Row; London: W.H. Allen, 1974. 428p.,
        illus., bibliog. notes.
        Author's brother performed with Beiderbecke.

Beiderbecke, Bix (cont.)

1976. James, Burnett. Bix Beiderbecke. London: Cassell, 1959;
       New York: A.S. Barnes, 1961. 90p., illus., discog. (Kings
       of Jazz, 4)
          Incorporated into item 1566.

1977. Sudhalter, Richard M., and Philip R. Evans. Bix: Man and
       Legend. New Rochelle, New York: Arlington House; London:
       Quartet, 1974; New York: Schirmer Books, 1975. 512p., illus.,
       discog., indexes.
          Written with the assistance of William Dean-Myatt.
       Discography uses musical notation to delineate different
       takes.

1978. Wareing, Charles Hodson, and George Garlick. Bugles For
       Beiderbecke. London: Sidgwick and Jackson, 1958. 333p.,
       illus., discog.

                         Discographies

1979. Castelli, Vittorio, Evert Ted Kaleveld, and Liborio Pusateri.
       The Bix Bands: a Bix Beiderbecke Disco-Biography. Milan:
       Raretone, 1972. 227p., illus.
          Includes chronology.

1980. Venables, Ralph G.V., and Clifford Jones. Bix. London:
       Discographical Society, 1945. 24p., illus.

BELAFONTE, HARRY

1981. Shaw, Arnold. Belafonte: an Unauthorized Biography. Phila-
       delphia: Chilton Book Company; London: Mayflower, 1960.
       338p., illus., discog. New York: Pyramid Publications, 1960.
       287p., illus., discog.

1982. Steirman, Hy (ed.). Harry Belafonte: His Complete Life
       Story. Associate editor: Anne E. Knoll. New York: Hillman
       Periodicals; London: Strato, 1957. 74p., illus.

BENATAR, PAT

1983. Magee, Doug. Benatar. London; New York: Proteus, 1985.
       128p., illus., discog.

BENEKE, TEX

1984. Garrod, Charles. <u>Tex Beneke and His Orchestra</u>. Spotswood,
       New Jersey: Joyce, 1973.   p.
          Discography.

BENNETT, RICHARD RODNEY, AND MARIAN MONTGOMERY

1985. Bennett, Richard Rodney, and Marian Montgomery. <u>Just Friends</u>
       <u>in Print</u>. London: Novello, 1979.   p., illus.
          The duo tell their story in words, music, and photographs.

BENNETT, TONY

1986. Jasper, Tony. <u>Tony Bennett: a Biography</u>. London: W.H.
       Allen, 1984. 191p., illus., discog.

BERKELEY, BUSBY

1987. Martin, David. <u>The Films of Busby Berkeley</u>. San Francisco:
       The Author, 1965. 28p.

1988. Pike, Bob, and David Martin. <u>The Genius of Busby Berkeley</u>.
       Reseda, California: C.F.S. Books, 1973. 194p., illus.

1989. Thomas, Tony, and Jim Terry. <u>The Busby Berkeley Book</u>. With
       Busby Berkeley. Foreword by Ruby Keeler. Greenwich, Conn.:
       New York Graphic Society; New York: A. and W. Visual Library;
       London: Thames and Hudson, 1973. 184p., illus., index.

BERLIN, IRVING

1990. Ewen, David. <u>The Story of Irving Berlin</u>. Illustrated by
       Jane Castle. New York: Henry Holt, 1950. 179p., illus.

1991. Freedland, Michael. <u>Irving Berlin</u>. London: W.H. Allen;
       New York: Stein and Day, 1974 (Reissued: 1978). 307p.,
       illus., index.

1992. Salsini, Barbara. <u>Irving Berlin: Master Composer of</u>
       <u>Twentieth-Century Songs</u>. Charlotteville, New York: SamHar
       Pr., 1972. 32p., illus. (Outstanding Personalities, 15)
          Aimed at younger readers.

1993. Woollcott, Alexander. <u>The Story of Irving Berlin</u>. New York:
       Putnam's, 1925. 237p., illus., discog. Harmondsworth,
       Middlesex: Penguin, 1939.   p., illus.
          Originally published in <u>The Saturday Evening Post</u>, 1925.

Berlin, Irving (cont.)

Songs

1994. Berlin Music Corporation. The Songs of Irving Berlin.
Arranged Alphabetically, Chronologically, Categorically;
Stage, Screen. New York: Berlin Music Corporation, 1957.
76p., illus.
    Catalog.

1995. Jay, Dave. The Irving Berlin Songography, 1907-1966. New
Rochelle, New York: Arlington House, 1969. 172p., discog.
    Chronological listing of his songs, and their recordings.
No indexes.

BERNSTEIN, LEONARD

1996. Bernstein, Leonard. Findings. London: Macdonald, 1982.
376p., illus.
    Autobiographical and philosophical musings. Includes
classified listing of his works.

1997. ————. The Joy of Music. New York: Simon and Schuster,
1959; London: Weidenfeld and Nicolson, 1960. 303p., illus.
New York: New American Library, 1967. 299p., illus. London:
White Lion, 1974. 303p., illus.
    Collection of his writings, 1954-58.

1998. Briggs, John. Leonard Bernstein: the Man, His Work, and His
World. Cleveland: World Publishing Company, 1961. 274p.,
illus., discog.

1999. Cone, Molly. Leonard Bernstein. Illustrated by Robert
Galster. New York: Crowell, 1970. 30p., illus.
    Aimed at younger readers.

2000. Ewen, David. Leonard Bernstein: a Biography For Young
People. Philadelphia: Chilton, 1960; London (as Leonard
Bernstein): W.H. Allen, 1967. 175p., illus.

2001. Gruen, John, and Ken Heyman. The Private World of Leonard
Bernstein. New York: Viking Pr.; London: Weidenfeld and
Nicolson, 1968. 191p., illus. (A Ridge Pr. Book)
    Profiles Bernstein on vacation in Italy, 1967, and
working in New York.

2002. Robinson, Paul. Bernstein. London: Macdonald, 1982. 152p.,
illus., bibliog., discog. (The Art of the Conductor)

Works

2003. Gottlieb, Jack (comp.). <u>Leonard Bernstein: a Complete</u>
       <u>Catalog of His Works</u>. New York: Amberson Enterprises, 1978.
       68p., illus., bibliog., index.

BERRIGAN, BUNNY

2004. Danca, Vince. <u>Bunny: a Bio-Discography of Jazz Trumpeter</u>
       <u>Bunny Berrigan</u>. Rockford, Illinois: The Author, 1978.   p.,
       illus.

BERRY, CHUCK

2005. Reese, Krista. <u>Chuck Berry: Mister Rock 'n' Roll</u>. London;
       New York: Proteus, 1982. 127p., illus., discog.

BERRY, LEON "CHU"

   *   Evensmo, Jan. <u>The Tenor Saxophone of Leon "Chu" Berry</u>.
          * Cited above as item 1548.

BIERMANN, WOLF

2006. Posadas, J. <u>The Singer Biermann, the Function of Criticism,</u>
       <u>and the Construction of Socialism</u>. London: Revolutionary
       Workers' Party (Trotskyist), 1977. 8p. (A <u>European Marxist</u>
       Publication)
          Marxist attack on East German political protest singer,
       now based in West Germany, after being refused readmission
       to East Germany.

BIG COUNTRY

2007. May, John. <u>Big Country: an Official Biography</u>. London:
       Omnibus Pr., 1985.   p., illus., discog.

BILK, BERNARD "ACKER"

2008. Leslie, Peter, and Patrick Gwynn-Jones. <u>The Book of Bilk</u>;
       <u>or, Forty-One Characters In Search of an Acker</u>. London:
       MacGibbon and Kee, 1961. 96p., illus.

Bilk, Bernard "Acker" (cont.)

2009. Williams, Gordon. <u>Acker Bilk</u>. London: My Fair, 1962. 128p.,
       illus.

BLACK SABBATH

2010. Welch, Chris. <u>Black Sabbath</u>. London; New York: Proteus,
       1982. 96p., illus., discog.

BLACKBURN, TONY

2011. Blackburn, Tony. <u>"The Living Legend." An Autobiography</u>.
       London: W.H. Allen; London: Comet, 1985.   p., illus.
           Autobiography of failed popular singer, now successful
       British disk-jockey.

BLAKE, EUBIE, AND NOBLE SISSLE

2012. Kimball, Robert, and William Bolcom. <u>Reminiscing With
       Sissle and Blake</u>. New York: Viking Pr., 1973. 256p., illus.,
       discog., filmog.
           Includes listings of their songs and productions, with
       full details. Discography includes piano rolls.

2013. Rose, Al. <u>Eubie Blake</u>. Foreword by Eubie Blake. New York:
       Schirmer Books, 1979. 256p., illus., discog., index.

BLAND, JAMES A.

2014. Bland, James A. <u>James A. Bland's De Golden Wedding Songster</u>.
       New York: New York Popular Publishing Company, 1880. 64p.
       (Favorite Dime Songbook, 114)
           Texts of songs. No music.

2015. Daly, John Jay. <u>A Song In His Heart</u>. Illustrated by Marian
       Larer. Philadelphia: Winston, 1951. 102p., illus.
           Includes music of eight of his best-known songs.

2016. Haywood, Charles. <u>James A. Bland: Prince of the Colored
       Songwriters</u>. Flushing, New York: Flushing Historical
       Society, 1944. 8p.

BLISS, PHILIP PAUL

2017. Whittle, Daniel W. (ed.). Memoirs of Philip P. Bliss.
       Contributions by E.P. Goodwin, Ira D. Sankey, and George F.
       Root. Introduction by D.L. Moody. New York; London: Barnes,
       1877. 367p., illus. Rev. ed.: New York: Barnes, 1878.
       374p., illus.
           Includes hymns and other music composed by Bliss.

BLONDIE

2018. Harry, Deborah, Chris Stein, and Victor Bockris. Making
       Tracks: the Rise of Blondie. New York: Dell; London: Elm
       Tree Books, 1982. 192p., illus.
           Leading band members tell its story. Photographs by
       Chris Stein.

Biographies

2019. Bangs, Lester. Blondie. New York: Simon and Schuster (A
       Fireside Book); London: Omnibus, 1980. 96p., illus.

2020. Muir, John (ed.). Blondie. Manchester, England: Babylon
       Books, 1979. unpaged, illus., discog.
           Compilation of press cuttings, with other items.

2021. Schruers, Fred. Blondie. New York: Tempo Books; London:
       Star Books, 1980. 134p., illus.

2022. Wergan, Raymond (ed.). Blondie Gift Book. London: Brown,
       Watson by arrangement with The Blondie Fan Club, 1980.
       unpaged, illus.
           Collection of features on the group.

BLOOD, SWEAT, AND TEARS

2023. Alterman, Lorraine. Blood, Sweat, and Tears. New York:
       Quick Fox, 1971.   p., illus., discog.

BLOOMFIELD, MICHAEL

2024. Ward, Ed. Michael Bloomfield: the Rise and Fall of an
       American Guitar Hero. New York: Cherry Lane Books, 1983.
       135p., illus., discog.

BLUES BROTHERS

2025. Jacklin, Judith, and Tino Insana. Blues Brothers: Private.
       New York: Putnam's, 1980. 150p., illus. (Perigee Books)
            Singing duo John Belushi and Dan Ackroyd. Linked to
       motion picture, The Blues Brothers.

BLUMENTHAL, GEORGE

2026. Blumenthal, George. My Sixty Years in Show Business. As
       told to Arthur H. Menkin. New York: Frederick C. Osberg,
       1936. 336p., illus.
            Associate of Oscar Hammerstein. Involved in straight
       theater, vaudeville, light opera, and grand opera.

BOLAN, MARC (pseud. of Mark Feld)

2027. Bolan, Marc. The Warlock of Love. London: Lupus Music,
       1969. 63p.
            Collection of his poems.

2028. Dicks, Ted, and Paul Platz (comps). Marc Bolan: a Tribute.
       Foreword by Elton John. Introduction by Steve Turner.
       London: Essex House Publishing/Springwood Books, 1978 (Re-
       issued: 1982). 128p., illus., discog.
            Includes words and music of nineteen of his songs.

2029. Melody Maker. Bolan: the Story of a Superstar. London:
       Melody Maker, 1972.   p., illus.

2030. Sinclair, Paul. Marc Bolan. Margate, Kent: The Author, 1979.
       74p., illus., discog.

            ————. Electric Warrior: the Marc Bolan Story. London:
       Omnibus Pr., 1982.   p., illus., discog.

2031. Tremlett, George. The Marc Bolan Story. London: Futura,
       1975. 126p., illus., discog.

2032. Welch, Chris. Marc Bolan: Born To Boogie. With Simon Napier-
       Bell. London: Eel Pie, 1982. 128p., illus.
            Napier-Bell was Bolan's manager.

                           Discographies

2033. Bramley, John, and Shan (pseud.). Marc Bolan: the Illustrated
       Discography. London: Omnibus Pr., 1983. 95p., illus.
            Includes bootleg records.

2034. Williams, Dave. A Wizard in the Underworld. Gloucester,
       England: The Author, 1980.   p.
              Coverage includes John's Children group, and Gloria Jones.

Periodicals

2035. Beyond the Rising Sun. 33 Grove Park Road, Nottingham,
       England. irreg., 1980- .

2036. Cosmic Dancer. Edited by Paul Sinclair. Margate, Kent.
       irreg., (?) 1979-80.

2037. Explosive Mouth. Edited by Ray Sullivan. 20b Powell Road,
       London E5. irreg., 1984- .

2038. Marc Bolan Collectors' Magazine. 236 Torbrex Road, Cumber-
       nauld, Glasgow, Scotland. irreg., 1984- .

2039. The Marc Bolan Magazine. Edited by Gordon Christer.
       Newcastle-upon-Tyne, England. irreg., 1979-80.

2040. Rarn. 72 Paxcroft Way, Ashton Park, Trowbridge, Wiltshire.
       irreg., 1980- .

BOLDEN, BUDDY

2041. Marquis, Donald B. In Search of Buddy Bolden, First Man of
       Jazz. Baton Rouge; London: Louisiana State University Pr.,
       1978; New York: Da Capo Pr., 1980. 176p., illus., bibliog.,
       index.

2042. ———. Finding Buddy Bolden. Goshen, Indiana: Pinchpenny
       Pr., 1978.   p.
              Account of the writing of item 2041.

2043. Ondaatje, Michael. Coming Through Slaughter. New York:
       Norton; Toronto: Anansi, 1976; London: Marion Boyars, 1979.
       159p.
              Novelized biography.

BOND, CARRIE JACOBS

2044. Bond, Carrie Jacobs. The Roads of Melody. New York: D.
       Appleton, 1927. 223p., illus.
              Songwriter's autobiography.

BOND, JESSIE

2045. Bond, Jessie. <u>The Life and Reminiscences of Jessie Bond,</u>
       <u>the Old Savoyard.</u> As told to Ethel MacGeorge. London: John
       Lane, 1930. 243p., illus.

BONEY M

2046. Shearlaw, John, and David Brown. <u>Boney M.</u> London: Hamlyn,
       1979. 140p., illus.

BOOMTOWN RATS

2047. Stone, Peter. <u>The Boomtown Rats: Having Their Picture Taken.</u>
       London: Star Books, 1980. 96p., illus.
          Tour photographs by Stone.

BOONE, DEBBY

2048. Boone, Debby, and Dennis Baker. <u>Debby Boone: So Far.</u> New
       York: Jove Publications, 1982. 240p., illus.
          Autobiography.

BOONE, PAT

2049. Boone, Pat. <u>Between You, Me, and the Gatepost.</u> Englewood
       Cliffs, New Jersey: Prentice-Hall; New York: Dell, 1960.
       153p., illus. Kingswood, Surrey: World's Work, 1961. 167p.,
       illus.
          Memoirs and reflections.

2050. ————. <u>A New Song.</u> Carol Stream, Illinois: Creation House,
       1970. 156p., illus. London (as <u>A Miracle Saved My Family</u>):
       Oliphants, 1971. Nashville: Impact Books, 1981. 192p.,
       illus.
          Reflections on Christian life.

2051. ————. <u>The Pat Boone Book.</u> London: Amalgamated Pr., 1958.
       62p., illus. (Fans' Star Library, 3)

2052. ————. <u>Together: Twenty-Five Years With the Pat Boone</u>
       <u>Family.</u> Photographs selected by Shirley Boone and Laury
       Boone. Nashville: T. Nelson, 1979.   p., illus.

2053. Boone, Shirley. <u>One Woman's Liberation.</u> Carol Stream,
       Illinois: Creation House, 1972. 230p., illus.
          By wife of Pat Boone.

BOWIE, DAVID (pseud. of David Robert Hayward-Jones)

2054. Bowie, David. Bowie In His Own Words. Compiled by Miles.
      London: Omnibus Pr., 1980; New York: Quick Fox, 1981;
      London: W.H. Allen, 1982. 128p., illus.
      Compiled from press and radio interviews.

                              Biographies

2055. Annema, S. Rotterdam, 1983. Leeuwarden, Holland: The
      Author, 1983. 28p., illus.
      Performances described.

2056. Bowie, Angie. Free Spirit. Edited by Don Short. London:
      Mushroom Books, 1981. 176p., illus.
      Account of her failed marriage to Bowie.

2057. Bowie Photomagazine. Manchester, England: Babylon Books,
      1982. unpaged, illus.

2058. Cann, Kevin. David Bowie: a Chronology. London: Vermilion,
      1983. 240p., illus., bibliog., discog., filmog.

2059. Charlesworth, Chris. David Bowie: Profile. London: Proteus;
      New York: Savoy, 1981. 96p., illus., discog.

2060. Claire, Vivian. David Bowie. New York: Flash Books, 1977.
      80p., illus., discog.

2061. Douglas, David. Presenting David Bowie! New York: Pinnacle
      Books, 1975. 212p., illus., discog.

2062. Flippo, Chet. David Bowie's Serious Moonlight: the World
      Tour. Photographs by Denis O'Regan. Garden City, New York:
      Doubleday (Dolphin Books); London: Sidgwick and Jackson,
      1984. 256p., illus.
      Account of his 1983 world tour.

2063. Hopkins, Jerry. Bowie. London: Elm Tree Books, 1985. 255p.,
      illus., discog., filmog.

2064. Kamin, Philip, and Peter Goddard. David Bowie: Out of the
      Cool. New York: Beaufort Books, 1983; London (as David
      Bowie Live): Virgin Books, 1984. 128p., illus.
      Photographs by Kamin; text by Goddard. Account of Bowie's
      1983 appearances in the United States.

2065. Kamp, Thomas R. The Wild-Eyed Boy: a Press Account. The
      Factual, and Sometimes Fictional, Biography of David Bowie.
      Lakewood, Ohio: Country Productions, 1982. 178p., illus.

2066. The Life and Times of Bowie. Manchester, England: Babylon
      Books, 1980. unpaged, illus., discog.
      Chiefly press cuttings, and illustrations.

Bowie, David (cont.)

2067.   Lynch, Kate. David Bowie: a Rock 'n' Roll Odyssey. London;
        New York: Proteus, 1984. 181p., illus., discog.

2068.   Marchbank, Pearce (comp.). Bowiepix. London; New York:
        Omnibus Pr., 1983. 32p., illus.
            Pictures and quotations from various stages of his career.

2069.   Matthew-Walker, Robert. David Bowie: Theatre of Music.
        Bourne End, Buckinghamshire: Kensal, 1985. 192p., illus.,
        discog.
            Critical study.

2070.   Melody Maker. The Book of Bowie. London: I.P.C. Magazines,
        1978. 65p., illus.

2071.   Miles (pseud. of Barry Miles). David Bowie Black Book: the
        Illustrated Biography. With Full Discography. London:
        Omnibus Pr.; New York: Quick Fox, 1981. 128p., illus.,
        discog.

2072.   Pitt, Kenneth. David Bowie: the Pitt Report. London:
        Design Music, 1983. 224p., illus. Rev. ed.: London:
        Omnibus Pr., 1985.   p., illus.
            Account of Bowie's early career, by his ex-manager.

2073.   Tremlett, George. The David Bowie Story. London: Futura;
        New York: Warner Paperback Library, 1975. 158p., illus.

                        Discographies

2074.   Bruna, Robert. David Bowie: a Collectors' Discography,
        1964-1982. Aubagne, France: The Author, 1983.   p.
            Text in French and English. Lists every known variant
        release; with record values in French, British, and United
        States currencies.

2075.   Carr, Roy, and Charles Shaar Murray. David Bowie: an
        Illustrated Record. London: Eel Pie; New York: Avon, 1981.
        120p., illus., discog.
            Bio-discography.

2076.   Fletcher, David Jeffrey. David Robert Jones Bowie: the
        Discography of a Generalist. Chicago: F. Fergeson Product-
        ions, 1979. 123p., illus., filmog. Rev. ed.: Chicago: F.
        Fergeson Productions, 1980. 165p., illus., filmog.

2077.   Hoggard, Stuart. David Bowie: an Illustrated Discography.
        London: Omnibus Pr., 1980; New York: Quick Fox, 1981. 93p.,
        illus. Rev. ed.: London: Omnibus Pr., 1982. 93p., illus.
            Critical discography. Includes bootleg recordings.

————. _Bowie-Changes: the Illustrated David Bowie Story._
Revised and updated by Chris Charlesworth. London: Omnibus
Pr., 1984. 83p., illus.
　　Text completely revised.

Periodicals

2078. _Ashes._ Edited by D. Banks. 9 Barfolds, North Mymms, Hat-
field, Hertfordshire. irreg., 1983- .

2079. _Missing Link._ Edited by Pete and Julia. 5 Braybrooke
Terrace, Hastings, East Sussex. irreg., 1984- .

2080. _Starzone: the International Magazine of David Bowie._ Edited
by David Currie. Box 225, Watford, Hertfordshire. irreg.,
1981- .

BOWLLY, AL

2081. Colin, Sid, and Tony Staveacre. _Al Bowlly._ Foreword by
Denis Norden. London: Elm Tree Books, 1979. 164p., illus.,
discog., index.

2082. Pallett, Ray. _Al Bowlly Pictorial Souvenir._ Leigh-on-Sea,
Essex: The Author, 1975. 48p., illus.

Discographies

* Craigie, Wemyess, and Ray Pallett. _The "Memory Lane" Tribute
to Roy Fox and Al Bowlly._
　　* Cited below as item

2083. Harvey, Clifford M., and Brian Arthur Lovell Rust. _The Al
Bowlly Discography._ Hatch End, Middlesex: Rust's Rare Records,
1965. 52p. _Rev. ed._: 1965.

BOYCE, MAX

2084. Boyce, Max. _"I Was There!"_ Drawings by Gren. London:
Weidenfeld and Nicolson, 1979. 94p., illus.
　　Material by the Welsh singer and entertainer.

2085. ————. _Max Boyce: His Songs and Poems._ Introduction by
Barry John. St. Albans, Hertfordshire: Panther, 1976. 63p.,
illus., discog.
　　Texts of his songs, and other material.

BRADFORD, PERRY

2086. Bradford, Perry. <u>Born With the Blues: the True Story of the</u>
       <u>Pioneering Blues Singers and Musicians in the Early Days of</u>
       <u>Jazz</u>. New York: Oak Publications, 1965. 175p., illus.,
       index.
            Autobiography. Includes words and music of ten of his
       songs.

BRAFF, RUBY

2087. McCarthy, Albert John. <u>Ruby Braff: a Biography, Appreciation,</u>
       <u>Record Survey, and Discography</u>. London: National Jazz Fed-
       eration, 1958. 20p., discog.

BRAXTON, ANTHONY

2088. Rissi, Mathias. <u>Anthony Braxton: a Discography</u>. Adliswil,
       West Germany: The Author, 1977. 16p.

BRECHT, BERTOLT

2089. Brecht, Bertolt. <u>Brecht On Theatre: the Development of an</u>
       <u>Aesthetic</u>. Translation and notes by John Willett. London:
       Methuen; New York: Hill and Wang, 1964. 294p., illus.,
       bibliog.
            Essays extracted from his theatrical writings.

Threepenny Opera

2090. ———. <u>Bertolt Brechts Dreigroschenbuch: Texte, Materialen,</u>
       <u>Dokumente</u>. Edited by Siegfried Unseld. Frankfurt/Main:
       Suhrkamp Verlag, 1973. <u>2 vols</u>., 711p., illus.
            Includes discussion of his sources; and his use of music.

2091. ———. <u>A Penny For the Poor</u>. London: Hale, 1937. 341p.

       ———. <u>Threepenny Novel</u>. Translated by Desmond I. Vesey.
       Verses translated by Christopher Isherwood. London: Bernard
       Harrison, 1958. 396p. Harmondsworth, Middlesex: Penguin,
       1961. 364p. London: Granada, 1981.   p.
            Originally published in Germany as <u>Dreigroschenroman</u>.
       Novelization of the play.

Biographies

2092. Ewen, Frederic. _Bertolt Brecht: His Life, His Art, and His_
       Times. Secaucus, New Jersey: Citadel Pr., 1969; London:
       Calder and Boyars, 1970. 573p., illus.

2093. Hayman, Ronald. _Brecht: a Biography_. London: Weidenfeld
       and Nicolson, 1983. 423p., illus., bibliog., index.

2094. Needle, Jan, and Peter Thomson. _Brecht_. London: Blackwell,
       1981. 252p., illus.

2095. Völker, Klaus. _Brecht: a Biography_. Translated by John
       Howell. New York: Seabury Pr., 1980. 412p., illus.

BREL, JACQUES

2096. Hongre, Brunot, and Paul Lidsky. _"Chansons" Jacques Brel:_
       analyse critique. Paris: Hatier, 1976.   p.

BRICE, FANNY

2097. Katkov, Norman. _The Fabulous Fanny: the Story of Fanny_
       Brice. New York: Knopf, 1953. 337p., illus.
          Includes discussion of other Ziegfeld stars.

BRIDGES, HENRY

  *   Evensmo, Jan. _The Tenor Saxophones of Henry Bridges, Robert_
       Carroll, Hershel Evans, and Johnny Russell.
          * Cited above as item 1548.

BRITTAN, BELLE

2098. Fuller, Hiram. _Belle Brittan On a Tour, At Newport, and Here_
       and There. New York: Derby and Jackson, 1858. 359p.

BROONZY, WILLIAM "BIG BILL"

2099. Broonzy, William. _Big Bill Blues: William Broonzy's Story_.
       As told to Yannick Bruynoghe. Illustrated by Paul Oliver.
       London: Cassell, 1955. 139p., illus., discog. _2nd. ed._:
       New York: Oak Publications, 1964. 176p., illus., discog.
          Autobiography. Discography for Cassell edition by Albert
       John McCarthy; for Oak Publications edition by McCarthy, Ken
       Harrison, and Ray Asbury.

BROWN, CLIFFORD

2100.   Montalbano, Pierre. <u>Clifford Brown: Biography and Discog-</u>
        <u>raphy</u>. Marseille, France: Jazz Club Aix-Marseille, 1969.
        12p.

BROWN, LES

2101.   Edwards, Ernie, George Hall, and Bill Korst. <u>Les Brown</u>
        <u>Discography, 1936-1964</u>. Whittier, California: Jazz Discog-
        raphies Unlimited, 1965. 52p.

        ————. <u>Les Brown and His Bands of Renown</u>. Whittier,
        California: Jazz Discographies Unlimited, 1966. 53p.

2102.   Garrod, Charles. <u>Les Brown and His Orchestra</u>. Spotswood,
        New Jersey: Joyce, 1973.   p.
            Discography.

BROWNE, JACKSON

2103.   Wiseman, Rich. <u>Jackson Browne: the Story of a Hold Out</u>.
        Garden City, New York: Doubleday, 1982. 192p., illus.
        (Dolphin Books)

BRUBECK, DAVE

2104.   <u>Dave Brubeck</u>. New York: Broadcast Music, 1961. 20p.

BRUMAS

2105.   Freuh, Joanna. <u>Brumas</u>. Oberlin, Ohio: Fresh Cut Pr., 1983.
        36p., illus.

BRUNIES, GEORGE

2106.   Gaze, Richard, and Dorothy Gaze. <u>George Brunies: His Story</u>.
        Edited by William H. Miller. Melbourne, Victoria: William
        H. Miller, 1946. 8p.

2107.   Miller, William H. <u>George Brunies Special</u>. Melbourne,
        Victoria: The Author, 1945. 8p.

BRYANT, ANITA

2108. Bryant, Anita. <u>Amazing Grace</u>. Old Tappan, New Jersey:
       Revell, 1971. 127p. New York: Bantam, 1974. 132p.
       Autobiography. Emphasis on her Christian outlook.

2109. ———. <u>Bless This House</u>. Old Tappan, New Jersey: Revell,
       156p., illus.
       Her Christian life.

2110. ———. <u>Mine Eyes Have Seen the Glory</u>. Old Tappan, New
       Jersey: Revell, 1970. New York: Bantam, 1972. 159p., illus.
       Autobiography.

BRYANT, BILLY

2111. Bryant, Billy. <u>Children of Ol' Man River: the Life and
       Times of a Show-Boat Trouper</u>. New York: L. Furman, 1936.
       303p., illus.

BUCHANAN, JACK

2112. Marshall, Michael. <u>Top Hat and Tails: the Story of Jack
       Buchanan</u>. Foreword by Fred Astaire. London: Elm Tree
       Books, 1978. 271p., illus., bibliog., discog., index.

BUCKS FIZZ

2113. Barrow, Tony. <u>Bucks Fizz</u>. London; New York: Proteus, 1984.
       32p., illus., discog.

BUE, PAPA (<u>pseud. of</u> Arne Bue Jensen)

2114. Bendix, Ole. <u>Papa Bue</u>. Copenhagen: Erichsen, 1962. 72p.

BUSH, KATE

2115. Bush, Kate. <u>Leaving My Tracks</u>. London: Sidgwick and Jack-
       son, 1982. 144p., illus., discog.
       Autobiography.

2116. Kerton, Paul. <u>Kate Bush: an Illustrated Biography</u>. London;
       New York: Proteus, 1980. 111p., illus., discog.

Bush, Kate (cont.)

2117. Vermorel, Fred, and Judy Vermorel. <u>Kate Bush: Princess of
       Suburbia</u>. London: Target Books, 1980. 34p., illus.

2118. ─────. <u>The Secret Life of Kate Bush</u>. London; New York:
       Omnibus Pr., 1983.   p., illus.
          Attempts to find common threads within her life and work.
       Little biographical information.

                              Periodicals

2119. <u>Homeground</u>. 55 Whippendell Way, Orpington, Kent. bi-monthly,
       1984- .

BYGRAVES, MAX

2120. Bygraves, Max. <u>"I Wanna Tell You a Story!" An Autobiography</u>.
       London: W.H. Allen, 1976. 195p., illus., index.

  *   ─────. <u>The Milkman's On His Way</u>.
          * Cited below as item 4544.

BYNG, DOUGLAS

2121. Byng, Douglas. <u>As You Were: Reminiscences</u>. London: Duck-
       worth, 1970. 176p., illus., index.

BYRDS

2122. Rogan, John. <u>Timeless Flight: the Definitive Biography of
       The Byrds</u>. London: Scorpion Publications, 1980. 160p.,
       illus., discog.

CAHN, SAMMY

2123. Cahn, Sammy. <u>I Should Care: the Sammy Cahn Story</u>. New York:
       Arbor House, 1974. 318p., illus., index. London: W.H. Allen,
       1975. 253p., illus., index.

  *   ─────. <u>The Songwriter's Rhyming Dictionary</u>.
          * Cited below as item 3831.

CALLOWAY, CAB

2124.   Calloway, Cab, and Bryant Rollins. Of Minnie The Moocher
        and Me. Illustrations selected and edited by John Shearer.
        New York: Crowell, 1976. 282p., illus.
            Autobiography. Incorporates item 718.

CAMPBELL, GLEN

2125.   Kramer, Freda. The Glen Campbell Story. New York: Pyramid
        Publications, 1970. 125p., illus.

CANTOR, EDDIE

2126.   Cantor, Eddie. As I Remember Them. New York: Duell, Sloan,
        and Pearce, 1963. 144p., illus.
            Memoir, and reminiscences of other performers.

2127.   ———. My Life Is In Your Hands. As told to David Freedman.
        New York; London: Harper and Brothers, 1928. 300p., illus.
            Autobiography.

            ———. ———. With a New Chapter Bringing the Story Up
        To 1932. New York: Blue Ribbon Books, 1932. 309p., illus.

2128.   ———. One Man Show: Forty Years of Show Business. (Place;
        Publisher unknown), 1950. 8p., illus.

2129.   ———. Take My Life. With Jane Kesner Ardmore.   Garden
        City, New York: Doubleday, 1957. 288p., illus.
            Memoirs.

2130.   ———. The Way I See It. Edited by Phyllis Rosenteur.
        Englewood Cliffs, New Jersey: Prentice-Hall, 1959. 204p.,
        illus.
            Memoirs.

CARLISLE, ELSIE

2131.   Walker, Edward Samuel. Elsie Carlisle, With a Different
        Style: a Discography. Chesterfield, Derbysshire: The Author,
        1974. 30p., illus.

CARMICHAEL, HOAGY

2132.   Carmichael, Hoagy. The Stardust Road. New York: Rinehart,
        1946 (Reprinted: Westport, Conn.: Greenwood Pr., 1969);
        London: Musicians Pr., 1947. 156p., illus.
            Autobiography.

Carmichael, Hoagy (cont.)

2133. Carmichael, Hoagy. Sometimes I Wonder: the Story of Hoagy
       Carmichael. With Stephen Longstreet. New York: Farrar,
       Straus, and Giroux, 1965; London: Alvin Redman; Rexdale,
       Ontario: Ambassador, 1966; New York: Da Capo Pr., 1976
       (Roots of Jazz). 314p., illus.
           Autobiography. Repeats some material from item 2132;
       continues his story.

2134. Indiana University. Lilly Library. An Exhibition Honoring
       the Seventy-Fifth Birthday of Hoagland Howard Carmichael,
       LLB. 1926, D.M. 1972, Indiana University. Bloomington,
       Indiana: Lilly Library, Indiana University, 1974. 38p.,
       illus.
           Exhibition catalog. Includes brief biography.

CARPENTERS

2135. Carpenters Quarterly. 2912 Simondale, Fort Worth, Texas
       76109. quarterly, 1979-?

CARROLL, ROBERT

  *   Evensmo, Jan. The Tenor Saxophones of Henry Bridges, Robert
       Carroll, Herschel Evans, and Johnny Russell.
           * Cited above as item 1548.

CARTER, BENNY

2136. Berger, Morroe, Edward Berger, and James Patrick. Benny
       Carter: a Life In American Music. Metuchen, New Jersey;
       London: Scarecrow Pr. and The Institute of Jazz Studies,
       Rutgers University, 1982. 2 vols., 873p., illus., bibliog.,
       discog., filmog., indexes. (Studies in Jazz, 1)

  *   Evensmo, Jan. The Alto Saxophone and Other Instruments of
       Benny Carter, 1927-1942.
           * Cited above as item 1548.

CARTER FAMILY

2137. Atkins, John (ed.). The Carter Family. By John Atkins, Bob
       Coltman, Alec Davidson, and Kip Lornell. London: Old Time
       Music, 1973. 63p., illus., discog. (Old Time Music Booklet, 1)

*   Carson, Gerald. <u>The Roguish World of Doctor Brinkley</u>.
       * Cited below as item 4035.

2138.   John Edwards Memorial Foundation. <u>The Carter Family On</u>
<u>Border Radio</u>. Los Angeles: John Edwards Memorial Foundation,
1972. 58p., illus., bibliog., discogs.
      Accompanies long-playing record, same title.

2139.   Orgill, Michael. <u>Anchored In Love: the Carter Family Story</u>.
Old Tappan, New Jersey: Revell, 1975. 192p., illus.

CASEY, TERANCE

2140.   Bevan, Sydney Gerald, and Bryan James Prevett. <u>Terance</u>
<u>Casey</u>. Brighton, Sussex: Cinema Organ Publications, 1953.
16p., illus. (Stars of the Console, 1)
      Biography of British theater organist. Played in the
intervals between movies.

CASH, JOHNNY

2141.   Cash, Johnny. <u>Man In Black</u>. Grand Rapids, Michigan: Zondervan, 1975; London: Hodder and Stoughton, 1976 (Reissued:
1977). 244p., illus. New York: Warner Books, 1976. 222p.,
illus.
      Autobiography. Concentrates on his personal problems.

2142.   Cash, June Carter. <u>Among My Klediments</u>. Grand Rapids,
Michigan: Zondervan, 1979.   p., illus.
      By wife of Johnny Cash. Empasis on their Christian life.

Biographies

2143.   Carpozi, George. <u>The Johnny Cash Story</u>. New York: Pyramid
Publications, 1970. 128p., illus.

2144.   Govoni, Albert. <u>A Boy Named Cash</u>. New York: Lancer Books,
1970. 190p., illus.
      Includes listing of his songs.

2145.   Wren, Christopher S. <u>Winners Got Scars, Too: the Life and</u>
<u>Legends of Johnny Cash</u>. New York: Dial Pr., 1971. 229p.,
illus. London (as <u>Johnny Cash: Winners Got Scars, Too</u>): W.H.
Allen, 1973. 229p., illus. New York: Ballantine, 1974.
252p., illus. (A <u>Country Music</u> Book). London: Abacus, 1974.
221p., illus.

Cash, Johnny (cont.)

Songs and Discographies

2146. Danker, Frederick C. The Repertory and Style of a Country
       Singer: Johnny Cash. Los Angeles: John Edwards Memorial
       Foundation, 1973. 20p., bibliog. notes, discog. notes.
       (J.E.M.F. Reprints, 28)
           Reprinted from the Journal of American Folklore, October-
       December, 1972. Sees Cash as bridging traditional and pop-
       ular cultures.

2147. Smith, John L. The Johnny Cash Discography and Recording
       History, 1955-1968. Los Angeles: John Edwards Memorial
       Foundation, 1969. 48p.

2148. ————. The Johnny Cash Discography. Westport, Conn.:
       Greenwood Pr., 1985.   p. (Discographies, 13)

CASSIDY, DAVID

2149. Cassidy, David. David In Europe: Exclusive! David's Own
       Story In David's Own Words. London: Daily Mirror Books,
       1973. 47p., illus.

2150. Daily Mirror. Darling David. London: Daily Mirror Books,
       1972. 64p., illus.

2151. Deck, Carol. The David Cassidy Story. Philadelphia: Curtis
       Books; Manchester, England: World Distributors, 1974.   p.,
       illus. (Ensign Books)

Periodicals

2152. The Official David Cassidy Magazine. London. monthly, June
       1971-December 1975.

CASSIDY, SHAUN

2153. Berman, Connie. The Shaun Cassidy Scrapbook: an Illustrated
       Biography. New York: Sunridge Pr., 1978. 123p., illus.

CASTLE, VERNON AND IRENE

2154. Castle, Irene. Castles In the Air. As told to Bob and Wanda
       Duncan. Garden City, New York: Doubleday, 1958; New York
       (with a new foreword by Ginger Rogers): Da Capo Pr., 1980.
       264p., illus.

2155. ———. My Husband. London: John Lane, 1919; New York: Scribner's, 1920; New York (with a new introduction by Iris M. Fange): Da Capo Pr., 1978 (Series in Dance). 264p., illus.
    Biography of Vernon Castle, by his wife. Da Capo edition is a reprint, with minor changes.

* Castle, Vernon, and Irene Castle. Modern Dancing.
   * Cited above as item 1278.

CASTON, LEONARD

2156. Caston, Leonard. From Blues to Pop: the Autobiography of Leonard "Baby Doo" Caston. Edited by Jeff Titon. Los Angeles: John Edwards Memorial Foundation, 1974. 29p., illus. (J.E.M.F. Special Series, 4)
    Transcribed interview.

CHARISSE, CYD, AND TONY MARTIN

2157. Martin, Tony, and Cyd Charisse. The Two Of Us. As told to Dick Kleiner. New York: Mason/Charter, 1976. 286p., illus.
    Memoirs.

CHARLES, RAY

2158. Charles, Ray, and David Ritz. Brother Ray: Ray Charles' Own Story. New York: Dial Pr., 1978; London: Macdonald and Jane's, 1979. 340p., illus., discog. New York: Warner Books, 1979. 366p., illus., discog.

CHER

2159. Carpozi, George. Cher. New York: Berkley Publishing, 1975. 178p., illus. (A Berkley Medallion Book)

CHERRY, DON

2160. Hames, Mike, and Roy Wilbraham. The Music of Don Cherry On Disc and Tape: a Discography. Wimbourne, Dorset: The Authors, 1980. 35p.

CHESTER, BOB

2161.   Garrod, Charles. Bob Chester Orchestra/Teddy Powell Orch-
        estra. Spotswood, New Jersey: Joyce, 1974.   p.
           Discography.

CHEVALIER, ALBERT

2162.   Chevalier, Albert. Albert Chevalier: a Record By Himself.
        Biographical and other chapters by Brian Daly. London:
        John MacQueen, 1895. 295p., illus.

2163.   ———. Before I Forget: the Autobiography of a Chevalier
        d'Industrie. London: T. Fisher Unwin, 1901. 257p., illus.

2164.   Chevalier, Florence. Albert Chevalier Comes Back. London:
        Rider, 1927. 199p., illus.
           Spiritualistic experiences described.

CHEVALIER, MAURICE

2165.   Chevalier, Maurice. Bravo Maurice! A Compilation From the
        Autobiographical Writings of Maurice Chevalier. Translated
        from the French by Mary Fitter. London: Allen and Unwin,
        1973. 240p., illus.
           Originally published as Bravo Maurice!, Paris: Julliard,
        1968.

2166.   ———. I Remember It Well. Preface by Marcel Pagnol.
        Translated from the French by Cornelia Higginson. London:
        W.H. Allen, 1970; New York: Macmillan, 1970; Boston: G.K.
        Hall, 1972. 221p., illus.
           Autobiography. Originally published as Môme à cheveux
        blancs, Paris: Presses de la Cité, 1969.

2167.   ———. Ma Route et mes chansons. Paris: Julliard, 1946-57.

        Ma Route et mes chansons. 1946. 275p.
        Londres, Hollywood, Paris. 1947. 241p.
        Tempes grises. 1948. 239p.
        Par ci, par là. 1950. 208p.
        Y a tant d'amour. 1952. 222p.
        Noces d'or. 1954. 277p.
        Artisan de France. 1957. 220p.

           Reminiscences.

2168.   ———. Maurice Chevalier's Own Story. As told to Percy
        Cudlipp. London: Nash and Grayson, 1930. 92p., illus.

2169.   ———. With Love: the Autobiography of Maurice Chevalier.
        As told to Eileen and Robert Mason Pollock. London: Cassell,
        1960. 336p., illus.

Biographies

2170. Boyer, William. The Romantic Life of Maurice Chevalier.
London: Hutchinson, 1937. 254p., illus.

2171. Freedland, Michael. Maurice Chevalier. London: Arthur
Barker, 1982. 292p., illus.

2172. Harding, James. Maurice Chevalier: His Life, 1888-1972.
With illustrations from the collection of André Bernard.
London: Secker and Warburg, 1982. 220p., illus., bibliog.,
index.

2173. Ringgold, Gene, and Dewitt Bodeen. Chevalier: the Films and
Career of Maurice Chevalier. Foreword by Rouben Mamoulian.
Secaucus, New Jersey: Citadel Pr., 1973. 242p., illus.

2174. Rivollet, André. Maurice Chevalier: de Menilmontant au
Casino de Paris. Paris: Grasset, 1927. 260p., illus.

CHIRGWIN, GEORGE

2175. Chirgwin, George H. Chirgwin's Chirrup: Being the Life and
Reminiscences of George Chirgwin, the "White-Eyed Musical
Kaffir." London: J. and J. Bennett, 1912. 134p.

CHISHOLM, GEORGE

2176. Clutten, Michael N. A George Chisholm Discography. Introduction by Syd R. Gallichan. Leicester, England: The Author,
1977. 49p.

————. Supplement One. By Syd R. Gallichan. Leicester,
England: Michael N. Clutten, 1980. 13p.

CHRISTIAN, CHARLIE

2177. Callis, John. Charlie Christian, 1939-1941: Discography.
London: Middleton, 1977. 51p.

   *   Evensmo, Jan. The Guitars of Charlie Christian, Robert
Normann, and Oscar Aleman (in Europe).
          * Cited above as item 1548.

CHURCHILL, SARAH

2178. Churchill, Sarah. <u>Keep On Dancing: an Autobiography</u>. Ed-
      ited by Paul Medlicott. London: Weidenfeld and Nicolson,
      1981. 243p., illus., index.
      The third daughter of Winston S. Churchill, she danced
      in stage and movie musicals.

CLAPTON, ERIC

2179. Clapton, Eric. <u>Conversations With Eric Clapton</u>. With Steve
      Turner. London: Abacus, 1976. 116p., illus., discog.
      Long interviews, conducted as he was resuming his career
      after a long period of drug addiction.

2180. Pidgeon, John. <u>Eric Clapton: a Biography</u>. St. Albans,
      Hertfordshire: Panther, 1976. 144p., illus., discog. <u>Rev.
      and updated ed.</u>: London: Vermilion, 1985. 224p., illus.,
      discog., index.

2181. Shapiro, Harry. <u>Slowhand: the Story of Eric Clapton</u>.
      London; New York: Proteus, 1982. 160p., illus., discog.

                          Discography

2182. Roberty, Marc. <u>Eric Clapton: the Illustrated Disco/Biography</u>.
      London: Omnibus Pr., 1984.   p., illus.
      Includes bootleg records.

CLARIBEL (<u>pseud. of</u> Charlotte Alington Barnard)

2183. Smith, Phyllis Mary. <u>The Story of Claribel (Charlotte Aling-
      ton Barnard)</u>. Assisted by Margaret Godsmark. Lincoln,
      England: J.W. Ruddock and Sons, 1965. 167p., illus.

CLARK, DICK

2184. Clark, Dick, and Richard Robinson. <u>Rock, Roll, and Remember</u>.
      New York: Crowell, 1976. 276p., illus., index. New York:
      Popular Library, 1978. 350p., illus., index.
      Autobiography of emcee of long-running television rock
      show, <u>American Bandstand</u>.

CLARK, PETULA

2185. Kon, Andrea. "This Is My Song." A Biography of Petula
       Clark. London: W.H. Allen, 1983. 256p., illus., index.

CLASH

2186. Clash, The. The Clash By The Clash. London: Wise Publicat-
       ations, 1978. 68p., illus.
           Lyrics, illustrations, music, and comment by the group.

2187. Smith, Pennie. The Clash, Before and After. With passing
       comments by Joe Strummer, Mick Jones, Paul Simoron, and
       Topper Headon. London: Eel Pie, 1980. 158p., illus.
       Boston: Little, Brown, 1982. unpaged, illus.
           Photographic study by Smith, before and during the group's
       first tour of the United States. With comment by its
       members.

2188. Tobler, John, and Miles (pseud. of Barry Miles). The Clash.
       London; New York: Omnibus Pr., 1981. 50p., illus., discog.

2189. ————. The Clash: a Visual Documentary. London: Omnibus
       Pr., 1984.   p., illus.

                         Periodicals

2190. Armagideon Times. London. irreg., 1980-?

CLAYDERMAN, RICHARD

2191. Rawlinson, Christine. Richard Clayderman: a Celebration.
       London: Zomba Books, 1983. 64p., illus., discog.

CLINE, PATSY

2192. Nassour, Ellis. Patsy Cline: an Intimate Biography. Intro-
       duction by Dottie West. New York: Tower Books, 1981. 416p.,
       illus., discog., index.

CLINTON, LARRY

2193. Garrod, Charles. Larry Clinton and His Orchestra. Spots-
       wood, New Jersey: Joyce, 1973.   p.
           Discography.

CLOONEY, ROSEMARY

2194.   Clooney, Rosemary. This For Remembrance: the Autobiography
        of Rosemary Clooney, an Irish-American Singer. With Ray-
        mond Strait. Foreword by Bing Crosby. Chicago: Playboy Pr.,
        1977; London: Robson Books, 1978. 257p., illus. New York:
        Berkley Publishing, 1982. 352p., illus.

COASTERS

2195.   Millar, Bill. The Coasters. London: Star Books, 1975.
        206p., illus., discog.

COBB, ARNETT

2196.   Demeusy, Bertrand, and Otto Flückinger (comps.). Arnett
        Cobb: the Wild Man of the Tenor Sax. Basle, Switzerland:
        Jazz Publications, 1962. 21p., illus.
            Bio-discography.

COBURN, CHARLES

2197.   Coburn, Charles. The Man Who Broke the Bank. London:
        Hutchinson, n.d.   p., illus.
            Autobiography.

COCHRAN, CHARLES BLAKE

2198.   Cochran, Charles Blake. The Secrets of a Showman. London:
        Heinemann, 1925. 436p., illus.
            First volume of his memoirs.

2199.   ———. Review of Revues, and Other Matters. London: Cape,
        1930. 94p., illus.
            Second volume of his memoirs.

2200.   ———. I Had Almost Forgotten. London: Hutchinson, 1932.
        304p., illus.
            Third volume of his memoirs.

2201.   ———. Cock-a-Doodle-Doo. London: Dent, 1941. 367p., illus
        illus.
            Fourth volume of his memoirs.

2202.   ———. A Showman Looks On. London: Dent, 1945. 323p.,
        illus. London: Dent, 1949. 256p., illus. (Guild Books, 404)
            Last volume of his memoirs.

Biographies

2203. Graves, Charles Patrick Ranke. <u>The Cochran Story: a Biog-</u>
       <u>raphy of Sir Charles Blake Cochran, Knight.</u> London: W.H.
       Allen, 1951. 282p., illus.

2204. Heppner, Sam. "<u>Cockie.</u>" Foreword by Noël Coward. London:
       Leslie Frewin, 1969. 288p., illus., index.

COCHRAN, EDDIE

2205. Muir, Eddie, and Tony Scott. <u>Something Else: a Tribute to</u>
       <u>Eddie Cochran.</u> Prescot, Merseyside: Vintage Rock 'n' Roll
       Appreciation Society, 1979. 45p., illus.
           Essays on Cochran.

CODY, COMMANDER (<u>pseud. of</u> George Frayn)

2206. Stokes, Geoffrey. <u>Star-Making Machinery: the Odyssey of an</u>
       <u>Album.</u> Indianapolis: Bobbs-Merrill, 1976; New York: Vantage
       Pr., 1977. 234p., illus., index.
           Account of country-rock group, Commander Cody and His Lost
       Planet Airmen, and its break-up during the making of an
       unsuccessful album.

COFFIN, CHARLES HAYDEN

2207. Coffin, Hayden. <u>Hayden Coffin's Book. Packed With Acts and</u>
       <u>Facts.</u> Foreword by T.P. O'Connor. Illustrated by John
       Hassall. London: Alston Rivers, 1930. 303p., illus.
           Includes texts and music of songs.

COHAN, GEORGE MICHAEL

2208. Cohan, George Michael. <u>Twenty Years On Broadway, and the</u>
       <u>Years It Took To Get There: the True Story of a Trouper's</u>
       Life From the Cradle To the "Closed Shop." New York; London:
       Harper and Brothers, 1925; Westport, Conn.: Greenwood Pr.,
       1971. 264p., illus.
           Autobiography. Emphasis on his early vaudeville career.

Biographies

2209. McCabe, John H. <u>George M. Cohan: the Man Who Owned Broadway.</u>
       Garden City, New York: Doubleday, 1973; New York: Da Capo Pr.,
       1980. 296p., illus., index.

Cohan, George Michael (cont.)

2210.   Morehouse, Ward. George M. Cohan: Prince of the American
        Theater. Philadelphia: Lippincott, 1944; Westport, Conn.:
        Greenwood Pr., 1971. 240p., illus.

2211.   Winders, Gertrude Hecker. George M. Cohan: Boy Theater Genius.
        Indianapolis: Bobbs-Merrill, 1968. 200p., illus. (Childhood
        of Famous Americans)
            Aimed at younger readers. Concentrates on his childhood
        and early career.

COHEN, LEONARD

Literary Works

2212.   Cohen, Leonard. Beautiful Losers. Toronto: McClelland and
        Stewart; New York: Viking Pr., 1966; London: Cape, 1970.
        243p. St. Albans, Hertfordshire: Panther, 1972. 239p.
            Novel.

2213.   ———. The Book of Mercy. New York: Villard Books; London:
        Cape, 1984. 88p., index.
            Sequence of poems, prose, meditations, and thoughts on
        love.

2214.   ———. Choosing To Work. Reston, Virginia: Reston Publish-
        ing, 1979.   p.

2215.   ———. Death of a Lady's Man. Toronto: McClelland and
        Stewart, 1978; London: Deutsch; New York: Penguin, 1979.
        216p.
            Poems, prose, musings, and lyrics (from long-playing
        record, same title).

2216.   ———. The Energy of Slaves. London: Cape, 1972. 127p.
            Poems.

2217.   ———. The Favorite Game. New York: Viking Pr., 1963. 244p.
        London: Secker and Warburg, 1963. 222p. New York: Avon,
        1965 (Reissued: 1970). 192p. London: Cape, 1970. 244p.
        Toronto (with introduction by Rowland J. Smith): McClelland
        and Stewart, 1970. 222p. (New Canadian Library, 73). St.
        Albans, Hertfordshire: Panther, 1973 (Reissued: St. Albans,
        Hertfordshire: Triad/Panther, 1979). 219p.
            Semi-autobiographical novel.

2218.   ———. Flowers For Hitler. Toronto: McClelland and Stewart,
        1964. 128p. London: Cape, 1973. 154p.
            Poems.

2219.   ———. Let Us Compare Mythologies. Drawings by Freda
        Guttman. Toronto: Contact Pr., 1956. 84p., illus. (McGill
        Poetry Series, 1)
            Poems.

2220. ————. Parasites of Heaven. Toronto: McClelland and
       Stewart, 1966. 80p.
            Poems.

2221. ————. Selected Poems, 1956-1968. Toronto: McClelland
       and Stewart; New York: Viking Pr., 1968; London: Cape,
       1969. 245p., illus., index.

            ————. Poems, 1956-1968. London: Cape, 1969. 94p.,
       index. (Cape Poetry Paperbacks)
            Abridgment.

2222. ————. The Spice-Box of Earth. New York: Viking Pr.,
       1965; Toronto: McClelland and Stewart, 1971. 88p. London:
       Cape, 1973. 93p.
            Poems.

                        Biographies

2223. Ondaatje, Michael. Leonard Cohen. Toronto: McClelland
       and Stewart, 1971. 64p. (New Canadian Library. Canadian
       Writers, 5)

2224. Scobie, Stephen. Leonard Cohen. Vancouver: Douglas and
       McIntyre, 1978. 192p., bibliog. (Studies in Canadian Lit-
       erature)

            ————. ————. Seattle: University of Washington Pr.,
       1978. 294p., bibliog. (Studies in Canadian Literature)

COLE, NAT "KING"

2225. Cole, Maria. Nat King Cole: an Intimate Biography. With
       Louie Robinson. New York: Morrow, 1971; London: W.H. Allen,
       1972; London: Star Books, 1982. 184p., illus., discog.
            By his widow. Includes extensive discography.

2226. Hall, George (ed.). The Nat "King" Cole Trio. Whittier,
       California: Jazz Discographies Unlimited, 1965. 18p.
            Discography.

COLEMAN, BILL

2227. Chilton, John. Bill Coleman On Record. London: The Author,
       1966. 18p.
            Discography.

   *   Evensmo, Jan. The Trumpets of Bill Coleman, 1929-1945; and
       Frankie Newton.
            * Cited above as item 1548.

COLETTE, SIDONIE GABRIELLE

2228. Colette, Sidonie Gabrielle. L'Envers du Music-Hall. Illustrated by Henri Mirande. Paris: (publisher unknown), 1929.
172p., illus.
Account of her appearances on the stage.

2229. ————. Journey For Myself: Selfish Memories. Translated
from the French by David Le Vay. London: Peter Owen, 1971.
156p., illus.
Autobiographical and other pieces.

2230. ————. Letters From Colette. Selected and translated by
Robert Phelps. New York: Farrar, Straus and Giroux, 1980.
214p. London: Virago, 1982. 224p.

2231. ————. Looking Backwards: Recollections. Translated from
the French by David Le Vay. Introduction by Maurice Goudeket.
London: Peter Owen, 1975. 214p.
Originally published: Paris: Fayard, 1941, as Journal à
rebours; and De ma fenêtre, 1942. Reminiscences, and other
pieces.

2232. ————. Mitsou; and, Music-Hall Sidelights. New York:
Farrar, Straus, and Cudahy, 1958. 260p.
Incorporates item 2228. Mitsou translated by Raymond
Postgate; Music-Hall Sidelights translated by Anne-Marie
Callimachi.

2233. ————. My Apprenticeships; and, Music-Hall Sidelights.
London: Secker and Warburg, 1957. 260p. (Uniform Edition of
Works by Colette, 4)
My Apprenticeships translated by Helen Beauclerk; Music-
Hall Sidelights translated by Anne-Marie Callimachi. Incorp-
orates item 2228.

                              Biographies

2234. Richardson, Joanna. Colette. London: Methuen, 1983. 276p.,
illus., bibliog., index.

2235. Sarde, Michele. Colette: Free and Fettered. Translated
from the French by Richard Miller. London: Michael Joseph,
1981. 479p., illus., bibliog., index.

COLLINS, JOSÉ (pseud. of Josephine Charlotte Cooney)

2236. Collins, José. The Maid of the Mountains: Her Story. The
Reminiscences of José Collins. London: Hutchinson, 1932.
287p., illus.

2237. Miss José Collins: Facts and Photos. Manchester, England:
Popular Favourites, 1920. 27p., illus. (Popular Favourites, 1)

COLLINS, JUDY

2238.   Claire, Vivian. Judy Collins. New York: Flash Books, 1977.
        78p., illus., discog.

COLLINS, LEE

2239.   Collins, Lee. Oh, Didn't He Ramble: the Life Story of Lee
        Collins. As told to Mary Collins. Edited by Frank J. Gillis
        and John W. Miner. Urabana; London: University of Illinois
        Pr., 1974. 159p., illus., bibliog., discog., index. (Music
        in American Life)
            Discography of commercial recordings compiled by Brian
        Rust; that of private recordings compiled by Gillis.

COLTRANE, JOHN

2240.   Cole, Bill (pseud. of William Shadrack Cole). John Coltrane.
        New York: Schirmer Books; London: Collier-Macmillan, 1976.
        264p., illus., bibliog., index.
            Includes transcribed excerpts from his solos. Based on
        the author's PhD. dissertation The Style of John Coltrane,
        1955-1967, Wesleyan University, 1975.

2241.   Harper, Michael S. Dear John, Dear Coltrane. Pittsburgh:
        University of Pittsburgh Pr., 1970. 88p.
            Poems inspired by Coltrane's music.

2242.   Kofsky, Frank, Bob Thiele, and John Norris. John Coltrane
        Memorial. Toronto: Coda, 1968. p., illus.
            Essays.

2243.   Priestley, Brian. John Coltrane. Speldhurst, Kent: Spell-
        mount; New York: Hippocrene Books, 1985. p., illus.,
        bibliog., discog., index. (Jazz Masters, 11)

2244.   Simpkins, Cuthbert Ormond. Coltrane: a Musical Biography.
        New York: Herdon House, 1975. 287p., illus., bibliog. refs.

2245.   Thomas, J.C. Chasin' the Trane: the Music and Mystique of
        John Coltrane. Garden City, New York: Doubleday, 1975 (Re-
        printed: New York: Da Capo Pr., 1976). 252p., illus.,
        discog., index. London: Elm Tree Books, 1976. 188p., illus.,
        discog., index.

                         Discographies

2246.   Davis, Brian, and Ray Smith. John Coltrane Discography.
        Hockley, Essex: Collet's, 1976. 43,(6)p.

Coltrane, John (cont.)

Discographies (cont.)

* Jepsen, Jorgen Grunnet. <u>Discography of Cannonball Adderley/</u>
  <u>John Coltrane</u>.
    * Cited above as item 1683.

2247. ———. <u>A Discography of John Coltrane</u>. Copenhagen: Knudsen,
      1969. 35p.

2248. Rissi, Mathias. <u>John Coltrane: Discography</u>. Adliswil, West
      Germany: The Author, 1977. 39p.

2249. Swoboda, Herbert. <u>The John Coltrane Discography, 1949-1967</u>.
      Stuttgart, West Germany: Modern Jazz Series, 1968. 40p.

2250. Wild, David Anthony. <u>The Recordings of John Coltrane: a</u>
      <u>Discography</u>. Ann Arbor, Michigan: Wildmusic, 1977. 72p.,
      16p. supplement.

COLYER, KEN

2251. Reddihough, John. <u>Ken Colyer: a Biography, Appreciation,</u>
      <u>Record Survey, and Discography</u>. London: National Jazz Fed-
      eration, 1958. 20p., discog.

COMPTON, FAY (<u>pseud. of</u> Virginia Compton Mackenzie)

2252. Compton, Fay. <u>Rosemary: Some Reminiscences</u>. Introduction
      by Compton Mackenzie. London: Alston Rivers, 1926. 264p.,
      illus.

CONDON, EDDIE

* Condon, Eddie. <u>We Called It Music: a Generation of Jazz</u>.
    * Cited above as item 800.

CONNOLLY, BILLY

2253. Connolly, Billy. <u>Gullible's Travels</u>. Compiled, and intro-
      duction by Duncan Campbell. Illustrated by Steve Bell.
      London: Pavilion Books, 1982. 184p., illus.
        Account of his experiences while touring.

COOKE, SAM

2254. McEwen, Joe. <u>Sam Cooke: a Biography in Words and Pictures</u>.
      Edited by Greg Shaw. New York: Sire Books, 1977.   p.,
      illus.

COOPER, ALICE (<u>pseud. of</u> Vincent Furnier)

2255. Cooper, Alice. <u>Me, Alice: the Autobiography of Alice Cooper</u>.
      With Steven Gaines. New York: Putnam's, 1975. 254p., illus.

2256. Demorest, Steve. <u>Alice Cooper</u>. New York: Popular Library,
      1974.   p., illus. (<u>Circus</u> Magazine Rock Books, 1)

2257. Greene, Bob. <u>Billion Dollar Baby</u>. New York: Atheneum,
      1974. 364p., illus. New York: New American Library, 1975.
      339p., illus. (A Signet Book)
          Behind-the-scenes view of the Alice Cooper band's 1973
      tour of the United States, immediately before its disband-
      ment.

COOPER, GLADYS

2258. Cooper, Gladys. <u>Gladys Cooper</u>. London: Hutchinson, 1931.
      288p., illus.
          Autobiography.

2259. Morley, Sheridan. <u>Gladys Cooper: a Biography</u>. London:
      Heinemann; New York: McGraw-Hill, 1979. 313p., illus.

2260. Stokes, Sewell. <u>Without Veils: the Intimate Biography of
      Gladys Cooper</u>. Introduction by William Somerset Maugham.
      London: Peter Davies, 1953. 243p., illus.

COOPER CLARKE, JOHN

2261. Cooper Clarke, John. <u>Directory 1979</u>. London: Omnibus Pr.,
      1979. 48p., illus.
          Autobiographical piece, plus eleven poems (from his long-
      playing record <u>Disguise In Love</u>, 1979).

CORVAN

2262. Gregson, Keith. <u>**Corvan: a Victorian Entertainer and His
      Songs**</u>. Foreword by Roy Palmer. Banbury, Oxfordshire: Kemble,
      1983. 52p., illus., bibliog., index.
          Includes texts and music of his songs.

COSLOW, SAM

2263. Coslow, Sam. Cocktails For Two: the Many Lives of Giant
       Songwriter Sam Coslow. New Rochelle, New York: Arlington
       House, 1977. 304p., illus., discog.
         Autobiography.

COSTELLO, ELVIS (pseud. of Declan Patrick MacManus)

2264. Reese, Krista. Elvis Costello: a Completely False Biography
       Based On Rumor, Innuendo, and Lies. London; New York:
       Proteus, 1981. 128p., illus., discog.

                        Discography

2265. Parkyn, Geoff. Elvis Costello: the Illustrated Disco/Biog-
       raphy. London: Omnibus Pr., 1984.   p., illus.
         International coverage. Includes bootleg and promotional
       records; also guest appearances with other artists.

                        Periodicals

2266. Elvis Costello Information Service. Edited by Richard
       Groothuizen. Primulastraat 46, 1441 HC, Purmerend, Holland.
       bi-monthly, 1981- .

2267. On The Beat. 1433 Reisterstown Road, Pikesville, Maryland.
       irreg., April 1979-?

COTTON, BILLY

2268. Cotton, Billy. I Did It My Way: the Life Story of Billy
       Cotton. London: Harrap, 1970. 192p., illus., index.

2269. Maxwell, John. The Greatest Billy Cotton Band Show. London:
       Jupiter Books, 1976. 155p., illus., index.
         Includes record in pocket.

COURTNEIGE, CICELY

2270. Courtneige, Cicely. Cicely. London: Hutchinson, 1953. 224p.,
       illus.
         Autobiography. See also HULBERT, Jack.

COURTNEIGE, ROBERT

2271. Courtneige, Robert. "I Was an Actor Once." London:
       Hutchinson, 1930. 287p., illus.
              Autobiography. Father of Cicely Courtneige.

COWARD, **NOEL**

2272. Coward, Noël. Australia Visited. London: Heinemann, 1941.
       60p., illus.
              Texts of radio broadcasts by Coward. His impressions.

2273. ————. Future Indefinite. London: Heinemann, 1954. 336p.,
       illus. New York: Doubleday, 1954. 352p., illus.
              Second volume of his memoirs. Covers 1939-45. See also
       item 2277.

2274. ————. A Last Encore: Words by Noël Coward; Pictures From
       His Life and Times. Edited by John Hadfield. Boston:
       Little, Brown, 1973. 144p., illus.
              Text compiled from previously published material.

2275. ————. Middle East Diary. London: Heinemann, 1944. 119p.
       New York: Doubleday, Doran, 1944. 155p.
              Covers July-October, 1943.

2276. ————. The Noël Coward Diaries. Edited by Graham Payn
       and Sheridan Morley. London: Weidenfeld and Nicolson, 1982.
       698p., index.
              Covers April 19, 1941 to December 31, 1969. Includes
       chronology.

2277. ————. Present Indicative. Garden City, New York: Double-
       day, Doran, 1937. 371p., illus.
              Limited edition of 301 copies.

       ————. ————. Garden City, New York: Doubleday, Doran,
       1937. 371p., illus. London; Toronto: Heinemann, 1937.
       431p., illus. New York: Garden City Publishing Company,
       1939. 371p., illus. London; Toronto: Heinemann, 1951 (Re-
       issued: 1974). 431p., illus.
              First volume of his memoirs. Continued by item 2273.

2278. ————. The Wit of Noël Coward. Compiled by Dick Richards.
       London: Leslie Frewin, 1968. 112p., illus. London: Sphere,
       1969. 113p., illus.
              Humorous quotations.

Coward, Noël (cont.)

Theatrical Works

2279. Coward, Noël. <u>Cowardy Custard: the World of Noel Coward.</u>
       <u>Based on the Mermaid Theatre Entertainment.</u> Devised by
       Gerald Frow, Alan Strachan, and Wendy Toye. Edited by John
       Hadfield. London: Heinemann, 1973. 144p., illus., index.
          Texts, lyrics, and illustrations from the stage show
       based on Coward's writings and musical and other shows.

2280. Mander, Raymond, and Joe Mitchenson. <u>Theatrical Companion</u>
       <u>to Coward: a Pictorial Record of the First Performances of</u>
       <u>the Theatrical Works of Noel Coward. With an Appreciation</u>
       <u>of Coward's Work in the Theatre, by Terence Rattigan.</u>
       London: Rockliff; New York: Macmillan, 1957. 407p., illus.
          Includes cast listings, and production details.

Lyrics

2281. Coward, Noël. <u>Collected Sketches and Lyrics.</u> London:
       Hutchinson, 1931. 288p., illus.

2282. ————. <u>The Lyrics of Noël Coward.</u> London: Heinemann, 1965;
       Garden City, New York: Doubleday, 1967. 418p., index.
          Chronologically-arranged collection of song texts. Intro-
       ductions for each decade by Coward.

       ————. <u>The Lyrics.</u> London: Methuen, 1983. 418p., index.

2283. ————. <u>The Noël Coward Songbook.</u> Introduced and annotated
       by the Author. Illustrated by Gladys Calthrop. London:
       Michael Joseph; New York: Simon and Schuster, 1953. 309p.,
       illus.
          Includes extensive comment by the author.

Biographies

2284. Braybrooke, Patrick. <u>The Amazing Mister Noël Coward.</u> London:
       Denis Archer, 1933; Folcroft, Pennsylvania: Folcroft Library
       Editions, 1974. 168p., illus.

2285. Castle, Charles. <u>Noël.</u> London: W.H. Allen, 1972; Garden
       City, New York: Doubleday, 1973; London: Abacus, 1974. 272p.,
       illus., index.

2286. Greacen, Robert. <u>The Art of Noël Coward.</u> Lympne, Kent: Hand
       and Flower Pr., 1953; Folcroft, Pennsylvania: Folcroft Pr.,
       1970. 86p., illus.

2287. Lesley, Cole. The Life of Noël Coward. London: Cape; New
York (as Remembered Laughter: the Life of Noël Coward):
Knopf, 1976. 499p., illus., bibliog., index. Harmondsworth,
Middlesex: Penguin, 1978. 560p., illus., bibliog., index.
By his companion of nearly forty years.

2288. ————, Graham Payn, and Sheridan Morley. Noël Coward and
His Friends. Designed by Craig Dodd. London: Weidenfeld
and Nicolson; New York: Morrow, 1979. 216p., illus.
Scrapbook.

2289. Marchant, William. The Privilege of His Company: Noël
Coward Remembered. Indianapolis: Bobbs-Merrill, 1975. 276p.,
illus. London: Weidenfeld and Nicolson, 1975. 248p., illus.

2290. Morley, Sheridan. A Talent To Amuse: a Biography of Noël
Coward. London: Heinemann, 1969. 359p., illus., bibliog.,
index. Garden City, New York: Doubleday, 1969. 453p.,
illus., bibliog., index. Harmondsworth, Middlesex: Penguin,
1974. 447p., illus., bibliog., index. London: Pavilion
Books, 1985. 363p., illus., bibliog., index.
Includes detailed chronological table.

2291. Morse, Clarence Ralph. Mad Dogs and Englishmen: a Study of
Noël Coward. Emporia, Kansas: School of Graduate and Pro-
fessional Studies, Kansas State Teachers' College, 1973.
52p., bibliog. (Emporia State Research Studies, vol. 21, 4)
Based on the author's thesis A Study of Noël Coward,
Kansas State Teachers' College, 1954.

COWELL, SAM

2292. Cowell, Emilie Marguerite. The Cowells in America: Being the
Diary of Mrs. Sam Cowell During Her Husband's Concert Tour in
the Years 1860-1861. Edited by Maurice Willson Disher.
London: Oxford University Pr., 1934. 426p., illus.
Cowell was one of the earliest music hall stars.

CRAWFORD, JESSE

2293. Landon, John W. Jesse Crawford: Poet of the Organ, Wizard of
the Mighty Wurlitzer. Vestal, New York: Vestal Pr., 1974.
372p., illus., bibliog.
Movie theater organist.

CREEDENCE CLEARWATER REVIVAL

2294. Hallowell, John. Inside Creedence. New York; London: Bantam,
1971. 88p., illus., discog.
Includes song lyrics, and sixty-four pages of photographs.

Creedence Clearwater Revival (cont.)

Periodicals

2295. Who'll Stop the Rain. Edited by Kevin Cooper. 60 Black-
ledge Street, Daubhill, Bolton, Lancashire. irreg., 1983-

CRICKETS see HOLLY, BUDDY

CROSBY, BING

2296. Crosby, Bing. Call Me Lucky. As told to Pete Martin. New
York: Simon and Schuster, 1953. 344p., illus., index.
London: Frederick Muller, 1953. 253p., illus., index. New
York: Pocket Books, 1954. 309p., illus.
Autobiography.

Biographies

2297. Barnes, Ken. The Crosby Years. London: Elm Tree Books/
Chappell; New York: St. Martin's Pr., 1980. 216p., illus.,
discog., filmog.
Includes fifty-page discography; twenty-eight page filmography. Appendix lists his major songs.

2298. Carpozi, George, Jr. The Fabulous Life of Bing Crosby. New
York: Woodhill Pr., 1975.   p., illus.

2299. Crosby, Kathryn. Bing, and Other Things. New York: Meredith
Pr.; London: Herbert Jenkins, 1967. 214p., illus.
By his wife.

2300. ————. My Life With Bing. Wheeling, Illinois: Collage;
London: Quartet, 1983. 355p., illus.

2301. Crosby, Edward J. ("Ted"), and Larry Crosby. Bing. Los
Angeles: Bolton Printing Company, 1937. 205p., illus.
By his brothers.

————. The Story of Bing Crosby. Foreword by Bob Hope.
Cleveland: World Publishing Company, 1946. 239p., illus.,
discog.
Revised and augmented.

2302. Mize, John Townsend Hinton. Bing Crosby and the Bing Crosby
Style: Crosbyana thru Biography, Photography, Discography.
Chicago: Published for The Academy of American Music by Who's
Who in Music, 1946. 170p., illus., discog. (Biographical
Bookettes)

2303.   Shepherd, Don, and Robert F. Slatzer. Bing Crosby: the
        Hollow Man. London: W.H. Allen, 1981; London: Star Books,
        1982. 326p., illus., bibliog., discog., filmog., index.
             Emphasis on the seamier side of his life.

2304.   Thomas, Bob. The One and Only Bing. New York: Grosset and
        Dunlap; London: Michael Joseph, 1977. 152p., illus., discog.,
        filmog.

2305.   Thompson, Charles. Bing: the Authorized Biography. London:
        W.H. Allen, 1975. 249p., illus., index. London: Star Books,
        1976. 223p., illus.

        ————. The Complete Crosby. Rev. and augmented ed. London:
        W.H. Allen; London: Star Books, 1978. 280p., illus., index.

2306.   Ulanov, Barry. The Incredible Crosby. New York: Whittlesey
        House, 1948. 336p., illus., discog.

                          Discographies

2307.   Bassett, John D., and Bishop, Albert S. The Bing Crosby LP-
        ography. Introduction by Bing Crosby. Cwmbran, Wales:
        International Crosby Circle, 1973. 81p.
             Alphabetically arranged by label names, then catalog order.

2308.   ————. The Bing Crosby Mini-Discography, 1926-1974. With
        Leslie Gaylor. Cwmbran, Wales: International Crosby Circle,
        1974. 40p.
             Chronological listing. Omits personnel details.

2309.   ————. The A-Z of Bing Crosby: a Title Listing. Cwmbran,
        Wales: International Crosby Circle, 1971. 66p.
             Complements items 2307 and 2308. Has personnel details;
        also acts as title index.

2310.   Mello, Edward J., and Tom McBride. Bing Crosby Discography.
        San Francisco: The Authors, 1947. 80p.

        ————. Crosby on Record, 1926-1950. With the following
        collectors: John Abercrombie (and others). Edited by Thomas
        Gleeson. San Francisco: Mello's Music, 1950. 101p., illus.

2311.   Zwisohn, Laurence J. Bing Crosby: a Lifetime of Music. Los
        Angeles: Palm Tree Library, 1978. 147p., illus., discog.

                         Motion Pictures

2312.   Bauer, Barbara. Bing Crosby. New York: Pyramid Publications,
        1977. 159p., illus., bibliog., index. (Pyramid Illustrated
        History of the Movies)

Crosby, Bing (cont.)

Motion Pictures (cont.)

2313. Bookbinder, Robert. The Films of Bing Crosby. Secaucus,
       New Jersey: Citadel Pr., 1977.   p., illus., bibliog.,
       index.

Periodicals

2314. Bing. Edited by John Bassett. International Crosby Circle,
       7 Greenmeadow Close, Cwmbran, Gwent, Wales. quarterly,
       1966- .

CROSBY, BOB

2315. Chilton, John. Stomp Off, Let's Go! The Story of Bob
       Crosby's Bob Cats and Big Band. London: Jazz Book Service,
       1983. 284p., illus.
           Includes biographies of his sidemen.

2316. Jones, Clifford (ed.). The Bob Crosby Band. London: Disco-
       graphical Society, 1946. 32p., illus.
           Discography.

CROSBY, GARY

2317. Crosby, Gary, and Ross Firestone. Going My Own Way. London:
       Robson Books, 1983. 304p., illus.
           Autobiography of Bing Crosby's eldest son.

CROSBY, STILLS, AND NASH

2318. Zimmer, Dave, and Henry Diltz. Crosby, Stills, and Nash:
       the Authorized Biography. Foreword by Graham Nash. New
       York: St. Martin's Pr.; London: Omnibus Pr., 1984. 256p.,
       illus., discog.
           Text by Zimmer; photographs by Diltz.

CROUCH, ANDRAE

2319. Crouch, Andrae. Through It All. With Nina Ball. Waco,
       Texas: Word Books, 1974. 148p., illus.
           Autobiography.

CUGAT, XAVIER

2320. Cugat, Xavier. <u>Rumba Is My Life</u>. Illustrated by the
       author. New York: Didier Publications, 1948. 210p., illus.
       London: Sampson Low; Toronto: Oxford University Pr., 1949.
       183p., illus.
       Autobiography.

CULTURE CLUB

2321. O'Dowd, George. <u>Culture Club: Boy George In His Own Words</u>.
       Compiled by Pearce Marchbank. London: Omnibus Pr., 1984.
       32p., illus.
       Compiled from press and other interviews.

2322. ————. <u>A Parade of Assumptions</u>. London: Sidgwick and
       Jackson, 1985. 128p., illus., discog.
       Autobiography.

                              Biographies

2323. Brompton, Sally. <u>Chameleon: the Boy George Story</u>. Tunbridge
       Wells, Kent: Spellmount, 1984. 157p., illus.

2324. David, Maria. <u>Boy George and Culture Club</u>. Guildford,
       Surrey: Colour Library Books, 1984. 59p., illus.
       Chiefly illustrated.

2325. De Graaf, Kasper, and Malcolm Garrett. <u>When Cameras Go
       Crazy: Culture Club</u>. London: Virgin Books; New York: St.
       Martin's Pr., 1983. 96p., illus.

2326. Dietrich, Jo. <u>Boy George and Culture Club</u>. London: Proteus,
       Port Chester, New York: Cherry Lane Books, 1984. 32p., illus.

2327. Gill, Anton. <u>Mad About the Boy: the Life and Times of Boy
       George and Culture Club</u>. London: Century Publishing, 1984.
       128p., illus., discog., filmog.

2328. Ginsberg, Merle. <u>Boy George</u>. New York: Dell; London: New
       English Library, 1984. 171p., illus.

2329. Norman, Neil. <u>Boy George and Culture Club</u>. London; New York:
       Proteus, 1984. 32p., illus.

2330. Tobler, John, and Pete Frame. <u>Culture Club</u>. London: Zomba
       Books, 1984. 96p., illus. (Rock Masters)

2331. Winder, Wayne, and Gerardine Winder. <u>The Boy George Fashion
       and Make-Up Book</u>. With Christina Saunders. London: Hamlyn,
       1984. 64p., illus.
       Practical guide. Some biographical information.

CURTIS, KING

2332. Simmonds, Roy. _King Curtis: a Discography_. Edgware, Middle-
       sex: The Author, 1984.   p.
          Covers 1952-71. Includes solo and other recordings.

DANIELS, MIKE

2333. Bowen, Michael. _Mike Daniels and The Delta Jazzmen_. North
       Ferriby, Humberside: Victor Houseman, 1982. 190p., illus.,
       bibliog., index.

DANKWORTH, JOHN, AND CLEO LAINE

2334. Collier, Graham. _Cleo and John: a Biography of the Dank-
       worths_. London: Quartet, 1976. 187p., illus., index.

DARBY AND TARLTON

2335. Wickman, Graham. _Darby and Tarlton_. Denver, Colorado: _Blue
       Yodeler_, 1967.   p., illus.
          Tom Darby and Jimmie Tarlton, early country duo.

DARE, PHYLLIS

2336. Dare, Phyllis. _From School To Stage_. London: Collier and
       Company, 1907. 146p., illus.
          Autobiography.

2337. _Miss Phyllis Dare: an Appreciation_. Manchester, England:
       Popular Favourites, 1921. 24p., illus. (Popular Favourites,
       2)

2338. W., T. (pseud.). _Musings on Miss Phyllis Dare as "Cinderella"_,
       Theatre Royal, Newcastle-on-Tyne, 1905-6. Newcastle-on-Tyne,
       England: The Author, 1906. 16p.

DARIN, BOBBY

2339. Diorio, Al. _Borrowed Time: the Thirty-Seven Years of Bobby
       Darin_. Philadelphia: Running Pr., 1980.   p., illus.,
       filmog., index.

DAVIS, CLIVE

2340.   Davis, Clive. Clive: Inside the Record Business. With
        James Willwerth. New York: Morrow, 1975; New York: Ballan-
        tine, 1976. 300p., illus.
        Autobiography of one-time president of Columbia Records.

DAVIS, JIMMIE.

2341.   Weill, Gus. You Are My Sunshine: the Jimmie Davis Story.
        An Affectionate Biography. Waco, Texas: Word Books, 1977.
        187p., illus.

DAVIS, MILES

2342.   Davis, Miles. Self Portrait of the Artist. New York:
        Columbia Records, Press and Public Information, 1968.   p.,
        illus.

                            Biographies

2343.   Carr, Ian. Miles Davis: a Critical Biography. London:
        Quartet, 1982. 310p., illus., bibliog., discog., index.
        New York: Morrow, 1984. 336p., illus., bibliog., discog.,
        index. London: Paladin, 1984. 367p., illus., bibliog.,
        discog., index.
        Includes complete discography compiled by Brian Priestley.

2344.   Cole, Bill. Miles Davis: a Musical Biography. New York:
        Morrow, 1974 (Reissued: 1980). 256p., bibliog., discog.,
        index.
        Emphasis on his music; includes thirteen transcriptions,
        1949-69. Also has detailed listing of his recording sessions.
        Based on the author's M.A. thesis, same title, University of
        Pittsburgh.

2345.   James Sydney Michael James. Miles Davis. London: Cassell;
        New York: A.S. Barnes, 1961. 90p., illus., discog. (Kings
        of Jazz, 9)
        Musical biography based on his recordings. Incorporated
        into item 1566.

                           Discographies

2346.   Jepsen, Jorgen Grunnet. A Discography of Miles Davis. Bio-
        graphical notes by Knud H. Ditlevsen. Brande, Denmark: Debut
        Records, 1959. 19p. 2nd. ed.: 1960. 21p. 3rd. ed.: Copen-
        hagen: Knudsen, 1969. 40p.

DAVIS, SAMMY, JR.

2347.   Davis, Sammy, Jr. Yes, I Can: the Story of Sammy Davis, Jr.
        With Jane and Burt Boyar. New York: Farrar, Straus, and
        Giroux; London: Cassell, 1965. 612p., illus. New York:
        Pocket Books, 1966. 626p., illus.
            Autobiography.

2348.   ————. Hollywood In a Suitcase. New York: Morrow; London:
        Granada, 1980; London: Star Books, 1981. 255p., illus.
            Second volume of his autobiography. Illustrated with
        photographs by the author.

DAY, DORIS

2349.   Day, Doris. Doris Day: Her Own Story. With Aeron Edward
        Hotchner. New York: Morrow; London: W.H. Allen, 1976;
        London: Star Books, 1977. 365p., illus., filmog., index.

2350.   Gelb, Alan. The Doris Day Scrapbook. New York: Grosset and
        Dunlap, 1977. 159p., illus.

2351.   Morris, George. Doris Day. New York: Pyramid Publications,
        1976. 159p., illus., filmog., index. (Pyramid Illustrated
        History of the Movies)

2352.   Young, Christopher. The Films of Doris Day. Secaucus, New
        Jersey: Citadel Pr., 1977. 253p., illus.

DE COURVILLE, ALBERT

2353.   De Courville, Albert. I Tell You. London: Chapman and Hall,
        1928. 253p., illus.
            Autobiography.

DE KOVEN, REGINALD

2354.   De Koven, Anna. A Musician and His Wife. New York; London:
        Harper and Brothers, 1926. 259p., illus.
            Biography, by his wife.

DE MILLE, AGNES

2355.   De Mille, Agnes George. And Promenade Home. Boston: Atlantic
        Monthly Pr., 1958 (Reprinted: New York: Da Capo Pr., 1980.
        Series in Dance). 301p., illus. London: Hamish Hamilton,
        1959. 293p., illus.
            Reminiscences.

2356. ————. Dance To the Piper. Boston: Atlantic Monthly Pr.,
       1951. 342p., illus. London (as Dance To the Piper: Memoirs
       of the Ballet): Hamish Hamilton, 1951. 318p., illus. New
       York: Bantam, 1964. 326p., illus. (Bantam Pathfinder Edit-
       ions). With a new preface by Cynthia Gregory. New York:
       Da Capo Pr., 1980. 342p., illus. (Series in Dance)
       Autobiography.

2357. ————. Dance To the Piper; and, Promenade Home: a Two-
       Part Autobiography. New York: Da Capo Pr., 1982. 643p.,
       illus.
       Combination of items 2355 and 2356.

2358. ————. Reprieve: a Memoir. Garden City, New York: Double-
       day, 1981. 288p., illus.

DEEP PURPLE

2359. Charlesworth, Chris. Deep Purple: the Illustrated Biography.
       London: Omnibus Pr., 1983.   p., illus., discog.

2360. Deep Purple. London: Omnibus Pr., 1984. 96p., illus. (H.M.
       Photobooks)
       Chiefly illustrated.

2361. Robinson, Simon. Deep Purple. Sheffield, Yorkshire: The
       Author, 1983.   p., illus.
       Discography.

DEF LEPPARD

2362. McGilly, Willy. Def Leppard. London; New York: Proteus,
       1984. 128p., illus., discog.

DEL RIO, DOLORES

2363. Woll, Allen L. The Films of Dolores Del Rio. New York:
       Gordon Pr., 1977.   p., illus., filmog. (Gordon Film Series)

DENE, TERRY

2364. Wooding, Dan. I Thought Terry Dene Was Dead. London: Cover-
       dale House, 1974. 160p., illus.

DENVER, JOHN

2365. Dachs, David. John Denver. New York: Pyramid Publications,
       1976. 93p., illus., bibliog., discog., filmog.

2366. Fleischer, Leonore. John Denver. New York: Flash Books,
       1976. 80p., illus., discog.

2367. Martin, James. John Denver: Rocky Mountain Wonderboy. New
       York: Pinnacle Books; London: Everest, 1977. 148p., illus.

DESMOND, FLORENCE

2368. Desmond, Florence. Florence Desmond, By Herself. London:
       Harrap, 1953. 303p., illus.

DEXTER, DAVE

2369. Dexter, Dave. Playback: a Newsman-Record Producer's Hits
       and Misses, From the Thirties To the Seventies. New York:
       Billboard Publications, 1976. 239p., illus., index.
          Memoirs of the popular music business, by former Capitol
       Records producer.

DIETRICH, MARLENE

2370. Carr, Larry. Four Fabulous Faces: the Evolution and
       Metamorphosis of Garbo, Swanson, Crawford, Dietrich. New
       Rochelle, New York: Arlington House, 1970. 492p., illus.

          ————. Four Fabulous Faces: Swanson, Garbo, Crawford,
       Dietrich. New York: Galahad Books, 1970; Harmondsworth,
       Middlesex; New York: Penguin, 1978. 492p., illus.

2371. Dickens, Homer. The Films of Marlene Dietrich. Secaucus,
       New Jersey: Citadel Pr., 1968. 223p., illus. (Citadel Film
       Series)

2372. Frewin, Leslie Ronald. Blonde Venus: a Life of Marlene
       Dietrich. London: MacGibbon and Kee, 1955. 159p., illus.

          ————. Dietrich: the Story of a Star. London: Leslie
       Frewin; New York: Stein and Day, 1967. 191p., illus.,
       filmog. Rev. ed.: London: Coronet, 1974. 187p., illus.,
       filmog.

2373. Higham, Charles. Marlene: the Life of Marlene Dietrich.
       New York: Norton, 1977; London: Hart-Davis, MacGibbon; Lon-
       don: Mayflower, 1978. 320p., illus., filmog., index. New
       York: Pocket Books, 1979. 261p., illus., filmog., index.

2374. Kobal, John. <u>Marlene Dietrich</u>. London: Studio Vista, 1968.
       160p., illus., bibliog.

2375. Morley, Sheridan. <u>Marlene Dietrich</u>. London: Elm Tree Books,
       1976; New York: McGraw-Hill, 1977. 128p., illus., filmog.,
       index. London: Sphere, 1978. 93p., illus., filmog., index.

2376. Navacelle, Thierry de. <u>Sublime Marlene</u>. Photographs from
       The Kobal Collection. Translated from the French by Carey
       L. Smith. London: Sidgwick and Jackson, 1984. 158p., illus.,
       index.

2377. Walker, Alexander. <u>Dietrich</u>. London: Thames and Hudson,
       1984. 209p., illus., index.

DIETZ, HOWARD

2378. Dietz, Howard. <u>Dancing In the Dark: Words by Howard Dietz</u>.
       New York: Quadrangle, 1974. 370p., illus.
          Autobiography. Withdrawn from sale.

          ————. <u>Dancing In the Dark: an Autobiography</u>. New York:
       Quadrangle, 1974; New York; London: Bantam, 1976. 366p.,
       illus., index.
          One chapter of original edition omitted.

DIRE STRAITS

2379. Nicholls, Mike. <u>Dire Straits</u>. London; New York: Proteus,
       1984.   p., illus., discog.

2380. Oldfield, Michael. <u>Dire Straits</u>. London: Sidgwick and
       Jackson; New York: Morrow, 1984. 152p., illus., discog.,
       index.

DIXON, REGINALD

2381. Dixon, Reginald. "<u>Mister Blackpool</u>." Sheffield, Yorkshire:
       Turntable Publications, 1977. 188p., illus.
          Autobiography of popular concert and radio organist.

DODDS, JOHNNY

2382. Lambert, George Edmund. <u>Johnny Dodds</u>. London: Cassell; New
       York: A.S. Barnes, 1961. 90p., illus., discog. (Kings of
       Jazz, 10)
          Incorporated into item 1566.

DODDS, WARREN "BABY"

2383. Dodds, Warren "Baby". The Baby Dodds Story. As told to
       Larry Gara. Los Angeles: Contemporary Pr., 1959. 109p.,
       illus., index.
          Taped autobiography, transcribed and edited by Gara.

DOLPHY, ERIC

2384. Kraner, Dietrich Heinz. The Eric Dolphy Discography, 1958-
       1964. Graz, Austria: Modern Jazz Series, 1967. 16p.

2385. Rissi, Mathias. Eric Dolphy: Discography. Adliswil. West
       Germany: The Author, 1977. 29p.

2386. Simosko, Vladimir, and Barry Tepperman. Eric Dolphy: a
       Musical Biography and Discography. Washington, D.C.:
       Smithsonian Institution Pr., 1974; New York: Da Capo Pr.,
       1979; Ann Arbor, Michigan: Books Demand/U.M.I., 1984. 132p.,
       illus.
          Lists all known recordings, including radio broadcasts.
       Chronological arrangement.

DOONICAN, VAL

2387. Doonican, Val. The Special Years: an Autobiography. London:
       Elm Tree Books, 1980. 157p., illus. London: Sphere, 1981.
       181p., illus.

DOORS

2388. Jahn, Mike. Jim Morrison and The Doors: an Unauthorized
       Book. New York: Grosset and Dunlap, 1969. 95p., illus.

2389. Sugerman, Danny. The Doors. London: Vermilion, 1983.   p.,
       illus.

2390. Tobler, John, and Andrew Doe. The Doors. London; New York:
       Proteus, 1984. 127p., illus., discog., filmog.

                              Periodicals

2391. Moonlight Drive. 2A, Page-Heath Villas, Bromley, Kent. bi-
       monthly, 1983- .

Individual Group Members

Morrison, Jim

Literary Works

2392. Morrison, Jim. <u>An American Prayer</u>. Los Angeles: Doors Inc-
       orporated, 1970. unpaged.
           Poems. Limited edition.

2393. ————. <u>The Lords; and, Notes On Vision</u>. Los Angeles: The
       Author, 1969. unpaged.
           Poems.

2394. ————. <u>The Lords; and, The New Creatures</u>. New York: Simon
       and Schuster, 1970; London: Omnibus Pr., 1985. 141p.
           Poems.

Biographies

2395. Hopkins, Jerry, and Daniel Sugerman. <u>No One Here Gets Out
       Alive</u>. New York: Warner Books; London: Plexus Publishing,
       1980. 387p., illus., discog.
           Includes motion picture credits, lyrics, and afterword by
       Michael McClure. Originally researched and written by
       Hopkins; rewritten by Sugerman.

2396. Kunstler, James Howard. <u>The Life of Byron James</u>. New York:
       Norton, 1982.   p.
           Novel based on life of Morrison. Instead of dying,
       protagonist goes underground; later being interviewed.

2397. Lisciandro, Frank. <u>Jim Morrison: an Hour For Magic</u>. New
       York: Delilah; London: Eel Pie, 1982. 160p., illus.
           Includes poetry by Morrison. Chiefly illustrated.

DORSEY, TOMMY AND JIMMY

2398. Allen, Stuart S. <u>The Fabulous Dorseys</u>. Edited by Julien
       Vedey. London: Venture Publications, 1947. 32p., illus.
       (2nd. ed.: 1948)

2399. Sanford, Herb. <u>Tommy and Jimmy: the Dorsey Years</u>. Introduct-
       ion by Bing Crosby. New Rochelle, New York: Arlington House;
       London: Ian Allan, 1972; New York: Da Capo Pr., 1980. 305p.,
       illus., index.
           Based on author's personal knowledge. Includes listings
       of their leading sidemen and arrangers; also their 1935 tour
       itinerary.

Dorsey, Tommy and Jimmy (cont.)

Discographies

2400. Edwards, Ernie, George Hall, and Bill Korst. Jimmy Dorsey
       and His Orchestra: a Complete Discography, 1953-1957.
       Whittier, California: Jazz Discographies Unlimited, 1966.
       30p. 2nd. ed.: Whittier, California: Erngeobil Publications,
       1968. 30p.

DRAGONETTE, JESSICA

2401. Dragonette, Jessica. Faith Is a Song: the Odyssey of an
       American Artist. New York: McKay, 1951. 322p., illus.
          Autobiography.

DRESSER, PAUL

2402. Dreiser, Theodore. The Songs of Paul Dresser. New York:
       Boni and Liveright, 1927. 263p.
          Collection of songs by Dresser, prefaced by detailed
       memoir by his brother.

DRESSLER, MARIE

2403. Dressler, Marie. The Eminent American Comedienne Marie
       Dressler In The Life Story of an Ugly Duckling: an Autobio-
       graphical Fragment. New York: McBride; London: Hutchinson,
       1925. 234p., illus.

2404. ————. My Own Story. As told to Mildred Harrington.
       Boston: Little, Brown, 1934; London: Hurst and Blackett,
       1935. 256p., illus.

DRIFTERS

2405. Millar, Bill. The Drifters: the Rise and Fall of the Black
       Vocal Group. London: Studio Vista, 1971. 112p., illus.,
       bibliog., discog. New York: Macmillan, 1971; New York:
       Collier-Macmillan, 1972. 180p., illus., bibliog., discog.
          Includes coverage of similar groups, The Inkspots onwards.

DUBIN, AL

* Dubin, Al. The Art of Songwriting.
  * Cited below as item 3836.

2406. McGuire, Patricia D. The Lullaby of Broadway: a Biography
of Al Dubin. Secaucus, New Jersey: Citadel Pr., 1983.
256p., illus.

DUBLINERS

2407. Hardy, Mary (comp.). The Dubliners Scrapbook: an Intimate
Journal. London: Wise Publications, 1978. 96p., illus.
Includes press cuttings, and letters.

DUKE, VERNON (pseud. of Vladimir Dukelsky)

2408. Duke, Vernon. Listen Here! A Critical Essay On Music
Depreciation. New York: Ivan Obolensky, 1963. 406p.
Vitriolic denunciation of modern musical trends, and of
other musicians.

2409. ———. Passport To Paris. Boston: Little, Brown, 1955.
502p., illus.
Autobiography.

DURAN DURAN

2410. Duran Duran. Duran Duran In Their Own Words. Compiled by
Pearce Marchbank. London: Omnibus Pr., 1984. 32p., illus.
From press and other interviews.

2411. ———. Duran Duran: the Official Lyric Book. The Complete
Words To All Their Songs. London: Music Sales, 1983. 32p.,
illus.

Biographies

2412. Burnett-Foster, Adam. The Complete Duran Duran. London:
Zomba Books, 1984. 96p., illus. (Rock Masters)

2413. David, Maria. Duran Duran. Produced by Ted Smart and Gerald
Hughes. Edited by David Gibbon. Designed by Philip Clucas.
Guildford, Surrey: Colour Library Books, 1984. 61p., illus.
(Coombe Books)
Chiefly illustrated.

Duran Duran (cont.)

2414. De Graaf, Kasper, and Malcolm Garrett. <u>Duran Duran: Their
       Story</u>. London; New York: Proteus, 1982. 32p., illus.,
       discog., filmog.

2415. Flans, Robyn. <u>Inside Duran Duran</u>. New York: Sharon Pub-
       lications, 1984. 64p., illus. (Star Books)

2416. Gaiman, Neil. <u>Duran Duran: the First Four Years of the Fab
       Five</u>. London; New York: Proteus, 1984. 126p., illus.,
       discog.

2417. Kamin, Philip, and Peter Goddard. <u>Duran Duran Live</u>. New
       York: St. Martin's Pr.; London: Virgin Books, 1984. 96p.,
       illus.
          Performance photographs by Kamin; text by Goddard.

2418. Norman, Neil. <u>Suburban Heroes: the Rise and Rise of Duran
       Duran</u>. London: Elm Tree Books, 1985. 160p., illus., discog.

2419. Simmons, William. <u>Duran Duran</u>. Skokie, Illinois: Publicat-
       ions International; London: Octopus, 1984. 65p., illus.,
       discog.
          Chiefly illustrated.

DURANTE, JIMMY

2420. Fowler, Gene. <u>Schnozzola: the Story of Jimmy Durante</u>. New
       York: Viking Pr., 1951. 261p., illus. London: Hammond, 1952.
       254p., illus.

DYLAN, BOB (<u>pseud. of</u> Robert Zimmerman)

2421. Dylan, Bob. <u>Bob Dylan In His Own Words</u>. Compiled by Miles.
       Edited by Pearce Marchbank. Designed by Perry Neville.
       London: Omnibus Pr.; New York: Quick Fox, 1978. 126p., illus.
          From press and other interviews.

2422. ————. <u>Bob Dylan In His Own Write</u>. London: Aloes seolA,
       196? p.
          Letters and poems from the early 1960's. Pirated edition.

2423. ————. <u>Eleven Outlined Epitaphs</u>. London: Aloes seolA,
       196? p.
          Poems. Originally published as sleeve notes to his long-
       playing record <u>The Times They Are A-Changin'</u>. Pirated edition.

2424. ————. <u>Poem To Joanie</u>. London: Aloes seolA, 196? p.
          Poem in honor of Joan Baez. Originally published as part
       of the sleeve notes for her album <u>Joan Baez in Concert</u>.
       Pirated edition.

2425. ———. <u>Tarantula</u>. Hibbing, Minnesota: Wimp Pr., 1970.
54p.
     Pirated, mimeographed, edition of his novel. Text from
proofs. Actually published in San Francisco; real publisher
unknown.

     ———. ———. San Francisco: Space Pr., 1971. 95p.
     Pirated edition.

     ———. ———. New York: Macmillan; London: MacGibbon and
Kee, 1971. 137p. St. Albans, Hertfordshire: Panther, 1973.
124p.
     Avant-garde novel. Written 1965-66; delayed by the
author's accident and convalescence.

Lyric Collections

2426. ———. <u>Approximately Complete Works</u>. Amsterdam: De Bezige
Bij Thomas Rap, 1970. 218p.
     His song texts in English. No music.

2427. ———. <u>Blues, Ballate, e Canzoni</u>. Introduction by Fernanda
Pivano. Edited and tranlated by Stefano Rizzo. Rome: Newton
Compton Italiana, 1972. 304p. (Paperbacks Poeti, 9)
     His song texts in English and Italian. No music.

2428. ———. <u>Damer i Regn</u>. Oslo, Norway: Den Norske Bokklubben,
1977.   p., illus.
     Texts of songs, in English and Norwegian.

2429. ———. <u>Lily, Rosemary, and the Jack of Hearts, and Other
Poems</u>. London: Duophonic Print, 1978.   p., illus.
     Lyrics from his album <u>Blood On the Tracks</u>.

2430. ———. <u>Writings and Drawings</u>. New York: Knopf; London:
Cape, 1973. 315p., illus., index. St. Albans, Hertfordshire:
Panther, 1974. 479p., illus., index.
     Lyrics, 1962-72. Chronological, album-by-album arrange-
ment. Transcripts have some variation from recordings.

Criticism

2431. Downley, Tim, and Barry Dunnage. <u>Bob Dylan: From a Hard
Rain To a Slow Train</u>. Tunbridge Wells, Kent: Midas Book,
1982; London; New York: Omnibus Pr., 1983 (Studies in Modern
Music). 177p., illus., bibliog., discog.
     Consideration of recurrent themes in his lyrics.

2432. Gray, Michael. <u>Song and Dance Man: the Art of Bob Dylan</u>.
London: Hart-Davis; New York: Dutton, 1972. 337p., illus.,
bibliog., discog., index. London: Abacus, 1973. 332p., illus.,
bibliog., discog., index. <u>New ed.</u>: London: Hamlyn, 1981.
236p., illus., bibliog., discog., index.

Dylan, Bob (cont.)

Criticism (cont.)

2433. Herdman, John. <u>Voice Without Restraint: a Study of Bob
       Dylan's Lyrics and Their Background</u>. Edinburgh: Paul Harris
       Publishing, 1982. 164p., bibliog., index.

2434. Mellers, Wilfred. <u>A Darker Shade of Pale: a Backdrop To
       Bob Dylan</u>. London: Faber and Faber, 1984. 255p., illus.,
       bibliog., index.
          Musicological study.

2435. Pickering, Stephen. <u>Bob Dylan Approximately: a Portrait of
       the Jewish Poet In Search of God--a Midrash</u>. New York:
       David McKay, 1975. 204p., illus., bibliog. refs.
          Dylan's 1974 tour linked to religious considerations.

2436. ———— (ed.). <u>Dylan: a Commemoration</u>. Assistant editor:
       Scott Sullivan. Berkeley, California: Book People, 1971.
       70p., illus.
          Critical and other articles. Emphasis on religious and
       philosophical aspects of his work.

2437. ————. <u>Praxis One: Existence, Men, and Realities</u>. Berk-
       eley, California: Book People, 1971. 152p., illus., bibliog.
          Essays and articles on the Judaic aspects of Dylan's
       work. Seen as "Hasidic existentialism."

2438. Thomson, Elizabeth M. (ed.). <u>Conclusions on the Wall: New
       Essays on Bob Dylan</u>. Manchester, England: Thin Man, 1980.
       108p., illus., bibliog.

                             Biographies

2439. Cott, Jonathan. <u>Dylan</u>. New York: Doubleday; London:
       Vermilion, 1984. 246p., illus., discog. (A <u>Rolling Stone</u>
       Pr. Book)

2440. Gross, Michael, and Robert Alexander. <u>Bob Dylan: an Illus-
       trated History</u>. New York: Grosset and Dunlap; London: Elm
       Tree Books, 1978; New York: Ace Books, 1980. 150p., illus.,
       bibliog.

2441. Kramer, Daniel. <u>Bob Dylan</u>. Secaucus, New Jersey: Citadel
       Pr., 1967; Secaucus, New Jersey: Castle Books, 1968. 150p.,
       illus. New York: Pocket Books, 1968. 210p., illus.
          Photographic study of the two years of Dylan's transition
       from folk to rock.

2442. McGregor, Craig (ed.). <u>Bob Dylan: a Retrospective</u>. New
       York: Morrow, 1972. 408p., illus. <u>Abridged ed.</u>: Sydney,

New South Wales; London: Angus and Robertson, 1972. 169p.
London: Pan, 1975. 281p., illus. (Picador Books). Rev. ed.:
Sydney, New South Wales; London: Angus and Robertson, 1980.
237p., illus.
   Chronological collection of significant biographical and
other articles.

2443. Miles (pseud. of Barry Miles). Bob Dylan. London: Big O
       Publishing, 1978. 64p., illus.

2444. Pickering, Stephen. Tour 1974. Berkeley, California: Echo
       Echo Publications, 1974.   p., illus.
          Limited edition. Published immediately prior to Dylan's
       1974 tour.

2445. Ribakove, Sy, and Barbara Ribakove. Folk-Rock: the Bob
       Dylan Story. New York: Dell, 1966. 124p., discog.

2446. Rolling Stone. Knockin' On Dylan's Door: On the Road In '74.
       By The Editors of Rolling Stone. New York: Pocket Books,
       1974; London (as Knockin' On Dylan's Door): Dempsey/Cassell,
       1975. 137p., illus.

2447. Rowley, Chris. Blood On the Tracks: the Story of Bob Dylan.
       London; New York: Proteus, 1984. 160p., illus., discog.

2448. Scaduto, Anthony. Bob Dylan: an Intimate Biography. New
       York: Grosset and Dunlap; London: W.H. Allen; London: Abacus,
       1972. 280p., illus., discog. New York: New American Lib-
       rary, 1973. 351p., illus., discog. (A Signet Book)

       ————. Bob Dylan. Updated, with a new afterword by
       Stephen Gaines. New York: New American Library, 1979. 366p.,
       illus., discog., index. (A Signet Book)

2449. Shepard, Sam. Rolling Thunder Logbook. New York: Viking Pr.,
       1977; Harmondsworth, Middlesex: Penguin, 1978. 184p., illus.
          Diary of Dylan's 1975-76 tour.

2450. Sloman, Larry. On the Road With Bob Dylan: Rolling With the
       Thunder. New York: Bantam, 1978. 412p., illus.
          Account of his 1975-76 tour.

2451. Thompson, Toby. Positively Main Street: an Unorthodox View
       of Bob Dylan. New York: Coward, McCann and Geoghegan;
       London: New English Library, 1971. 188p.
          The author visits Dylan's birthplace; talks to people who
       knew him before achieving fame. Originally published serially
       in the Village Voice and U.S. 2.

2452. Williams, Paul. Dylan: What Happened? South Bend, Indiana:
       and Books/Entwhistle Books, 1979. 128p., illus.
          Account of Dylan's brief conversion to Christianity.

2453. Yenne, Bill (ed.). One Foot On the Highway: Bob Dylan On
       Tour, 1974. San Francisco: Klonh Books, 1974.   p., illus.
          Chiefly illustrated.

Dylan, Bob (cont.)

Discographies

2454. Barrett, G. My Back Pages. Stoke-on-Trent, Staffordshire:
The Author, 1982.   p.
Concentrates on rare recordings.

2455. Cable, Paul. Bob Dylan: His Unreleased Recordings. London:
Scorpion Publications, 1978. 192p., illus. Rev. ed.: New
York: Schirmer Books, 1980.   p., illus.

2456. Dorman, James. Recorded Dylan. Pinedale, California: Soma
Pr., 1983.   p.

2457. Hoggard, Stuart, and Jim Shields. Bob Dylan: an Illustrated
Discography. Dumbarton, Scotland: Transmedia Express, 1978.
108p., illus., bibliog., index. (Rev. ed.: 1979)
In chronological order. Includes bootleg recordings.

2458. Krogsgaard, Michael. Twenty Years of Recording: the Bob
Dylan Reference Book. Copenhagen: Scandinavian Institute
for Rock Research, 1981. 608p., index.
The definitive discography. Includes details of every
recording session, formal and informal; also concert and
other appearances where recordings are known to exist.

2459. ————. Rain Unravelled Tales. Copenhagen: Scandinavian
Institute for Rock Research, 1981.   p.
Supplements item 2458. Details of one hundred tapes of
Dylan recordings that are rumored to exist.

2460. Rinzler, Alan. Bob Dylan: the Illustrated Record. New York:
Harmony Books; London: Music Sales, 1979. 120p., illus.,
bibliog., discog.
Bio-discography.

Motion Pictures

2461. Pennebaker, D.A. Bob Dylan: Don't Look Back. New York:
Ballantine, 1968. 152p., illus.
Complete dialog and over two hundred illustrations from
Pennebaker's cinema-verité record of Dylan's 1965 tour of
Britain, Don't Look Back.

Miscellanea

2462. Fletcher, Alan, and Robert Litchfield. How Many Roads? A Bob
Dylan Quiz Book. London: Plexus Publishing, 1984. 128p.,
illus.

Periodicals

2463. <u>Bob Dylan Occasionally</u>. Wolverhampton, England. irreg.,
      December 1981-?

2464. <u>The Telegraph</u>. Post Office Box 18, Bury, Lancashire. irreg.,
      1981- .
          Published by the Bob Dylan Information Service. Includes
      irreg. information sheet, <u>The Wicked Messenger</u>, as supple-
      ment.

2465. <u>Zimmerman Blues</u>. St. Louis, Missouri. quarterly, 1975-79.
          Continued as <u>Changin'</u> as of issue 10, 1979-?

EDDY, NELSON <u>see</u> MACDONALD, JEANETTE, AND NELSON EDDY

EDMONDS, NOEL

2466. Edmonds, Noel. <u>The Multi-Coloured Noel Edmonds</u>. With
      Michael Cable. London: W.H. Allen, 1978. 96p., illus.
          Autobiography of British disk-jockey.

EDWARD H. DAFIS

2467. Wyn, Hefin. <u>Doeod Neb Yn Becso Dam: Hanes, Llunian a</u>
      <u>Chaneuon Edward H. Dafis</u>. Penygroes, Gwynnedd, Wales: Sain
      (Recordian) Cyf, 1977. 79p., illus.
          In Welsh. Story of Edward H. Dafis rock group.

EDWARDES, GEORGE

2468. Bloom, Ursula Harvey. <u>Curtain Call For The Guv'nor: a</u>
      <u>Biography of George Edwardes</u>. London: Hutchinson, 1954.
      238p., illus.

ELDRIDGE, ROY

  *   Evensmo, Jan. <u>The Trumpet of Roy Eldridge, 1933-1943</u>.
          * Cited above as item 1548.

ELECTRIC LIGHT ORCHESTRA

2469. Bevan, Bev. <u>The Electric Light Orchestra Story</u>. London:
      Mushroom Publishing, 1980; New York: Quick Fox, 1981. 175p.,
      illus., discog.
          By band member.

ELLINGTON, EDWARD KENNEDY "DUKE"

* Ellington, Duke. <u>How To Write a Song</u>.
  * Cited below as item 3849.

2470. ———. <u>Music Is My Mistress</u>. Garden City, New York:
Doubleday, 1973; London: W.H. Allen, 1974; London: Quartet,
1977; New York: Da Capo Pr., 1976. 523p., illus., bibliog.,
discog.
      Autobiography. Includes listing of his compositions.
Da Capo Pr. edition has revised discography, compiled by
Stanley Dance.

                          Biographies

2471. Arnaud, Noel, Jacques Bureau, and Michel Philippot. <u>Duke
Ellington</u>. Paris: Messager Boiteux, Gizard, 1950. 18p.,
illus.

2472. Dance, Stanley. <u>The World of Duke Ellington</u>. New York:
Scribner's; London: Macmillan, 1971; New York: Da Capo Pr.,
1980. 311p., illus., discog., index.

2473. Darrell, Robert Donaldson. <u>Black Beauty</u>. Philadelphia:
(Publisher unknown), 1933.   p.

2474. Ellington, Mercer. <u>Duke Ellington In Person: an Intimate
Memoir</u>. With Stanley Dance. Boston: Houghton Mifflin;
London: Hutchinson, 1978. 236p., illus., discog., index.
      By his son. Includes listing of Ellington's compositions.

2475. Gammond, Peter (ed.). <u>Duke Ellington: His Life and Music</u>.
Foreword by Hugues Panassié. London: Phoenix House, 1958;
New York: Roy, 1959; New York: Da Capo Pr., 1977 (Roots of
Jazz). 255p., illus., discog.
      Pieces by fifteen contributors, mostly British.

2476. ———. <u>Duke Ellington</u>. Tunbridge Wells, Kent: Spellmount;
New York: Hippocrene Books, 1984. 96p., illus., discog.
(Jazz Masters)

2477. George, Don. <u>The Real Duke Ellington</u>. London: Robson Books,
1982. 272p., illus., index.
      By his companion and collaborator of over thirty years.

2478. Gutman, Bill. <u>Duke: the Musical Life of Duke Ellington</u>.
New York: Random House, 1977. 185p., illus., discog., index.
      Aimed at younger readers.

2479. Jewell, Derek. <u>Duke: a Portrait of Duke Ellington</u>. London:
Elm Tree Books, 1977. 192p., illus., discog., index. New
York: Norton, 1977. 264p., illus., bibliog., discog., index.
London: Sphere, 1978. 302p., illus., bibliog., discog., index.

2480. Lambert, George Edmund. Duke Ellington. London: Cassell;
       New York: A.S. Barnes, 1959. 90p., illus., bibliog.,
       discog. (Kings of Jazz, 1)
       Incorporated into item 1566.

2481. Trazegnies, Jean de. Duke Ellington: Harlem Aristocrat of
       Jazz. Brussels: Hot Club de Belgique, 1946. 80p., illus.

2482. Ulanov, Barry. Duke Ellington. New York: Creative Age Pr.,
       1946 (Reprinted: New York: Da Capo Pr., 1975. Roots of Jazz);
       London: Musicians Pr., 1947. 322p., illus., discog., index.

                         Discographies

2483. Aaslund, Benny H. The "Wax Works" of Duke Ellington.
       Stockholm, Sweden: Foliotryck, 1954. 164p.
       Coverage to 1954. Supplemented by item 2489.

2484. Bakker, Dick M. Duke Ellington On Microgroove, 1923-1942.
       Alphen aan den Rijn, Holland: Micrography, 1974. unpaged,
       index.
       Lists all known recordings (including radio broadcasts),
       1923-42; gives all known microgroove releases of these.

2485. Connor, Donald Russell. Twenty Years of The Duke, 1933-1955.
       Carnegie, Pennsylvania: Pope's Records Unlimited, 1966. 12p.

2486. Jepsen, Jorgen Grunnet. Discography of Duke Ellington.
       Biographical notes by Knud H. Ditlevsen. Brande, Denmark:
       Debut Records, 1959.
       Vol. 1: 1925-37. p.
       Vol. 2: 1937-47. p.
       Vol. 3: 1948-60. p.

2487. Massagli, Luciano, Liborio Pusateri, and Giovanni M. Volote.
       Duke Ellington's Story on Records. Milan: Musica Jazz,
       1966- . p., indexes.
       Detailed recording information. Each volume has separate
       index.

2488. Preston, Denis. Mood Indigo. Egham, Surrey: Citizen Pr.,
       1946. 84p.
       Bio-discography.

2489. Sanfilippo, Luigi. General Catalog of Duke Ellington's
       Recorded Music. Palermo, Italy: Centro Studi di Musica
       Contemporanea, 1964. 70p., index. 2nd. ed.: Palermo, Italy:
       Centro Studi di Musica Contemporanea, 1966. 112p., index.
       Continues item 2483. Lists 1,472 titles; chronological
       sequence. Includes V-disks, motion picture, radio, and
       television transcriptions.

ELLIS, MARY

2490. Ellis, Mary. <u>Those Dancing Years: an Autobiography</u>. London:
       John Murray, 1982. 182p., illus., index.

ELLIS, VIVIAN

2491. Ellis, Vivian. <u>I'm On a See-Saw</u>. London: Michael Joseph,
       1953; Bath, Avon: Cedric Chivers, 1974. 270p., illus.,
       index.
           Autobiography.

EMMETT, DANIEL DECATUR

2492. Galbreath, Charles Burleigh. <u>Daniel Decatur Emmett, Author
       of "Dixie."</u> Columbus, Ohio: Fred J. Heer, 1904. 66p.,
       illus., index.
           Based on personal knowledge.

2493. Nathan, Hans. <u>Dan Emmett and the Rise of Early Negro Min-
       strelsy</u>. Norman, Oklahoma: University of Oklahoma Pr.,
       1962. 496p., illus., bibliog., index.
           Includes words and music of some of his songs.

2494. <u>The Origin of Negro Minstrelsy and the Birth of Emmett's
       "Dixie."</u> Mount Vernon, Oklahoma: Christian Music Publishing
       Company, n.d.   p.

EMNEY, FRED

2495. Fairlie, Gerard. <u>The Fred Emney Story</u>. London: Hutchinson,
       1960. 190p., illus.

ENGEL, LEHMAN

2496. Engel, Lehman. <u>This Bright Day: an Autobiography</u>. New York:
       Macmillan, 1974. 366p., illus.
           Includes behind-the-scenes accounts of Broadway musical
       productions.

ESSEX, DAVID

2497. Tremlett, George. <u>The David Essex Story</u>. London: Futura,
       1974. 144p., illus. London: White Lion, 1976. 140p., illus.

ETHIOPIAN SERENADERS

2498. Ethiopian Serenaders, The. The Ethiopian Serenaders' Own
       Book. Philadelphia; New York: Fisher and Brothers, 1857.
       256p.

EURYTHMICS

2499. Eurythmics. Eurythmics In Their Own Words. Compiled by
       London: Omnibus Pr., 1983. 32p., illus.
          Compiled from press and other interviews.

2500. Jasper, Tony. Eurythmics. London: Zomba Books, 1985.
       128p., illus., discog. (Rock Masters)

2501. Roland, Paul. Eurythmics. London; New York: Proteus, 1984.
       p., illus., discog.

2502. Waller, Johnny, and Steve Rapport. Eurythmics: Sweet
       Dreams. The Official Biography. Foreword by Dave Stewart
       and Annie Lennox. London: Virgin Books, 1985. 128p., illus.,
       discog.

EVANS, BILL

2503. Feather, Leonard Geoffrey. Bill Evans. Discography by
       Bruno Schiozzi. Milan: Fratelli Fabbri, 1968. 16p., discog.
       (Il Jazz, 14)
          In Italian.

EVANS, GIL

2504. Hentoff, Nat. Gil Evans. New York: Broadcast Music, 1960.
       20p.

2505. Horricks, Raymond. Svengali, or, The Orchestra Called Gil
       Evans. Selected discography by Tony Middleton. Tunbridge
       Wells, Kent: Spellmount; New York: Hippocrene Books, 1984.
       95p., illus., bibliog., discog. (Jazz Masters)

EVERLY BROTHERS

2506. Denis, Paul. Meet The Everly Brothers: an Informal Date In
       Words and Personal Album Pictures. London: Amalgamated Pr.,
       195?   p., illus. (Star Special, 2)

2507. White, Roger. Walk Right Back: the Story of The Everly
       Brothers. London: Plexus Publishing, 1984. 160p., illus.,
       discog.

Everly Brothers (cont.)

Periodicals

2508. Everly Brothers International. Edited by Martial F. Bekkers.
Hoge Gouwe 107, Gouda 2300, Holland. irreg., 1980- .

FAIRPORT CONVENTION

2509. Humphries, Patrick. Meet On the Ledge: a History of Fairport Convention. London: Eel Pie, 1983.   p., illus.,
discog.

Periodicals

2510. The Ledge. Edited by Martyn Kenny. 85 Woodlands Way,
Kingswood, Bristol, Avon. quarterly, 1984- .

FAITH, ADAM

2511. Faith, Adam. Adam: His Fabulous Year. Adam's Personal
Story, and His Own Selection of Photos. London: Picture
Story Publications, 1960. unpaged, illus.
Includes record.

2512. ———. Poor Me. London: Four Square Books, 1961. 95p.,
illus.
Autobiography.

FAYE, ALICE

2513. Moshier, W. Franklyn. The Alice Faye Movie Book. Harrisburg, Pennsylvania: Stackpole Books, 1974. 192p., illus.,
discog.

FELSENSTEIN, WALTER

2514. Fuchs, Peter P. (ed.). The Musical Theater of Walter Felsenstein. New York: Norton, 1975.   p., illus.

FENSTON, JOSEPH

2515. Fenston, Joseph. Never Say Die: an Impresario's Scrapbook.
       London: Alexander Moring, 1958. 206p., illus.

FIEDLER, ARTHUR

2516. Dickson, Harry E. Arthur Fiedler and The Boston Pops.
       Boston: Houghton Mifflin, 1981. 256p., illus.

2517. Holland, James R. Mister Pops. Barre, Massachusetts: Barre
       Publishers, 1972. 96p., illus.
           Photographic essay.

2518. Moore, Robert Lowell. Fiedler, the Colorful Mister Pops:
       the Man and His Music. Boston: Little, Brown, 1968; New
       York: Da Capo Pr., 1980. 372p., illus., discog., index.

2519. Wilson, Carol Green. Arthur Fiedler: Music For the Millions.
       The Story of the Conductor of The Boston Pops Orchestra.
       New York: Evans Publishing, 1968. 223p., illus.

FIELD, AL

2520. Field, Alfred Griffith. Watch Yourself Go By: a Book by
       Al. G. Field. Columbus, Ohio: Printed by Spohr and Glenn,
       1912. 537p., illus.

FIELD, SID

2521. Fisher, John. What a Performance! A Life of Sid Field.
       London: Seeley Service, 1975. 236p., illus., index.

FIELDS, GRACIE

2522. Fields, Gracie. Sing As We Go: the Autobiography of Gracie
       Fields. London: Frederick Muller, 1960. 203p., illus.
       Garden City, New York: Doubleday, 1961. 216p., illus.
       Manchester, England: World Distributors, 1962. 188p., illus.

                              Biographies

2523. Aza, Bert. Our Gracie: the Story of Gracie Fields. London:
       Pitkins, 1951. 32p., illus.

Fields, Gracie (cont.)

2524. Burgess, Muriel. <u>Gracie Fields</u>. With Tommy Keen. London:
       W.H. Allen, 1980; London: Star Books, 1980. 125p., illus.

2525. Moules, Joan. <u>Gracie</u>. Emsworth, Hampshire: The Author,
       1980. 55p., illus., discog.

2526. ————. <u>Our Gracie: the Life of Dame Gracie Fields</u>. Fore-
       word by Roy Hudd. London: Hale, 1983. 247p., illus.,
       discog., filmog., index.
           Elaboration of item 2525.

2527. Rochdale Museum. <u>Our Gracie</u>. Text by Elizabeth Pollitt.
       Rochdale, Lancashire: Rochdale Arts and Entertainment
       Services, 1978. 25p., illus., bibliog.
           Accompanies exhibition at Rochdale Museum, 1978.

FISHER, EDDIE

2528. Fisher, Eddie. <u>Eddie: My Life, My Loves</u>. New York: Harper
       and Row, 1981; London: Star Books, 1982. 429p., illus.

2529. Greene, Myrna. <u>The Eddie Fisher Story</u>. Middlebury, Vermont:
       P.S. Eriksson, 1979. 210p., illus., index.

FITZGERALD, ELLA

2530. Green, Benny. <u>Ella</u>. London: Elm Tree Books, 1979.   p.,
       illus.

FLANAGAN, BUD (<u>pseud. of</u> Robert Winthrop Flanagan)

2531. Flanagan, Bud. <u>My Crazy Life</u>. London: New English Library,
       1962. 160p., illus. (Four Square Books)

FLEETWOOD MAC

2532. Clarke, Steve. <u>Fleetwood Mac</u>. London; New York: Proteus,
       1984. 128p., illus., discog.

2533. Graham, Samuel. <u>Fleetwood Mac: the Authorized History</u>.
       New York: Warner Books, 1978; Poole, Dorset: Blandford Pr.,
       1980. 175p., illus., discog.

           ————. <u>Fleetwood Mac: Rumours 'n' Fax</u>. New York: Harmony
       Books; London: Book Sales, 1979. 120p., illus., discog.
           Larger format; text identical.

2534. Williams, Mark. <u>Fleetwood Mac</u>. London; New York: Proteus, 1983. 128p., illus., discog.

FLEMMING, HERB

2535. Biagioni, Egino. <u>Herb Flemming</u>. Cologne: The Author, 1976. p.
    In English.

FLESHTONES

2536. <u>Watch This</u>! Edited by Bryan Gregory. 10 Dochart Path, Grangemouth, Stirlingshire, Scotland. irreg., November 1984- .

FLETCHER, TOM

2537. Fletcher, Tom. <u>One Hundred Years of the Negro In Show Business! The Tom Fletcher Story</u>. New York: Burdge, 1954. 337p., illus.
    Autobiography. Includes comment on other artists and on show business life.

FLOREN, MYRON

2538. Floren, Myron, and Randee Floren. <u>Accordion Man</u>. Brattleboro, Vermont: Stephen Greene Pr., 1981. 256p., illus.
    Memoirs.

FORD, TENNESSEE ERNIE

2539. Ford, Tennessee Ernie. <u>This Is My Story, This Is My Song</u>. Line drawings by Lorin Thompson. Englewood Cliffs, New Jersey: Prentice- Hall, 1963. 177p., illus.

FORMBY, GEORGE

2540. Fisher, John. <u>George Formby</u>. London: Woburn Pr., 1975. 96p., illus. (The Entertainers)

2541. Randall, Alan, and Ray Seaton. <u>George Formby: a Biography</u>. London: W.H. Allen, 1974. 192p., illus., discog., filmog.

FORREST, HELEN

2542. Forrest, Helen, and Bill Libby. I Had the Craziest Dream:
       Helen Forrest and the Big Band Era. New York: Coward,
       McCann, and Geoghegan, 1982. 256p., illus.

FOSTER, POPS (pseud. of George Foster)

2543. Foster, Pops. Pops Foster: the Autobiography of a New
       Orleans Jazzman. As told to Tom Stoddard. Introduction by
       Bertram Turetzky. Interchapters by Ross Russell. Discog-
       raphy by Brian Rust. Berkeley, California; London: Univ-
       ersity of California Pr., 1971. 208p., illus., bibliog.,
       discog., index.
           Transcribed from interviews.

FOSTER, STEPHEN COLLINS

                         Bibliographies

2544. Fuld, James J. A Pictorial Bibliography of the First
       Editions of Stephen C. Foster. Philadelphia: Musical
       Americana, 1957. 206p., illus.
           Twenty-five pages of text; rest is plates. Continues
       item 2546.

2545. Howard, John Tasker. The Literature On Stephen Foster.
       Pittsburgh: Foster Hall, 1944. 8p.
           Reprinted from Notes, and other journals.

2546. Whittlesey, Walter R., and O.G. Sonneck. Catalog of First
       Editions of Stephen C. Foster (1826-1864). Washington, D.C.:
       Library of Congress, 1915; New York: Da Capo Pr., 1971. 79p.,
       indexes.
           Continued by item 2545.

                             Lyrics

2547. Foster, Stephen Collins. Biography, Songs, and Musical
       Compositions of Stephen Collins Foster. Compiled by his
       brother, Morrison Foster. Pittsburgh: Percy F. Smith, 1896.
       312p., illus.
           Collection of his works. Includes words and music. Bio-
       graphical preface published separately as item 2552.

2548. ———. Songs. Prepared especially for the Armed Forces by
       the Staff of the Foster Hall Collection of the University of
       Pittsburgh. Pittsburgh: University of Pittsburgh Pr., 1942.
       (Reprinted: 1944; 1952). 24p.
           Words only.

2549. ———. Songs of Stephen Foster. Pittsburgh: University of
       Pittsburgh Pr., 1952. 24p.
          Words only.

                              Biographies

2550. Barnes, Edwin N.C. The Bard of Pittsburgh: Tuning In On
       American Music. Washington, D.C.: Music Education Public-
       ations, 1936. 13p., bibliog. (Tuning In On American Music)

2551. ———. Near Immortals? Stephen Foster, Edward MacDowell,
       Victor Herbert. Washington, D.C.: Music Education Publicat-
       ions, 1940. 48p. (Tuning In On American Music, 5)
          Includes revision of item 2550.

2552. Foster, Morrison. My Brother Stephen. Preface by Josiah
       Kirby Lilly. Indianapolis: Privately printed by Hollenbeck
       Pr., 1932. 56p., illus.
          Limited edition of two thousand copies. Originally
       published as part of item 2547.

2553. Gaul, Harvey Bartlett. The Minstrel of the Alleghenies.
       Pittsburgh: Issued by The Friends of Harvey Gaul, 195? 86p.,
       illus.

2554. Higgins, Helen Boyd. Stephen Foster, Boy Minstrel. Illus-
       trated by Clothilde Embree Funk. Indianapolis: Bobbs-Merrill,
       1944. 201p., illus. (Childhood of Famous Americans)
          Aimed at younger readers.

2555. Hodges, Fletcher. Stephen Foster, Democrat. Pittsburgh:
       University of Pittsburgh Pr., 1946. 30p., illus.
          His political activities. First published in the Lincoln
       Herald, June, 1945.

2556. Howard, John Tasker. Stephen Foster: America's Troubadour.
       New York: Crowell, 1934. 445p., illus., bibliog., index.
       Rev. ed.: New York: Crowell, 1953. 433p., illus., bibliog.,
       index.
          The standard biography. Includes chronology and listing
       of his published works. Rev. ed. has new information on his
       last years.

2557. Lamme, Louise, and Vernon Lamme. Stephen Foster: a Florida
       Minstrel. Illustrated by Bob Lamme. Boynton Beach, Florida:
       Star Pr., 1969. 62p., illus.
          Includes words and histories of his songs.

2558. MacGowan, Robert. The Significance of Stephen Collins Foster.
       Indianapolis: The Author, 1932. 25p.

2559. Milligan, Harold Vincent. Stephen Collins Foster: a Biography
       of America's Folk-Song Composer. New York: Schirmer, 1920;
       New York: Gordon Pr., 1977. 116p., illus.

Foster, Stephen Collins (cont.)

2560. Morneweck, Evelyn Foster. Chronicles of Stephen Foster's
       Family. Pittsburgh: University of Pittsburgh Pr. for the
       Foster Hall Collection, 1944. 2 vols., 767p., illus.
       index. Port Washington, New York: Kennikat Pr., 1973.
       2 vols., 768p., illus., index.
            By niece of Stephen Foster. Includes letters, newspaper
       articles, prints, and other illustrations.

2561. Peare, Catherine Owens. Stephen Foster: His Life. Illus-
       trated by Margaret Ayer. New York: Holt, 1952. 87p.,
       illus.
            Aimed at younger readers.

2562. Purdy, Claire Lee. He Heard America Sing: the Story of
       Stephen Foster. New York: J. Messner, 1940. 236p., illus.
            Aimed at younger readers. Includes words and music of
       songs by Foster.

2563. Smith, Earl Hobson. Stephen Foster; or, Weep No More, My
       Lady: a Biographical Play On the Life of Stephen Collins
       Foster, Father of American Folk Song. Knoxville, Tennessee:
       The Foster Players, 1935. 67p.

2564. Walters, Raymond W. Stephen Foster: Youth's Golden Gleam.
       A Sketch of His Life and Background in Cincinnati, 1846-
       1850. Princeton, New Jersey: Princeton University Pr., 1936.
       160p., illus., bibliog.

                              Miscellanea

2565. Hodges, Fletcher, Jr. A Pittsburgh Composer and His Memorial.
       Pittsburgh: Historical Society of Western Pennsylvania, 1938.
       32p., illus.
            On his memorial at the University of Pittsburgh. Reprinted
       from The Western Pennsylvania Historical Magazine, vol. 21,
       1938.

2566. ─────. The Stephen Collins Foster Memorial of the Univers-
       ity of Pittsburgh, Dedicated June 2, 1937. A Tribute to the
       Composer Whose Melodies Have Become the Heart Songs of the
       American People. Pittsburgh: University of Pittsburgh Pr.,
       1941. 15p., illus., bibliog. (Reprinted: 1941; 1944)

                              Foster Hall

2567. ─────. The Research Work of the Foster Hall Collection.
       Philadelphia: University of Pennsylvania Pr., 1948. 13p.,
       illus.
            Reprinted from Pennsylvania History, July, 1948.

2568. Jillson, Willard Rouse. In Memory of Stephen Collins
       Foster, 1826-1864. Frankfort, Kentucky: The State Journal
       Company, 1940. 19p., illus.
           Describes rare items held by the Foster Hall.

2569. Lilly, Josiah Kirby. Foster Hall: a Reminder of the Life
       and Work of Stephen Collins Foster, 1826-1864. Indianapolis:
       The Author, 1932. 7p.

                         Periodicals

2570. Lilly Bulletin; later Lilly-Foster Bulletin; later Foster
       Hall Bulletin. Edited by Josiah Kirby Lilly. Indianapolis.
       irreg., 1931-5; 1940.
           Twelve issues published.

FOUNTAIN, PETE

2571. Fountain, Pete. A Closer Walk: the Pete Fountain Story.
       With Bill Neely. Chicago: Regnery, 1972. 202p., illus.,
       discog.

FOX, ROY

2572. Fox, Roy. Hollywood, Mayfair, and All That Jazz: the Roy
       Fox Story. London: Leslie Frewin, 1975. 248p., illus.
           Autobiography.

                        Discography

2573. Craigie, Wemyess, and Ray Pallett. The "Memory Lane" Trib-
       ute to Roy Fox and Al Bowlly. Leigh-on-Sea, Essex: Memory
       Lane, 1982. 35p., illus.

FRAMPTON, PETER

2574. Adler, Irene. Peter Frampton. New York: Quick Fox, 1979.
       96p., illus.

2575. Daly, Marsha. Peter Frampton. New York: Grosset and Dunlap,
       1978. 167p., illus., discog. Abridged ed.: New York: Tempo
    • Books, 1979. 92p., illus.

2576. Katz, Susan. Frampton! An Unauthorized Biography. New York:
       Jove Publications, 1978. 190p., illus., discog.

FRANCIS, CONNIE

2577. Francis, Connie. Who's Sorry Now? Connie Francis Tells Her
       Own Story. Introduction by Dick Clark. New York: St.
       Martin's Pr.; London (as Who's Sorry Now?): W.H. Allen,
       1984. 332p., illus., discog.

FRANKIE GOES TO HOLLYWOOD

2578. Anthony, Dean. Frankie Goes To Hollywood. Guildford,
       Surrey: Colour Library Books, 1984. unpaged, illus. (Coombe
       Books).
           Chiefly illustrated.

2579. Hizer, Bruno. Give It Loads: the Story of Frankie Goes To
       Hollywood. London; New York: Proteus, 1984.   p., illus.
           Chiefly illustrated.

2580. Jackson, Danny. Frankie Say: the Rise of Frankie Goes To
       Hollywood. London: Omnibus Pr., 1985.   p., illus.,
       discog.

FRANKLIN, ARETHA

2581. Nemeroff, David. Glory. New York: Pocket Books, 1980.
       309p.
           Novel, loosely based on Aretha Franklin.

FREED, ARTHUR

   *   Fordin, Hugh. The World of Entertainment! Hollywood's
       Greatest Musicals.
           * Cited above as item 1074.

FREEMAN, LAWRENCE "BUD"

2582. Freeman, Bud. If You Know of a Better Life, Please Tell Me.
       Dublin: Bashall Eaves, 1976. 62p.
           Reminiscences.

2583. ———. You Don't Look Like a Musician. Detroit: Balamp
       Publications, 1974. 135p.
           Autobiography.

FROHMAN, CHARLES

2584.   Barrie, James Matthew. Charles Frohman: a Tribute. London:
        Clement Shorter, 1915.   p.
            Limited edition of twenty copies. Reprinted from the
        Daily Mail.

2585.   Frohman, Daniel, and Isaac F. Marcosson. Charles Frohman,
        Manager and Man. With an appreciation by James M. Barrie.
        New York: Harper; London: John Lane, 1916. 439p., illus.
            Memoir by his brother.

FROHMAN, DANIEL

2586.   Frohman, Daniel. Daniel Frohman Presents: an Autobiography.
        New York: Claude Kendall and Willoughby Sharp, 1935; New
        York: Lee Furman, 1937. 397p., illus., index.
            Continues item 2588.

2587.   ————. Encore. New York: Lee Furman, 1937. 295p., illus.

2588.   ————. Memories of a Manager: Reminiscences of the Old
        Lyceum, and of Some Players of the Last Quarter Century.
        London: Heinemann; New York: Doubleday, Page, 1911. 235p.,
        illus., index.
            Autobiography. Includes listing of productions by him.
        Continued by item 2586.

FURY, BILLY

2589.   The Billy Fury Monthly. Edited by Albert Hand. Heanor,
        Derbysshire. monthly, 1963-64.

GARLAND, JUDY

2590.   Deans, Mickey, and Ann Pinchot. Weep No More, My Lady.
        New York: Hawthorn Books, 1972. 247p., illus.

            ————. Weep No More, My Lady: an Intimate Biography of
        Judy Garland. London: W.H. Allen, 1972. 238p., illus.
        St. Albans, Hertfordshire: Mayflower, 1973. 221p., illus.
            Memoir by her last husband.

2591.   DiOrio, Al, Jr. Little Girl Lost: the Life and Hard Times
        of Judy Garland. New Rochelle, New York: Arlington House,
        1974; London: Robson Books, 1975. 298p., illus., discog.,
        filmog., index. New York: Manor Books, 1975. 221p., illus.,
        discog., filmog., index. London: Coronet, 1976. 190p.,
        illus., discog., filmog., index.

Garland, Judy (cont.)

2592. Edwards, Anne. Judy Garland: a Biography. New York:
       Simon and Schuster; London: Constable, 1975; London: Corgi,
       1976. 350p., illus., discog., filmog.

2593. Finch, Christopher. Rainbow: the Stormy Life of Judy
       Garland. New York: Grosset and Dunlap; London: Michael
       Joseph, 1975. 255p., illus., index.

2594. Frank, Gerold. Judy. New York: Harper and Row; London:
       W.H. Allen, 1975. 654p., illus., index. New York: Dell,
       1976. 716p., illus., index.

2595. Juneau, James. Judy Garland. New York: Pyramid Publicat-
       ions, 1974. 159p., illus., filmog., index. London: Star
       Books., 1976. 160p., illus., filmog., index.

2596. Melton, David. Judy: a Remembrance. Hollywood, California:
       Stanyan Books, 1972. 58p., illus.

2597. Meyer, John. Heartbreaker: Two Months With Judy. London:
       W.H. Allen, 1983. 322p., index.
          By lover/secretary/business manager.

2598. Smith, Lorna. Judy, With Love: the Story of "Miss Show
       Business." London: Hale, 1975. 208p., illus., filmog.,
       index.

2599. Spada, James. Judy and Liza. New York: Doubleday; London:
       Sidgwick and Jackson, 1983. 216p., illus., bibliog.
          Garland and her daughter, Liza Minelli.

2600. Tormé, Mel. The Other Side of the Rainbow. London; New
       York: W.H. Allen, 1971. 241p., illus.

                        Motion Pictures

2601. Baxter, Brian. The Films of Judy Garland. Bembridge, Isle
       of Wight: B.C.W. Publishing, 1974 (Reissued: 1977). 47p.,
       illus., bibliog., discog., filmog.

2602. Dahl, David, and Barry Kehoe. Young Judy. New York: Mason/
       Charter, 1975; London: Hart-Davis, MacGibbon, 1976. 250p.,
       illus., bibliog. St. Albans, Hertfordshire: Mayflower,
       1977. 238p., illus., bibliog.
          Her screen career to 1935.

2603. Morella, Joe, and Edward Z. Epstein. Judy: the Films and
       Career of Judy Garland. Secaucus, New Jersey: Citadel Pr.,
       1969. 216p., illus. London: Leslie Frewin, 1969. 218p.,
       illus.

GAYE, MARVIN

2604. Davis, Sharon. <u>Marvin Gaye</u>. London; New York: Proteus,
      1984. 124p., illus., discog.
      Written before his death.

2605. Vermorel, Fred, and Judy Vermorel. <u>On the Grapevine</u>.
      London: Sidgwick and Jackson, 1985.   p., illus.

GENESIS

2606. Genesis. <u>Genesis In Their Own Words</u>. Compiled by Pearce
      Marchbank. London: Sidgwick and Jackson, 1983. 32p.,
      illus.
      Compiled from press and other interviews.

2607. ————. <u>Genesis Lyrics</u>. Illustrated by Kim Poor. Intro-
      duction to Genesis by Chris Welch. Introduction to Kim
      Poor by Jo Durden-Smith. London: Sidgwick and Jackson,
      1979. 100p., illus., discog., index.
      Artwork in various media illustrating their lyrics.

Biographies

2608. Fielder, Hugh. <u>The Book of Genesis</u>. London: Sidgwick and
      Jackson; New York: St. Martin's Pr., 1984. 128p., illus.

2609. Gallo, Armando. <u>Genesis: the Evolution of a Rock Band</u>.
      London: Sidgwick and Jackson, 1978. 148p., illus., discog.,
      index.

2610. ————. <u>Genesis: From One Fan To Another</u>. Edited by Dan
      Dan Jones. Los Angeles: D.I.Y. Books; London: Omnibus Pr.,
      1984. unpaged, illus.
      Chiefly photographs by Gallo.

      ————. <u>Genesis: I Know What I Like</u>. Introduction by Mike
      Rutherford. Los Angeles: D.I.Y. Books, 1980. 176p., illus.
      Rewritten and redesigned.

2611. Kamin, Philip, and Peter Goddard. <u>Genesis: Peter Gabriel,
      Phil Collins, and Beyond</u>. Introduction by Phil Collins.
      New York: Beaufort Books; London: Sidgwick and Jackson, 1984.
      128p., illus.
      Performance photographs by Kamin; text by Goddard.

2612. Schacht, Janis. <u>Genesis</u>. London; New York: Proteus, 1984.
      128p., illus., discog.

Genesis (cont.)

Discographies

2613. Parkynn, Geoff. <u>Genesis: the Illustrated Discography</u>.
       London: Omnibus Pr., 1983. 96p., illus.
           Includes bootleg recordings; also lists videos.

       ————. <u>Genesis: Turn It On Again</u>. London: Omnibus Pr.,
       1984.   p., illus.
           Revised, with additional material and a short history of
       the group by Steve Clarke.

Periodicals

2614. <u>Gabbleratchet</u>. Box 35, Bath, Avon. irreg., 198?- .
           Emphasis on Peter Gabriel, ex-member of the group.

2615. <u>Genesis Magazine</u>. Box 107, London N6. quarterly, 198?- .

GERRY AND THE PACEMAKERS

2616. <u>Gerry and The Pacemakers Monthly</u>. Edited by Pete Goodman.
       London. monthly, March 1964-June 1964.

GERSHWIN, GEORGE AND IRA

2617. Gershwin, Ira. <u>Lyrics on Several Occasions: a Selection of
       Stage and Screen Lyrics</u>. New York: Knopf, 1959; New York:
       Viking Pr., 1973; London: Elm Tree Books, 1977. 362p., index.
       London: Omnibus Pr., 1978. 384p., index.

Biographies

2618. Altman, Frances. <u>George Gershwin: Master Composer</u>. Minnea-
       polis: T.S. Denison, 1968. 235p., illus., bibliog. (Men of
       Achievement)

2619. Armitage, Merle (ed.). <u>George Gershwin</u>. London; New York:
       Longmans, 1938. 252p., illus., discog.
           Thirty-eight pieces by and about Gershwin; the majority
       commissioned for the volume.

2620. ————. <u>George Gershwin: Man and Legend</u>. New York: Duell,
       Sloan, and Pearce, 1958; Freeport, New York: Books for Lib-
       raries Pr., 1970. 188p., illus., bibliog., discog.
           Essays by Armitage.

2621. Ewen, David. A Journey To Greatness: the Life and Music of
       George Gershwin. New York: Holt, 1956. 384p., illus.,
       bibliog., discog. London: W.H. Allen, 1956. 255p., illus.,
       bibliog., discog.

       ————. George Gershwin: His Journey To Greatness. Engle-
       wood Cliffs, New Jersey; London: Prentice-Hall, 1970;
       Westport, Conn.: Greenwood Pr., 1977. 354p., illus., index.
       Completely rewritten; bibliography and discography dropped.

2622. ————. The Story of George Gershwin. New York: Holt, 1943.
       211p., illus., discog.
       Aimed at younger readers. Contains invented dialog.

2623. Goldberg, Isaac. George Gershwin: a Study in American Music.
       New York: Simon and Schuster, 1931. 310p., illus.

       ————. ————. Supplemented by Edith Garson. Foreword and
       discography by Alan Dashiell. New York: Frederick Ungar,
       1958. 287p., illus., discog.
       Expanded from three articles first published in the Ladies'
       Home Journal, 1931.

2624. ————. George Gershwin and American Music. Girard, Kansas:
       Haldeman-Julius, 1936. 32p.

2625. Jablonski, Edward. George Gershwin. Introduction by Harold
       Arlen. New York: Putnam, 1962. 190p., discog. (Lives To
       Remember)
       Aimed at younger readers.

2626. ————, and Lawrence D. Stewart. The Gershwin Years. Garden
       City, New York: Doubleday, 1958. 313p., illus., bibliog.,
       discog., index. 2nd. ed.: Garden City, New York: Doubleday,
       1973; London: Robson Books, 1974. 416p., illus., bibliog.,
       discog., index.
       Includes listing of their published works, and description
       of the Gershwin Archives.

2627. Kimball, Robert, and Alfred Simon. The Gershwins. New York:
       Atheneum, 1973; London: Cape, 1974; London: Book Sales, 1980.
       292p., illus., bibliog., discog.
       Includes reproductions of diaries, letters, programs, and
       other material. Also has listings of compositions, and piano
       rolls.

2628. Museum of the City of New York. Gershwin: George, the Music;
       Ira, the Words. A Catalog of the Exhibition, May 6 Through
       September 2, 1968. New York: Museum of the City of New York,
       1968. 30p., illus.

2629. Payne, Robert. Gershwin. New York: Pyramid Books, 1960.
       157p., illus. London: Hale, 1962. 128p., illus., bibliog.,
       discog., index.
       Hale edition has discography of British releases, compiled
       by Peter Watt.

Gershwin, George and Ira (cont.)

2630. Rushmore, Robert. The Life of George Gershwin. New York:
       Crowell-Collier; London: Collier-Macmillan, 1966. 177p.,
       illus., discog., index. (America in the Making)
           Aimed at younger readers.

2631. Schwartz, Charles M. Gershwin: His Life and Music.
       Indianapolis: Bobbs-Merrill, 1973; London: Abelard-Schuman,
       1974; New York: Da Capo Pr., 1979. 428p., illus., bibliog.,
       discog., index.
           Includes listing of his compositions, and motion picture
       use of his music. Based on the author's M.A. thesis,
       Elements of Jewish Music in Gershwin's Melody, New York
       University, 1965; and his PhD. dissertation, The Life and
       Orchestral Works of George Gershwin, New York University,
       1969. Bibliography and discography published separately as
       item 2633.

2632. Warner Brothers. Rhapsody in Blue: the Jubilant Story of
       George Gershwin and His Music. Hollywood, California:
       Warner Brothers, 1945.   p., illus.
           Promotional brochure.

                    Bibliography/Discography

2633. Schwartz, Charles M. George Gershwin: a Selective Bibliog-
       raphy and Discography. Detroit: Published for The College
       Music Society by Information Coordinators, 1974. 118p.,
       illus. (Bibliographies in American Music, 1)
           Bibliography lists 654 items. Includes books, parts of
       books, periodical articles, reviews, dissertations, and
       other material. Arranged in single alphabetical sequence.
       Discography chiefly of long-playing records. Bibliography
       and discography both essentially identical to those in item
       2631.

GETZ, STAN

2634. Astrup, Arne. The Stan Getz Discography. Introduction by
       Jerry L. Atkins. Texarkana, Texas: Jerry L. Atkins, 1979.
       119p.

2635. Walker, Malcolm. Stan Getz: a Discography, 1944-1955.
       London: The Author, 1957. 20p.

GILLESPIE, JOHN BIRKS "DIZZY"

Bibliography

*   Morgenstern, Dan, Ira Gitler, and Jack Bradley. <u>Bird and
      Diz: a Bibliography</u>.
         * Cited below as item 3215.

Biographies

2636. Gillespie, Dizzy. <u>To Be, Or Not...To Bop: Memoirs</u>. With Al
       Fraser. Garden City, New York: Doubleday, 1979; London (as
       <u>Dizzy: the Autobiography of Dizzy Gillespie</u>): W.H. Allen,
       1980; London (as <u>Dizzy: To Be, Or Not To Bop: the Autobiog-
       raphy of Dizzy Gillespie</u>): Quartet, 1982. 553p., illus.,
       discog., filmog., index. New York: Da Capo Pr., 1985. 574p.,
       illus., discog., filmog., index.
          Includes listings of his honors and awards.

2637. Horricks, Raymond. <u>Dizzy Gillespie and the Be-Bop Revolution</u>.
       Selected discography by Tony Middleton. Tunbridge Wells,
       Kent: Spellmount; New York: Hippocrene Books, 1984. 95p.,
       illus., bibliog., discog. (Jazz Masters)

2638. James, Michael. <u>Dizzy Gillespie</u>. London: Cassell, 1959; New
       York: A.S. Barnes, 1961. 89p., illus., discog. (Kings of
       Jazz)
          Incorporated into item 1566.

Discographies

2639. Edwards, Ernie, George Hall, and Bill Korst. <u>The Dizzy
       Gillespie Big Bands, 1945-1950, 1955-1957</u>. Whittier,
       California: Jazz Discographies Unlimited, 1966. 12p.

2640. Jepsen, Jorgen Grunnet. <u>Discography of Dizzy Gillespie</u>.
       Biographical notes by Knud H. Ditlevsen. Brande, Denmark:
       Debut Records, 1961. 33p.

          ————. <u>A Discography of Dizzy Gillespie</u>. Copenhagen:
       Knudsen, 1969.
       <u>Vol. 1: 1937-1952</u>. 41p.
       <u>Vol. 2: 1953-1968</u>. 32p.

GILMORE, PATRICK

2641. Darlington, Marwood. <u>Irish Orpheus: the Life of Patrick S.
       Gilmore, Bandmaster Extraordinary</u>. Philadelphia: Olivier-
       Nancy-Klein, 1950. 135p., illus.

GINGOLD, HERMIONE

2642. Gingold, Hermione. The World Is Square. Illustrated by
       James Bowling. London: Horne and Van Thal, 1945; New York:
       Athene Pr., 1958. 66p., illus.
          Autobiography.

GIUFFRE, JIMMY

2643. Nelson, Don. Jimmy Giuffre. New York: Broadcast Music,
       1961. 24p.

GLEASON, JACKIE

2644. Bishop, James Alonzo. The Golden Ham: a Candid Biography of
       Jackie Gleason. New York: Simon and Schuster, 1956. 298p.,
       illus.

GLITTER, GARY (pseud. of Paul Gadd)

2645. Tremlett, George. The Gary Glitter Story. London: Futura,
       1974. 144p., illus.

GLOVER, JIMMY (pseud. of James Mackey Glover)

2646. Glover, Jimmy. Hims Ancient and Modern: Being the Third
       Book of Jimmy Glover. London: T. Fisher Unwin, 1926. 256p.,
       illus.
          Reminiscences.

2647. ———. Jimmy Glover and His Friends. London: Chatto and
       Windus, 1913. 325p., illus.
          Reminiscences. Includes descriptions of other music hall
       acts.

2648. ———. Jimmy Glover: His Book. London: Methuen, 1911.
       299p., illus.

GODDARD, GEOFF

2649. Goddard, Geoff. Geoff Goddard: the Other Half of the Joe Meek
       Legend. Basingstoke, Hampshire: Deleted Sound, 1983. 43p.,
       discog.
          Memoirs of British songwriter; worked as Joe Meek's partner.

GONZALES, BABS

*   Gonzales, Babs. Be-Bop Dictionary, and History of its
    Famous Stars.
        * Cited above as item 721.

*   ————, and Paul Weston. Boptionary: What is Bop?
        * Cited above as item 722.

2650. ————. I Paid My Dues: Good Times, No Bread. A Story of
    Jazz. New York: Lancer Books; East Orange, New York:
    Expubidence Publishing, 1967. 160p., discog.
        Memoirs.

GOODMAN, BENNY

2651. Goodman, Benny, and Stanley Baron. Benny: King of Swing. A
    Pictorial Biography Based on Benny Goodman's Personal Arch-
    ives. Introduction by Stanley Baron. London: Thames and
    Hudson, 1979. 206p., illus.
        Chiefly illustrated.

2652. Goodman, Benny. The Benny Goodman Story: Adapted From the
    Universal-International Film. Foreword by Steve Race.
    London: Beverley Books, 1956. 40p., illus. (Beverley Books
    of the Film)

2653. ————, and Irving Kolodin. The Kingdom of Swing. Harris-
    burg, Pennsylvania: Stackpole; London: W.H. Allen, 1939; New
    York: Frederick Ungar; London: Constable, 1961. 265p.,
    illus.
        Autobiography.

                        Biographies

2654. Caen, Herbert Eugene. Benny Goodman: an Album. New York:
    Putnam, 1976.   p., illus.

2655. Russell, D. Benny Goodman: the Record of a Legend. New
    York; Bicester, Oxfordshire: Facts on File, 1985.   p.,
    illus., discog.

                        Discographies

2656. Connor, Donald Russell, and Warren W. Hicks. B.G.--Off the
    Record: a Bio-Discography of Benny Goodman. Fairless Hills,
    Pennsylvania: Gaildonna Publishers, 1958. 305p., illus.,
    index.

Goodman, Benny (cont.)

Discographies (cont.)

> Connor, Donald Russell, and Warren W. Hicks. B.G.--On the
> Record: a Bio-Discography of Benny Goodman. New Rochelle,
> New York: Arlington House, 1969. 691p., illus., index.
>> Extended, and thoroughly revised.

2657. Cruise, Patrick F. The Benny Goodman Record Circle. New
York: The Author, 1948.   p.

2658. Fry, John G. Benny Goodman: an English Discography. Kingswood, Bristol, Somerset: The Author, 1957. 66p.
   Supplements published November 1957, and January 1958.

GOODMAN, HAPPY

2659. Buckingham, James R. O, Happy Day: the Happy Goodman Story.
Waco, Texas: Word Books, 1973. 224p., illus.

GORDON, DEXTER

2660. Britt, Stan. Long Tall Dexter. London: Millington, 1982.
   p., illus., discog.

GORDON, MAX

2661. Gordon, Max. Max Gordon Presents. With Lewis Funke. New
York: Bernard Geis Associates, 1963. 314p., illus.
   Autobiography.

GORDON, TAYLOR

2662. Gordon, Taylor. Born To Be. Introduction by Muriel Draper.
Foreword by Carl Van Vechten. Illustrated by Covarrubias.
New York: Covici-Friede, 1929; Seattle: University of Wash-
ington Pr., 1975. 236p., illus.
   University of Washington Pr. edition has new introduction
by Robert Hemenway.

GORMAN, LARRY

2663. Ives, Edward Dawson. Larry Gorman: the Man Who Made the Songs.
Bloomington: Indiana University Pr., 1964; New York: Arno Pr.,
1977. 225p., bibliog., index.

GRAPPELLI, STEPHANE

2664.   Horricks, Raymond. Stephane Grappelli; or, The Violin With
        Wings: a Profile. Selected discography by Tony Middleton.
        Tunbridge Wells, Kent: Midas Books; New York: Hippocrene
        Books, 1983. 134p., illus., discog., index.

GRATEFUL DEAD

2665.   Grushkin, Paul. The Grateful Dead: the Official Book of the
        Deadheads. New York: Morrow, 1983. 224p., illus. (Quill
        Paperbacks)

2666.   Harrison, Hank. The Dead Book: a Social History of The
        Grateful Dead. New York; London: Links Books, 1973. 177p.,
        illus.
             Includes acetate disk of 1967 Neal Cassady speech (with
        the group in background). Based on personal knowledge.

        ————. The Grateful Dead. London: Star Books, 1975.
        175p., illus.
             Revised and rewritten.

        ————. The Dead. Millbank, California: Celestial Arts,
        1980. 322p., illus.
             Revised; rewritten.

2667.   Jackson, Blair. The Grateful Dead: the Music Never Stopped.
        New York: Delilah; London: Plexus Publishing, 1983. 256p.,
        illus.

                          Periodicals

2668.   Dead Heads Newsletter. San Rafael, California. irreg.,
        197?-?

2669.   Dead Relix. Brooklyn, New York. bi-monthly, 1972- .
             Name changed to Relix, 197? See item 5115.

2670.   Spiral Light: the Official Newsletter of the Deadheads Infor-
        mation Exchange. Edited by Ken Ingham. 8c Highmoor Court,
        Amersham, Buckinghamshire. irreg., 1984- .

                          Jerry Garcia

2671.   Garcia, Jerry. Garcia: the Rolling Stone Interview; plus,
        A Stoned Sunday Rap With Jerry Garcia and Mountain Girl.
        San Francisco: Straight Arrow Books, 1972. 254p., illus.
             Interviews conducted by Charles Reich and Jann Wenner.
        First published in Rolling Stone, 1971.

GRAY, HECTOR

2672. Gray, Hector. <u>Memories of a Variety Artist</u>. Melbourne,
       Victoria: Hawthorne Pr., 1975. 106p., illus.

GREEN, BENNY

2673. Green, Benny. <u>Swingtime in Tottenham</u>. Illustrated by Ross.
       London: Lemon Tree Pr., 1976. 107p., illus.
       Memoir of his jazz career.

GROSSMITH, GEORGE

2674. Grossmith, George. "<u>G.G.</u>" London: Hutchinson, 1933. 288p.,
       illus.
       Autobiography.

  *   Naylor, Stanley. <u>The Gaiety and George Grossmith: Random</u>
       <u>Reflections on the Serious Business of Enjoyment</u>.
       * Cited above as item 1221.

GUILBERT, YVETTE

2675. Guilbert, Yvette. <u>Autres temps, autres chants</u>. Paris: (Pub-
       lisher unknown), 1946. 218p., illus.
       Memoirs.

2676. ————. <u>La Chanson de ma vie: mes mémoires</u>. Paris: B.
       Grasset, 1927 (Reissued: 1945). 320p., illus.

       ————. <u>The Song of My Life: My Memories</u>. Translated by
       Béatrice de Holthoir. London: Harrap, 1929. 328p., illus.
       Contents partially published in item 2681.

  *   ————. <u>How To Sing a Song</u>.
       * Cited below as item

2677. ————. <u>Mes Lettres d'amour</u>. Paris: Denoël et Steele, 1933.
       279p., illus.

2678. ————. <u>La Passante emerveillée: mes voyages</u>. Paris: B.
       Grasset, 1929. 334p.
       Memoirs of her travels.

2679. ————. <u>La Vedette: roman</u>. Paris: H. Simonis Empis, 1902.
       366p.
       Autobiographical novel.

2680. ———. The Virgin and The Devil. New York: J.D. McGuire,
       1917. 19p.

2681. ———, and Harold Simpson. Yvette Guilbert: Struggles and
       Victories. London: Mills and Boon, 1910. 348p., illus.
          Contains Struggles and Victories of My Life, by Guilbert;
       and The Life of Yvette Guilbert, by Simpson. Partially
       republished in item 2676.

2682. Knapp, Bettina Liebowitz, and Myra Chipman. That Was Yvette:
       the Biography of a Great Diseuse. New York: Holt, Rinehart
       and Winston, 1964; London: Muller, 1966. 319p., illus.,
       bibliog., index.

2683. Toulouse-Lautrec, Henri de. Yvette Guilbert. Text by
       Gustave Geffroy. Paris: L'Estampe Originale, 1894. 19p.,
       illus.
          Limited edition of one hundred copies.

       ———. ———. Described by Arthur Byl. Translated by
       A. Teixeira de Mattos. London: Bliss, Sands, 1898.   p.,
       illus.
          Limited edition of 350 copies.

       ———. ———. Text by Claude Roger-Marx. Paris: Pont
       des Arts, 1950. 45p., illus.

GUTHRIE, ARLO

2684. Herndon, Venable, and Arthur Penn. Alice's Restaurant: a
       Screenplay. Garden City, New York: Doubleday, 1970. 141p.,
       illus.
          Script of the motion picture based on Guthrie's song,
       Alice's Restaurant Massacree.

GUTHRIE, WOODROW "WOODY"

Bibliography

2685. Reuss, Richard A. A Woody Guthrie Bibliography, 1912-1967.
       New York: Guthrie Children's Trust Fund, 1967. 94p.
          Annotated.

Biographies

2686. Guthrie, Woody. Born To Win. Edited by Robert Shelton.
       New York: Macmillan, 1967. 256p., illus.
          Collection of autobiographical and other writings.

Guthrie, Woodrow "Woody" (cont.)

2687. Guthrie, Woody. <u>Bound For Glory</u>. New York: Dutton, 1943
       (Reissued: 1968); London: Dent, 1969. 430p., illus. New
       York: New American Library, 1970 (Reissued: 1976) (Signet
       Books); London: Pan, 1974 (Picador Books). 320p., illus.
       Autobiography. Illustrated with sketches by Guthrie.

2688. ————. <u>Seeds of Man: an Experience Lived and Dreamed</u>.
       New York: Dutton, 1976. 401p. New York: Pocket Books,
       1977. 434p. (A Kangaroo Book)
          Memoirs.

2689. Klein, Joe. <u>Woody Guthrie: a Life</u>. New York: Knopf, 1980;
       London: Faber and Faber, 1981. 476p., illus., index.

2690. Yurchenco, Henrietta. <u>A Mighty Hard Road: the Woody Guthrie
       Story</u>. Assisted by Marjorie Guthrie. Introduction by Arlo
       Guthrie. New York: McGraw-Hill, 1970. 159p., illus.,
       discog., index.

HAGGARD, MERLE

2691. Haggard, Merle, and Peggy Russell. <u>Sing Me Back Home</u>. New
       York: Times Books, 1981. 288p., illus.
          Autobiography.

HAIRCUT ONE HUNDRED

2692. Marchbank, Pearce, and Sally Payne. <u>The Haircut One Hundred
       Catalogue</u>. London: Omnibus Pr., 1982.   p., illus., discog.

HALEY, BILL

2693. Gardner, Chris. <u>Crazy, Man, Crazy</u>. Coniston, Merseyside:
       Vintage Rock 'n' Roll Appreciation Society, 1980.   p.,
       illus., discog.

2694. Swenson, John. <u>Bill Haley</u>. London: W.H. Allen, 1982; London:
       Star Books, 1983. 174p., illus., discog., index. New York
       (as <u>Bill Haley: the Daddy of Rock and Roll</u>): Stein and Day,
       1983. 200p., illus., discog., index.

HALL, HENRY

2695. Hall, Henry. <u>Here's To the Next Time: the Autobiography of
       Henry Hall</u>. London: Odhams Pr., 1955. 240p., illus.

HALL, TOM T.

2696. Hall, Tom T. The Storyteller's Nashville. Garden City,
       New York: Doubleday, 1979. 221p., illus.
          Autobiography.

HALL AND OATES

2697. Tosches, Nick. Darryl Hall/John Oates--Dangerous Dances:
       the Authorized Biography. New York: St. Martin's Pr.;
       London: Sidgwick and Jackson, 1984. 144p., illus.

HAMMERSTEIN, OSCAR, II see RODGERS, RICHARD

HAMMOND, JOHN

2698. Hammond, John. John Hammond On Record: an Autobiography.
       With Irving Townsend. New York: Ridge Pr., 1977. 416p.,
       illus., discog., index. (Summit Books). New York; London:
       Penguin, 1981. 432p., illus., discog., index.
          Autobiography.

HAMPTON, LIONEL

2699. Hampton, Lionel. Lionel Hampton's Swing Book. Edited by
       Alice C. Browning. Chicago: Lionel Hampton/Negro Story Pr.,
       1946. 106p., illus.
          Chiefly illustrated. Memoir; includes comment on other
       musicians.

                          Discographies

2700. Demeusy, Bertrand, and Otto Flückiger. Discography of
       Lionel Hampton and His Orchestra, 1951-1953. Basle, Switz-
       erland: Jazz Publications, 1961. 22p. (Jazz Publications, 2)

2701. ————. Discography of Lionel Hampton, 1954-1958. Basle,
       Switzerland: Jazz Publications, 1962. 29p., illus. (Jazz
       Publications, 6)

HANDY, WILLIAM CHRISTOPHER

2702. Handy, William Christopher. Father of the Blues: an Auto-
       biography. Edited by Arna Bontemps. Foreword by Abbe Niles.

Handy, William Christopher (cont.)

New York: Macmillan, 1941; London: Sidgwick and Jackson,
1957. 317p., illus., bibliog., index. New York: Collier
Books, 1970. 320p., illus., bibliog., index.

2703. Montgomery, Elizabeth Rider. William C. Handy: Father of
the Blues. Illustrated by David Hodges. Champaign, Illinois:
Garrad Publishing, 1968 (Americans All); New York: Dell,
1972. 95p., illus.
Aimed at younger readers.

HANSON, JOHN

2704. Hanson, John. Me and My Red Shadow: the Autobiography of
John Hanson. London: W.H. Allen, 1980; London: Star Books,
1981. 218p., illus., index.

HARKREADER, SIDNEY J.

2705. Harkreader, Sidney J. Fiddlin' Sid's Memoirs: the Autobiography of Sidney J. Harkreader. Edited by Walter D. Haden.
Los Angeles: John Edwards Memorial Foundation, 1976. 37p.,
illus., discog. (J.E.M.F. Special Series, 9)
Country musician.

HARPER, ROY

2706. Hors d' Oeuvres. Edited by P. Cunliffe. The Rectory, Gol-
borne, Warrington, Lancashire. irreg., 1984- .

HARRIGAN AND HART

2707. Kahn, Ely Jacques, Jr. The Merry Partners: the Age and Stage
of Harrigan and Hart. New York: Random House, 1955. 302p.,
illus.
Story of musical comedy team, Edward "Ned" Harrigan, and
partner Tony Hart.

HARRIOTT, JOE

2708. Cotterrell, Roger. The Joe Harriott Memorial: a Bio-Discography. Discography by Barry Tepperman. Gants Hill, Essex:
The Author, 1974. 26p., discog.

HARRIS, BILL

2709. Edwards, Ernie, George Hall, and Bill Korst. Bill Harris
       Discography. Whittier, California: Jazz Discographies
       Unlimited, 1966. 30p.

HARRIS, CHARLES KASSELL

2710. Harris, Charles Kassell. After the Ball: Forty Years of
       Melody. An Autobiography. New York: Frank-Maurice, 1926.
       376p., illus.

   *   ————. How To Write a Popular Song.
       * Cited below as item 3844.

HART, LORENZ see RODGERS, RICHARD

HART, MOSS

2711. Hart, Moss. Act One: an Autobiography. New York: Random
       House, 1959; London: Secker and Warburg, 1960. 444p.
       London: New English Library, 1962. 383p. (Four Square Books)

HAWES, HAMPTON

2712. Hawes, Hampton. Raise Up Off Me: a Portrait of Hampton Hawes.
       With Don Asher. New York: Coward, McCann and Geoghegan,
       1974; New York: Da Capo Pr., 1979. 179p.
          Da Capo edition has new introduction by Gary Giddins.

HAWKINS, COLEMAN

2713. James, Burnett. Coleman Hawkins. Selected discography by
       Tony Middleton. Tunbridge Wells, Kent: Spellmount; New York:
       Hippocrene Books, 1984. 93p., illus., bibliog., discog.
       (Jazz Masters)

2714. McCarthy, Albert John. Coleman Hawkins. London: Cassell;
       New York: A.S. Barnes, 1963. 90p., illus., discog. (Kings
       of Jazz, 12)
          Incorporated into item 1566.

Hawkins, Coleman (cont.)

Discography

   *   Evensmo, Jan. The Tenor Saxophone of Coleman Hawkins, 1929-
       1942.
          * Cited above as item 1548.

HAWKINS, ERSKINE

2715. Edwards, Ernie, George Hall, and Bill Korst. Erskine
       Hawkins-Horace Henderson Discography. Whittier, California:
       Jazz Discographies Unlimited, 1965. 10p.

HAWKINS, RONNIE

2716. The Camel Walk, later The Camel Walker. Edited by Brian
       T. Simmons. 41 Amundson Road, North Heath Farm Estate,
       Littlehaven, West Sussex. irreg., 1978- .

HAWKWIND

2717. Moorcock, Michael, and Michael Butterworth. Time of The
       Hawklords. Henley-on-Thames, Oxfordshire: Aidan Ellis,
       1976. 255p.
         Science-fiction novel, featuring the group.

Robert Calvert

2718. Calvert, Robert. Centigrade 232. London: Quasar Books,
       1977.   p.
         Poetry collection by Hawkwind member.

    *   ———. Hype.
        * Cited below as item 4545.

HAYES, ROLAND

2719. Helm, MacKinley. Angel Mo' and Her Son, Roland Hayes.
       Boston: Little, Brown, 1942; Westport, Conn.: Greenwood Pr.,
       1969. 289p., illus.
         Written in the first person.

HEATH, TED

2720. Heath, Ted. Listen To My Music: an Autobiography. London:
       Frederick Muller, 1957. 176p., illus.

                          Biography

2721. Charles, E. The Full Story of Ted Heath and His Music.
       London: Fletcher, 1945.   p.

                          Periodicals

2722. The Beat. London. monthly, 1947-49.
           Continued as The New Beat: the World' Brightest Modern
       Music Magazine. London. monthly, 1949-50.

HELD, ANNA

2723. Held, Anna. Mémoires: une étoile française au ciel de
       l'Amérique. Preface by Charles Jacques. Brussels: G.
       Houyoux, 1954. 210p., illus.
           In French. Autobiography of Ziegfeld Star.

HENDERSON, FLETCHER

2724. Allen, Walter Charles. Hendersonia: the Music of Fletcher
       Henderson and His Musicians: a Bio-Discography. Highland
       Park, New Jersey: The Author, 1973. 651p., illus., bibliog.,
       discog., index. (Jazz Monographs, 4)

2725. Gray-Clarke, G.F., and Eric S. Tonks. Deep Henderson.
       Newark, Nottinghamshire: Jazz Appreciation Society, 1944.
       24p.

HENDERSON, HORACE

  *   Edwards, Ernie, George Hall, and Bill Korst. Erskine Hawkins-
       Horace Henderson Discography.
            * Cited above as item 2715.

HENDRIX, JIMI

2726. Henderson, David. Jimi Hendrix: Voodoo Child of the
       Aquarian Age. Garden City, New York: Doubleday, 1978.
       514p., illus., discog.

       ———. 'Scuse Me While I Kiss the Sky: the Life of Jimi
       Hendrix. New York; London: Bantam, 1981. 384p., illus.,
       discog.
              Revised version.

2727. Hopkins, Jerry. Hit and Run: the Jimi Hendrix Story. New
       York: Perigee Books, 1983; London (as The Jimi Hendrix
       Story): Sphere, 1984. 240p., illus., discog.

2728. Knight, Curtis. Jimi: an Intimate Biography of Jimi Hendrix.
       New York: Praeger; London: W.H. Allen, 1974; London: Star
       Books, 1975. 223p., illus., discog., index.
              Based on personal knowledge. Discography compiled by
       John McKellar. Star Books edition has fewer illustrations.

2729. Nolan, Tom. Jimi Hendrix: a Biography in Words and Pictures.
       Edited by Greg Shaw. New York: Sire Books, 1977.   p.,
       illus.

2730. Sampson, Victor. Hendrix: an Illustrated Biography. London;
       New York: Proteus, 1984. 126p., illus., discog.

2731. Welch, Chris. Hendrix: a Biography. London: Ocean Books,
       1972; New York: Flash Books, 1973. 104p., illus., discog.
       Rev. ed.: London: Ocean Books, 1984.   p., illus., discog.

                         Discography

2732. Glebbeck, Caesar, and Dan Foster. Jimi Hendrix: Stay Free.
       A Comprehensive Discography. Amsterdam: Hendrix Information
       Center, 1980.   p., illus.

                         Periodicals

2733. Are You Experienced? Newton Crt., Massachusetts. irreg.,
       1980-?

HENRY COW

2734. Cutler, Chris, and Tim Hodginson (comps.). The Henry Cow
       Book. London: The Authors, 1981. 115p., illus.

HENSON, LESLIE LINCOLN

2735. Henson, Leslie Lincoln. My Laugh Story: the Story of My
      Life. London: Hodder and Stoughton, 1926. 293p., illus.

2736. ———. Well! Well! Well! London: Hutchinson, 1926. 221p.
      Reminiscences.

2737. ———. Yours Faithfully: an Autobiography. London: John
      Long, 1948. 180p., illus.

HERBERT, VICTOR

  *   Barnes, Edwin N.C. Near Immortals? Stephen Foster, Edward
      MacDowell, Victor Herbert.
        * Cited above as item 2551.

2738. Kaye, Joseph. Victor Herbert: the Biography of America's
      Greatest Composer of Romantic Music. New York: G. Howard
      Watt, 1931; Freeport, New York: Books for Libraries Pr.,
      1970. 271p., illus., index.

2739. Purdy, Claire Lee. Victor Herbert: American Music-Master.
      New York: J. Messner, 1945. 271p., illus.

2740. Waters, Edward Neighbor. Victor Herbert: a Life in Music.
      New York: Macmillan, 1955; New York: Da Capo Pr., 1978.
      653p., illus., bibliog., index.
        Includes listing of his compositions.

HERGEST

2741. Dyddiau da Hergest, 1971-1979. Aberystwyth, Wales: Hergest/
      O'r Niwl, 1979. 20p., illus., discog.
        In Welsh. Story of the Welsh rock group.

HERMAN, WOODROW WILSON "WOODY"

2742. Edwards, Ernie, George Hall, and Bill Korst. Discography
      of Woody Herman. Brande, Denmark: Debut Records, 1959-61;
      Whittier, California: Jazz Discographies Unlimited,
      1965-66. 3 vols.,   p.

2743. Voce, Steve. Woody Herman. Speldhurst, Kent: Spellmount;
      New York: Hippocrene Books, 1985.   p., illus., bibliog.,
      discog., index. (Jazz Masters, 10)

HERRMAN, BERNARD

2744. Johnson, Edward. Bernard Herrman, Hollywood's Music-Drama-
       tist: a Biographical Sketch. With a Filmography, Catalogue
       of Works, Discography, and Bibliography. Foreword by Miklōs
       Rōzsa. Rickmansworth, Hertfordshire: Triad Pr., 1977. 60p.,
       illus., bibliog., discog., filmog. (Bibliographical Series,
       6)

HEYWARD, DU BOSE

2745. Durham, Frank. Du Bose Heyward: the Man Who Wrote "Porgy."
       Columbia: University of South Carolina Pr., 1954. 152p.,
       illus.
          Includes account of Heyward's collaboration with Gershwin.
       Based on the author's PhD. dissertation, Du Bose Heyward:
       the Southerner As Artist: a Critical and Biographical Study,
       Columbia University, 1953.

HICKS, SEYMOUR

2746. Hicks, Seymour. Between Ourselves. London: Cassell, 1930.
       252p., illus.
          Memoirs

2747. ———. Me and My Missus: Fifty Years on the Stage. London:
       Cassell, 1939. 276p., illus.
          Memoirs. Hicks was husband of Ellaline Terriss.

2748. ———. Twenty-Four Years of an Actor's Life. London:
       Alston Rivers, 1910. 321p.

2749. ———. Vintage Years: When King Edward the Seventh Was
       Prince of Wales. London: Cassell, 1943. 184p.
          Memoirs.

HIGGINBOTHAM, J.C.

2750. Jones, Clifford (ed.). J.C. Higginbotham. London: Disco-
       graphical Society, 1944. 24p., illus.

HINES, EARL

2751. Dance, Stanley. The World of Earl Hines. New York: Scrib-
       ner's, 1977 (Reprinted: New York: Da Capo Pr., 1983); London:
       Sidgwick and Jackson, 1980. 324p., illus., bibliog., discog.,
       index.

HODES, ART

2752. Fairchild, Ralph. <u>Art Hodes Discography</u>. Ontaria, Calif-
       ornia: The Author, 1962. 36p.

HOLIDAY, BILLIE

2753. Holiday, Billie. <u>Lady Sings the Blues</u>. With William Dufty.
       New York: Doubleday, 1956. 250p., illus., discog. London:
       Barrie Books, 1958. 226p., illus. New York: Popular Lib-
       rary, 1958; New York: Lancer Books, 1965. 192p. London:
       Barrie and Jenkins, 1973. 234p., illus., discog. London:
       Sphere, 1973. 188p., illus., discog. London; New York:
       Penguin, 1984. 199p., discog.
       Autobiography.

Biographies

2754. Chilton, John. <u>Billie's Blues: a Survey of Billie Holiday's
       Career, 1933-1959</u>. Foreword by Buck Clayton. London:
       Quartet; New York: Stein and Day, 1975. 259p., illus.,
       bibliog., discog., index.
       Biographical items from her friends and associates; plus
       an account of her recording career.

2755. Deveaux, Alexis. <u>Don't Explain: a Song of Billie Holiday</u>.
       New York: Harper and Row, 1980.   p., bibliog.
       Prose-poem form.

2756. James, Burnett. <u>Billie Holiday</u>. Selected discography by
       Tony Middleton. Tunbridge Wells, Kent: Spellmount; New
       York: Hippocrene Books, 1984. 95p., illus., discog. (Jazz
       Masters)

2757. Kuehl, Linda, and Ellie Shokert. <u>Billie Holiday Remembered</u>.
       New York: New York Jazz Museum, 1973. 20p.

Discographies

2758. Bakker, Dick M. <u>Billie and Teddy on Microgroove, 1932-1944</u>.
       Alphen aan den Rijn, Holland: Micrography, 1975. 52p.,
       indexes.
       Lists records by Holiday and Teddy Wilson, made separately
       and together, that have been reissued on long-playing albums.

2759. Jepsen, Jorgen Grunnet. <u>Discography of Billie Holiday</u>. Bio-
       graphical notes by Knud H. Ditlevsen. Brande, Denmark: Debut
       Records, 1960. 29p. <u>Rev. ed.</u>: Copenhagen: Knudsen, 1969.
       37p.

Holiday, Billie (cont.)

Discographies (cont.)

2760. Millar, Jack. Born To Sing: a Discography of Billie Holiday.
       Copenhagen: Jazzmedia, 1980. 150p., illus., index.
           Includes bootleg records.

HOLLIES

   *   Hollies, The. How To Run a Beat Group.
           * Cited below as item 4088.

HOLLY, BUDDY (pseud. of Charles Harden Holley)

2761. Clark, Alan. Buddy Holly and The Crickets. West Corvina,
       California: The Author, 1980.   p, illus., discog.

2762. Firminger, John (comp.). The Crickets File. Sheffield,
       Yorkshire: The Author, 1980.   p., illus., discog.

2763. Goldrosen, John J. Buddy Holly: His Life and Music. Bowling
       Green, Ohio: Bowling Green University Popular Pr.; London:
       Spice Box Books; London: Charisma Books, 1975.   p., illus.,
       discog., index. St. Albans, Hertfordshire: Panther, 1978.
       258p., illus., discog., index.

           ————. The Buddy Holly Story. Brockton, Massachsetts: The
       Author, 1979.   p., illus., discog. With an introduction
       by Dave Marsh. Foreword by Ralph M. Newman. New York:
       Quick Fox, 1979. 257p., illus., discog.
           Expanded and completely rewritten.

2764. Laing, Dave. Buddy Holly. London: Studio Vista, 1971.
       111p., illus., discog. New York: Macmillan, 1971; New York:
       Collier Books, 1972. 144p., illus., discog.

2765. Peer, Ralph, and Elizabeth Peer. Buddy Holly: a Biography
       in Words, Photographs, and Music. New York: Peer Internat-
       ional, 1972.   p., illus.

2766. Tobler, John. The Buddy Holly Story. London: Plexus Pub-
       lishing, 1979. 96p., illus., discog.

                            Periodicals

2767. Buddy: the Original Texas Music Magazine. Box 8366, Dallas,
       Texas 75205. monthly, June 1978-

HOLMAN, BILL

2768. Hentoff, Nat. **Bill Holman.** New York: Broadcast Music, 1960.
16p.

HONRI FAMILY

2769. Honri, Peter. **Peter Honri Presents--Working the Halls: the**
Honris in One Hundred Years of British Music Hall. Intro-
duction by Spike Milligan. Farnborough, Hampshire: D.C.
Heath, 1973; London: Futura, 1974. 215p., illus., bibliog.,
index.
D.C. Heath edition includes record in pocket.

HOPKINS, SAM "LIGHTNING"

2770. Holt, John, and Frank Scott. **Lightning Hopkins' Story and**
Discography. With Paul Oliver. London: John Holt, 1965.
43p., discog.

HORNE, LENA

2771. Horne, Lena. **In Person: Lena Horne.** As told to Helen
Arstein and Carlton Moss. New York: Greenberg, 1950. 249p.,
illus.
Autobiography.

2772. ———, and Richard Schickel. **Lena.** Garden City, New York:
Doubleday, 1965; London: Deutsch, 1966. 300p., illus. New
York: New American Library, 1966. 224p., illus. (Signet
Books)
Further autobiography.

HUGHES, PATRICK C. "SPIKE"

2773. Hughes, Spike. **Opening Bars: Beginning an Autobiography.**
London: Pilot Pr., 1946. 382p.

2774. ———. **Second Movement: Continuing the Autobiography of**
Spike Hughes. London: Museum Pr., 1951. 346p., illus.

HULBERT, JACK

2775. Hulbert, Jack. **The Little Woman's Always Right.** London:
W.H. Allen, 1975. 244p., illus., index.
Husband of Ciceley Courtneige. See also item 2270.

HUMAN LEAGUE

2776. Nash, Peter. _The Human League_. London: Star Books, 1982.
       143p., illus., discog.

2777. Ross, Alaska. _The Story of a Band Called The Human League_.
       London; New York: Proteus, 1983. 128p., illus., discog.

HUMPERDINCK, ENGELBERT (pseud. of Gerald Dorsey)

2778. Short, Don. _Engelbert Humperdinck: the Authorised Biography_.
       London: New English Library, 1972. 97p., illus.

HUNTER, IAN

2779. Hunter, Ian. _Diary of a Rock 'n' Roll Star_. St. Albans,
       Hertfordshire: Panther, 1974. 159p., illus. New York (as
       Reflections of a Rock Star): Flash Books, 1976. 104p., illus.
          Written 1972, during Mott The Hoople U.S.A. tour.

HUTCHINSON FAMILY

2780. Brink, Carol. _Harps in the Wind: the Story of the Singing
       Hutchinsons_. New York: Macmillan, 1947; New York: Da Capo
       Pr., 1980. 312p., illus., bibliog., index.

2781. _The Granite Songster: Comprising the Songs of The Hutchinson
       Family_. Boston: A.B. Hutchinson; New York: Charles Holt,
       1847. 69p.
          Words only.

2782. Hutchinson, John Wallace. _The Story of The Hutchinsons
       (Tribe of Jesse)_. Introduction by Frederick Douglass. Boston:
       Lee and Shepard, 1896; New York: Da Capo Pr., 1977. 2 vols.,
       p., illus.

2783.1 Jordan, Philip Dillon. _Singin' Yankees_. Minneapolis: Univ-
       ersity of Minnesota Pr., 1946. 305p., illus., index.

INK SPOTS

2783.2 Watson, Deek. _The Story of the Ink Spots_. With Lee Stephen-
       son. New York: Vantage Pr., 1967. 72p., illus.

INTERNATIONAL SWEETHEARTS OF RHYTHM

2784. Handy, D. Antoinette. _The International Sweethearts of Rhythm_.

Metuchen, New Jersey; London: Scarecrow Pr., 1983. 258p.,
illus., bibliog., index.

IRON MAIDEN

2785. Bushell, Gary, and Ross Halfin. Iron Maiden, Running Free:
the Official Story of Iron Maiden. London: Zomba Books,
1984; Port Chester, New York: Cherry Lane Books, 1985.
128p., illus., discog. (Rock Masters)

IRVINE, BILL, AND BOBBIE IRVINE

2786. Irvine, Bill, and Bobbie Irvine. The Dancing Years. London:
W.H. Allen, 1970. 176p., illus.
British ballroom dancing duo tell their story.

IVES, BURL

2787. Ives, Burl. Wayfaring Stranger. New York: Whittlesey House,
1948. 253p.
Autobiography.

JACKSON, MAHALIA

2788. Jackson, Mahalia. Movin' On Up: the Mahalia Jackson Story.
With Evan McLeod Wylie. New York: Hawthorn Books, 1966; New
York: Avon, 1969. 217p., illus., discog.

Biographies

2789. Goreau, Laurraine R. Just Mahalia, Baby. Waco, Texas: Word
Books, 1975. 611p., illus. Berkhamstead, Hertfordshire:
Lion Publishing/Aslan, 1976. 592p., illus.

2790. Jackson, Jesse. Make a Joyful Noise Unto The Lord! The
Life of Mahalia Jackson, Queen of Gospel Singers. New York:
Crowell, 1974. 160p., illus., bibliog. New York: Dell,
1975. 126p., illus., bibliog.

2791. Memorial Tribute: Mahalia Jackson, World's Greatest Gospel
Singer. (Place; publisher unknown), 1972. unpaged, illus.,
discog.
Commemorates her funeral, January 1972.

JACKSON FIVE/JACKSONS

2792. The Jackson Five. Hitchin, Hertfordshire: B.C. Enterprises, 1972. 24p., illus.

2793. Manning, Steve. The Jackson Five. Indianapolis: Bobbs-Merrill, 1976.   p., illus.

2794. Pitts, Leonard, Jr. Papa Joe's Boys: the Jacksons Story. Cresskill, New Jersey: Sharon Publications, 1983. 96p., illus., discog. (Starbooks)

Michael Jackson

2795. Bego, Mark. Michael! The Michael Jackson Story. London: Zomba Books, 1984. 125p., illus., discog.

2796. ————. On the Road With Michael Jackson. London: Zomba Books, 1985.   p., illus.

2797. Brown, Geoff. Michael Jackson, Body and Soul: an Illustrated Biography. London: Virgin Books, 1984. 128p., illus.

2798. Garland, Phyl. Michael: In Concert, With Friends, At Play. London: Pan, 1984. 65p., illus.

2799. George, Nelson. The Michael Jackson Story. New York: Dell; London: New English Library, 1984. 128p., illus., discog.

2800. Honeyford, Paul. Michael Jackson: the Golden Touch. London: Plexus Publishing, 1984. 64p., illus.

2801. Kamin, Philip, and Peter Goddard. Michael Jackson and The Jacksons: Live On Tour in 1984. London: Virgin Books, 1984. 95p., illus.

2802. Latham, Caroline. Michael Jackson: Thriller. New York: Zebra Books, 1984.   p., illus.

2803. Magee, Doug. Michael Jackson. London; New York: Proteus, 1984. 62p., illus., discog.

2804. The Magic of Michael Jackson. Cresskill, New Jersey: Sharon Publications, 1984.   p, illus.

2805. Marchbank, Pearce (comp.). Michael Jackson. London: Omnibus Pr., 1984. 32p., illus.

2806. Matthew, Gordon. Michael Jackson. New York: J. Messner, 1984.   p., illus. (In the Spotlight Series)

2807. Regan, Stewart. Michael Jackson. Guildford, Surrey: Colour Library Books, 1984. unpaged, illus.

JAM

2808. Hewitt, Paulo. <u>The Jam: a Beat Concerto. The Authorised
       Biography</u>. Introduction by Paul Weller. London: Omnibus
       Pr., 1983.   p., illus., discog.

2809. Honeyford, Paul. <u>The Jam: the Modern World By Numbers</u>.
       London: Eel Pie, 1980. 112p., illus., discog. <u>Rev. ed</u>.:
       London: Star Books, 1982. 125p., illus., discog.

2810. <u>The Jam</u>. London: Kelmoss, 1980. 34p., illus.

2811. Miles (<u>pseud. of</u> Barry Miles). <u>The Jam</u>. London: Omnibus
       Pr., 1981. 49p., illus., discog.

2812. Nicholls, Mike. <u>About the Young Idea: the Story of The Jam,
       1972-1982</u>. London; New York: Proteus, 1984. 126p., illus.,
       discog.

JAMES, BURNETT

2813. James, Burnett. <u>Living Forwards: the Autobiography of
       Burnett James</u>. London: Cassell, 1961. 243p.
            British jazz writer.

JAMES, HARRY

2814. Stacy, Frank. <u>Harry James' Pin-Up Life Story</u>. New York:
       Arco, 1944. 32p., illus., discog.

                          Discographies

2815. Garrod, Charles, and Peter Johnston. <u>Harry James and His
       Orchestra</u>. Zephyr Hills, Florida: Joyce, 1975.   p.

2816. Hall, George. <u>Harry James and His Orchestra</u>. Laurel,
       Maryland: Jazz Discographies Unlimited, 1971.   p.

JANIS, ELSIE

2817. Janis, Elsie. <u>Counter Currents</u>. With Marguerite Aspinall.
       New York: Putnam, 1926. 350p.
            Reminiscences.

2818. ————. <u>If I Know What I Mean</u>. New York; London: Putnam,
       1925. 132p., illus.
            Reminiscences.

2819. ————. <u>Love Letters From an Actress</u>. New York; London:
       Appleton, 1913. 97p. London: Pearson, 1915. 115p.

Janis, Elsie (cont.)

2820.   Janis, Elsie. Poems Now and Then. Colorado Springs: The
        Author, 193? 60p.

2821.   ————. So Far, So Good! An Autobiography. New York:
        Dutton, 1932. 344p., illus. London: John Long, 1935.
        287p., illus.

JAPAN

2822.   Bamboo. Slough, Berkshire. irreg., 1984- .

JARA, VICTOR

2823.   Jara, Joan. Victor: an Unfinished Song. London: Cape, 1983.
        278p., illus., index.

JEFFERSON, BLIND LEMON

2824.   Jefferson, Blind Lemon. Blind Lemon Jefferson. Compiled by
        Bob Groom. Knutsford, Cheshire: Blues World, 1970. 35p.,
        illus., discog.
            Song lyrics transcribed.

JEFFERSON AIRPLANE

2825.   Gleason, Ralph J. The Jefferson Airplane and the San
        Francisco Sound. New York: Ballantine, 1969. 340p., illus.

                            Grace Slick

2826.   Rowes, Barbara. Grace Slick: the Biography. Garden City,
        New York: Doubleday, 1980. 215p., illus.

JENKINS, DEWITT, AND HOMER SHERRILL

2827.   Ahrens, Pat J. A History of the Musical Careers of Dewitt
        "Snuffy" Jenkins, Banjoist, and Homer "Pappy" Sherrill,
        Fiddler. Columbia, South Carolina: The Author, 1970. 24p.

JENNINGS, WAYLON

2828.   Allen, Bob. Waylon and Willie: the Full Story in Words and

Pictures of Waylon Jennings and Willie Nelson. New York: Quick Fox, 1979. 127p., illus., discog.

2829. Denisoff, R. Serge. Waylon: a Biography. Knoxville: University of Tennessee Pr., 1983. 368p., illus., discog.

2830. Smith, John L. Waylon Jennings: Recording History and Complete Discography, 1959-1972. Des Moines: The Author, 1972. 34p.

JETHRO TULL

2831. Meyers, Brian. To Be the Play. Kansas City: Spectacles, 1978. 152p., illus., discog.

JOEL, BILLY

2832. Gambaccini, Peter. Billy Joel: a Personal File. New York: Quick Fox, 1979. 128p., illus., discog.

2833. Geller, Debbie, and Tom Hibbert. Billy Joel: an Illustrated Biography. London: Virgin Books, 1985. 128p., illus., discogs.

2834. Myers, Donald. Billy Joel. New York: Ace Books, 1981. 192p., illus.

JOHN, ELTON (pseud. of Reginald Dwight), AND BERNIE TAUPIN

2835. John, Elton. The Elton John Tapes: Elton John in Conversation with Andy Peebles. London: British Broadcasting Corpion; New York: St. Martin's Pr., 1981. 54p., illus.

2836. ———, and Bernie Taupin. A Conversation With Elton John and Bernie Taupin. Edited by Paul Gambaccini. New York: Flash Books, 1975. 112p., illus., discog.

Biographies

2837. Gambaccini, Paul. Elton John and Bernie Taupin. New York: Quick Fox, 1975. 104p., illus., discog. London: Star Books, 1975. 117p., illus., discog.

2838. Newman, Gerald. Elton John. With Joe Bivona. New York: New American Library, 1976. 188p., illus., discog. (Signet Books). London: New English Library, 1976. 159p., illus., discog.

John, Elton, and Bernie Taupin (cont.)

2839. Taupin, Bernie, and David Nutter. <u>Elton: It's a Little Bit
        Funny</u>. Dedication by Elton John. Harmondsworth, Middlesex:
        Penguin, 1977. 144p., illus. New York: Viking Pr., 1977.
        143p., illus.
            Text by Taupin; photographs by Nutter.

2840. Roland, Paul. <u>Elton John</u>. London; New York: Proteus, 1984.
        128p., illus., discog.

2841. Shaw, Greg (ed.). <u>Elton John</u>. New York: Sire Books, 1977.
        p., illus.

2842. Stein, Cathi. <u>Elton John</u>. New York: Popular Library, 1975.
        159p., illus., discog. London: Futura, 1975. 144p., illus.,
        discog.

2843. Tatham, Dick, and Tony Jasper. <u>Elton John</u>. London: Octopus,
        1976. 92p., illus., discog.

                        Bernie Taupin

2844. Taupin, Bernie. <u>Bernie Taupin, the One Who Writes the Words
        For Elton John: Complete Lyrics From 1968 Through To "Good-
        bye, Yellow Brick Road."</u> Introduction by Elton John. Ed-
        ited by Alan Aldridge and Mike Dempsey. London: Cape; New
        York: Knopf, 1976. 144p., illus.

                        Discographies

2845. Finch, Alan. <u>Elton John: the Illustrated Discography</u>.
        London: Omnibus Pr., 1981. 96p., illus.
            Includes bootleg recordings.

            ————, and Chris Charlesworth. <u>Elton John:"Only the Piano
        Player</u>." London: Omnibus Pr., 1984.   p., illus.
            Updated by Charlesworth, who also added a biographical
        chapter.

JOHNSON, JAMES P.

2846. Trolle, Frank. <u>James P. Johnson: Father of the Stride Piano</u>.
        Alphen aan der Rijn, Holland: Micrography, 1981. <u>2 vols</u>.,
        96p., discog.

JOHNSON, JAY JAY

2847.   Fini, Francesco. <u>The Jay Jay Johnson Complete Discography</u>.
        Imola, Italy: Galeati, 1962. 26p.

JOHNSON, PETE

2848.   Mauerer, Hans J. (ed.). <u>The Pete Johnson Story</u>. New York;
        Frankfurt/Main: The Author, 1965. 78p., illus., discog.
           Biographical and other pieces.

JOHNSON, ROBERT

2849.   Charters, Samuel Barclay. <u>Robert Johnson</u>. New York: Oak
        Publications, 1973. 87p., illus., discog.
           Includes song transcriptions.

JOHNSON, TOMMY

2850.   Evans, David. <u>Tommy Johnson</u>. London: Studio Vista; New
        York: Stein and Day, 1971. 112p., illus., bibliog., discog.
           Based on the author's dissertation, <u>The Blues of Tommy
        Johnson: a Study of a Tradition</u>, University of California at
        Los Angeles, 1967.

JOHNSON, WILLIAM GEARY "BUNK"

2851.   Sonnier, Austin M., <u>Jr</u>. <u>Willie Geary "Bunk" Johnson: the
        New Iberia Years</u>. New York: Crescendo Publishing, 1977.
        81p., illus., discog.

JOLSON, AL (<u>pseud. of</u> Asa Yoelson)

2852.   Anderton, Barrie. <u>Sonny Boy! The World of Al Jolson</u>. London:
        Jupiter Books, 1975. 160p., illus., discog., filmog.

2853.   Freedland, Michael. <u>Al Jolson</u>. London: W.H. Allen, 1972.
        318p., illus., index. New York (as <u>Jolson</u>): Stein and Day,
        1972. 256p., illus., index. London: Abacus, 1975. 268p.,
        illus., index.

2854.   Jolson, Harry (<u>pseud. of</u> Hirsch Yoelson). <u>Mistah Jolson</u>.
        As told to Alban Emley. Hollywood, California: House-Warren,
        1957. 257p., illus.
           Autobiography of Al Jolson's brother, one-time vaudeville
        partner.

Jolson, Al (cont.)

2855. Oberfirst, Robert. <u>Al Jolson: You Ain't Heard Nothing Yet!</u>
       San Diego, California: A.S. Barnes; London: Tantivity Pr.,
       1980. 341p., illus., discog.

2856. Sieben, Pearl. <u>The Immortal Jolson: His Life and Times.</u>
       New York: Frederick Fell, 1962. 231p., illus.

                         Discographies

2857. Jay, Dave. <u>Jolsonography</u>. Washington, D.C.: Big Time Pr.,
       1966. 320p., illus., bibliog., discogs., filmog.

       ————. <u>Jolsonography: the World's Greatest Reference Book
       on the World's Greatest Entertainer.</u> <u>2nd. ed.</u> Bournemouth,
       Dorset: Barrie Anderton, 1974. 284p., illus., bibliog.,
       discogs., filmog.
          Updated to April, 1969. Limited edition of 250 numbered
       copies.

2858. Kiner, Larry F. <u>The Al Jolson Discography</u>. Foreword by
       Peter Tatchell. Westport, Conn.: Greenwood Pr., 1983.
       194p., illus., bibliog., index. (Discographies, 8)
          Includes unissued recordings.

                          Periodicals

2859. <u>Jolson Journal</u>. Edited by Irvan Warwick. Brownsburg,
       Quebec. 3 per year, 1958- .

JONES, GRACE

2860. Gonde, Jean Paul. <u>Jungle Fever</u>. London: Quartet, 1982.
       144p., illus.
          Chiefly illustrated.

JONES, HOWARD

2861. Jones, Howard. <u>Jazz Was My Life</u>. Oradell, New Jersey: Amer-
       ican Tract Society, n.d. 4p.

JONES, QUINCY

2862. Horricks, Raymond. Quincy Jones. Discography by Tony
       Middleton. Speldhurst, Kent: Spellmount; New York: Hippo-
       crene Books, 1985.   p., illus., bibliog., discog., index.
       (Popular Musicians, 2)

JONES, TOM

2863. Jones, Peter. Tom Jones: Biography of a Great Star. London:
       Arthur Barker, 1970. 120p., illus. Chicago: Regnery, 1970.
       161p., illus.

2864. Schwartz, Bert. Tom Jones. New York: Grosset and Dunlap,
       1969.   p., illus.

JOPLIN, JANIS

2865. Caserta, Peggy. Going Down With Janis. As told to Dan
       Knapp. Secaucus, New Jersey: Lyle Stuart, 1973. 298p.
       London: Talmy Franklin, 1975. 271p., illus. London: Fut-
       ura, 1975. 267p.
           Account, by her lover, of their relationship.

2866. Dalton, David (comp.). Janis. New York: Simon and Schuster,
       1971; London: Calder and Boyars/New English Library, 1972.
       154p., illus. New York: Popular Library, 1973. 317p., illus.
           Contents reprinted from Rolling Stone. Simon and Schuster
       edition has record in pocket.

   *   Fleischer, Leonore. The Rose: a Novel.
           * Cited above as item 1184.

2867. Friedman, Myra. Buried Alive: the Biography of Janis Joplin.
       New York: Morrow, 1973; London: W.H. Allen, 1984. 333p.,
       illus. New York: Bantam, 1974. 398p., illus. London: Star
       Books, 1975. 284p., illus. London: Plexus Publishing, 1984.
       336p., illus.
           By her press agent.

2868. Landau, Deborah. Janis Joplin: Her Life and Times. New
       York: Paperback Library, 1971. 160p., illus., discog.

   *   Watson, Diana Masters. The Rose.
           * Cited above as item 1185.

JOPLIN, SCOTT

2869. Joplin, Scott. The Collected Works. New York: New York Pub-
       lic Library, 1971. 2 vols.,   p., illus.

Joplin, Scott (cont.)

Biographies

2870. Evans, Mark. <u>Scott Joplin and the Ragtime Years</u>. New York:
Dodd, Mead, 1976. 120p., illus., index.
Aimed at younger readers.

2871. Gammond, Peter. <u>Scott Joplin and the Ragtime Era</u>. Foreword by Eubie Blake. London; Sydney: Angus and Robertson;
New York: St. Martin's Pr.; London: Sphere; London: Abacus,
1975. 223p., illus., bibliog., discog. <u>Rev. ed.</u>: New
York: St. Martin's Pr., 1976.   p., illus., bibliog.,
discog.
Includes listing of his works.

2872. Haskins, James. <u>Scott Joplin: the Man Who Made Ragtime</u>.
With Kathleen Benson. Garden City, New York: Doubleday,
1978; London: Robson Books, 1979; New York: Stein and Day,
1980. 248p., illus., bibliog., index.

JOYSTRINGS

2873. Gilliard, Alfred James. <u>Joy and The Joystrings: the Sal-
vation Army's Pop Group</u>. London: Lutterworth Pr., 1967.
90p., illus.

2874. Webb, Joy. <u>And This Is Joy</u>. London: Hodder, 1969. 95p.,
illus.

JUBILEE SINGERS

2875. Marsh, J.B.T. <u>The Story of The Jubilee Singers, With Their
Songs</u>. London: Hodder and Stoughton, 1875. 227p., illus.
<u>Rev. ed.</u>: London: Hodder and Stoughton, 1876. 248p., illus.
Boston: Houghton Mifflin, 1880 (Reprinted: New York: Negro
Universities Pr., 1969; New York: A.M.S. Pr., 1971; Westport,
Conn.: Greenwood Pr., 1979). London: Hodder and Stoughton,
1885. 265p., illus. <u>With Supplement Containing an Account
of Their Six Years' Tour Around the World, and Many New
Songs; by F.J. Londin</u>. Cleveland: Cleveland Printing and
Publishing Company, 1892; London: Hodder and Stoughton,
1898. 311p., illus.
Includes songs.

2876. Pike, Gustavus D. <u>The Jubilee Singers and Their Campaign
For Twenty Thousand Dollars</u>. Boston: Lee and Shepard, 1873;
New York: A.M.S. Pr., 1974. 219p., illus.
Includes sixty-one songs, edited by Theo F. Seward.

2877. ———. The Singing Campaign For Ten Thousand Pounds; or,
The Jubilee Singers in Great Britain. With an Appendix
Containing Slave Songs, Compiled and Arranged by Theodore
F. Seward. London: Hodder and Stoughton, 1874; New York:
American Missionary Association, 1875. 219p., illus.
Includes seventy-one songs.

Thomas Rutling

2878. Rutling, Thomas. "Tom:" an Autobiography. With Revised
Negro Melodies. Torrington: T.J. Dyer, 1907. 64p., illus.
Tenor with The Jubilee Singers. Remained in Hamburg,
1878; went to England, 1890.

JUNE (pseud. of June Hillman)

2879. June. The Glass Ladder. London: Heinemann, 1960. 336p.,
illus., index.
Autobiography.

KAJAGOOGOO

2880. Kajagoogoo. Kajagoogoo: the Official Lyric Book. Introduction by Paul Gambaccini. London: Omnibus Pr., 1983.
32p., illus.

KAMINSKY, MAX

2881. Kaminsky, Max. My Life in Jazz. With V.E. Hughes. New
York: Harper and Row, 1963; London: Deutsch, 1964. 242p.,
illus., index. New ed.: New York (as Jazz Band: My Life in
Jazz): Da Capo Pr., 1982. 242p., illus., index.

KATZ, MICKEY (pseud. of Myron Katz)

2882. Katz, Myron. Papa, Play For Me: the Hilarious, Heartwarming
Autobiography of Comedian and Bandleader Mickey Katz. As
told to Hannibal Coons. Introduction by Joel Grey. New
York: Simon and Schuster, 1977. 223p., illus.

KAUFMAN, GEORGE S.

2883. Meredith, Scott. George S. Kaufman and His Friends. Garden
City, New York: Doubleday, 1974.   p., illus.

Kaufman, George S. (cont.)

2884. Teichman, Howard. <u>George S. Kaufman: an Intimate Portrait</u>.
       New York: Atheneum; London: Angus and Robertson, 1972.
       372p., illus., index.

KAUFMAN, MURRAY

2885. Kaufman, Murray. <u>Murray The K Tells It Like It Is, Baby</u>.
       Foreword by Tony Bennett. New York: Holt, Rinehart and
       Winston, 1966. 127p., illus.
           Disk-jockey's autobiography. The self-appointed "Fifth
       Beatle."

KAYE, DANNY (<u>pseud. of</u> David Daniel Kominsky)

2886. Singer, Kurt Deutsch. <u>The Danny Kaye Story</u>. London: Hale,
       1957. 206p., illus., bibliog. New York: Nelson, 1958.
       241p., illus., bibliog.

KELLY, GENE

2887. Basinger, Jeanine. <u>Gene Kelly</u>. New York: Pyramid Publicat-
       ions, 1976. 160p., illus., bibliog., filmog., index. (Illus-
       trated History of the Movies)

2888. Burrows, Michael. <u>Gene Kelly: Versatility Personified</u>.
       St. Austell, Cornwall: Primestyle, 1972. 40p., illus.

2889. Hirschhorn, Clive. <u>Gene Kelly: a Biography</u>. Chicago:
       Regnery; London: W.H. Allen, 1974. 334p., illus., filmog.,
       index. London: Comet Books, 1984. 296p., illus., filmog.,
       index.

2890. Thomas, Tony. <u>The Films of Gene Kelly, Song and Dance Man</u>.
       Foreword by Fred Astaire. Secaucus, New Jersey: Citadel
       Pr., 1974. 243p., illus.

KENTON, STAN

2891. Dietzel, Hans-Joachim, and Horst Heinz Lange. <u>Stan Kenton
       Biography; Stan Kenton Discography</u>. Berlin: New Jazz Circle,
       1959. 27p., illus.
           Biography by Dietzel; discography by Lange.

2892. Easton, Carol. Straight Ahead: the Story of Stan Kenton.
       New York: Morrow, 1973. 252p., illus.

2893. Lee, William F. Stan Kenton: Artistry in Rhythm. Edited
       by Andree Coke. Los Angeles: Creative Pr., 1980. 727p.,
       illus., discog.
            Appendix lists his sidemen.

2894. New Musical Express. The Stan Kenton Story. London: New
       Musical Express, 1953. 21p., illus. (Star Series, 1)

                          Discographies

2895. Edwards, Ernie. Discography of Stan Kenton and His Orch-
       estra. Brande, Denmark: Debut Records, 1963.
       Vol.1: 1941-52.   p.
       Vol.2: 1952-62.   p.

2896. Jepsen, Jorgen Grunnet. Discography of Stan Kenton. Bio-
       graphical notes by Knud H. Ditlevsen. Brande, Denmark:
       Debut Records, 1950. 22p. Rev. ed.: 1960. 25p.

2897. Pirie, Christopher A., and Siegfried Mueller. Artistry in
       Kenton: a Bio-Discography of Stan Kenton and His Music.
       Vienna: Siegfried Mueller, 1969. 289p., index. 2nd. ed.:
       1969. 3rd. ed.: 1972.
            Includes radio transcriptions.

2898. Sparke, Michael, Pete Venudor, and Jack Hartley. Kenton on
       Capitol: a Discography. Compiled with the cooperation of
       Capitol Records, Inc. Hounslow, Middlesex: Michael Sparke,
       1966. 134p.

2899. Venudor, Pete, and Michael Sparke. The Standard Kenton
       Directory. Amsterdam: Pete Venudor, 1968. 52p.
            Annotated. Includes commercials, soundtracks, and
       broadcasts.

KERN, JEROME

2900. Bordman, Gerald. Jerome Kern: His Life and Music. New
       York; London: Oxford University Pr., 1980. 438p., illus.,
       indexes.

2901. Ewen, David. The Story of Jerome Kern. New York: Holt;
       Toronto: Clark, Irwin, 1953. 148p., illus.

       ————. The World of Jerome Kern: a Biography. New York:
       Holt, 1960. 178p., illus., discog., index.

2902. Fordin, Hugh. Jerome Kern: the Man and His Music. Santa
       Monica, California: T.B. Harms, 1974.   p., illus.

Kern, Jerome (cont.)

2903. Freedland, Michael. <u>Jerome Kern: a Biography</u>. London:
      Robson Books, 1978. 182p., illus., index.

2904. Lamb, Andrew. <u>Jerome Kern in Edwardian London</u>. Littlehamp-
      ton, West Sussex: The Author, 1981. 32p., bibliog.
         Account of his visit, 1905-10.

KID CREOLE (<u>pseud. of</u> August Darnell)

2905. Goldman, Vivien. <u>Kid Creole and The Coconuts: Indiscreet</u>.
      London: Zomba Books, 1983.   p., illus.

KING, B.B. (<u>pseud. of</u> Riley King)

2906. King, B.B. <u>B.B. King: the Blues, the Wellspring of Today's</u>
      <u>American Popular Music, and Its Greatest Performer, B.B.</u>
      <u>King, in an Unusual and Beautiful Collection of Articles,</u>
      <u>Music, Lyrics, Photos, and Quotes</u>. New York: Amsco, 1970.
      60p., illus.

2907. Sawyer, Charles. <u>The Arrival of B.B. King: the Authorized</u>
      <u>Biography</u>. Garden City, New York: Doubleday, 1980. 274p.,
      illus., discog., index.

         ————. <u>B.B. King: the Authorized Biography</u>. Poole, Dorset:
      Blandford Pr., 1981; London: Quartet, 1982. 274p., illus.,
      discog., index.

KING, CAROLE

2908. King, Carole. <u>You've Got a Friend: Poetic Selections From</u>
      <u>the Songs of Carole King</u>. Edited by Susan Polis Schutz.
      Boulder, Colorado: Blue Mountain Pr., 1978. 61p., illus.

                              Biography

2909. Cohen, Mitchell S. <u>Carole King: a Biography in Words and</u>
      <u>Pictures</u>. Edited by Greg Shaw. New York: Sire Books, 1976.
      56p., illus., discog.

KINKS

2910. Mendelssohn, John. <u>The Kinks Kronikles</u>. New York: Morrow,
      1984. 192p., illus., discog.

2911. Rogan, Johnny. The Kinks: the Sound and the Fury. London:
      Elm Tree Books, 1984. 242p., illus., discog.

2912. Savage, Jon. The Kinks: the Official Biography. London:
      Faber and Faber, 1984. 178p., illus., bibliog., discog.

2913. Schruers, Fred. The Kinks. London: Hutchinson, 1984.
      p., illus., discog.

2914. Skidmore, Mike. Survivors. Dagenham, Essex: The Author,
      1979.   p., illus., discog.

                              Periodicals

2915. Kinky Mirror. Edited by W. Hagspiel. Maastrichterstrasse
      22, D-5000, Cologne, West Germany. irreg., 1983- .
      In German, with English translation insert.

KIRK, ROLAND

2916. Tarrant, Don. Roland Kirk Discography. Southsea, Hampshire:
      The Author, 1970. 11p.

KISS

2917. Swenson, John. Kiss. New York: Delilah; London: Hamlyn,
      1979. 185p., illus.

2918. Tomarkin, Peggy. Kiss: the Real Story, Authorized. New
      York: Dell, 1980. 111p., illus. (A Delta Special)

KITT, EARTHA

2919. Kitt, Eartha. Alone With Me. Chicago: Regnery, 1976.   p.,
      illus.
          Memoirs.

2920. ———. Thursday's Child. New York: Duell, 1956; London:
      Cassell, 1957. 250p., illus. London: Landsborough Public-
      ations, 1958. 192p., illus. (Four Square Books)

KOLLER, HANS

2921. Kraner, Dietrich Heinz. Die Hans Koller Discographie, 1947-
      1966. Graz, Austria: Modern Jazz Series, 1967. 20p.

KOOPER, AL

2922. Kooper, Al. Backstage Passes: Rock 'n' Roll Life in the
       Sixties. With Ben Edmonds. New York: Stein and Day, 1977.
          p., illus.
       Memoirs.

KRISTOFFERSON, KRIS

2923. Kalet, Beth. Kris Kristofferson. New York: Quick Fox,
       1979. 96p., illus., discog.

KRUPA, GENE

2924. Shaw, Arnold. Gene Krupa. New York: Pin-Up Press Company,
       1945. 32p., illus., discog.

                            Discographies

2925. Edwards, Ernie, George Hall, and Bill Korst. Gene Krupa and
       His Orchestra, 1938-1951. Whittier, California: Jazz Discog-
       raphies Unlimited, 1968. 36p.

2926. Hall, George, and Stephen A. Kramer. Gene Krupa and His
       Orchestra. Laurel, Maryland: Jazz Discographies Unlimited,
       1975. 90p., indexes.

   *   Strateman, Klaus. Buddy Rich and Gene Krupa: a Filmo-Discog-
       raphy.
          * Cited below as item 3399.

LANZA, MARIO

2927. Bernard, Matt. Mario Lanza. New York: MacFadden-Bartell,
       1971. 224p., illus.

2928. Burrows, Michael. Mario Lanza; and, Max Steiner. St. Aust-
       ell, Cornwall: Primestyle, 1971. 44p., bibliog., filmog.

2929. Strait, Raymond, and Terry Robinson. Lanza: His Tragic Life.
       Englewood Cliffs, New Jersey; London: Prentice-Hall, 1980.
       181p., illus., discog., index.

Discographies

2930.   British Mario Lanza Society. <u>Mario Lanza Discography</u>.
Banbury, Oxfordshire: British Mario Lanza Society, 1980.
52p.

LAST, JAMES

2931.   Last, James. <u>James Last Story</u>. Hamburg: R. Gloss, 1975.
304p., illus., discog.
Autobiography. In German.

Biographies

2932.   Elson, Howard. <u>James Last</u>. London; New York: Proteus,
1982. 64p., illus., discog.

2933.   Willox, Bob. <u>James Last</u>. London: Everest, 1976. 207p.,
illus., discog.

LAUDAN, STANLEY

2934.   Laudan, Stanley. <u>The White Baton</u>. As told to Kendall
McDonald. London: Wingate, 1957. 196p.   .
Autobiography.

LAUDER, HARRY

2935.   Lauder, Harry. <u>Between You and Me</u>. New York: McCann, 1919.
324p.
Memoirs.

2936.   ———. <u>Harry Lauder at Home and On Tour: by Ma' Sel'</u>.
London: Greening, 1906. 126p.

2937.   ———. <u>A Minstrel in France</u>. London: Andrew Melrose; New
York: Hearst's International Library, 1918. 338p., illus.
Touring experiences.

2938.   ———. <u>My American Travels</u>. London: Newnes, 1910. 114p.

2939.   ———. <u>Roamin' in the Gloamin'</u>. London: Hutchinson, 1928;
Wakefield, Yorkshire: E.P. Publishing, 1976. 287p., illus.,
index.
Autobiography.

Lauder, Harry (cont.)

2940. Lauder, Harry. Ticklin' Talks. London: D.C. Thomson, 1934.
352p.
Reminiscences.

Biographies

2941. Irving, Gordon. Great Scot: the Life Story of Sir Harry
Lauder, Legendary Laird of the Music Hall. London: Leslie
Frewin, 1968. 184p., illus., index.
Includes listing of his songs.

2942. Quigley, Joseph. The Slogan: Side-Lights on Recruiting With
Harry Lauder's Band. Edited by T.S. Dickson. Illustrated
by George Whitelaw. London: Simpkin, Marshall, 1916. 157p.,
illus.
Account of his World War I army recruiting campaigns.

LAWRENCE, ELLIOT

2943. Garrod, Charles. Elliot Lawrence and His Orchestra. Spotswood, New Jersey: Joyce, 1973.   p.
Discography.

LAWRENCE, GERTRUDE

2944. Lawrence, Gertrude. A Star Danced. London: W.H. Allen;
Garden City, New York: Doubleday, Doran; Garden City, New
York: Star Books, 1946. 238p.
Autobiography.

Biographies

2945. Aldrich, Richard. Gertrude Lawrence as Mrs. A: an Intimate
Biography of the Great Star. Foreword by Daphne Du Maurier.
New York: Greystone Pr., 1954. 320p., illus. London: Odhams
Pr., 1955. 351p., illus. New York; London: Bantam, 1968.
378p.
By her husband.

2946. Morley, Sheridan. Gertrude Lawrence. London: Weidenfeld and
Nicolson, 1981. 228p., illus., bibliog., discog., filmog.,
index.

2947. Thomas, Bob. Star! From the Screenplay by William Fairchild.
London: Corgi, 1968. 150p., illus.
Novelization of the motion picture based on her life.

LAYE, EVELYN

2948. Laye, Evelyn. <u>Boo, To My Friends</u>. London: Hurst and
       Blackett, 1958. 180p., illus., index.
          Autobiography.

LEADBELLY (<u>pseud. of</u> Huddie Ledbetter)

2949. Garvin, Richard M., and Edmond G. Addeo. <u>The Midnight</u>
       <u>Special: the Legend of Leadbelly</u>. New York: Bernard Geis
       Associates, 1971. 312p., illus.

2950. Jones, Max, and Albert John McCarthy (eds.). <u>A Tribute to</u>
       <u>Huddie Ledbetter</u>. London: Jazz Music Books, 1946. 26p.,
       illus., discog.

LED ZEPPELIN

2951. Led Zeppelin. <u>Led Zeppelin In Their Own Words</u>. Compiled by
       Paul Kendall. London: Omnibus Pr., 1982. 128p., illus.
          Compiled from press and other interviews.

Biographies

2952. Bunton, Richard. <u>Led Zeppelin: In the Light, 1968-1980</u>.
       With Howard Mylett. London; New York: Proteus, 1981. 96p.,
       illus., discog. (Proteus Rocks)

2953. Davis, Stephen. <u>Hammer of the Gods: the Led Zeppelin Saga</u>.
       London: Sidgwick and Jackson, 1985. 224p., illus., bibliog.

2954. Hoffer, John. <u>Led Zeppelin: the Road Album</u>. London; New
       York: Proteus, 1984.   p., illus.
          Performance photographs.

2955. Kendall, Paul. <u>Led Zeppelin: a Visual Documentary</u>. London:
       Omnibus Pr.; New York: Delilah, 1983. 96p., illus.

2956. <u>Led Zeppelin</u>. Milwaukee: Ideals Publishing, 1979. 52p.,
       illus.

2957. Lewis, Dave. <u>Led Zeppelin: the Final Acclaim</u>. Birmingham,
       England: Babylon Books, 1984. 144p., illus., discog., filmog.

2958. Mylett, Howard. <u>Led Zeppelin</u>. St. Albans, Hertfordshire:
       Panther, 1976. 156p., illus. <u>Rev. ed.</u>: London: Panther,
       1978. 172p., illus. <u>3rd. ed.</u>: London: Panther, 1981. 205p.,
       illus. (Panther Rock Series)

Led Zeppelin (cont.)

2959. Mylett, Howard (comp.). Led Zeppelin: On-Stage Action, 1970-
       75. Photographs by Carl Dunn. Brighton, West Sussex: The
       Author, 1984. 56p., illus.
          Chiefly illustrated.

2960. Preston, Neal. Led Zeppelin: Portraits. Introduction by
       Cameron Crowe. New York: Rock-at-Home, 1983.   p., illus.
          Photographs by the group's official tour photographer,
       1973-79. Limited edition of five thousand signed copies.

2961. Welch, Chris. Led Zeppelin. London: Omnibus Pr., 1984.
       96p., illus. (H.M. Photobooks)
          Chiefly illustrated.

2962. ───────. Led Zeppelin: the Book. London; New York: Proteus,
       1984. 157p., illus., discog.

2963. Yorke, Ritchie. The Led Zeppelin Biography. New York:
       Two Continents/Methuen, 1976.   p., illus.

                              Periodicals

2964. P.B. Edited by Claudia Chapman. Wolcottville, Indiana.
       bi-monthly, 1979-?

2965. Proximity. Seattle, Washington. irreg., 1980-?

2966. Tight But Loose. Edited by Dave Lewis. 52 Dents Road,
       Bedford, England. irreg., 1980- .

                         Individual Band Members

Page, Jimmy

2967. Mylett, Howard. Jimmy Page: Tangents Within a Framework.
       London: Omnibus Pr., 1983.   p., illus.

Plant, Robert

2968. Gross, Michael. Robert Plant. New York: Popular Library,
       1975. 160p., illus.

LEIBER AND STOLLER

2969. Leiber, Jerry. Selected Lyrics, 1950-1980. New York:
Urizen Books, 1980.   p.

2970. Palmer, Robert, and John Lahr. Baby, That Was Rock and Roll:
the Legendary Leiber and Stoller. New York: Urizen Books;
New York; London: Harcourt, Brace, Jovanovich, 1978. 181p.,
illus., discog.
Story of songwriting team of Jerry Leiber and Mike Stoller. Includes lyrics of thirty-four songs.

LENYA, LOTTE see WEILL, KURT

LERNER, ALAN JAY

2971. Lerner, Alan Jay. The Street Where I Live: the Story of
"My Fair Lady", "Gigi", and "Camelot." New York: Norton,
1978. 336p., illus., index. London: Hodder and Stoughton,
1980. 303p., illus., index. London: Coronet, 1980. 346p.,
illus., index.
Autobiography. Includes lyrics.

LEVANT, OSCAR

2972. Levant, Oscar. Memoirs of an Amnesiac. New York: Putnam,
1965. 320p.

2973. ————. A Smattering of Ignorance. Garden City, New York:
Doubleday, Doran, 1940; Garden City, New York: Doubleday,
1959. 181p., illus.
Autobiography.

2974. ————. The Unimportance of Being Oscar. New York: Putnam,
1968. 255p., illus.
Further memoirs.

LEWIS, GEORGE

2975. Bethell, Tom. George Lewis: a Jazzman From New Orleans.
Berkeley; London: University of California Pr., 1977. 387p.,
illus., bibliog., discog., index.

2976. Stuart, Jay Allison (pseud. of Dorothy Tait). Call Him
George. London: Peter Davies; New York: Crown, 1961. 285p.,
illus. New ed.: New York: Crown, 1969. 303p., illus.
Based on information from Lewis. 1969 edition published
under the pseudonym "Ann Fairbairn."

LEWIS, JERRY LEE

2977. Cain, Robert. Whole Lotta Shakin' Going On. Bromley,
       Kent: Columbus Books, 1981.   p., illus., discog.

2978. Lewis, Myra. Great Balls of Fire! The True Story of Jerry
       Lee Lewis. Santa Barbara, California: Quill Publications;
       London: Virgin Books, 1982. 319p., illus., index.
          By his ex-wife.

2979. Palmer, Robert. Jerry Lee Lewis Rocks. New York: Delilah,
       1981; London: Omnibus Pr., 1982. 128p., illus., discog.

2980. Tosches, Nick. Hellfire: the Jerry Lee Lewis Story. New
       York: Delacorte Pr.; London: Plexus Publishing, 1982. 276p.,
       illus., index.

LIBERACE, WLADZIU VALENTINO

2981. Liberace. Liberace: an Autobiography. New York: Putnam;
       London: W.H. Allen, 1973; New York: Popular Library, 1976.
       316p., illus. London: Star Books, 1974. 307p., illus.

2982. ────────. The Things I Love. Edited by Tony Palmer. New
       York: Grosset and Dunlap, 1976. 224p., illus.
          Memoirs.

Biographies

2983. Burney, Anton. The Liberace Story. Foreword by Liberace.
       London: Beverley Pr., 1955. 52p., illus.

2984. Guild, Leo. The Loves of Liberace. New York: Avon Books,
       1956. 160p., illus.

LIGHTFOOT, GORDON

2985. Lightfoot, Gordon. I Wish You Good Spaces. Edited by
       Susan P. Schutz. Kalamazoo, Michigan: Blue Mountain Pr.,
       1977.   p., illus.
          Poetry.

2986. ────────. The Pony Man. New York: Harper and Row, 1972.
       32p., illus.
          Poetry.

Biography

2987. Gabiou, Alfrieda. <u>Gordon Lightfoot</u>. New York: Quick Fox,
      1979. 128p., illus., discog.

LILLIE, BEATRICE

2988. Lillie, Beatrice. <u>Every Other Inch a Lady</u>. Aided and
      abetted by John Philip. With James Brough. Garden City,
      New York: Doubleday, 1972. 360p., illus. London: W.H.
      Allen, 1973. 318p., illus. New York: Dell, 1973. 363p.,
      illus.
      Autobiography.

LIND, JENNY

2989. Lind, Jenny. <u>The Lost Letters of Jenny Lind</u>. Translated
      from the German, and edited with commentaries by W. Porter
      Ware and Thaddeus C. Lockard, <u>Jr</u>. London: Gollancz, 1966.
      159p., illus.

Songs

2990. <u>The Jenny Lind Forget-Me-Not Songster</u>. New York: R. Marsh,
      185? 739p., illus.

2991. <u>Jenny Lind; or, Songs of The Swedish Nightingale. Together
      With a Collection of Sentimental, Comic, and Temperance
      Songs, With All the Late Negro Melodies</u>. Philadelphia:
      J.B. Perry, 1850. 297p., illus.
      Texts only.

Biographies

2992. Benét, Laura. <u>The Enchanting Jenny Lind</u>. New York: Dodd,
      Mead, 1940. 452p., illus.

2993. Bulman, Joan Carroll Boone. <u>Jenny Lind: a Biography</u>. Lon-
      don: Barrie, 1956. 326p., illus., bibliog.

2994. Foster, George G. <u>Memoir of Jenny Lind: Compiled From the
      Most Authentic Sources</u>. New York: Dewitt and Davenport,
      1850. 64p.

2995. Gleason, F. <u>Jenny Lind</u>. Boston: The Author, 185? 4p.

Lind, Jenny (cont.)

2996. Godwin, Parke. Vala: a Mythological Tale. New York: Putnam, 1851. 46p., illus.
Novel based on Lind. Originally published in shorter form in the New York Evening Post.

2997. Holland, Henry Scott, and William Smyth Rockstro. A Memoir of Madame Jenny Lind Goldschmidt: Her Early Art-Life and Dramatic Career, 1820-1851. From Original Documents, Letters, Manuscript Diaries, etc., Collected by Mr. Otto Goldschmidt. London: John Murray, 1891 (Reprinted: Boston: Longwood Pr., 1978). 2 vols., 478p., illus. New and abridged ed.: London: John Murray; New York: Scribner's, 1893. 473p., illus.
Based on material provided by her husband. Includes words and music of songs.

2998. Jenny Lind Association, New York. The Jenny Lind Association, New York. New York: Paragon Pr., 1923. 64p.
Includes biographical information.

2999. Jenny Lind Foundation. Souvenir Magazine of the Jenny Lind Centennial Celebration, Minneapolis and St. Paul, Minnesota, October 9th and 10th, 1920. Minneapolis: Jenny Lind Foundation, 1920. 12p., illus.
Includes biographical information.

3000. Kyle, Elisabeth (pseud. of Agnes Mary Robertson Dunlop). Girl With a Song: the Story of Jenny Lind. Illustrations by Charles Mozley. London: Evans, 1964. 189p., illus. New York (as The Swedish Nightingale: Jenny Lind): Holt, 1965. 223p., illus., bibliog.

3001. Lindiana: an Interesting Narrative of the Life of Jenny Lind. Arundel, Sussex: Mitchell and Son; London: J. Thomas, 1847. 52p., illus.

3002. Maude, Jenny Maria Catherine Goldschmidt. The Life of Jenny Lind, Briefly Told by Her Daughter, Mrs. Raymond Maude. London: Cassell, 1926; New York: Arno Pr., 1977. 222p., illus., index.

3003. Memoir of Jenny Lind. London: J. Ollivier, 1847. 20p., illus.

3004. Myers, Elisabeth P. Jenny Lind: Songbird From Sweden. Champaign, Illinois: Garrard Publishing, 1968. 143p., illus.
Aimed at younger readers.

3005. Reach, Angus Bethune. Jenny Lind At Last; or, The Swedish Nightingale: an Apropos Operatic Bagatelle. London: Barth, 1847; Boston: W.V. Spencer, 1856. 16p. New York: Samuel French, 1864. 12p.
One-act play on the Lind craze.

3006. Rockstro, William Smyth. Jenny Lind: a Record and Analysis
of the "Method" of Madame Jenny Lind-Goldschmidt. London:
Novello, 1894. 20p.
        Includes musical examples.

3007. Rosenberg, Charles G. Jenny Lind: Her Life, Her Struggles,
and Her Triumphs. New York: Stringer and Townsend, 1850.
82p., illus.

3008. ————. Jenny Lind in America. New York: Stringer and
Townsend, 1851. 226p., illus.
        Account of her tour.

3009. Schultz, Gladys. Jenny Lind: The Swedish Nightingale.
Philadelphia: Lippincott, 1962.   p., illus.

3010. Wagenknecht, Edward Charles. Jenny Lind. Boston: Houghton
Mifflin, 1931; New York: Da Capo Pr., 1980. 230p., illus.,
bibliog., index.

3011. Ware, W. Porter, and Thaddeus C. Lockard, Jr. P.T. Barnum
Presents Jenny Lind: the American Tour of The Swedish Nightingale. Baton Rouge; London: Louisiana State University Pr.,
1980. 204p., illus., bibliog., index.

3012. Westervelt, Leonidas. The Jenny Lind Medals and Tokens.
New York: American Numismatic Society, 1921. 25p., illus.
(Numismatic Notes and Monographs, 5)

3013. Willis, Nathaniel Parker. Memoranda of the Life of Jenny
Lind. Philadelphia: R.E. Peterson, 1851. 236p., illus.

                        Phineas Taylor Barnum

3014. Werner, Morris Robert. Barnum. New York: Harcourt, Brace;
London: Cape, 1923. 381p., illus.
        Includes account of his promotion of Lind.

LINDSAY AND CROUSE

3015. Skinner, Cornelia Otis. Life With Lindsay and Crouse.
Boston: Houghton Mifflin, 1976. 242p., illus., index.
        Account of musical comedy librettists, Howard Lindsay and
Russell Crouse.

LISTER, MOIRA

3016. Lister, Moira. The Very Merry Widow Moira. London: Hodder
and Stoughton, 1969. 189p., illus.
        Autobiography.

LLOYD, MARIE

3017. Farson, Daniel. <u>Marie Lloyd and Music Hall</u>. London: Tom
       Stacey, 1972. 176p., illus., index.

3018. Jacob, Naomi. <u>"Our Marie" (Marie Lloyd): a Biography</u>.
       London: Hutchinson, 1936; Bath, Somerset: Chivers, 1972.
       287p., illus., index.
           Includes genealogical table.

3019. MacQueen-Pope, Walter James. <u>Queen of the Music Halls:
       Being the Dramatized Story of Marie Lloyd</u>. London: Oldbourne,
       1957. 186p., illus. (Close-Up Biographies)

LLOYD WEBBER, ANDREW

3020. McKnight, Gerald. <u>Andrew Lloyd Webber</u>. London: Granada,
       1984. 278p., illus., discog., index.

LOGAN, JOSHUA

3021. Logan, Joshua. <u>Josh: My Up and Down, In and Out Life</u>. New
       York: Delacorte Pr., 1976; London: W.H. Allen, 1977. 408p.,
       illus., index.

LOMAX, JOHN AVERY

3022. Lomax, John Avery. <u>Adventures of a Ballad Hunter</u>. New
       York: Macmillan, 1947; New York: Hafner Publishing, 1971.
       302p., illus.
           Autobiography.

LOMBARDO, GUY

3023. Lombardo, Guy. <u>Auld Acquaintance</u>. With Jack Altshul.
       Introduction by Jules Stein. Garden City, New York: Double-
       day, 1975. 295p., illus.
           Autobiography.

LONGHAIR, PROFESSOR (<u>pseud. of</u> Roy Byrd)

3024. Crosby, John. <u>Professor Longhair: a Bio-Discography</u>.
       London: The Author, 1983. 11p., discog.

LOVE, BESSIE

3025. Love, Bessie. <u>From Hollywood With Love</u>. London: Elm Tree
Books, 1977. 160p., illus., filmog., index.
Autobiography.

LUNCEFORD, JIMMIE

3026. Demeuldre, Leon. <u>Discography of the Jimmie Lunceford Orch-
estra</u>. Brussels: The Author, 1961. 9p.

3027. Edwards, Ernie, George Hall, and Bill Korst. <u>The Jimmie
Lunceford Band</u>. Whittier, California: Jazz Discographies
Unlimited, 1965. 12p.

LYMAN, MEL

3028. Lyman, Mel. <u>Mirror at the End of the Road</u>. Illustrated by
Ebon Given. New York: Ballantine, 1971. unpaged, illus.
Autobiography.

LYNN, LORETTA

3029. Lynn, Loretta. <u>Loretta Lynn: Coal Miner's Daughter</u>. With
George Vecsey. Chicago: Regnery, 1976. 204p., illus.,
index.

————. <u>Coal Miner's Daughter</u>. With George Vecsey. New
York: Warner Books, 1976; London: Panther, 1979. 256p.,
illus., discog., index.

Biographies

3030. Krishef, Robert K. <u>Loretta Lynn</u>. Minneapolis: Lerner
Publications, 1978. 64p., illus., discog., index.
Aimed at younger readers.

3031. Zwisohn, Laurence J. <u>Loretta Lynn's World of Music</u>. Los
Angeles: Palm Tree Library, 1980. 116p., illus.

LYNN, VERA

3032. Lynn, Vera. <u>Vocal Refrain: an Autobiography</u>. London: W.H.
Allen, 1975. 192p., illus., index.

LYTTELTON, HUMPHREY

3033. Lyttelton, Humphrey. I Play As I Please: the Memoirs of an
       Old Etonian Trumpeter. London: MacGibbon and Kee, 1954.
       200p., illus. London: Pan, 1959. 188p., illus.

3034. ———. Second Chorus. London: MacGibbon and Kee, 1958.
       198p., illus.
           More autobiography.

3035. ———. Take It From the Top: an Autobiographical Scrap-
       book. London: Robson Books, 1975. 164p., illus.

3036. ———. Why No Beethoven? The Diary of a Vagrant Musician.
       London: Robson Books, 1984. 176p., illus.
           Account of tours to Poland, 1976; and the Middle East,
       1979 and 1982.

                              Discography

3037. Purser, Julian. "Humph" A Discography of Humphrey Lyttel-
       ton, 1945-1983. Walton-on-Thames, Surrey: Collectors' Items,
       1983. 60p.

McCLAREN, MALCOLM

3038. Vermorel, Fred, and Judy Vermorel. Malcolm McClaren: an
       In-Depth Biography. London: Virgin Books, 1985. 192p.,
       illus., discog.

McCORMACK, JOHN

3039. McCormack, John. John McCormack: His Own Life Story. As
       told to Pierre V. Key. New York: Vienna House, 1973. 443p.,
       illus.
           Written in 1918.

                             Biographies

3040. Foxall, Raymond. John McCormack. Foreword by Compton
       Mackenzie. London: Hale, 1963. 186p., illus.

3041. Ledbetter, Gordon T. The Great Irish Tenor. London: Duck-
       worth, 1977; New York: Scribner's, 1978. 160p., illus.,
       bibliog., index.

3042. McCormack, Lily Foley. <u>I Hear You Calling Me</u>. Milwaukee:
       Bruce Publishing, 1949; Westport, Conn.: Greenwood Pr.,
       1975. 201p., illus., discog.
          By his wife.

                          Discographies

3043. McDermott Roe, Leonard Francis Xavier. <u>John McCormack: the
       Complete Discography</u>. London: C. Jackson, 1956. 93p.,
       illus. <u>Rev. ed.</u>: Lingfield, Surrey: Oakwood Pr., 1972.
       93p., illus.

MACDONALD, JEANETTE, AND NELSON EDDY

3044. Castanza, Philip. <u>The Films of Jeanette MacDonald and
       Nelson Eddy</u>. Introduction by Eleanor Powell. Secaucus,
       New Jersey: Citadel Pr., 1978. 224p., illus., discogs.
          Details of every production, together and separately.

3045. Knowles, Eleanor. <u>The Films of Jeanette MacDonald and
       Nelson Eddy</u>. Film credits by John Robert Cocchi. Music
       credits and discography by J. Peter Bergman. South Bruns-
       wick, New York: A.S. Barnes; London: Tantivity Pr., 1975.
       469p., illus., discog., index.

                       Jeanette MacDonald

3046. Parish, James Robert. <u>The Jeanette MacDonald Story</u>. New
       York: Mason/Charter, 1976. 181p., illus.

3047. Rich, Sharon. <u>Jeanette MacDonald: a Pictorial Treasury</u>.
       Presented by Tom Hartzog. Los Angeles: Times Mirror Pr.,
       1973. 253p., illus.

3048. Stern, Lee Edward. <u>Jeanette MacDonald</u>. New York: Jove
       Publications, 1977.   p., illus., bibliog., index.

McKUEN, ROD

3049. McKuen, Rod. <u>Finding My Father: One Man's Search For
       Identity</u>. New York: Coward, McCann, and Geoghegan, 1976;
       London: Elm Tree Books, 1977. 255p., illus., bibliog.,
       index.
          Autobiography.

3050. ————. <u>New Ballads</u>. Los Angeles: Stanyan Books, 1970.
       44p.
          Song lyrics.

McKuen, Rod (cont.)

3051. McKuen, Rod. <u>Pastorale: a Collection of Lyrics</u>. Photo-
       graphs by Wayne Massie. Hollywood, California: Stanyan
       Books, 1971. 61p., illus.

                           Biographies

3052. Nutter, David. <u>Rock Hudson/Rod McKuen: First Recordings,
       London, March 1970</u>. Hollywood, California: Cheval Books,
       1970. 56p., illus.
          Chiefly photographs by Nutter.

McLEAN, JACKIE

3053. Wilbraham, Roy. <u>Jackie McLean: a Discography, With Biog-
       raphy</u>. London: The Author, 1967. 16p., index.

MACON, DAVID HARRISON "UNCLE DAVE"

3054. Rinzler, Ralph, and Norm Cohen. <u>Uncle Dave Macon: a Bio-
       Discography</u>. Los Angeles: John Edwards Memorial Foundation,
       1970. 50p., illus., bibliog., discog. (J.E.M.F. Special
       Series, 3)

MADNESS

3055. Waller, Johnny. <u>Madness: the Official Biography</u>. London:
       Omnibus Pr., 1985.   p., illus., discog.

3056. Williams, Mark. <u>A Brief History of Madness</u>. London; New
       York: Proteus, 1983. 32p., illus.

MAIRANTS, IVOR

3057. Mairants, Ivor. <u>My Fifty Fretting Years: a Personal History
       of the Twentieth-Century Guitar Explosion</u>. Gateshead: Ash-
       ley Mark, 1980. 392p., illus.
          Autobiography. Includes discussion of other performers.

MANILOW, BARRY

3058. Bego, Mark. <u>Barry Manilow: an Unauthorized Biography</u>. New

York: Grosset and Dunlap, 1977. 139p., illus., discog.

————. Barry Manilow. Edited by Barbara Williams Prabhu.
New York: Grosset and Dunlap, 1979. 88p., illus. (Tempo
Books)
    Abridged edition.

3059. Clarke, Alan. The Magic of Barry Manilow. London: Prize
       Books, 1981. 48p., illus., discog.

3060. Elson, Howard. Barry. London; New York: Proteus, 1984.
       125p., illus., discog.

3061. Jasper, Tony. Barry Manilow. London: Star Books, 1981.
       160p., illus., discog.

3062. Peters, Richard. The Barry Manilow Scrapbook: His Magical
       World in Words and Pictures. London: Pop Universal/Souvenir
       Pr., 1982. 95p., illus., discog. New York: Delilah, 1983.
       104p., illus., discog.

MANONE, JOSEPH "WINGY"

3063. Manone, Wingy, and Paul Vandervoort. Trumpet On the Wing.
       Foreword by Bing Crosby. Garden City, New York: Doubleday,
       1948. 256p., illus., discog.

MARKS, EDWARD BENNET

3064. Marks, Edward Bennet. They All Sang: From Tony Pastor to
       Rudy Vallee. As told to Abbott J. Liebling. New York:
       Viking Pr., 1934. 321p., illus., index.
           Autobiography of song publisher. Includes account of
       turn-of-Century popular music scene. Also includes listing
       of leading songs.

MARLEY, BOB

3065. Clarke, Sebastian. Bob Marley: Rasta Vision of a New World.
       London: Heinemann Educational, 1982. 156p., illus.

3066. Dalrymple, Henderson. Bob Marley: Music, Myth, and the
       Rastas. Sudbury, Middlesex: Carib-Arawak Publishers, 1976.
       77p., illus.

3067. Davis, Stephen. Bob Marley: the Biography. London: Arthur
       Barker, 1983; London: Granada, 1984; Garden City, New York:
       Doubleday, 1985 (Dolphin Books). 248p., illus., bibliog.,
       index.

Marley, Bob (cont.)

3068. Goldman, Vivien, and Adrian Boot. Bob Marley: Soul Rebel,
       Natural Mystic. London: Eel Pie; New York: St. Martin's
       Pr., 1981. 96p., illus., discog.
           Text by Goldman; photographs by Boot.

3069. McKnight, Cathy, and John Tobler. Bob Marley: Roots of
       Reggae. London: Star Books, 1977.   p., illus., discog.

3070. White, Timothy. Catch a Fire: the Life of Bob Marley.
       London: Elm Tree Books, 1983. 380p., illus., bibliog.,
       discog., index.

3071. Whitney, Monika Lee, and Dermott Hussey. Bob Marley: Reggae
       King of the World. Foreword by Rita Marley. London: Plexus
       Publishing, 1984. 192p., illus.

                              Discography

3072. Station, Observer. Bob Marley: the Illustrated Disco/Biog-
       raphy. London: Omnibus Pr., 1985.   p., illus.

                              Periodicals

3073. No Chains Around My Feet. Edited by Martin J. Rowbotham.
       7 Glenfield Road, Herton Chapel, Stockport, Cheshire.
       irreg., May 1984- .

MARTIN, DEAN

3074. Freedland, Michael. Dino: the Dean Martin Story. London:
       W.H. Allen, 1984. 191p., illus., index.

3075. Marx, Arthur. Everybody Loves Somebody Sometime (Especially
       Himself): the Story of Dean Martin and Jerry Lewis. New
       York: Hawthorn Books, 1974; London: W.H. Allen, 1975. 288p.,
       illus., bibliog., index.
           Martin's screen comedy career with partner Lewis, prior
       to his solo career.

MARTIN, GEORGE

3076. Martin, George. All You Need Is Ears. With Jeremy Hornsby.
       London: Macmillan, 1979; New York: St. Martin's Pr., 1980.
       285p., illus., index.
           Autobiography.

MARTIN, MARY

3077. Martin, Mary. My Heart Belongs. New York: Morrow, 1976;
       London: W.H. Allen, 1977. 320p., illus., index.
          Autobiography.

3078. Newman, Shirlee Petkin. Mary Martin On Stage. Philadelphia:
       Westminster Pr., 1969. 126p., illus., bibliog.

MASCHWITZ, ERIC

3079. Maschwitz, Eric. No Chip On My Shoulder. London: Herbert
       Jenkins, 1957. 208p., illus.
          Autobiography.

MATHIS, JOHNNY

3080. Jasper, Tony. Johnny: the Authorised Biography of Johnny
       Mathis. London: W.H. Allen, 1983. 268p., illus., discog.

MATTHEWS, JESSIE

3081. Matthews, Jessie. Over My Shoulder: an Autobiography. As
       told to Muriel Burgess. London: W.H. Allen, 1974; New
       Rochelle, New York: Arlington House, 1975. 240p., illus.,
       index.
          Autobiography.

3082. Thornton, Michael. Jessie Matthews: a Biography. London:
       Hart Davis, MacGibbon, 1974. 359p., illus., bibliog.,
       discog., filmog., index.

MEATLOAF (pseud. of Marvin Lee Aday)

3083. Robertson, Sandy. Meatloaf: Jim Steinman and the Phenomen-
       ology of Excess. London: Omnibus Pr., 1981. 50p., illus.,
       discog., filmog.
          Steinman is his librettist and catalyst.

MEEK, JOE

3084. Whitehouse, Adrian. Joe Meek: the R.G.M. Legend. Tadley,
       Hampshire: The Author, 1982.   p., illus., discog.
          Bio-discography.

MELLY, GEORGE

3085. Melly, George. <u>Mellymobile: 1970-1981</u>. Illustrated by
      Trog. London: Robson Books, 1982; London: New English
      Library, 1983. 168p., illus.
          Articles based on his touring experiences; contents
      first published in <u>Punch</u>.

3086. ———. <u>Owning-Up</u>. Illustrated by Trog. London: Weiden-
      feld and Nicolson, 1965. 204p., illus. Harmondsworth,
      Middlesex: Penguin, 1970. 251p., illus.
          Memoir of his jazz career during the 1950's.

3087. ———. <u>Rum, Bum, and Concertina</u>. London: Weidenfeld and
      Nicolson, 1977. 183p.
          Memoir of his World War II navy experiences, and his
      early encounters with jazz and blues.

3088. ———. <u>Scouse Mouse</u>. London: Weidenfeld and Nicolson,
      1984. 208p.
          Memoir of his early life.

MELVILLE, ALAN (<u>pseud. of</u> William Melville Caverhill)

3089. Melville, Alan. <u>Merely Melville: an Autobiography</u>. London:
      Hodder and Stoughton, 1970. 223p., index.

3090. ———. <u>Myself When Young</u>. London: Max Parrish, 1955.
      106p., illus.
          Memoirs.

MENUDO

3091. Greenberg, Keith. <u>Menudo</u>. New York: Pocket Books, 1983.
      64p., illus.
          Text in English and Spanish.

3092. Molina, Maria. <u>Menudo</u>. New York: J. Messner, 1984.   p.,
      illus. (In the Spotlight Series)
          Aimed at younger readers.

MERCER, JOHNNY

3093. Bach, Bob, and Ginger Mercer. <u>Our Huckleberry Friend: the
      Life, Times, and Lyrics of Johnny Mercer</u>. Secaucus, New
      Jersey: Lyle Stuart, 1982. 256p., illus.

MERMAN, ETHEL

3094. Merman, Ethel. <u>Who Could Ask For Anything More</u>. As told
       to Pete Martin. Garden City, New York: Doubleday, 1955.
       252p., illus. London (as <u>Don't Call Me Madam</u>): W.H. Allen,
       1955. 215p., illus.
           Autobiography.

3095. ————. <u>Merman</u>. With George Eells. New York: Simon and
       Schuster, 1978.   p., illus.
           Memoirs.

MEZZROW, MILTON "MEZZ"

3096. Mezzrow, Milton "Mezz", and Bernard Wolfe. <u>Really the Blues</u>.
       Preface by Henry Miller. New York; Toronto: Random House;
       London: Secker and Warburg, 1946; London: Musicians Pr.,
       1947. 388p., index. New York: Dell, n.d. 384p., index.
       <u>New ed.</u>: London: Secker and Warburg, 1957. 388p., index.
       London: Transworld Publishers, 1961. 381p., index. (Corgi
       Books). New York: New American Library, 1964. 320p.,
       index. (Signet Books). Garden City, New York: Doubleday,
       1972. 348p., index.
           Autobiography. Includes glossary of jazz terms.

3097. Panassié, Hugues. <u>Histoire des disques swing enregistrés à
       New York par Tommy Ladnier, Mezz Mezzrow, Frank Newton, etc</u>.
       Geneva: Charles Grasset, 1944. 117p., illus., discog.
           Account of notable 1939 recording session. In French.

       ————. <u>Quand Mezzrow enregistre: histoire des disques de
       Milton Mezzrow et Tommy Ladnier</u>. Preface by Milton Mezzrow.
       Paris: Robert Laffont, 1952. 142p., illus., discog.

MIDLER, BETTE

3098. Midler, Bette. <u>A View From a Broad</u>. Photography by Sean
       Russell. New York: Simon and Schuster; London: Angus and
       Robertson, 1980. 160p., illus.
           Account of her concert tour of Europe and Australasia,
       1979.

                          Biographies

3099. Baker, Robb. <u>Bette Midler</u>. New York: Fawcett Publications,
       1976; Sevenoaks, Kent: Coronet, 1980. 256p., illus. <u>Rev</u>.
       <u>ed</u>.: London: Angus and Robertson, 1980. 160p., illus.

MILLER, ALTON GLENN

3100. Boulton, Derek. Dedication to Glenn Miller and His Orch-
       estra. New York: Metronome; London: Fanfare Musical Pub-
       lications, 1948. 28p., illus.

3101. Howard, George Sallade. The Big Serenade. Evanston, Ill-
       inois: Instrumenalist, 1961. 242p., illus.
       The story of Miller's United States Air Force Band.

3102. Simon, George Thomas. Glenn Miller and His Orchestra.
       Introduction by Bing Crosby. New York: Crowell; London:
       W.H. Allen, 1974; New York: Da Capo Pr., 1980. 473p.,
       illus., discog., index.
       By his first drummer; later editor of Metronome.

3103. Snow, George, and Jonathon Green. Glenn Miller and the Age
       of Swing. Conceived, designed and produced by George Snow;
       written by Jonathon Green. London: Dempsey and Squires,
       1976. 128p., illus., discog., index.

                          Discographies

3104. Bedwell, Stephen Frederick. A Glenn Miller Discography and
       Biography. Edited, and with additional material, by Geoff-
       rey E. Butcher. London: Glenn Miller Appreciation Society,
       1955. 102p., illus. Rev. ed.: London: Glenn Miller
       Appreciation Society, 1956. 102p., illus.

3105. Edwards, Ernie, George Hall, and Bill Korst. Glenn Miller
       Alumni. Whittier, California: Jazz Discographies Unlimited,
       1965. 2 vols., p.

3106. Flower, John. Moonlight Serenade: a Bio-Discography of the
       Glenn Miller Civilian Band. Introduction by George T. Simon.
       New Rochelle, New York: Arlington House, 1972. 554p., illus.,
       index.

3107. Glenn Miller Society. Miller Discs: the Glenn Miller Orch-
       estra, 1935 to 1942. New Malden, Surrey: Glenn Miller
       Society, 1968. 38p.

   *   Strateman, Klaus. The Films of Artie Shaw, Glenn Miller,
       and Tony Pastor: a Filmo-Discography.
         * Cited below as item 3548.

MILLINDER, LUCKY

3108. Demeusy, Bertrand, Otto Flückiger, and Jorgen Grunnet Jepsen.
       Discography of Lucky Millinder, 1941-1960. Foreword by Rudy
       Powell and Johnny Simmen. Basle: Jazz Publications, 1962.
       26p.

MINELLI, LIZA

3109.   Owen, Michael. <u>Liza Minelli</u>. Tunbridge Wells, Kent:
        Spellmount; New York: Hippocrene Books, 1984. 96p., illus.
        (Film and Theatre Stars)

3110.   Parish, James Robert. <u>Liza! An Unauthorized Biography</u>.
        New York: Pocket Books, 1974. 176p., illus., discog.,
        filmog. London (as <u>Liza: Her Cinderella Nightmare</u>): W.H.
        Allen, 1975. 186p., illus., discog., filmog.

   *   Spada, James. <u>Judy and Liza</u>.
        * Cited above as item 2599.

                        Motion Pictures

3111.   D'Arcy, Susan. <u>The Films of Liza Minelli</u>. Bembridge, Isle
        of Wight: B.C.W. Publishing, 1973. 2nd. ed.: Bembridge,
        Isle of Wight: B.C.W. Publishing, 1977. 47p., illus.,
        filmog.

MINELLI, VINCENTE

3112.   Minelli, Vincente. <u>I Remember It Well</u>. With Hector Arce.
        Foreword by Alan Jay Lerner. Garden City, New York: Double-
        day, 1974; London: Angus and Robertson, 1975. 392p., illus.,
        filmog., index.
           Autobiography. Author was married to Judy Garland; is
        father of Liza Minelli.

                          Biography

3113.   Casper, Joseph Andrew. <u>Vincente Minelli and the Film
        Musical</u>. South Brunswick, New York: A.S. Barnes; London:
        Yoseloff, 1977. 192p., illus., bibliog., index.

MINGUS, CHARLES

3114.   Mingus, Charles. <u>Beneath the Underdog: His World as Comp-
        osed by Mingus</u>. New York: Knopf; London: Weidenfeld and
        Nicolson, 1971. 366p. Harmondsworth, Middlesex: Penguin,
        1971 (Reissued: 1980). 263p. New York: Bantam, 1972.   p.
        New York: St. Martin's Pr., 1975.   p.

Mingus, Charles (cont.)

Biographies

3115. Coss, Bill. <u>Charles Mingus</u>. New York: Broadcast Music,
       1961. 20p.

3116. Priestley, Brian. <u>Mingus: a Critical Biography</u>. London:
       Quartet, 1982; New York: Da Capo Pr., 1984; London: Paladin,
       1985. 308p., illus., discog., index.

Discography

3117. Wilbraham, Roy J. <u>Charles Mingus: a Biography and Discog-
       raphy</u>. London: The Author, 1967. 28p.

MISTINGUETT, JEANNE

3118. Mistinguett, Jeanne. <u>Mistinguett and Her Confessions</u>.
       Translated and edited by Hubert Griffith. London: Hurst,
       1938. 286p., illus.

3119. ————. <u>Mistinguett, Queen of the Paris Night</u>. Translated
       by Lucienne Hill. London: Paul Elek, 1954. 247p., illus.
          Originally published as <u>Toute ma vie</u>, Paris: Julliard,
       1954.

MITCHELL, GUY

3120. Foster, Ivan. <u>Guy Mitchell Discography</u>. Newcastle-upon-
       Tyne, England: The Author, 1983.   p.

Periodicals

3121. <u>Mitchell Music</u>. Edited by Ivan Foster. 47 Granville Drive,
       Forest Hall, Newcastle-upon-Tyne, England. irreg., 1983- .

MITCHELL, JONI

3122. Fleischer, Leonore. <u>Joni Mitchell</u>. New York: Flash Books;
       London: Book Sales, 1976. 79p., illus., discog.

MITCHELL, LOUIS A.

3123. Gillet, André V. The European Recordings by Louis A. Mitchell. Brussels: The Author, 1957. 8p. 2nd. ed.: 1957. 10p.

3124. ————. The Mitchell's Jazz Kings: Discographie critique. Brussels: The Author, 1966. 20p.

MODE

3125. Millidge, Gary (ed.). The Mode. Leigh-on-Sea, Essex: Opal, 1983. 8p., illus.

MODERN JAZZ QUARTET

Milt Jackson

3126. Wilbraham, Roy J. Milt Jackson: a Discography and Biography (Including Recordings Made With The Modern Jazz Quartet). London: The Author, 1968. 40p.

John Lewis

3127. Hentoff, Nat. John Lewis. New York: Broadcast Music, 1960. 16p.

MONK, THEOLONIUS

3128. Hentoff, Nat. Theolonius Monk. New York: Broadcast Music, 1960. 20p.

3129. Jepsen, Jorgen Grunnet. A Discography of Theolonius Monk and Bud Powell. Copenhagen: Knudsen, 1969. 65p.

3130. ————. Discography of Theolonius Monk; Sonny Rollins. Biographical notes by Knud H. Ditlevsen. Brande, Denmark: Debut Records, 1960. 28p.

MONKEES

3131. Adler, Bill (ed.). Love Letters to the Monkees. Illustrated by Jack Davis. New York: Popular Library, 1967. 127p., illus. Letters from fans.

Monkees (cont.)

3132. Baker, Glenn A., Peter Hogan, and Tom Czarnota. Monkee-
       mania! The Story of The Monkees. London: Plexus Publishing,
       1985. 128p., illus., discog.

3133. Daily Mirror. Meet The Monkees. London: Daily Mirror,
       1967. 80p., illus.

3134. Mirabelle. The Monkees: a "Mirabelle" Colour Photo Souvenir.
       London: Newnes, 1967. 16p., illus.

3135. O'Connor, Patrick (ed.). The Monkees Go Mod. Contributing
       editor: Carolyn Fireside. New York: Popular Library, 1967.
       unpaged, illus.
           Chiefly illustrated.

                              Periodicals

3136. Monkees. Edited by P. Muncey. Impington, Cambridgeshire.
       irreg., 1979-?

3137. Monkees Monthly. London. monthly, February 1967 - September
       1969.

                            Michael Nesmith

3138. Foster, Anne. Michael Nesmith, From Musician to Video
       Producer: a Michael Nesmith Biography. Hull, England: The
       Author, 1983. 403p.

MONROE, BILL

3139. Rooney, James. Bossmen: Bill Monroe and Muddy Waters. New
       York: Dial Pr., 1971; Rochelle Park, New Jersey: Hayden Book
       Company, 1972. 159p., illus., discogs.
           Separate biographical interviews, linked with comment by
       Rooney.

3140. Rosenberg, Neil V. Bill Monroe and His Blue Grass Boys: an
       Illustrated Discography. Nashville: Country Music Foundation
       Pr., 1974. 120p., illus., bibliog. notes, index.
           Annotated.

MONTGOMERY, LITTLE BROTHER

3141. Zur Heide, Karl Gert. Deep South Piano: the Story of Little

Brother Montgomery. London: Studio Vista, 1970; Hatboro, Pennsylvania: Legacy Books, 1983 (The Paul Oliver Blues Series)
   Includes information on musicians who worked or encountered Montgomery.

MONTGOMERY, MARIAN see BENNET, RICHARD RODNEY, AND MARIAN MONTGOMERY

MORGAN, HELEN

3142. Maxwell, Gilbert. Helen Morgan: Her Life and Legend. New York: Hawthorn Books, 1974. 192p., illus.

MORMON TABERNACLE CHOIR

3143. Calman, Charles. The Mormon Tabernacle Choir. New York: Harper and Row, 1979.   p., illus., index.

3144. Petersen, Gerald A. More Than Music: The Mormon Tabernacle Choir. Provo, Utah: Brigham Young University Pr., 1979. 103p., illus., bibliog. refs.

3145. Thomas, Warren John. Salt Lake Mormon Tabernacle Choir Goes to Europe, 1955. Salt Lake City, Utah: Deseret News Pr., 1957. 277p., illus.

MORRISON, VAN (pseud. of George Ivan Morrison)

3146. DeWitt, Howard A. Van Morrison: the Mystic's Music. New York: Horizon Books, 1983.   p., illus., discog.

3147. Rogan, Johnny. Van Morrison: a Portrait of the Artist. London: Elm Tree Books, 1984. 160p., illus., discog.

3148. Yorke, Ritchie. Into the Music. London: Charisma Books/Futura, 1979.   p., illus., discog.

Discography

3149. Van Morrison: Them and Now. Kingston, Surrey: Rock Revelations, 1976.   p.
   Covers his recordings 1963-76; solo and with group Them.

MORTON, CHARLES

3150. Morton, William H., and Henry Chance Newton. Sixty Years'
       Stage Service: Being a Record of the Life of Charles Morton,
       "The Father of the Halls." London: Gale and Polden, 1905.
       208p.

MORTON, JELLY ROLL (pseud. of Ferdinand Joseph La Menthe Morton)

3151. Hood, Mary Allen, and Helen M. Flint. "Jelly Roll" Morton:
       the Original Mister Jazz. New York: E.H. Morris, 1975.
       143p., illus.

3152. Lomax, Alan. Mister Jelly Roll: the Fortunes of Jelly Roll
       Morton, New Orleans Creole and "Inventor of Jazz." Drawings
       by David Stone Martin. New York: Duel, Sloan, and Pearce;
       New York: Grosset and Dunlap, 1950. 318p., illus., discog.
       London: Cassell, 1952. 296p., illus., discog. New York:
       Grove Pr., 1956. 301p., illus., discog. London: Pan,
       1959. 253p., illus. 2nd. ed.: Berkeley; London: Univers-
       ity of California Pr., 1973. 318p., illus., discog.
          Based on interviews conducted with Morton, 1938. Includ-
       es listing of his compositions.

3153. Smith, Charles Edward. Jelly Roll Morton's New Orleans
       Memories. New York: Consolidated Records, 194? 16p.

3154. Williams, Martin T. Jelly Roll Morton. London: Cassell,
       1962; New York: A.S. Barnes, 1963. 89p., illus., bibliog.
       notes, discog., index. (Kings of Jazz, 2)
          Incorporated into item 1566.

                              Discographies

3155. Cusack, Thomas. Jelly Roll Morton: an Essay in Discography.
       London: Cassell, 1952. 40p.

3156. Davies, John R.T., and Laurie Wright. Morton's Music.
       London: Storyville Publications, 1968. 38p.
          Includes listing of piano rolls.

3157. Jepsen, Jorgen Grunnet. Discography of Jelly Roll Morton.
       Biographical notes by Knud H. Ditlevsen. Brande, Denmark:
       Debut Records, 1959.
       Vol.1: 1922-1929. 18p.
       Vol.2: 1930-1940. 21p.

3158. Wright, Laurie (ed.). Mister Jelly Lord. Chigwell, Essex:
       Storyville, 1980. 245p., illus., bibliog., discog., index.

MOTORHEAD

3159. Burridge, Alan. <u>Motorhead: Born To Lose</u>. Manchester,
       England: Babylon Books; London (as <u>Motorhead</u>): Omnibus Pr.,
       1982. 48p., illus., discog.

3160. <u>Motorhead Magazine</u>. Edited by Alan Burridge. Poole, Dorset.
       irreg., 1980-?

MULLIGAN, GERRY

3161. Horricks, Raymond. <u>Gerry Mulligan</u>. Discography by Tony
       Middleton. Speldhurst, Kent: Spellmount; New York: Hippo-
       crene Books, 1985.   p., illus., bibliog., discog., index.
       (Jazz Masters, 12)

3162. Jepsen, Jorgen Grunnet. <u>Discography of Gerry Mulligan and
       Lee Konitz</u>. Biographical notes by Knud H. Ditlevsen.
       Brande, Denmark: Debut Records, 1960.   p.

3163. Morgan, Alun, and Raymond Horricks. <u>Gerry Mulligan: a
       Biography, Appreciation, Record Survey, and Discography</u>.
       London: National Jazz Federation, 1958. 16p.

MUSICAL YOUTH

3164. Musical Youth. <u>Musical Youth: Their Own Story</u>. London:
       Omnibus Pr., 1983. 32p., illus., discog.

3165. Thompson, Caro. <u>Musical Youth: the Official Biography</u>.
       London: Virgin Books, 1983. 48p., illus., discog.

NAPIER-BELL, SIMON

3166. Napier-Bell, Simon. <u>You Don't Have To Say You Love Me</u>.
       London: New English Library, 1982; London: Coronet, 1984.
       178p., illus.
          Autobiography. Includes comment on British rock scene
       of the 1960's.

NASH, "JOLLY" JOHN

3167. Nash, John F.B. <u>The Merriest Man Alive: Stories, Anecdotes,
       Adventures</u>. London: General Publishing Company, 1891. 192p.
          Autobiography. Nash was early exponent of the "laughing
       song."

NAVARRO, THEODORE "FATS"

3168. Jepsen, Jorgen Grunnet. Discography of Fats Navarro; Clifford Brown. Biographical notes by Knud H. Ditlevsen. Brande, Denmark: Debut Records, 1960. 27p.

NELSON, WILLIE

* Allen, Bob. Waylon and Willie.
  * Cited above as item 2828.

3169. Fowler, Lana Nelson (comp.). The Willie Nelson Family Album. Amarillo, Texas: H.M. Poirot, 1980. 160p., illus., bibliog.
       Includes song lyrics.

3170. Scobey, Lola. Willie Nelson: Country Outlaw. New York: Zebra Books, 1982.   p., illus.

NEW ORDER (formerly JOY DIVISION)

3171. Edge, Brian. Joy Division and New Order: Pleasures and Wayward Distractions. London: Omnibus Pr., 1984.   p., illus., discog.

3172. Johnson, Mark. An Ideal For Living: a History of Joy Division and New Order. London; New York: Proteus, 1984. 128p., illus., discog.

NEW YORK DOLLS

3173. Morissey (pseud.). The New York Dolls. Manchester, England: Babylon Books, 1983. unpaged, illus., discog.

NEWTON, FRANKIE

* Evensmo, Jan. The Trumpets of Bill Coleman, 1939-1945; and Frankie Newton.
  * Cited above as item 1548.

NEWTON-JOHN, OLIVIA

3174. Ruff, Peter. Olivia Newton-John. New York: Quick Fox, 1979. 96p., illus., discog.

NICHOLLS, ERNEST LORING "RED"

3175. Johnson, Grady. <u>The Five Pennies: the Biography of Jazz</u>
       <u>Band Leader Red Nicholls</u>. New York: Dell, 1959. 192p.
           Text based on biographical motion picture, <u>The Five</u>
       <u>Pennies</u>.

3176. Lange, Horst Heinz. <u>Loring "Red" Nicholls: ein Porträt</u>.
       Wetzlar, West Germany: Pegasus Verlag, 1960. 48p., illus.,
       discog. (Jazz-Bücherei, 5)
           In German.

                        Discographies

3177. Venables, Ralph G.V., and C.W.A. Langston White. <u>Reminting</u>
       <u>The Pennies</u>. Tilford, Surrey: Jazz Appreciation Society,
       1942. 8p.

3178. ————, Clifford Jones, and C.W.A. Langston White. <u>A Comp-</u>
       <u>lete Discography of Red Nicholls and His Five Pennies</u>. Ed-
       ited by William H. Miller. Melbourne, Victoria: <u>Australian</u>
       <u>Jazz Quarterly</u>, 1946. 16p. 2nd. ed.: 1947. 16p.

NIGHTINGALE, ANNE

3179. Nightingale, Anne. <u>Chase the Fade: Music, Memories, and</u>
       <u>Memorabilia</u>. Poole, Dorset: Blandford Pr., 1981. 121p.,
       illus.
           Memoirs of British disk-jockey and rock journalist.

NOLANS

3180. Treasurer, Kim. <u>In the Mood For Stardom: The Nolans</u>. Tun-
       bridge Wells, Kent: Midas Books; New York: Hippocrene Books,
       1982. 128p., illus., discog.

NORMANN, ROBERT

  *   Evensmo, Jan. <u>The Guitars of Charlie Christian, Robert</u>
       <u>Normann, and Oscar Aleman (in Europe)</u>.
           * Cited above as item 1548.

NOVELLO, IVOR

3181. MacQueen-Pope, Walter James. <u>Ivor, the Story of an Achieve-</u>

Novello, Ivor (cont.)

ment: a Biography of Ivor Novello. London: W.H. Allen,
1951. 550p., illus. New ed.: London: Hutchinson, 1954.
317p., illus.

3182. Noble, Peter. Ivor Novello: Man of the Theatre. Foreword
by Noël Coward. London: Falcon Pr., 1951; London: White
Lion, 1975. 306p., illus.

3183. Rose, Richard. Perchance To Dream: the World of Ivor
Novello. London: Leslie Frewin, 1974. 199p., illus.
By his partner.

3184. Wilson, Sandy. Ivor. London: Michael Joseph, 1975. 288p.,
illus., discog.

NUMAN, GARY

3185. Coleman, Ray. Gary Numan: the Authorised Biography. London:
Sidgwick and Jackson, 1982. 128p., illus., discog., index.

3186. Gilbert, Peter, and Francis Drake. Gary Numan: Into the
Eighties. London: In The City, 1980. 16p., illus.

3187. Vermorel, Fred, and Judy Vermorel. Gary Numan By Computer.
London: Omnibus Pr., 1981. 64p., illus.
Chiefly illustrated.

OCHS, PHIL

3188. Eliot, Marc. Death of a Rebel: Starring Phil Ochs and a
Small Circle of Friends. Garden City, New York: Anchor Pr.,
1979. 316p., illus., discog., index.
Written from personal knowledge.

O'CONNOR, HAZEL

3189. O'Connor, Hazel. Hazel O'Connor Uncovered Plus. With Judith
Simons. London; New York: Proteus, 1981. 127p., illus.,
discog.

O'DAY, ANITA

3190. O'Day, Anita. High Times, Hard Times. With George Eells.
Discography compiled by Robert A. Siksmith and Alan Eichler.
New York: Berkley Publishing, 1982; London: Corgi, 1983.
327p., illus., discog.

O'HARA, MARY

3191. O'Hara, Mary. The Scent of Roses. London: Michael Joseph,
       1980. 253p., illus. London: Fontana, 1981. 318p., illus.,
       index.
           Autobiography.

OLIVER, JOE "KING"

3192. Allen, Walter Charles, and Brian Arthur Lovell Rust. King
       Joe Oliver. Belleville, New Jersey: Walter C. Allen, 1955.
       162p., illus., discog., index. (Jazz Monographs, 1). London:
       Sidgwick and Jackson, 1958. 224p., illus., bibliog., discog.

3193. Williams, Eugene. King Oliver. New York: Brunswick Radio,
       1946. 12p.

3194. Williams, Martin T. King Oliver. London: Cassell, 1960;
       New York: A.S. Barnes, 1961. 90p., illus., discog. (Kings
       of Jazz, 8)
           Incorporated into item 1566.

ORCHESTRAL MANOEUVRES IN THE DARK

3195. West, Mike. Orchestral Manoeuvres in the Dark. London:
       Omnibus Pr., 1982. 48p., illus., discog.

ORIGINAL DIXIELAND JAZZ BAND

3196. Brunn, Harry Otis. The Story of The Original Dixieland Jazz
       Band. Baton Rouge: Louisiana State University Pr., 1960 (Re-
       printed: New York: Da Capo Pr., 1977. Roots of Jazz); London:
       Sidgwick and Jackson, 1961. 268p., illus., index.

3197. Lange, Horst Heinz. Nick LaRocca: ein Porträt. Wetzlar,
       West Germany: Pegasus Verlag, 1960. 48p., illus., discog.
       (Jazzbücherei, 8)
           In German. The group's story through the life and career
       of its leading member.

OSBOURNE, OZZY

3198. Osbourne, Ozzy. Ozzy Osbourne by Ozzy Osbourne. As told to
       Brian Harrigan. London: Zomba Books, 1985. 128p., illus.,
       discog.
           Autobiography.

Osbourne, Ozzy (cont.)

Biographies

3199.   Johnson, Gary. <u>Ozzy Osbourne</u>. London; New York: Proteus,
        1985.   p., illus., discog.

3200.   <u>Ozzy Osbourne</u>. London: Omnibus Pr., 1983.   96p., illus.
        (H.M. Photobooks)
             Chiefly illustrated.

3201.   Welch, Chris. <u>Ozzy Osbourne</u>. London: Zomba Books, 1984.
        96p., illus., discog. (Rock Masters)

OSMONDS

3202.   Daily Mirror. <u>The Fantastic Osmonds</u>! London: <u>Daily Mirror</u>
        Books, 1972. 48p., illus.
             Chiefly illustrated.

3203.   Daly, Marsha. <u>The Osmond Family Biography</u>. New York: St.
        Martin's Pr., 1983. 144p., illus.

3204.   Dunn, Paul H. <u>The Osmonds: the Official Story of The Osmond
        Family</u>. Salt Lake City, Utah: Bookcraft, 1974; Garden City,
        New York: Doubleday; London: W.H. Allen, 1975. 246p., illus.
        New York: Avon Books, 1977. 255p., illus. London: Star
        Books, 1977. 189p., illus.

3205.   Gregory, James. <u>Donny and The Osmonds Backstage</u>. Manchest-
        er, England: World Distributors, 1974. 127p., illus.
             Cover title: <u>Backstage With The Osmonds</u>. Aimed at young-
        er readers.

3206.   <u>Osmonds' World: the Official Year Book of The Osmonds</u>. Lon-
        don: I.P.C. Magazines. annual, 1976-77.

3207.   Tremlett, George. <u>The Osmonds Story</u>. London: Futura; New
        York: Warner Paperback Library, 1975. 158p., illus.

Periodicals

3208.   <u>Osmonds' World: the Official Magazine of The Osmonds</u>. Lon-
        don. monthly, 1973-74.

Donny Osmond

3209.   Gregory, James. <u>Donny</u>! Manchester, England: World Distrib-
        utors, 1974. 125p., illus. (Ensign Books)

OSTERWALD, HAZY

3210. Grieder, Walter. <u>Die Hazy Osterwald Story</u>. Zürich:
       Schweizer Druck- und Verlagshaus, 1961. 160p., illus.

OTIS, JOHNNY

3211. Otis, Johnny. <u>Listen To the Lambs</u>. New York: Norton, 1968.
       256p., illus.
          Autobiography.

PAGE, DREW

3212. Page, Drew. <u>Drew's Blues: a Sideman's Life With the Big
       Bands</u>. Baton Rouge; London: Louisiana State University Pr.,
       1980. 226p., illus., index.

PAGE, ORAN THADDEUS "HOT LIPS"

3213. Demeusy, Bertrand, Otto Flückiger, Jorgen Grunnet Jepsen,
       and Kurt Mohr. <u>Hot Lips Page</u>. Basle: Jazz Publications,
       1961. 30p., illus.
          Discography.

PANASSIÉ, HUGUES

3214. Panassié, Hugues. <u>Monsieur Jazz</u>. Paris: Editions Stock,
       1975. 379p., illus.
          In French. Autobiography of influential jazz critic.

PARKER, CHARLIE

Bibliography

3215. Morgenstern, Dan, Ira Gitler, and Jack Bradley. <u>Bird and
       Diz: a Bibliography</u>. New York: New York Jazz Museum, 1973.
       19p.
          Separate bibliographies of Parker and Dizzy Gillespie.

Biographies

3216. Harrison, Max. <u>Charlie Parker</u>. London: Cassell; New York:

Parker, Charlie (cont.)

A.S. Barnes, 1960. 88p., illus., bibliog. notes, discog.
(Kings of Jazz, 6)
    Incorporated into item 1566.

3217. Hentoff, Nat. Charlie Parker. New York: Broadcast Music,
        1960. 16p.

3218. Paudras, Francis, and Chan Parker. To Bird With Love.
        Sawbridgeworth, Hertfordshire: Spotlite Records, 1981.
        424p., illus.
            Limited edition. Includes reproductions of documents
        and other original material.

3219. Priestley, Brian. Charlie Parker. Tunbridge Wells, Kent:
        Spellmount; New York: Hippocrene Books, 1984. 96p., illus.,
        bibliog., discog. (Jazz Masters)

3220. Reisner, Robert George. Bird: the Legend of Charlie Parker.
        New York: Citadel Pr.; New York: Bonanza Books, 1962; London:
        MacGibbon and Kee, 1963; London: Quartet, 1974; New York: Da
        Capo Pr., 1975. 256p., illus., discog.
            Biographical account, followed by interviews with eighty
        individuals who knew Parker.

3221. Russell, Ross. Bird Lives: the High Life and Hard Times of
        Charlie (Yardbird) Parker. New York: Charterhouse; London
        (as Bird Lives!): Quartet, 1973. 405p., illus., bibliog.,
        discog., index.
            By founder of Dial Record company, founded in order to
        record Parker. Written in style of a novel.

3222. ———————. The Sound. New York: Dutton, 1961; London: Cassell,
        1962. 287p.
            Novelization of Parker's life.

3223. Watts, Charlie. Ode To a High-Flying Bird. Compiled by One
        Charlie To a Late and Great Charlie. Dedicated To Charles
        Christopher Parker. London: Beat Publications, 1965. 32p.,
        illus.
            Cartoons and brief biography of Parker. Author is member
        of The Rolling Stones group.

                               Discographies

3224. Bettonville, Albert, and André V. Gillet. Dial Records
        Long-Playing Discography of Charlie Parker. Brussels: The
        Authors, 1957. 18p.

3225. Edwards, Ernie, George Hall, and Bill Korst. Charlie Parker.
        Whittier, California: Jazz Discographies Unlimited, 1965.   p.

3226. Gillet, André V. <u>Essays in Discography of Charlie Parker.</u>
       Brussels: The Author, 1957. 42p.

3227. Jepsen, Jorgen Grunnet. <u>Discography of Charlie Parker.</u>
       Biographical notes by Knud H. Ditlevsen. Brande, Denmark:
       Debut Records, 1959. 23p. <u>2nd. ed.:</u> 1960. 30p. <u>3rd. ed.:</u>
       Copenhagen: Knudsen, 1968. 38p.

3228. Koster, Piet, and Dick Bakker. <u>Charlie Parker.</u> Alphen aan
       den Rijn, Holland: Micrography, 1974-76.
       <u>Vol. 1: 1940-47.</u> 1974. 34p., indexes.
       <u>Vol. 2: 1948-50.</u> 1975. 36p., indexes.
       <u>Vol. 3: 1951-54.</u> 1975.   p., indexes.
       <u>Vol. 4: 1940-55.</u> 1976.   p., indexes.
          Volume 4 covers omissions, corrections, and additions.
       Also combined indexes to all volumes.

PARTON, DOLLY

3229. Berman, Connie. <u>Dolly Parton: a Personal Portrait.</u> New
       York: Quick Fox; London: Book Sales, 1979. 96p., illus.

3230. ————. <u>The Official Dolly Parton Scrapbook.</u> Foreword by
       Dolly Parton. New York: Grosset and Dunlap, 1978. 96p.,
       illus., discog. <u>Abridged ed.:</u> New York: Grosset and Dunlap,
       1978. 79p., illus., discog. (A Target Book)

3231. Caraeff, Ed, and Richard Amdur. <u>Dolly: Close Up/Up Close.</u>
       London: Sidgwick and Jackson, 1983. 90p., illus.
          Photographs by Caraeff; text by Amdur.

3232. James, Otis. <u>Dolly Parton.</u> New York: Quick Fox, 1978.
       95p., illus., discog.

3233. Nash, Alanna. <u>Dolly.</u> Los Angeles: Reed Books, 1978. 275p.,
       illus., discog. (A <u>Country Music</u> Magazine Book)

3234. ————. <u>Dolly: the Intimate Biography of Dolly</u> Parton.
       Danbury, New Hampshire: Addison House, 1978; St. Albans,
       Hertfordshire: Panther, 1979. 397p., illus., discog.
          Not the same as item 3233.

PASTOR, TONY (1837-1908)

3235. Zellers, Parker Richardson. <u>Tony Pastor, Dean of the Vaude-
       ville Stage.</u> Ypsilanti, Michigan: Eastern Michigan Univers-
       ity Pr., 1971. 155p., illus., bibliog., index.
          Based on the author's PhD. dissertation, <u>Tony Pastor:
       Manager and Impresario of the American Variety Stage,</u> State
       University of Iowa, 1964.

PASTOR, TONY (Bandleader)

3236.   Garrod, Charles. Tony Pastor and His Orchestra. Spotswood,
        New Jersey: Joyce, 1973.   p.
            Discography.

   *   Strateman, Klaus. The Films of Artie Shaw, Glenn Miller,
        and Tony Pastor: a Filmo-Discography.
            * Cited below as item 3548.

PATTON, CHARLIE

3237.   Evans, David. Charlie Patton. Knutsford, Cheshire: Blues
        World, 1969. 20p., illus.

3238.   Fahey, John. Charley Patton. London: Studio Vista; New
        York: Stein and Day, 1970; Hatboro, Pennsylvania: Legacy
        Books, 1983 (The Paul Oliver Blues Series). 112p., illus.,
        bibliog., discog.
            Includes appendix of song transcriptions (words and
        music). Based on the author's M.A. thesis, A Textual and
        Musicological Analysis of the Repertoire of Charlie Patton,
        University of California at Los Angeles, 1966. Fahey
        is himself a composer and performer.

PAYNE, JACK

3239.   Payne, Jack. Signature Tune. London: Stanley Paul, 1947.
        143p., illus.
            Memoirs.

3240.   ———. "This Is Jack Payne." London: Sampson Low, 1932.
        148p., illus.
            Memoirs.

                            Biography

3241.   Cochrane, Peggy. We Said It With Music: the Story of Peggy
        Cochrane and Jack Payne. Foreword by Frank Chacksfield.
        Bognor Regis, West Sussex: New Horizon, 1979. 142p., illus.
            By his wife, a musician in her own right.

PEARL, MINNIE (pseud. of Ophelia Colley Cannon)

3242.   Cannon, Ophelia Colley. Minnie Pearl: an Autobiography.
        With Joan Dew. New York: Simon and Schuster, 1980.   p.,
        illus.

PEPPER, ART

3243. Pepper, Art, and Laurie Pepper. <u>Straight Life: the Story
       of Art Pepper</u>. New York: Schirmer Books; London: Collier-
       Macmillan, 1979. 517p., illus., discog., index.
            Includes detailed discography, compiled by Todd Selbert.

                              Discography

3244. Edwards, Ernie, George Hall, and Bill Korst. <u>Art Pepper:
       a Complete Discography</u>. Whittier, California: Jazz Discog-
       raphies Unlimited, 1965. 22p.

PERKINS, CARL

3245. Perkins, Carl. <u>A Disciple in Blue Suede Shoes</u>. With Don
       Rendleman. Grand Rapids, Michigan: Zondervan, 1978.   p.,
       illus.
            Autobiography.

PETERSON, OSCAR

3246. Palmer, Richard. <u>Oscar Peterson</u>. Tunbridge Wells, Kent:
       Spellmount; New York: Hippocrene Books, 1984. 93p., illus.,
       discog. (Jazz Masters)

PIAF, EDITH

3247. Piaf, Edith. <u>The Wheel of Fortune: the Autobiography of
       Edith Piaf</u>. Translated by Peter Trewartha and Andree
       Masoin de Virton. London: Peter Owen, 1965. 138p., illus.
       Philadelphia: Chilton Book Company, 1965. 192p., illus.
       Bath, Avon: Chivers, 1983. 138p., illus. (A New Portway
       Book)
            Originally published as <u>Au bal de la chance</u>, Paris:
       Jeheber, 1958.

                              Biographies

3248. Berteaut, Simone. <u>Piaf: a Biography</u>. London: W.H. Allen,
       1970. 440p., illus., index. New York: Harper and Row,
       1972. 488p., illus., index. Harmondsworth, Middlesex:
       Penguin, 1973. 434p., illus., index.
            By her sister. Originally published as <u>Piaf: récit</u>,
       Paris: Laffont, 1969.

Piaf, Edith (cont.)

3249. Grimault, Dominique, and Patrick Mahe. Piaf and Cerdan: a
       Hymn to a Love. Translated by Barbara Mitchell. London:
       W.H. Allen, 1984. 236p., illus., bibliog.
           Story of Piaf and her lover, Marcel Cerdan. Originally
       published, Paris: Laffont, 1983.

3250. Lange, Monique. Piaf. Translated from the French by Rich-
       ard S. Woodward. New York: Seaver Books; London: W.H. Allen,
       1981. 256p., illus. London: Plexus Publishing, 1981. 240p.,
       illus.
           Originally published as Histoire de Piaf, Paris: Editions
       Ramsay, 1979.

PINK FLOYD

3251. Waters, Roger. The Pink Floyd Lyric Book. Poole, Dorset:
       Blandford Pr., 1983. 79p., illus.

                          Biographies

3252. Dallas, Karl. Bricks In the Wall. London: Baton Pr., 1984.
       160p., illus., discog.

3253. Miles (pseud. of Barry Miles). Pink Floyd. London: Omnibus
       Pr., 1980. 117p., illus. Rev. ed.: London: Omnibus Pr.;
       New York: Quick Fox, 1981; New York: Delilah, 1982. 120p.,
       illus.

3254. Sanders, Rick. Pink Floyd. London: Futura, 1976. 143p.,
       illus., discog. (A Contact Book)

                          Discographies

3255. Miles (pseud. of Barry Miles). Pink Floyd: the Illustrated
       Discography. London: Omnibus Pr.; New York: Quick Fox, 1981.
       64p., illus.
           Includes bootleg recordings.

       ————. Pink Floyd: Another Brick. London: Omnibus Pr., 1984.
       p., illus.
           Updated and extended edition.

Motion Pictures

3256. Pink Floyd. <u>The Wall</u>. London: Avon, 1982.   p., illus.
       Book of the production; illustrated with stills. Incl-
       udes lyrics.

Syd Barrett

3257. Jones, Malcolm. <u>Syd Barrett: the Making of "The Madcap
       Laughs."</u> London: The Author, 1983. 30p., illus.
       Account of Barrett's solo activities, and his 1969
       recording sessions. Author was his producer.

3258. <u>Terrapin</u>. Edited by Bernard White. London. irreg., 1973-?

PINZA, EZIO

3259. Pinza, Ezio. <u>Ezio Pinza: an Autobiography</u>. With Robert
       Magidoff. New York: Rinehart, 1958; New York: Arno Pr.,
       1977. 307p., illus., index.

PLAYFAIR, NIGEL

3260. Playfair, Nigel. <u>Hammersmith Hoy: a Book of Minor Revelat-
       ions</u>. London: Faber and Faber, 1930. 310p., illus.
       Autobiography. Author was best-known as manager-director
       of London's Lyric Theatre, Hammersmith.

POLICE

3261. Summers, Andy. <u>Throb</u>. New York: Morrow; London: Sidgwick
       and Jackson, 1984.   p., illus.
       Photographs by group member Summers; chiefly taken during
       the band's tours.

Biographies

3262. Goldsmith, Lynn. <u>The Police: Photographed by Lynn Goldsmith</u>.
       London: Vermilion; New York: St. Martin's Pr., 1983. 112p.,
       illus.

3263. Kamin, Philip, and Peter Goddard. <u>The Police Chronicles</u>.
       New York: Beaufort Books; London: Virgin Books, 1984. 128p.,
       illus.
       Photographs by Kamin; text by Goddard.

Police (cont.)

3264. Lowe, Jacques. The Police. London: Quartet, 1983.   p.,
       illus.

3265. Miles (pseud. of Barry Miles). The Police: a Visual Doc-
       umentary. London: Omnibus Pr., 1981. 128p., illus., discog.

3266. The Police Released. London; New York: Proteus, 1980. 96p.,
       illus., discog. (A Big O Publication)

3267. Sutcliffe, Phil, and Hugh Fielder. The Police: l'Historia
       Bandido. London; New York: Proteus, 1981. 96p., illus.,
       discog.

                            Periodicals

3268. The Official Police File. London. monthly, May 1980-Decem-
       ber 1981.

                    Sting (pseud. of Gordon Sumner)

3269. Cohen, Barney. Sting: Every Breath He Takes. New York:
       Berkley Publishing, 1984. 192p., illus.

POOLE, CHARLIE

3270. Rorrer, Clifford Kinney. Charlie Poole and The North
       Carolina Ramblers. Eden, North Carolina: Tar Heel Printing,
       1968. 22p., illus., discog.

POP, IGGY (pseud. of James Jewell Osterberg)

3271. Pop, Iggy, and Anne Wehrer. I Need More. Foreword by Andy
       Warhol. Princeton, New Jersey: Karz-Cohl Publishing, 1982.
       128p., illus., discog.
          Autobiography. Includes song lyrics and poems.

PORTER, COLE

3272. Porter, Cole. The Cole Porter Story. As told to Richard G.
       Hubler. Introduction by Arthur Schwartz. Cleveland: World
       Publishing Company, 1965. 140p., illus., bibliog.
          Based on interviews recorded in 1954. Publication delayed
       until after Porter's death in 1964.

3273. ———. The Complete Lyrics of Cole Porter. Edited by
       Robert Kimball. Foreword by John Updike. London: Hamish
       Hamilton, 1983. 354p., illus., index.

3274. ———. One Hundred and Three Lyrics. Selected, with an
       introduction and commentary by Fred Lounsberry. New York:
       Random House, 1954. 224p.

                              Biographies

3275. Eells, George. The Life That Late He Led: a Biography of
       Cole Porter. New York: Putnam; London: W.H. Allen, 1967.
       383p., illus. New York: Berkley Medallion Books, 1972.
       447p., illus., index.
       Includes listing of his compositions.

3276. Ewen, David. The Cole Porter Story. New York: Holt,
       Rinehart and Winston, 1965. 192p., illus., bibliog.,
       discog.

3277. Gill, Brendan. Cole: a Biographical Essay. Edited by
       Robert Kimball. New York: Holt, Rinehart and Winston,
       1971; London: Michael Joseph, 1972; London: Book Sales,
       1980. 283p., illus., discog.
       Includes reproductions of letters, music manuscripts,
       and other documents. Two hundred song lyrics also included.

3278. Schwartz, Charles. Cole Porter: a Biography. New York:
       Dial Pr., 1977; London: W.H. Allen, 1978; New York: Da Capo
       Pr., 1979. 365p., illus., bibliog., discog., index.
       Includes listing of his compositions.

POWELL, BUD

  *   Jepsen, Jorgen Grunnet. Discography of Art Tatum; Bud Powell.
          * Cited below as item 3686.

  *   ———. Discography of Theolonius Monk and Bud Powell.
          * Cited above as item 3129.

POWELL, SANDY

3279. Powell, Sandy. "Can You Hear Me, Mother?" Sandy Powell's
       Lifetime of Music Hall. As told to Harry Stanley. London:
       Jupiter Books, 1975. 192p., illus.

POWELL, TEDDY

* Garrod, Charles. <u>Bob Chester Orchestra/ Teddy Powell</u>
  <u>Orchestra</u>.
     * Cited above as item 2161.

PRENDERGRASS, TEDDY

3280. Stone, Eddie. <u>Teddy Prendergrass</u>. Los Angeles: Holloway
       House, 1980. 96p., illus., discog.

PRESLEY, ELVIS AARON

(i) Bibliographies

3281. Hammontree, Patsy Guy. <u>Elvis Presley: a Bio-Bibliography</u>.
       Westport, Conn.: Greenwood Pr., 1985.   p., bibliog.,
       discog., filmog. (Popular Culture Bio-Bibliographies)

3282. Whisler, John A. <u>Elvis Presley: Reference Guide and</u>
       <u>Discography</u>. Metuchen, New Jersey; London: Scarecrow Pr.,
       1981. 258p., bibliog., discog., index.

(ii) Autobiographical Works

3283. Presley, Elvis. <u>Elvis In His Own Words</u>. Compiled by Mick
       Farren and Pearce Marchbank. London: Omnibus Pr., 1977;
       London: W.H. Allen, 1981. 124p., illus.
          Compiled from press and other interviews.

(iii) Biographies

3284. <u>The Amazing Elvis Presley</u>. London: Amalgamated Pr., 1958.
       62p., illus. (Fans' Star Library, 2)

3285. Barlow, Roy, David T. Cardwell, and Albert Hand. <u>The Elvis</u>
       <u>Presley Elcyclopedia: Bringing You Everything You Wish To</u>
       <u>Know About Elvis, In Concise Chronological Order</u>. Heanor,
       Derbysshire: Albert Hand, 1964. 52p. <u>2nd. ed</u>.: 1964. 57p.

3286. Bates, Graham, and John Tobler (comps.). <u>The A-Z of Elvis</u>.
       Hastings, East Sussex: Mason's Music, 1982.   p., illus.

3287. Buckle, Philip (<u>pseud. of</u> Desmond Elliott). <u>All Elvis: an</u>
       <u>Unofficial Biography of the "King of Discs."</u> London: <u>Daily</u>
       <u>Mirror</u>, 1962. 64p., illus.

3288. Cocke, Marian J. <u>I Called Him Babe: Elvis Presley's Nurse
       Remembers</u>. Memphis: Memphis State University Pr., 1979.
       160p., illus. (Twentieth-Century Reminiscences)
       Account of his hospitalization, 1975.

3289. Cortez, Diego (ed.). <u>Private Elvis</u>. Text by Duncan Smith.
       Photographs by Rudolf Paulini. Stuttgart: Jochen Fey; New
       York: Two Continents, 1978; London: Book Sales, 1979.
       199p., illus.
       Photographs taken in Germany during his army service.

3290. Crumbaker, Marge. <u>Up and Down With Elvis Presley</u>. With Gabe
       Tucker. New York: Putnam, 1981; London: New English Library,
       1982. 209p., illus.

3291. Dundy, Elaine. <u>Elvis and Gladys: the Genesis of The King</u>.
       London: Weidenfeld and Nicolson, 1985. 362p., illus.,
       bibliog., index.
       Investigation of his relationship with his mother.

3292. <u>Elvis: a Tribute to The King of Rock 'n' Roll--Remembering
       You</u>. London: I.P.C. Magazines, 1977. 62p., illus., discog.,
       filmog.

3293. <u>Elvis Lives</u>! London: Galaxy Publications, 1978. 49p.,
       illus. (A Galaxy Special)

3294. <u>Elvis Presley, 1935-1977: a Tribute</u>. Wednesbury, West
       Midlands: Bavie Publications, 1977.
       <u>Vol. 1</u>. 30p., illus.
       <u>Vol. 2</u>. 33p., illus.
       <u>Vol. 3</u>. 33p., illus.
       <u>Vol. 4</u>. 31p., illus.
       <u>Vol. 5</u>. 32p., illus.
          Chiefly illustrated.

3295. <u>Elvis Presley Picture Parade Album</u>. London: Stanley Ilkin,
       1958. 23p., illus.

3296. <u>Elvis Special</u>. Compiled by Albert Hand. Manchester,
       England: World Distributors. annual, 1962-75.
       Special issues of <u>Elvis Monthly</u>.

3297. Gehman, Richard. <u>Elvis Presley: Hero or Heel</u>? Edited by
       Mary Callahan. London: L. Miller and Sons, 1957. 66p.,
       illus.

3298. Goldman, Albert. <u>Elvis</u>. New York: McGraw-Hill; London:
       Allen Lane, 1981. 598p., illus., index. London: Penguin,
       1982. 727p., illus., index.

3299. Gregory, James. <u>The Elvis Presley Story</u>. New York: Hillman
       Books, 1960; London: May Fair Books, 1961. 160p., illus.

3300. Hand, Albert. <u>A Century of Elvis</u>. Heanor, Derbysshire: The
       Author, 1959. 34p., illus.

Presley, Elvis (cont.)

3301. Hand, Albert. The Elvis Pocket Handbook. Heanor, Derbysshire: The Author, 1961. 64p., illus.

3302. ———. The Elvis They Dig. Heanor, Derbysshire, 1959. 35p., illus.

3303. Hanna, David. Elvis: Lonely Star At the Top. New York: Nordon Publications, 1977. 224p., illus. (A Leisure Book)

3304. Harbinson, William Allen. Elvis Presley. New York: Grosset and Dunlap, 1975. 160p., illus. 2nd. ed.: The Illustrated Elvis. New York: Grosset and Dunlap; New York: Today Pr./ Madison Square Pr.; London (as Elvis Presley: an Illustrated Biography): Michael Joseph, 1976. 160p., illus., discog., filmog. Rev. ed.: The Life and Death of Elvis Presley. London: Michael Joseph, 1977. 160p., illus.

3305. Harper, Betty. Elvis: Newly Discovered Drawings of Elvis Presley. New York; London: Bantam, 1979. 59p., illus. Chiefly illustrated. Collection of pencil drawings, by Tennessee artist Harper.

3306. Holmes, Robert. The Three Loves of Elvis Presley: the True Story of the Presley Legend. London: Charles Buchan's Publications/Hulton Pr., 1959. 63p., illus.

3307. Holzer, Hans. Elvis Presley Speaks. New York: Manor Books, 1978; London: New English Library, 1980. 255p. Author claims spiritualistic contact beyond the grave.

3308. Hopkins, Jerry. Elvis: a Biography. New York: Simon and Schuster, 1971; London: Open Gate Books, 1972; New York: Warner Books, 1973. 448p., illus., discog., filmog. London: Abacus, 1974. 365p., illus., discog., filmog.

3309. ———. Elvis: the Final Years. New York: St. Martin's Pr.; London: W.H. Allen; London: Omnibus Pr., 1980; London: Star Books, 1981. 258p., illus.

3310. Jones, Peter. Elvis. London: Octopus, 1976. 88p., illus.

3311. Jones, V. (comp.). Elvis Presley: the Official F.B.I. File. Beaconsfield, Quebec: The Author, 1978. 100p. Reproductions of Federal Bureau of Investigation documentation.

3312. Lacker, Marty, Patsy Lacker, and Leslie S. Smith. Elvis: Portrait of a Friend. Memphis: Wimmer Books, 1979; New York; London: Bantam, 1980. 369p., illus. Authors worked from late 1950's to late 1960's as aides to Presley.

3313. Levy, Alan. Operation Elvis. London: Andre Deutsch, 1960. 117p., illus. Army induction.

3314. Lichter, Paul. <u>The Boy Who Dared To Rock: the Definitive Elvis</u>. Garden City, New York: Doubleday, 1978 (Dolphin Books); London (as <u>Elvis: the Boy Who Dared To Rock</u>): Sphere, 1980. 304p., illus., discog., filmog., index.

3315. Mann, May. <u>Elvis and The Colonel</u>. New York; London: Drake, 1975. 273p., illus. New York: Pocket Books, 1976. 249p., illus.
    Story of Presley and his manager, Tom Parker.

3316. ————. <u>Elvis, Why Won't They Leave You Alone?</u> New York: New American Library, 1982. 214p., illus. (A Signet Book)
    Movie actress Mann worked with Presley.

3317. Mansfield, Rex, and Elisabeth Mansfield. <u>Elvis, the Soldier</u>. Bamberg, West Germany: Collectors' Service, 1983.   p., illus.
    Account of Presley's army service in Germany. By friend.

3318. Marchbank, Pearce (ed.). <u>Elvis Aaron Presley, 1935-1977: the Memorial Album</u>. London: Wise Publications, 1977. 64p., illus.
    Biographical and other articles. Includes reproductions of newspaper accounts of his death; also words and music of many of his hits.

3319. Marsh, Dave. <u>Elvis</u>. Art direction by Bea Feitler. New York: Times Books; London: Elm Tree Books, 1982. 246p., illus., bibliog., discog., filmog. (A <u>Rolling Stone</u> Pr. Book)

3320. Matthew-Walker, Robert. <u>Elvis Presley: a Study In Music</u>. Tunbridge Wells, Kent: Midas Books, 1979; London: Omnibus Pr., 1983. 154p., illus., bibliog., discog., filmog., indexes.

3321. Naphray, A.R. <u>Goodbye</u>. Photographs by J. Rock Caile and John Herman. Wednesbury, West Midlands: Bavie Publications, 1977. <u>5 vols.</u>,   p., illus.
    Poems about Presley.

3322. ————. <u>Pyromania</u>. Wednesbury, West Midlands: Bavie Publications, 1976. <u>5 vols.</u>,   p., illus.
    Poems about Presley.

3323. Panta, Ilona. <u>Elvis Presley, King of Kings</u>. Hicksville, New York: Exposition Pr., 1979. 247p., illus.

3324. Parish, James Robert. <u>The Elvis Presley Scrapbook</u>. New York: Ballantine, 1975. 185p., illus., discog. <u>Rev. ed.</u>: New York: Ballantine, 1977. 218p., illus., discog.

3325. Parker, Edmund K. <u>Inside Elvis</u>. Orange, California: Rampart House, 1978. 197p., illus.
    By friend.

Presley, Elvis (cont.)

3326. Peters, Richard. <u>Elvis: the Golden Anniversary Tribute.</u>
       <u>Fifty Fabulous Years, 1935-1985, In Words and Pictures.</u>
       London: Pop Universal/Souvenir Pr., 1984. 128p., illus.
       Includes chronological listing of his songs.

3327. Photoplay. <u>Elvis Presley: His Complete Life Story In Words</u>
       <u>and Illustrated With More Than One Hundred Pictures.</u> London:
       Illustrated Publications, 1956. 64p., illus.

3328. Presley, Dee, Billy Stanley, Rick Stanley, and David Stanley.
       <u>Elvis, We Love You Tender.</u> As told to Martin Torgoff. New
       York: Delacorte Pr.; London: New English Library, 1980.
       426p., illus., index.

3329. Presley, Vester. <u>A Presley Speaks.</u> As told to Deda Bonura.
       Memphis: Wimmer Books, 1978. 150p., illus.
       By his uncle.

3330. Reggero, John. <u>Elvis In Concert.</u> Introduction by David
       Stanley. New York: Dell, 1979. 128p., illus. (A Delta
       Special)
       Performance photographs by Reggero.

3331. Slaughter, Todd. <u>The A-Z of Elvis Presley.</u> Heanor, Derbys-
       shire: Albert Hand Publications, 1976.   p., illus.
       Dictionary format.

3332. ————. <u>Elvis Presley.</u> London: Wyndham Publications, 1977.
       60p., illus.

3333. Staten, Vince. <u>The Real Elvis: Good Old Boy.</u> Dayton, Ohio:
       Media Ventures, 1978.   p., illus.

3334. Tharpe, Jac L. (ed.). <u>Elvis: Images and Fancies.</u> Columbia,
       Mississippi: University Pr. of Mississippi, 1979; London:
       Star Books, 1983. 188p., illus.
       Biographical and critical essays contributed by staff of
       the University of Southern Mississippi.

3335. Thornton, Mary Ann. <u>Ever Elvis.</u> Harrison, Arkansas: New
       Leaf Pr., 1979. 128p., illus.

3336. Torgoff, Martin (ed.). <u>The Complete Elvis.</u> New York:
       Delilah; London: Sidgwick and Jackson; London: Virgin Books,
       1982. 253p., illus., bibliog., discog., filmog.
       Collection of biographical and other articles.

3337. Wallraf, Rainer, and Heinz Prehn. <u>Elvis Presley: an Illus-</u>
       <u>trated Biography.</u> Translated by Judith Waldman. London:
       Omnibus Pr., 1978. 118p., illus., discog., filmog.
       Originally published in West Germany.

3338. Wertheimer, Alfred, and Gregory Martinelli. <u>Elvis '56: in
       the Beginning</u>. New York: Collier Books; London: Cassell,
       1980. 149p., illus.
          Photographs taken in 1956 by Wertheimer, prior to Presley's
       Presley's rise to success.

3339. West, Red, Sonny West, and Dave Hebler. <u>Elvis: What
       Happened?</u> As told to Steve Dunleavy. New York: Ballantine,
       1977. 332p., illus.
          By his former bodyguards, fired in 1976.

3340. Wootton, Richard. <u>Elvis Presley: King of Rock and Roll</u>.
       London: Hodder and Stoughton, 1982. 128p., illus., index.
       (Twentieth Century People)
          Aimed at younger readers.

3341. Worth, Fred L., and Steve D. Tamerius. <u>All About Elvis:
       the King of Rock and Roll, From A to Z</u>. New York: Bantam;
       London: Corgi, 1981. 414p., illus., bibliog., discog.,
       filmog.

3342. Yancey, Becky. <u>My Life With Elvis: the Fond Memories of a
       Fan Who Became Elvis's Private Secretary</u>. With Clive
       Linedecker. New York: St. Martin's Pr.; London: W.H. Allen,
       1977; London: Mayflower, 1978. 254p., illus.
          Author worked for the Presley organization, 1962-75.

                         (iv) Discographies

3343. Barry, Ron. <u>The Elvis Presley American Discography</u>.
       Phillipsburg, New Jersey: Spectator Service/Maxigraphics,
       1976. 221p., illus.

3344. Carr, Roy, and Mick Farren. <u>Elvis: the Illustrated Record</u>.
       New York: Harmony Books, 1980; New York: Crown, 1982;
       London: Eel Pie, 1983. 192p., illus., bibliog., discog.
          Bio-discography.

3345. Cotten, Lee, and Howard DeWitt. <u>Jailhouse Rock</u>. Ann Arbor,
       Michigan: Pierian Pr., 1984.   p.
          Bootleg recordings detailed.

3346. <u>The Elvis Presley U.K. Discography</u>. London: Vintage Record
       Centre, 1980.   p.
          Complete listing of his British releases. Annotated.

3347. Escott, Colin, and Martin Hawkins. <u>Elvis Presley: the
       Illustrated Discography</u>. London: Omnibus Pr., 1981. 120p.,
       illus., filmog.
          Includes bootleg recordings.

3348. Jorgensen, Ernst, Erik Rasmussen, and Johnny Mikkelsen.
       <u>Elvis Presley: Recording Sessions</u>. Stenlose, Denmark: Jee
       Productions, 1977.   p., illus.
          Includes unreleased recordings.

Presley, Elvis (cont.)

Discographies (cont.)

3349. Osborne, Jerry, and Randy Jones. The Complete Elvis.
       Phoenix, Arizona: Jellyroll Productions, 1977.   p., illus.
          Includes bootleg recordings; foreign and variant releases;
       and unreleased material.

3350. Osborne, Jerry, and Bruce Hamilton. Presleyana. Phoenix,
       Arizona: O'Sullivan Woodside, 1981.   p.
          Price guide to rare Presley material.

                         (v) Motion Pictures

3351. Aros, Andrew A. Elvis: His Films and Recordings. Diamond
       Bar, California: Applause Publications, 1980. 64p., bibliog.,
       discog., indexes.

3352. Lichter, Paul. Elvis in Hollywood. New York: Simon and
       Schuster, 1975 (A Fireside Book); London: Hale, 1977. 188p.,
       illus., discog.

3353. Zmijewsky, Steven, and Boris Zmijewsky. The Films and
       Career of Elvis Presley. Secaucus, New Jersey: Citadel Pr.,
       1976. 224p., illus., discog., filmog.

                         (vi) Miscellanea

3354. Adler, Bill (comp.). Bill Adler's Love Letters To Elvis.
       New York: Grosset and Dunlap, 1978. 96p., illus.
          Fan letters.

3355. Cohn, Nik. King Death. New York: Harcourt, Brace, Jovano-
       vich, 1975.   p.
          Novel. The relationship of Presley with his twin brother
       Jesse, who died at birth.

3356. Nash, Bruce M. The Elvis Presley Quizbook. New York:
       Warner Books; London: New English Library, 1978. 205p.,
       illus.

3357. Rooks, Nancy, and Vester Presley. The Presley Family
       Cookbook. Memphis: Wimmer Books, 1980.   p., illus.
          Their favorite recipes.

                         (vii) Periodicals

3358. Elvis: Today, Tomorrow, and Forever. Gloucester, England.
       monthly, 1979-?

3359. Elvis Monthly. Edited by Todd Slaughter. Heanor, Derbys-
       shire; later Nottingham. monthly, 1959- .

3360. Elvis Presley Spearheads. Stourbridge, Worcestershire.
       irreg., 1961-?

3361. Strictly Elvis. Edited by Rocky Bara. Livonia, Michigan.
       monthly, 1967-?

PRETENDERS

3362. Miles (pseud. of Barry Miles). The Pretenders. London:
       Omnibus Pr., 1981. 49p., illus., discog.

3363. Salewicz, Chris. The Pretenders. London; New York: Proteus,
       1983. 128p., illus., discog.

PREVIN, ANDRE

3364. Bookspan, Martin, and Ross Yockey. Andre Previn: a Biography.
       London: Hamish Hamilton, 1981. 398p., illus., index.

3365. Greenfield, Edward. Andre Previn. New York: Drake Publish-
       ers, 1973. 96p., illus., discog.

PREVIN, DORY

3366. Previn, Dory. Bog-Trotter: an Autobiography, With Lyrics.
       Drawings by Joby Baker. Garden City, New York: Doubleday;
       London: Weidenfeld and Nicolson, 1980. 383p., illus.
          Her second volume of memoirs. Includes song lyrics.

3367. ———. Midnight Baby: an Autobiography. New York: Mac-
       millan, 1976; London: Elm Tree Books, 1977. 246p. London:
       Corgi, 1978. 140p.
          Her first volume of memoirs.

3368. ———. On My Way To Where. New York: McCall Publishing,
       1971. 117p., illus.
          Poems.

PRINCE (pseud. of Prince Rogers Nelson)

3369. Prince. Prince In His Own Words. Edited by Dave Fudger.
       London: Omnibus Pr., 1984. 32p., illus.
          Compiled from interviews.

Prince (cont.)

Biographies

3370. Ivory, Steven. <u>Prince</u>. New York; London: Bantam, 1985.
       175p., illus., discog.

3371. Olmeca (<u>pseud.</u>). <u>Prince</u>. London; New York: Proteus, 1984.
       32p., illus., discog.

3372. <u>The Year of the Prince</u>. New York: Sharon Publications;
       London: Sphere, 1984. 64p., illus.
           Chiefly illustrated.

PRINCE, HAROLD SMITH

3373. Prince, Harold Smith. <u>Contradictions</u>. New York: Dodd, Mead,
       1974.   p., illus.
           Autobiography.

PRINTEMPS, YVONNE

3374. O'Connor, Patrick. <u>Yvonne Printemps, 1894-1977</u>. Richmond,
       Surrey: The Author, 1978. 22p., illus., discog.
           Limited edition of three hundred numbered copies.

PROCTOR, F.F.

3375. Marston, William Moulton, and J.H. Feller. <u>F.F. Proctor,
       Vaudeville Pioneer</u>. New York: Richard R. Smith, 1943. 191p.,
       illus.

PROCUL HARUM

3376. <u>Procul Harum: Shine On</u>. Edinburgh, 1980.   p., illus.,
       discog.

QUEEN

3377. Davis, Judith. <u>Queen: an Illustrated Biography</u>. London;
       New York: Proteus, 1981. 144p., illus., discog.

3378. Lowe, Jacques (ed.). <u>Queen's Greatest Pix</u>. Text by Ray
       Bonici, Ray Coleman, Ray Connolly, Paul Gambaccini, and Ziggy.
       London: Quartet, 1981. 95p., illus., discog.

3379. Pryce, Larry. Queen. London: Star Books, 1976. 124p.,
      illus., discog.

3380. Tremlett, George. The Queen Story. London: Futura, 1978.
      p., illus., discog.

3381. West, Mike. Queen. London: Omnibus Pr., 1982. 112p.,
      illus., discog.

RAEBURN, BOYD

3382. Edwards, Ernie, George Hall, and Bill Korst. Boyd Raeburn
      and His Orchestra. Introduction by Jack McKinney. Whittier,
      California: Jazz Discographies Unlimited, 1960. 20p.

RAINEY, MA (pseud. of Gertrude Malissa Pridgett)

3383. Lieb, Sandra R. Mother of the Blues: a Study of Ma Rainey.
      Amherst, Massachusetts: University of Massachusetts Pr.,
      1983. 256p., illus., discog.

3384. Stewart-Baxter, Derrick. Ma Rainey and the Classic Blues
      Singers. London: Studio Vista; New York: Stein and Day,
      1970. 112p., illus., bibliog., discog., index. Amherst,
      Massachusetts: University of Massachusetts Pr., 1983. 248p.,
      illus., bibliog., discog., index.
         Includes discussion of other artists.

RAMONES

3385. Miles (pseud. of Barry Miles). The Ramones. London:
      Omnibus Pr., 1981. 51p., illus., discog.

RAY, JOHNNIE

3386. Sonin, Ray. The Johnnie Ray Story. London: Horace Marshall,
      1955. 83p., illus.

REDDING, OTIS

3387. Schiesel, Jane. The Otis Redding Story. Garden City, New
      York: Doubleday, 1973. 143p., illus., discog.

Redding, Otis (cont.)

Periodicals

3388. <u>The Otis File</u>. Edited by John Stuart. Swindon, Wiltshire.
       irreg., 1984-85.
          Continued 1985 as <u>Sweet Soul Music</u>. Coverage altered to
       general soul.

REEVE, ADA

3389. Reeve, Ada. <u>Take It For a Fact: a Record of My Seventy-
       Five Years On the Stage</u>. Foreword by Compton Mackenzie.
       London: Heinemann, 1954. 263p., illus.
          Autobiography.

REEVES, JIM

3390. Cackett, Alan (ed.). <u>Jim Reeves and His Friends</u>. Maidstone,
       Kent: The Author, 1974.   p., illus., discog.

3391. Reeves, Mary. <u>The Jim Reeves Memorial and Souvenir Photo
       Album</u>. Madison, Tennessee: Mary Reeves Incorporated, 1959.
          p., illus.
          By his widow.

REINHARDT, DJANGO

3392. Delaunay, Charles. <u>Django Reinhardt</u>. Foreword by Jean
       Cocteau. Translated by Michael James. London: Cassell,
       1961; New York: Da Capo Pr., 1982. 247p., illus., discog.
       <u>2nd. ed.</u>: Gateshead, Tyne and Wear: Ashley Mark, 1981. 300p.,
       illus., discog., index.
          Originally published as <u>Django Reinhardt: souvenirs</u>, Paris:
       Editions <u>Jazz-Hot</u>, 1954.

Discographies

3393. Abrams, Max. <u>The Book of Django</u>. Los Angeles: The Author,
       1973. 188p., illus.
          Limited edition of seventy-five copies.

3394. Neill, Billy, and E. Gates. <u>Discography of the Recorded
       Works of Django Reinhardt and The Quintette du Hot Club de
       France</u>. London: Clifford Essex Music, 1944. 24p., illus.

REYNOLDS, MALVINA

3395. Reynolds, Malvina. Not In Ourselves, Nor In Our Stars
       Either. San Rafael, California: Schroder Music, 1975. 40p.
       Autobiography.

RICH, BUDDY

3396. Balliett, Whitney. Super Drummer: a Profile of Buddy Rich.
       Photographs by Fred Seligo. Indianapolis: Bobbs-Merrill,
       1968. 128p., illus.
       Originally published in the New Yorker.

                        Discographies

3397. Cooper, David J. A Buddy Rich Discography. Blackburn,
       Lancashire: The Author, 1974. 48p.
       Includes radio broadcasts.

3398. Meriwether, Doug. The Buddy Rich Orchestra and Small Groups.
       Spotswood, New Jersey: Joyce, 1974.   p.

3399. Strateman, Klaus. Buddy Rich and Gene Krupa: a Filmo-
       Discography. Lübeck, West Germany: Uhle und Kleimann, 1980.
       76p., illus. (Jazzfreund Publikation)
       Documentation of their motion picture appearances; plus
       discography of long-playing records taken from them.

RICHARD, CLIFF (pseud. of Harry Webb)

3400. Richard, Cliff. Cliff Richard's Top Pops. Presented by
       Patrick Doncaster. London: Daily Mirror Newspapers, 1963.
       63p., illus.

3401. ————. Cliff In His Own Words. Compiled by Kevin St. John.
       London: W.H. Allen, 1981; London: Omnibus Pr., 1982. 128p.,
       illus.
       Compiled from interviews.

3402. ————. Happy Christmas From Cliff. London: Hodder and
       Stoughton, 1980. 100p., illus.
       Proposed annual; only issue.

3403. ————. It's Great To Be Young: My Teenage Story and Life
       in Show Business. London: Souvenir Pr., 1960. 128p., illus.
       Manchester, England (as It's Great To Be Young): World
       Distributors, 1961. 127p., illus. (Consul Books)

Richard, Cliff (cont.)

3404.   Richard, Cliff. Me and My Shadows. London: Daily Mirror
         Newspapers, 1961. 64p., illus.

3405.   ———. Questions. London: Hodder and Stoughton, 1970.
         96p., illus.
              Answers to fans' queries on Richard's Christian beliefs.

3406.   ———. The Way I See It. London: Hodder and Stoughton,
         1968. 95p. London: Hodder and Stoughton, 1970. 187p.
         (Square Books). Rev. ed.: The Way I See It Now. London:
         Hodder and Stoughton, 1973. 92p., illus.
              Personal observations on Christianity.

3407.   ———. Which One's Cliff? With Bill Latham. London:
         Hodder and Stoughton, 1977. 156p., illus., discog.
              Autobiography.

         ———. The Illustrated "Which One's Cliff?" London:
         Hodder and Stoughton, 1978. 192p., illus., discog.
              Text updated; many illustrations added.

         ———. Which One's Cliff? The Autobiography. Sevenoaks,
         Kent: Coronet, 1981. 218p., illus., discog.

                              Biographies

3408.   Cliff Richard. London: Amalgamated Pr., 1959. 63p., illus.
         (Fans' Star Library, 28)

3409.   Cliff With the Kids in America. Leicester, England: Empire
         Records, 1981.   p., illus.
              Account of his 1981 tour.

3410.   Doncaster, Patrick, and Tony Jasper. Cliff. Written in
         cooperation with Cliff Richard. London: Sidgwick and Jack-
         son, 1981. 240p., illus., bibliog., discog., index. London:
         New English Library, 1982. 253p., illus., bibliog., discog.,
         index.

3411.   Ferrier, Bob. Cliff Around the Clock. London: Daily Mirror
         Newspapers, 1964. 24p., illus.

3412.   ———. The Wonderful World of Cliff Richard. London:
         Peter Davies, 1964. 247p., illus.

3413.   Harris, Jet, and Royston Ellis. Driftin' With Cliff Richard:
         the Inside Story of What Really Happens On Tour. London:
         Charles Buchan's Publications, 1959. 63p., illus.
              Harris was bassist in Richard's backing group, The Drift-
         ers (later The Shadows).

3414. Hoffman, Dezo. Cliff Richard and The Shadows. London:
       Virgin Books, 1985.   p., illus.
           Photographs by Hoffman.

3415. Jasper, Tony. Silver Cliff: a Twenty-Five Year Journal,
       1958-1983. London: Sidgwick and Jackson, 1983. 136p.,
       illus., discog., index.

3416. Life With Cliff Richard. London: Charles Buchan's Public-
       ations, 1963.   p., illus.

3417. Sutter, Jack. Cliff: the Baron of Beat. Blackpool: Valex
       Products, 1960. 20p., illus.

3418. Tobler, John. Cliff Richard. London: Deans International
       Publishing, 1983.   p., illus., bibliog., discog., index.
           For sale only in W.H. Smith bookstores.

3419. Tremlett, George. The Cliff Richard Story. London: Futura,
       1975. 156p., illus.

3420. Winter, David. New Singer, New Song: the Cliff Richard
       Story. London: Hodder and Stoughton; Waco, Texas: Word
       Books, 1968. 192p., illus., discog., filmog.

RICHARD, LITTLE (pseud. of Richard Wayne Penniman)

3421. Courtney, Tez. Little Richard. New York: Macmillan, 1972.
       p., illus., discog. (Rockbooks)

3422. White, Charles. The Life and Times of Little Richard, the
       Quasar of Rock. Foreword by Paul McCartney. New York:
       Harmony, 1984; London: Pan, 1985.   p., illus., discog.

RICHARDS, JOHNNY

3423. Hentoff, Nat. Johnny Richards. New York: Broadcast Music,
       1960. 16p.

RICHIE, LIONEL

3424. Nathan, David. Lionel Richie: an Illustrated Biography.
       London: Virgin Books, 1985. 127p., illus., discog.

RICHMAN, HARRY

3425. Richman, Harry. A Hell of a Life. New York: Duell, Sloan,
       and Pearce, 1966. 242p., illus.
           Autobiography. Ghosted by Richard Gehman.

RILEY, JEANNIE C.

3426. Riley, Jeannie C. From Harper Valley To the Mountain Top.
       With Jamie Buckingham. Lincoln, Virginia: Chosen Books;
       Eastbourne, East Sussex: Kingsway, 1981. 211p.
            Autobiography.

ROBESON, PAUL

3427. Robeson, Paul. Here I Stand. New York: Othello Associates;
       London: Dobson, 1958; Boston: Beacon Pr., 1971. 128p.
            Autobiography and statement of his political philosophy.

3428. ———. Paul Robeson Speaks: Writings, Speeches, Interviews;
       1918-1974. Edited, with an introduction and notes, by
       Philip S. Foner. Larchmont, New York: Brunner/Mazel, 1978.
            p., bibliog., index.

                         Bibliography

3429. Davis, Lenwood G. A Paul Robeson Research Guide: a Selected
       Annotated Bibliography. Westport, Conn.: Greenwood Pr.,
       1982. 879p., illus., index.

                         Biographies

3430. Brown, Lloyd Louis. Paul Robeson Rediscovered. New York:
       American Institute for Marxist Studies, 1976. 23p., bibliog.
       refs. (Occasional Papers, 19)
            Text of lecture, delivered April 22, 1976, at the North
       Conference on Paul Robeson, Purdue University, Indiana.

3431. Du Bois, Shirley Graham. Paul Robeson, Citizen of the World.
       Foreword by Carl van Doren. New York: J. Messner, 1946;
       Westport, Conn.: Negro Universities Pr., 1971. 264p., illus.,
       bibliog.
            Aimed at younger readers.

3432. Freedomways. Paul Robeson: the Great Forerunner. By the
       Editors of Freedomways. New York: Dodd, Mead, 1978. 383p.,
       illus., bibliog., index.
            Essays on Robeson's life and politics.

3433. Gilliam, Dorothy Butler. Paul Robeson, All-American.
       Washington, D.C.: New Republic Book Company, 1976.   p.,
       bibliog. refs., index.

3434. Greenfield, Eloise. Paul Robeson. Illustrated by George
       Ford. New York: Crowell, 1975. 32p., illus. (Crowell Biog-
       raphies)
            Aimed at younger readers.

3435. Hamilton, Virginia. Paul Robeson: the Life and Times of a
       Free Black Man. New York: Harper and Row, 1974. 217p.,
       illus., bibliog., index. New York: Dell, 1979. 224p.,
       illus., bibliog., index. (A Laurel Leaf Book)
          Aimed at younger readers.

3436. Hoyt, Edwin Palmer. Paul Robeson, the American Othello.
       Cleveland: World, 1967; London (as Paul Robeson): Cassell,
       1968. 228p., bibliog. notes.

3437. Nazel, Joseph. Paul Robeson: the Biography of a Proud Man.
       Los Angeles: Holloway House, 1980. 216p., bibliog.

3438. Robeson, Eslanda Goode. Paul Robeson, Negro. New York:
       Harper; London: Gollancz, 1930. 153p., illus.
          By his wife.

3439. Robeson, Susan. The Whole World In His Hands: a Pictorial
       Biography of Paul Robeson. Secaucus, New Jersey: Citadel
       Pr., 1981. 224p., illus.

3440. Seton, Marie. Paul Robeson. Foreword by Arthur Bryant.
       London: Dobson, 1958. 254p., illus., index.

RODGERS, JIMMIE

3441. Paris, Mike, and Chris Comber. Jimmie the Kid: the Life of
       Jimmie Rodgers. London: Eddison Pr./Old Time Music Magazine,
       1977; New York: Da Capo Pr., 1981. 211p., illus., bibliog.,
       discog., index.

3442. Porterfield, Nolan. Jimmie Rodgers: the Life and Times of
       America's Blue Yodeler. Urbana; London: University of
       Illinois Pr., 1979. 460p., illus., bibliog., discog., index.
       (Music in American Life)

3443. Rodgers, Carrie Cecil Williamson. My Husband, Jimmie Rodgers.
       San Antonio, Texas: Southern Literary Institute, 1935;
       Nashville: Country Music Foundation Pr., 1975. 264p., illus.
          1975 edition has new introduction and chronology, by
       Nolan Porterfield.

                          Discography

3444. Bond, Johnny. The Recordings of Jimmie Rodgers: an Annotated
       Discography. Los Angeles: John Edwards Memorial Foundation,
       1978.   p.

RODGERS, RICHARD, LORENZ HART, AND OSCAR HAMMERSTEIN II

3445. Rodgers, Richard. <u>Musical Stages: an Autobiography</u>. New
       York: Random House, 1975; London: W.H. Allen, 1976. 341p.,
       illus., index.

Theatrical Works

3446. <u>The Rodgers and Hammerstein Fact Book</u>. New York: Richard
       Rodgers and Oscar Hammerstein II, 1955. 678p., illus.,
       bibliogs., discog.

       ————. <u>With Supplement</u>. New York: Lynn Farnol Group,
       1959-61. <u>2 vols</u>., 659p., illus., bibliogs., discog.
       Full details of all their productions.

       <u>Richard Rodgers Fact Book</u>. New York: Lynn Farnol Group,
       1965. 582p., illus., bibliog., discog.

       ————. <u>With Supplement</u>. New York: Lynn Farnol Group,
       1968. 659p., illus., bibliog., discog.
       Omits all references to Hammerstein's independent works.

Biographies

3447. Ewen, David. <u>Richard Rodgers</u>. New York: Holt, 1957. 378p.,
       illus., bibliog., discog.

3448. Green, Stanley. <u>The Rodgers and Hammerstein Story</u>. New
       York: J. Day, 1963 (Reprinted: New York: Da Capo Pr., 1980).
       189p., illus., bibliog., index. London: W.H. Allen, 1963.
       170p., illus., bibliog., index.

3449. Marx, Samuel, and Jan Clayton. <u>Rodgers and Hart: Bewitched,
       Bothered, and Bedevilled</u>. New York: Putnam's, 1976; London:
       W.H. Allen, 1977. 287p., illus., index.

3450. Nolan, Frederick. <u>The Sound of Their Music: the Story of
       Rodgers and Hammerstein</u>. London: Dent, 1978; London: Unwin
       Paperbacks, 1979. 272p., illus., bibliog., index.

3451. Rodgers, Dorothy. <u>A Personal Book</u>. New York: Harper and
       Row, 1977. 188p., illus.
       Memoir by wife of Richard Rodgers.

3452. Taylor, Deems. <u>Some Enchanted Evenings: the Story of Rodgers
       and Hammerstein</u>. New York: Harper, 1953 (Reprinted: Westport,
       Conn.: Greenwood Pr., 1972). 244p., illus., bibliog. London:
       MacDonald, 1955. 195p., illus., bibliog.

Lorenz Hart

3453. Hart, Lorenz. Thou Swell, Thou Witty: the Life and Lyrics
of Lorenz Hart. Edited, with a memoir, by Dorothy Hart.
New York; London: Harper and Row, 1976. 192p., illus.,
bibliog., filmog. London: Elm Tree Books, 1978. 254p.,
illus., bibliog., filmog., index.

Oscar Hammerstein II

3454. Hammerstein, Oscar, II. Lyrics. New York: Simon and
Schuster, 1949. 215p.

Biography

3455. Fordin, Hugh. Getting To Know Him: a Biography of Oscar
Hammerstein II. New York: Random House, 1977.   p., illus.,
bibliog., index.

ROGERS, KENNY

3456. Hume, Martha. Gambler, Dreamer, Lover: the Kenny Rogers
Story. New York: Delilah/Tower Books, 1982. 160p., illus.

ROGERS, ROY (pseud. of Leonard Slye), AND DALE EVANS

3457. Rogers, Roy. Happy Trails: the Story of Roy Rogers and
Dale Evans. With Carlton Stowers. Waco, Texas: Word Books,
1979. 213p., illus., filmog.

Biography

3458. Davis, Elise Miller. The Answer is God: the Inspiring
Personal Story of Dale Evans and Roy Rogers. London: Peter
Davies, 1956. 250p., illus.

Dale Evans

3459. Rogers, Dale Evans. Dale: My Personal Picture Album. Old
Tappan, New Jersey: Revell, 1971; London: Oliphants, 1972.
127p., illus.

Rogers, Roy, and Dale Evans (cont.)

3460. Rogers, Dale Evans. The Woman At the Well. Old Tappan, New
      Jersey: Revell, 1970; London: Oliphants, 1971. 191p., illus.
      Observations on their Christian life and outlook.

ROLLING STONES

3461. Rolling Stones, The. Our Own Story. As told to Pete Good-
      man. Illustrated by Bob Gibson. London: Transworld Pub-
      lishers, 1964. 188p., illus. Rev. ed.: New York: Bantam,
      1970.   p., illus.

3462. ————. The Rolling Stones Complete Works. Amsterdam:
      Thomas Rap, 1971. 120p.
      Lyric collection. Chronological arrangement.

3463. ————. The Rolling Stones In Their Own Words. Compiled
      by David Dalton and Mick Farren. London: Omnibus Pr., 1982;
      New York: Delilah, 1983. 128p., illus.
      Compiled from press and other interviews.

                           Bibliography

3464. Dimmick, Mary Laverne. The Rolling Stones: an Annotated
      Bibliography. Pittsburgh: University of Pittsburgh, Grad-
      uate School of Library and Information Sciences, 1972. 73p.
      (Pittsburgh Studies in Library and Information Sciences, 4)
      Rev. and enlarged ed.: Pittsburgh: University of Pittsburgh
      Pr., 1978.   p., index.
      Classified arrangement. Revised edition cites 455 items.

                           Biographies

3465. Booth, Stanley. Dance With The Devil: The Rolling Stones
      and Their Times. New York: Random House; London (as The
      True Adventures of The Rolling Stones): Heinemann, 1985.
      385p., illus.
      Centered on their 1969 American tour.

3466. Dalton, David (ed.). The Rolling Stones: an Unauthorized
      Biography in Words, Photographs, and Music. New York: Amsco
      Music Publishing; London: Music Sales, 1972. 352p., illus.,
      discogs.
      Collection of biographical and critical pieces. Includes
      words and music of key songs.

      ————. The Rolling Stones. London: Star Books, 1975.
      186p., illus., discog.
      Songs omitted; text partially revised.

————. The Rolling Stones: an Unauthorized Biography in Words and Photographs. New York: Quick Fox, 1979. 126p., illus., discog.

3467. ————. The Rolling Stones: the First Twenty Years. New York: Knopf; London: Thames and Hudson, 1982. 192p., illus., discog.
Collection of contemporary newspaper and other articles.

3468. Downley, Tim. The Rolling Stones. Tunbridge Wells, Kent: Midas Books; New York: Hippocrene Books, 1983. 156p., illus., bibliog., discog., filmog.

3469. Elman, Richard M. Uptight With The Stones: a Novelist's Report. New York: Scribner's, 1973. 119p., illus.
Account of their 1972 American tour.

3470. Greenfield, Robert. S.T.P. A Journey Through America With The Rolling Stones. New York: Saturday Review Pr.; London (as Stones Touring Party: a Journey Through America With The Rolling Stones): Michael Joseph, 1974. 337p., illus. St. Albans, Hertfordshire (as A Journey Through America With The Rolling Stones): Panther, 1975. 287p., illus.

3471. Hewat, Tim (ed.). The Rolling Stones File. St. Albans, Hertfordshire: Panther, 1967. 128p., illus. (Panther Record, 2)
Includes facsimiles of newspaper stories.

3472. Hoffman, Dezo. The Rolling Stones. With Norman Jopling. Introduction by Mick Jagger. London: Vermilion, 1984. 126p., illus.
Photographs by Hoffman, chiefly from the 1960's.

3473. Jasper, Tony. The Rolling Stones. London: Octopus, 1976. 92p., illus., discogs. Rev. ed.: London: Bounty Books, 1984. p., illus., discogs.

3474. Kamin, Philip. The Rolling Stones: Live. Text by Peter Goddard. London: Sidgwick and Jackson, 1982. 125p., illus.
Performance photographs.

3475. ————. The Rolling Stones: the Last Tour. Text by James Karnbach. London: Sidgwick and Jackson, 1983. 128p., illus.
Performance photographs of their 1982 American tour.

3476. Leibovitz, Annie. The Rolling Stones On Tour. With Christopher Sykes. Text by Terry Southern. Cheltenham, Gloucestershire: Phin Publishing, 1978. 143p., illus.
Photographs of their 1975 American tour, by Leibovitz and Sykes.

3477. Luce, Philip Carmelo. The Stones. London: Howard Baker, 1970. 117p., illus., discogs.

Rolling Stones (cont.)

3478.   Mankowitz, Gered. Satisfaction: the Rolling Stones Photo-
        graphs of Gered Mankowitz. Edited and designed by Pearce
        Marchbank. Foreword by Andrew Loog Oldham. London:
        Sidgwick and Jackson; New York: St. Martin's Pr., 1984.
        104p., illus.
            By their official photographer. Most of the photographs
        are from the 1960's.

3479.   Martin, Linda. The Rolling Stones In Concert. New Malden,
        Surrey: Colour Library Books, 1982. 96p., illus., discog.
            Chiefly illustrated.

3480.   Norman, Philip. The Stones. London: Elm Tree Books; New
        York (as Symphony For The Devil): Linden/Simon and Schuster,
        1984. 372p., illus., index. London: Corgi, 1985. 432p.,
        illus., index.

3481.   Palmer, Robert. The Rolling Stones. Garden City, New York:
        Doubleday/Rolling Stone Pr.; London: Sphere, 1984. 256p.,
        illus., bibliog.

3482.   Pascall, Jeremy. The Rolling Stones. London; New York:
        Hamlyn, 1977. 96p., illus., discog.

3483.   Sanchez, Tony. Up and Down With The Rolling Stones: the
        Inside Story. New York: Morrow, 1979. 310p., illus.
            By ex-staff member. Emphasis on their drug abuse.

3484.   Tabori, Paul. Song of The Scorpions: a Novel. London: New
        English Library, 1971 (Reissued: 1972). 189p.
            Thinly-disguised novelization of their career.

3485.   Tremlett, George. The Rolling Stones Story. London: Futura,
        1974; London: White Lion, 1976. 190p., illus. New York:
        Warner Books, 1976. 174p., illus.

3486.   Weiner, Sue, and Lisa Howard. The Rolling Stones, A-Z. New
        York: Grove Pr., 1983 (Evergreen Editions); London: Omnibus
        Pr., 1984. 149p., illus., discog.
            In dictionary form.

                            Discographies

3487.   Carr, Roy. The Rolling Stones: an Illustrated Record.
        London: New English Library; New York: Harmony Books, 1976.
        120p., illus., discogs., filmog.
            Bio-discography.

3488.   Lazell, Barry, and Daffydd Rees. The Stones Bootlegs.
        London; New York: Proteus, 1984.   p., illus. (Bootleg
        Series)

3489. Miles (pseud. of Barry Miles). The Rolling Stones: an
       Illustrated Discography. London: Omnibus Pr., 1980. 92p.,
       illus.
           Includes bootleg recordings.

                          Periodicals

  *   Beatles/Stones Newsletter and Collectors' Guide.
           * Cited above as item 1897.

3490. The Rolling Stones Book. London. monthly, June 1964-
       December 1966.

                   Individual Group Members

Jagger, Michael "Mick"

3491. Jagger, Mick. Mick Jagger In His Own Words. Compiled by
       Miles. London: Omnibus Pr., 1982; New York: Delilah, 1983.
       128p., illus.
           Compiled from press and other interviews.

                         Biographies

3492. Aldridge, John. Satisfaction: the Story of Mick Jagger.
       London; New York: Proteus, 1984. 126p., illus., discog.

3493. Blake, John. His Satanic Majesty: Mick Jagger. London:
       Plexus Publishing, 1985. 192p., illus.

3494. Littlejohn, David. The Man Who Killed Mick Jagger: a Novel.
       New York: Pocket Books, 1978. 294p. (A Kangaroo Book)

3495. Marks, J. Mick Jagger: the Singer, Not the Song. New York:
       Curtis Books, 1973; London: Abacus, 1974. 155p., illus.
           Biographical account, mixed with personal reminiscences
       and musings.

3496. Scaduto, Anthony. Mick Jagger: Everybody's Lucifer. New
       York: David McKay, 1974. 376p., illus. New York: Berkley
       Publishing, 1975. 297p., illus. (Berkley Medallion Books)

       ————. Mick Jagger. London: W.H. Allen, 1974; London:
       Mayflower, 1975. 290p., illus.

3497. Schofield, Carey. Jagger. London: Methuen, 1983. 248p.,
       illus., bibliog., index. London: New English Library, 1984.
       256p., illus., bibliog., index.

Rolling Stones (cont.)

Jagger, Michael "Mick" (cont.)

3498. Time Out. Performance: the Full Story of Mick Jagger's
       First Feature Film. London: Time Out, 1970.   p., illus.

3499. Whitaker, Robert. Mick Jagger Is Ned Kelly. London: Corgi,
       1970. 32p., illus.
          Photographs by Whitaker taken during the production of
       Jagger's second motion picture, Ned Kelly.

                            Brian Jones

3500. Aftel, Mandy. Death of a Rolling Stone: the Brian Jones
       Story. New York: Delilah, 1982; London: Sidgwick and
       Jackson, 1983. 208p., illus.

                           Keith Richards

3501. Charone, Barbara. Keith Richards. London: Futura, 1979;
       Garden City, New York (as Keith Richards: Life as a Rolling
       Stone): Doubleday, 1982 (Anchor Books). 192p., illus.,
       discog.

ROLLINS, SONNY

3502. Blancq, Charles. Sonny Rollins: the Journey of a Jazzman.
       Boston: Twayne, 1982. 148p., illus., discog. (Music Series)

   *   Jepsen, Jorgen Grunnet. Discography of Theolonius Monk;
       Sonny Rollins.
          * Cited above as item 3130.

ROMBERG, SIGMUND

3503. Arnold, Elliott. Deep In My Heart: a Story Based On the
       Life of Sigmund Romberg. New York: Duell, Sloan, and Pearce,
       1949. 511p.
          Fictionalized biography.

RONSTADT, LINDA

3504. Berman, Connie. Linda Ronstadt: an Illustrated Biography.
       London; New York: Proteus, 1979. 117p., illus., discog.

3505. Claire, Vivian. <u>Linda Ronstadt</u>. New York: Flash Books,
1978. 72p., illus., discog.

3506. Kanakaris, Richard. <u>Linda Ronstadt: a Portrait</u>. Los Angeles:
Los Angeles Pop Publishing, 1977. 79p., illus., discog.

3507. Moore, Mary Ellen. <u>The Linda Ronstadt Scrapbook: an Illustrated Biography</u>. New York: Sunridge Pr., 1978. 122p.,
illus. New York: Ace Books, 1978. 154p., illus. New York:
Grosset and Dunlap; London: Blandford Pr., 1979. 122p.,
illus.

ROOT, GEORGE FREDERICK

3508. Root, George Frederick. <u>The Story of a Musical Life: an
Autobiography</u>. Cincinnati: J. Church, 1891; New York: Da
Capo Pr., 1970; New York: A.M.S. Pr., 1973. 256p., illus.

ROSE, BILLY

3509. Conrad, Earl. <u>Billy Rose: Manhattan Primitive</u>. Cleveland:
World Publishing, 1968. 272p., illus.

3510. Gottlieb, Polly Rose. <u>The Nine Lives of Billy Rose</u>. New
York: Crown, 1968. 290p., illus. New York: New American
Library, 1969. 240p., illus. (A Signet Book)
   By his sister.

ROSENKRANTZ, TIMME

3511. Rosenkrantz, Timme. <u>Das med jazzen: mine jazzmemoiren. En
bog om jazz--og andet godtfolk</u>. Copenhagen: Erickson, 1965.
149p., illus.
   Memoirs of Danish jazz writer and enthusiast.

ROSS, DIANA

3512. Brown, Geoff. <u>Diana Ross</u>. London: Sidgwick and Jackson,
1981. 144p., illus., discog., index.

3513. Itzkowitz, Leonore K. <u>Diana Ross</u>. New York: Random House,
1974.   p., illus.

3514. Pitts, Leonard, <u>Jr</u>. <u>Reach Out: the Diana Ross Story</u>. Bromley,
Kent: Columbus Books, 1983.   p., illus., discog.

3515. Taraborelli, J. Randy. <u>Diana</u>. London: W.H. Allen, 1985.
   p., illus., discog.

ROXY MUSIC

3516. Lazell, Barry, and Daffydd Rees. Bryan Ferry and Roxy
      Music. London; New York: Proteus, 1982. 96p., illus.,
      discog. (Proteus Rocks)
          Coverage of the group and its members' solo careers.

3517. Rogan, Johnny. Roxy Music: Style With Substance. Roxy's
      First Ten Years. London: Star Books, 1982. 219p., illus.,
      discog.
          Includes coverage of group members' solo activities.

3518. Williams, Kit. Roxy Music. London; New York: Proteus,
      1982. 128p., illus., discog.

                        Bryan Ferry

3519. Balfour, Rex. The Bryan Ferry Story. London: Michael
      Dempsey, 1976. 128p., illus., discog.

RUSH

3520. Harrigan, Brian. Rush. London: Omnibus Pr., 1982. 80p.,
      illus.
          Author was once their British press officer.

RUSSELL, GEORGE

3521. Hentoff, Nat. George Russell. New York: Broadcast Music,
      1960. 12p.

RUSSELL, HENRY

3522. Russell, Henry. Cheer! Boys, Cheer! Memories of Men and
      Music. London: J. Macqueen, 1895. 276p., illus.
          Autobiography of British entertainer and songwriter.
      Russell wrote Woodman, Spare That Tree, A Life On the
      Ocean Wave, and other standards.

RUSSELL, JOHNNY

*   Evensmo, Jan. The Tenor Saxophones of Henry Bridges, Robert
       Carroll, Herschel Evans, and Johnny Russell.
          * Cited above as item 1548.

RUSSELL, LILLIAN

3523. Burke, John. Duet In Diamonds. New York: Putnam, 1972.
          p., illus.

3524. Morell, Parker. Lillian Russell: the Era of Plush. New
       York: Random House, 1940. 319p., illus.

RUSSELL, ROSALIND

3525. Russell, Rosalind. Life Is a Banquet. With Chris Chase.
       New York: Random House, 1977; London: W.H. Allen, 1978.
       260p., illus., filmog., index.
          Autobiography.

SAVITT, JAN

3526. Hall, George. Jan Savitt and His Top Hatters. Whittier,
       California: Jazz Discographies Unlimited, n.d. (196?).   p.

       ————. Jan Savitt and His Orchestra. Spotswood, New Jersey:
       Joyce, 1974.   p.

SAVO, JIMMY

3527. Savo, Jimmy. I Bow To the Stones: Memories of a New York
       Childhood. Introduction by George Freedley. Drawings by
       Victor J. Dowling. New York: H. Frisch, 1963. 144p., illus.

SCOBEY, BOB

3528. Scobey, Jan. Jan Scobey Presents He Rambled! Till Cancer
       Cut Him Down: Bob Scobey, Dixieland Jazz Musician and Band-
       leader, 1916-1963. Northridge, California: Pal Publishing,
       1976. 344p., illus., index.
          Includes Cancer? What Can You Do!

SCOTT, CECIL

* Evensmo, Jan. The Tenor Saxophones of Cecil Scott, Elmer
  Williams, and Dick Wilson.
    * Cited above as item 1548.

SEDAKA, NEIL

3529. Sedaka, Neil. Laughter In the Rain: My Own Story. New
      York: Putnam's, 1982; London: Elm Tree Books, 1983. 252p.,
      illus., discog.
          Includes listing (partial) of his compositions.

SEEGER, PETE

3530. Seeger, Pete. The Incompleat Folksinger. Edited by Jo
      Metcalf Schwartz. New York: Simon and Schuster, 1972.
      596p., illus., bibliogs., discogs., index.
          Collection of his writings. Includes autobiographical
      material, profiles of other artists, practical advice, and
      social comment.

                              Biographies

3531. Citizens' Committee of California. The Communist Seeger
      Sings. Los Angeles: Citizens' Committee of California,
      1964.   p.
          Political attack.

3532. Dunaway, David King. How Can I Keep From Singing: Pete
      Seeger. New York: McGraw-Hill, 1982; London: Harrap, 1985.
         p., illus.

SELVIN, BEN

3533. Backensto, Woody. A Ben Selvin Discography. Woodbury, New
      Jersey: The Author, 1954. 53p.

SEX PISTOLS

3534. Moorcock, Michael. The Great Rock 'n' Roll Swindle. London:
      Virgin Books, 1980.   p., illus. (Reissued: 1981)
          Novelization of their story, loosely based on the motion
      picture account, same title; itself tenuously connected to
      the facts. 1980 edition is in newspaper format.

3535. Stevenson, Ray (comp.). The Sex Pistols File. London:
       Omnibus Pr., 1978. 64p., illus. Updated ed.: London:
       Omnibus Pr., 1979. 64p., illus.
          Compilation of press cuttings; with photographs by
       Stevenson.

3536. Vermorel, Fred, and Judy Vermorel. The Sex Pistols: the
       Inside Story. London: Universal, 1978.   p., illus. Rev.
       ed.: London: Star Books, 1981. 287p., illus.

                          Sid Vicious

3537. The Sid Vicious Family Album. London: Virgin Books, 1980.
       unpaged, illus.
          Family snapshots.

3538. Spungen, Deborah. And I Don't Want To Live This Life.
       London: Corgi, 1984.   p., illus.
          Mother of Nancy Spungen, girlfriend of Vicious, tells of
       her daughter's involvement with him, her drug abuse, and
       her death while in his company.

SHADOWS

3539. Shadows, The. The Story of The Shadows: an Autobiography.
       With Mike Read. Foreword by Cliff Richard. London: Elm
       Tree Books, 1983. 246p., illus., discog.
          Includes genealogical chart of the group.

                        Discographies

3540. Geddes, George Thomson. Foot Tapping: The Shadows, 1958-
       1978. Glasgow: The Author, 1978. 54p., bibliog.

              ————. The Shadows: a History and Discography. Glasgow:
       The Author, 1981. 178p., bibliog.

SHAND, JIMMY

3541. Phillips, David. Jimmy Shand. Dundee: D. Winter and Son,
       1976. 166p., illus., discog.

SHAPIRO, HELEN

3542. Janson, John S. Helen Shapiro, Pop Princess. London: New
       English Library, 1963. 126p., illus.

SHAW, ARTIE (pseud. of Abraham Isaac Arshawsky)

3543. Shaw, Artie. I Love You, I Hate You, Drop Dead! Variations
On a Theme. London: Phoenix House, 1966. 192p.
Short stories.

3544. ————. The Trouble With Cinderella: an Outline of Ident-
ity. New York: Farrar, Straus, and Young, 1952 (Reprinted:
New York: Da Capo Pr., 1979). 394p., illus. London:
Jarrolds, 1955. 279p., illus. New York: Collier, 1963.
352p., illus.
Autobiography.

Discographies

3545. Blandford, Edmund L. Artie Shaw: a Bio-Discography. Hastings, Sussex: Castle Books, 1973. 229p., illus., discog.

3546. Korst, Bill, and Charles Garrod. Artie Shaw and His Orchestra. Spotswood, New Jersey: Joyce, 1974.   p.

3547. Robertson, A. Artie Shaw, '36 to '55. (Place unknown): The
Author, 1971.   p.

3548. Strateman, Klaus. The Films of Artie Shaw, Glenn Miller,
and Tony Pastor: a Filmo-Discography. Menden, West Germany:
Jazzfreund, 1980. 53p., illus., discog., filmog.
Account of their appearances; with discography of long-
playing records taken from the soundtracks.

SHEA, GEORGE BEVERLY

3549. Shea, George Beverly. Songs That Lift the Heart: a Personal
Story. With Fred Bauer. Old Tappan, New Jersey: Revell,
1972. 125p., illus. London: Lakeland, 1973. 96p., illus.

3550. ————. Then Sings My Soul. With Fred Bauer. Old Tappan,
New Jersey: Revell, 1968. 168p., illus. London: Hodder and
Stoughton, 1968. 176p., illus.
Memoirs.

SHEPP, ARCHIE

3551. Cooke, Jack. Archie Shepp. Discography by Bruno Schiozzi.
Milan: Fratelli Fabbri, 1968. 16p., discog. (Il jazz, 24)
In Italian.

3552. Rissi, Mathias. Archie Shepp: Discography. Adliswil, West
Germany: The Author, 1977. 21p.

SHORE, DINAH

3553. Cassidy, Bruce. Dinah! a Biography. New York: Franklin
       Watts, 1979; New York: Berkley Publishing, 1980. 215p.,
       illus.

SHUBERT BROTHERS

3554. Stagg, Jerry. A Half-Century of Show Business and the
       Fabulous Empire of the Brothers Shubert. New York: Random
       House, 1968. 431p., illus., index.
           Includes listing of productions staged by Sam, J.J., and
       Lee Shubert.

SILLMAN, LEONARD DEXTER

3555. Sillman, Leonard Dexter. Here Lies Leonard Sillman,
       Straightened Out At Last: an Autobiography. Secaucus, New
       Jersey: Citadel Pr., 1959. 377p., illus.

SILVER, HORACE

3556. Kazan, Max. Horace Silver. Brussels: Dialogue, 1964.
       164p., illus., discog.

SILVESTER, VICTOR

3557. Silvester, Victor. Dancing Is My Life: an Autobiography.
       London: Heinemann, 1958. 230p., illus.

SIMON, PAUL, AND ARTHUR GARFUNKEL

3558. Cohen, Mitchell S. Simon and Garfunkel: a Biography In Words
       and Pictures. Edited by Greg Shaw. New York: Sire Books,
       1977.   p., illus.

3559. Humphries, Patrick. Bookends: the Simon and Garfunkel Story.
       London; New York: Proteus, 1982. 128p., illus., discog.

3560. Matthew-Walker, Robert. Simon and Garfunkel. Tunbridge
       Wells, Kent; New York: Hippocrene Books, 1984. 165p., illus.,
       discog., filmog., index.

3561. Swenson, John. Simon and Garfunkel: a Musical Biography.
       London: W.H. Allen, 1984. 222p., illus., discog., index.
       (Comet Books)

Simon, Paul, and Arthur Garfunkel (cont.)

Paul Simon

3562. Leigh, Spencer. Paul Simon: Now and Then. Liverpool:
       Raven Books, 1973. 110p., illus., bibliog., discog.

3563. Marsh, Dave. Paul Simon. New York: Quick Fox, 1978.   p.,
       illus.

SIMPLE MINDS

3564. Bos, Alfred. Simple Minds: the Race Is the Prize. London:
       Virgin Books, 1984. 128p., illus., discog.

3565. Thompson, Dave. Simple Minds. London: Omnibus Pr., 1985.
          p., illus., discog.

SIMS, JOHN HALEY "ZOOT"

3566. Astrup, Arne. The John Haley Sims (Zoot Sims) Discography.
       Lyngby, Denmark: Dansk Historisk Handbogsforlag, 1980.
       104p., illus.
          Bio-discography.

SINATRA, FRANK (pseud. of Francis Albert Sinatra)

3567. Sinatra, Frank. Sinatra on Sinatra. Compiled by Guy Yarwood.
       London: W.H. Allen, 1982. 128p., illus.
          Compiled from interviews and other sources.

Biographies

3568. Cariozi, George, Jr. Frank Sinatra: Is This Man Mafia?
       New York: Woodhill Pr., 1979.   p., illus.

3569. Douglas-Home, Robin. Sinatra. London: Michael Joseph; New
       York: Grosset and Dunlap, 1962. 64p., illus. London:
       Transworld Publishers, 1963. 110p., illus.

3570. Frank, Alan. Sinatra. London: Hamlyn, 1978 (Reissued: 1984).
       176p., illus., bibliog., discog., filmog., index.

3571. Goldstein, Norm. Frank Sinatra: Ol' Blue Eyes. New York:
       Holt, Rinehart, and Winston, 1983.   p., illus.

3572. Howlett, John. Frank Sinatra. London: Plexus Publishing,
       1980. 176p., illus., discog., filmog.

3573. Kahn, Ely Jacques, Jr. The Voice: the Story of an American
       Phenomenon (Francis Albert Sinatra). New York: Harper;
       London: Musicians Pr., 1947. 125p., illus.
           Material originally published in the New Yorker, October-
       December, 1946.

3574. Lonstein, Albert. Sinatra. New York; Bicester, Oxfordshire:
       Facts On File, 1985.   p., illus.
           Chronology.

3575. Moore, Thurston. The Complete Life of Frank Sinatra. New
       York: Pocket Magazines, 1955. 65p., illus. (Pocket
       Celebrity Scrapbooks, 1)

3576. Peters, Richard. The Frank Sinatra Scrapbook: His Life and
       Times in Words and Pictures. Incorporating The Sinatra
       Sessions: a Complete Listing of All His Recording Sessions,
       1939-1982, by Ed O'Brien and Scott P. Sayers, Jr. London:
       Pop Universal/Souvenir Pr., 1982. 160p., illus., discog.
           Incorporates item 3588. Appendix lists Sinatra societies.

3577. Rockwell, John. Sinatra: an American Classic. New York:
       Random House; London: Elm Tree Books, 1984. 253p., illus.,
       bibliog., discog., index. (A Rolling Stone Pr. Book)

3578. Romero, Jerry. Sinatra's Women. New York: Manor Books,
       1975.   p., illus.

3579. Scaduto, Anthony. Frank Sinatra. New York: Pinnacle Books;
       London: Michael Joseph, 1976; London: Sphere, 1977. 159p.,
       illus.
           Pinnacle Books edition published under the pseudonym
       "Tony Sciacca."

3580. Shaper, Hal. Sinatra: the Man and His Music. London: Wise
       Publications, 1975. 176p., illus., discog.
           Includes song lyrics.

3581. Shaw, Arnold. Sinatra: Twentieth Century Romantic. New
       York: Holt, Rinehart, and Winston, 1968. 371p., illus.,
       discog., filmog., index.

       ————. Sinatra: Retreat of the Romantic. London: W.H.
       Allen, 1968. 392p., illus., discog., filmog., index.
       London: Hodder and Stoughton, 1970. 381p., illus., discog.,
       filmog., index.

3582. The Sinatra Story. London: Amalgamated Pr., 1958. 66p.,
       illus. (Fans' Star Library)

3583. Turner, John Frayn. Frank Sinatra: a Personal Portrait.
       Tunbridge Wells, Kent: Midas Books; New York: Hippocrene
       Books, 1983. 160p., illus., discog., filmog., index.

Sinatra, Frank (cont.)

3584. Wilson, Earl. Sinatra. New York: Macmillan; London: W.H.
       Allen; New York: Collier Books, 1976; London: Star Books,
       1978. 380p., illus.

                            Discographies

3585. Deacon, John. The Frank Sinatra Discography. (Place
       unknown): The Author, 1961. 116p.

3586. Hainsworth, Brian. Songs By Sinatra, 1939-1970. Leeds,
       Yorkshire: The Author, 1973. 92p.
          Chronological arrangement. Lists all known recordings.

3587. Lonstein, Albert I., and Vito R. Marino. The Compleat
       Sinatra: Discography, Filmography, Television Appearances,
       Motion Picture Appearances, Radio Appearances, Concert
       Appearances, Stage Appearances. Ellenville, New York:
       Cameron Publications, 1970. 383p., illus., bibliogs.

3588. O'Brien, Ed, and Scott P. Sayers, Jr. The Sinatra Sessions:
       a Complete Listing of All His Recording Sessions, 1939-
       1980. Dallas, Texas: The Sinatra Society of America, 1980.
       125p., illus.
          Incorporated (with updating to 1982) into item 3576.

3589. Ridgway, John. The Sinatra File. Birmingham England: The
       Author.
       Part One: Non Commercial. 1977. 310p., illus.
       Part Two: Commercial. 1978. 309p., illus., bibliog.
          Limited edition of one thousand copies.

                          Motion Pictures

3590. Ringgold, Gene, and Clifford McCarty. The Films of Frank
       Sinatra. Secaucus, New Jersey: Citadel Pr., 1971. 249p.,
       illus.

SINFIELD, PETE

3591. Sinfield, Pete. Under the Sky. Illustrated by Julia Fayer.
       Ipswich, Suffolk: Boydell Pr., 1974. 72p., illus.
          Poems and song lyrics by ex-member of King Crimson group.

SIOUXIE AND THE BANSHEES

3592. Stevenson, Ray. <u>Ray Stevenson's Siouxie and The Banshees
      Photo Book</u>. London: Symbiosis, 1983. 64p., illus.

SISSLE, NOBLE <u>see</u> BLAKE, EUBIE

SLACK, FREDDIE

3593. Edwards, Ernie. <u>Freddie Slack: a Complete Discography</u>.
      Whittier, California: Jazz Discographies Unlimited, 1965.
      17p. (Spotlight Series, 3)

SLADE

3594. Charlesworth, Chris. <u>Slade: Feel the Noize! An Illustrated
      Biography</u>. London: Omnibus Pr., 1984. 128p., illus.,
      discog.

3595. <u>Slade</u>. Hitchin, Hertfordshire: B.C. Enterprises, 1972.
      26p., illus.

3596. Tremlett, George. <u>The Slade Story</u>. London: Futura, 1975.
      128p., illus.

                              Periodicals

3597. <u>Slade News</u>. Edited by Dave Kemp. London. bi-monthly,
      1979-?

SLIK

3598. Tremlett, George. <u>Slik</u>. London: Futura, 1976. 144p.,
      illus.

SMALL FACES

   * Pidgeon, John. <u>Rod Stewart and the Changing Faces</u>.
         * Cited below as item 3663.

3599. Rawlings, Terry. <u>The Small Faces: All Our Yesterdays</u>.
      London: Riot Stories, 1982.   p., illus., discog.

SMITH, BESSIE

3600. Albertson, Chris. <u>Bessie: a Biography</u>. New York: Stein
       and Day; London: Barrie and Jenkins, 1972. 253p., illus.,
       bibliog., discog., index. London: Abacus, 1975. 224p.,
       illus., bibliog., discog., index.

3601. Moore, Carman. <u>Somebody's Angel Child: the Story of Bessie</u>
       Smith. New York: Crowell, 1969. 121p., illus., bibliog.,
       discog., index. New York: Dell, 1975. 126p., illus.,
       bibliog., discog., index. (Women in America)

3602. Oliver, Paul. <u>Bessie Smith</u>. London: Cassell, 1959; New
       York: A.S. Barnes, 1961. 83p., illus., bibliog., discog.
       (Kings of Jazz, 3)
           Incorporated into item 1566.

                          Discographies

3603. Brooks, Edward. <u>The Bessie Smith Companion: a Critical and</u>
       <u>Detailed Appreciation of the Recordings</u>. Wheathampstead,
       Hertfordshire: Cavendish, 1982; New York: Da Capo Pr.,
       1983. 229p., illus., bibliog., discog., index.

SMITH, HARRY BACHE

3604. Smith, Harry Bache. <u>First Nights and First Editions</u>.
       Boston: Little, Brown, 1931. 325p., illus., indexes.
           Autobiography.

SMITH, JABBO

3605. Flückiger, Otto. <u>Discography of Jabbo Smith</u>. Including a
       note on Jabbo Smith by Johnny Simmen. Basle: Jazz Publicat-
       ions, 1962. 8p.

SMITH, PATTI

3606. Smith, Patti. <u>Babel</u>. New York: Putnam's; London: Virago,
       1978. 205p., illus.
           Collection of old and new poems; prose; lyrics; and
       reminiscences.

3607. ———. <u>Early Morning Dreams</u>. (Place unknown): The Author,
       1972. 8p.
           Poems. Limited edition of one hundred copies.

3608.   ————. Kodak. Philadlephia: Middle Earth Bookshop, 1972.
         16p. (Middle Earth Pamphlet Series, 3)
              Poems. Limited edition of one hundred signed copies.

3609.   ————. Seventh Heaven. Folcroft, Pennsylvania: Folcroft
         Pr.; Yeadon, New York: Telegraph Books, 1972. 47p., illus.
         Poems.

3610.   ————. Witt. New York: Gotham Book Mart, 1973. 43p.
              Poems.

3611.   ————, and Tom Verlaine. The Night. London: Aloes Books,
         1976.   p.
              Poem. Limited edition of five hundred copies.

                              Biographies

3612.   Patti Smith: High On Rebellion. Manchester, England:
         Babylon Books, 1980. unpaged, illus., discog.

SMITH, WILLIE "THE LION"

3613.   Smith, Willie. Music On My Mind: the Memoirs of an American
         Pianist. With George Hoefer. Foreword by Duke Ellington.
         Garden City, New York: Doubleday, 1964; London: MacGibbon
         and Kee, 1965; New York (with a new introduction by John S.
         Wilson): Da Capo Pr., 1975 (Roots of Jazz). 318p., illus.,
         bibliog., discog., index.
              Includes listing of his compositions.

SNOW, JIMMIE RODGERS

3614.   Snow, Jimmie Rodgers. I Cannot Go Back. Plainfield, New
         Jersey: Logos International, 1977.   p., illus.
              Memoir, by son of Hank Snow, himself a performer.

SOFT CELL

3615.   Tebbutt, Simon. Soft Cell: the Authorized Biography. Fore-
         word by Marc Almond. London: Sidgwick and Jackson, 1984.
         136p., illus., discog., index.

SONDHEIM, STEPHEN

3616.   Zadan, Craig. Sondheim and Company. New York: Macmillan;
         London: Collier-Macmillan, 1976. 279p., illus., discog.,
         index.

SONNY AND CHER see CHER

SONS OF THE PIONEERS

3617. Griffis, Ken. Hear My Song: the Story of the Celebrated
       Sons of the Pioneers. Los Angeles: John Edwards Memorial
       Foundation, 1974. 148p., illus., bibliog., discog. (J.E.M.F.
       Special Series, 5)

SOTHERN, GEORGIA

3618. Sothern, Georgia. Georgia: My Life In Burlesque. New York:
       New American Library, 1972. 351p., illus. (A Signet Book)

SOUSA, JOHN PHILIP

3619. Sousa, John Philip. Marching Along: Recollections of Men,
       Women, and Music. Boston: Hale, Cushman, and Flint, 1928
       (Reissued: 1941). 384p., illus.
            Autobiography. Includes listing of his works.

3620. ———. Through the Year With Sousa: Excerpts From the
       Operas, Marches, Miscellaneous Compositions, Novels, Letters,
       Magazine Articles, Songs, Sayings, and Rhymes of John Philip
       Sousa. New York: Crowell, 1910. 209p.
            Day-by-day arrangement.

                              Works

3621. Bierley, Paul E. John Philip Sousa: a Descriptive Catalog
       of His Works. Urbana; London: University of Illinois Pr.,
       1973. 177p., illus., bibliog. (Music In American Life)
            Brief biography, followed by listing of approximately
       five hundred musical and literary works. Classified.

                           Biographies

3622. Berger, Kenneth Walter. The March King and His Band: the
       Story of John Philip Sousa. New York: Exposition Pr., 1957.
       95p., illus., discog.
            Includes listing of his works, and band rosters.

3623. Bierley, Paul E. John Philip Sousa: American Phenomenon.
       New York: Appleton-Century-Crofts, 1973. 261p., illus.,
       bibliog., index.
            Includes listing of his musical and literary works.

3624. Lewiton, Mina. <u>John Philip Sousa: the March King</u>. Illus-
       trated by Howard Simon. New York: Didier, 1944. 60p.,
       illus.

3625. Lingg, Ann M. <u>John Philip Sousa</u>. New York: Holt, Rinehart,
       and Winston, 1954. 250p., illus.

Discographies

3626. Smart, James R. <u>The Sousa Band: a Discography</u>. Washington,
       D.C.: Library of Congress, 1970. 123p.
              Lists 1,052 items.

SPAETH, SIGMUND

3627. Spaeth, Sigmund. <u>Fifty Years With Music</u>. New York: Fleet,
       1959; Westport, Conn.: Greenwood Pr., 1977. 288p., illus.
              Memoir of his career with popular and other music forms.

SPANDAU BALLET

3628. Spandau Ballet. <u>Spandau Ballet In Their Own Words</u>. Comp-
       iled by Pearce Marchbank. London: Omnibus Pr., 1983. 32p.,
       illus.
              Compiled from interviews.

Songs

3629. Kemp, Gary. <u>Spandau Ballet: the Official Lyric Book. The
       Complete Words to All of Spandau Ballet's Songs</u>. London:
       Reformation, 1983. 32p., illus.
              Texts of songs by group member Kemp.

Biographies

3630. Johnson, David, and Robert Elms. <u>Angel Boys: the Authorised
       Biography of Spandau Ballet</u>. London: Sidgwick and Jackson,
       1985. 144p., illus., discog.

3631. Sutherland, Steve. <u>Spandau Ballet: the Full Story</u>. London:
       I.P.C., 1983. 18p., illus., discog.
              Issued as supplement to <u>Melody Maker</u>, September 24, 1983.

SPECTOR, PHIL

3632. Finnis, Rob. The Phil Spector Story. London: Rock On Books,
      1975.   p., illus., discogs.

3633. Williams, Richard. Out Of His Head: the Sound of Phil
      Spector. New York: Outerbridge and Lazard; New York: Dutton,
      1972. 206p., illus., bibliog. refs., discog. London:
      Abacus, 1974. 156p., illus., discog.
          Includes listing of his compositions.

                            Periodicals

3634. Philately. Edited by Mick Patrick. 21D Grove Park Road,
      London W.4. irreg., 1984- .

SPEER FAMILY

3635. Becker, Paula. Let the Song Go On: Fifty Years of Gospel
      Singing With the Speer Family. Nashville: Impact Books,
      1971. 175p., illus.

SPINNERS

3636. Stuckey, David. The Spinners: Fried Bread and Brandy-O.
      London: Robson Books, 1983. 157p., illus.
          British folk group.

SPIVAK, CHARLIE

3637. Hall, George. Charlie Spivak and His Orchestra. Laurel,
      Maryland: Jazz Discographies Unlimited, 1972.   p.

SPRINGSTEEN, BRUCE

3638. Gambaccini, Peter. Bruce Springsteen. New York: Quick Fox,
      1979. 127p., illus., discog.

3639. Goldsmith, Lynn. Springsteen. London: Sidgwick and Jackson,
      1985. 96p., illus., discog.

3640. Humphries, Patrick, and Chris Hunt. Blinded By the Light.
      London: Plexus Publishing, 1985.   p., illus., discog.

3641. Kamin, Philip, and Peter Goddard. Springsteen Live. Toronto:

Stoddart, 1984; London: New English Library, 1985.   128p.,
illus.
Performance photographs by Kamin; text by Goddard.

3642. Lynch, Kate. Springsteen. London; New York: Proteus, 1984.
128p., illus., discog.

3643. Marsh, Dave. Born To Run: the Bruce Springsteen Story.
Garden City, New York: Doubleday, 1979. 176p., illus.
(Dolphin Books). Rev. ed.: London: Omnibus Pr., 1981.
192p., illus.
Revised edition includes extra chapter.

Periodicals

3644. Backstreets. Seattle, Washington. irreg., 198?-?

3645. Candy's Room. Edited by Gary Desmond. Liverpool. irreg.,
1981-?

3646. Thunder Road. Bogota, New Jersey. irreg., 1977-81.

SQUIER, BILLY

3647. Atkinson, Terry, and Martin Cerf. Billy Squier: an Illustrated History. Port Chester, New York: Cherry Lane, 1983.
48p., illus., discog.

STARDUST, ALVIN

3648. Tremlett, George. The Alvin Stardust Story. London: Futura,
1976. 144p., illus.

STATUS QUO

3649. Hibbert, Tom. Status Quo. London: Omnibus Pr., 1982.
81p., illus., discog.

3650. Jeffries, Neil. Status Quo: Rockin' All Over the World.
London; New York: Proteus, 1985.   p., illus., discog.

3651. Shearlaw, John. Status Quo: the Authorized Biography. Fore-
face by the Band. London: Sidgwick and Jackson, 1979. 152p.,
illus., discog., index. Rev. ed.: London: Sidgwick and
Jackson, 1982. 168p., illus., discog., index.

3652. Young, Bob, and John Shearlaw. Status Quo Again and Again.
London: Sidgwick and Jackson, 1984. 104p., illus., discog.

STEELE, TOMMY (pseud. of Thomas Hicks)

3653. Kennedy, John. Tommy Steele: the Facts About a Teenage
      Idol, and an "Inside" Picture of Show Business. London:
      Souvenir Pr., 1958. 166p., illus. London (as Tommy Steele):
      Transworld Publishers, 1959. 189p., illus. (Corgi Books)
          By his manager.

3654. Tommy Steele. London: Amalgamated Pr., 1959. 64p., illus.
      (Fans' Star Library, 25)

3655. The Wonderful Tommy Steele: Picture-Story Album. Text by
      Dick Tatham. London: Record Mirror/Cardfont Publishers,
      1957. 28p., illus.

STEVENS, CAT (pseud. of Steven Demetri Georgiou, later Yusuf Islam)

3656. Stevens, Cat. Teaser and the Firecat. London: B. Jacobson,
      1972. 43p., illus.
          Children's book; text and illustrations by Stevens.

                          Biography

3657. Charlesworth, Chris. Cat Stevens. London; New York:
      Proteus, 1984. 94p., illus., discog.

STEVENS, SHAKIN' (pseud. of Michael Barratt)

3658. Barrett, Paul. Shakin' Stevens. With Hilary Hayward.
      London: Star Books, 1983. 160p., illus., discog.

3659. Leese, Martyn. Shakin' Stevens. London; New York: Proteus,
      1981. 48p., illus., discog. (Prize Books)

STEWART, ROD

3660. Burton, Peter. Rod Stewart: a Life On the Town. London:
      New English Library, 1977. 120p., illus., discog.
          Includes songs.

3661. Jasper, Tony. Rod Stewart. London: Octopus, 1977. 94p.,
      illus., discog.

3662. Nelson, Paul, and Lester Bangs. Rod Stewart. New York:
      Delilah, 1981; London: Sidgwick and Jackson, 1982. 159p.,
      illus., discog.

3663. Pidgeon, John. Rod Stewart and the Changing Faces. St.
       Albans, Hertfordshire: Panther, 1976. 144p., illus.,
       discog.

3664. Tremlett, George. The Rod Stewart Story. London: Futura,
       1976. 143p., illus.

STONE, LEW

3665. Trodd, Kenith. Lew Stone: a Career In Music. London:
       Joyce Stone, 1971. 150p., illus., index.

STONEMAN, ERNEST V. "POP"

3666. John Edwards Memorial Foundation. The Early Recording
       Career of Ernest V. "Pop" Stoneman: a Bio-Discography.
       Los Angeles: John Edwards Memorial Foundation, 1968. 20p.,
       illus. (J.E.M.F. Special Series, 1)

STRANGLERS

3667. Black, Jet (pseud.). Much Ado About Nothing. London:
       Stranglers Information Service, 1981.   p.
          Group member's account of 1980 riot at Stranglers'
       performance, Nice University, France.

3668. Cornwell, Hugh. Inside Information. London: Stranglers
       Information Service, 1980. 28p.
          Account of group member's 1980 prison sentence on drug
       charge.

                          Periodicals

3669. Strangled. Edited by Tony Moon. London. irreg., 1978-?

STREISAND, BARBRA

3670. Black, Jonathan. Streisand. New York: Leisure Books,
       1975. 187p., illus.

3671. Brady, Frank. Barbra: an Illustrated Biography. New York:
       Grosset and Dunlap; London: Blandford Pr., 1979. 152p.,
       illus.

Streisand, Barbra (cont.)

3672. Jordan, René. The Greatest Star: the Barbra Streisand
       Story. An Unauthorized Biography. New York: Putnam, 1975;
       London (as Streisand: an Unauthorised Biography): W.H. Allen,
       1976. 253p., discog., filmog., index. New York: Berkley
       Publishing, 1977. 242p., discog., filmog., index.

3673. Spada, James. Streisand: the Woman and the Legend. With
       Christopher Nickens. Garden City, New York: Doubleday,
       1981; London: W.H. Allen, 1982; London: Comet Books, 1983.
       250p., illus.

3674. Teti, Frank, and Karen Moline. Streisand Through the Lens.
       New York: Delilah; London: Sidgwick and Jackson, 1982.
       144p., illus.
           Photographs edited by Teti; text by Moline. Includes
       interviews with the photographers.

3675. Zec, Donald, and Anthony Fowles. Barbra: a Biography of
       Barbra Streisand. London: New English Library, 1981. 253p.,
       illus., discog., filmog., index. 2nd. ed.: London: New
       English Library, 1982. 384p., illus., discog., filmog.,
       index.

                        Motion Pictures

3676. Castell, David. The Films of Barbra Streisand. Bembridge,
       Isle of Wight: B.C.W. Publishing, 1975. Rev. ed.: Bembridge,
       Isle of Wight: B.C.W. Publishing, 1977. 47p., illus.,
       filmog.

3677. Spada, James. Barbra: the First Decade. The Films and
       Career of Barbra Streisand. Secaucus, New Jersey: Citadel
       Pr., 1974. 224p., illus., filmog.

                        Periodicals

3678. Barbra. Edited by Christopher Nickens. 7985 Santa Monica
       Boulevard, Suite 109, Hollywood, California 90046. quarterly,
       197?- .

STYNE, JULE (pseud. of Julius Kerwin Stein)

3679. Taylor, Theodore. Jule: the Story of Composer Jule Styne.
       A Revue in Many Acts and Scenes. New York: Random House,
       1978.   p., illus.

SUMNER, JOHN DANIEL

3680. Sumner, John Daniel. _J.D. Sumner: Gospel Music Is My Life._
       With Bob Terrell. Nashville: Impact Books, 1971. 208p.,
       illus.

SUTTON, RALPH

3681. Shacter, James D. _Piano Man: the Story of Ralph Sutton._
       Chicago: Jaynar Pr., 1975. 244p., illus., discog., index.

SWIFT, KAY

3682. Swift, Kay. _Who Could Ask For Anything More?_ New York:
       Simon and Schuster, 1943. 211p., illus.
          Autobiography of songwriter.

TALKING HEADS

3683. Miles (_pseud. of_ Barry Miles). _Talking Heads._ London:
       Omnibus Pr., 1981; New York: Delilah, 1982. 49p., illus.,
       discog.

3684. Reese, Krista. _The Name of This Book is Talking Heads._
       London; New York: Proteus, 1983.   p., illus., discog.

                          Periodicals

3685. _Talking Heads._ Edited by Simon Robinson. 8 Herbert Road,
       Nether Edge, Sheffield, Yorkshire. irreg., 1984- .

TATUM, ARTHUR "ART"

3686. Jepsen, Jorgen Grunnet. _Discography of Art Tatum; Bud
       Powell._ Biographical notes by Knud H. Ditlevsen. Brande,
       Denmark: Debut Records, 1961. 28p.

3687. Laubich, Arnold, and Ray Spencer. _Art Tatum: a Guide to His
       Recorded Music._ Metuchen, New Jersey; London: Scarecrow Pr./
       Institute of Jazz Studies, Rutgers University, 1982. 359p.
       (Studies in Recorded Jazz, 2)
          Chronological arrangement.

TAUBER, RICHARD

3688.   Castle, Charles. <u>This Was Richard Tauber</u>. With Diana
        Napier Tauber. London: W.H. Allen, 1971. 209p., illus.,
        index.

3689.   Tauber, Diana Napier. <u>My Heart and I</u>. London: Evans,
        1959. 208p., illus.
            By his wife.

3690.   ————. <u>Richard Tauber</u>. Foreword by Charles B. Cochran.
        Glasgow: Art and Educational Publishers, 1949; New York: Da
        Capo Pr., 1980.   p., illus., index.

TEAGARDEN, JACK

3691.   Smith, Jay D., and Len Guttridge. <u>Jack Teagarden: the Story
        of a Jazz Maverick</u>. London: Cassell, 1960; New York: Da
        Capo Pr., 1976. 208p., illus., discog., index.

                          Discographies

3692.   Smith, Jay D. <u>Big Gate: a Chronological Listing of the
        Recorded Works of Jack Teagarden From 1928 to 1950</u>. Wash-
        ington, D.C.: The Author, 1951. 36p., illus.

3693.   Waters, Howard J., <u>Jr</u>. <u>Jack Teagarden's Music, His Career,
        and Recordings</u>. Foreword by Paul Whiteman. Stanhope, New
        Jersey: Walter C. Allen, 1960. 222p., illus., bibliog.,
        index. (Jazz Monographs, 3)
            Bio-discography.

TEARDROP EXPLODES

3694.   Cooper, Mark. <u>Liverpool Explodes: The Teardrop Explodes;
        Echo and The Bunnymen</u>. London: Sidgwick and Jackson, 1982.
        96p., illus., discog., index.
            Includes the story of Echo and The Bunnymen group.

TEMPEST, MARIE (<u>pseud. of</u> Marie Susan Etherington)

3695.   Bolitho, Hector. <u>Marie Tempest</u>. London: Cobden Sanderson,
        1936. 345p., illus.

3696.   <u>The Marie Tempest Birthday Book</u>. With an introductory
        appreciation by Sidney Dark. London: Stanley Paul, 1913.
        142p., illus.

TEMPLE, SHIRLEY

3697. Temple, Shirley. <u>My Young Life</u>. Garden City, New York:
       Doubleday, 1945.   p., illus.

Biographies

3698. Basinger, Jeannie. <u>Shirley Temple</u>. New York: Pyramid
       Publications, 1975. 160p., illus., bibliog.

3699. Burdick, Loraine. <u>The Shirley Temple Scrapbook</u>. Middle
       Village, New York: Jonathan David Publishers, 1975.   p.,
       illus.

3700. David, Lester, and Irene David. <u>The Shirley Temple Story</u>.
       New York: Putnam's, 1983; London: Robson Books, 1984. 224p.,
       illus., bibliog., filmog., index.

3701. Eby, Lois. <u>Shirley Temple</u>. Derby, Conn.: Monarch Books,
       1962.   p., illus.

3702. Smith, Patricia R. <u>Shirley Temple Dolls and Collectibles</u>.
       Paducah, Kentucky: Collector Books, 1977. 144p., illus.

3703. Windeler, Robert. <u>Shirley Temple</u>. London: W.H. Allen,
       1976; Secaucus, New Jersey (as <u>The Films of Shirley Temple</u>):
       Citadel Pr., 1978. 160p., illus., filmog., index.

TEN C.C.

3704. Creme, Lol, and Kevin Godley. <u>The Fun Starts Here: Out-
       Takes From a Rock Memoir</u>. London: Arrow Books, 1981.   p.,
       illus.
           Group members Creme and Godley satirize the rock business.

3705. Tremlett, George. <u>The 10 c.c. Story</u>. London: Futura, 1975.
       p., illus.

TERRISS, ELLALINE (<u>pseud. of</u> Ellaline Lewin)

3706. Terriss, Ellaline. <u>Ellaline Terriss, By Herself and With
       Others</u>. London: Cassell, 1928. 305p., illus.
           Autobiography. Terriss was married to Seymour Hicks.

3707. ———. <u>Just a Little Bit of String</u>. Foreword by Beverley
       Nicholls. London: Hutchinson, 1955. 296p., illus.
           Further autobiography.

TERRY, CLARK

3708. Radzitzky, Carlos. A 1960-1967 Clark Terry Discography.
       With bibliographical notes. Antwerp: The Author, 1968.
       48p. (United Hot Club of Europe Publications, 1)

TERRY, ELLEN

3709. Terry, Ellen. The Story of My Life. Woodbridge, Suffolk:
       Boydell Pr., 1982. 240p. (Bookmarks)

Biography

3710. Fecher, Constance. Bright Star: a Portrait of Ellen Terry.
       New York: Farrar, Straus, and Giroux, 1970; London: Gollancz,
       1971. 236p., illus., bibliog., index.

THEODORAKIS, MIKIS

3711. Giannaris, George. Mikis Theodorakis: Music and Social
       Change. New York: Praeger, 1972; London: Allen and Unwin,
       1973. 322p., illus., bibliog., discog., index.

THOMAS, B.J.

3712. Thomas, B.J. Home Where I Belong. As told to Jerry B.
       Jenkins. Waco, Texas: Word Books, 1978. 150p., illus.
          Autobiography.

THOMPSON TWINS

3713. Thompson Twins. Thompson Twins In Their Own Words. Compiled
       by Pearce Marchbank. London: Omnibus Pr., 1984. 32p., illus.

Biographies

3714. Hizer, Bruno. Thompson Twins. London; New York: Proteus,
       1984. 32p., illus., discog.

3715. Rouse, Rose. The Thompson Twins: an Official Biography.
       London: Virgin Books, 1985. 128p., illus., discog.

THORNHILL, CLAUDE

3716.1 Edwards, Ernie, George Hall, and Bill Korst. <u>The Sound of</u>
<u>Claude Thornhill and His Orchestra</u>. Introduction by Jack
McKinney. Whittier, California: Jazz Discographies Unlim-
ited, 1965. 25p. <u>Rev. ed.</u>: Whittier, California: Erngeobil
Publications, 1967. 25p.

3716.2 Garrod, Charles. <u>Claude Thornhill and His Orchestra</u>.
Spotswood, New Jersey: Joyce, 1975.   p.

TILLEY, VESTA

3716.3 Tilley, Vesta. <u>Recollections of Vesta Tilley</u>. Foreword by
Oswald Stoll. Appreciation by Alfred Butt. London: Hutchinson, 1934. 295p., illus.

TINY TIM

3716.4 Tiny Tim (<u>pseud</u>.). <u>Beautiful Thoughts</u>. Garden City, New
York: Doubleday, 1969. 44p., illus.

                        Biographies

3716.5 Larkin, Rochelle, and Barry Weiser. <u>The True, Fantastic</u>
<u>Story of Tiny Tim</u>. New York: Corncob, 1968. 74p., illus.

3716.6 Stein, Harry. <u>Tiny Tim</u>. Chicago: <u>Playboy</u> Pr., 1976. 243p.,
illus.

TIOMKIN, DIMITRI

3716.7 Tiomkin, Dimitri. <u>Please Don't Hate Me</u>. With Prosper
Buranelli. Garden City, New York: Doubleday, 1959. 261p.,
illus.
        Autobiography.

TODD, MICHAEL

3716.8 Cohn, Art. <u>The Nine Lives of Michael Todd</u>. New York: Random
House, 1958. 396p., illus. London: Hutchinson, 1959. 304p.,
illus.

TOPOL, CHAIM

3716.9 Topol, Chaim. _Topol_. London: Weidenfeld and Nicolson,
        1981. 222p., illus., index.

TOYAH (_pseud. of_ Toyah Willcox)

3716.10 Evans, Gayna. _Toyah_. London; New York: Proteus, 1984.
        32p., illus., discog.

3716.11 West, Mike. _Toyah!_ Manchester, England: Babylon Books;
        London: Omnibus Pr., 1982. 80p., illus., discog.

TRAPP FAMILY SINGERS

3716.12 Trapp, Maria Augusta von. _Maria_. Carol Stream, Illinois:
        Creation House, 1972. 203p., illus. London: Coverdale
        House, 1973. 188p., illus.
           Autobiography.

3716.13 ———. _The Story of The Trapp Family Singers_. Philadel-
        phia: Lippincott, 1949. 309p., illus. London: Geoffrey
        Bles, 1953. 287p., illus. Garden City, New York: Doubleday,
        1957. 312p., illus. (Image Books). New York: Scholastic,
        1965. 380p., illus.

        ———. _The Sound of Music: Based on The Story of The Trapp
        Family Singers_. London: Fontana, 1965. 253p., illus.

        ———. _The Sound of Music: The Story of The Trapp Family
        Singers_. London: White Lion, 1976. 287p., illus.

3716.14 ———. _The Trapp Family On Wheels_. With Ruth T. Murdoch.
        Philadelphia: Lippincott, 1959. 309p., illus. Garden City,
        New York: Doubleday, 1959. 199p., illus. (Image Books).
        London: Geoffrey Bles, 1960. 190p., illus. London: Fontana,
        1966. 192p.

3716.15 ———. _Yesterday, Today, and For Ever_. Philadelphia:
        Lippincott, 1952. 220p. London: Geoffrey Bles, 1956. 192p.
        London: Fontana, 1967. 160p.
           Emphasis on the Family's Christian outlook and life.

3716.16 Wilhelm, Hans. _The Trapp Family Book_. London: Heinemann,
        1983. 88p., illus.
           Aimed at younger readers. Includes music.

TRAVOLTA, JOHN

3716.17 Munshower, Suzanne. <u>Meet John Travolta</u>. New York: Sunridge
         Pr., 1976.   p., illus.

         ————. <u>The John Travolta Scrapbook: an Illustrated Bio-
         graphy</u>. London: Pop Universal/Souvenir Pr., 1978. 121p.,
         illus.
            Adaption.

         ————. <u>John Travolta</u>. With Barbara Williams Prabhu. New
         York: Grosset and Dunlap, 1979. 92p., illus.
            Abridgement.

3716.18 Reeves, Michael. <u>Travolta! A Photo Biography</u>. New York:
         Jove Publications, 1978. 272p., illus.

3716.19 <u>Travolta Superstar Special</u>! London: I.P.C. Magazines, 1978.
         48p., illus.

                              Periodicals

3716.20 <u>John Travolta</u>. London. monthly, September 1978-October
         1979.

TUCKER, SOPHIE (<u>pseud. of</u> Sonia Kalish)

3716.21 Tucker, Sophie. <u>Some of These Days: an Autobiography</u>. With
         Dorothy Giles. Garden City, New York: Doubleday, 1945.
         309p., illus. London: Hammond, 1948. 293p., illus.

                              Biography

3716.22 Freedland, Michael. <u>Sophie: the Sophie Tucker Story</u>. London:
         Woburn Pr., 1978. 221p., illus.

TURNER, BRUCE

3716.23 Turner, Bruce. <u>Hot Air, Cool Music</u>. London: Quartet, 1984.
         248p., illus., discog., index.
            Autobiography of British jazzman.

TURNER, TINA

3716.24 Agee, Philip. <u>Tina Pie</u>. New Haven, Conn.: The Author, 1968.
         unpaged, illus.

Turner, Tina (cont.)

3716.25 Olmeca (pseud.). <u>Tina Turner</u>. London; New York: Proteus,
         1985.   p., illus., discog.

U2

3716.26 Thomas, Dave. <u>U2: Stories For Boys</u>. London; New York:
         Proteus, 1985.   p., illus., discog.

UB 40

3716.27 <u>Portraits: a Photojournal of UB 40 On Tour</u>. Solihull, West
         Midlands: Fairline, 1984. 112p., illus.

ULTRAVOX

3716.28 Ultravox. <u>Ultravox In Their Own Words</u>. London: Omnibus Pr.,
         1984. 32p., illus.
            Compiled from interviews.

                              Biography

3716.29 The Past, Present, and Future of Ultravox. London: <u>In The
         City</u>, 1980. 33p., illus.

VALLÉE, RUDY

3716.30 Vallée, Rudy. <u>Let the Chips Fall</u>. Harrisburg, Pennsylvania:
         Stackpole Books, 1975. 320p., illus., index.
            Autobiography.

3716.31 ————. <u>Vagabond Dreams Come True</u>. New York: Dutton, 1930.
         262p., illus.
            Autobiography.

3716.32 ————, and Gil McKean. <u>My Time Is Your Time: the Story of
         Rudy Vallée</u>. New York: Ivan Obolensky, 1962. 244p., illus.
            Autobiography.

VANBRUGH, IRENE

3716.33 Vanbrugh, Irene. <u>To Tell My Story</u>. London: Hutchinson,
         1948. 217p., illus.

VAN HALEN, EDDIE

3716.34 Kamin, Philip, and Peter Goddard. <u>Van Halen</u>. Toronto:
        Stoddart Publishing; London: Sidgwick and Jackson, 1984.
        128p., illus.
            Performance photographs by Kamin; text by Goddard.

3716.35 Shearlaw, John. <u>Van Halen: Jumpin' For the Dollar</u>. London:
        Zomba Books, 1984. 96p., illus., discog. (Rock Masters)

VAN PALLANDT, NINA

3716.36 Van Pallandt, Nina. <u>Nina</u>. New York: Walker, 1973; London:
        Hale, 1974. 221p., illus.
            Autobiography of member of folk duo Nina and Frederick.

VAUGHAN, FRANKIE (<u>pseud. of</u> Frank Ableson)

3716.37 Vaughan, Frankie. <u>The Frankie Vaughan Story. By Himself</u>.
        London: Pemrow, 1957. 66p., illus.

VAUGHAN, SARAH

3716.38 Leydi, Roberto. <u>Sarah Vaughan</u>. Milan: Ricordi, 1961.
        100p., illus.
            In Italian.

VECSEY, ARMAND

3716.39 Vecsey, Armand. <u>The Fiddler of The Ritz</u>. New York:
        William F. Payson, 1931. 308p.
            Memoir of his career as bandleader at London's Savoy
        Hotel, and later at New York's Ritz.

VELVET UNDERGROUND

3716.40 Bockris, Victor, and Gerard Malanga. <u>Up-Tight: the Velvet
        Underground Story</u>. London: Omnibus Pr., 1983.   p., illus.

3716.41 Clapton, Diana. <u>Lou Reed and The Velvet Underground</u>.
        London; New York: Proteus, 1983. 128p., illus., discog.

3716.42 Trevena, Nigel. <u>Lou Reed and The Velvets</u>. Redruth, Corn-
        wall: The Author, 1973.   p., illus., discog. New York:
        Bantam, 1977.   p., illus., discog.

VINCENT, GENE (pseud. of Vincent Eugene Craddock)

3716.43 Foster, Neil. A Tribute To Gene Vincent. Prescott, Mersey-
         side: The Author, 1979.   p., illus., discog.

3716.44 Hagarty, Britt. The Day the World Turned Blue: a Biography
         of Gene Vincent. Vancouver: Talon, 1983; Poole, Dorset:
         Blandford Pr., 1984. 262p., illus., bibliog., discog.

3716.45 Lautrey, Gerard. The Gene Vincent Story. Saulon La Chapelle,
         France: The Author, 1979. 2 vols.,   p., illus., discog.
         Includes press cuttings.

VINTON, BOBBY

3716.46 Vinton, Bobby. The Polish Prince. With Robert E. Burger.
         New York: M. Evans, 1978.   p., illus.
         Autobiography.

WAKEMAN, RICK

3716.47 Wooding, Dan. Rick Wakeman: the Caped Crusader. Foreword
         by Elton John. London: Hale, 1978. 192p., illus., discog.,
         filmog., index. St. Albans, Hertfordshire: Panther, 1979.
         206p., illus., discog., filmog., index.

WALLER, THOMAS WRIGHT "FATS"

3716.48 Fox, Charles. Fats Waller. London: Cassell, 1960; New
         York: A.S. Barnes, 1961. 89p., illus., bibliog. notes,
         discog. (Kings of Jazz, 7)
         Incorporated into item 1566.

3716.49 Gee, John (ed.). Waller and Johnson. Hemel Hempstead,
         Hertfordshire: Society for Jazz Appreciation in the Younger
         Generation, 1945. 24p., illus.
         Includes account of Bunk Johnson.

3716.50 Kirkeby, W.T. (ed.). Ain't Misbehavin': the Story of Fats
         Waller. In collaboration with Duncan P. Schiedt and Sinclair
         Traill. London: Peter Davies; New York: Dodd, Mead, 1966;
         New York: Da Capo Pr., 1975. 248p., illus., discog.
         Kirkeby was his manager.

3716.51 Vance, Joel. Fats Waller: His Life and Times. Chicago:
         Contemporary Books, 1977; London: Robson Books, 1979. 179p.,
         illus., bibliog., index.

3716.52 Waller, Maurice. Fats Waller. With Anthony Calabrese.
        Foreword by Michael Lipskin. New York: Schirmer Books,
        1977; London: Cassell, 1978. 235p., illus., discog., index.
        By his son. Includes listing of piano rolls.

Biographies

3716.53 Davies, John R.T. The Music of Thomas "Fats" Waller. With
        Complete Discography. London: Jazz Journal Publications,
        1950. 26p., illus.

        ————. ————. Revised by R.M. Cooke. London: Friends of
        Fats, 1953. 40p., illus.
            Includes piano rolls.

WARREN, HARRY

3716.54 Thomas, Tony. Harry Warren and the Hollywood Musical.
        Foreword by Bing Crosby. Secaucus, New Jersey: Citadel Pr.,
        1975. 344p., illus., index.

WATERS, ETHEL

3716.55 Waters, Ethel. His Eye Is On the Sparrow: an Autobiography.
        With Charles Samuels. Garden City, New York: Doubleday,
        1951. 278p., illus. London: W.H. Allen, 1951. 260p.,
        illus. New York: Bantam, 1952. 342p., illus. New York:
        Pyramid Publications, 1967; Westport, Conn.: Greenwood Pr.,
        1978. 278p., illus.

3716.56 ————. To Me It's Wonderful. Introduction by Eugenia
        Price and Joyce Blackburn. New York: Harper and Row, 1972.
        162p., illus., discog.
            Her involvement with Billy Graham's Crusades.

Biography

3716.57 Dekorte, Juliann. Finally Home. Old Tappan, New Jersey:
        Revell, 1978.   p., illus.

WATERS, MUDDY (pseud. of McKinley Morganfield)

    *   Rooney, James. Bossmen: Bill Monroe and Muddy Waters.
            * Cited above as item 3139.

WEBSTER, BEN

* Evensmo, Jan. <u>The Tenor Saxophone of Ben Webster, 1931-</u>
<u>1942</u>.
* Cited above as item 1548.

WEEDON, BERT

3716.58 Geddes, George Thomson. <u>Mister Guitar: Bert Weedon</u>.
Glasgow: The Author, 1980. 10p.
Discography.

WELK, LAWRENCE

3716.59 Welk, Lawrence. <u>Ah-One, Ah-Two! Life With My Musical Family</u>.
With Bernice McGeehan. Englewood Cliffs, New Jersey:
Prentice-Hall, 1974. 215p., illus.
Memoir, with description of his orchestra.

3716.60 ————. <u>Lawrence Welk's Musical Family Album</u>. With Bernice
McGeehan. Englewood Cliffs, New Jersey: Prentice-Hall, 1977.
150p., illus.
Includes brief commentary on each of his musicians; also
has songs.

3716.61 ————. <u>My America, Your America</u>. With Bernice McGeehan.
Englewood Cliffs, New Jersey: Prentice-Hall, 1976. 182p.,
illus. New York: Pocket Books, 1977. 205p., illus. (A
Kangaroo Book)
Memoirs.

3716.62 ————. <u>This I Believe</u>. With Bernice McGeehan. Englewood
Cliffs, New Jersey: Prentice-Hall, 1979.   p., illus.

3716.63 ————. <u>Wunnerful, Wunnerful: the Autobiography of Lawrence</u>
<u>Welk</u>. With Bernice McGeehan. Englewood Cliffs, New Jersey:
Prentice-Hall, 1971. 294p., illus. New York: Bantam, 1973.
404p., illus.

Biographies

3716.64 Govoni, Albert. <u>The Lawrence Welk Story</u>. New York: Pocket
Books, 1966. 122p., illus.

3716.65 Schwienher, William K. <u>Lawrence Welk: an American Institut-</u>
<u>ion</u>. Chicago: Nelson-Hall, 1980.   p., illus., bibliog.,
index.

3716.66 Zehnpfennig, Gladys. <u>Lawrence Welk, Champagne Music Man</u>.
Minneapolis: T.S. Denison, 1968. 390p., illus.

WEILL, KURT, AND LOTTE LENYA

3716.67 Weill, Kurt. <u>Ausgewählte Schriften</u>. Edited, with a foreword, by David Drew. Frankfurt/Main: Suhrkamp Verlag, 1975.
239p., illus., bibliog.

Biographies

3716.68 Drew, David. <u>Ueber Kurt Weill</u>. Frankfurt/Main: Suhrkamp
Verlag, 1975. 186p.
In German. Collection of biographical and critical items.

3716.69 Jarman, Douglas. <u>Kurt Weill: an Illustrated Biography</u>.
London: Orbis, 1982. 160p., illus., bibliog., discog.,
index.

3716.70 Kotschenreuther, Hellmut. <u>Kurt Weill</u>. Berlin: Wunsiedel,
1962. 103p., illus.

3716.71 Kowalke, Kim H. <u>Kurt Weill in Europe, 1900-1935: a Study of
His Music and Writings</u>. Ann Arbor, Michigan: U.M.I. Research
Pr., 1980. 589p., bibliog., index. (Studies in Musicology,
14)
Includes listing of his compositions, 1900-35.

3716.72 Marx, Henry (ed.). <u>Weill-Lenya</u>. New York: Goethe House,
1976. 46p., illus.
Linked with exhibition at New York's Lincoln Center,
November 1976 to June 1977.

3716.73 Sanders, Ronald. <u>The Days Grow Short: the Life and Music of
Kurt Weill</u>. New York: Holt, Rinehart, and Winston, 1979;
London: Weidenfeld and Nicolson, 1980. 469p., illus.,
bibliog., discog., index.

WELLS, DICKY

3716.74 Wells, Dicky. <u>The Night People: Reminiscences of a Jazzman</u>.
As told to Stanley Dance. Foreword by Count Basie. Boston:
Crescendo; London: Hale, 1971. 122p., illus., index.

WHAM

3716.75 Grant, Barry. <u>Wham: Young and Gunning</u>. London: Zomba Books,
1985. 64p., illus., discog.

Wham (cont.)

3716.76 Hizer, Bruno. <u>Wham</u>. London; New York: Proteus, 1985. 32p.,
        illus., discog.

3716.77 Rees, Daffydd, and Luke Crampton. <u>Wham! An Official Bio-
        graphy</u>. London: Virgin Books, 1985. 96p., illus., discog.

WHEATSTRAW, PEETIE

3716.78 Garon, Paul. <u>The Devil's Son-In-Law: the Story of Peetie
        Wheatstraw and His Songs</u>. London: Studio Vista, 1971;
        Hatboro, Pennsylvania: Legacy Books, 1983 (The Paul Oliver
        Blues Series). 111p., illus., bibliog., discog.

WHITCOMB, IAN

3716.79 Whitcomb, Ian. <u>Rock Odyssey: a Chronicle of The Sixties</u>.
        Garden City, New York: Doubleday, 1983 (Dolphin Books);
        London: Hutchinson, 1984. 376p., illus., index.
            Memoir. Includes detailed personal account of the rock
        business.

WHITEMAN, PAUL

   *   Whiteman, Paul, and Leslie Lieber. <u>How To Be a Bandleader</u>.
        * Cited below as item 4093.

3716.80 ————, and Margaret McBride. <u>Jazz</u>. New York: J.H. Sears,
        1926; New York: Arno Pr., 1974. 298p., illus.
            Autobiography.

                            Biographies

3716.81 Delong, Thomas A. <u>Pops: Paul Whiteman, King of Jazz</u>.
        Piscataway, New Jersey: New Century Pr., 1983. 352p., illus.

3716.82 Marx, Samuel. <u>Paul Whiteman</u>. Girard, Kansas: Haldeman-
        Julius, 1929. 32p. (Little Blue Books)

WHITESNAKE

3716.83 Hibbert, Tom. <u>Whitesnake</u>. London: Omnibus Pr., 1982. 48p.,
        illus., discog.

WHITMAN, OTIS DEWEY "SLIM"

3716.84 Gibble, Kenneth L. Mister Songman: the Slim Whitman Story.
        Elgin, Illinois: Brethren, 1982. 160p., illus., discog.
        Naperville, Illinois: Caroline House, 1982.   p., illus.,
        discog.

WHO

3716.85 Who, The. The Who In Their Own Words. Compiled by Steve
        Clarke. London: Omnibus Pr.; New York: Quick Fox, 1979;
        New York: Delilah, 1982. 128p., illus.
        Compiled from interviews.

                          Biographies

3716.86 Ashley, Brian. Whose Who? A Who Retrospective. London:
        New English Library, 1978. 128p., illus., discog.

3716.87 Barnes, Richard. The Who: Maximum R and B. London: Eel
        Pie; New York: St. Martin's Pr., 1982. 168p., illus.,
        discog.
            Includes flexidisk, containing demonstration recordings
        of their songs, My Generation, and Pinball Wizzard.

3716.88 Charlesworth, Chris. The Who: the Illustrated Biography.
        London: Omnibus Pr., 1982. 96p., illus., discog.

3716.89 Herman, Gary. The Who. London: Studio Vista, 1971; New
        York: Macmillan, 1972. 112p., illus., bibliog., discog.

3716.90 Kamin, Philip, and Peter Goddard. The Who: the Farewell
        Tour. Toronto: General Publishing; London: Sidgwick and
        Jackson, 1983. 126p., illus.
            Performance photographs by Kamin; text by Goddard.

3716.91 Marsh, Dave. Before I Get Old: the Story of The Who.
        London; New York: Plexus Publishing, 1983. 546p., illus.,
        bibliog., index.

3716.92 Stein, Jeff, and Chris Johnston. The Who. New York: Stein
        and Day, 1973. 96p., illus. With a new introduction: New
        York: Stein and Day, 1979. 96p., illus.
            Chiefly illustrated.

3716.93 Swenson, John. The Who. New York: Tempo Books, 1979;
        London: Star Books, 1981. 167p., illus., discog.

3716.94 Tremlett, George. The Who. London: Futura, 1975. 125p.,
        illus. New York: Warner Books, 1975. 142p., illus.

Who (cont.)

3716.95 Turner, Steve, and John Davis. <u>A Decade of The Who: an Authorised History In Music, Paintings, Words, and Photographs</u>. Edited by Ted Dicks. London: Elm Tree Books/Fabulous Music, 1977. 239p., illus., discog.
        Includes eighty song lyrics; plus words and music of a further forty.

Discographies

3716.96 Hanel, Ed. <u>The Who: the Illustrated Discography</u>. London: Omnibus Pr., 1981. 176p., illus.
        Includes bootleg recordings.

Motion Pictures

3716.97 Barnes, Richard, and Pete Townshend. <u>The Story of "Tommy."</u> London: Eel Pie, 1977. 129p., illus.

3716.98 Fletcher, Alan. <u>Quadrophenia</u>. London: Corgi, 1979. 190p.
        Novelization of the production.

Periodicals

3716.99 <u>Who's News</u>. Framingham, Massachusetts. irreg., 1979-?

Individual Group Members

Moon, Keith

3716.100 Butler, Dougal. <u>Moon the Loon: the Rock and Roll Life of Keith Moon, the Most Spectacular Drummer the World Has Ever Seen</u>. With Chris Trengrove and Peter Lawrence. London: Star Books, 1981. 231p., illus.

          ————. <u>Full Moon: the Amazing Rock and Roll Life of the Late Keith Moon</u>. With Chris Trengrove and Peter Lawrence. New York: Morrow, 1981. 269p., illus.

3717.   Waterman, Ivan. <u>Keith Moon: the Life and Death of a Rock Legend</u>. London: Arrow Books, 1979. 142p., illus.

Pete Townshend

3718. Townshend, Pete. <u>Horse's Neck</u>. London: Faber and Faber,
       1985.   p.
          Collection of his autobiographical and other writings.

Biography

3719. Charlesworth, Chris. <u>Townshend: a Career Biography</u>. London;
       New York: Proteus, 1984. 175p., illus., bibliog., discog.
          Includes listing of his compositions.

WILK, MAX

3720. Wilk, Max. <u>Every Day's a Matinee: Memoirs Scribbled On a
       Dressing-Room Door</u>. New York: Norton, 1975. 288p., illus.

WILLIAMS, ANDY, AND DAVID

3721. Daily Mirror. <u>Andy and David On the Beach</u>. London: <u>Daily
       Mirror</u> Books, 1973. 48p., illus.
          Account of abortive teeny-bop duo. Sons of Andy Williams.

WILLIAMS, BERT (<u>pseud. of</u> Egbert Austin Williams)

3722. Charters, Ann. <u>Nobody: the Story of Bert Williams</u>. New
       York: Macmillan; London: Collier-Macmillan, 1970. 157p.,
       illus., discog.
          Includes words and music of ten of his songs.

3723. Rowland, Mabel (ed.). <u>Bert Williams, Son of Laughter: a
       Symposium of Tribute to the Man and His Work, by His Friends
       and Associates</u>. Preface by David Belasco. New York: The
       English Crafters, 1923; New York: Negro Universities Pr.,
       1969. 218p., illus.

WILLIAMS, BILLY

3724. Andrews, Frank, and Ernie Bayly. <u>Billy Williams' Records: a
       Study in Discography</u>. Bournemouth, Dorset: <u>Talking Machine
       Review</u>, 1982. 86p., illus.

WILLIAMS, CLARENCE

3725. Lord, Tom. Clarence Williams. London, Storyville, 1976.
       p., illus., discog.

Discographies

3726. Bakker, Dick. Clarence Williams on Microgroove. Alphen
       aan den Rijn, Holland: Micrography, 1977.   p.

3727. Goldman, Elliott. A Clarence Williams Discography. Fore-
       word by Alex Clayman. London: Jazz Music Books, 1947. 24p.

WILLIAMS, ELMER

   *   Evensmo, Jan. The Tenor Saxophones of Cecil Scott, Elmer
       Williams, and Dick Wilson.
          * Cited above as item 1548.

WILLIAMS, HANK (pseud. of Hiram King Williams)

Bibliography

3728. Koon, George William. Hank Williams: a Bio-Bibliography.
       Westport, Conn.: Greenwood Pr., 1983. 180p., illus.,
       bibliog., discog. (Popular Culture Bio-Bibliographies)
          Includes reproductions of interviews.

Biographies

3729. Caress, Jay. Hank Williams, Country Music's Tragic King.
       New York: Stein and Day, 1979.   p., illus., bibliog.,
       index.

3730. Deal, Babs H. High Lonesome World: the Death and Life of a
       Country Music Singer. Garden City, New York: Doubleday,
       1969; London (as High Lonesome World): New English Library,
       1974. 300p.
          Novel, loosely based on Williams.

3731. Flippo, Chet. Your Cheatin' Heart: a Biography of Hank
       Williams. New York: Simon and Schuster, 1981. 251p.,
       illus., index.

3732. Moore, Thurston (ed.). Hank Williams: the Legend. Denver:
       Heather Enterprises, 1972. 63p., illus., bibliog., discog.

3733. Rivers, Jerry. <u>Hank Williams: From Life To Legend</u>. Edited
        by Thurston Moore. Denver: Heather Enterprises, 1967. 40p.,
        illus., bibliog., discog.
            Author was member of Williams' band.

3734. Williams, Lillian. <u>Our Hank Williams</u>. (Place unknown): The
        Author, 1953.   p., illus.
            Reminiscences by his mother. Omits Williams' alcoholism,
        and his divorce.

3735. Williams, Roger M. <u>Sing a Sad Song: the Life of Hank
        Williams</u>. Garden City, New York: Doubleday, 1970; New York:
        Ballantine, 1973. 276p., illus., discog. 2nd. ed.: Urbana;
        Chicago; London: University of Illinois Pr., 1981. 318p.,
        discog., index. (Music in American Life)
            Discography by Bob Pinson. Second edition omits illus-
        trations.

WILLIAMS, HANK, <u>JR</u>.

3736. Williams, Hank, <u>Jr</u>. <u>Living Proof: an Autobiography</u>. With
        Michael Bane. New York: Putnam, 1979. 222p., illus.

WILLIAMS, JOE

3737. Gourse, Leslie. <u>Everyday: a Biography of Joe Williams</u>.
        London: Quartet, 1984. 256p., illus., discog.

WILLIAMSON, ROBIN

3738. Williamson, Robin. <u>Home Thoughts From Abroad</u>. London:
        Deepdown, 1972. 96p., illus.
            Verse and other writings, 1966-71.

WILLIE AND DWIKE

3739. Zinsser, William. <u>Willie and Dwike: an American Profile</u>.
        New York; London: Harper and Row, 1984. 170p., illus.
            Jazz duo Willie Ruff and Dwike Mitchell.

WILLS, BOB

3740. Latham, Jimmy. <u>The Life of Bob Wills: the King of Western
        Swing</u>. Odessa, Texas: Latham Publishing, 1974. 129p., illus.,
        discogs.

Wills, Bob (cont.)

3741. Sheldon, Ruth. <u>Hubbin' It: the Life of Bob Wills</u>. Kings-
       port, Tennessee: Kingsport Pr., 1938. 147p., illus.

3742. Stricklin, Al. <u>My Years With Bob Wills</u>. With John McConal.
       San Antonio, Texas: Naylor, 1976. 153p., illus.

3743. Townsend, Charles R. <u>"San Antonio Rose." The Life and
       Music of Bob Wills</u>. Discography and filmusicography by Bob
       Pinson. Urbana; London: University of Illinois Pr., 1976.
       395p., illus., bibliog., discog., filmog., index. (Music in
       American Life)

WILLSON, MEREDITH (<u>pseud. of</u> Robert Meredith Reiniger)

3744. Willson, Meredith. <u>And There I Stood With My Piccolo</u>.
       Westport, Conn.: Greenwood Pr., 1976. 255p.
          Memoirs.

3745. ———. <u>"But He Doesn't Know the Territory."</u> New York:
       Putnam, 1959. 190p.
          Autobiography.

WILSON, DICK

    * Evensmo, Jan. <u>The Tenor Saxophones of Cecil Smith, Elmer
       Williams, and Dick Wilson</u>.
          * Cited above as item 1548.

WILSON, SANDY

3746. Wilson, Sandy. <u>I Could Be Happy: an Autobiography</u>. London:
       Michael Joseph; New York: Stein and Day, 1975. 283p., illus.,
       index.

WILSON, TEDDY

       Bakker, Dick M. <u>Billie and Teddy on Microgroove</u>.
          * Cited above as item 2758.

WINFIELD, GEORGE

3747. Winfield, George. <u>You Don't Know Me, But... George Winfield's
       Story</u>. As told to Peter Carr. Chigwell, Essex: Storyville,
       1978. 49p., illus.

WINNER, SEPTIMUS

3748. Claghorn, Charles Eugene. <u>The Mocking Bird: the Life and
Diary of Its Author, Septimus Winner</u>. Philadelphia: Magee
Pr., 1937. 66p., illus.
Includes listing of his compositions. Limited edition
of three hundred copies.

WODEHOUSE, PELHAM GRENVILLE

3749. Wodehouse, Pelham Grenville. <u>America, I Like You</u>. New
York: Simon and Schuster, 1956. 212p.
Observations. Based on series of articles for <u>Punch</u>.

———. <u>Over Seventy</u>. London: Herbert Jenkins, 1957. 190p.
Rewritten. Less on the United States; more autobiography.
Incorporated into item 3752.

3750. ———. <u>Performing Flea: a Self-Portrait in Letters</u>.
Introduction, and additional notes, by William Townend.
London: Herbert Jenkins, 1953. 224p. New York (as <u>Author!
Author!</u>): Simon and Schuster, 1962. 192p.
Letters to his friend, William Townend. Simon and
Schuster edition has revised text; additional material.
Incorporated into item 3752.

3751. ———, and Guy Reginald Bolton. <u>Bring On the Girls! The
Improbable Story of Our Life In Musical Comedy. With
Pictures To Prove It</u>. New York: Simon and Schuster, 1953.
278p., illus. London: Herbert Jenkins, 1954. 248p., illus.
British edition rewritten; with different illustrations.
Incorporated into item 3752.

3752. ———. <u>Wodehouse On Wodehouse</u>. London: Hutchinson, 1980;
London: Penguin, 1981. 655p., bibliog., index.
Compilation of items 3749-51.

Theatrical Works

3753. Jasen, David A. <u>The Theatre of P.G. Wodehouse</u>. London:
Batsford, 1979. 120p., illus.
Chronological arrangement. Casts, plots, staging.

Biographies

3754. Connolly, Joseph. <u>P.G. Wodehouse: an Illustrated Biography.
With Complete Bibliography and Collectors' Guide</u>. London:
Orbis, 1979. 160p., illus., bibliog., index.
Emphasis on his literary career. Bibliography is annot-
ated.

Wodehouse, Pelham Grenville (cont.)

3755.   Donaldson, Frances. P.G. Wodehouse: the Authorized
        Biography. London: Weidenfeld and Nicolson, 1982. 399p.,
        illus., bibliog., index. London: Futura, 1983. 432p.,
        illus., bibliog., index.

3756.   Wind, Herbert Warren. The World of P.G. Wodehouse. New
        York: Praeger, 1972. 102p., illus. Rev. ed.: London:
        Hutchinson, 1981. 93p., illus., index.

WONDER, STEVIE (pseud. of Steveland Morris)

3757.   Dragonwagon, Crescent. Stevie Wonder. New York: Flash
        Books, 1977. 95p., illus., discog.

3758.   Elsner, Constanze. Stevie Wonder. London: Everest, 1977.
        360p., illus., discog., index.

3759.   Fox-Cumming, Ray. Stevie Wonder. London: Mandabrook Books,
        1977. 123p., illus., discog.

3760.   Haskins, James. The Story of Stevie Wonder. New York:
        Lothrop, Lee, and Shepard, 1976.   p., illus., discog.,
        index. St. Albans, Hertfordshire: Panther, 1978. 93p.,
        illus., discog., index. New York: Dell, 1979. 112p.,
        illus., discog., index. (Laurel Leaf Library)
            Aimed at younger readers.

3761.   ————, and Kathleen Benson. The Stevie Wonder Scrapbook.
        New York: Grosset and Dunlap, 1978; London: Cassell, 1979.
        159p., illus.

3762.   Swenson, John. Stevie Wonder. London: Plexus Publishing,
        1985. 128p., illus., discog.

                        Discography

3763.   Taylor, Rick. Stevie Wonder: the Illustrated Disco-Biography.
        London: Omnibus Pr., 1985.   p., illus.
            Includes bootleg recordings.

WOOD, PEGGY

3764.   Wood, Peggy. Actors--and People: Both Sides of the Footlights.
        New York; London: D. Appleton, 1930. 177p., illus.
            Memoirs.

3765.   ————. How Young You Look: Memoirs of a Middle-Sized
        Actress. New York; Toronto: Farrar and Rinehart, 1941. 277p.,
        illus.

WYNETTE, TAMMY (pseud. of Wynette Pugh)

3766. Wynette, Tammy. Stand By Your Man: an Autobiography. With
       Joan Dew. New York: Simon and Schuster, 1979; London:
       Hutchinson, 1980; New York: Pocket Books; London: Arrow,
       1981. 349p., illus.

YANKOVIC, FRANKIE

3767. Yankovic, Frankie. The Polka King: the Life of Frankie
       Yankovic. As told to Robert Dolgan. Cleveland: Dillon/
       Liederbach, 1977. 226p., illus.

YARDBIRDS

3768. Platt, John, Chris Dreja, and Jim McCarty. Yardbirds.
       London: Sidgwick and Jackson, 1983. 160p., illus., discog.,
       index.
           Dreja and McCarty were members of the group.

YES

3769. Hedges, Dan. Yes: the Authorized Biography. London:
       Sidgwick and Jackson, 1981. 147p., illus., discog., index.

YOUMANS, VINCENT MILLIE

3770. Bordman, Gerald. Days To Be Happy, Years To Be Sad: the
       Life and Music of Vincent Youmans. New York; London:
       Oxford University Pr., 1982. 266p., illus., index.

YOUNG, JIMMY

3771. Young, Jimmy. J.Y. The Autobiography of Jimmy Young.
       London: W.H. Allen, 1973; London: Star Books, 1974. 176p.,
       illus.
           Singer; later became disk jockey.

3772. ————. Jimmy Young. London: Michael Joseph/Rainbird,
       1982. 176p., illus. London: New English Library, 1983.
       208p., illus., index.
           Further memoirs.

YOUNG, LESTER

3773. Gelly, Dave. <u>Lester Young</u>. Tunbridge Wells, Kent: Spell-
       mount; New York: Hippocrene Books, 1984. 96p., illus.,
       discog. (Jazz Masters)

                          Discographies

   *   Evensmo, Jan. <u>The Tenor Saxophone and Clarinet of Lester
       Young, 1936-1942</u>.
            * Cited above as item 1548.

3774. Jepsen, Jorgen Grunnet. <u>A Discography of Lester Young</u>.
       Biographical notes by Knud H. Ditlevsen. Copenhagen:
       Knudsen, 1968. 45p.

YOUNG, NEIL

3775. Dufrechou, Carole. <u>Neil Young</u>. New York: Quick Fox, 1978;
       London: Book Sales, 1979; London: Omnibus Pr., 1982. 126p.,
       illus., discog.

3776. Rogan, Johnny. <u>Neil Young: the Definitive Biography of His
       Career</u>. London; New York: Proteus, 1982. 160p., illus.,
       discog.
            Discography includes bootleg and unreleased recordings.

                           Periodicals

3777. <u>Broken Arrow</u>. Edited by Alan Jenkins. 2-A Llnfi Street,
       Bridgend, Mid Glamorgan, Wales. bi-monthly, 1981- .

ZAPPA, FRANCIS VINCENT "FRANK"

3778. Fisher, Trevor (ed.). <u>Frank Zappa and The Mothers</u>.
       Manchester, England: Babylon Books, 1980. unpaged, illus.
            Includes reproductions of press cuttings.

3779. Gray, Michael. <u>Mother! Is the Story of Frank Zappa</u>.
       London; New York: Proteus, 1984. 128p., illus., discog.

3780. Groening, Matt. <u>Zappa</u>. London; New York: Proteus, 1983.
       128p., illus., discog.

3781. Walley, David. <u>No Commercial Potential: the Saga of Frank
       Zappa and The Mothers of Invention</u>. New York: Outerbridge
       and Lazard, 1972. 184p., illus., bibliog., discog.
       (A <u>Fusion</u> Book)

Discographies

3782. Stoplar, Justin. Frank Zappa/The Mothers. London: The
       Author, 1984. 10p.
           Brief listing. Includes unreleased recordings.

Periodicals

3783. Hot Rats Times. Zürich. irreg., 1976-?

ZIEGFELD, FLORENZ

3784. Cantor, Eddie, and David Freedman. Ziegfeld, the Great
       Glorifier. New York: A.H. King, 1934. 166p., illus.
           Originally published serially in Collier's.

3785. Carter, Randolph. The World of Flo Ziegfeld. New York:
       Praeger; London: Paul Elek, 1974. 176p., illus., bibliog.,
       index.
           Includes listing of his shows.

3786. Farnsworth, Marjorie. The Ziegfeld Follies. Introduction
       by Billie Burke Ziegfeld. New York: Putnam; London: Peter
       Davies; New York: Bonanza Books, 1956. 194p., illus., index.

3787. Higham, Charles. Ziegfeld. Chicago: Regnery, 1972; London:
       W.H. Allen, 1973. 245p., illus., index.

3788. Phillips, Julien. Stars of the Ziegfeld Follies. Minneapol-
       is: Lerner Publications, 1972. 79p., illus. (A Pull Ahead
       Book)
           Brief biography of Ziegfeld; plus profiles of his leading
       performers. Aimed at younger readers.

3789. Santon, Frederick. M.G.M.'s Ziegfeld Trilogy: a Literary
       and Pictorial Treasury. South Brunswick, New Jersey: A.S.
       Barnes, 1979.   p., illus., bibliog., index.
           Accounts of the biographical motion pictures, The Great
       Ziegfeld, The Ziegfeld Girl, and The Ziegfeld Follies.

3790. Ziegfeld, Patricia. The Ziegfelds' Girl: Confessions of an
       Abnormally Happy Childhood. Boston: Little, Brown, 1964.
       210p., illus.
           Memoir by his daughter.

Billie Burke

3791. Burke, Billie. With a Feather On My Nose. With Cameron
       Shipp. New York: Appleton, Century, 1949. 272p., illus.
       London: Peter Davies, 1950. 236p., illus.
           Autobiography of his wife, performer in his shows.

ZWERIN, MIKE

3792. Zwerin, Mike. <u>Close Enough For Jazz</u>. London: Quartet,
       1983. 246p., illus., index.
            Autobiography of British jazzman and journalist.

PART THREE: TECHNICAL

A. MUSIC EDUCATION AND APPRECIATION

(i) Popular

3793. Attwood, Tony, and Paul Farmer. Pop Workbook. London:
Edward Arnold, 1978. 96p., illus., bibliog., discog., index.

3794. Cooper, B. Lee. Images of American Society in Popular
Music: a Guide to Reflective Teaching. Chicago: Nelson-
Hall, 1982.   p., bibliog., discog.

3795. Swanwick, Keith. Popular Music and the Teacher. Oxford;
London; New York: Pergamon, 1968. 140p., illus., bibliog.,
discog., index.

3796. Tarshis, Steve. Teach Yourself Rock Theory. New York;
London: Music Sales, 1983. 72p., illus.

3797. Vulliamy, Graham, and Edward Lee. Pop Music in School.
Cambridge; London; New York: Cambridge University Pr.,
1976. 207p., illus., bibliog., discog., index. (Resources
of Music). Rev. ed.: 1980. 229p., illus., bibliog.,
discog., index. (Resources of Music.

————. Pop, Rock, and Ethnic Music in School. Cambridge;
London: Cambridge University Pr., 1982. 240p., illus.,
bibliog., discog. (Resources of Music)

3798. ————. Popular Music: a Teacher's Guide. London: Routledge
and Kegan Paul, 1982. 127p., illus., bibliog., discog.
(Routledge Popular Music)

(ii) Jazz

3799. Armando, Don. Artistry in Jazz: an Educative Essay. Los
Angeles: Premier Music Enterprises, 1960. 32p.

3800. Coker, Jerry. The Jazz Idiom. Englewood Cliffs, New Jersey;
London: Prentice-Hall, 1975. 84p., bibliog. refs. (A Spect-
rum Book)
    Comprehensive overview, from educational standpoint.
Includes literature evaluations.

3801. Collier, Graham. Jazz: a Student's and Teacher's Guide.
Cambridge; London; New York: Cambridge University Pr., 1975.
167p., illus., bibliogs., discogs. (Resources of Music)
    Part One: History of jazz; Part Two: Performance.

Jazz (cont.)

3802. Dankworth, Avril. Jazz: an Introduction To Its Musical
       Basis. London; New York: Oxford University Pr., 1968.
       91p., bibliog., index.

3803. Jaffe, Andrew. Jazz Theory. Duboque, Iowa: William C.
       Brown, 1983. 208p.
          Includes teacher's supplement.

3804. Mecklenburg, Carl Gregor, Herzog zu, and Waldemar Scheck.
       Die Theorie des Blues im modernen Jazz. Strasbourg, France;
       Baden-Baden: Heitz, 1963. 131p., bibliog., discog.
       (Sammlung musikwissenschaftlichen Abhandlungen/Collection
       d'Etudes musicologiques, 45)
          Analysis of use in modern instrumental jazz of blues
       elements. In German.

3805. Nanry, Charles. The Jazz Text. With Edward Berger. New
       York; London: Van Nostrand Reinhold, 1979; New York: Trans-
       action Books, 1982. 276p., illus., bibliog., index.
          Technical aspects introduced for listeners and performers.

3806. Schenkel, Steven M. The Tools of Jazz. Englewood Cliffs,
       New Jersey; London: Prentice-Hall, 1983. 144p., illus.

3807. Scott, Allen. Jazz Educated, Man: a Sound Foundation.
       Washington, D.C.: American International Publishers, 1973.
       136p., illus., bibliog.
          Discusses courses in jazz studies at American universities.
       Includes brief history of jazz, and account of jazz in educ-
       ation.

3808. Stanton, Kenneth. Introduction to Jazz Theory. Dallas:
       Crescendo Publishing, 1977.   p.

3809. ───────. Jazz Theory: a Creative Approach. Dallas: Crescendo
       Publishing, 1982. 192p.

3810. Tanner, Paul, and Maurice Gerow. A Study of Jazz. Duboque,
       Iowa: William C. Brown, 1964. 83p., illus., bibliog.,
       discog. 2nd. ed.: 1973. 189p., illus., bibliog., discog.
       3rd. ed.: 1977. 211p., illus., bibliog., discog. 4th. ed.:
       1981. 240p., illus., bibliog., discog. 5th. ed.: 1984.
       242p., illus., bibliog., discog.
          Includes record of musical examples recorded by the
       authors. Based on Tanner's M.A. dissertation, A Technical
       Analysis of the Development of Jazz, University of Calif-
       ornia at Los Angeles, 1962.

3811. Viera, Joe. Jazz Education in Europe: a Summary. Munich:
       The Author, 1968. 12p.

B. TECHNIQUE

(1) GENERAL WORKS

(i) Popular

3812. Stewart, Dave. <u>Introducing the Dots: a Rock Musician's
Guide to Reading and Writing Music</u>. Poole, Dorset: Bland-
ford Pr., 1982. 128p., illus.
Originally published serially in <u>Sound International</u>.
Author is member of Eurythmics group.

(ii) Jazz

3813. Baresel, Alfred. <u>Das Jazz-Buch: Anleitung zum Spielen,
Improvisieren, und Komponieren moderner Tanzstücke</u>.
Leipzig: J.H. Zimmermann, 1926. 34p.

————. <u>Das Neue Jazzbuch: ein praktisches Handbuch für
Musiker, Komponisten, Arrangeure, Tänzer, und Freunde der
Jazzmusik</u>. Leipzig: W. Zimmermann, 1929. 98p.
Comprehensive practical guide. In German.

3814. Bryce, Owen, and Alex McLaren. <u>Let's Play Jazz: a Beginner's
Guide to Jazz</u>. Bushey, Hertfordshire: The Authors, 1965.   p.

3815. Henry, Robert E. <u>The Jazz Ensemble: a Guide to Technique</u>.
Englewood Cliffs, New Jersey; London: Prentice-Hall, 1981.
117p., illus., bibliog. (A Spectrum Book)

3816. Traill, Sinclair (ed.). <u>Play That Music: a Guide to Playing
Jazz</u>. London: Faber and Faber, 1956. 113p., illus.
Essays by British performers.

(2) SPECIFIC TECHNIQUES

(i) Composition

(a) Popular

3817. Adams, Charles F. <u>How To Put a Melody On Paper</u>. Hollywood,
California: Musicraft Material, 1966. 207p.

3818. Adams, Chick. <u>Song Success</u>. New York: Adams-Payne Printing
Service, 1938. 119p., illus.

3819. Armstrong, Neville. <u>How To Sell Your Songs</u>. Foreword by
Montague Ross. London: Neville Spearman, 1940. 55p.

3820. Ascott, Dennis. <u>The Christian Songwriter's Handbook</u>. With
Mal Grosch. Maidstone, Kent: Third Day Enterprises, 1977.
12p.

Composition (cont.)

Popular (cont.)

3821. Attwood, Tony. _British Songwriters' Guide_. Totnes, Devon:
      R.S. Productions, 1981. 10p., bibliog.

3822. Autry, Gene. _The Art of Writing Songs; and, How To Play a
      Guitar_. Evanston, Illinois: Frontier Publishers, 1933.
      32p., illus.

3823. Bart, Teddy. _Inside Music City, U.S.A_. Nashville: Aurora
      Publishers, 1970. 164p., illus., bibliog.
      Nine Nashville songwriters on composition of songs.

3824. Bender, Leta S. _Short Cut Method To Successful Songwriting_.
      Friend, Nebraska: _Studio News_, 1948.   p.

3825. Bennett, Roy C. _The Songwriter's Guide To Writing and
      Selling Hit Songs_. Englewood Cliffs, New Jersey; London:
      Prentice-Hall, 1983. 161p.

3826. Bolte, Carl E. _Secrets of Successful Songwriting_. New York:
      Arco Publishing, 1984. 208p.

3827. Boyce, Tommy. _How To Write a Hit Song and Sell It_. North
      Hollywood, California: Melvin Powers, 1975. 151p., illus.

3828. Boye, Henry. _How To Make Money Selling the Songs That You
      Write_. New York: Frederick Fell, 1970. 176p. _Rev. ed._:
      New York: Frederick Fell, 1975. 192p.

3829. Bruce, Robert. _How To Write a Song Hit and Sell It_. New
      York: Lexington Pr., 1945 (Reprinted: New York: Paragon Music
      Publishers, 1949). 208p., illus.

3830. ————. _So You Want To Write a Song?_ Introduction by
      Arthur Schwartz. Brooklyn, New York: P.L. Schwartz, 1935.
      90p., illus.

3831. Cahn, Sammy. _The Songwriter's Rhyming Dictionary_. New York:
      Facts on File; London: Souvenir Pr.; New York: New American
      Library, 1984. 208p., illus.

3832. Cartman, Shirley E. _Begin Your Song-Writing Career_. Wash-
      ington, D.C.: Car-Mitch Associates, 1976. 106p., illus.

3833. Davis, Sheila. _The Craft of Lyric Writing_. Cincinnati:
      Writer's Digest, 1984. 252p.

3834. Day, Julius Edgar. _How To Write Words For Songs_. London:
      Reynolds, 1936. 81p., illus.

3835. Decker, Tom W. _So You Wrote a Song, Now What? A Complete
      Guide For Songwriters_. Dallas: Mecca Pr., 1973. 121p.,
      illus., bibliog.

3836. Dubin, Al. The Art of Song Writing. New York: Jack Mills,
       1928. 53p.

3837. Frankel, Aaron. Writing the Broadway Musical. New York:
       Drama Book Publishers, 1977.   p.

3838. Garland, Wallace Graydon. Popular Songwriting Methods: the
       Unit System For Composing Melody, Harmony, Rhythm, and
       Lyrics. New York: American Music Guild, 1942. 324p.

3839. George, Nelson. Top of the Charts. Piscataway, New Jersey:
       New Century, 1983. 448p., illus.
           Includes publishing information.

3840. Glaser, Hy. How To Write Lyrics That Make Sense...and
       Dollars. Hicksville, New York: Exposition Pr., 1977. 110p.

3841. Gornston, David, and Louis Herscher. Practical Songwriting:
       a Method Dealing With the Construction of the Words and the
       Music. New York: Harry Engel, 1936. 32p.

3842. Green, Abel. Inside Stuff On How To Write Popular Songs.
       Introduction by Paul Whiteman. New York: Paul Whiteman
       Publications, 1927; New York: Robbins Music, 1928. 70p.

3843. Hall, Tom T. How I Write Songs. New York: Chappell, 1976.
           p., illus.

3844. Harris, Charles Kassell. How To Write a Popular Song.
       Chicago: The Author, 1906. 123p.

3845. Harris, Rolf. Write Your Own Pop Song. London: Wolfe/Keith
       Music, 1973. 111p., illus.

3846. Herscher, Louis. Successful Songwriting: the Magic Key To
       Words and Melody. Including a Handy Rhyming Dictionary.
       Beverley Hills, California: Accadia Music, 1963. 64p.
       2nd. ed.(as Successful Songwriting: How To Succeed In Writing
       Songs): Beverley Hills, California: Solo Music, 1966. 60p.

3847. Hutchinson, Larry. Rock and Roll Songwriter's Handbook.
       New York: Scholastic Book Services, 1972.   p.

3848. Jones, Arthur. How To Crash Tin-Pan Alley: the Authoritat-
       ive Handbook For a Successful Songwriting Career. As told
       to Louise Howard and Jeron Criswell. Foreword by Sammy Kaye.
       New York: Howard and Criswell, 1939. 137p., illus. (Read-
       to-Succeed Books, 2)

3849. Kane, Henry (ed.). How To Write a Song. As Told To Henry
       Kane by Duke Ellington (and Others). New York: Macmillan,
       1962. 219p. New York: Avon Books, 1964. 224p.
           Interviews giving advice.

3850. Kasha, Al, and Joel Hirschhorn. If They Ask You, You Can
       Write a Song. New York: Simon and Schuster, 1979.   p.,
       index.

Composition (cont.)

Popular (cont.)

3851. Kenny, Nick A. (ed.). How To Write, Sing, and Sell Popular Songs. New York: Hermitage Pr., 1946. 255p.

3852. Knight, George Morgan. How To Construct and Write Song Hits of Today and Tomorrow. Edited by Leta S. Bender. Leonard-town, Maryland: Knight Publishing, 1948. 42p.

3853. ————. How To Write and Publish That Song In Your Heart. Leonardtown, Maryland: Knight Publishing, 1943. 43p.
         Ten revisions issued, 1943-53.

3854. Korb, Arthur. How To Write Songs That Sell. New York: Greenberg, 1949. 179p., illus. New rev. ed.: Boston: Plymouth Publishing, 1957. 179p., illus.

3855. Kosser, Michael. How To Become a Successful Nashville Songwriter. Nashville: Porch Swing, 1981. 100p., illus.

3856. Lewis, Al. From Rhymes To Riches. Preface by Rudy Vallee. New York: Donaldson, Douglas, and Gumble, 1935. 94p., illus.

3857. Lincoln, Harry J. How To Write and Make a Success Publishing Music. Cincinnati: Union Music, 1919. 48p. Rev. ed. (as How To Write and Publish Music): Cincinnati: Otto Zimmerman and Son, 1926. 119p.

3858. Lindsay, Martin. Teach Yourself Songwriting. London: English Universities Pr., 1956. 164p., bibliog.

3859. McMahon, Jack. Practical Song Writing and Composition. South Norwalk, Conn.: Cromat Publishing, 1935. 40p.

3860. McNeel, Kent, and Mark Luther. How To Be a Successful Songwriter. New York: St. Martin's Pr., 1978.   p.

3861. Neal, Roy. Compose Your Own Tunes: the Roy Neal Tune-Tutor. Peterborough, Cambridgeshire: Sceptre Publishers, 1981. 32p., illus.

3862. Nelson, Margaret (ed.). Lyrics For Song Hits. New York: Avon House, 1942. 504p.
         Includes biographical notes on songwriters.

3863. Nichols, Horatio. How To Write a Successful Song. Bognor Regis; London: Crowther, 1943.   p.

3864. O'Connor, Desmond. How To Write the Words of a Hit Song. London: Cosmo Music, 1947. 28p., illus.

3865. Peacock, Alan, and Ronald Weir. The Composer in the Market Place. Preface by Asa Briggs. London: Faber and Faber, 1975. 172p., illus., index.

3866. Pincus, Lee. The Songwriter's Success Manual. New York:
       Music Pr., 1974. 160p., illus. 2nd. ed.: New York: Music
       Pr., 1976. 160p., illus.

3867. Rachlin, Harvey. The Songwriter's Handbook. New York:
       Funk and Wagnalls, 1977. 172p., illus., index.

3868. Raja, Om Prakash. As I Wrote Songs, So You Can. Far
       Rockaway, New York: Modern Publishers, 1974. 133p.

3869. Reubens, Aida (ed.). Songwriters' Desk Book. London:
       Neville Spearman, 193? p.
          Also issued in sections, 1938-42.

3870. Robbins, Johnny. You Can Be a Country Music Songwriter.
       Carthage, Tennessee: Green Block, 1982. 84p., illus.

3871. Sabas, Frankie. How To Make a Million Dollars Writing Songs.
       New York: Fortuny's, 1940. 77p.

3872. Sheppard, Leslie. How To Compose Popular Songs That Will
       Sell. London: Foulsham, 1935. 61p.

3873. Sherwin, Sterling (pseud. of John Milton Hagen). Song-
       writing and Selling Secrets: a Manual of Popular Songwriting.
       Upland, Indiana: A.D. Freese and Son, 1935. 39p.

3874. Silver, Abner, and Robert Bruce. How To Write and Sell a
       Song Hit. Foreword by Sigmund Spaeth. New York: Prentice-
       Hall, 1939. 203p., illus.

3875. Songwriter's Action Manual. Baton Rouge: Red River Music,
       1979.   p.

3876. Songwriter's Guide. Staverton, Devon: R.S. Productions,
       1979.   p.

3877. Songwriter's Market. Cincinnati: Writer's Digest Books.
       annual, 1978- .

3878. Spaeth, Sigmund Gottfried, and Robert Bruce. The Fundament-
       als of Popular Songwriting. New York: The Songmart, 1939
       7 vols., 116p.

          ————. How To Write Popular Songs. New York: The Songmart,
       1939. 116p.
          One-volume edition.

3879. Spiers, Caleb. How To Write a Song-Waltz. Leeds: Leedham
       Tutorial, 1954. 60p.

3880. ————. How To Write Melody. Leeds: Leedham Tutorial,
       1955. 70p.

3881. Stiner, E.J. What Every Amateur Songwriter Should Know
       About Songwriting and Publishing. Edited by George Morgan
       Knight. Leonardtown, Maryland: Knight Publishing, 1948. 21p.

Composition (cont.)

Popular (cont.)

3882. Stoddard, Harry. <u>Secrets of Successful Song Writing</u>. Los
      Angeles: Musicrest Publications, 1949. 100p.

3883. Warner, Jay. <u>How To Have Your Hit Song Published</u>.
      Hollywood, California: Almo Publications, 1983.   p.

3884. Weir, William J., and Uno Goddard. <u>The Songwriting Racket
      and How To Beat It</u>. North Palm Springs, California:
      Cherokee Publishing, 1977. 187p., illus.

3885. Whitfield, Jane. <u>Songwriters' Rhyming Dictionary</u>. North
      Hollywood, California: Wilshire Book Company, 1974.   p.

3886. Wickes, Edward Michael. <u>The Song Writer's Guide</u>. New York:
      Morrison Music, 1931. 188p.
           Includes biographical appendix of songwriters.

3887. ————. <u>Writing the Popular Song</u>. Springfield, Massachus-
      etts: The Home Correspondence School, 1916. 181p. (The
      Writer's Library)

3888. ————, and Richard H. Gerard. <u>Popular Songs: How To Write
      and Where To Sell</u>. New York: Hannis Jordan, 1913. 47p.

3889. Wilbur, L. Perry. <u>How To Write Songs That Sell</u>. Chicago:
      Regnery; New York: Contemporary Books, 1977. 200p., index.

3890. Williams, George J., III. <u>The Songwriter's Demo Manual</u>.
      Edited by Bill Dalton. Riverside, California: Tree By
      River, 1983. 200p., illus.

3891. Willis, Samuel L. <u>Turn Professional In Your Lyric Song
      Writing</u>. Hicksville, New York: Exposition Pr., 1960.
      55p., bibliogs.

3892. Young, Shirley. <u>How To Market Your Songs To the Artists Who
      Sing the Hits</u>. Santa Rosa, California: Youngjohn Publicat-
      ions, 1983. 150p.

                              (b) Jazz

3893. Collier, Graham. <u>Compositional Devices</u>. Based On "Songs
      For My Father." Boston: Berklee, 1974.   p.
           Analysis of the material on his long-playing album, <u>Songs
      For My Father</u>.

3894. Goldstein, Gil. <u>The Jazz Composer's Companion</u>. New York:
      Music Sales, 1983. 144p., illus.

3895.   Russo, William. <u>Composing For the Jazz Orchestra</u>. Chicago;
        London: University of Chicago Pr., 1961 (Reissued: 1973).
        90p., illus.
        Author was composer and arranger for Stan Kenton.

3896.   ————. <u>Jazz Composition and Orchestration</u>. Chicago;
        London: University of Chicago Pr., 1968. 825p., bibliog.,
        index. <u>New ed.</u>: Chicago; London: University of Chicago
        Pr., 1975. 848p., bibliog., index.

(ii) Harmony

3897.   Amadie, Jimmy. <u>Harmonic Foundation For Jazz and Popular
        Music</u>. Bala Cynwyd, Pennsylvania: Thornton Publications,
        1981. 168p.

3898.   Bobbitt, Richard. <u>Harmonic Technique in the Rock Idiom:
        the Theory and Practice of Rock Harmony</u>. Belmont, Calif-
        ornia: Wadsworth Publishing, 1976.   p., bibliog., index.

3899.   Evans, George. <u>Modern Dance Band Harmony. With Three
        Thousand Chords</u>. London: Fanfare Musical Publications,
        1948. 155p.

3900.   Markewich, Reese. <u>Substitute Harmony in Modern Jazz and
        Pop Music</u>. Riverdale, New York: The Author, 1967. 93p.

3901.   Ricigliano, Daniel Anthony. <u>Popular and Jazz Harmony For
        Composers, Arrangers, Performers</u>. New York: Donato Music
        Publishing, 1967. 197p. <u>Rev. ed.</u>: New York: Donato Music
        Publishing, 1969. 192p.

3902.   Stanton, Kenneth. <u>Introduction to Jazz Theory: a Beginning
        Text in Jazz Harmony in Workbook Form</u>. Boston: Crescendo
        Publishing, 1976. 48p.

(iii) Rhythm

3903.   Winick, Steven D. <u>Rhythm: an Annotated Bibliography</u>.
        Metuchen, New Jersey; London: Scarecrow Pr., 1974. 157p.,
        index.
            Approximately five hundred citations. Includes books,
        periodical articles, theses, dissertations; 1900-72.

(iv) Arrangement

3904.   Baker, David N. <u>Arranging and Composing For the Small
        Ensemble: Jazz/R-and-B/Jazz-Rock</u>. Chicago: Maher Public-
        ations, 1970. 184p., illus., bibliogs., discogs.

Arrangement (cont.)

3905. Charlton, Andrew, and John DeVries. Jazz and Commercial
       Arranging. Englewood Cliffs, New Jersey; London: Prentice-
       Hall, 1982. 2 vols., 384p.

3906. Dedrick, Art, and Al Polhamus. How the Dance Band Swings.
       East Aurora, New York: Kendor Music, 1958.   p.

3907. Ellis, Norman. Instrumentation and Arranging For the Radio
       and Dance Orchestra. New York: Roell Publications, 1936.
       209p., illus.

3908. Lange, Arthur. Arranging For the Modern Dance Orchestra.
       New York: The Author, 1926. 238p., illus.

3909. Lapham, Claude. Scoring For the Modern Dance Band. London;
       New York: Pitman, 1937. 164p.

3910. Miller, Alton Glenn. Glenn Miller's Method For Orchestral
       Arranging. New York: Mutual Music Society, 1943; London:
       Chappell, 1956. 116p., illus.

3911. Owen, Reg. The Reg Owen Arranging Method. New York:
       Robbins Music; London: Francis, Day, and Hunter, 1956.
       77p., illus.
          For the light orchestra.

3912. Skinner, Frank. Frank Skinner's New Methods For Orchestra
       Scoring. New York: Robbins Music, 1935. 171p.
          For dance bands.

3913. Weirick, Paul. Dance Arranging: a Guide to Scoring Music
       For the American Dance Orchestra. New York: Witmark
       Educational Publications, 1934. 142p.

                        (v) Improvisation

3914. Baker, David N. Advanced Improvisation. Chicago: Maher
       Publications, 1974. 256p., illus., bibliog.
          Accompanied by cassette of musical examples.

3915. ————. Jazz Improvisation: a Comprehensive Study For All
       Players. Chicago: Maher Publications, 1969. 184p., bibliog.

3916. ————. Techniques of Improvisation. Libertyville,
       Illinois: National Educational Services/Chicago: Maher
       Publications, 1968-71. 4 vols.,   p., illus.
          Volumes one and two published by National Educational
       Services; volumes three and four published by Maher Publicat-
       ions.

3917. Balliett, Whitney. Improvising: Sixteen Jazz Musicians
and Their Art. New York; London: Oxford University Pr.,
1977. 272p., index.
   Mary Lou Williams, Sid Catlett, Buddy Rich, Henry Allen,
Earl Hines, Red Norvo, and others give advice and opinions.

3918. Benward, Bruce, and Joan Wildman. Jazz Improvisation in
Theory and Practice. Duboque, Iowa: William C. Brown,
1984. 224p.

3919. Bettonville, Albert. Paranoia du jazz: l'improvisation
dans la musique de jazz. Paris: Les Cahiers du Jazz, 1939.
40p., illus.
   Limited edition of four hundred numbered copies.

3920. Coker, Jerry. Improvising Jazz. Forewords by Stan Kenton
and Gunther Schuller. Englewood Cliffs, New Jersey; London:
Prentice-Hall, 1964. 116p., illus. (A Spectrum Book)
   Based on his M.A. dissertation, An Introduction to the
Theory of Jazz Improvisation, Sam Houston State University,
1960.

3921. ————. Listening to Jazz. Englewood Cliffs, New Jersey;
London: Prentice-Hall, 1978. 148p., illus., discog.
(A Spectrum Book)
   For both performers and listeners.

3922. Kynaston, Trent P., and Robert J. Ricci. Jazz Improvisation.
Englewood Cliffs, New Jersey; London: Prentice-Hall, 1978.
218p.

3923. Mehegan, John. Jazz Improvisation. New York: Watson-
Guptill.
   Vol. 1: Tonal and Rhythmic Principles. Introduction by
            Leonard Bernstein. 1959. 207p.
   Vol. 2: Jazz Rhythm and the Improvised Line. Introduction
            by Harold Arlen. 1962. 207p.
   Vol. 3: Swing and Early Progressive Piano Styles. Intro-
            duction by Horace Silver. 1964.   p.
   Vol. 4: Contemporary Piano Styles. 1965. 287p.

3924. Oestereich, James. Improvising and Arranging on the Keyboard. With Earl Pennington. Englewood Cliffs, New Jersey;
· London: Prentice-Hall, 1981. 182p. (A Spectrum Book)

3925. Phillips, Alan. Jazz Improvisation and Harmony. Hialeah,
Florida: Columbia Pictures Publications, 1973. 96p., illus.

3926. Sudnow, David. Ways of the Hand: the Organization of
Improvised Conduct. Cambridge, Massachusetts: Harvard
University Pr.; London: Routledge and Kegan Paul, 1978.
155p., illus., bibliog.
   Jazz piano.

(vi) Recording

3927. Anderton, Craig. <u>Home Recording For Musicians</u>. Saratoga, California: <u>Guitar Player</u> Books, 1978. 183p., illus., bibliog., index.
Includes record of recording techniques demonstrated.

3928. Connelly, Will. <u>The Musician's Guide to Independent Record Production</u>. Chicago: Contemporary Books, 1981.   p., index.

3929. Jahn, Mike. <u>How To Make a Hit Record</u>. Scarsdale, New York: Bradbury Pr., 1976. 118p.

3930. Lambert, Dennis. <u>Producing Hit Records</u>. With Ronald Zalkind. Foreword by Al Coury. New York: Schirmer Books; London: Collier-Macmillan, 1980. 196p., illus.
Includes record demonstrating production techniques.

3931. Miller, Fred. <u>Studio Recording For Musicians</u>. New York: Music Sales, 1983. 144p., illus.

3932. Rapaport, Diane Sward. <u>How To Make and Sell Your Own Record: the Complete Guide To Independent Recording</u>. New York: Harmony Books, 1979.   p., bibliog., index.

   * Stokes, Geoffrey. <u>Star-Making Machinery: the Odyssey of an Album</u>.
         * Cited above as item 2206.

3933. Talmy, Shel. <u>How To Succeed in Recording By Really Trying</u>. London: Mills Music, 1964. 19p., illus.
By successful producer.

C. INSTRUMENTS

(1) Comprehensive Works

3934. Bacon, Tony (ed.). <u>Rock Hardware: the Instruments, Equipment, and Technology of Rock</u>. Poole, Dorset: Blandford Pr.; New York: Harmony Books, 1981. 224p., illus., discog., index.

3935. Fox, Lilla Margaret. <u>Instruments of Popular Music: a History of Musical Instruments</u>. London: Lutterworth Pr., 1966; New York: Roy, 1968. 112p., illus., bibliog.

(2) Specific Instruments

(i) Voice

3936. Anderson, Doug. The Swing and Show Choir and Vocal Jazz Ensemble Handbook. Studio City, California: First Place Music Publications, 1974. 127p., illus., discog.

3937. Burman, Jean. Modern Pop Singing: a Manual Specially Prepared to Help Both Beginners and Advanced Students. London: Lorna Music, 1962. 24p.

3938. Guilbert, Yvette. How To Sing a Song: the Art of Dramatic and Lyric Interpretation. Introduction by Clayton Hamilton. New York: Macmillan, 1918. 136p., illus.

3939. Rowe, John (ed.). Vocal Jazz: About Jazz and Dance Band Vocalists. London: Jazz Tempo Publications, 1945. 24p.
      Styles examined.

3940. Spier, Miriam. The Why and How of Popular Singing: a Guide for Vocalists. Introduction by Peggy Lee. New York: Marks, 1950. 53p., illus.

3941. Whitley, Roger Dee. How To Get Started Singing. Kannapolis, North Carolina: Reveal Publications, 1979. 50p., illus.

(ii) Wind

3942. Baker, David N. Jazz Styles and Analyses: Trombone. A History of the Jazz Trombone Via Recorded Solos, Transcribed and Annotated. Chicago: Down Beat/Music Workshop Publications, 1973. 144p., illus.

3943. McCarthy, Albert John. The Trumpet in Jazz. London: Citizen Pr., 1945. 82p., illus., discog.
      Styles and leading performers examined.

3944. Rowe, John (ed.). Trombone Jazz. London: Jazz Tempo Publications, 1944. 32p.
      Styles examined.

3945. Viera, Joe. Das Saxophon im Jazz. Vienna: Universal Edition, 1977. 88p. (Reihe Jazz, 8)
      In German.

(iii) String

3946. Rasof, Henry. The Folk, Country, and Bluegrass Musician's
Catalog: a Complete Sourcebook For Guitar, Banjo, Fiddle,
Bass, Dulcimer, Mandolin, Autoharp, Harmonica, Ukelele, and
More. New York: St. Martin's Pr., 1982. 272p., illus.

Guitar

(a) General Works

3947. Achard, Ken. The History and Development of the American
Guitar. London: Guitar Magazine, 1980.   p., illus.

3948. Bellow, Alexander. The Illustrated History of the Guitar.
Garden City, New York: Rockville House/Franco Colombo Publications, 1970. 215p., illus.

3949. Brosnac, Donald. The Electric Guitar: Its History and
Construction. San Francisco: Panjandrum Pr.; London:
Omnibus Pr., 1975. 96p., illus., bibliog. Rev. ed.: Fresno,
California: Bold Strummer, 1979. 96p., illus., bibliog.

3950. Denyer, Ralph, and Isaac Guillory. The Guitar Handbook.
With Alastair M. Crawford. Foreword by Andy Summers. London:
Dorling Kindersley; London: Pan, 1982. 256p., illus., index.

3951. Evans, Tom, and Mary Anne Evans. Guitars: Music, History,
Construction, and Players From the Renaissance to Rock.
New York; London: Paddington Pr., 1977; London: Oxford
University Pr., 1983. 479p., illus., bibliog., index.

3952. Grunfeld, Frederic V. The Art and Times of the Guitar: an
Illustrated History of Guitars and Guitarists. New York:
Macmillan, 1969. 340p., illus., bibliog.

3953. Guitar Player. Guitar Player. Saratoga, California: Guitar
Player Productions, 1975. 140p., illus.
        Facsimile reproduction of the first year (1967-8) of
Guitar Player.

3954. ———. The Guitar Player Book. By The Editors of Guitar
Player Magazine. Introduction by Les Paul. Saratoga,
California: Guitar Player Books, 1978. 403p., illus., index.
Revised and updated ed.: Cupertino, California: Guitar Player
Books, 1983. 403p., illus., index.
        Technical and other articles reprinted from Guitar Player.

3955. Kozinn, Allan, Pete Welding, Dan Forte, and Gene Santoro.
The Guitar: the History, the Music, the Players. Bromley,
Kent: Columbus Books, 1983.   p., illus.

  * Summerfield, Maurice J. The Jazz Guitar: Its Evolution and
Its Players.
        * Cited above as item 1600.

3956. Wheeler, Tom. American Guitars: an Illustrated History.
       Foreword by Les Paul. New York; London: Harper and Row,
       1983. 370p., illus., index.

3957. ————. The Guitar Book: a Handbook for Electric and
       Acoustic Guitarists. New York: Harper and Row, 1974; London:
       Macdonald and Janes, 1975. 269p., illus., index. Rev. ed.:
       New York: Harper and Row, 1978; London: Macdonald and Janes,
       1981. 343p., illus., index.

(b) Individual Marques

3958. Achard, Ken. The Fender Guitar. London: Musical New Serv-
       ices, 1977. 68p., illus. (A Guitar Magazine Project)

3959. Bellson, Julius. The Gibson Story. Kalamazoo, Michigan:
       The Author, 1973. unpaged, illus.

3960. Bishop, Ian Courtney. The Gibson Guitar. London: Musical
       New Services, 1977. 2 vols.,   p., illus. (A Guitar
       Magazine Project)

3961. Day, Paul (comp.). The Burns Book. Newton Abbot, Devon:
       P.P. Publishing, 1979.   p., illus.

3962. Longworth, Mike. Martin Guitars: a History. Cedar Knolls,
       New Jersey: Colonial Pr., 1975. 219p., illus. London:
       Omnibus Pr., 1977. 160p., illus.

(iv) Keyboard

(a) Organ

3963. Foort, Reginald. The Cinema Organ: a Description in Non-
       Technical Language of a Fascinating Instrument and How It Is
       Played. London: Pitman, 1932. 126p., illus. 2nd. ed.:
       Vestal, New York: Vestal Pr., 1970. 199p., illus.

3964. Landon, John W. Behold the Mighty Wurlitzer: the History of
       the Theater Pipe Organ. Westport, Conn.: Greenwood Pr., 1983.
       231p., illus., bibliog., index. (Contributions to the Study
       of Popular Culture, 6)
       Includes listing of installations worldwide.

3965. Roehl, Harvey N. The World's Greatest Achievement in Music
       For Theaters: the Wurlitzer Hope-Jones Unit Orchestra.
       Vestal, New York: Vestal Pr., 1964. unpaged, illus.

3966. Whitworth, Reginald. The Cinema and Theatre Organ. London:
       Musical Opinion, 1932. 112p., illus.

3967. Wyatt, Geoffrey. At the Mighty Organ. Oxford: Oxford Illus-
       trated Pr., 1974. 98p., illus., bibliog.
       Theater organs. Includes listing of installations.

Keyboard (cont.)

(b) Piano

* McCarthy, Albert John, and Max Jones (eds.). Piano Jazz.
  * Cited above as item 1577.

3968. Schwanniger, Armin, and André Gurwitsch. Le Jazz au piano.
Lausanne: Editions de l'Echiquier, 1946.   p.
In French. Styles and performers examined.

* Taylor, Billy. Jazz Piano.
  * Cited above as item 832.

(v) Electronic

3969. Crombie, David. The Complete Synthesizer: a Comprehensive
Guide. London: Omnibus Pr., 1982. 104p., illus.
Emphasis on popular music applications.

3970. ————. The Synthesizer and Electronic Keyboard Handbook.
Foreword by Thomas Dolby. London: Dorling Kindersley, 1984.
160p., illus., index.
Guide to selection and performance.

3971. Devarahi (pseud.). The Complete Guide to Synthsizers.
Englewood Cliffs, New Jersey; London: Prentice-Hall, 1982.
214p., illus., bibliog., discog., index.

3972. Mackay, Andy. Electronic Music: the Instruments, the Music,
the Musicians. London: Phaidon, 1981. 124p., illus., index.
Comprehensive survey; emphasis on popular music. Author
is member of Roxy Music group.

3973. Norman, Michael. The Complete Synthesizer Handbook. London:
Zomba Books, 1984. 144p., illus.
Guide to selection and performance.

3974. Yelton, Geary. The Rock Synthesizer Manual. Woodstock,
Georgia: Rock Technical Publications, 1983. 124p., illus.

(vi) Mechanical

3975. Bowers, Q. David. Encyclopedia of Automatic Musical Instruments. Vestal, New York: Vestal Pr., 1972. 1,008p., illus.
Includes glossary of terms.

3976. ————. A Guidebook of Automatic Musical Instruments.
Vestal, New York: Vestal Pr., 1967.   p., illus.

3977. ————. Put Another Nickel In: a History of Coin-Operated
Pianos and Orchestrions. Vestal, New York: Vestal Pr.,
1966. 243p., illus.

3978. Buchner, Alexander. Mechanical Musical Instruments.
Westport, Conn.: Greenwood Pr., 1978.   p., illus.

3979. Crowley, Terence Eldon. Discovering Mechanical Music.
Aylesbury, Buckinghamshire: Shire Publications, 1975. 48p.,
illus., bibliog., index. (Discovering Series, 200)

3980. De Ward, Romke. From Music Boxes to Street Organs. Vestal,
New York: Vestal Pr., 1967.   p., illus.

3981. Ord-Hume, Arthur W. Clockwork Music: an Illustrated History
of Mechanical Musical Instruments. From the Music Box to the
Pianola, From Automaton Lady Virginal Players to Orchestrion.
London: Allen and Unwin, 1973. 334p., illus.

3982. ————. Pianola: the History of the Self-Playing Piano.
London: Allen and Unwin, 1984. 395p., illus., bibliog.,
index.
      Includes listing of makers, patentees, and agents.

3983. ————. Player Piano: the History of the Mechanical Piano,
and How to Repair It. With Wolfgang Julius Gerald. London:
Allen and Unwin, 1970. 296p., illus., bibliog., index.

3984. Roehl, Harvey N. Keys To a Musical Past. Being an Illus-
trated Treatise on the Various Types of Mechanical Musical
Instruments Which Have Enlightened the Spirits of Mankind
Over Many Decades. With Particular Attention Paid to
Pictures and Advertising Material From the Early Days, and
Special Emphasis on the Remarkable Musical Characteristics
of These Devices. Vestal, New York: Vestal Pr., 1968.
48p., illus.

PART FOUR: THE MUSIC BUSINESS

A. BUSINESS ASPECTS

(1) REFERENCE MATERIALS

3985. Christensen, Roger, and Karen Christensen. <u>The Ultimate Movie, T.V., and Rock Directory</u>. Cardiff-by-the-Sea, California: Cardiff, 1984. 372p.
      Contact directory.

3986. Hurst, Walter E., and William Storm Hale. <u>The Music Industry Book: Stories, Texts, Forms, Contracts</u>. Los Angeles: Seven Arts Pr., 1963.   p., illus.

      ————. <u>The Music Industry Book: Protect Yourself Before You Lose Your Rights and Royalties</u>. Edited by Annette Kargodorian. Los Angeles: Seven Arts Pr., 1983.   p., illus. (The Entertainment Industry, 2)

3987. ————. <u>Your Introduction to Music/Record Copyright, Contracts, and Other Business and Law</u>. Los Angeles: Seven Arts Pr., 1974.   p.

3988. Shemel, Sidney, and M. William Krasilovsky. <u>This Business of Music</u>. Edited by Paul Ackerman. New York: Billboard Publications, 1964. <u>Rev. ed.</u>:New York: Billboard Publications, 1971. 420p., illus., bibliog., index. <u>Rev., enlarged (New Copyright Act) ed.</u>: New York: Billboard Publications, 1977. 578p., illus., bibliog., index. <u>4th ed.</u>: New York: Billboard Publications, 1979. 596p., illus., bibliog., index.
      Emphasis on popular music.

3989. ————. <u>More About This Business of Music</u>. Edited by Lee Zhito. New York: Billboard Publications, 1967. 160p., illus. <u>Rev., enlarged ed.</u>: New York: Billboard Publications, 1974.   p., illus. <u>3rd. ed.</u>: New York: Billboard Publications, 1982. 204p., illus.

(2) ANNUALS AND YEARBOOKS

3990. <u>Artistes and Their Agents</u>. Eastbourne, East Sussex: John Offord Publications. annual, 1979- .
      Musicians.

3991. Billboard. <u>International Directory of Recording Studios</u>. Edited by Lee Zhito. New York: Billboard Publications. annual, 1968- .

Annuals and Yearbooks (cont.)

3992. Billboard. International Buyer's Guide of the Music-Record
       Industry. Cincinnati: Billboard Publications. annual,
       1955-59.

       ————. International Buyer's Guide of the Music, Record,
       and Tape Industry. New York: Billboard Publications.
       annual, 1960- .
            Title varies.

3993. ————. International Record and Talent Showcase: Who's
       Who in the World of Music. Cincinnati: Billboard Publicat-
       ions. annual, 1954-59.

       ————. International Talent Directory. New York: Bill-
       board Publications. annual, 1960- .
            Title varies.

3994. ————. Music On Campus. New York: Billboard Publications.
       annual, 1964-68.

       ————. Campus Attractions: Survey of the College Music
       Industry. Edited by Lee Zhito. New York: Billboard Public-
       ations. annual, 1969- .

3995. ————. The Billboard Music Year Book. Cincinnati: Bill-
       lishing. annual, 1939-46.
            1946 ed. published as The Billboard Encyclopedia of Music.

3996. British Phonographic Industry. B.P.I. Year Book: a Review
       of the British Record and Tape Industry. London: British
       Phonographic Industry. annual, 1976- .

3997. Hot Press. Hot Press Industry Yearbook. Dublin: Hot Press.
       annual, 1979- .

3998. Kemp's Music and Record Industry Yearbook. London: Kemp's
       Printing and Publishing. annual, 1965- .

3999. Melody Maker. Melody Maker Yearbook. London: Longacre Pr.
       annual, 1968-70; London: I.P.C. annual, 1971- .
            Title varies. Published as Melody Maker File, 1973-75;
       as Melody Maker Yearbook and Desk Diary, 1976- .

4000. The Music Business Yearbook. Edited by Gary Gee. London:
       Eccentric Music; Bromley, Kent: Columbus Books, 1981. 104p.
            Only issue.

4001. Music Week. "Music Week" Yearbook. London: Tell-Time.
       annual, 1972-74.

       ————. "Music Week" Industry Yearbook. London: Billboard
       Publications. annual, 1975- .

4002. <u>Music Industry Directory</u>. Chicago: Who's Who. annual,
       1977- .

4003. <u>The Music World Directory</u>. Rickmansworth, Hertfordshire:
       Turret/Wheatland. annual, 1981- .

4004. <u>Official Talent and Booking Directory</u>. Los Angeles:
       Speciality Publications. annual, 1975- .

4005. <u>Record and Tape Directory</u>. London: Parkway Publications,
       1981. 328p.
           Only issue.

4006. Variety. <u>"Variety" International Show Business Reference</u>.
       New York: Garland Publishing. annual, 1981- .

4007. <u>The White Book: the International Entertainment Industry
       Buyers' Guide</u>. Shepperton, Middlesex: Birdhurst. annual,
       1984- .

                   (3) GENERAL GUIDES AND OVERVIEWS

4008. Cable, Michael. <u>The Pop Industry Inside Out</u>. London: W.H.
       Allen, 1977. 228p., index. (Inside Out Series)

   *   Dachs, David. <u>Anything Goes: the World of Popular Music</u>.
           * Cited above as item 55.

4009. Leslie, Peter. <u>Fab: the Anatomy of a Phenomenon</u>. London:
       MacGibbon and Kee, 1965. 187p., illus.
           The British popular music industry.

4010. Meyer, Hazel. <u>The Gold in Tin Pan Alley</u>. New York:
       Lippincott, 1958; Westport, Conn.: Greenwood Pr., 1977.
       258p.

4011. Michel, Trudi. <u>Inside Tin Pan Alley</u>. New York: F. Fell,
       1948. 172p.

4012. Plimmer, Martin. <u>The Rock Factory</u>. London; New York:
       Proteus, 1981. 160p., illus.

4013. Rogers, Eddie. <u>Tin Pan Alley</u>. As told to Mike Hennessey.
       London: Hale, 1964. 196p., illus., index.
           The British scene.

   *   Rublowsky, John. <u>Popular Music</u>.
           * Cited above as item 73.

4014. Shepherd, John. <u>Tin Pan Alley</u>. London: Routledge and
       Kegan Paul, 1982. 154p. (Routledge Popular Music)

4015. Silver, Caroline. <u>The Pop Makers</u>. New York: Scholastic
       Book Services, 1967. 127p., illus.

General Guides and Overviews (cont.)

4016. Spitz, Robert Stephen. The Making of Superstars: the
       Artists and Executives of the Rock Music World. Garden
       City, New York: Doubleday, 1978.   p., index. (Anchor
       Books)

4017. Wale, Michael. Voxpop: Profiles of the Pop Process.
       London: Harrap, 1972. 320p., illus.
          Based on British radio program. Interviews with
       industry figures.

4018. Watson, Pat. Inside the Pop Scene. Gloucester, England:
       Thornhill Pr., 1977. 45p., illus., bibliog.

4019. Wattis, Roger, and Krister Malm. Big Sounds From Small
       People: the Music Industry in Small Countries. London:
       Constable; New York: Pendragon, 1984. 419p., illus.,
       bibliog., index. (Sociology of Music)
          Emphasis on popular music from the Third World, and its
       exploitation.

                        (4) CRITICISM

4020. Barnard, Emmett. The Rock 'n' Roll Rip-Off. New York:
       Carlton, 1981.   p.

4021. Chapple, Steve, and Reebee Garofalo. Rock 'n' Roll is Here
       To Pay: the History and Politics of the Music Industry.
       Chicago: Nelson-Hall, 1978. 354p., illus., bibliog., index.
       Leftist anti-industry polemic.

                        Language

4022. Huntley, Leston. The Language of the Music Business: a
       Handbook of Its Customs, Practices, and Procedures.
       Nashville: Del Capo Publications, 1966. 465p.

   *   Shaw, Arnold. The Lingo of Tin-Pan Alley.
          * Cited above as item 84.

                     (5) SPECIFIC FIELDS

                       (i) Publishing

                      (a) General Works

4023. Dranov, Paula. Inside the Music Publishing Industry. White
       Plains, New York; London: Knowledge Industry Publications,
       1980. 185p., bibliog., index. (Communications Library)

4024. Fisher, William Arms. One Hundred and Fifty Years of Music
       Publishing in the United States: an Historical Sketch. With
       Special Reference to the Pioneer Publisher, Oliver Ditson
       Company, Inc., 1783-1933. Boston: Oliver Ditson Company,
       1933; New York: Gordon Pr., 1983. 146p.
            Based on his Notes On Music in Old Boston, Boston: Oliver
       Ditson Company, 1918.

4025. Harwell, Richard B. Confederate Music. Chapel Hill, North
       Carolina: University of North Carolina Pr., 1980. 184p.,
       illus., bibliogs.
            Account of music publishing in the Confederacy. Includes
       detailed listings of over 650 sheet music items.

4026. Humphries, Charles, and William C. Smith. Music Publishing
       in the British Isles, from the Beginning until the Middle
       of the Nineteenth Century: a Dictionary of Engravers,
       Printers, Publishers, and Music Sellers. With a Historical
       Introduction. London: Cassell, 1954. 354p., illus.
       2nd. ed.: Oxford: Blackwell, 1970. 392p., illus.

4027. Hurst, Walter E., and Don Rico. How To Be a Music Publisher.
       Los Angeles: Seven Arts Pr., 1979.   p., index. (The
       Entertainment Industry, 11)

4028. Sanjek, Russell. From Print to Plastic: Publishing and
       Promoting America's Popular Music, 1900-1980. Brooklyn,
       New York: Institute for Studies in American Music, 1984.
       76p., illus. (I.S.A.M. Monographs, 20)

                    (b) Individual Organizations

American Society of Composers, Authors, and Publishers (ASCAP)

4029. American Society of Composers, Authors, and Publishers.
       The Story of ASCAP, an American Institution, 1914-1944:
       Thirty Years of Service. New York: ASCAP, 1944. 16p.

            ————. The Story of ASCAP, an American Institution: More
    . Than Thirty Years of Service. New York: ASCAP, 1946. 16p.

4030. New York Times. The ASCAP Story, 1914-1964. New York: New
       York Times, 1964. 24p., illus.
            Published as a supplement to the newspaper, February 16,
       1964.

Chappell

4031. Mair, Carlene. The Chappell Story, 1811-1961. London:
       Chappell, 1961. 89p.

Individual Organizations (cont.)

Ditson, Oliver

   *   Fisher, William Arms. One Hundred and Fifty Years of Music
        Publishing in the United States.
             * Cited above as item 4024.

Francis, Day, and Hunter

4032.   Abbott, John. The Story of Francis, Day, and Hunter.
        London: Francis, Day, and Hunter, 1952. 84p., illus.

Witmark

4033.   Witmark, Isidore, and Isaac Goldberg. The Story of The
        House of Witmark: From Ragtime to Swingtime. New York:
        Leslie Furman, 1939 (Reprinted: New York: Da Capo Pr.,
        1975). 480p., illus.
             Witmark was the Company's founder. Emphasis on its
        activities in the popular music field. Includes listing
        of Witmark publications.

                          (ii) Broadcasting

4034.   Billboard. The Facts About Television Record and Dance
        Programs: an Analysis of Television's Highest-Rated
        Programs For Teenagers and Young Adults. New York:
        Billboard Publications, 1960. 92p.
             Business emphasis.

4035.   Carson, Gerald. The Roguish World of Doctor Brinkley.
        New York: Rinehart, 1960. 280p., illus., bibliog.
             Biography of medical quack and political huckster. He
        operated high-power Mexican border radio station, XERA;
        broadcast country and hillbilly programs to the United
        States in the late 1930's. XERA was a key outlet for The
        Carter Family.

4036.   DeLong, Thomas. The Mighty Music Box: the Golden Age
        of Musical Radio. Southport, Conn.: Sasco, 1980. 335p.,
        illus.
             History of popular and jazz broadcasting in the United
        States.

 *   Eberly, Phillip K. Music in the Air: America's Changing
        Taste in Popular Music, 1920-1980.
             * Cited above as item 184.

4037.   Harris, Paul. Broadcasting From the High Seas: the History
        of Offshore Radio in Europe, 1958-1976. Edinburgh: Paul
        Harris Publishing, 1977. 361p., illus.

4038.   ————. When Pirates Ruled the Waves. London: Impulse,
        1968. 206p., illus.
             British offshore broadcasting.

4039.   Henry, Stuart, and Mike Von Joel. Pirate Radio: Then and
        Now. Poole, Dorset: Blandford Pr., 1984. 128p., illus.
             Offshore and British internal illicit broadcasting.
        Includes appendix of stations and frequencies.

4040.   Krieger, Susan. Hip Capitalism. Beverly Hills, California:
        Sage Publications, 1979. 340p.
             Account of idealistic San Francisco radio station, and
        its gradual change in values.

4041.   MacFarland, David T. The Development of the Top Forty Radio
        Format. New York: Arno Pr., 1979.   p., bibliog. (Diss-
        ertations in Broadcasting)
             Based on the author's thesis, same title, University of
        Wisconsin, 1972.

4042.   Nichols, Richard. Radio Luxembourg: the Station of the
        Stars: an Affectionate History of Fifty Years of Broadcast-
        ing. London: W.H. Allen, 1983. 192p., illus., index.
        (Comet Books)
             Account of European radio station, noted for its trans-
        missions to Britain.

4043.   Noakes, Bob. Last of the Pirates: a Saga of Everyday Life
        On Board Radio Caroline. Edinburgh: Paul Harris Publishing,
        1984. 237p., illus.
             Author was engineer with British offshore stations Radio
        Caroline, and Radio Nordzee International.

4044.   Passman, Arnold. The Deejays. New York: Macmillan, 1971.
        315p., illus.
             History of United States disk-jockeys influential in the
        development of rock and pop.

4045.   Perry, Dick. Not Just a Sound: the Story of WLW. Engle-
        wood Cliffs, New Jersey: Prentice-Hall, 1971. 242p., illus.
             Influential Cincinnati radio station.

4046.   Record Industry Association of America. Radio and Records.
        New York: Record Industry Association of America, 1964.   p.

4047.   Rusling, Paul. The Lid Off Laser 558. Herne Bay, Kent:
        The Author, 1984. 128p., illus.
             Account of British offshore radio station.

4048. Skues, Keith. Radio Onederland: the Story of Radio One.
       Lavenham, Suffolk: Landmark Pr., 1968. 224p., illus.
             Account of British radio station, founded 1967. By one
       of its disk-jockeys.

4049. Williams, John R. This Was Your Hit Parade. Camden, Maine:
       The Author, 1973. 209p.
             Account of American radio (later television) program.

4050. Williamson, Bill. The Dee Jay Book. London: Purnell, 1969.
       156p., illus.
             Cover title: Radio One Annual. Account of Britain's
       Radio One station, and its disk-jockeys.

                              B. CAREERS

                        (1) REFERENCE MATERIALS

4051. Baskerville, David. Music Business Handbook and Career
       Guide. Los Angeles: Sherwood, 1979. 669p., illus., bibliog.
       2nd. ed.: Denver, Colorado: Sherwood, 1980.   p., illus.,
       bibliog. 3rd. ed.: Denver, Colorado: Sherwood, 1981.   p.,
       illus., bibliog.

4052. The Gigster's Guide: Dance Musicians' Handbook. Gateshead-
       on-Tyne, England: Charles G. Hazell, 1950. 27p., illus.

4053. Given, Dave F. The Dave Given Rock 'n' Roll Star's Handbook.
       New York: Exposition Pr., 1980.   p., illus. (Banner Books)

4054. Record Company and Music Industry Employment Guide.
       Totnes, Devon: Hamilton House Productions, 1979. 11p.
             Chiefly address listings.

                        (2) COMPREHENSIVE WORKS

4055. Bennett, H. Stith. On Becoming a Rock Musician. Amherst:
       University of Massachusetts Pr., 1980. 272p., bibliog.,
       index.

4056. Burton, Gary. A Musician's Guide to the Road. New York:
       Billboard Publications, 1981. 164p.

4057. Collier, James Lincoln. Rock Star. Englewood Cliffs, New
       Jersey: Four Winds, 1970. 192p., illus.
             Aimed at younger readers.

4058. Dann, Allan, and John Underwood. How To Succeed in the Music
       Business: a Guide For Singers, Songwriters, and Musicians
       to the Business Side of the Music World. London; New York:
       Wise Publications, 1978. 87p., illus., bibliog., index.
             Emphasis on popular music.

4059. Davidson, John, and Cort Casady. The Singing Entertainer.
       Sherman Oaks, California: Alfred Publishing, 1979.   p.,
       bibliog. refs., index.
          Vocational guidance.

4060. Dearing, James. Making Money Making Music. Cincinnati:
       Writer's Digest, 1982. 320p.

4061. Edmunds, Alice (ed.). Who Puts the Grooves in the Record?
       New York: Random House, 1976. 74p., illus. (Adventures in
       the World of Work)
          Aimed at younger readers. Accounts of the various jobs
       involved in popular music recording.

4062. Faulkner, Robert Roy. Hollywood Studio Musicians: Their
       Work and Careers in the Recording Industry. Chicago: Aldine
       Atherton, 1971. 218p., bibliog. (Observations Series)
          Sociological study. Based on the author's PhD. dissert-
       ation, Studio Musicians: Their Work and Career Contingencies
       in the Hollywood Film Industry, University of California at
       Los Angeles, 1968.

4063. Gammond, Peter, and Raymond Horricks (eds.). The Music Goes
       Round and Round: a Cool Look at the Record Industry. London:
       Quartet, 1980. 183p., illus.
          Collection of essays on various aspects of the recording
       industry, by participants.

4064. Hammond, Ray. How To Get a Hit Record. Poole, Dorset:
       Javelin Books, 1985. 200p., illus., bibliog., index.
          Practical guide to the business of popular music, based
       on case histories.

4065. ————. Working in the Music Business. Poole, Dorset:
       Blandford Pr., 1983. 158p., illus., bibliog., index.
          Emphasis on popular music.

4066. Harris, Herby, and Lucien Farrar. How To Make Money in Music:
       a Guidebook for Success in Today's Music Business. New York:
       Arco Publishing, 1978.   p.

4067. Hatch, Tony. So You Want To Be in the Music Business.
       London: Everest, 1976. 240p., illus.
          Popular music. By leading arranger and composer.

4068. Hayward, Hilary. Careers in the Music Business. London:
       Kogan Page, 1983. 100p., illus.
          Popular music.

4069. Horn, Yvonne Michie. Sing For Your Supper: Earning Your
       Living as a Singer. New York: Harcourt, Brace, Jovanovich,
       1979.   p.
          Aimed at younger readers. Based on interviews with
       performers. Emphasis on popular music forms.

Comprehensive Works (cont.)

4070. Lawrence, S. So You Want To Be a Rock and Roll Star. New
      York: McGraw-Hill, 1983. 224p.

4071. Lecky, Zip (pseud.). How T' Make It as a Rock Star.
      Assistant editor: Tony Benyon. London: I.P.C. Magazines,
      1977.   p., illus.

4072. Martin, George (ed.). Making Music: the Guide to Writing,
      Performing, and Recording. London: Frederick Muller; Santa
      Barbara, California: Quill; London: Pan, 1983. 352p.,
      illus., bibliog., index.
         Emphasis on popular music. Contributions from practit-
      ioners.

4073. Mitz, Rick. Aim For a Job in the Record Business. New
      York: Richards Rosen Pr., 1977. 126p., illus., bibliog.
      (Aim High Vocational Series)

4074. Palmer, Tony. How To Make a Million Out of Pop Music.
      London: Hansen Publications, 1972. 28p.

4075. Pearcey, Leonard. The Musician's Survival Kit: How To Get
      Work With Music. Foreword by Peter Pears. London: Barrie
      and Jenkins, 1979. 120p., illus.
         Comprehensive guide to self-employment in music. Includ-
      es popular music forms.

4076. Rappoport, Victor D. Making It in Music. Englewood Cliffs,
      New Jersey; London: Prentice-Hall, 1979.   p., index.
      (A Spectrum Book)
         Popular music. Chapters 1-4 first published as The Sing-
      er's and Songwriter's Survival Kit, 1974.

4077. Rogers, Kenny, and Len Epand. Making It With Music: Kenny
      Rogers' Guide To the Music Business. New York: Harper and
      Row, 1978.   p., illus.

4078. Shankman, Ned N., and Larry A. Thompson. How To Make a
      Record Deal and Have Your Songs Recorded. Los Angeles:
      Barrister House Publishing, 1975. 192p., illus.

4079. Shinn, Duane. How People Make Money in Music. Central
      Point, Oregon: The Author, 1971. 40p.

4080. Siegel, Alan H. Breakin' in to the Music Business. Port
      Chester, New York: Cherry Lane Books, 1983.   p.
         Rock.

4081. ———. How To Become a Professional Pop Singer. Secaucus,
      New Jersey: Citadel Pr., 1963. 121p., illus.

4082. Weissman, Dick. The Music Business: Career Opportunities
      and Self-Defense. New York: Crown, 1979. 246p., illus.,
      bibliog., index.

4083. Young, Jean, and Jim Young. <u>Succeeding in the Big World of</u>
       <u>Music</u>. Boston: Little, Brown, 1977. 300p.
          Popular music.

4084. Zalkind, Ronald. <u>Getting Ahead in the Music Business</u>. New
       York: Schirmer, 1979.   p.
          Popular music.

                    (3) SPECIFIC FIELDS

              (i) Organization and Administration

4085. Antrim, Doron Kemp (ed.). <u>Paul Whiteman, Jimmy Dorsey,</u>
       <u>Rudy Vallee, Freddy Rich, Glen Gray, Frank Skinner, Enric</u>
       <u>Madriguera, Jimmy Dale, Merle Johnston, Guy Lombardo, Uriel</u>
       <u>Davis, and Duke Ellington Give Their Secrets of Dance Band</u>
       <u>Success</u>. New York: Famous Stars Publishing, 1936. 87p.
          How they ran their bands.

4086. Dagnall, Cynthia. <u>Starting Your Own Rock Band</u>. Chicago:
       Contemporary Books, 1983. 96p., illus.

4087. Guitar Player. <u>Putting a Band Together</u>. By the Editors of
       <u>Guitar Player</u> magazine. Saratoga, California: <u>Guitar Player</u>
       Productions, 1978. 32p.

4088. Hollies, The. <u>How To Run a Beat Group</u>. As told to Anne
       Nightingale. London: <u>Daily Mirror</u>, 1964. 100p., illus.

4089. Lieber, Leslie. <u>How To Form a Rock Group</u>. New York:
       Grosset and Dunlap, 1968. 112p., illus.

4090. Robinson, Richard. <u>Electric Rock</u>. New York: Pyramid Books,
       1972. 224p., illus.
          Comprehensive guide to starting and running a rock band.

4091. Specht, Paul L. <u>How They Became Name Bands: the Modern</u>
       <u>Technique of a Dance Band Maestro</u>. New York: Fine Arts
       Publications, 1941. 175p., illus.
          Advice, based on personal experience, from the first
       bandleader to broadcast.

4092. Turnbull, Stanley. <u>How To Run a Small Dance Band For Profit</u>.
       London: Nelson, 1937. 86p.

4093. Whiteman, Paul, and Leslie Lieber. <u>How To Be a Bandleader</u>.
       New York: R.M. McBride, 1941. 144p., illus., discog.

4094. Williams, Ralph Rex. <u>How To Build a Band and Make It Pay</u>.
       Chicago: Down Beat Publishing Company, 1940. 188p.

4095. Wise, Herbert H. (ed.). <u>Professional Rock and Roll</u>. New
       York: Collier Books; London: Collier-Macmillan, 1967. 94p.,
       illus.
          Fifteen experts advise the beginner.

(ii) Management

4096. Frascogna, Xavier M., and H. Lee Hetherington. <u>Successful</u>
       <u>Artist Management</u>. New York: Billboard Publications, 1978.
       p., index.

4097. Godbolt, Jim. <u>All This and Ten Per Cent</u>. London: Hale,
       1976. 208p., illus., index.
           Anecdotal memoir by former British agent, promoter, and
       manager. Author was in the music business from the 1930's
       to 1970.

(iii) Broadcasting/Disk Jockeys

4098. Attwood, Tony. <u>How To Become a Successful Disk Jockey</u>.
       Northampton, England: Hamilton House, 1984. 39p.

4099. <u>Radio Industry Business and Employment Guide</u>. Totnes,
       Devon: R.S. Productions, 1979. 8p.
           Advice on entering the business, plus addresses.

4100. Rosko, Emperor (<u>pseud</u>.). <u>Emperor Rosko's DJ Book</u>. Ideas
       by Rosko; translated into English, and written down by
       Johnny Beerling. London: Everest, 1976. 224p., illus.,
       index.
           Advice from leading disk-jockey on French (later British)
       radio.

4101. See, David J. <u>How To Be a Disk Jockey</u>. London: Hamlyn,
       1980. 87p., illus., index.

   *   Shannon, Doug. <u>Off the Record: Everything Related To Play-</u>
       <u>ing Recorded Dance Music in the Entertainment Business</u>.
           * Cited above as item 1269.

(iv) Folk Music

4102. Nye, Hermes. <u>How To Be a Folksinger: How To Sing and</u>
       <u>Present Folksongs; or, The Folksinger's Guide; or, Eggs I</u>
       <u>Have Laid</u>. New York: Oak Publications, 1965. 160p., illus.,
       bibliog.
           Includes words and music of twenty-three songs.

4103. Traum, Happy (<u>pseud</u>.). <u>Folk Guitar as a Profession</u>. Fore-
       word by John Sebastian. Saratoga, California: <u>Guitar Player</u>
       Books, 1977. 68p.

(v) Country Music

*   Bart, Teddy. <u>Inside Music City, U.S.A.</u>
       * Cited above as item 3823.

4104.   Levine, Arthur D. <u>The Nashville Number System: a Guide to
How It Works</u>. Nashville: Gibraltar, 1981. 74p., illus.

4105.   Sadler, Barry. <u>Everything You Want To Know About the
Record Industry in Nashville, Tennessee, Country Music
Capital of the World</u>. Nashville: Aurora Publishers, 1978.
119p., illus.

PART FIVE: PRODUCT

A. SONGS

(1) REFERENCE MATERIALS

(i) Bibliographies

4106. Denisoff, R. Serge. <u>American Protest Songs of War and Peace:</u>
<u>a Selected Bibliography and Discography.</u> Los Angeles:
Center for the Study of Armament and Disarmament, California
State College, 1970. 15p. (Bibliography Series, 1). <u>Rev.</u>
<u>ed.</u> (as <u>Songs of Protest, War, and Peace: a Bibliography and</u>
<u>Discography</u>): Santa Barbara, California: A.B.C.-Clio, 1973.
70p.

Sheet Music

4107. Board of Music Trade of the United States of America.
<u>Complete Catalog of Sheet Music and Musical Works Published</u>
<u>by the Board of Music Trade.</u> New York: Board of Music Trade
of the United States of America, 1870; New York: Da Capo Pr.,
1973. 575p.
Classified title listing of works published by consortium
of twenty companies. Da Capo Pr. edition has new introduction
by Dena J. Epstein.

4108. Dichter, Harry. <u>Handbook of American Sheet Music: a Catalog</u>
<u>of Sheet Music For Sale by the Compiler and Publishers.</u>
Philadelphia: The Author, 1947. 100p., illus. <u>2nd. ed.</u>:
Philadelphia: The Author, 1953.   p., illus.
Classified listing, with bibliographical data. 1953
edition prepared with the assistance of Bernice Larrabee.

4109. ————, and Elliott Shapiro. <u>Early American Sheet Music:</u>
<u>Its Lure and Its Lore, 1768-1889. Including a Directory of</u>
<u>Early American Music Publishers.</u> New York: Bowker, 1941;
New York: Dover; London: Constable (as <u>Handbook of Early</u>
<u>American Sheet Music, 1768-1889</u>), 1977. 287p., illus., index.
Classified. Dover/Constable edition has revised illustrat-
ions section.

4110. Klamkin, Marian. <u>Old Sheet Music.</u> New York: Hawthorn Books,
1975.   p., illus.
Aimed at collectors.

4111. Priest, Daniel B. <u>American Sheet Music: a Guide to Collect-</u>
<u>ing Sheet Music, From 1775 to 1975. With Prices.</u> Des Moines,
Iowa: Wallace-Homestead Book Company, 1978. 82p., illus.

Bibliographies (cont.)

Sheet Music (cont.)

4112. Library Company. <u>American Song Sheets, Slip Ballads, and</u>
<u>Poetical Broadsides, 1850-1870: a Catalog of the Collection</u>
<u>of the Library Company of Philadelphia.</u> Compiled by Edwin
Wolf. New York: Kraus Reprint, 1963. 232p., illus.,
indexes.

Sheet Music Covers and Illustrations

4113. Pearsall, Ronald. <u>Victorian Sheet Music Covers.</u> Newton
Abbot, Devon: David and Charles, 1972. 112p., illus., index.

4114. Spellman, Doreen, and Sidney Spellman. <u>Victorian Music</u>
<u>Covers.</u> Foreword by Sacheverell Sitwell. London: Evelyn,
Adams, and Mackay, 1969. 72p., illus.

4115. Tatham, David. <u>The Lure of the Striped Pig: the Illustrat-</u>
<u>ion of Popular Music in America, 1820-1870.</u> Barre, Mass-
achusetts: Imprint Society, 1973. 157p., illus.

4116. Wilk, Max (ed.). <u>Memory Lane, 1890 to 1925: Ragtime, Jazz,</u>
<u>Foxtrot, and Other Popular Music and Music Covers.</u> London:
<u>Studio International,</u> 1973; New York: Ballantine, 1976.
124p., illus.
      Full-color reproductions of over one hundred covers.

(ii) Indexes and Directories

4117. Blacklock, Robert Shedden. <u>Which Song and When: a Handbook</u>
<u>of Selected Song Titles From 1880 to 1974.</u> Edinburgh:
Bandparts Music Stores, 1975. 84p.

4118. Burton, Jack. <u>The Blue Book of Broadway Musicals.</u> Watkins
Glen, New York: Century House, 1952. 320p., illus., discog.,
index. <u>Rev. ed., with additions by Larry Freeman:</u> Watkins
Glen, New York: Century House, 1969. 327p., illus., discog.,
index.
      Arranged chronologically, in decades. Guide to songs in
approximately 1,500 Broadway musicals.

4119. ————. <u>The Blue Book of Hollywood Musicals: Songs From the</u>
<u>Sound Tracks, and the Stars Who Sang Them, Since the Birth</u>
<u>of the Talkies a Quarter-Century Ago.</u> Watkins Glen, New
York: Century House, 1953. 296p., illus., discog., index.
      Guide to musical items in approximately three thousand
motion pictures, 1927-52. Includes information about the
productions. Chronological, classified arrangement.

4120.   ———. The Blue Book of Broadway Musicals, and Hollywood.
Watkins Glen, New York: Century House, 1974.   344p., illus.,
discog., index.
        Revised compilation of items 4118 and 4119.

4121.   ———. The Blue Book of Tin Pan Alley: a Human Interest
Anthology of American Popular Music. Watkins Glen, New
York: Century House, 1950. 520p., illus., discogs., index.

        ———. ———. Deluxe ed.: Watkins Glen, New York:
Century House, 1951. 520p., illus., discogs., index.

        ———. The Blue Book of Tin Pan Alley: a Human Interest
Encyclopedia of American Popular Music. Expanded new ed.,
1950-1965. Supplement by Larry Freeman. Watkins Glen, New
York: Century House, 1962-65. 2 vols.,   p., illus.,
discogs., index.
        Covers 1776 to date. Guide to composers and lyricists;
and their songs.

4122.   ———. Index of American Popular Music: Thousands of
Titles Cross-Referenced to Our Basic Anthologies of Popular
Songs: "The Blue Book of Tin Pan Alley", "The Blue Book of
Broadway Musicals", "The Blue Book of Hollywood Musicals",
"The Melodies Linger On". Watkins Glen, New York: Century
House, 1957 (Reissued: 1981). 231p.
        Alphabetical index of song titles. References are to
page numbers of items 4118, 4119, 4121, and

4123.   Chipman, John H. Index to Top-Hit Tunes, 1900-1950. Foreword by Arthur Fiedler. Boston: B. Humphries, 1962. 249p.,
bibliog.
        Includes over three thousand best-selling songs; gives
key, also publishing details.

4124.   Cleveland Public Library. Index to Negro Spirituals.
Cleveland: Cleveland Public Library, 1937. 149p.

4125.   Colbert, Warren E. Who Wrote That Song? Or, Who in the
Hell is J. Fred Coots? An Informal Survey of American
Popular Songs, and Their Composers. New York: Revisionist
Pr., 1975. 195p., illus.
        Alphabetical listing of best-selling songs, with details
of their composers.

4126.   Ewen, David. American Popular Songs From the Revolutionary
War to the Present. New York: Random House, 1966. 507p.,
discog.
        Listing of over 3,600 songs by title, with their histories.

4127.   Fuld, James J. American Popular Music Reference Book, 1875-
1950. Philadelphia: Musical Americana, 1955; South Benfleet,
Essex: Swift Musical Service, 1956. 94p., illus., index.
        Descriptive listing of popular songs, with details of
first editions. Supplement, giving corrections, issued 1956.

Indexes and Directories (cont.)

4128. Fuld, James J. <u>The Book of World-Famous Music: Classical,
       Popular, and Folk</u>. New York: Crown, 1966. 564p., index.
       <u>Rev., enlarged ed</u>.: New York: Crown, 1971. 688p., illus.,
       bibliog., index.
           Alphabetical title arrangement. Gives publishing details
       and histories of a "fair sample of well-known melodies."
       Includes library locations.

4129. Gargan, William, and Sue Sharman. <u>Find That Tune: an Index
       to Rock, Folk-Rock, Disco, and Soul in Collections</u>. New
       York: Neal-Schuman Publishers; London: Mansell, 1984. 303p.,
       indexes.
           Indexes over four thousand songs in 203 published sheet
       music collections.

4130. Havlice, Patricia Pate. <u>Popular Song Index</u>. Metuchen, New
       Jersey; London: Scarecrow Pr., 1975. 933p., bibliog.

       ————. ————. <u>First Supplement</u>. Metuchen, New Jersey;
       London: Scarecrow Pr., 1978. 386p., bibliog.

4131. Leigh, Robert. <u>Index to Songbooks: a Title Index to Over
       Eleven Thousand Copies of Almost 6,800 Songs in 111 Song
       Books Published Between 1933 and 1962</u>. Stockton, California:
       The Author, 1964; New York: Da Capo Pr., 1973. 237p.

4132. Lewine, Richard, and Alfred Simon. <u>Encyclopedia of Theater
       Music: a Comprehensive Listing of More Than Four Thousand
       Songs From Broadway and Hollywood, 1900-1960</u>. New York:
       Random House, 1961 (Reissued: 1971). 248p., index.

       ————. <u>Songs of the American Theater: a Comprehensive
       Listing of More Than Twelve Thousand Songs, Including
       Selected Titles From Film and Television Productions</u>.
       Introduction by Stephen Sondheim. New York: Dodd, Mead,
       1973. 820p., index.

4133. Lindstrom, Robert C. <u>Songs For Remembrance: a Compilation
       of Song Titles and Information. Jazz-Popular. Musicians'
       Guide, Song and Folio Reference</u>. Great Falls, Montana:
       Lindstrom Publications, 1961. 80p., illus.

4134. Lowe, Leslie. <u>Directory of Popular Music, 1900-1965</u>.
       Droitwich, Worcestershire: Peterson Publishing, 1975.
       1,034p., index.

4135. Mackean, Bob, Peter Fornatale, and Bill Ayers. <u>The Rock
       Music Source Book</u>. Garden City, New York: Anchor Pr., 1980.
       600p.
           Listing of rock songs according to their subject matter.

4136. Markewich, Reese. <u>Bibliography of Jazz and Pop Tunes
       Sharing the Chord Progressions of Other Compositions</u>.
       Riverdale, New York: The Author, 1970. 58p. <u>Rev. ed</u>.: 1974.

4137. Morgan, Sophia. That's an Old One: a Compilation of Song
       Titles and Their Copyright Dates. Glendale, California:
       Morgan Mimeographing, 1950. 145p.

4138. Parsons, Denys. The Directory of Tunes and Musical Themes.
       Introduction by Bernard Levin. Cambridge, England: Spencer
       Brown, 1975. 286p.
            Guide to song identification, using non-notational coding
       system.

4139. Sears, Minnie Earl, and Phyllis Crawford. Song Index: an
       Index to More Than Twelve Thousand Songs in 177 Song Collect-
       ions Comprising 262 Volumes. New York: H.W. Wilson, 1926.
       648p.

            ————. Supplement: an Index to More Than Seven Thousand
       Songs in 104 Song Collections Comprising 124 Volumes. New
       York: H.W. Wilson, 1934. 366p.

            ————. Song Index: an Index to More Than Twelve Thousand
       Songs in 177 Song Collections Comprising 262 Volumes; and,
       Supplement: an Index to More Than Seven Thousand Songs in
       104 Song Collections Comprising 124 Volumes. Hamden, Conn.:
       Shoe String Pr., 1966. 1,014p.

4140. Stecheson, Anthony, and Anne Stecheson. The Stecheson
       Classified Song Directory. Hollywood, California: Music
       Industry Pr., 1961. 503p.

            ————. ————: with Supplement Thru 1978. Hollywood,
       California: Criterion Music, 1979.   p.

4141. Turpie, Mary C. American Music for the Study of American
       Civilization. Minneapolis: University of Minnesota, 1954.
       91p., discogs., index. (Program in American Studies)
            Includes listing of some 350 folk and popular songs;
       indicates collections in which they appear.

4142. Warner, Alan. Who Sang What On the Screen. Foreword by
       Tim Rice. London: Angus and Robertson, 1984. 168p., illus.,
       index.
            Guide, with background information, to popular songs
       from Hollywood musicals. Includes background and theme songs.

4143. Whitter, John, and Ruth Worth. Song Index: Popular Songs,
       and Where to Find Them. London: Association of Assistant
       Librarians, 1981. 111p., bibliog.

4144. Woll, Allen L. Songs From Hollywood Musical Comedies,
       1927 to the Present: a Dictionary. New York: Garland
       Publishing, 1976. 251p., bibliog. refs., index. (Garland
       Reference Library in the Humanities, 44)

(iii) Chronologies

4145. American Society of Composers, Authors, and Publishers.
       <u>Forty Years of Hit Tunes</u>. New York: ASCAP, 1956. 64p.
       Year-by-year listing of compositions by ASCAP members.
       Covers 1915-55.

       ———. ———. New York: ASCAP, 1958. 80p.
       Reprint of previous item, with supplemental listings for
       1956 and 1957.

       ———. <u>ASCAP Hit Tunes</u>. New York: ASCAP, 1967. 110p.
       Updated and expanded.

       ———. <u>ASCAP Hit Tunes, 1892-1970</u>. New York: ASCAP,
       1971.   p.

4146. ———. <u>Forty Years of Show Tunes: the Big Broadway Hits</u>,
       <u>1917-1957</u>. New York: ASCAP, 1959. 149p.
       Year-by-year listing of compositions by ASCAP members.

4147. ———. <u>Thirty Years of Motion Picture Music: the Big</u>
       <u>Hollywood Hits, 1928-1958</u>. New York: ASCAP, 1958. 122p.
       Year-by-year listing of compositions by ASCAP members.

4148. <u>Eighty Years of American Song Hits, 1892-1972: a Comprehen-</u>
       <u>sive Yearly Reference Book Listing America's Major Hit Songs</u>
       <u>and Their Writers</u>. New York: Chappell, 1973. 106p.

4149. Mattfield, Julius. <u>"Variety" Music Cavalcade, 1620-1950</u>:
       <u>a Chronology of Vocal and Instrumental Music Popular in the</u>
       <u>United States</u>. New York: Prentice-Hall, 1952. 637p., index.

       ———. <u>"Variety" Music Cavalcade, 1620-1961</u>. Englewood
       Cliffs, New Jersey: Prentice-Hall, 1962. 713p., index.

       ———. <u>"Variety" Music Cavalcade, 1620-1969</u>. Additional
       information by Herm Schoenfeld. Englewood Cliffs, New
       Jersey; London: Prentice-Hall, 1971. 766p., index.
       Begun as a library card index; originally published in
       <u>"Variety" Radio Directory, 1938-39</u>. Lists (3rd. ed.) some
       five thousand compositions.

4150. Shapiro, Nat. <u>Popular Music: an Annotated Index of American</u>
       <u>Popular Songs</u>. New York: Adrian Pr., 1964-73; Detroit: Gale
       Research, 1964- .
       Vol. 1: <u>1950-1959</u>. 1964. 350p.
       Vol. 2: <u>1940-1949</u>. 1965. 350p.
       Vol. 3: <u>1960-1964</u>. 1967. 350p.
       Vol. 4: <u>1930-1939</u>. 1968. 350p.
       Vol. 5: <u>1920-1929</u>. 1969. 350p.
       Vol. 6: <u>1965-1969</u>. 1973. 350p.
       Vol. 7: <u>1970-1974</u>. 1975. 350p.
       Vol. 8: <u>1975-1979</u>. 1984. 350p.

       Year-by-year treatment within each volume.

(2) CRITICISM

4151. Dennison, Sam. <u>Scandalize My Name: Black Imagery in American</u>
       <u>Popular Music</u>. New York: Garland Publishing, 1980. 608p.,
       bibliog., indexes.
           Examines the image (usually negative) of Blacks as
       presented in White popular music.

4152. Niemoeller, Adolph Frederick. <u>Sex Ideas in Popular Songs</u>.
       Girard, Kansas: Haldeman-Julius, 1946. 32p.

4153. Rimler, Walter. <u>Not Fade Away: a Comparison of Two Gener-</u>
       <u>ations of Composers of Contemporary Popular Music</u>. Ann
       Arbor, Michigan: Pierian Pr., 1983.   p.

4154. Spaeth, Sigmund Gottfried. <u>The Facts of Life in Popular</u>
       <u>Song</u>. New York: Whittlesey House, 1934. 148p.
           The influence of current mores and social concerns on the
       topics of popular songs.

4155. ————. <u>They Still Sing of Love</u>. New York: Horace
       Liveright, 1929. 234p.
           Essays on the lyrical content of popular songs.

(3) GENERAL HISTORIES

(i) Comprehensive Works

4156. Ewen, David. <u>Songs of America: a Cavalcade of Popular Songs</u>.
       Arranged for voice and piano by Mischa and Wesley Portnoff.
       Chicago: Ziff-Davis, 1947; Westport, Conn.: Greenwood Pr.,
       1978. 246p.
           Fifty-eight representative songs. Includes much commentary.

  *   ————. <u>Panorama of American Popular Music</u>.
            * Cited above as item 188.

  *   Finck, Henry Theophilus. <u>Songs and Songwriters</u>.
            * Cited above as item 1650.

4157. Fitz-Gerald, Shafto Justin Adair. <u>The Stories of Famous</u>
       <u>Songs</u>. London: J.C. Nimmo; Philadelphia: Lippincott, 1898.
       426p.

4158. Freeman, Larry (<u>pseud. of</u> Graydon La Verne Freeman). <u>The</u>
       <u>Melodies Linger On: Fifty Years of Popular Song</u>. Watkins
       Glen, New York: Century House, 1951. 212p., illus.
           The stories of popular songs, 1900-50. Indexed by item
       4122.

4159. Geller, James J. <u>Famous Songs and Their Stories</u>. New York:
       Macauley, 1931. 248p.
           Fifty-five songs (words and music); each with detailed
       account of its origin.

General Histories (cont.)

4160. Gilbert, Douglas. <u>Lost Chords: the Diverting Story of
       American Popular Songs</u>. Garden City, New York: Doubleday,
       Doran, 1942; New York: Cooper Square Publishers, 1971.
       377p., indexes.

4161. Greenway, John. <u>American Folksongs of Protest</u>. Philadelphia:
       University of Pennsylvania Pr.; London: Oxford University Pr.,
       1953; Gloucester, Massachusetts: Peter Smith, 1962; New York:
       Octagon Books, 1970. 348p., illus., bibliog., discog.,
       indexes.

4162. Kobbe, Gustav. <u>Famous American Songs</u>. New York: Crowell,
       1906. 168p., illus.

4163. Luther, Frank. <u>Americans and Their Songs</u>. New York: Harper,
       1942. 323p., index.
           Song collection. Illustrates connections between folk
       and popular songs, and historical events, 1620-1900.

4164. Marcuse, Maxwell F. <u>Tin Pan Alley in Gaslight: a Saga of
       the Songs That Made the Gray Nineties "Gay."</u> Watkins Glen,
       New York: Century House, 1959. 448p., illus.

4165. Montgomery, Elizabeth Rider. <u>The Story Behind Popular Songs</u>.
       Illustrated by Ernest Norling. New York: Dodd, Mead, 1958.
       253p., illus.
           Aimed at younger readers.

4166. Rosen, David M. <u>Protest Songs in America</u>. Foreword by David
       Manning White. Westlake Village, California: Aware Pr.,
       1972. 159p., bibliog., discog.

4167. Stevens, Denis. <u>A History of Song</u>. London: Hutchinson,
       1960; New York: Norton, 1961. 491p., bibliog., index.
           Includes consideration of popular songs.

4168. Wickes, Edward Michael. <u>True Stories of Famous Songs</u>.
       New York: De Sylva, Brown, and Henderson, 192? (Reissued:
       1930). 32p.

4169. Wilk, Max. <u>They're Playing Our Song: From Jerome Kern to
       Stephen Sondheim. The Stories Behind the Words and Music of
       Two Generations</u>. New York: Atheneum, 1973; London: W.H.
       Allen, 1974. 295p.
           The stories of twenty-one standard popular songs, by
       twenty-one composers. Based on first-hand knowledge.

4170. Wolfe, William E. <u>Music You Wear</u>. Nashville: Tidings, 1975.
       111p.

4171. Yerbury, Grace Helen Davies. <u>Song in America, From Early
       Times to About 1850</u>. Metuchen, New Jersey; London: Scarecrow
       Pr., 1971. 305p., illus., bibliog.

(ii) Individual Songs

4172. Foner, Philip S. <u>The Case of Joe Hill</u>. New York: International Publishers, 1965. 127p., illus., bibliog. notes.
Account of the labor leader; inspiration for songwriters.

4173. Jackson, Carlton. <u>The Great Lili</u>. San Francisco: Strawberry Hill Pr., 1978.   p., bibliog. refs.
Story of World War II song, <u>Lili Marleen</u>, and its
writers, Norbert Schultze and Hans Leip.

4174. Owens, Harry. <u>Sweet Leilani: the Story Behind the Song. An
Autobiography</u>. Pacific Palisades, California: Hula House,
1970. 313p., illus.
By its composer.

4175. Turner, Martha Anne. <u>The Yellow Rose of Texas: the Story of
a Song</u>. El Paso, Texas: Texas Western Pr., 1971. 19p.,
illus. (South Western Studies Monographs, 31)

———. <u>The Yellow Rose of Texas: Her Saga and Her Song;
with, The Santa Anna Legend</u>. Austin: Shoal Creek Publishers,
1976. 136p., illus., bibliog. refs., index.

(4) PERIODS AND STYLES

(a) Popular

Lyric Collections

4176. Chipman, Bruce L. (comp.). <u>Hardening Rock: an Anthology of
the Adolescence of Rock 'n' Roll</u>. With an appreciative
essay by X.J. Kennedy. Boston: Little, Brown, 1972. 154p.,
illus.

4177. Damsker, Matt (comp.). <u>Rock Voices: the Best Lyrics of an
Era</u>. Foreword by Paul Gambaccini. New York: St. Martin's
Pr.; London: Arthur Barker, 1980. 139p.

4178. Goldstein, Richard (comp.). <u>The Poetry of Rock</u>. New York:
Bantam, 1969. 147p., illus.

4179. Nickoll, Peter (comp.). <u>Juke Box: Thirty-Three Pop Songs
From the Fifties, Sixties, and Seventies</u>. London: Black,
1984. 48p., illus., index.

4180. Pichaske, David R. (comp.). <u>The Poetry of Rock: the Golden
Years</u>. Peoria, Illinois: Ellis Pr., 1981. 192p.

4181. Pollock, Bruce (comp.). <u>In Their Own Words: Lyrics and
Lyricists, 1955-1974</u>. New York: Macmillan; New York:
Collier Books; London: Collier-Macmillan, 1975. 231p.,
illus.

Lyric Collections (cont.)

4182. Spinner, Stephanie (comp.). Rock is Beautiful: an Anthology
       of American Lyrics, 1953-1968. Introduction by Nat Hentoff.
       New York: Dell, 1970. 158p.

                              (b) Folk

4183. Green, Archie. Only a Miner: Studies in Recorded Coal-
       Mining Songs. Urbana; Chicago; London: University of
       Illinois Pr., 1971. 480p., illus., bibliog., discog.,
       index. (Music in American Life)
            Examines, through study of the songs, the change from
       folk to wider popular culture.

                         Lyric Collections

4184. Silber, Irwin, and Fred Silber (comps.). The Folksinger's
       Wordbook. New York: Oak Publications, 1973. 430p., illus.,
       bibliog.

                            (c) Country

4185. McCulloh, Judith. Hillbilly Records and Tune Transcriptions.
       Los Angeles: John Edwards Memorial Foundation, 1968. 19p.,
       bibliog., discog. (J.E.M.F. Reprint Series, 9)
            History of published transcriptions of early country
       performances on record. Urges folklorists to pay more
       regard to such sources. Reprinted from Western Folklore,
       1967.

4186. White, John Irwin. Git Along, Little Dogies: Songs and
       Songmakers of the American West. Urbana; Chicago; London:
       University of Illinois Pr., 1975. 221p., illus., bibliog.,
       discog., index. (Music in American Life)
            Memoir by early singer of cowboy songs; with critical
       study of the genre. Includes sample songs, and record.

                         Lyric Collections

4187. Horstman, Dorothy A. (comp.). Sing Your Heart Out, Country
       Boy. New York: Dutton, 1975; New York: Pocket Books, 1976.
       455p., bibliog., discog., index.

4188. Offen, Carol (comp.). Country Music: the Poetry. New York:
       Ballantine, 1977. 120p., illus.

(d) Black Music

(i) Comprehensive Works

4189. Odum, Howard Washington, and Guy Benton Johnson. <u>The Negro
        and His Songs: a Study of Typical Negro Songs in the South</u>.
        Chapel Hill, North Carolina: University of North Carolina
        Pr., 1925; Hatboro, Pennsylvania: Folklore Associates,
        1964; New York: Negro Universities Pr., 1968; Westport,
        Conn.: Greenwood Pr., 1969. 306p., bibliog.
        Includes over 250 songs (words and music.)

(ii) Black Folksongs

(a) Bibliography

4190. Ferris, William R. <u>Mississippi Black Folklore: a Research
        Bibliography</u>. Hattiesburg: University and College Pr. of
        Mississippi, 1971. 61p., illus., discog.
        Not annotated.

(b) General Guides and Overviews

4191. Courlander, Harold. <u>Negro Folk Music, U.S.A.</u> New York;
        London: Columbia University Pr., 1963. 324p., illus.,
        bibliogs., discog., index.
        Includes appendix of songs (words and music.)

4192. Jackson, Clyde Owen. <u>The Songs of Our Years: a Study of
        Negro Folk Music</u>. New York: Exposition Pr., 1968. 54p.,
        bibliog.
        Includes consideration of use of Black folk music in
        concert works.

4193. Ramsey, Frederic, <u>Jr</u>. <u>Been Here and Gone</u>. New Brunswick,
        New Jersey: Rutgers University Pr., 1960; London: Cassell,
        1961. 178p., illus.
        Account, compressed from five 1950's field trips, of
        song collection in the Deep South. Includes song texts.

4194. Scarborough, Dorothy. <u>On the Trail of Negro Folk-Songs</u>.
        With Ola Lee Gulledge. Cambridge, Massachusetts: Harvard
        University Pr., 1925; Hatboro, Pennsylvania: Folklore
        Associates, 1963. 295p.
        Includes song texts; also words and music of 108 songs.

4195. Work, John Wesley. <u>Folk Song of the American Negro</u>. Nash-
        ville: Fisk University Pr., 1915; New York: Negro Universities
        Pr., 1969. 131p.

Black Folksongs (cont.)

(c) General Histories

4196. Epstein, Dena J. <u>Sinful Tunes and Spirituals: Black Folk
       Music to the Civil War</u>. Urbana; Chicago; London: Univers-
       ity of Illinois Pr., 1977. 433p., illus., bibliog., index.
       (Music in American Life)

4197. Fisher, Miles Mark. <u>Negro Slave Songs in the United States</u>.
       Ithaca, New York: Cornell University Pr. for The American
       Historical Association, 1953; New York: Russell and Russell,
       1968. 223p., bibliog., index.
          Based on his dissertation, <u>The Evolution of Slave Songs
       in the United States</u>, University of Chicago, 1949.

4198. Krehbiel, Henry Edward. <u>Afro-American Folk Songs: a Study
       in Racial and National Music</u>. New York; London: Schirmer,
       1914; New York: Frederick Ungar, 1962; Portland, Maine:
       Longwood Pr., 1976. 176p., index.
          Contends that the folk music of Blacks in the United
       States is predominantly of African origin.

                       Lyric Collections

4199. White, Newman Ivey (comp.). <u>American Negro Folk-Songs</u>.
       Foreword by Bruce Jackson. Cambridge, Massachusetts: Harvard
       University Pr., 1928; Hatboro, Pennsylvania: Folklore
       Associates, 1965. 501p., illus., bibliog., indexes.
          Texts of over eight hundred black folksongs; also has
       specimin tunes.

       (iii) Sacred (including White Spirituals)

4200. Cone, James H. <u>The Spirituals and the Blues: an Interpretat-
       ion</u>. New York: Seabury Pr., 1972; Westport, Conn.: Green-
       wood Pr., 1980. 152p., bibliog. refs.

4201. Dett, Robert Nathaniel. <u>The Development of the Negro
       Spiritual</u>. Minneapolis: Schmitt, Hall, and McCreary, 1936.
          p.

4202. Dixon, Christa R. <u>Negro Spirituals: From Bible to Folk Song</u>.
       Philadelphia: Fortress Pr., 1976. 117p., indexes.

4203. Djedje, Jacqueline C. <u>American Black Spirituals and Gospel
       Songs From Southeast Georgia: a Comparative Study</u>. Los
       Angeles: Center for Afro-American Study, 1978. 105p.

4204. Friedel, L.M. <u>The Bible and the Negro Spirituals</u>. St.
       Louis: St. Augustine Seminary, 1947. 24p.

4205. Jackson, George Pullen. <u>White and Negro Spirituals: Their
Life Span and Kinship. Tracing Two Hundred Years of
Untrammeled Song Making and Singing Among Our Country Folk.
With 116 Songs as Sung by Both Races.</u> Locust Valley, New
York: J.J. Augustin, 1943; New York: Da Capo Pr., 1975.
349p., illus., bibliog., index.
    Discards the concept of African origins; contends that
Black forms derive from White forms through borrowings and
adaptions.

4206. ———. <u>White Spirituals in the Southern Uplands: the Story
of the Fasola Folk, Their Songs, Singings, and "Buckwheat
Notes."</u> Chapel Hill, North Carolina: University of North
Carolina Pr.; London: Oxford University Pr., 1933; New York:
Dover, 1965. 444p., illus., bibliog.
    Study of the shape-note forms. Includes discussion of
Black spirituals; contends that their source lies in White
forms.

4207. Lehman, Theo. <u>Negro Spirituals: Geschichte und Theologie.</u>
Berlin: Eckart, 1965. 414p., bibliog., index.
    In German. Based on the author's Dissertation, same
tile, Halle University, 1963.

4208. Lovell, John. <u>Black Song: the Forge and the Flame. The
Story of How the Afro-American Spiritual Was Hammered Out.</u>
New York: Macmillan; London: Collier-Macmillan, 1972. 686p.,
illus., bibliog.

4209. Owens, James Garfield. <u>All God's Children: Meditations on
Negro Spirituals.</u> Nashville: Abingdon Pr., 1971. 144p.

4210. Ricks, George Robinson. <u>Some Aspects of the Religious Music
of the United States Negro. An Ethnomusicological Study,
With Special Emphasis on the Gospel Tradition.</u> Edited by
Richard Dorson. New York: Arno Pr., 1977.   p., bibliog.
    Based on the author's Thesis, same title, Northwestern
University, 1960.

4211. Thurman, Howard. <u>Deep River: Reflections On the Religious
Insight of Certain of the Negro Spirituals.</u> New York:
Harper, 1955; Port Washington, New York: Kennikat Pr., 1969.
93p., illus.

4212. ———. <u>The Negro Spiritual Speaks of Life and Death. Being
the Ingersoll Lecture on the Immortality of Man.</u> New York;
London: Harper, 1947; New York: Harper and Row, 1969. 55p.
    Delivered at Harvard University, 1947.

4213. ———. <u>Deep River; and, The Negro Spiritual Speaks of Life
and Death.</u> Richmond, Indiana: Friends United Pr., 1975.
136p.

4214. Yoder, Don. <u>Pennsylvania Spirituals.</u> Lancaster: Pennsylvania
Folklife Society, 1961. 528p., illus.
    Includes discussion of Black forms; has 150 song texts.

Sacred (cont.)

Lyric Collections

4215. Lehman, Theo (comp.). <u>Nobody Knows: Negro Spirituals</u>.
       Leipzig: Koehler und Amslang, 1961. 211p.

4216. Lilje, Hans, Kurt Heinrich Hansen, and Siegfried Schmidt-
       Joos. <u>Das Buch der Spirituals und Gospelsongs: Texte der
       Spirituals und Gospelsongs in deutscher und englischer
       Sprache</u>. Hamburg: Furche, 1961. 232p.
          Original texts, with German translations. Includes
       record.

(iv) Blues

4217. Charters, Samuel Barclay. <u>The Poetry of the Blues</u>. With
       photographs by Ann Charters. New York: Oak Publications,
       1963. 111p., illus., bibliog.
          Critical analysis of blues lyrics.

  *   Cone, James H. <u>The Spirituals and the Blues: an Interpret-
       ation</u>.
          * Cited above as item 4200.

4218. Greenberg, Alan. <u>Love in Vain</u>. Garden City, New York:
       Doubleday, 1983. 388p., illus. (Dolphin Books)

4219. Oliver, Paul. <u>Blues Fell This Morning: the Meaning of the
       Blues</u>. Foreword by Richard Wright. London: Cassell; New
       York: Horizon Pr., 1960. 336p., illus., bibliog., discog.

          —————. <u>The Meaning of the Blues</u>. Foreword by Richard
       Wright. New York: Collier Books, 1963; New York: Horizon
       Pr., 1983. 383p., illus., bibliog., discog.
          Lyrics analyzed through transcriptions of 350 examples
       taken from records.

4220. —————— (ed.). <u>Conversations With the Blues</u>. Photographs by
       the author. London: Cassell; New York: Horizon Pr., 1965.
       217p., illus., discog., index.
          Sequel to item 4219. Verbatim extracts from conversations
       with some seventy bluesmen on the nature of the blues as a
       means of expression.

4221. Scarborough, Dorothy. <u>The "Blues" as Folk Songs</u>. Austin:
       Texas Folklore Society, 1923. 13p. (Texas Folklore Society
       Publications, 2)

4222. Wiser, William. <u>Ballads, Blues, and Swan Songs</u>. New York:
       Atheneum, 1982.   p.

Lyric Collections

4223.   Berendt, Joachim Ernst (comp.). Blues: ein Essay. Foreword
        by Arrigo Polillo. Munich: Nymphenburger Varlagshandlung,
        1957. 122p., illus., discog.
            Forty-eight blues lyrics in English, with German trans-
        lations. Includes twenty-seven songs with words and music.

        ————. Blues: Englisch-deutsch. Munich: Nymphenburger
        Verlagshandlung, 1962. 116p., illus., discog. (Schwartzer
        Gesang, 2)

4224.   Jahn, Janheinz (comp.). Blues und Work Songs. Introductory
        essay by Alfons Michael Dauer. Frankfurt/Main: Fischer,
        1964. 185p., bibliog., discog.
            Essay by Dauer on the nature of blues lyrics, followed by
        texts in English, with German translations. Includes forty
        songs with words and music.

4225.   Nicholas, A.X. (comp.). Woke Up This Mornin': the Poetry of
        the Blues. New York: Bantam, 1973. 122p.

4226.   Sackheim, Eric (comp.). The Blues Line: a Collection of
        Blues Lyrics. Illustrations by Jonathan Shahn. New York:
        Grossman, 1969 (A Munshinsha Book); New York: Schirmer Books,
        1975; London: Collier-Macmillan, 1977. 500p., illus.
            Classified arrangement. Lyrics of 270 songs.

4227.   Taft, Michael (comp.). Blues Lyric Poetry: an Anthology.
        New York: Garland Publishing, 1982. 407p., index.
            Over two thousand transcribed lyrics, representing the
        work of over 350 inter-war artists.

4228.   ————. Blues Lyric Poetry: a Concordance. New York:
        Garland Publishing, 1983. 3 vols., 3,196 p.
            Accompanies item 4227. Key word in context format.
        Includes word-frequency list; also historical and discograph-
        ical details of each song.

(v) Soul

Lyric Collections

4229.   Nicholas, A.X. (comp.). The Poetry of Soul. New York:
        Bantam, 1971. 103p., illus., discog.
            Lyrics of forty-three songs.

(vi) Caribbean

4230.   Espinet, Charles S., and Harry Pitts. Land of the Calypso:
        the Origin and Development of Trinidad Folksong. Port of
        Spain: Guardian Commercial Printery, 1944. 74p., illus.

Caribbean (cont.)

4231. Warner, Keith Q. The Trinidad Calypso: a Study of the
       Calypso as Oral Literature. London: Heinemann, 1983. 152p.,
       illus., bibliog., discog.

                         Lyric Collections

4232. Quevedo, Raymond (comp.). Victory Calypsos: Popular
       Compositions by the Leading Calypso Artists of Trinidad.
       Port of Spain: Trinidad Publishing Company, 1944. 31p.,
       illus.

                      (e) Stage and Screen

                        (i) Music Hall

4233. Pulling, Christopher. They Were Singing, and What They
       Sang About. London: Harrap, 1952. 276p., illus.
          Music hall songs related to their social context.

                         Lyric Collections

4234. Davidson, Peter (comp.). Songs of the British Music Hall.
       With a Critical History of the Songs and Their Times. New
       York: Oak Publications; London: Music Sales, 1971. 244p.,
       illus., bibliog., discog., index.
          Words and music of the principal songs, each preceded by
       a long commentary.

4235. Gammond, Peter (comp.). Best Music Hall and Variety Songs.
       London: Wolfe, 1972. 512p.

                         (ii) Musicals

   *   Engel, Lehman (comp.). Their Words Are Music: the Great
       Theater Lyricists and Their Lyrics.
          * Cited above as item 1647.

4236. ————. Words With Music: the Broadway Musical Libretto.
       New York: Macmillan, 1972; New York: Schirmer Books, 1981.
       358p.

   *   Root, Deane L. American Popular Stage Music, 1860-1880.
          * Cited above as item 1117.

B. RECORDS

(a) RECORD INDUSTRY

(1) REFERENCE MATERIALS

4237. Dearling, Robert, and Celia Dearling. <u>The Guinness Book of
Recorded Sound</u>. With Brian Rust. Enfield, Middlesex:
Guinness Superlatives, 1984. 225p., illus., bibliog., index.

4238. Hurst, Walter E., and William Storm Hale. <u>The Record Industry Book</u>. Los Angeles: Seven Arts Pr., 1961- .
Regularly updated.

4239. ─────. <u>The U.S. Master Producers and British Music Scene
Book: Stories, Texts, Forms, Contracts</u>. Los Angeles: Seven
Arts Pr., 1968. 402p. (The Entertainment Industry, 4)

4240. Leggett, Pete, and Richard Buckle. <u>The London Recording
Studio Guide</u>. London: Knockabout, 1982. unpaged, illus.
Guide to facilities.

(2) GENERAL GUIDES AND OVERVIEWS

4241. Denisoff, R. Serge. <u>Solid Gold: the Popular Record Industry</u>.
New Brunswick, New Jersey: Transaction Books, 1975. 504p.,
illus., bibliog.

4242. Doncaster, Patrick (ed.). <u>Discland: a Panorama of the
Fabulous World of the Gramophone Record</u>. London: <u>Daily
Mirror</u>, 1956. 94p., illus.
Popular record industry.

4243. Dunn, Lloyd. <u>On the Flip Side</u>. New York: Billboard Publications, 1975.   p.
Emphasis on popular music.

4244. Hirsch, Paul Morris. <u>The Structure of the Popular Music
Industry: the Filtering Process By Which Records Are Pre-
Selected For Public Consumption</u>. Ann Arbor, Michigan:
Survey Research Center, Institute for Social Research,
University of Michigan, 1970. 72p., bibliog.

4245. Karshner, Roger. <u>The Music Machine</u>. Los Angeles: Nash
Publishing, 1971. 196p.
Ex-executive of record company exposes the workings of
the industry.

(b) RECORDS

(1) REVIEWS AND CRITICISM

(i) Indexes

4246. Annual Index to Popular Music Record Reviews. Metuchen,
New Jersey; London: Scarecrow Pr. annual, 1973- .
Guide to record releases and their reviews. Covers jazz,
rock, folk, stage, middle-of-the-road pop, and humor, U.S.
and foreign. Gives ratings.

(ii) Reviews

4247. Aranza, Jacob. Backward Masking Unmasked: Backward Satanic
Messages of Rock and Roll Exposed. Lambertville, New Jersey:
Huntingdon House, 1983. 118p.
Claims that concealed messages can be deciphered by
playing certain rock records backwards.

4248. Christgau, Robert. Christgau's Guide to Rock Albums of the
Seventies. New Haven, Conn.: Ticknor and Fields, 1981;
London: Vermilion, 1982. 472p.

4249. Collis, John. The Rock Primer. Harmondsworth, Middlesex:
Penguin, 1980. 335p., index.
Reviews of 120 key rock albums; also some singles.

4250. Down Beat. "Down Beat" Jazz Record Reviews. Chicago:
Maher Publications. annual, 1957-64.
Reviews reprinted from Down Beat.

4251. Gambaccini, Paul (ed.). Critics' Choice Top Two Hundred
Albums. With Susan Ready. London: Omnibus Pr.; New York:
Quick Fox, 1978. 96p., illus.
Listing by major rock critics of their favorite records.

4252. Hibbert, Tom (comp.). The Perfect Collection. London; New
York: Proteus, 1983. 96p., illus.
Lists two hundred albums and ninety-nine singles, 1950's
to 1980's. Compiled from lists solicited by the author.

4253. Jakubowski, Maxim. The Rock Album: the Year's Rock Releases
Reviewed. London: Frederick Muller, 1983. 160p., illus.,
index.
Arranged by three-month sections of 1982. Aims to
assess all rock album releases.

————. The Rock Album, Volume Two. London: Zomba Books,
1984. 194p., illus., index.

4254. Jones, Lesley-Ann, Robin Eggar, and Phil Swern (eds.). The
Sony Tape Rock Review. Foreword by Bill Wyman. London:
Rambletree/Pelham, 1984. 128p., illus.

4255. Larkin, Philip. <u>All What Jazz: a Record Diary, 1961-68</u>.
London: Faber and Faber; New York: St. Martin's Pr., 1970.
272p., index.
Reviews first published in London's <u>Daily Telegraph</u>
newspaper.

4256. Marcus, Greil (ed.). <u>Stranded: Rock and Roll For a Desert
Island</u>. New York: Knopf, 1979. 306p., discog.
"Twenty leading rock and roll writers, forced to choose,
pick the <u>one</u> album they would take to a desert island"--
cover. Essays.

4257. O'Neal, Hank (ed.). <u>The Best of Jazz: Noted Writers on
Great Jazz Records</u>. New York: Horizon Pr., 1984. 300p.,
illus.

4258. Rolling Stone. <u>The "Rolling Stone" Jazz Record Guide</u>.
Edited by John Swenson. New York: Random House, 1984. 320p.,
illus. (A <u>Rolling Stone</u> Pr. Book)

4259. ————. <u>The "Rolling Stone" Record Review</u>. By the Editors
of <u>Rolling Stone</u>. San Francisco: Straight Arrow Books,
1971. 500p., index.

————. <u>The "Rolling Stone" Record Review: the Authoritative
Guide to Contemporary Records, Volume Two</u>. New York: Pocket
Books, 1974. p., index.
Reviews first published in <u>Rolling Stone</u>.

————. <u>The "Rolling Stone" Record Guide: Reviews and
Ratings of Almost Ten Thousand Currently-Available Rock, Pop,
Soul, Country, Blues, Jazz, and Gospel Albums</u>. Edited by
Dave Marsh, with John Swenson. New York: Random House, 1979;
London: Virgin Books, 1980 (Reissued: 1983). 631p., illus.,
bibliog. (A <u>Rolling Stone</u> Pr. Book). 2nd. ed.: New York:
Random House, 1983. p., illus., bibliog. (A <u>Rolling Stone</u>
Pr. Book)
Based on reviews from <u>Rolling Stone</u>, with other sources.
Arranged in categories; with ratings. Limited to United
States releases, with some imports. Supersedes previous
editions.

* Tudor, Dean, and Nancy Tudor. <u>Popular Music: an Annotated
Guide to Recordings</u>.
* Cited below as item 4363.

(2) ILLUSTRATION COLLECTIONS

4260. <u>The Album Cover Album</u>. Edited by Roger Dean and Storm
Thorgerson. Introduction by Dominy Hamilton. Limpsfield,
East Sussex: Dragon's World; New York: A. and W. Publishers,
1977. 160p., illus.
Reproduction of some seven hundred album covers, with
commentary. Technical aspects discussed in appendix.

Illustration Collections (cont.)

> The Album Cover Album: the Second Volume. Edited by Storm
> Thorgerson, Roger Dean, and David Howells. Limpsfield,
> East Sussex: Dragon's World, 1983.   p., illus.

> The Album Cover Album, 3. Edited by Roger Dean and David
> Howells; text by Colin Greenland and Bob Fisher. Limpsfield,
> East Sussex: Dragon's World; New York: St. Martin's Pr.,
> 1984. 140p., illus., index.

4261. Benedict, Brad, and Linda Barton. Phonographics: Contemp-
      orary Album Cover Art and Design. New York: Collier Books;
      London: Collier-Macmillan, 1977. 142p., illus., index.
          Reproductions of covers, with credits. No commentary.

4262. Dean, Roger. Views. Text by Dominy Hamilton and Carla
      Capalbo. Limpsfield, East Sussex: Dragon's Dream, 1976.
      155p., illus.
          Record sleeves and other artwork by Dean. Includes
      critical assessment by Donald Lehmkuhl.

4263. Errigo, Angie, and Steve Leaning. The Illustrated History
      of the Rock Album Cover. London: Octopus, 1979. 160p.,
      illus., indexes.

4264. Herdeg, Walter (ed.). Record Covers: the Evolution of
      Graphics Reflected in Record Packaging. Zürich: Graphis Pr.;
      New York: Hastings House, 1974. 192p., illus.

4265. Herman, Gary (ed.). Rock Album Art. London: Octopus, 1979.
          p., illus.

4266. Hipgnosis. The Work of Hipgnosis: "Walk Away, René." Comp-
      iled by Hipgnosis and George Hardis; text by Storm Thorgerson.
      Limpsfield, East Sussex: Dragon's World; New York: A. and W.
      Publishers, 1978. 160p., illus., index.
          Record sleeves and other artwork by the Hipgnosis design
      team. Technical aspects discussed in appendix.

4267. ———. The Photodesigns of Hipgnosis: the Goodbye Look.
      Edited by Peter Christopherson, Aubrey Powell, and Storm
      Thorgerson; text by Storm Thorgerson. General editor: Nick
      Sedgwick. London: Vermilion, 1982. 128p., illus.
          Record sleeves and other artwork.

4268. Pollock, Bruce (ed.). The Face of Rock and Roll: Images of
      a Generation. Foreword by Pete Fornatale. New York: Holt,
      Rinehart, and Winston; London: New English Library, 1978.
      184p., illus., indexes.
          History of rock, as presented through album covers.

4269. Saleh, Dennis (ed.). Rock Art: Fifty-Two Album Covers.
      Seaside, California: Comma Books, 1977.   p., illus.

4270. Wiedeman, Kurt (ed.). <u>Book Jackets and Record Covers: an</u>
       <u>International Survey</u>. New York: Praeger, 1969.   p., illus.

(3) MISCELLANEA

4271. Barnes, Ken. <u>Twenty Years of Pop</u>. London: Kenneth Mason,
       1973. 96p., illus.
            Chronicles "significant" pop singles in attempt to show
       trends.

4272. Goldmann, Frank, and Klaus Hiltscher (eds.). <u>The Gimmix</u>
       <u>Book of Records: an Almanac of Unusual Records, Sleeves,</u>
       <u>and Picture Discs</u>. London: Virgin Books, 1981. 128p.,
       illus.

(4) RECORD CHARTS

4273. Albert, George, and Frank Hoffman (comps.). <u>The "Cash Box"</u>
       <u>Country Singles Charts, 1958-1982</u>. Metuchen, New Jersey;
       London: Scarecrow Pr., 1984. 595p.

4274. Billboard. <u>Music/Records Two Hundred</u>. Los Angeles:
       Billboard Publications, 1976. 150p.
            Published to coincide with the Bicentennial celebrations,
       1976. Lists the top two hundred records (singles and albums),
       also top two hundred artists "of our time."

4275. Gillett, Charlie (ed.). <u>Rock File</u>. London: Pictorial
       Presentations/New English Library, 1972. 156p., illus.
            British record charts reprinted; plus general articles.

       ————. <u>Rock File 2</u>. St. Albans, Hertfordshire: Panther,
       1974. 169p., illus.

       ————, and Simon Frith (eds.). <u>Rock File 3</u>. St. Albans,
       Hertfordshire: Panther, 1975. 224p., illus.

       ————. <u>Rock File 4</u>. St. Albans, Panther, 1976. 400p.,
       illus.
            Incorporates some material from <u>Rock File</u> (1972).

       ————. <u>Rock File 5</u>. St. Alban's, Hertfordshire: Panther,
       1978. 286p., illus.

4276. Hoffman, Frank, and Lee Ann Hoffman (comps.). <u>The "Cash Box"</u>
       <u>Singles Charts, 1950-1981</u>. Metuchen, New Jersey; London:
       Scarecrow Pr., 1983. 860p.

4277. Jasper, Tony (comp.). <u>Twenty Years of British Record Charts,</u>
       <u>1955-1975</u>. With commentary by Peter Jones and Tony Jasper.
       London: Queen Anne Pr., 1975. 208p.

Record Charts (cont.)

Jasper, Tony (comp.). British Record Charts, 1955-1978.
London: Macdonald and Janes, 1978. 288p.

———. British Record Charts, 1955-1979. London: Futura,
1979. 296p.
Includes first two months of 1979 only.

———. The Top Twenty Book: the Official British Record
Charts, 1955-1982. Published in association with Music and
Video Week. Poole, Dorset: Blandford Pr., 1983. 351p.

———. The Top Twenty Book: the Official British Record
Charts, 1955-1983. Published in association with Music and
Video Week. Poole, Dorset: Blandford Pr., 1984. 367p.

4278. Kaplan, Fred (comp.). The Music Bible. Brroklyn, New York:
The Author, 1971. 164p.
Singles charts, taken from Billboard, 4 November, 1955 to
27 June, 1970.

4279. Kasem, Casey. Casey Kasem's American Top Forty Yearbook.
Researched, compiled, and prepared by the Staff of American
Top Forty. Editor: Jay Goldsworthy; Editor-in-Chief: Don
Bustany. New York: Grosset and Dunlap, 1979. 203p., illus.
(Target Books)
Based on the Billboard charts, 1978. Linked with Kasem's
syndicated radio program.

4280. The Miles Chart Display of Popular Music. Boulder, Colorado:
Convex Industries. irreg., 1971- .
Editors vary.

4281. Miron, Charles (comp.). Rock Gold: All the Hit Charts, From
1955 to 1976. New York: Drake Publishers, 1977. 160p., illus.

4282. Murrells, Joseph (comp.). The "Daily Mail" Book of Golden
Discs: the Story of Every Million-Selling Disc in the World
Since 1903. Edited by Norris and Ross McWhirter. London:
McWhirter Twins on behalf of the Daily Mail, 1966. 374p.,
illus., index.
Chronological presentation, by artist within each year.

———. The Book of Golden Discs. London: Barrie and
Jenkins, 1974. 503p., illus., index.
Revised to cover 1903-69.

———. The Book of Golden Discs. Completely rev. ed.
London: Barrie and Jenkins, 1978. 413p., illus., index.
Revised to cover 1903-77.

———. Million-Selling Records, From the 1900's to the
1980's: an Illustrated Directory. London: Batsford, 1984.
530p., illus., index.
Revised to cover 1903-83.

4283. Nugent, Stephen, and Charlie Gillett (eds.). Rock Almanac:
Top Twenty American and British Singles and Albums of the
Fifties, Sixties, and Seventies. Garden City, New York:
Doubleday, 1978.   p. (Anchor Books)
       Prepared in 1974. Based on item 4275.

4284. Rice, Jo, and Tim Rice (comps.). The Guinness Book of
British Hit Singles (The Guinness Book of Records Records.)
Enfield, Middlesex: Guinness Superlatives, 1977. 277p.,
illus., index. 2nd. ed. (compiled by Jo Rice, Tim Rice,
Paul Gambaccini, and Mike Read): Enfield, Middlesex:
Guinness Superlatives, 1979. 318p., illus., index. 3rd.
ed.: Enfield, Middlesex: Guinness Superlatives, 1981. 352p.,
illus., index.

       ————, Paul Gambaccini, and Mike Read (comps.). The
Guinness Book of British Hit Singles. 4th. ed. Enfield,
Middlesex: Guinness Superlatives, 1983. 313p., illus.,
index. 5th. ed.: Enfield, Middlesex: Guinness Superlatives,
1985. 312p., illus., index.
       Chart entries, 1952 to date. Arranged alphabetically by
artist, with background information.

4285. ————. The Guinness Book of British Hit Albums. Editorial
associate: Steve Smith. London: GRRR Books/Enfield, Middlesex: Guinness Books, 1983. 216p., illus.
       Chart albums listed, with background information.

4286. ————. The Guinness Book of Five Hundred Number One Hits.
Enfield, Middlesex: Guinness Superlatives, 1982. 263p.,
illus.
       Includes detailed information on the items included.

4287. ————. The Guinness Book of Hits of the Sixties. Editorial associate: Steve Smith. Enfield, Middlesex: Guinness
Books, 1984. 256p., illus.
       Includes singles, extended-play, and long-playing records,
with detailed background information on selected disks.

4288. ————. The Guinness Book of Hits of the Seventies. Enfield,
Middlesex: Guinness Superlatives, 1980. 239p., illus.
       Same format as item 4287.

4289. Rohde, H. Kandy (comp.). The Gold of Rock and Roll, 1955-
1967. Research assistance by Laing Ned Kandel. New York:
Arbor House, 1970. 352p., illus., bibliog., discog.
       Year-by-year chart compilations.

4290. Savile, Jimmy, and Tony Jasper. The Nostalgia Book of Hit
Singles. London: Frederick Muller, 1982. 320p., illus.
       Detailed background information on selected British hits.

4291. Solomon, Clive (comp.). Record Hits: the British Top Fifty
Charts, 1954-76. Index compiled by Martin Watson. London:
Omnibus Pr., 1977. 263p., index.

Record Charts (cont.)

Solomon, Clive, Howard Pizzey, and Martin Watson (comps.).
Record Hits: the British Top Fifty Charts, 1952-1977. Plus
U.S. Chart Positions. London: Omnibus Pr., 1979. 270p.,
index.

4292. Star File Annual: Incorporating the Year's Record Information From "Music Week" and "Billboard." Compiled by Daffydd
Rees. Introduction by John Tobler. London: Hamlyn, 1978.
439p., index.

Chart File, 1982. Compiled by Alan Jones, with Barry Lazell
and Daffydd Rees. London: Virgin Books, 1982. 224p.
Continues previous item. British and American charts.

Chart File, Volume 2. Compiled by Daffydd Rees, Barry
Lazell, and Alan Jones. London: Virgin Books, 1983.   p.

4293. Whitburn, Joel (comp.). The "Billboard" Book of U.S. Top
Forty Hits, 1955 to the Present. Introduction by Casey
Kasem. New York: Billboard Publications; Enfield, Middle-
sex: Guinness Superlatives, 1983. 509p., illus. 2nd. ed.:
New York: Billboard Publications; Enfield, Middlesex:
Guinness Superlatives, 1985.   p., illus.

4294. ————. Bubbling Under the Hot Hundred, 1959-1981.
Menomonee Falls, Wisconsin: Record Research, 1982. 234p.,
index.
Based, like Whitburn's other volumes, on the Billboard
charts.

4295. ————. Joel Whitburn's Top Easy Listening Records, 1961-
1974. Menomonee Falls, Wisconsin: Record Research, 1975.
152p., illus., index.
Annual supplements published 1976- .

4296. ————. Joel Whitburn's Top LP's, 1945-1972. Menomonee
Falls, Wisconsin: Record Research, 1973. 224p., illus.,
index.
Annual supplements published 1974- .

4297. ————. Top Country and Western Records, 1949-1971.
Menomonee Falls, Wisconsin: Record Research, 1972. 152p.,
illus., index.
Annual supplements published 1973- .

4298. ————. Top Pop Records, 1940-1955. Menomonee Falls,
Wisconsin: Record Research, 1973. 88p., index.

————. Record Research: Compiled From "Billboard" Magazine's
"Hot Hundred" Charts, 1955-1969. Menomonee Falls, Wisconsin:
Record Research, 1970. 104p., index.
Supplement published 1971.

———. Top Pop Records, 1955-1970: Facts About 9,800
Recordings Listed in "Billboard's" "Hot Hundred" Charts,
Grouped Under the Names of the 2,500 Recording Artists.
Detroit: Gale Research, 1972. unpaged.
  Reprint of Record Research, plus supplement, in one
sequence.

———. Top Pop Records, 1955-1972. Menomonee Falls,
Wisconsin: Record Research, 1973. 416p., illus., index.
  Annual supplements published 1974- .

———. Pop Annual, 1955-1977. Menomonee Falls, Wisconsin:
Record Research, 1978. 623p., index.

———. Joel Whitburn's Top Pop Artists and Singles, 1955-
1978. Compiled from "Billboard's" Pop Singles Charts, 1955-
1978. Menomonee Falls, Wisconsin: Record Research, 1979.
662p., illus., index.

———. Joel Whitburn's Top Pop, 1955-1982. Compiled from
"Billboard's" Pop Singles Charts, 1955-1982. Menomonee
Falls, Wisconsin: Record Research, 1983. 692p., index.

4299. ———. Top Rhythm and Blues Records, 1949-1971. Menomonee
Falls, Wisconsin: Record Research, 1973. 184p., illus.,
index.
  Annual supplements published 1974- .

(5) RECORD COLLECTING

4300. Anderson, Andy. Helpful Hints to Jazz Collectors; Combined
With Jazz Men and Their Records. Baraboo, Wisconsin: Andoll
Publishing, 1957. 107p., bibliog., discog.

4301. Bannister, Lawrence H. (ed.). International Jazz Collectors'
Directory. Malvern Link, Worcestershire: The Author, 1948.
76p.
  Contact listing.

4302. Black, Douglas C. Matrix Numbers. Edited by William H.
Miller. Melbourne, Victoria: Australian Jazz Quarterly,
1946. 24p.
  Jazz. Not the same as item 4303.

4303. ———. Matrix Numbers: Their Meaning and History. Edited
by William H. Miller. Melbourne, Victoria: Australian Jazz
Quarterly, 1946. 23p. (A.J.Q. Handbook, 1)
  Not the same as item 4302.

4304. Charlie The Collector (pseud.). When Was That Old Record
Made? Dating List For Popular, Ten-Inch, 78-rpm Records,
1908-1958. Dallas: The Author, 1973.   p., illus.

Record Collecting (cont.)

4305.   Dealers' Directory, 1984. Chaddesden, Derby, England:
        Dealers' Directory, 1984.   p.

4306.   Deitch, Gene, and George Avakian. The Cat. New York: The
        Record Changer, 1948. 32p., illus.
             Cartoons by Deitch; text by Avakian. Humorous aspects of
        being a collector of jazz records; also advice.

4307.   Felton, Gary S. The Record Collector's International
        Directory. New York: Crown, 1980.   p., index.
             Contacts listing.

4308.   Hearne, Will Roy (comp.). American Record Collectors'
        Directory. Hollywood, California: Hollywood Premium Record
        Guide, 1953. 24p.
             Contact directory, for jazz collectors.

4309.   ————. World-Wide Record Collectors' Directory. Hollywood,
        California: Hollywood Premium Record Guide, 195? 27p.

4310.   Langridge, Derek. Your Jazz Collection. London: Bingley;
        Hamden, Conn.: Shoestring Pr. (Archon Books), 1970. 162p.,
        bibliog., index.
             How to collect and arrange jazz records. Includes
        cumbersome scheme for classifying and indexing literature
        and recordings.

4311.   Martin, James. The £-s-d of Record Collecting: a Manual For
        the Collector-Dealer. Lingfield, Surrey: Oakwood Pr., 1956.
        48p.

4312.   Peterson, Bill, and Howard E. Penny. Good Diggin'. Portland,
        Oregon: Portland Record Collectors' Club, 1948. 80p., illus.
             Jazz.

4313.   Record Collector's Source Book. Peoria, Illinois: Recorded
        Sound Research. irreg., 1973- .

4314.   Rowe, John (ed.). Record Information: a Book For the Record
        Collector. London: Jazz Tempo Publications, 1945. 24p.,
        illus.
             Jazz.

4315.   Semeonoff, Boris. Record Collecting: a Guide For Beginners.
        With a Chapter on Collecting Jazz Records, by Alexander
        Ross. Chislehurst, Kent: Oakwood Pr., 1949. 100p., illus.
        2nd. ed.: South Godstone, Surrey: Oakwood Pr., 1951. 101p.,
        illus.

4316.   Stilwell, Arnold B. Record Dating Chart: Part One (Up to
        1930.) New York: The Record Changer, 1948.   p.
             Jazz. No further parts issued.

4317. <u>Who's Who in Jazz Collecting</u>. Compiled by William C. Love. Nashville: The Author, 1942. 52p. <u>2nd. ed.</u>: Compiled by William C. Love and Bill Rich. Nashville: The Authors, 1949. 150p.

4318. Williams, Stewart (ed.). <u>Jazz Information</u>. Cardiff, Wales: The Author, 1945. 24p.

4319. ————, and Tom Cundall (eds.). <u>Junking in the Land of Jazz</u>. Cardiff, Wales: Jazz Information, 1946. 28p. (Jazz Information Book, 4)

(6) DISCOGRAPHIES

(i) Bibliographies

4320. Allen, Daniel. <u>Bibliography of Discographies, Volume 2: Jazz</u>. New York: Bowker, 1981. 239p., index.
Includes books and periodical articles, 1935-80. Record company catalogs excluded.

4321. Cooper, David E. <u>International Bibliography of Discographies, Classical Music, and Jazz and Blues, 1962-1972: a Reference Book For Record Collectors, Dealers, and Libraries</u>. Littleton, Colorado: Libraries Unlimited, 1975. 272p., index. (Keys to Music Bibliography, 2)
Includes books and periodical articles.

4322. Gray, Michael H., and Gerald D. Gibson. <u>Bibliography of Discographies, Volume 3: Popular Music</u>. New York: Bowker, 1983. 200p., index.

4323. Moon, Pete A. <u>A Bibliography of Jazz Discographies Published Since 1960</u>. Edited by Barry Witherden. London: British Institute of Jazz Studies, 1969. unpaged. <u>2nd. ed.</u>: South Harrow, Middlesex: British Institute of Jazz Studies, 1972. 40p.
Arranged by artists.

(ii) Discographies

(a) Popular

4324. Abbott, Kingsley. <u>British Beach Music</u>. London: The Author, 1982. 52p.
All known examples from Britain of surf music style rock.

4325. Anderson, Ian. <u>Rock Record Collectors' Guide</u>. London: M.R.P. Books, 1977. 177p., illus.
Arbitrary listing of two thousand "all-time classic albums."

Popular (cont.)

4326. Arf Arf. <u>The Catalog of 45's</u>. <u>2nd. ed</u>.: New York: Arf Arf,
      1982.   p., illus.
         Lists over twenty-five thousand out-of-print rock, soul,
      pop, and country singles, 1948-date. Updated by supplements.

4327. Blair, John. <u>The Illustrated Discography of Surf Music,
      1959-1965</u>. Riverside, California: J. Bee Productions, 1978.
      52p., illus. Rev. ed. (as <u>The Illustrated Discography of
      Surf Music, 1961-1965</u>): Ann Arbor, Michigan: Pierian Pr.,
      1984.   p., illus.

4328. <u>Collectable EP's</u>. London: Vintage Record Centre, 1982-4.
      <u>Part 1</u>: <u>Artists A-F</u>. unpaged.
      <u>Part 2</u>: <u>Artists G-M</u>. unpaged.
      <u>Part 3</u>: <u>Artists N-Z</u>. unpaged.

4329. <u>Collectable 45's: a Price Reference Guide to Singles</u>.
      London: Vintage Record Centre, 1981.
      <u>Part 1</u>: <u>Artists A-K</u>. unpaged.
      <u>Part 2</u>: <u>Artists L-Z</u>. unpaged.
         Covers deleted singles, 1950's to 1960's. With prices.

4330. <u>Collectable 45's of the Swinging Sixties</u>. Compiled by Peter
      Dickerson and Mike Gordon. London: Vintage Record Centre,
      1984. unpaged.
         Lists over five thousand British singles, January 1965 to
      December 1969, on 250 labels.

4331. <u>The Complete Bootlegs Checklist and Discography</u>. Manchester,
      England: Babylon Books, 1980. 116p., illus.

      <u>The Bootleg Bible</u>. Manchester, England: Babylon Books, 1982.
      272p.
         Complete revision.

4332. Davis, Lloyd E. <u>Collectors' Price Guide to 45-rpm Picture
      Sleeves</u>. With Marvin Davis. Ashland, Oregon: Winema Pub-
      lications, 1977.   p., illus.

4333. Dellar, Fred, and Barry Lazell (comps.). <u>The Essential Guide
      to Rock Records</u>. London: Omnibus Pr., 1983. 256p., illus.,
      index.
         Comprehensive listing of releases. Arranged by artists.

   * Denisoff, R. Serge. <u>American Protest Songs of War and Peace:
      a Selected Bibliography and Discography</u>.
         * Cited above as item 4106.

      ————. <u>Songs of Protest, War, and Peace: a Bibliography
      and Discography</u>.
         * Cited above as item 4106.

4334. Docks, L.R. <u>1915-1965 American Premium Record Guide:</u>
       <u>Identification and Values: 78's, 45's, and LP's</u>. Florence,
       Alabama: Books Americana, 1980. 737p., illus., bibliog.,
       index.
           Lists 45,000 recordings, by over 6,200 artists.

4335. Duxbury, Janell R. <u>Rockin' the Classics, and Classicizin'</u>
       <u>the Rock: a Selectively Annotated Discography</u>. Westport,
       Conn.: Greenwood Pr., 1985.   p., index. (Discographies,
       14)
           Covers Britain and the United States.

4336. Engel, Lyle Kenyon. <u>Popular Record Directory</u>. Edited by
       Fred Honig. Greenwich, Conn.: Fawcett; London: Frederick
       Muller, 1958. 143p., illus.

  *   Ferlingere, Robert D. <u>A Discography of Rhythm and Blues,</u>
       <u>and Rock and Roll Vocal Groups, 1945-1965</u>.
           * Cited below as item 4383.

4337. Gibbon, Peter. <u>Discofile: Vocal Group Discography</u>. Welwyn,
       Hertfordshire: The Author, 1981. 396p.

4338. Goldstein, Stewart, and Alan Jacobson. <u>Oldies But Goldies:</u>
       <u>the Rock 'n' Roll Years</u>. New York: Mason/Charter, 1977.
       328p., illus., indexes.

4339. Gonzalez, Fernando L. <u>Disco-File: the Discographical Catalog</u>
       <u>of American Rock and Roll, and Rhythm and Blues Vocal Groups</u>.
       Flushing, New York: The Author, 1974. 200p. <u>2nd. ed.</u>:
       Flushing, New York: The Author, 1977. 496p. <u>3rd. ed.</u>:
       Flushing, New York: The Author, 1984.   p.

4340. Gramophone. <u>The "Gramophone" Long-Playing Popular Record</u>
       <u>Catalogue</u>. Harrow, Middlesex: General Gramophone Company.
       quarterly (later 2 p.a.), 1957- .
           Listing of currently-available record and tape releases.
       Title later changed to <u>Popular Record Catalogue</u>.

4341. ————. <u>Gramophone Records of the First World War: an H.M.V.</u>
       <u>Catalogue, 1914-1918</u>. Introduction by Brian Rust. Newton
       Abbot, Devon: David and Charles, 1975.   p.
           Includes popular records.

4342. Hibbert, Tom. <u>Rare Records: Wax Trash and Vinyl Treasures</u>.
       London; New York: Proteus, 1982. 128p., illus.
           Guide to collecting 1960's rock records. Includes advice,
       and price indications.

4343. Hill, Randal C. <u>The Official Price Guide to Collectible</u>
       <u>Rock Records</u>. Orlando, Florida: House of Collectibles,
       1979. 391p., illus. (Collector Series). <u>2nd. ed.</u>: Orlando,
       Florida: House of Collectibles, 1980. 544p., illus.
       (Collector Series)

Popular (cont.)

4344. Hounsome, Terry, and Tim Chambre (eds.). Rockmaster 1978.
       Southampton, Hampshire: Rockmaster, 1978. 309p., index.
           Listing of all known releases on album, Britain and U.S.A.
       Artist sequence. Employs extensive cross-referencing.

       ————. Rock Record: Collectors' Catalogue of Rock Albums
       and Musicians. Southampton, Hampshire: Rock Record, 1979.
       386p., index.

       ————. New Rock Record: a Collectors' Directory of Rock
       Albums and Musicians. Poole, Dorset: Blandford Pr.; New
       York: Facts on File, 1981. 526p., index. 2nd. ed.: Poole,
       Dorset: Blandford Pr.; New York: Facts on File, 1983. 700p.,
       index.

4345. Leibowitz, Alan. The Record Collector's Handbook. New York:
       Everest House, 1980.   p.
           Listing of popular records; with prices.

4346. Music Master. Hastings, East Sussex: John Humphries.
       annual, 1974- .
           Lists currently available popular records sold in Britain.
       Updated by monthly supplements.

4347. Osborne, Jerry. Record Collector's Price Guide. Edited by
       Bruce Hamilton. Phoenix, Arizona: O'Sullivan Woodside, 1976.
       196p., illus. 2nd. ed. (as Popular and Rock Records, 1948-
       1978): Phoenix, Arizona: O'Sullivan Woodside, 1978. 252p.,
       illus.

4348. ————. Thirty-Three and One-Third, and Forty-Five Extended-
       Play Record Album Pricing Guide. Edited by Bruce Hamilton.
       Phoenix, Arizona: O'Sullivan Woodside, 1977. 165p., illus.
       2nd. ed. (as Record Albums, 1948-1978): Phoenix, Arizona:
       O'Sullivan Woodside, 1978. 256p., illus. 3rd. ed. (as The
       Record Albums Price Guide): Phoenix, Arizona: O'Sullivan
       Woodside, 1980.   p., illus.

4349. ————, and Bruce Hamilton. A Guide to Record Collecting.
       Phoenix, Arizona: O'Sullivan Woodside, 1979.   p., index.
           Listing of valuable popular records, with advice on
       collecting.

4350. Propes, Steve. Golden Goodies: a Guide to Fifties and Six-
       ties Popular Rock and Roll Collecting. Philadelphia: Chilton
       Book Company, 1975. 208p.
           Discography of valuable records. Condensed from items
       4351 and 4352.

4351. ————. Golden Oldies: a Guide to Sixties Record Collecting.
       Philadelphia: Chilton Book Company, 1974. 240p.

4352. ————. Those Oldies But Goodies: a Guide to Fifties Record

Collecting. New York: Macmillan; London: Collier-Macmillan, 1973. 192p.

4353. Rees, Daffydd (comp.). Heavy Metal Bootlegs. London; New York: Proteus, 1984.   p., illus.

4354. Rees, Tony. Rare Rock: a Collector's Guide. Poole, Dorset: Blandford Pr., 1985. 352p.
       Lists valuable records not generally released. Includes promotional, limited-edition, flexidisk, one-off, motion picture soundtrack compilations, and cassette-format magazine material.

4355. Robbins, Ira (ed.). The "Trouser Press" Guide to New Wave Records. New York: Scribner's, 1983. 288p., illus.

4356. Rust, Brian Arthur Lovell. The American Dance Band Discography, 1917-1942. New Rochelle, New York: Arlington House, 1975. 2 vols., 2,066p., index.

4357. ————, and Leo Walker. The British Dance Bands Discography, 1912-1939. Leigh-on-Sea, Essex: Storyville, 1973. p.

4358. ————, and Allen G. Debus. The Complete Entertainment Discography, From the Mid-1890's to 1942. New Rochelle, New York: Arlington House, 1973. 677p., illus.

4359. Schleman, Hilton R. Rhythm on Record: a Who's Who and Complete Register of Recorded Dance Music, 1906-1936. London: Melody Maker, 1936; Westport, Conn.: Greenwood Pr., 1978. 333p., illus.
       Arranged by artists. Includes biographical information.

4360. Singles Master. London: John Humphries. annual, 1976- .
       Listing of currently available popular singles sold in Britain. Updated by weekly and monthly cumulative supplements.

4361. Soderberg, Peter A. Seventy-Eight R.P.M. Records and Prices. Des Moines: Wallace-Homestead, 1977. 116p., illus.

4362. Tudor, Dean, and Nancy Tudor. Contemporary Popular Music. Littleton, Colorado: Libraries Unlimited, 1979. 314p.
       Annotated. Incorporated into item 4363.

4363. ————. Popular Music: an Annotated Guide to Recordings. Littleton, Colorado: Libraries Unlimited, 1983. 900p.
       Compilation, with amendments and additions, of items 4362,

4364. Volume: International Discography of the New Wave. Edited by Bob George and Martha Defoe. New York: One-Ten Records, 1980. 264p. Rev. ed. (as International Discography of the New Wave: Volume 1982/83): New York: One-Ten Records; London: Omnibus Pr., 1982. 736p.

Popular (cont.)

4365. Whiteman, Paul, and David A. Stein. Records For the
       Millions. New York: Hermitage, 1948. 331p.
          Listing of Whiteman's own records; plus popular dance
       bands recordings.

                          (b) Folk Music

   *   Haywood, Charles. Bibliography of North American Folklore
       and Folksong.
          * Cited above as item 4.

   *   Lawless, Ray McKinley. Folksingers and Folksongs in America.
          * Cited above as item 1465.

4366. Lifton, Sarah. The Listener's Guide to Folk Music. New
       York: Facts on File; Poole, Dorset: Blandford Pr., 1983.
       140p., illus., bibliog., index.
          Emphasis on American forms.

4367. Lumpkin, Ben Gray. Folksongs on Records. Boulder, Colorado:
       Folksongs on Records; Denver, Colorado: Alan Swallow, 1960.
          p.

                          (c) Country

4368. American Society of Authors, Composers, and Publishers.
       Country and Western Music: ASCAP Music on Records. New
       York: ASCAP, 196? 122p.

4369. Haglund, Urban, and Lillies Ohlsson. A Listing of Bluegrass
       LP's. Vasteras, Sweden: Kountry Korral, 1971. 71p.
          Includes American and foreign long-playing records.
       Arranged by artists.

4370. Oermann, Robert K. The Listener's Guide to Country Music.
       With Douglas B. Green. New York: Facts on File; Poole,
       Dorset: Blandford Pr., 1983. 137p., illus., bibliog., index.

4371. Osborne, Jerry. Fifty-Five Years of Recorded Country and
       Western Music. Phoenix, Arizona: O'Sullivan Woodside, 1976.
       208p., illus.
          Includes interview with Gene Autry.

4372. Russell, Tony. The Complete Country Music Discography,
       1922-1942. Nashville: Country Music Foundation, 1983.   p.

4373. Tudor, Dean, and Nancy Tudor. Grass Roots Music. Littleton,
       Colorado: Libraries Unlimited, 1979. 367p., index. (American
       Popular Music on Elpee)
          Incorporated into item 4363.

(d) Black Music

(i) Comprehensive Works

4374.   Dain, Bernice, and David Nevin.   The Black Record: a Select-
        ive Discography of Afro-Americana on Audio Disks Held by the
        Audio-Visual Department, John M. Olin Library.   St. Louis:
        Washington University, Library Studies Department, 1973.   p.

4375.   Tudor, Dean, and Nancy Tudor.   Black Music.   Littleton,
        Colorado: Libraries Unlimited, 1979.   262p., index. (Amer-
        ican Popular Music on Elpee)
            Annotated.   Incorporated into item 4363.

(ii) Sacred

4376.   Hayes, Cedric J.   A Discography of Gospel Records, 1937-1971.
        Copenhagen: Knudsen, 1973.   116p.
            Selective.

(iii) Ragtime

4377.   Jasen, David A.   Recorded Ragtime, 1897-1958.   Hamden, Conn.:
        Shoestring Pr., 1973.   155p., illus., bibliog., index.
        (Archon Books)

4378.   Walker, Edward S., and Steven Walker.   English Ragtime: a
        Discography, 1898-1920.   Woodthorpe, Derbysshire: The Authors,
        1971.   104p., illus.
            Includes recordings by American artists who performed in
        England.

(iv) Blues

    *   Cooper, David E.   International Bibliography of Discographies:
        Classical Music, and Jazz and Blues.
            * Cited above as item 4321.

4379.   Dixon, Robert Malcolm Ward, and John Godrich.   Blues and
        Gospel Records, 1902-1942.   Kenton, Middlesex: Steve Lane
        (Music and Publicity Services), 1964.   765p.

        Godrich, John, and Robert Malcolm Ward Dixon.   Blues and
        Gospel Records, 1902-1942.   Rev. ed.   London: Storyville,
        1969.   912p.   3rd. ed.: Chigwell, Essex: Storyville, 1982.
        898p., index.

4380.   ————.   Recording the Blues.   London: Studio Vista; New
        York: Stein and Day, 1970.   112p., illus., bibliog., discog.,
        index.
            Complements item 4379.

Blues (cont.)

4381. Guralnick, Peter. The Listener's Guide to the Blues. New
York: Facts on File; Poole, Dorset: Blandford Pr., 1982.
154p., illus., bibliog., index.

4382. Leadbitter, Mike, and Neil Slaven. Blues Records, January
1943 to December 1966. London: Hanover Books, 1968; New
York: Oak Publications, 1969. 381p. Rev. ed.: London:
Storyville, 1971; London: Music Sales; New York: Oak Publications, 1975. 381p.
      Continues item 4379.

   * McCarthy, Albert John. Jazz and Blues on Record.
         * Cited below as item 4427.

   * Townley, Eric. Tell Your Story: a Dictionary of Jazz and
      Blues Recordings, 1917-1950.
         * Cited below as item 4451.

                    (v) Rhythm and Blues

4383. Ferlingere, Robert D. A Discography of Rhythm and Blues,
and Rock and Roll Vocal Groups, 1945-1965. Pittsburgh: The
Author, 1976. 600p.
      Chronological arrangement.

   * Gibbon, Peter. Discofile: Vocal Group Discography.
         * Cited above as item 4337.

   * Gonzales, Fernando L. Disco-File: the Discographical Catalog
      of American Rock and Roll, and Rhythm and Blues Vocal Groups.
         * Cited above as item 4339.

4384. Topping, Ray. New Orleans Rhythm and Blues: Record Label
Listings. Bexhill-on-Sea, East Sussex: Flyright Records,
1978.   p.

                        (vi) Soul

4385. Collector's Guide to Rare British Soul Releases. Newcastle,
Staffordshire: Soul Cargo Publications and Records, 1980.
      p.

(e) Jazz

(i) General Works

4386. Allen, Walter C. (ed.). Studies in Jazz Discography:
Proceedings of the First and the Second Annual Conferences
on Discographical Research, 1968-69; and of the Conference
on the Preservation and Extension of the Jazz Heritage,
1969. New Brunswick, New Jersey: Rutgers University,
Institute of Jazz Studies, 1971; Westport, Conn.: Greenwood
Pr., 1978. 112p., bibliog. notes.

 *   Cooper, David E. International Bibliography of Discographies: Classical Music, and Jazz and Blues.
* Cited above as item 4321.

4387. Rust, Brian Arthur Lovell. Brian Rust's Guide to Discography. Westport, Conn.: Greenwood Pr., 1980. 133p.,
bibliog., index. (Discographies, 4)
The theory and methods of discography outlined.

(ii) Discographies

4388. Asman, James, and Bill Kinnell. Jazz on Record. Chilwell,
Nottinghamshire: Jazz Appreciation Society, 1944. 20p.

4389. Barazetta, Giuseppe. Jazz Inciso in Italia. Milan:
Messaggerie Musicali, 1960. 189p. (Musica Jazz, 1)
In Italian. Lists jazz records made in Italy.

4390. Blackstone, Orin. Index to Jazz: Jazz Recordings, 1917-1944.
Fairfax, Virginia: The Record Changer, 1945-48 (Reprinted:
New Orleans: Gordon Gullickson, 1948; Ann Arbor, Michigan:
University Microfilms, 1965; Westport, Conn.: Greenwood Pr.,
1978). 4 vols., 443p. 2nd. ed.: Vol. 1: A-E. New Orleans:
The Author, 1949. 312p.
Arranged by artists. Original edition was loose-leaf
format. Second edition abandoned after first volume.

4391. Brown, Kenneth, and Ralph G.V. Venables. Collectors'
Catalogue. With Jackson D. Hale and Cedric H. White.
Glasgow: Kenneth Brown, 1943. 24p.

4392. Bruyninckx, Walter. Fifty Years of Recorded Jazz, 1917-1967.
Mechelen, Belgium: The Author, 1961-75. 40 vols., loose-
leaf.

———. Sixty Years of Recorded Jazz, 1917-1977. Mechelen,
Belgium: The Author, 1978-80. 6 vols., 6,000p.
Loose-leaf format.

4393. Cabanowski, Marek, and Henryk Cholinski. Polska dyskografia
jazzowa, 1955-1972. Warsaw: The Authors, 1974. 187p.
In Polish.

Jazz (cont.)

4394. Carey, Dave, Albert John McCarthy, and Ralph G.V. Venables.
       The Directory of Recorded Jazz and Swing Music (Including
       Gospel and Blues Records.) Fordingbridge, Hampshire: Delphic
       Pr., 1950-52; London: Cassell, 1955-57. 6 vols., 1,112p.
       Vol. 1: A-B. 1950.
       Vol. 2: C-D. 1950. 2nd. ed.: London: Cassell, 1955.
       Vol. 3: E-G. 1951. 2nd. ed.: London: Cassell, 1956.
       Vol. 4: G-I. 1952. 2nd. ed.: London: Cassell, 1957.
       Vol. 5: J-K. 1955.
       Vol. 6: K-L. 1955.
          Last entry: Longshaw. Loose-leaf format; listing of
       commercially available jazz records. Arranged by artists.
       Supplemented by item 5203. Continued by items 4428 and 4411.

4395. Cerri, Livio. Jazz in microsolco: raesegna di quasi tutti
       i microsolco di jazz pubblicati in Italia. Pisa: Nistri-
       Lischi, 1962. 505p.
          In Italian. Long-playing jazz releases in Italy listed.

4396. Cullaz, Maurice. Guide des disques de jazz: les mille
       meilleurs disques de spirituals, Gospel songs, blues,
       rhythm and blues, jazz; et leur histoire. Paris: Buchet-
       Chastel, 1971. 351p.
          In French.

4397. Dansk Jazz. Ordrup, Denmark: Nationalmuseet, 1961. 4 vols.,
       102p.

4398. Delaunay, Charles. Hot discographie. Forewords by Hugues
       Panassié, Lucienne Panassié, and Henri Bernard. Paris: Hot
       Jazz, 1936. 271p. 2nd. ed.: Paris: Hot Jazz, 1938. 408p.

       ———— . Hot Discography. New York: Commodore Music Shop,
       1940. 416p.

       ———— . Hot Discography. Edited by Hot Jazz. 3rd. ed.:
       New York: Commodore Record Company, 1943. 416p.

       ———— . Hot discographie, 1943. Paris: Collection du Hot
       Club de France, 1944. 538p.

       ———— . New Hot Discography: the Standard Directory of
       Recorded Jazz. Edited by Walter E. Schaap and George
       Avakian. New York: Criterion Music Corporation, 1948
       (Reprinted: New York: Wehman, 1963). 608p., index.

       ———— . Hot discographie encyclopédique. With Kurt Mohr.
       Paris: Editions Jazz Disques, 1951-53. 3 vols.,   p.
          Early editions arranged in complex historical-stylistic
       sequence; 1951-53 edition altered to alphabetical artist
       order. Last published edition covers A-Hefti: publication
       abandoned (too many jazz records.)

Gullickson, Gordon. <u>Numerical Index to Delaunay's "Hot Discography.</u>" Washington, D.C.: The Author, 1941. 28p.

4399. Elmenhorst, Gernot Wolfram, and Walter von Bebenburg. <u>Die Jazz-Diskothek</u>. Reinbek bei Hamburg: Rowohlt, 1961. 362p., illus.
  In German; international coverage.

* Evensmo, Jan. <u>Jazz Solography</u>.
  * Cited above as item 1548.

* ————. <u>The Tenor Saxophonists of the Period 1930-1942</u>.
  * Cited above as item 1549.

4400. Gainsbury, Arthur J. <u>Guide For Junk Shoppers, 1956 ed.</u> Harrow, Middlesex: The Author, 1956. 53p., illus.
  Lists deleted jazz records.

4401. Gammond, Peter, and Raymond Horricks. <u>Big Bands</u>. London: Patrick Stephens, 1981. 183p., illus., bibliog. (Music on Record, 2)
  Alphabetically arranged bio-discography.

4402. Gammond, Peter, and Peter Clayton. <u>Fourteen Miles on a Clear Night: an Irreverent, Sceptical, and Affectionate Book About Jazz Records</u>. London: Peter Owen, 1966; Westport, Conn.: Greenwood Pr., 1978. 128p., illus.

4403. Gee, John, and Michael Wadsley. <u>Jazzography</u>. Tring, Hertfordshire: Society for Jazz Appreciation in the Younger Generation, 1944. 24p.

4404. Harris, Rex, and Brian Arthur Lovell Rust. <u>Recorded Jazz: a Critical Guide</u>. Harmondsworth, Middlesex: Penguin, 1958.
  Selective; includes British and American records. Emphasis on traditional jazzmen.

4405. Harrison, Max, Charles Fox, and Eric Thacker. <u>The Essential Jazz Records</u>. London: Mansell; Westport, Conn.: Greenwood Pr., 1984- .
Vol. 1: <u>Ragtime to Swing</u>. 1984. 595p., index.
  First of planned two-volume set. Critical annotations.

4406. Harrison, Max, Alun Morgan, Ronald Atkins, Michael James, and Jack Cooke. <u>Modern Jazz: the Essential Records: a Critical Selection</u>. London: Aquarius Books, 1975. 140p., index.

4407. Hippenmeyer, Jean Roland. <u>Swiss Jazz Disco</u>. Yverdon, Switzerland: Editions de la Thiele, 1977. 214p.
  Lists some five thousand titles made/sold in Switzerland, 1926-76.

4408. <u>Jazz Catalogue: a Discography of All British Jazz Releases, Complete With Full Personnels and Recording Dates.</u> Compiled (1960-66) by George Cherrington and Brian Knight; (1967-71) by Ralph Laing, Michael Coates and Bernard Shirley). London:

Jazz (cont.)

       Jazz Journal. annual, 1960-71
         Releases chronicled as they appeared. Arranged by
       artists.

4409. Jazz 'n' Pops: a Comprehensive Catalog of Jazz and Popular
       Long-Play Records. New York: Long Player Publications.
       irreg., March 1957- ?

4410. Jazz on Record: a Critical Guide. Compiled by Charles Fox,
       Peter Gammond, and Alun Morgan; with additional material by
       Alexis Korner. London: Hutchinson (Reprinted: Westport,
       Conn.: Greenwood Pr., 1978); London: Arrow Books, 1960.
       352p., bibliogs., index.

       Jazz on Record: a Critical Guide of the First Fifty Years,
       1917 to 1967. Compiled by Albert John McCarthy, Alun Morgan,
       Paul Oliver, and Max Harrison. 2nd. ed. London: Hanover
       Books; New York: Oak Publications, 1968; New York: Quick
       Fox, 1969. 416p., bibliogs., index.
         Covers jazz, blues, gospel, and ragtime records available
       in Britain. Arranged by artists. Second edition retains
       original format, with entirely new text.

4411. Jepsen, Jorgen Grunnet. Jazz Records, 1942-1967: a Discog-
       raphy. Holte, Denmark: Knudsen/Copenhagen: Nordisk
       Tidskrift Forlag, 1963-70.
       Vol. 1: 1966. unpaged.
       Vol. 2: 1966. unpaged.
       Vol. 3: 1967. unpaged.
       Vol. 4: 1968. unpaged.
       Vol. 4-A: 1968. unpaged.
       Vol. 4-B: 1969. unpaged.
       Vol. 4-C: 1970. unpaged.
       Vol. 5: 1963. unpaged.
       Vol. 6: 1963. unpaged.
       Vol. 7: 1964. unpaged.
       Vol. 8: 1965. unpaged.

         Volumes 4-6 published by Nordisk Tidskrift Forlag; rest
       by Knudsen. Arranged by artists. Published out of sequence
       in order to continue item 4394. Supplements item 4428.

4412. Jones, Clifford. Hot Jazz. London: Discographical Society,
       1944. 24p., illus.

4413. ———. Jazz in New York. London: Discographical Society,
       1944. 24p., illus.

4414. ———. New Orleans and Chicago Jazz. London: Discograph-
       ical Society, 1944. 24p., illus.

4415. ———, and Ralph G.V. Venables. Black and White. London:
       Discographical Society, 1945-46. 2 vols., 40p., illus.

4416.   Katalog der Jazz-Schallplatten (later Bielefelder Jazz
        Katalog). Bielefeld, West Germany: Bielefelder Verlags-
        anstalt. annual, 1959- .
             Lists releases in West Germany.

    *   Kraner, Dietrich Heinz, and Klaus Schulz. Jazz in Austria:
        Historische Entwicklung und Diskographie des Jazz in Oester-
        reich.
             * Cited above as item 909.

4417.   Laing, Ralph, and Chris Sheridan. Jazz Records. New York:
        Billboard Publications, 1978.   p.

4418.   ———. Jazz Records: the Specialist Labels. Copenhagen:
        Jazz Media, 1981. 2 vols.,   p.
             Lists currently available long-playing records. Arranged
        by label and number. Includes addresses, including pirate
        labels.

4419.   Lange, Horst Heinz. Die deutsche Jazz-Discographie: eine
        Geschichte des Jazz auf Schallplatten, von 1902-1955.
        Berlin/Wiesbaden: Bote und Bock, 1955. 651p.
             Text in German.

4420.   ———. Die deutsche Siebenundachtziger: Discographie der
        Jazz-und Hot-Dance-Musik, 1903-1958. Berlin: Colloquium
        Verlag, 1966. 775p. 2nd. ed.: Berlin: Colloquium Verlag,
        1978. 1,056p.
             Listing of 78-rpm records issued in Germany.

4421.   ———. The Fabulous Fives. Lübecke, West Germany: Uhle
        und Kleimann, 1959. 32p.

        ———. Horst H. Lange's "The Fabulous Fives." Revised by
        Ron Jewson, Derek Hamilton-Smith, and Ray Webb. Chigwell,
        Essex: Storyville Publications, 1978. 150p., illus.,
        bibliog., index.
             Discographies of The Original Dixieland Jazz Band, The
        Louisiana Five, The New Orleans Jazz Band, Earl Fuller's
        Famous Jazz Band, The Original Georgia Five, The Original
        Indiana Five, The Original Memphis Five, and The Southern
        Five.

4422.   ———. Die G.J.C.-Disco. Berlin: The Author, 1951-53.
        3 vols., 204p.

4423.   Litchfield, Jack. The Canadian Jazz Discography, 1916-1980.
        Toronto; London: University of Toronto Pr., 1982. 945p.,
        index.

4424.   Lucas, John. Basic Jazz on Long-Play: the Great Soloists.
        Ragtime, Folksong, Blues, Jazz, Swing, and the Great Bands:
        New Orleans, Swing, Dixieland. Northfield, Minnesota:
        Carleton Jazz Club, Carleton College, 1954. 103p. (Carleton
        Jazz Club Bulletin, 1)

Jazz (cont.)

4425. Lucas, John. The Great Revival on Long-Play. Northfield,
       Minnesota: Carleton Jazz Club, Carleton College, 1957. 56p.
       (Carleton Jazz Club Bulletin, 2)
           Dixieland revival.

4426. Lyons, Leonard. The One Hundred and One Best Jazz Albums:
       a History of Jazz on Records. New York: Morrow, 1980.
       476p., illus., bibliog.

4427. McCarthy, Albert John. Jazz and Blues on Record. London:
       Quartet, 1985. 250p., bibliog., index.

4428. ———. Jazz Discography: an International Discography of
       Recorded Jazz. Including Blues, Gospel, and Rhythm-and-
       Blues. London: Cassell.
       Vol. 1: January-December, 1958. 1960. 271p.
           Abortive attempt to continue item 4394. Only volume
       issued; continued as supplement to Jazz Monthly (1962-66.)
       Aim was to document new releases worldwide as they appeared.
       Superseded by item 4411.

4429. McCoy, Meredith, and Barbara Parker (eds.). Catalog of the
       John D. Reid Collection of Early American Jazz. Advisor:
       John D. Reid. Little Rock, Arkansas: Arkansas Arts Center,
       1975. 112p., illus.
           Guide to record collection.

4430. Mellor, Richard N. One Thousand and One Best Recordings.
       Auburndale, Massachusetts: The Author, 1948. 51p.

4431. Miller, William H. A Discography of the "Little" Recording
       Companies. Melbourne, Victoria: The Author, 1943. 20p.
       Rev. ed. (as The Little Discography): Melbourne, Victoria:
       The Author, 1945. 64p.

4432. Mitchell, Jack. The Australian Discography. Edited by
       William H. Miller. Melbourne, Victoria: Australian Jazz
       Quarterly, 1950. 16p. (A.J.Q. Booklet, 3). 2nd. ed.:
       Lithgow, New South Wales: The Author, 1960. 78p.
           Jazz records made in Australia.

4433. Moeller, Borge J.C. Dansk jazzdiscografi: komplet fortegnelse
       over samtlige i Danmark indspillende jazzpladen. Med
       indspillende orkestr og deres sammensaetning, indspilningsaar,
       melodier, komponister, arrangorer, sangere, matrice-numre,
       grammofonmaeker, bestillingsnumer, m.m. Copenhagen: Artum
       Musikforlag, 1945. 94p.
           In Danish. Listing of Danish jazz records.

4434. Nicolausson, Harry. Svensk Jazz Diskografi. Stockholm:
       Nordiska Musikförlaget, 1953. 115p.
           In Swedish. Listing of Swedish jazz records.

4435. Panassié, Hugues. Discographie critique des meilleurs
       disques de jazz. Geneva: Charles Grasset, 1948. 322p.,
       index. Rev. ed. (as Discographie critique des meilleurs
       disques de jazz, 1920-1951): Paris: Côrrea, 1951. 371p.,
       illus., index. 3rd. ed.: Paris: Laffont, 1958. 624p.,
       indexes.

4436. ———. Petit guide pour une discothèque de jazz: les
       meilleurs disques du jazz publiés en France. Paris: Laffont,
       1955. 153p.

   *   Pernet, Robert. Jazz in Little Belgium: Historique (1881-
       1966); Discographie (1894-1966.)
          * Cited above as item 910.

4437. Personeault, Ken, and Carl M. Sales. Jazz Discography.
       Jackson Heights, New York: The Needle, 1944. 145p.

4438. Philpot, Sam H. Jazz, 1919-1947. Atlanta, Georgia: Jazz
       Catalogue, 1948. 64p.

4439. Raben, Erik. A Discography of Free Jazz: Albert Ayler, Don
       Cherry, Ornette Coleman, Pharoah Sanders, Archie Shepp,
       Cecil Taylor. Copenhagen: Knudsen, 1969. 38p.

4440. Ramsey, Frederic, Jr. A Guide to Longplay Jazz Records.
       New York: Long Player Publications, 1954. 263p., illus.,
       bibliog., index.

          ———. ———. With a new introduction by the Author, and
       supplementary record listings. New York: Da Capo Pr., 1977.
       282p., illus., bibliog., index. (Roots of Jazz)

4441. Rich, Alan, and Morley Jones. The Listener's Guide to Jazz.
       New York: Facts on File; Poole, Dorset: Blandford Pr., 1980.
       134p., illus.

4442. Rowe, John, and Ted Watson. Junkshoppers' Discography.
       London: Jazz Tempo Publications, 1945. 36p., illus.
          Guide to pseudonymous and other jazz bands, on "out-of-
       the-way British labels."

4443. Rust, Brian Arthur Lovell. Jazz Records, A-Z: 1897-1931.
       Hatch End, Middlesex: The Author, 1961. 844p. 2nd. ed.:
       Hatch End, Middlesex: The Author, 1962. 736p., index.
          Loose-leaf format.

          ———. ———: Index. Compiled by Richard Grandorge.
       Hatch End, Middlesex: Brian Rust, 1963. 63p.

4444. ———. Jazz Records, A-Z: 1932-1942. Hatch End, Middlesex:
       The Author, 1965. 680p., index.

4445. ———. Jazz Records, 1897-1942. London: Storyville Pub-
       lications, 1970. 2 vols., 1968p., index. Rev. ed.: London:
       Storyville Publications; New Rochelle, New York: Arlington

Jazz (cont.)

> House, 1978. 2 vols., 1,996p., index. 5th. rev. ed.:
> Chigwell, Essex: Storyville Publications, 1984. 2 vols.,
> 1,998p., index.
> Combination, with revisions and additions, of items
> 4443 and 4444. Continued by item 4411.

4446. Schwanniger, Armin, and André Gurwitsch. Swing discographie.
Geneva: Charles Grasset, 1945. 200p.
Text in French.

4447. Seidel, Richard. A Basic Record Library of Jazz. Boston:
Schwann, 1974.   p.

4448. Smith, Charles Edward, Frederic Ramsey, Jr., Charles Payne
Rogers, and William Russell. The Jazz Record Book. New
York: Smith and Durrell, 1942; New York: Crown, 1950;
Westport, Conn.: Greenwood Pr., 1978; New York: Scholarly
Pr., 1983. 515p., illus., bibliog., index.
Annotated guide, categorized to show the development of
jazz.

4449. Stagg, Tom, and Charlie Crump. New Orleans: the Revival.
A Tape and Discography of Negro Traditional Jazz Recorded
in New Orleans, or by New Orleans Bands, 1937-1972. Dublin:
Bashall Eaves, 1973. 307p., illus., index.
Includes private and other unreleased recordings.

4450. Stiassi, Ruggiero. The Modern Jazz Basic Index. Bologna,
Italy: The Author, 1977.   p.
Lists two hundred key recordings, 1941-70.

4451. Townley, Eric. Tell Your Story: a Dictionary of Jazz and
Blues Recordings, 1917-1950. Chigwell, Essex: Storyville
Publications, 1977. 432p.
Lists approximately 2,700 recordings. Includes study of
song titles and their meanings.

4452. Tudor, Dean, and Nancy Tudor. Jazz. Littleton, Colorado:
Libraries Unlimited, 1979. 302p., index. (American Popular
Music on Elpee)
Annotated. Incorporated into item 4363.

4453. Venables, Ralph G.V., and Clifford Jones. Cream of the
White Clarinets. London: Discographical Society, 1946.
16p., illus.

4454. ———. Eye Witness Jazz. London: Discographical Society,
1946. 2 vols., 48p.

4455. Westerberg, Hans. Suomalaiset jazzlevytykset, 1932-1976.
Helsinki: The Author, 1977. 104p.
Lists Finnish jazz records. In Finnish.

4456. Williams, Martin T. The Smithsonian Institution Collection
       of Classic Jazz. Washington, D.C.: Smithsonian Institution;
       New York: Norton, 1973. 48p.
            Annotated. Accompanied by set of long-playing records.

4457. Wilson, John Stewart. The Collector's Jazz: Modern.
       Philadelphia: Lippincott, 1959. 318p. (Keystone Books in
       Music)
            Annotated listing of long-playing recordings.

4458. ───. The Collector's Jazz: Traditional and Swing.
       Philadelphia: Lippincott, 1958. 319p. (Keystone Books in
       Music.

                  (iii) V-Disks and Transcriptions

4459. Heider, Wally. Transcography: a Discography of Jazz and
       Pop Music Issued on Sixteen-Inch Transcriptions. San
       Francisco: The Author, 1970. 106p.

4460. Sears, Richard S. V-Disks: a History and Discography.
       Prepared under the auspices of the Association for Recorded
       Sound Collections. Westport, Conn.: Greenwood Pr., 1980.
       1,166p., illus., indexes. (Discographies, 5)

4461. V-Disc Catalogue, Volume One: Numbers 1-500. Compiled by
       Stephan Wante and Walter DeBlock. Antwerp, Belgium: Willem
       van Laernstraat, 1954. 83p.

       V-Disc Catalogue: Discography (Numbers 500-904). Compiled
       by Klaus Teubis. Berlin: Deutscher Bibliotheksverband,
       Arbeitsstelle für das Bibliothekswesen, 1976. 155p.
       (Musikbibliothek Aktuell, 5)

                       (f) Stage and Screen

4462. Hodgins, Gordon W. The Broadway Musical: a Complete LP
       Discography. Metuchen, New Jersey; London: Scarecrow Pr.,
       1980. 183p., indexes.

4463. Hummel, David. The Collector's Guide to the American Musical
       Theater. Metuchen, New Jersey; London: Scarecrow Pr., 1984.
       2 vols., 940p.

4464. Pitts, Michael R., and Louis R. Harrison. Hollywood on
       Record: the Film Stars' Discography. Metuchen, New Jersey;
       London: Scarecrow Pr., 1978. 911p., illus.

4465. Preston, Mike. Tele-Tunes: the Book of T.V. and Film Music.
       Television and Film Music on Record. Kidderminster, Worcest-
       ershire: Record Information Centre, 1979. 108p.

Stage and Screen (cont.)

Preston, Mike. Tele-Tunes, 2: the Second Book of T.V. and
and Film Music. Kidderminster, Worcestershire: Record
Information Centre, 1979. 152p., index.

————. Tele-Tunes, 3. Hastings, East Sussex: Tele-Tunes
Publications, 1984.   p., index.

Tele-Tunes. Hastings, East Sussex: Tele-Tunes Publications.
quarterly, 1984- .
     Lists themes, advertising, and other screen music avail-
able on record; also background information; awards.

4466. Raymond, Jack. Show Music on Record, From the 1890's to
the 1980's: a Comprehensive List of Original Cast and Studio
Cast Performances Issued on Commercial Phonograph Records,
Covering Music of the American Stage, Screen, and Television.
With Composer Performances, and Other Selected Collateral
Recordings. New York: Frederick Ungar, 1982. 253p., illus.,
index.

4467. Rust, Brian Arthur Lovell. British Music-Hall on Record.
Harrow, Middlesex: General Gramophone Publications, 1979.
301p.
     Arranged by artists. Covers 1895-1960.

4468. ————. London Musical Shows on Records, 1894-1954.
London: British Institute of Recorded Sound, 1958. 207p.

————. London Musical Shows on Record, 1897-1976. Harrow,
Middlesex: General Gramophone Publications, 1977. 672p.

4469. Smolian, Steven. A Handbook of Film, Theater, and Television
Music on Record, 1948-1969. New York: The Record Undertaker,
1970. 2 vols., 128p., index.
     Classified listing of long-playing recordings.

                     (7) RECORDING COMPANIES

                     (i) Comprehensive Works

4470. Rust, Brian Arthur Lovell. The American Record Label Book.
New Rochelle, New York: Arlington House, 1978.   p.

4471. Ska to Reggae United Kingdom Label Discographies. Edited
by Roger Dalke. Weybridge, Surrey: Top Sounds International,
1983-84. 7 vols., p.
     Listing of individual labels, with their releases.

4472. Wyler, Michael. A Glimpse At the Past: an Illustrated
History of Some Early Record Companies That Made Jazz
History. West Moors, Dorset: Jazz Publications, 1957. 32p.,
illus.

(ii) Individual Companies

A & M

4473. Casell, Chuck. <u>A & M Records: the First Ten Years</u> (a Fairy Tale.) With design by Roland Young. Hollywood, California: A & M Records, 1972. 34p., illus.

Atlantic

4474. Gillett, Charlie. <u>Making Tracks: Atlantic Records and the Growth of a Multi-Billion-Dollar Industry</u>. London: W.H. Allen; New York: Dutton, 1974. 305p., illus., bibliog., index. St. Albans, Hertfordshire: Panther, 1975.   p., illus., bibliog., index.

4475. Ruppli, Michel (comp.). <u>Atlantic Records: a Discography</u>. Westport, Conn.: Greenwood Pr., 1979. <u>4 vols.</u>,   p., index. (Discographies, 1)
    Lists every Atlantic record, 1947-74.

Chess

4476. Fancourt, Leslie (comp.). <u>Chess Blues Discography</u>. Faversham, Kent: The Author, 1984.   p.

4477. ———. <u>Chess Rhythm and Blues Discography</u>. Faversham, Kent: The Author, 1984.   p.

4478. Ruppli, Michel (comp.). <u>The Chess Labels: a Discography</u>. Westport, Conn.: Greenwood Pr., 1983. <u>2 vols.</u>, 743p., index. (Discographies, 7)
    Lists every record issued by Chess and its associated labels, 1947-75.

Columbia

4479. Avakian, George. <u>Jazz From Columbia: a Complete Jazz Catalog</u>. New York: Columbia Records, 1956. 32p., illus.
    Record company advertising brochure. Classified arrangement, with introductions to each section by Avakian. Lists approximately 150 current releases.

4480. Mahoney, Dan (comp.). <u>The Columbia 13/14000-D Series: a Numerical Listing</u>. Stanhope, New Jersey: Walter C. Allen, 1961. 80p., illus., indexes. (Record Handbook, 1). <u>2nd. ed.</u>: Stanhope, New Jersey: Walter C. Allen, 1966. 80p., illus., indexes. (Record Handbook, 1)
    Lists output of Columbia's race label, September 1923-April 1933.

Individual Companies (cont.)

Columbia (British) <u>see</u> His Master's Voice

Decca Group

4481. Decca Record Company. <u>Jazz on LP's: a Collector's Guide to</u>
      <u>Jazz on Decca, Brunswick, London, Felsted, Ducretet-Thomson,</u>
      <u>Vogue, Coral, Telefunken, and Durium Long-Playing Records.</u>
      London: Decca Record Company, 1955. 212p. <u>2nd. ed.</u>:
      London: Decca Record Company, 1956; Westport, Conn.: Green-
      wood Pr., 1975. 282p.
         Arranged by artists. Includes critical assessments.

4482. ————. <u>Jazz on Seventy-Eights: a Guide to the Many</u>
      <u>Examples of Classic Jazz on Decca, Brunswick, and London</u>
      <u>78-rpm Records.</u> London: Decca Record Company, 1954. 83p.
         Arranged by artists. Includes critical assessments.

4483. Pelletier, Paul Maurice (comp.). <u>Decca Complete Singles</u>
      <u>Catalogue, 1954-1983.</u> Chessington, Surrey: Record Informat-
      ion Services, 1984. unpaged, illus.
         British issues.

                              Brunswick

4484. Hibbs, Leonard (comp.). <u>A Short Survey of Modern Rhythm on</u>
      <u>Brunswick Records.</u> London: Brunswick Record Company, 1934.
      23p.

4485. ————. <u>Twenty-One Years of Swing Music on Brunswick</u>
      <u>Records.</u> London: A. White/Brunswick Records, 1937. 80p.,
      illus.

4486. Pelletier, Paul Maurice (comp.). <u>Brunswick Complete Singles</u>
      <u>Catalogue, 1952-1967.</u> Chessington, Surrey: Record Informat-
      ion Services, 1982. unpaged., illus.
         British issues.

                                Coral

4487. ————. <u>Coral Atlantic Complete Singles Catalogue.</u> Chess-
      ington, Surrey: Record Information Services, 1984. unpaged,
      illus.

London

4488. Decca Record Company. Complete Catalogue of London
       "Origins of Jazz" Records. London: Decca Record Company,
       1957.   p., illus.

4489. Pelletier, Paul Maurice (comp.). British London (American)
       Complete Singles Catalogue, 1949-1980. Chessington, Surrey:
       Record Information Services, 1982. 128p., illus.
            British issues. Includes 78-rpm and 45-rpm recordings.

4490. ────. London (American) Complete E.P.'s, 1954-1967.
       Chessington, Surrey: Record Information Services, 1982.
       unpaged, illus.
            British extended-play issues.

Electrical and Musical Industries (E.M.I.)

4491. E.M.I. Records. The Jazz Scene, Volume One. London: E.M.I.
       Records, 1962.   p.

Excello

4492. Leadbitter, Mike. Crowley, Louisiana, Blues: the Story of
       J.D. Miller and His Blues Artists. With a Guide to Their
       Music. Bexhill-on-Sea, East Sussex: Blues Unlimited, 1968.
       32p., illus.

Gennett

4493. Gennett Records. Gennett Records of Old Time Tunes: a
       Catalog Reprint. Los Angeles: John Edwards Memorial Found-
       ation, 1975.   p. (J.E.M.F. Special Series, 6)
            Early country label.

Goldband

4494. Leadbitter, Mike, and Eddie Shuler. From the Bayou: the
       Story of Goldband Records. Bexhill-on-Sea, East Sussex:
       Blues Unlimited, 1969. 62p., illus., discog.
            Cajun label. Includes reproduction of its current
       catalog.

Individual Companies (cont.)

His Master's Voice (H.M.V.) Group

4495. Casteels, Raymond. Catalogue Pathe, Capitol, His Master's
      Voice, Columbia, Norman Granz: 33/45/78 tours. Brussels:
      Gramophone, 1955. 36p.
           Listing of jazz on the labels. Supplement published,
      1955.

4496. Jackson, Edgar (comp.). Swing Music. Hayes, Middlesex:
      The Gramophone Company, 1941. 100p., illus. 2nd. ed.:
      1942. 3rd. ed.: 1944. 4th. ed.: 1946. 5th. ed.: 1948.
           Listing of swing issued on the H.M.V. label.

4497. Rust, Brian Arthur Lovell (comp.). The H.M.V. House Bands,
      1912-1939. Chigwell, Essex: Storyville Publications, 1976.
      33p.
           Guide to their recordings.

                              Capitol

4498. Pelletier, Paul Maurice (comp.). British Capitol 45-rpm
      Singles Catalogue, 1954-1981. Chessington, Surrey: Record
      Information Services, 1982. 64p., illus.

London see Decca Group

Okeh

4499. Okeh Records. The Okeh Records Catalog, Circa 1920. Leigh-
      on-Sea, Essex: Storyville Publications, 1976.   p.
           Reprint.

Paramount

4500. Vreede, Max E. (comp.). The Paramount 12000/13000 Series.
      London: Storyville Publications, 1971. unpaged, illus.,
      index.
           Lists, in catalog-number order, blues and jazz releases
      on the label, 1920's and 1930's.

Parlophone/Odeon

4501. Grezzi, Juan Rafael. Estudios sobre la "New Rhythm Style

Series", disco "Odeon." Buenos Aires: Industrias Electricas
y Musicales Odeon, 1957. 127p., illus., discog.

4502. Jackson, Edgar (comp.). The Parlophone "Rhythm Style"
Series. Hayes, Middlesex: The Parlophone Company, 1936.
28p. 2nd. ed. (as The Rhythm Style Series, Number Two):
Hayes, Middlesex: The Parlophone Company, 1941. 36p.
3rd. ed. (as The Rhythm Style Series): Hayes, Middlesex: The
Parlophone Company, 1942. 112p. 4th. ed.: 1944. 112p.
5th. ed.: 1944. 112p. 6th. ed.: 1948. 112p.

4503. Moller, Borge J.C. (comp.). Parlophone Bio-Discografi.
Copenhagen: Irichs Bogtrykkeri, 1946. 64p.
        Jazz. Text in Danish.

Prestige

4504. Ruppli, Michel (comp.). Prestige Jazz Records, 1949-1969:
a Discography. Copenhagen: Knudsen, 1972. 399p., indexes.
New ed. (as The Prestige Label: a Discography. With
assistance from Bob Porter): Westport, Conn.: Greenwood Pr.,
1980. 377p., index. (Discographies, 3)
        Complete listing of the label's jazz, blues, and gospel
output.

Radio Corporation of America/Victor (R.C.A./Victor)

4505. Radio Corporation of America. The Fifty-Year Story of
R.C.A. Victor Records. New York: Radio Corporation of
America, Department of Information, 1953. 77p., illus.

                           Victor

4506. Fagan, Ted, and William R. Moran (comps.). The Encyclopedic
Discography of Victor Recordings: Pre-Matrix Series--The
Consolidated Talking Machine Company, Eldridge R. Johnson,
and The Victor Talking Machine Company, 12 January 1900 to
23 April 1903. With a Special Appendix: The Victor Talking
Machine Company, by B.L. Aldridge. Westport, Conn.: Greenwood Pr., 1983. 393p., illus., bibliog., index.

4507. Panassié, Hugues. Hugues Pannassié Discusses 144 Hot Jazz
Bluebird and Victor Records. Edited by John D. Reid.
Camden, New Jersey: Radio Corporation of America, 1939. 44p.
        Annotated discography.

4508. Rust, Brian Arthur Lovell (comp.). The Victor Master Book.
Volume Two (1925-1936). With indexes by Malcolm Shaw and
Nevil Skrimshire. Hatch End, Middlesex: The Author, 1969;
Stanhope, New Jersey: Walter C. Allen, 1970. 776p.
        In matrix-number order. No first volume published.

Individual Companies (cont.)

Savoy

4509. Ruppli, Michel (comp.). The Savoy Label: a Discography.
       With assistance from Bob Porter. Westport, Conn.: Green-
       wood Pr., 1980. 442p., illus., index. (Discographies, 2)
          Includes subsidiary labels.

Stateside see Top Rank/Stateside

Stiff

4510. Muirhead, Bert. Stiff: the Story of a Record Label. Poole,
       Dorset: Blandford Pr., 1983. 112p., illus., discog.

                         Periodicals

4511. Be Stiff. Edited by Michael Robson. 103 Ladybower, Newton
       Aycliffe, County Durham. irreg., 1984- .
          Aimed at collectors of the label's releases.

Sue

4512. Pelletier, Paul Maurice (comp.). Sue Complete Singles, EP's,
       and LP's, 1963-1968. Chessington, Surrey: Record Information
       Services, 1982. unpaged, illus.

Sun

4513. Escott, Colin, and Martin Hawkins. Catalyst: the Sun Records
       Story. London: Aquarius Books, 1975. 173p., illus., bibliog.,
       discog., index.

       ————. Sun Records: the Brief History of the Legendary
       Recording Label. London: Omnibus Pr.; New York: Quick Fox,
       1980. 184p., illus., bibliog., discog., index.

4514. ————. The Sun Sessions File. Ashford, Kent: The Authors,
       1973-74. 6 vols.,   p., index.
          All records made on Sun and Phillips International labels.

4515. Vernon, Paul. The Sun Legend. London: Stve Lane, 1969.
       64p., illus., index.
          Brief history; followed by numerical complete listing of
       releases on Sun and its subsidiary labels.

Tamla Motown

4516.   Benjaminson, Peter. The Story of Motown. New York: Grove
        Pr., 1980; Bromley, Kent: Columbus Books, 1981. 320p.,
        illus.

4517.   Davis, Sharon. The Motown Story: the Detroit Phenomenon.
        London; New York: Proteus, 1985. 96p., illus., discog.
           Based on personal knowledge.

4518.   Martin, Sandra Pratt. Inside Motown: the Million Dollar
        Story of the Black Sound. New York: Drake Publishers, 1974.
           p., illus.

4519.   Morse, David. Motown and the Arrival of Black Music.
        London: Studio Vista; New York: Macmillan, 1971. 111p.,
        illus.
           Critical history of Motown, and its influence.

4520.   Pelletier, Paul Maurice (comp.). Tamla Motown Complete
        Singles, EP's, and LP's, 1959-1970. Chessington, Surrey:
        Record Information Services, 1982. unpaged, illus.

4521.   ———. Tamla Motown Complete Singles and LP's, 1971-1978.
        Chessington, Surrey: Record Information Services, 1982.
        unpaged, illus.

Top Rank/Stateside

4522.   ———. Top Rank/Stateside Complete Singles and EP's
        Catalogue, 1959-1974. Chessington, Surrey: Record Informat-
        ion Services, 1982. unpaged, illus.

Victor see Radio Corporation of America/Victor

Vocalion

4523.   Pelletier, Paul Maurice (comp.). Vocalion Complete Singles
        Catalogue. Chessington, Surrey: Record Information Services,
        1984. unpaged, illus.

Vogue

4524.   ———. Vogue Complete Singles Catalogue. Chessington,
        Surrey: Record Information Services, 1984. unpaged, illus.

Individual Companies (cont.)

Warner Brothers

4525. Pelletier, Paul Maurice (comp.). Warner Brothers Complete
      Singles Catalogue. Chessington, Surrey: Record Information
      Services, 1984. unpaged, illus.

Zonophone

4526. Rust, Brian Arthur Lovell (comp.). The Zonophone Studio
      House Bands, 1924-1932. Chigwell, Essex: Storyville
      Publications, 1976. 35p.
          Guide to their recordings.

PART SIX: LITERARY WORKS

A. NOVELS

(1) POPULAR

4527. Adams, Seth. <u>Asparagus Tips and Honey: an Amusement</u>.
Northwood, Middlesex: Imprint, 1973. 200p., illus.

4528. Aldiss, Brian Wilson. <u>Brothers of the Head</u>. London:
Pierrot Publishing, 1977. p.

————. <u>Brothers of the Head; and, Where the Lines
Converge</u>. St. Albans, Hertfordshire: Panther, 1979. 156p.
(Panther Science Fiction)

4529. Allen, Richard. <u>Glam</u>. London: New English Library, 1973.
125p.

4530. ————. <u>Teeny Bopper Idol</u>. London: New English Library,
1973. p.

4531. Allsop, Kenneth. <u>The Leopard-Paw Orchid</u>. London: Quality
Pr., 1954. 222p.
Mystery set in the world of dance bands.

4532. Anderson, John Richard Lane. <u>Festival</u>. London: Gollancz,
1979. 203p.
Detective novel.

4533. Ashe, Gordon (<u>pseud. of</u> John Creasey). <u>A Blast of Trumpets</u>.
London: John Long, 1975. 184p.
Mystery.

4534. Baldwin, James. <u>Just Above My Head</u>. New York: Dial Pr.;
London: Michael Joseph, 1979; New York: Dell, 1980. 256p.
Gospel singer's life and death.

4535. Barker, Dudley Raymond. <u>The Voice</u>. London: Heinemann, 1953.
263p.

4536. Bentinck, Ray. <u>Golden Disc Girl</u>. London: Gresham, 1969.
158p.

4537. Boland, John. <u>Kidnap</u>. London: Cassell, 1970. 201p.
Mystery.

4538. Bradley, Carole. <u>Echoes</u>. London: Zomba Books, 1984. 600p.
Set in the record business, swing to rock eras.

4539. Breeze, Paul. <u>While My Guitar Gently Weeps</u>. London: Michael
Joseph, 1979. 222p.

Popular (cont.)

4540. Breeze, Paul. <u>Back Street Runner</u>. London: Michael Joseph,
       1980. 283p.
           Rock. Sequel to item 4539.

4541. Brown, Christy. <u>A Promising Career</u>. London: Secker and
       Warburg, 1981. 256p.

4542. Bush, Christopher. <u>The Case of the Extra Man</u>. London:
       Macdonald, 1956. 206p.
           Mystery.

4543. Butterworth, Michael. <u>Festival!</u> London: Collins, 1976.
       192p. (Crime Club)

4544. Bygraves, Max. <u>The Milkman's On His Way</u>. London: W.H.
       Allen, 1977. 160p. London: Star Books, 1978. 188p.
           Huorous account of instant pop stardom.

4545. Calvert, Robert. <u>Hype</u>. London: New English Library, 1981.
       221p.
           Machinations of the rock industry. Accompanied by long-
       playing album by Calvert, <u>Hype: the Songs of Tom Mahler</u>, 1981.

4546. Carlile, Richard. <u>Drummer</u>. London: Tandem, 1971. 123p.
           Rock fantasy.

4547. Charbonneau, Louis. <u>Way Out: a Novel</u>. London: Barrie and
       Rockliff, 1966. 189p.
           Mystery.

4548. Cleary, Jon. <u>Remember Jack Hoxie</u>. London: Collins, 1969.
       320p.

    * Cohen, Leonard. <u>Beautiful Losers</u>.
           * Cited above as item 2212.

    * ————. <u>The Favorite Game</u>.
           * Cited above as item 2217.

4549. Cohen, Sharleen Cooper. <u>Regina's Song</u>. New York: Dell;
       London: New English Library, 1980. 411p.
           Rock.

4550. Cohn, Nik. <u>I Am Still the Greatest, Says Johnny Angelo</u>.
       London: Secker and Warburg, 1967. 191p.
           Rock.

    * ————. <u>King Death</u>.
           * Cited above as item 3355.

4551. Collins, Jackie. <u>Lovers and Gamblers</u>. London: W.H. Allen,
       1977. 657p. New York: Warner Books, 1980. 592p.

* Connolly, Ray. <u>Stardust</u>.
  * Cited above as item 1191.

4552. ————. <u>A Sunday Kind of Woman</u>. London: Collins, 1980.
192p.

* ————. <u>That'll Be the Day</u>.
  * Cited above as item 1190.

4553. Courtis, Gerald. <u>The Big Noise</u>. London: Hale, 1977. 185p.
Mystery.

* Deal, Babs H. <u>High Lonesome World: the Death and Life of a</u>
  <u>Country Music Singer</u>.
  * Cited above as item 3730.

4554. De Lillo, Don. <u>Great Jones Street</u>. Boston: Houghton
Mifflin; London: Andre Deutsch; London: Wildwood House,
1973; New York: Paperback Library, 1974. 265p.
Rock.

4555. Ellis, Royston. <u>The Big Beat Scene</u>. London: Four Square
Books, 1961. 124p., illus.

4556. Eskow, John. <u>Smokestack Lightning</u>. New York: Delacorte Pr.,
1980. 310p.
Rock.

4557. Fabian, Jenny, and Johnny Byrne. <u>Groupie</u>. London: New
English Library, 1969. 220p. St. Albans, Hertfordshire:
Mayflower, 1970. 205p.
Rock.

4558. Fabian, Jenny. <u>A Chemical Romance</u>. London: Talmy, Franklin,
1971. 175p.
Sequel to item 4557.

4559. Farren, Mick. <u>The Tale of Willy's Rats</u>. St. Albans, Hertfordshire: Mayflower, 1975. 351p.
Rock.

4560. ————. <u>The Texts of Festival</u>. London: Hart-Davis, MacGibbon,
1973; St. Albans, Hertfordshire: Mayflower, 1975. 205p.
Rock fantasy.

* Fleischer, Leonore. <u>Fame: a Novel</u>.
  * Cited above as item 1151.

* ————. <u>The Rose</u>.
  * Cited above as item 1184.

4561. Fletcher, Chrys Paul. <u>Cry For a Shadow</u>. London: Barker,
1967. 160p. London: Panther, 1969. 176p.

4562. Galloway, David. <u>Melody Jones</u>. London: John Calder, 1980.
120p.

Popular (cont.)

4563. Gibson, M.A. Benny With Joy. Ilfracombe, Devon: Arthur H.
       Stockwell, 1968. 208p.

4564. Glanville, Brian. Never Look Back. London: Michael
       Joseph, 1980. 240p.
           Rock.

4565. Gonzales, Laurence. Jambeaux. New York: Harcourt, Brace,
       Jovanovich, 1979. 275p.
           Rock.

4566. Goyen, William. The Fair Sister. Garden City, New York:
       Doubleday, 1963. 104p. London (as Savata, My Fair Sister):
       Peter Owen, 1963. 145p.

4567. Grant, John. The Truth About The Flaming Ghoulies. London:
       Frederick Muller, 1984. 224p.
           Rock science fiction.

4568. Gray, Berkeley (pseud. of Edwy Searles Brooks). Death On
       the Hit Parade. London: Collins, 1958. 191p.
           Mystery.

4569. Grex, Leo (pseud. of Leonard Reginald Gribble). The Crooner's
       Swan Song. London: Hutchinson, 1935. 287p.
           Mystery.

   *   Guilbert, Yvette. La Vedette: roman.
           * Cited above as item 2679.

4570. Haas, Charlie, and Tim Hunter. The Soul Hit. New York:
       Harper and Row, 1977; London: Hale, 1978. 186p.
           Rock and crime.

4571. Hancock, Robert (pseud. of Douglas Naylor Howell). The A.
       and R. Man. London: Hutchinson, 1958. 159p. London: Four
       Square Books, 1961. 128p.

4572. Hasluck, Nicholas. The Blue Guitar. London: Macmillan, 1980.
       206p.
           Entrepreneur's attempts to market a self-playing guitar.

4573. Helton, David. King Jude. New York: Simon and Schuster,
       1969; London: New English Library, 1971. 124p.
           Rock.

4574. Henry, Clayton Russell. Not Dead Enough. London: Boardman,
       1965. 186p. (Bloodhound Mysteries)

   *   Hine, Al. The Unsinkable Molly Brown: a Novel Based Upon the
       Stage Play.
           * Cited above as item 1194.

4575. Hjortsberg, William. _Falling Angel_. New York: Harcourt, Brace, Jovanovich, 1978; London: Hutchinson, 1979; London: Arrow, 1980. 244p.
Mystery.

4576. Holden, Stephen. _Triple Platinum_. New York: Dell, 1979. 430p. London: New English Library, 1980. 317p.
Rock record industry.

4577. Hughes, Langston. _Tambourines To Glory: a Novel_. New York: John Day, 1958; London: Gollancz, 1959. 188p.
Gospel.

4578. Hughes, Megan. _Yesterday's Music_. New York: Leisure Books, 1980. 285p.
Rock.

4579. Jahn, Mike. _The Scene_. New York: Bernard Geis Associates, 1970. 210p.
Rock.

4580. Jenkins, Dan. _Baja, Oklahoma_. New York: Atheneum, 1981.
p.
Country music.

4581. ————, and Edwin Shrake. _Limo_. New York: Atheneum, 1976.
p.
Rock.

4582. Jesmer, Elaine. _Number One With a Bullet_. New York: Farrar, Straus, and Giroux; London: Weidenfeld and Nicolson, 1974; London: Futura, 1976. 424p.
Soul record industry.

4583. Jessup, Richard. _Lowdown_. London: Secker and Warburg, 1958. 160p. London: Pan, 1961. 154p.
Mystery.

4584. Jones, Arthur E. _It Makes You Think_. London: John Long, 1958. 191p.
Mystery.

4585. Jones, Mervyn. _Nobody's Fault_. London: Quartet, 1977. 198p.

4586. Kershaw, John. _Company and Co_. London: British Broadcasting Corporation, 1980. 208p. Reissued: London: British Broadcasting Corporation, 1980. 159p.
Based on British television series. Mystery.

4587. Keyes, Thom. _One Night Stand_. London: W.H. Allen, 1966. 216p.
Rock.

4588. Kosinski, Jerzy. _Pinball_. New York: Bantam; London: Michael Joseph, 1982. 236p.
Rock.

Popular (cont.)

* Kunstler, James Howard. The Life of Byron James.
   * Cited above as item 2396.

4589. Lantz, Frances L. Rock 'n' Roll Romance. New York: Ace
      Books, 1984. 160p. (Caprice Series)

4590. Lauder, Stuart. Break and Begin Again. London: Longmans,
      1966. 239p.

4591. Launay, Droo (pseud. of Andre Joseph Launay). The Scream.
      London: Boardman, 1965. 144p. (Bloodhound Mysteries)

4592. Lea, Timothy. Confessions From the Pop Scene. London:
      Futura, 1974. 156p. Reissued (as Confessions of a Pop
      Performer): London: Futura, 1975. 160p.

4593. Leslie, David Stuart. Bad Medicine. London: Macmillan,
      1971. 250p.

4594. ————. Snap, Crackle, Pop. London: Macmillan, 1970.
      214p.

* Littlejohn, David. The Man Who Killed Mick Jagger: a Novel.
   * Cited above as item 3494.

4595. McBain, Ed (pseud. of Evan Hunter). Calypso. London:
      Hamish Hamilton, 1979. 200p.
      Mystery.

4596. ————. Rumpelstiltskin. London: Hamish Hamilton, 1981.
      240p.
      Mystery.

4597. McGrath, Pat. Daybreak. London: W.H. Allen, 1977. 311p.
      Rock.

4598. McGuane, Thomas. Panama. New York: Penguin, 1980. 176p.
      Rock.

4599. MacInnes, Colin. Absolute Beginners. London: MacGibbon
      and Kee, 1959. 223p. London: New English Library, 1962.
      172p. (Four Square Books). Harmondsworth, Middlesex:
      Penguin, 1964. 235p.

4600. MacLeod, Sheila. The Moving Accident. London: Faber and
      Faber, 1968. 222p.

4601. Martin, George R.R. The Armageddon Rag. New York: Poseidon,
      1983.   p.
      Rock mystery.

4602. Masters, Simon. Scream a Little Louder. London: Longmans,
      1966. 185p.
      Rock.

4603. Moorcock, Michael. <u>The Condition of Muzak: a Jerry
Cornelius Novel</u>. Illustrated by Richard Glyn Jones.
London: Alison and Busby, 1977. 313p., illus. London:
Fontana, 1978. 272p., illus.

* ————. <u>The Great Rock 'n' Roll Swindle</u>.
  * Cited above as item 3534.

* ————, and Michael Butterworth. <u>Time of the Hawklords</u>.
  * Cited above as item 2717.

4604. Muller, Robert. <u>Cinderella Nightingale</u>. London: Arthur
Barker, 1958. 255p. London: Pan, 1962. 202p.

4605. Murray, Angus Wolfe. <u>Resurrection Shuffle: a Novel</u>. London:
Peter Owen, 1978. 190p.
Rock.

* Nemeroff, David. <u>Glory</u>.
  * Cited above as item 2581.

4606. Norman, Philip. <u>Wild Thing</u>. London: Heinemann, 1972. 192p.
Rock short stories.

4607. O'Connor, Mary. <u>The Blue Guitar</u>. London: Geoffrey Bles,
1966. 222p.

* O'Hara, John. <u>Pal Joey</u>.
  * Cited above as item 1178.

4608. Olds, Helen Diehl. <u>Lark, Radio Singer</u>. Illustrated by
Dorothy Wagstaff. New York: J. Messner, 1946. 256p., illus.
Aimed at younger readers.

4609. Parsons, Tony. <u>Platinum Logic</u>. London: Pan, 1981. 510p.
Rock record industry.

4610. Pearce, Garth. <u>One Too Many Midnights</u>. New York: Avon;
London: Arrow, 1979. 286p.
Rock.

4611. Peters, Ellis (<u>pseud. of</u> Edith Mary Parteger). <u>Black Is
the Colour of My True Love's Heart</u>. London: Collins, 1967.
224p.
Mystery.

* Potter, Dennis. <u>Pennies From Heaven</u>.
  * Cited above as item 1179.

4612. Raphael, Frederic. <u>Obbligato</u>. London: Macmillan, 1956.
219p.

* Rauch, Earl Mac. <u>New York, New York</u>.
  * Cited above as item 1175.

4613. Raymond, Mary (<u>pseud. of</u> Josephine Edgar). <u>The Bachelor
Girls</u>. London: Pan, 1968. 157p. (A Pan Romance)

Popular (cont.)

4614. Rendell, Ruth. <u>Some Lie and Some Die</u>. London: Hutchinson,
       1973. 192p.
           Rock mystery.

4615. Scott, Jack. <u>The Gospel Lamb</u>. London: Collins, 1980.
       178p.
           Rock mystery.

4616. Shaw, Arnold. <u>The Money Song</u>. New York: Random House,
       1953. 306p.

4617. Sheldon, Sidney. <u>The Other Side of Midnight</u>. New York:
       Morrow; London: Hodder and Stoughton, 1974. 440p. London:
       Pan, 1976. 462p.

   *   Shipper, Mark. <u>Paperback Writer</u>.
           * Cited above as item 1836.

4618. Smiley, Jane. <u>Duplicate Keys</u>. New York: Knopf, 1984.   p.
           Rock mystery.

4619. Smith, Joseph C. <u>The Day the Music Died: a Novel</u>. New
       York: Grove Pr., 1981. 576p. London: W.H. Allen, 1982.
       536p.
           Popular music industry.

4620. Sonin, Ray. <u>The Dance Band Mystery</u>. London: Quality Pr.,
       1940. 307p. London: Withy Grove Pr., 1941. 224p. (Cherry
       Tree Books). London: Kemsley Newspapers, 1951. 190p.
       (A Cherry Tree Novel)

4621. Squire, Robin. <u>Square One</u>. London: W.H. Allen, 1968.
       206p.
           Rock.

4622. Street, Arthur George. <u>Johnny Cowslip</u>. London: Hale, 1964.
       189p.

   *   Tabori, Paul. <u>Song of The Scorpions: a Novel</u>.
           * Cited above as item 3484.

   *   Tewkesbury, Joan. <u>Nashville</u>.
           * Cited above as item 1174.

   *   Thelwell, Michael. <u>The Harder They Come</u>.
           * Cited above as item 1163.

   *   Thomas, Bob. <u>Star! From the Screenplay by William Fairchild</u>.
           * Cited above as item 2947.

4623. Tormé, Mel. <u>Wynner</u>. New York: Stein and Day, 1978; London:
       Macdonald and Jane's, 1979. 348p.

4624. Villa-Gilbert, Mariana. _A Jingle-Jangle Song_. London:
Chatto and Windus, 1968. 165p.

4625. Wakefield, Maureen Ellen. _The Dollmaker_. London: Remploy;
New York: Lenox Hill Pr., 1974. 192p.
Romance.

4626. Walker, Leslie. _New Sound_. Illustrated by Marius Shafer.
London: Macdonald, 1969. 128p., illus.
Rock.

4627. Weatherall, Ernie. _Rock 'n' Roll Gal_. New York: Beacon,
1957. 187p.

4628. Whitcomb, Ian. _Lotus Land: a Story of Southern California_.
London: Wildwood House, 1979. 290p.

4629. Williams, Hugo. _No Particular Place To Go_. London: Cape,
1981; London: Picador, 1982. 190p.
Poet tours historic United States rock areas.

4630. Worsley-Gough, Barbara. _Lantern Hill_. London: Michael
Joseph, 1957. 285p.

4631. Young, Al. _Snakes: a Novel_. New York: Holt, Rinehart and
Winston, 1970; London: Sidgwick and Jackson, 1971. 149p.
Soul music.

(2) JAZZ

4632. Asher, Don. _Electric Cotillion_. Garden City, New York:
Doubleday, 1970; London: W.H. Allen, 1971; London: Pan, 1971.
215p.

4633. Avery, Robert. _Murder On the Downbeat_. New York: Mystery
House, 1943. 256p.

4634. Baird, Jack. _Hot, Sweet, and Blue_. New York: Fawcett
Publications, 1956. 160p. (A Gold Medal Book)

  * Baker, Dorothy. _Young Man With a Horn_.
    * Cited above as item 1974.

4635. Bird, Brandon. _Downbeat For a Dirge_. New York: Dodd, Mead,
1952. 237p. New York (as _Dead and Gone_): Dell, 1952. 192p.
Mystery.

4636. Brossard, Chandler. _Who Walk in Darkness_. New York: New
Directions, 1952. 192p. London: John Lehman, 1952. 224p.
New York: New American Library, 1954.   p. (A Signet Book)

4637. Bunyan, Pat. _The Big Blues_. London: Brown, Watson, 1963.
159p. (Digit Books)

Jazz (cont.)

4638. Catling, Patrick Skene. <u>Jazz, Jazz, Jazz</u>. London: Blond
       and Briggs, 1980. 320p., bibliog.
           The evolution of jazz in novelized form.

4639. Clapham, Walter. <u>Come Blow Your Horn</u>. London: Cape;
       Toronto: Clarke Irwin, 1958. 256p.

4640. Coxhead, Nona. <u>Big-Time Baby</u>. London: Magnum Books, 1981.
       343p.
           Includes words and music of song, <u>Big-Time Baby</u>, by Jill
       McManus and Nona Coxhead.

4641. Curran, Dale. <u>Dupree Blues</u>. New York: Knopf, 1948. 228p.
       New York: Berkley Publishing, 195? 156p.

4642. ————. <u>Piano in the Band</u>. New York: Reynal and Hitchcock,
       1940. 261p.

4643. Cuthbert, Clifton. <u>The Robbed Heart: a Novel</u>. New York:
       L.B. Fischer, 1945. 219p. New York: Dell, n.d. 191p.

4644. Duke, Osborn. <u>Sideman</u>. New York: Criterion, 1956. 448p.

4645. Ekwensi, Cyprian Odiatu Duaka. <u>People of the City</u>. London:
       Andrew Dakers, 1954. 237p. <u>Rev. ed.</u>: London; Ibadan,
       Nigeria: Heinemann Educational, 1963. 156p. (African
       Writers, 5)

4646. English, Richard. <u>Strictly Ding-Dong, and Other Swing
       Stories</u>. Garden City, New York: Doubleday, Doran, 1941.
       278p.

4647. Ewing, Annemarie. <u>Little Gate</u>. New York: Rinehart, 1947.
       278p.

4648. Feuser, W.F. (ed.). <u>Jazz and Palm Wine, and Other Stories</u>.
       New York: Longman, 1981. 224p.

4649. Flender, Harold. <u>Paris Blues</u>. New York: T. Allen; New York:
       Ballantine, 1957. 187p. London: Panther, 1961. 156p.
           Filmed, same title, 1961.

4650. Gant, Roland. <u>The World in a Jug</u>. London: Cape, 1959; New
       York: Vanguard Pr., 1961. 220p.

4651. Gilbert, Edwin. <u>The Hot and the Cool</u>. Garden City, New
       York: Doubleday, 1953. 280p. New York: Popular Library,
       1954. 288p.

4652. Gosling, Paula. <u>Loser's Blues</u>. London: Macmillan, 1980;
       London: Pan, 1981. 256p.

4653. Grant, James. <u>Don't Shoot the Pianist</u>. London: Piatkus,
       1980. 192p.

4654. Green, Benny. <u>Blame It On My Youth</u>. London: MacGibbon and Kee, 1967. 180p.

4655. Gwinn, William. <u>Jazz Bum</u>. New York: Lion Books, 1954. 158p.

4656. Hanley, Jack. <u>Hot Lips</u>. New York: Designs Publishing, 1952. 128p.

4657. Harvey, Charles (ed.). <u>Jazz Parody: an Anthology of Jazz Fiction</u>. London: Neville Spearman in association with The American Jazz Society, 1948. 109p., illus.

4658. Hentoff, Nat. <u>Jazz Country</u>. New York: Harper, 1965 (Reprinted: New York: Harper and Row, 1976); London: Hart-Davis, 1966. 146p.
   Aimed at younger readers.

4659. Holmes, John Clellon. <u>Go</u>. New York: Scribner's, 1952. 311p. London (as <u>The Beat Boys</u>): Harborough Publishing, 1959. 204p. (Ace Books)

4660. ————. <u>The Horn</u>. New York: Random House, 1958; London: Andre Deutsch, 1959. 243p.

4661. Hunter, Evan. <u>Second Ending</u>. New York: Simon and Schuster, 1956. 359p. London: Constable, 1956. 384p. London: Transworld Publishers, 1957. 380p. (Corgi Books). London: New English Library, 1968. 318p. (Four Square Books)

4662. ————. <u>Streets of Gold</u>. New York: Harper and Row, 1974; London: Macmillan; London: Pan, 1975. 473p. London: Corgi, 1982. 399p.

4663. Johnson, James Weldon. <u>The Autobiography of an Ex-Colored Man</u>. New York: Knopf, 1927 (Reprinted: New York: Hill and Wang, 1960). 211p. New York: New American Library, 1948. 142p. (Mentor Books)
   Originally published anonymously.

4664. Kanin, Garson. <u>Blow Up a Storm</u>. New York: Random House, 1959; London: Heinemann, 1960. 337p. London: Panther, 1961. 286p.

4665. Kelley, William Melvin. <u>A Drop of Patience</u>. Garden City, New York: Doubleday, 1965; London: Hutchinson, 1966. 237p.

4666. Kelly, Rod. <u>Just For the Bread</u>. London: Hale, 1976. 191p.
   Mystery.

4667. Kerouac, Jack. <u>On the Road</u>. New York: Viking Pr., 1957 (Reprinted: College Point, New York: Buccaneer Books, 1976); London: Andre Deutsch, 1958. 310p. New York: New American Library, 1958. p. (A Signet Book). London: Pan, 1961. 319p. Harmondsworth, Middlesex: Penguin, 1972. 291p.

Jazz (cont.)

4668. Kerouac, Jack. The Subterraneans. New York: Grove Pr.,
       1958. 111p. (Evergreen Books). London: Andre Deutsch,
       1960. 158p. New York: Ballantine, 1973.   p.

4669. Kundera, Milan. Farewell Party. Translated from the Czech
       by Peter Kussi. New York: Knopf, 1976; London: John Murray,
       1977. 209p.

4670. Lea, George. Somewhere There's Music. Philadelphia:
       Lippincott, 1958. 224p.

4671. Lee, George Washington. Beale Street Sundown. New York:
       House of Field, 1942. 176p.
           Short stories.

4672. McCabe, Cameron (pseud. of Ernest Borneman). Tremolo. New
       York: Harper; London: Jarrolds, 1948. 224p. London (as
       Something Wrong): Four Square Books, 1960. 223p.

4673. McKay, Claude. Home To Harlem. New York; London: Harper,
       1928. 340p.

4674. ————. Banjo: a Story Without a Plot. New York; London:
       Harper, 1929. 326p.
           Sequel to item 4673.

4675. Mandel, George. Flee the Angry Strangers. Indianapolis:
       Bobbs-Merrill, 1952; Indianapolis: Charter Books, 1962. 480p.

4676. Marsh, Ngaio. Swing, Brother, Swing. London: Collins, 1949.
       288p. Boston (as A Wreath For Rivera): Little, Brown, 1949.
       294p. London: Fontana, 1956. 255p.
           Mystery.

4677. Martucci, Ida. Jive Jungle. New York: Vantage Pr., 1956.
       161p.

4678. Millen, Gilmore. Sweet Man. London: Cassell, 1930. 301p.
       New York: Pyramid Books, 1952. 238p.

4679. Mitchell, Adrian. If You See Me Comin'. London: Cape, 1962.
       158p. New York: Macmillan, 1962. 168p.

4680. Nin, Anais. Seduction of the Minotaur. London: Peter Owen,
       1961. 159p.

4681. Nuttall, Jeff. Snipe's Spinster. London: Calder and Boyars,
       1975 (Reissued: 1976). 119p.

   *   Ondaatje, Michael. Coming Through Slaughter.
         * Cited above as item 2043.

4682. Quin, Ann. Tripticks. Illustrated by Carol Annand. London:

Calder and Boyars, 1972. 192p., illus.
Experimental; aims to fuse the techniques of jazz improvisation with those of the comic-strip.

4683. Rayner, Claire. Reprise. London: Hutchinson, 1980. 342p.

4684. Reed, Harlan. The Swing Music Murder. New York: Dutton, 1938. 320p.
Mystery.

4685. Rieman, Terry. Vamp Till Ready. New York: Harper, 1954; London: Gollancz, 1955. 312p.

4686. Rundell, Wyatt. Jazz Band. New York: Greenberg, 1935. 246p.

* Russell, Ross. The Sound.
* Cited above as item 3222.

* Shaw, Artie. I Love You, I Hate You, Drop Dead! Variations on a Theme.
* Cited above as item 3543.

4687. Shurman, Ida. Death Beats the Band. New York: Phoenix Pr., 1943. 256p.
Mystery.

4688. Simmons, Herbert Alfred. Man Walking on Eggshells. Boston: Houghton Mifflin; London: Methuen, 1962. 250p.

4689. Simon, George Thomas. Don Watson Starts His Band. Foreword by Benny Goodman. New York: Dodd, Mead, 1940. 306p.
Aimed at younger readers.

4690. Sinclair, Harold. Music Out of Dixie. New York: Rinehart, 1952. 306p. New York: Permabooks, 1953. 384p.

4691. Sklar, George. The Two Worlds of Johnny Truro. Boston: Little, Brown, 1947; Garden City, New York: Sun Dial Pr., 1948. 372p. Abridged ed.: New York: Popular Library, 1950. 224p.

4692. Skvorecky, Josef. The Bass Saxophone: Two Novellas. Translated by Kaca Polackova-Henley. London: Chatto and Windus, 1978. 186p. New York: Knopf, 1979. 208p. London: Picador, 1980. 125p.
Originally published separately as Legenda Emöke (1963), and Bassaxofon (1967), in Czech.

4693. Slovo, Gillian. Morbid Symptoms. London; Sydney, New South Wales: Pluto Pr., 1984. 147p. (Pluto Crime Fiction)
Marxist detective novel, set in jazz world.

4694. Smith, Robert Paul. So It Doesn't Whistle. New York: Harcourt, Brace, 1941. 234p. London: Nicholson and Watson, 1947. 132p. New York (as So It Doesn't Whistle; plus, Blood in Their Veins): Avon, 1952. 126p.

Jazz (cont.)

4695. Spicer, Bart. _Blues For the Prince_. New York: Dodd, Mead,
      1950. 249p. London: Collins, 1951. 192p. New York:
      Bantam, 1951. 212p. London: Transworld Publishers, 1954.
      220p. (Corgi Books)

4696. Steig, Henry Anton. _Send Me Down_. New York: Knopf, 1941.
      461p. New York: Avon, 194?   p. London: Jarrolds, 1943.
      255p. (Jay Novel Library)

4697. Sylvester, Robert. _Rough Sketch_. New York: Dial Pr., 1948.
      302p.

4698. Thurman, Wallace. _Infants of the Spring_. New York:
      Macaulay, 1932. 284p.

4699. Traill, Sinclair. _Way Down Yonder_. London: Parade, 1949.
      256p.

4700. Updyke, James. _It's Always Four O'Clock_. New York: Random
      House, 1956. 178p.

4701. Van Vechten, Carl. _Nigger Heaven_. New York; London: Knopf,
      1926. 286p. New York: Avon, n.d. 186p.
          Set in Harlem's night-life. Title is ironic.

4702. Wain, John. _Strike the Father Dead_. London: Macmillan,
      1962. 238p.

4703. Wainwright, John. _Do Nothing Till You Hear From Me_. London:
      Macmillan, 1977. 224p.
          Mystery.

4704. Wallop, Douglass. _Night Light_. New York: Norton, 1953.
      378p. New York: Pocket Books, 1955.   p.

4705. Whitmore, Stanford. _Solo_. New York: Harcourt, Brace, 1955.
      382p. London: Gollancz, 1956. 304p. London: Transworld
      Publishers, 1958. 318p. (Corgi Books)

4706. Williams, John Alfred. _Night Song_. New York: Farrar, Straus,
      and Giroux, 1961. 219p. London: Collins, 1962. 191p.

4707. Willis, George. _Little Boy Blues_. New York: Dutton, 1947.
      223p.

4708. ———. _Tangleweed_. Garden City, New York: Doubleday, 1943.
      182p.

4709. ———. _The Wild Faun_. New York: Greenberg, 1945. 179p.

    * Woodley, Richard. _The Jazz Singer_.
          * Cited above as item 1165.

4710. Yerby, Frank. Speak Now. New York: Dial Pr., 1969. 227p.
       London: Heinemann, 1970. 183p. London: Pan, 1980. 139p.

(3) STAGE

4711. Biggar, Joan. Edwina Alone. London: Pan, 1980. 189p.
       Music Hall.

4712. Brent, Madeleine. The Capricorn Stone. London: Souvenir
       Pr., 1979. 336p.
       Music Hall.

4713. Carstairs, John Paddy. Sunshine and Champagne. London:
       Hutchinson, 1955. 189p.
       Chorus girls.

4714. Chester, Charlie. Overture to Anthem. London: New English
       Library, 1977. 218p.
       Music Hall. Author was performer.

4715. Gilbert, Anthony (pseud. of Lucy Malleson). The Musical
       Comedy Crime. London: Collins, 1933. 255p.
       Mystery.

4716. Jacques-Charles (pseud. of Jacques Charles). Le Journal
       d'une figurante: roman de moeurs du music-hall. Paris:
       Gallimard, 1933. 251p.
       Paris Music Hall.

4717. Mackenzie, Compton. The Vanity Girl. London: Macdonald,
       1920. 369p. New ed.: London: Macdonald, 1954 (Reprinted:
       London: Remploy, 1973). 302p.
       Music Hall. Based on The Gaiety theater, London.

4718. Prior, Alan. Never Been Kissed In the Same Place Twice.
       London: Cassell, 1978; London: Arrow Books, 1980. 477p.
       Music Hall.

4719. Whitmee, Jeanne. A Lobster and a Lady. London: Hale, 1979.
       224p.
       Music Hall.

(4) DANCE

4720. Farraday, Chelsea. Disco. New York: Nordon Publishing,
       1978. 287p. (A Leisure Book)

   *   Fleischer, Leonore. Staying Alive: a Novel.
         * Cited above as item 1187.

4721. French, Michael. Rhythms. London: Hamlyn, 1981. 391p.
       Disco mystery.

Dance (cont.)

* Gilmour, H.B. <u>Saturday Night Fever: a Novelization</u>.
  * Cited above as item 1186.

* La Camara, Félix, <u>Comte de. Mon sang dans tes veines:
  roman d'après une idée de Joséphine Baker</u>.
  * Cited above as item 1748.

4722. Lewis, Stephen. <u>The Regulars</u>. New York: Leisure Books,
      1980. 476p.
          Popular music television show dancers reunite after
      twenty years for repeat show.

4723. Lipton, James. <u>Mirrors</u>. London: New English Library, 1982.
      352p.
          Broadway show dance.

* Stoddart, Bill. <u>The Music Machine</u>.
  * Cited above as item 1172.

                              B. VERSE

                            (1) POPULAR

4724. Cant, Adrian. <u>Swing and Go</u>. London: Riot Stories, 1983.
          p.
          Rock poems.

                             (2) JAZZ

4725. Goffin, Robert. <u>Jazz Band</u>. Brussels: Le Disque Vert, 1921.
          p.
          In French.

* Harper, Michael S. <u>Dear John, Dear Coltrane</u>.
  * Cited above as item 2241.

4726. Hollo, Paul Anselm Alexis (ed.). <u>Jazz Poems</u>. Chester
      Springs, Pennsylvania: Dufour; London: Vista Books, 1963.
      47p. (Pocket Poets)

4727. Hughes, Langston. <u>Ask Your Mama: Twelve Moods For Jazz</u>.
      New York: Knopf, 1961. 92p.
          Verse in jazz patterns.

4728. ———. <u>Fine Clothes To the Jew</u>. New York: Knopf, 1927.
      89p.
          Verse in blues patterns.

4729. ———. <u>Shakespeare in Harlem</u>. New York: Knopf, 1942. 124p.,

illus.
Verse in jazz patterns.

4730.   ————. The Weary Blues. New York: Knopf, 1926 (Reissued:
1929). 109p.
Verse in jazz and blues patterns.

4731. Joans, Ted. All of Ted Joans, and No More: Poems and
Collages by Ted Joans. Introduction by Ilizabeth D. Klar.
New York: Excelsior-Press Publishers, 1961. 100p., illus.
Collection of his jazz verse.

4732.   ————. A Black Manifesto in Jazz Poetry and Prose. London:
Calder and Boyars, 1971. 92p. (Signature Series, 8)

4733.   ————. Black Pow-Wow: Jazz Poems. New York: Hill and
Wang, 1969. 130p. (American Century Series)

4734.   ————. Jazz Poems. New York: Rhino Review, 1959.   p.

4735. Johnson, James Weldon. God's Trombones: Seven Negro
Sermons in Verse. Illustrated by Aaron Douglas. New York:
Viking Pr., 1927. 56p., illus. London (as God's Trombones:
Some Negro Sermons in Verse): Allen and Unwin, 1929. 58p.

4736. Kayton, George. Swing It High, Sweet Saxophones. Prairie
City, Illinois: Press of James A. Decker, 1944. 80p.
Poems on jazz themes.

4737. Marks, Jim. Jazz, Women, Soul. Millbrae, California:
Celestial Arts, 1974.   p.

4738. Robson, Jeremy Michael. Poems For Jazz. Leicester, England:
Leslie Weston, 1963. 16p.

4739.   ———— (ed.). Poems From "Poetry and Jazz in Concert."
Selections From the First to Two Hundred and Fiftieth
Performances: an Anthology. London: Souvenir Pr., 1969.
144p., illus.

————. Poems From "Poetry and Jazz in Concert": an Anthology. London: Panther, 1969. 144p., illus.

4740. Sinclair, John. This Is Our Music. Detroit: Artists'
Workshop Pr., 1965.   p.
Collection of jazz poems.

4741. Trussell, Jake. After-Hours Poetry. Kingsville, Texas: The
Author, 1958. 80p., illus.
Collection of jazz poems.

4742. Wolf, Howard Paulus. Tin Roof Anthology. Philadelphia:
The Author, 1952. unpaged.
Jazz poems.

(3) DANCE

4743. Ellis, Ron. <u>Diary of a Discotheque: a Selection of Poems,</u>
    <u>1970-78</u>. Southport, Merseyside: Nirvana Books, 1978. 48p.
       British discotheque operator's poetic observations on
    discos and their clients.

4744. Morgan, Pete (ed.). <u>C'mon Everybody: Poetry of the Dance.</u>
    London: Corgi, 1971. 144p.

PART SEVEN: PERIODICALS

A. NORTH AMERICA AND BRITAIN

4745. **Abe's Folke Musicke Almanacke**. Leeds, Yorkshire. irreg., May 1962-?

4746. **Acid Rock**. New York. bi-monthly, 1977-?

4747. **Acoustic Music and Folk Song and Dance News**. London. monthly, October 1979- .
Continues **Folk News**; incorporates **Folk Song and Dance News**. Title later changed to **Acoustic Music**.

4748. **Action Plus**! Bloomfield, Indiana. irreg., 1984-
Rock; emphasis on the 1960's.

4749. **Ad Lib**. Toronto. irreg., 1944-47
Jazz.

4750. **Album Tracking: the Music Buyer's Guide**. London. monthly, October 1976- .

4751. **American Folk Music Occasional**. Berkeley, California; later New York. irreg., 1964- .

4752. **American Jazz**. Chilwell, Nottinghamshire. irreg., 1946-?

4753. **American Jazz Monthly**. New York. monthly, ?-October 1944.
Continued by item 4754.

4754. **American Jazz Review**. New York. monthly, November 1944-?
Continues item 4753.

4755. **American Pie**. Toronto. irreg., 1978-?
Rock.

4756. **America's Oldies**. Anaheim, California. irreg., 197?-?
Popular record collecting.

4757. **Amusement Globe: Devoted to the Dramatic, Theatrical, Musical, Vaudeville, and Circus Professions**. New York. weekly, 1893-94.

4758. **And All That Jazz**. Kerrville, Texas. 4 per year, ?-?

4759.1 **Back Trax**. Margate, Kent. irreg., 1981-?
Popular record collecting.

4759.2 **Ballroom and Band**. London. monthly, 1934-36.

North America and Britain (cont.)

4760. Ballroom Dancing Times. London. monthly, 1956- .

4761. B.A.M. (Bay Area Music). Oakland, California/Hollywood,
        California. bi-weekly, 1983- .
            Popular. Separate editions for North and South California.

4762. Bam Balam. Dunbar, Scotland. irreg., 1976- .
            Emphasis on British popular music of the 1960's.

4763. Band Leaders. Mount Morris, Illinois. quarterly (monthly
        from 1944), April 1942-?

4764. Barba: the Rock Newspaper of Puerto Rico. Rio Piedras,
        Puerto Rico. monthly, 1969- .
            Text in English and Spanish.

4765. Basin Street. New Orleans. March 1945.
            Jazz. Only issue.

4766. The Baton. Chicago. monthly, March 1941-May 1944.
            Jazz. Continued as The New Baton, June 1944-?

4767. Beat. Los Angeles. Bi-weekly, 1964-?
            Rock.

4768. Beat Instrumental (later Beat Instrumental and International
        and International Recording Studio). London. monthly,
        November 1963- .
            Title varies; initial issues entitled Beat Monthly.

4769. Beatbox. London. monthly, 1983.
            Popular videos. Defunct after several issues.

4770. Bells. Berkeley, California. bi-monthly, 197?-?
            Avant-garde jazz.

4771. Big Beat. London. monthly, March 1964-65.
            Popular.

4772. Billboard Advertising (later Billboard). Cincinnati; later
        New York; later Los Angeles. monthly, 1984-May 1900; weekly,
        June 1900- .
            Trade.

4773. Bim Bam Boom: the Magazine Devoted to the History of Rhythm
        and Blues. New York. bi-monthly, July 1972- .

4774. Black Beat. Tonbridge, Kent. bi-monthly, January 1980- .
            Continued as Black Beat International, London. monthly,
        198?- .

4775. Black Dwarf. Bristol. irreg., 1978- .
            Rock.

4776. Black Echoes (later Echoes). London. weekly, 1976- .

4777. Black Music. London. monthly, December 1973-March 1978.
Incorporated into item 4778.

4778. Black Music and Jazz Review. London. monthly, April 1978- .
Continues item 4777.

4779. The Black Perspective in Music. New York. 2 per year,
1973- .

4780. Black Stars. Chicago. monthly, 1971- .

4781. Black Wax. London. irreg., 1973-7?
Listing of releases by Black recording artists.

4782. Blam! Chelmsford, Essex. irreg., 1981-83.
Rock.

4783. Blitz. Los Angeles. bi-monthly, 198?- .
Rock.

4784. Bluegrass Unlimited. Broad Run, Virginia. monthly, 1966-?

4785. Blues. Toronto. bi-monthly, 1975- .

4786. Blues: the Magazine of the New Rhythm. Columbus, Mississippi.
monthly, 1929-30.

4787. Blues and Rhythm: the Gospel Truth. London. 10 per year,
August 1984- .
Blues, rhythm-and-blues, gospel, soul, and zydeco.

4788. Blues and Soul (later Blues and Soul Music Review). London.
bi-weekly (later monthly), 1966- .

4789. Blues-Link. Hitchin, Hertfordshire. irreg., 1973-75.
Incorporated item 4792.

4790. Blues Research. Brooklyn, New York. irreg., 1959- .
Initial issues entitled Blues Research Record Mart.
Discographical. Subsidiary publication of item 5112.

4791. Blues Unlimited. London. monthly (later bi-monthly; later
quarterly), April 1963- .

Steenson, Martin. Blues Unlimited, 1-50: an Index. London:
The Author, 1971. 76p.

4792. Blues World. Knutsford, Cheshire; later Bristol. monthly,
1965-73.
Incorporated into item 4789.

4793. Bomp! Burbank, California. bi-monthly, 1966- .
Rhythm-and-blues; rock. Initial issues entitled Who Put
the Bomp.

North America and Britain (cont.)

4794. Boogie: the Gulf Coast's Rock Quarterly. Gulfport, Michigan.
       quarterly, 1972-?

4795. Boston Rock. Boston. monthly, 198?- .

4796. British Bluegrass Journal. Chelmsford, Essex. irreg.,
       1979- .

4797. British Songwriter and Dance Band. London. monthly,
       1947-48.
           Continues item 4798.

4798. British Songwriter and Poet. London. monthly, 1940-46.
           Continued by item 4797.

4799. Broadside Magazine: National Topical Song Monthly. Cambridge,
       Massachusetts; later New York. monthly (later bi-monthly),
       1962-70.

4800. Buffalo Jazz Report. Buffalo, New York. irreg., 1974- .

4801. Buy Gone. West Bridgford, Nottinghamshire. monthly, 1980- .
           Rock record collecting.

4802. Buzz. New Malden, Surrey. monthly, 1965-83.
           Christian popular music.

4803. Cadence: the American Review of Jazz and Blues. Redwood,
       New York. monthly, 1976- .

4804. Calypso Stars. London. monthly, September 1957-?

4805. Canawirl Music Reader: Canada's Pop Magazine. Hamilton,
       Ontario. monthly, 1965-

4806. Caravan: the Magazine of Folk Music. (Place unknown).
       bi-monthly, 1957-?

4807. Caribbeat: the Magazine of Reggae, Calypso, Steelpan, and
       Spooze. New York. monthly, 1973-?

4808. Cash Box: the International Music-Record Weekly. New York.
       weekly, 1942- .
           Trade.

4809. Changes. San Rafael, California. bi-weekly, 1970-?
           Rock.

4810. Chartwatch. Ilminster, Somerset; later Cambridge. quarterly,
       1981- .
           Popular record charts analyses and statistics.

4811. Cheetah. New York. monthly, 1967-6?
           Popular.

4812. <u>Christiansen's Ragtime Review</u> (later <u>Ragtime Review</u>).
Chicago. monthly, December 1914–January 1918.

4813. <u>Circus</u>. New York. monthly (later bi-weekly), September
1972– .
Rock. Continues <u>Hullaballoo</u>.

4814. <u>Circus Raves</u>. New York. monthly, 1973– .
Rock.

4815. <u>Clef</u>. Santa Monica, California. monthly, March–October
1946.
Traditional jazz.

4816. <u>Climax</u>. New Orleans. irreg., 1955–?
Jazz.

4817. <u>Coda: Canada's Jazz Magazine</u>. Toronto. bi-monthly, 1958– .

4818. <u>Collectors' Items</u>. Walton-on-Thames, Surrey. bi-monthly,
August 1980– .
Jazz discography and record collecting.

4819. <u>Combo</u>. Liverpool. monthly, February 1964–?

4820. <u>Comstock Lode</u>. London. quarterly, 1977– .
Rock and country-rock.

4821. <u>Contemporary Keyboard</u>. Saratoga, California; later Cupertino,
California. bi-monthly (later monthly), 1975– .
For players.

4822. <u>Country and Western Express</u>. London. quarterly, 1954– .

4823. <u>Country and Western Record Review</u> (later <u>Country and Western
Review</u>; later <u>Country-Western Express</u>). London; later Grays,
Essex. monthly (later bi-monthly), 1958– .

4824. <u>Country and Western Roundabout</u>. Loughton, Essex; later
Takeley, Essex. quarterly, 1962–?

4825. <u>Country and Western World</u>. New York. quarterly, 1972– .

4826. <u>Country Directory</u>. Cheswold, Delaware. irreg., 1960–67.

4827. <u>Country Music</u>. New York. monthly, 1972– .

4828. <u>Country Music Explorer</u>. Hamilton, Ohio. monthly, 197?–?

4829. <u>Country Music News</u>. Buffalo, New York; later Pittsburgh.
monthly, 1972– .

4830. <u>Country Music People</u>. Sidcup, Kent; later Orpington, Kent;
later Dartford, Kent. monthly, 1970– .

North America and Britain (cont.)

4831. Country Music Reporter. Nashville. weekly, August 1956-57.
       Continued, with widened scope, as Music Reporter.

4832. Country Music Review. London. monthly, 1971-7?

  *   Country Music Round-Up. (U.S.A.)
          * Cited below as item 4987.

4833. Country Music Round Up. Barking, Essex/North Hykeham,
       Lincolnshire; later Lincoln. monthly, 1976- .

4834. Country Music Trail. Kent, Washington. bi-monthly, 1970-?

4835. Country Music World. Arlington, Virginia; later Whitestone,
       New York. bi-monthly, January 1972- .

4836. Country News and Views. Lowestoft, Suffolk. quarterly,
       1962-?

4837. Country People. London. monthly, 1979-?

4838. Country Rambler. Niles, Illinois. bi-weekly, 1976-?
          Progressive country music.

4839. Country Rhythms. New York. monthly, 198?- .

4840. Country Style. Franklin Park, Illinois. bi-monthly, 1976- .

4841. Country Tune-Up. Santa Clara, California. monthly, November
       1969-?

  *   Country-Western Express.
          * Cited above as item 4823.

4842. Crawdaddy: the Magazine of Rock (later Crawdaddy/Feature).
       New York. bi-weekly (later monthly), 1966- .

4843. Cream. London. monthly, 1971-73.
          Rock.

4844. Creem. Birmingham, Michigan. monthly, 1969- .
          Rock.

4845. Crescendo (later Crescendo International). London. monthly,
       July 1962- .
          Jazz.

4846. The Cricket. Newark, New Jersey. bi-monthly, 1969-?
          Black music; jazz.

4847. Dance News. London; later Godalming, Surrey. weekly, 1937- .
          Ballroom dancing.

4848. Dark Star. Northolt, Middlesex. irreg. (later bi-monthly),
       November 1975- .
            Rock; country-rock; bluegrass.

4849. Debut. London. monthly, 1984- .
            Rock. Includes long-playing record with each issue.

4850. Dee Jay and Radio Monthly. Hitchin, Hertfordshire. monthly,
       October 1972-?
            British popular music radio and its personalities.

4851. Deeper and Deeper Soul Magazine. Birkenhead, Merseyside.
       quarterly, July 1977- .

4852. Different Drummer: the Magazine For Jazz Listeners.
       Rochester, New York. monthly, 1973-

4853. Disc (later Disc and Music Echo; later Disc). London.
       weekly, February 1958-1975.
            Popular. Absorbed Music Echo, 196?; incorporated into
       Record Mirror, 1975.

4854. Disc Jockey. London. monthly, 1980- .
            Trade.

4855. Disco. London. monthly, 1980-?

4856. Disco International and Club News (later Disco and Club News
       International). London. monthly, 1976- .
            Trade.

4857. Disco World. Buffalo, New York. monthly, 1976- .

4858. Disco World (Britain). London. monthly, 1978- .

4859. Disc-o-Graph. Baltimore. monthly, 1976- .
            Jazz record collecting.

4860. Discographical Forum. London. quarterly (later irreg.;
       later bi-monthly), 1960- .
            Jazz.

4861. Discography: For the Jazz Student. London. bi-weekly
       (later irreg.), October 1942-July 1946.
            Incorporated into Jazz Music, 1946.

4862. The Discophile: the Magazine For Record Information. Barking,
       Essex. bi-monthly, August 1948-1958.
            Incorporated into Matrix, 1958. Jazz discography.

4863. Discotheque and Dance. London. monthly, 197?-?
            Trade.

4864. The Dis-Counter. Evansville, Indiana. monthly, January
       1948-?
            Jazz.

North America and Britain (cont.)

4865. Down Beat. Chicago. monthly (later bi-monthly; later
       bi-weekly), July 1934- .
           Jazz.

4866. Easy Listening. London. monthly, January 1973-?
           Record reviews.

   *   Echoes.
           * Cited above as item 4776.

4867. The Encore: a Music Hall and Theatrical Review. London.
       weekly, 1892-1930.

4868. Eureka. London. monthly, 1960-61.
           New Orleans jazz.

4869. Eurock. Torrance, California. irreg., 1982- .
           New-wave rock.

4870. The Face. London. monthly, April 1980-
           Popular; also fashion.

4871. Fat Angel. Harrow, Middlesex. irreg., 1971-73.
           West-Coast rock.

4872. Fender Musician. Enfield, Middlesex. monthly, March 1981- .
           Popular; for performers.

4873. Flexipop. London. monthly, October 1980-1983.
           First twenty-six issues included free record with each
       issue.

4874. Flip. New York. monthly, 1964-6?
           Popular.

4875. Flipside. Whittier, California. irreg., 1983- .
           New-wave rock.

4876. Friday Morning Quarterback (later F.M.I.). Cherry Hill,
       New Jersey. weekly, 197?- .
           Trade, for radio stations. Compilation of reports from
       radio stations on popular records currently being aired.

4877. Folk News. London. bi-monthly, 1971-79.
           British folk. Continued as item 4747.

4878. Folk Review. Nantwich, Cheshire. monthly, 1971- .
           British folk.

4879. Folk Scene. Woodham Walter, Essex. monthly, October 1964-?

4880. Folk Song and Dance News. London. monthly, 197?-79.
           Incorporated into item 4747.

4881. Folk Style. London. irreg, 1958-?

4882. Folkscene Publication. Los Angeles. monthly, 1973- .

4883. Footnote: the Magazine For New Orleans Jazz. Royston,
       Hertfordshire; later Cambridge. bi-monthly, 1969- .
       Subtitle varies.

4884. Frets: For All Acoustic Stringed Instrument Players.
       Saratoga, California; later Cupertino, California. monthly,
       March 1979- .

4885. Fretwire Music. Middlewich, Cheshire. monthly, 198?- .
       For players.

4886. Friends of "Rolling Stone" (later Friends; later Frendz).
       London. irreg., 1969-72.
       Continues short-lived British edition of Rolling Stone.

4887. Fusion. Boston. bi-weekly, 1969-7?
       Rock.

4888. Gandy Dancer (later New Gandy Dancer). Gateshead, Tyne and
       Wear; later Newcastle-on-Tyne. irreg., 1977- .
       Popular.

4889. Gatcomb's Banjo and Guitar Gazette (later Gatcomb's Musical
       Gazette). Boston. monthly (later bi-monthly), 1887-99.

4890. Gig. New York. monthly, 197?-?
       Popular.

4891. Golden Oldies Times. Seattle. monthly, 1979- .
       For popular music record collectors.

4892. Golden Years. Cwmbran, Gwent, Wales. quarterly, 1970-?
       For collectors of vintage dance bands and swing records.

4893. Goldmine: the Record Collector's Marketplace. Fraser,
       Michigan; later Iola, Wisconsin. monthly, 1974- .
       For rock collectors.

   *   Good Listening and Record Collector.
          * Cited below as item 5104.

4894. Good News. Nashville. monthly, 1969- .
       Gospel.

4895. Good Times. Fort Lauderdale, Florida. bi-weekly, 1980- .
       Local rock. Published in regional editions.

4896. The Grackle. Brooklyn, New York. 3 per year, 197?- .
       Avant-garde jazz.

4897. 'Grass Seen. London. irreg., 1982- .
       Bluegrass.

North America and Britain (cont.)

4898. Groove. London. bi-monthly, 1971-?
           Popular.

4899. Grooves Presents. New York. bi-monthly, 1978-?
           Rock.

4900. Guitar: the Magazine For All Guitarists. London. monthly,
       June 1972- .

4901. Guitar Heroes. London. monthly, 1982- .
           Rock.

4902. Guitar Player. San Jose; later Saratoga, California; later
       Cupertino, California. monthly, 1967- .
           For players; emphasis on rock and jazz. Fasimile
       reproduction of the first year's issues published as item
       3953.

4903. Guitar World. New York. bi-monthly, 198?- .

4904. Guitarist. Cambridge, England. monthly, 1984- .

4905. Ha'ilono Mele. Honolulu. monthly, 1975- .
           Hawaiian music.

4906. Hawaiian Guitarist (later Guitarist; later Music Today).
       Cleveland. monthly, 1933-45.

4907. Hip: the Milwaukee Jazz Letter (later Hip: the Jazz Record
       Digest; later Jazz Digest). Milwaukee; later Sterling,
       Virginia; later McLean, Virginia. irreg., 1963-74.
           Chiefly record reviews.

4908. Hit Parade. London. monthly, June 1954-?

4909. Hit Parader. Derby, Conn. monthly, 1954- .
           Aimed at younger readers. Includes song texts.

4910. Hitsville, U.S.A. (later Rhythm and Soul, U.S.A.). Bexley-
       heath, Kent. monthly, January 1965-1966.

4911. Hoedown. Cincinnati. monthly, September 1953-?
           Country.

4912. Home Studio Recording. Cambridge, England. monthly, 1983-

4913. Hootenanny. New York. bi-monthly, 1964.
           Short-lived folk magazine.

4914. Hot Buttered Soul. Newcastle, Staffordshire. monthly,
       1971-77.

4915. Hot News (later Hot News and Rhythm Record Review). London.

weekly (later monthly), 1935-46.
Absorbed by item 4950.

4916. Hot Notes. Waterford, Eire. bi-monthly, March 1946-1948.
Jazz.

4917. Hot Notes: the Jazz Newsletter. New York. monthly, 1969-
78.
Published by the New York Jazz Museum.

4918. Hot Press. Dublin; later London. bi-weekly, June 1977- .
Rock.

4919. Hot Record Society Rag. New York. quarterly (later monthly),
July 1938-March 1941.
Jazz.

4920. Hot Wacks. Edinburgh. irreg., March 1974- .
Rock.

4921. Hot Wacks Quarterly. Kitchener, Ontario. quarterly, 1979-
Rock. Not the same as item 4920.

4922. Hullabaloo. New York. monthly, 1966-August 1972.
Popular. Continued by item 4813.

4923. Impetus: a Magazine on New Trends in Rock, Jazz, and Classical
Music. London. irreg., 1978-?

4924. In the City. London. irreg., 1977- .
New-wave rock.

4925. The Independent Songwriter. Somerville, New Jersey. bi-
monthly, 1948-?

4926. Instrumental Obscurities Unlimited (later Instrumental
Review). Ilford, Essex. irreg., 1983- .
Rock instrumental records. For collectors.

4927. International Art of Jazz. Stony Brook, New York. irreg.,
197?-?

4928. International Country Music News. Kegworth, Derbysshire.
monthly, 1984- .

4929. International Discophile. Los Angeles. irreg., 197?-?
Jazz.

4930. International Musician and Recording World. London; New
York. monthly, 1975- .
Trade. Emphasis on popular music business. Separate
editions published in London and New York; some common text.

4931. Into Jazz. London. monthly, 1974.
Two issues only.

North America and Britain (cont.)

4932. It Will Stand: Dedicated to the Preservation of Beach Music.
       Charlotte, North Carolina. irreg., 198?- .

4933. It's Only Rock and Roll. San Antonio, Texas. monthly,
       1982- .
          Emphasis on Texas developments.

4934. Jamming. London. bi-monthly, 1978- .
          New-wave rock.

4935. Jazz. Forest Hills, New York; later New York. irreg.,
       June 1942-December 1943. New series: monthly, December
       1944-January 1945.

4936. Jazz (later Jazz and Pop). New York. monthly, October
       1962-1971.

4937. Jazz. Northport, New York. quarterly, 1976- .

4938. Jazz: a Quarterly of American Music. Berkeley, California;
       later Albany, California. quarterly, October 1958-Winter
       1960.

4939. Jazz and Blues. London. monthly, 1971-73.
          Continues item 4949. Incorporated into item 4947, 1974.

   *   Jazz and Pop.
          * Cited above as item 4936.

4940. Jazz Commentary. Dalbeattie, Scotland. irreg., 1944-45.

   *   Jazz Digest.
          * Cited above as item 4907.

4941. Jazz Echo: Publication of the International Jazz Federation.
       New York. monthly, October 1978- .
          Continues item 5204.

4942. Jazz Fan. London. irreg., 195?-?

4943. Jazz Forum: Quarterly Review of Jazz and Literature.
       Fordingbridge, Hampshire. quarterly, May 1946-July 1947.

4944. Jazz Guide. London. irreg., 1964-?

4945. Jazz Illustrated. London. monthly, November 1949-1950.

4946. Jazz Information. New York. irreg., September 1939-November
       1941.

4947. Jazz Journal (later Jazz Journal International). London.
       monthly, May 1948- .
          Continues item 4949. Incorporated item 4939, 1974.

4948.   Jazz Junction Jive. London. annual, 1943-45.

4949.   Jazz Monthly. London; later St. Austell, Cornwall.
monthly, 1954-71.
        Included register of new record releases, Jazz Records,
as supplement, 1962-66. Incorporated into item 4939.

4950.   Jazz Music: the International Jazz Magazine. London.
monthly, October 1942-April 1944. New series: bi-monthly,
July 1946-1960.
        Incorporated items 4861, 4915, and 4965.

4951.   Jazz Music News. London. monthly, 1982- .

4952.   Jazz New England. Lawrence, Massachusetts. monthly, 1975- .
        Local emphasis.

4953.   Jazz News. London. weekly, 1956-63.
        Continued by item 4974.

4954.   Jazz Orchestras. London. irreg., 1946-?

4955.   Jazz Panorama. Toronto. monthly (later irreg.), December
1946-May 1948.

4956.   Jazz Quarterly. Chicago. quarterly, 1942-45.
        Local emphasis.

4957.   The Jazz Record. New York. irreg., February 1943-December
1947.
        Edited by jazz pianist Art Hodes.

4958.   Jazz Record (later Jazz; later Jazz Magazine). Newark,
Nottinghamshire. monthly, 1939-46.
        Temporarily incorporated into Vox Pop, 1944-45. Absorbed
by Keynote, 1947.

4959.   Jazz Report. Ventura, California. bi-monthly, 1958-61.
        Continued by item 5029.

4960.   Jazz Review. London. monthly, January 1948-?

4961.   The Jazz Review. New York. monthly, January 1958-1961.
        Reprinted as facsimile, Millwood, New York: Kraus Reprint,
1973.

4962.   Jazz Scene. London. monthly, May 1962-?

4963.   The Jazz Session. Chicago. monthly (later bi-monthly),
September 1944-1946.

4964.   Jazz Studies. London. quarterly, 1964- .

4965.   Jazz Tempo. London. irreg., March 1943-June 1946.
        Incorporated into item 4950.

North America and Britain (cont.)

4966. Jazz Tempo. Hollywood, California. January 1946.
         Only issue.

4967. Jazz Times. London. monthly, 1964- .

4968. Jazz Times (U.S.A.). Silver Springs, Maryland. monthly,
         198?- .

4969. Jazz Times Bulletin. Hemel Hempstead, Hertfordshire. irreg.,
         194?-?

4970. Jazz Today. New York. monthly, October 1956-November 1957.

4971. Jazz Wax. Birmingham, England. monthly, August-October
         1948.
         Discographical.

4972. Jazz World. New York. irreg., March 1957-?

4973. Jazz Writings. London. irreg., 1936-?

4974. Jazzbeat: the Lively Jazz Magazine. London. monthly,
         January 1964-1966.
         Continues item 4953.

4975. Jazzette. Boston. irreg., 1944-?

4976. The Jazz Finder. New Orleans. monthly, January-December
         1948.
         Continued by item 5077.

4977. Jazzmen News. London. monthly, 1945-45.

4978. Jazzocracy. Milton Keynes, Buckinghamshire. irreg., 1975-?

4979. Jazzography. Tring, Hertfordshire. irreg., 194?-?

4980. Jazzologist. Kerrville, Texas. irreg., 1963- .
         Emphasis on New Orleans jazz.

4981. Jazz-ology. London. monthly, 1944-February 1947.

4982. John Edwards Memorial Foundation Quarterly. Los Angeles.
         quarterly, 1965- .
         Early country music research.

4983. The Journal For Serious Record Collectors. Chicago. irreg.,
         1983- .
         Rock. Chiefly reprints from other journals.

4984. Journal of Jazz Discography. Newport, Gwent, Wales. irreg.,
         1976- .

4985. Journal of Jazz Studies: Incorporating Studies in Jazz Discography. New Brunswick, New Jersey. semi-annual, 1973- .
   Academic research.

4986. Just Jazz. Birmingham, England. monthly, 1963-?
   Local emphasis.

4987. K-Bar-T Country Roundup (later Country Music Roundup). Pueblo, Colorado. quarterly, 1960-6?

4988. Kent Beat. Rainham, Kent. monthly, July 1965-?
   Rock.

4989. Kerrang! London. monthly (later bi-weekly), June 1981- .
   Heavy-metal rock.

4990. Keynote: the Progressive Music Quarterly (later Keynote: the Music Magazine). London. quarterly, 1945-47.
   Incorporated items 4958 and 5230.

4991. Kommotion (later New Kommotion). Wembley, Middlesex. quarterly, 197?- .
   Early rock.

4992. The Lawrence Wright Bulletin. London, 1922-?
   Jazz.

4993. Let It Rock. London. monthly, 1972-75.
   Emphasis on discographical and historical coverage.

4994. Listen Easy. Hitchin, Hertfordshire. monthly, 1972-73.
   Chiefly record reviews.

4995. Little Sandy Review. Burbank, California. bi-monthly, 1961-6?
   Folk and topical songs.

4996. Living Blues. Chicago. bi-monthly (later quarterly), 1970- .
   Emphasis on Chicago blues, and other modern styles.

4997. Master. Evanston, Illinois. monthly, 198?- .
   Contemporary rock.

4998. Matrix: Jazz Record Research Magazine. Victoria, Australia; later Stoke-on-Trent, Staffordshire; later London. irreg., July 1954-December 1975.
   Incorporated item 4862.

4999. Maximum Rock 'n' Roll. Berkeley, California. irreg., 1983- .
   New-wave rock.

5000. Mecca: the Journal of Traditional Jazz. New Orleans. monthly, 1974.
   Three issues only.

North America and Britain (cont.)

5001. <u>Melody Maker</u>. London. monthly (later weekly), 1926- .
      Comprehensive coverage. Incorporated item 5117.

5002. <u>Melody World: the Songwriters' Review</u>. London. monthly,
      1940-?

5003. <u>Memory Lane</u>. Leigh-on-Sea, Essex. quarterly, 1968- .
      Vintage jazz and dance bands.

5004. <u>Mersey Beat</u>. Liverpool. bi-weekly, July 1961–September
      1963.
      Popular. Incorporated into item 4853.

5005. <u>Merseybeating</u>. Bristol. monthly, June 1964-?

5006. <u>Metal Fury</u>. London. monthly, 1983- .
      Heavy-metal rock.

5007. Metronome (later <u>Music, U.S.A.</u>). New York. monthly,
      January 1885-December 1961.
      Published (October 1914–January 1932) in two editions:
      <u>Metronome Orchestra Monthly</u> (later <u>Metronome Orchestra
      Edition</u>), and <u>Metronome Band Monthly</u> (later <u>Metronome Band
      Edition</u>). Not originally devoted to jazz; later largely
      jazz-oriented.

5008. <u>Midland Beat</u>. Birmingham, England. monthly, 1963-68.

5009. <u>Mississippi Rag</u>. Minneapolis. monthly, 1973- .
      Dixieland jazz.

5010. <u>The Modern Dance and the Dancer</u>. London. monthly, 1934-76.
      Ballroom dancing.

5011. <u>Modern Recording</u> (later <u>Modern Recording and Music</u>). Port
      Washington, New York. monthly, 1975- .
      Rock from the studio angle. Includes equipment reviews.

   * <u>Mojo Navigator: Rock and Roll News</u>.
      * Cited below as item 5123.

5012. <u>Muleskinner News</u> (later <u>Music Country: the Magazine of Blue-
      grass and Old Time Music</u>). Ruffin, North Carolina. monthly,
      1969- .

5013. <u>Music: the Alternative Music Paper</u>. London. weekly, 1983-83.
      Short-lived rock magazine.

5014. <u>Music America</u> (later <u>Musician, Player, and Listener</u>; later
      <u>Musician</u>). New York. monthly, 1976- .
      Rock, jazz, popular.

5015.1 <u>Music and Rhythm</u>. Chicago; later Los Angeles. monthly (later
      irreg.), November 1940-1945.
      Swing and jazz.

5015.2 <u>Music and Sound Output</u>. Carle Place, New York. monthly,
       1983- .
            Business and technical aspects; emphasis on rock.

5016. <u>Music and Video</u>. London. monthly, May 1980-?
            Popular music and videos.

5017. <u>Music Business Weekly</u>. London. weekly, September 1969-
       March 1971.
            Trade.

5018. <u>Music City News</u>. Nashville. monthly, 1963- .
            Country music.

5019. <u>Music Echo</u>. Liverpool. weekly, 196?-6?
            Popular. Incorporated into item 4853.

5020. <u>Music Gig: the Magazine For the Record-Buying Public</u>. New
       York. irreg., 197?-?
            Chiefly popular record reviews.

5021. <u>The Music Hall</u> (later <u>Hall and Theatre</u>; later <u>Hall and
       Theatre Review</u>). London. bi-monthly, 1889-1912.

5022. <u>The Music Hall Critic and Programme of Amusements</u>. London.
       monthly, 1870-70.
            Seven issues only published.

5023. <u>The Music Hall Pictorial and Variety Stage</u>. London. monthly,
       1904-05.

5024. <u>Music Hall Records</u>. London. bi-monthly, June 1978- .

5025. <u>The Music Halls' Gazette</u>. London. weekly, April-December
       1868.

5026. <u>Music Maker</u>. London. monthly, 1965-67.
            Popular. Some jazz coverage.

5027. <u>Music Makers of Stage, Screen, Radio</u>. New York. bi-monthly,
       May-December 1940.

5028. <u>Music Market Canada</u>. Toronto. bi-monthly, 1977- .
            Trade.

5029. <u>Music Memories</u> (later <u>Music Memories and Jazz Report</u>).
       Birmingham, Alabama. bi-monthly, 1961- .
            Jazz. Chiefly discographical. For collectors. Incorp-
       orated item 4959.

5030. <u>Music Now</u>. London. weekly, 1970-71.
            Rock.

5031. <u>Music Pictorial</u>. Birmingham, England. weekly, March 1959-?
            Popular.

North America and Britain (cont.)

5032. <u>Music Reporter</u>. Nashville. weekly, 1957- .
       Popular and country music. Continues, with broadened
       coverage, item 4831.

5033. <u>Music Scene</u>. London. monthly, November 1972-1974.
       Popular.

5034. <u>Music Star</u>. London. monthly, 1973-October 1974.
       Popular.

5035. <u>Music Studio News</u>. Oakland, California. monthly, 1946-?
       Emphasis on Hawaiian music.

5036. <u>Music U.K.</u> Bromley, Kent. monthly, 1983- .
       Trade and job advertising. Emphasis on popular and jazz
       musicians' news.

5037. <u>Music Week</u> (later <u>Music and Video Week</u>). London. weekly,
       1959- .
       Trade.

5038. <u>Music World</u>. Nashville. monthly, 1965- .
       Trade.

5039. <u>Music World and Superstar</u>. London. monthly, September 1971-?
       Popular.

5040. <u>Musical Express</u> (later <u>New Musical Express</u>). London. weekly,
       October 1946- .
       Popular; rock.

5041.1 <u>Musical News (News and Dance Band</u>). London. monthly, 1935-38.

5041.2 <u>Musical Show: Devoted to the Amateur Presentation of Broadway
       Musical Shows on the Stage</u>. New York. 6 per year, 1962- .

   *   <u>Musician</u>.
       * Cited above as item 5014.

   *   <u>Musician, Player, and Listener</u>.
       * Cited above as item 5014.

5041.3 <u>Musicians' Classified</u>. London. weekly, 1981- .
       Job advertising for rock musicians.

5042. <u>Musicians' News</u>. San Francisco. monthly, 1977- .
       For rock and jazz performers.

5043. <u>Musicians Only</u>. London. weekly, October 1979-8?
       Trade. Aimed at rock and jazz musicians.

5044. <u>Musigram</u>. Covina, California. 9 per year, 1963-66.
       Sheet music. For collectors and students.

5045. <u>N.A.J.E. Educator</u>. Manhattan, Kansas. quarterly, 1968–
April/May 1977.
  Published by the National Association of Jazz Educators.

5046. <u>National Blast</u>. New York. weekly, November 1965–?
  Popular.

5047. <u>National Rockstar</u>. London. weekly, October 1976–7?

5048. <u>The Needle</u>. Jackson Heights, New York. monthly, June 1944–
January 1945.
  Jazz.

  *   <u>The New Baton</u>.
         * Cited above as item 4766.

5049. <u>New Chartbusters</u>. London. monthly, 1980–8?
  Current rock stars.

5050. <u>New Christian Music</u>. London. quarterly, 1975– .
  Christian popular music.

  *   <u>New Gandy Dancer</u>.
         * Cited above as item 4888.

  *   <u>New Kommotion</u>.
         * Cited above as item 4991.

5051. <u>New Music News: the Independent Rock Weekly</u>. London. weekly,
1980–80.
  Short-lived tabloid.

  *   <u>New Musical Express</u>.
         * Cited above as item 5040.

5052. <u>New On the Charts</u>. White Plains, New York. monthly, 197?– .
  Popular playlist information for radio stations.

5053. <u>New Rockpile</u>. Brighton, East Sussex. irreg., 1972–?
  Vintage rock and roll.

5054. <u>The New Singles</u>. St. Austell, Cornwall. weekly, 1963– .
  Releases listed.

5055. <u>New Sounds, New Styles</u>. Market Harborough, Leicestershire.
monthly, March 1981–July 1982.
  Popular.

5056. <u>New York Rocker</u>. New York. monthly, 1977–82. <u>New series</u>:
monthly, 1984–84.

5057. <u>The Night</u>. New York. monthly, 198?–?
  Disco dancing; venues.

5058. <u>No. 1</u>. London. bi-weekly, 1983– .
  Popular. Includes song texts.

North America and Britain (cont.)

5059. Noise! London. monthly, May 1982-1983.
      Popular.

5060. Nostalgia. New Barnet, Hertfordshire. quarterly, 1969- .
      Vintage jazz and dance music. Continues item 5193.

5061. Not Fade Away. Prescott, Merseyside. irreg., 1971-83.
      Vintage rock and roll.

5062. Not Just Jazz. New York. bi-monthly, 1983- .
      Jazz; also other art forms.

5063. Note: Hollywood. Hollywood, California. monthly, March-
      July 1946.
      Jazz.

5064. Nuggets. Birmingham, England. irreg., 1977-?
      Rock.

   * Number One.
      * Cited above as item 5058.

5065. Oh, Play That Thing. San Francisco. irreg., July 1938-?
      Jazz discography.

5066. Old Time Music. London. quarterly, 1971- .
      Vintage country and western swing.

5067. Omaha Rainbow. Wallington, Surrey. irreg., November 1973- .
      Rock and country-rock.

5068. One, Two, Testing. London. irreg. (later monthly), October
      1982- .
      Rock hardware.

5069. Opry. Chislehurst, Kent. monthly, 1973-?
      Country music.

5070. Out of Print. Bexhill-on-Sea, East Sussex. irreg., 1979-?
      Rock.

5071. Outlet. Barkingside, Essex. irreg., 1982- .
      Rock discography. Emphasis on independent labels,
      particularly cassettes.

5072. People's Song Bulletin. New York. irreg., 1946-49.
      Political and topical folk songs. Continued by item 5155.

5073. Phonograph Record Magazine. Hollywood, California. monthly,
      1967- .
      Rock record reviews.

5074. Pickin' the Blues. East Calder, Scotland. bi-monthly, 1983-

5075. Pickup: the Record Collector's Guide. Birmingham, England.
       monthly, January 1946-December 1947.
            Jazz.

5076. Platter Chatter. Seattle, Washington. monthly, September
       1945-4?
            Jazz discography.

5077. Playback: the Jazz Record Magazine. New Orleans. monthly,
       January 1949-March/April 1952.
            Jazz discography. Continues item 4976.

5078. Pop Around Pictorial. London. monthly, 1963-?

5079. Pop Pix. London. monthly, 1981- .
            Chiefly illustrated.

5080. Pop Records. London. monthly, 1956-?
            Releases listed.

5081. Pop-Shop (later Pop-Shop and Teenbeat). Heanor, Derbysshire.
       monthly, October 1964-65.

5082. Pop Show International. Heanor, Derbysshire. monthly,
       March 1966-?

5083. Pop Singles: a Quarterly Cumulative Catalogue of All Pop
       Single Gramophone Records Available in Great Britain.
       London. quarterly, January 1967-?

5084. Pop Star Weekly. London. weekly, March 1979-80.

5085. Pop Ten Teenbeat (later Teenbeat Monthly). Heanor, Derbys-
       shire. monthly, October 1963-May 1965.
            Continued by item 5081.

5086. Pop Tops. London. monthly, 1982- .

5087. Pop Weekly. London. weekly, September 1962-?

5088. Popster: the New Poster Magazine. London. monthly,
       November 1972-?

5089. Pop-Swop. London. weekly, October 1972-1974.
            Incorporated into item 5110.

5090. Popular Music and Society. Bowling Green, Ohio. quarterly,
       1971- .
            Scholarly research.

5091. Popular Music Magazine. Dayton, Ohio. bi-monthly, 1970- .
            Initial issues entitled Best of Popular Music.

5092. Punk. New York. irreg., 1975- .
            New-wave rock.

North America and Britain (cont.)

5093. Quality Rock Reader. New York. quarterly, 1975-?

5094. R and B Magazine. Northridge, California. bi-monthly, 1970-?

5095. R and B Monthly. London. monthly, January 1964-1966.

5096. Radio and Record News. London. weekly, 1978-7?
       Trade. Station reports; playlists.

5097. Radio and Records. Los Angeles. weekly, 197?- .
       Trade. Station reports; playlists. Includes station audience ratings.

5098. Rag Times. Los Angeles. bi-monthly, 1967- .
       Ragtime.

   *   Ragtime Review.
       * Cited above as item 4812.

5099. The Record. New York. monthly, November 1981- .
       Rock.

5100. The Record Advertiser. Northolt, Middlesex. monthly (later bi-monthly), January 1948-?
       Jazz.

5101. Record Business. London. monthly, 1978- .
       Trade.

5102. Record Buyer. Manchester, England. monthly, February 1969-?
       Popular record reviews.

5103. The Record Changer. Fairfax, Virginia. monthly, July 1942-1957.
       Jazz. For collectors.

5104. Record Collector (later Good Listening and Record Collector).
       Heanor, Derbysshire. monthly, 1970-?

5105. Record Collector. London. monthly, September 1979- .
       Rock discography. Not the same as item 5104.

5106. Record Digest. Prescott, Arizona. bi-weekly, 1977- .
       Rock.

5107. The Record Exchange. Toronto. monthly, March 1948-?
       Jazz. For collectors.

5108. The Record Exchanger. Orange, California. bi-monthly, 1969- .
       Vintage Rhythm-and-Blues and rock discography. For collectors.

5109. Record Mart. Rayleigh, Essex. monthly, 1968- .
        Popular and rock sales listings. For collectors.

5110. Record and Show Mirror (later Record Mirror; later Record
        and Popswop Mirror; later Record Mirror). London. weekly,
        1953- .
        Incorporates items 4853 and 5089.

5111. Record Pictorial. London. monthly, November 1962-?
        Popular.

5112. Record Research: the Magazine of Record Statistics and
        Information. Brooklyn, New York. bi-monthly, February
        1955- .
        Jazz discography.

5113. Record Review. Los Angeles. bi-monthly, 1976- .
        Reviews, classified by genre.

5114. Record Week. Toronto. weekly, 1975- .
        Trade.

5115. Relix: Music For the Mind. Brooklyn, New York. bi-monthly,
        197?- .
        Continues, with broadened coverage, item 2669.

5116. Replay: a Professional Publication For the Music Amusement
        Industry. Woodland Hills, California. monthly, 1975- .

5117. Rhythm. London. monthly, 1927-39.
        Jazz and dance bands. Incorporated into item 5001.

    *   Rhythm and Soul, U.S.A.
        * Cited above as item 4910.

5118. Rhythm Rag. Edgware, Middlesex. quarterly, 1977-?
        Jazz.

5119. Right On! Hollywood, California. monthly, 1971- .
        Soul.

5120. Rock. New York. monthly, 1969-72.

5121. Rock. Los Angeles. bi-monthly, 197?- .

5122. Rock and Roll Confidential. Teaneck, New Jersey. monthly,
        1983- .

5123. Rock and Roll News (later Mojo Navigator: Rock and Roll News).
        San Francisco. monthly, 1966-?

5124. Rock 'n' Roll News. Sacramento, California. bi-weekly,
        1976- .
        Not the same as item 5123.

5125. Rock 'n' Roll Personality Parade. London. monthly, 1957-?

North America and Britain (cont.)

5126. Rock and Pop Stars. Whyteleafe, Surrey. monthly, 1979- .

5127. Rock and Soul Songs. Derby, Conn. monthly, 1956- .
        Includes song texts.

5128. Rock Guitar. Mentor, Ohio. monthly, 1980- .

5129. Rock Love. West Hempstead, New York. bi-monthly, 198?- .

5130. The Rock Marketplace. New York. bi-monthly, 1974-?
        For collectors.

5131. Rock On! London. monthly, May 1978-?

5132. Rock Scene. Bethany, Conn. 8 per year, 1973- .

5133. Rock Scene. Maidenhead, Berkshire. monthly, 1979-?

5134. Rock Video. New York. monthly, 198?- .
        Aimed at younger readers.

5135. Rock Wire Service Report. Rego Park, New York. bi-weekly,
        198?- .

5136. Rockbill. New York. monthly, 1983- .
        Current rock.

5137. The Rocket. Seattle, Washington. monthly, 198?- .
        Rock. Local emphasis.

5138. Rocking Chair: the Review Newsletter For Librarians and
        Popular Music Fans Who Buy Records. Philadelphia. monthly,
        1977- .

5139. Rockpool Newsletter. New York. bi-weekly, 198?- .
        Trade. Radio station and club playlists and reports.

5140. Rockstock. London. monthly, October 1974-?

5141. Rollin' Rock. Hollywood, California. irreg., 197?- .
        For rock record collectors.

5142. Rolling Stone. San Francisco; later New York. bi-weekly,
        1967- .
        Rock, and other topics. Separate British edition published
        in London, June-November 1969; this continued independently as
        item 4886. German-language edition published in Cologne,
        monthly, January 1982- .

5143. Rolling Stone College Papers. New York. irreg., October
        1979- .
        Aimed at the campus audience. Similar coverage to Rolling
        Stone.

5144. R.P.M. Weekly: Records-Promotion-Music. Toronto. weekly,
       197?- .
            Trade. Emphasis on popular music and record industry.

5145. R.S.V.P.: the Magazine For Record Collectors. London.
       monthly, 1973- .
            Vintage jazz and dance band records.

5146. Rumble: the Magazine For Collectors of Instrumental Records.
       Mansfield, Nottinghamshire; later Rising Brook, Staffordshire.
       irreg., 1972- .
            Rock records.

5147. Sailor's Delight: the World's Weirdest Blues Magazine.
       London. quarterly, 1978-83.
            For blues record collectors.

5148. Sandy Bell's Broadsheet. Edinburgh. irreg., August 1973-?
            British folk.

5149. Scene. Philadelphia. monthly, 196?-?
            Popular.

5150. Scottish Country Music Express. South Queensferry, Scotland.
       monthly, 1981- .
            American country music.

5151. Scream: Top Pop Parade of the Stars. London. quarterly,
       May 1964-?

5152. S.F.X. London. bi-weekly, November 1981-August 1982.
            Rock. Published in C-60 cassette format.

5153. Sheet Music. Oradell, New Jersey. 9 per year, 1976- .
            For collectors.

5154. Sheet Music Trade News (later Music Trade News; later The
       Music Trades). New York; later Englewood Cliffs, New Jersey.
       weekly (later monthly), 1890- .

  *   Shout.
            * Cited below as item 5168.

5155. Sing Out. New York. bi-monthly, 1950- .
            Folk and topical songs, and features. Continues item
       5072.

5156. Singing News: the Printed Voice of Gospel Music. Pensacola,
       Florida. monthly, 1969- .

5157. Small Axe. London. irreg., 1980- .
            Reggae.

5158. Smash Hits. Derby, Conn. monthly, 197?- .
            Includes song texts.

North America and Britain (cont.)

5159. Smash Hits (Britain). Peterborough, Northamptonshire;
       later London. bi-weekly, 1978- .
           Includes song texts. Not the same as item 5158.

5160. Sniffin' Glue. London. irreg., July 1976-February 1977.
           New-wave rock. Entire contents republished as item
       294.

5161. Solid Set. St. Joseph, Missouri. monthly, 1943-45.
           Jazz.

5162. Song Hits Magazine. Derby, Conn. monthly, 1942- .
           Chiefly song texts.

5163. Song Service Reporter. Leeds, Yorkshire. quarterly,
       1885-1982.

5164. Songsmith's Journal. Northbrook, Illinois. irreg., 1976- .

5165. The Songwriter. New York. monthly, 1895-96.

5166. Songwriter Magazine. Hollywood, California. monthly,
       197?- .

5167. Songwriter's Review. New York. bi-monthly, 1946- .

5168. Soul (later Soul Monthly; later Soul Music Monthly; later
       Shout). Plymouth, Devon; later Chislehurst, Kent; later
       London. monthly, 1967- .
           Soul and rhythm-and-blues; discographical emphasis.

5169. Soul (Canada). Toronto. monthly, October 1965-?

5170. Soul: America's Most Soulful Newspaper. Los Angeles.
       bi-weekly, 1975- .

5171. Soul and Jazz Records. Hollywood, California. monthly,
       197?- .

5172. Soul Cargo. Newcastle-under-Lyme, Staffordshire.
       bi-monthly, 1977-1982.
           Soul records.

5173. Soul For Sale. Eccles, Lancashire. monthly, January 1983- .
           For soul collectors; discographical emphasis.

5174. Soul In Review. New York. irreg., 1975-?
           Record reviews.

5175. Soul Sounds and Stars (later Soul Sounds). New York.
       monthly, 1973-76.

5176. Soul Survivor. Whitchurch, Shropshire. quarterly, 1984- .
           Discographical emphasis.

5177. Sound Engineer. Bromley, Kent. monthly, 1984- .
       Trade. Emphasis on popular music recording.

5178. Sound International. London. monthly, 1978-82.
       Rock technique, recording, and equipment; for performers.

5179. Soundcheck. London. bi-weekly (later weekly), 1983- .
       Popular and rock.

5180. Sounds. London. weekly, 1970- .

5181. Sounds Fine: the Rock Collector's Marketplace. Riverdale,
       Maryland. monthly, 197?-78.

5182. Sounds Magazine. New York. irreg., 1976-?
       Jazz.

5183. Sounds Vintage. Billericay, Essex. bi-monthly, 1979- .
       Vintage jazz and dance bands.

5184. Soundtrax. New York. bi-monthly, 1978- .

5185. Southern Rag (later Folk Roots: the Son of "Southern Rag").
       Farnham, Surrey. quarterly (later monthly), 197?- .
       British folk.

5186. Spin: the Folksong Magazine. Wallasey, Cheshire. bi-monthly,
       1961-?

5187. Star Hits. New York. bi-weekly, 198?- .
       Includes song texts.

5188. Story Untold. Bayside, New York. irreg., 1979-?
       Emphasis on 1950's rock.

5189. Storyville. Chigwell, Essex; later London; later Dagenham,
       Essex. bi-monthly, 1965- .
       Jazz and blues. Discographical emphasis.

5190. Strait. London. irreg., 1981-?
       Christian popular music.

5191. Strange Days: the British Rock Paper. London. bi-weekly,
       September-October 1970.

5192. Street Life. London. bi-weekly, November 1975-76.
       Rock.

5193. Street Singer. New Barnet, Hertfordshire. irreg., 196?-69.
       Vintage jazz and dance bands. Continued by item 5060.

5194. Studies in Jazz Discography. New Brunswick, New Jersey.
       semi-annual, 197?-73.
       Incorporated into item 4985.

North America and Britain (cont.)

5195. Studio Sound (later Studio Sound and Broadcast Engineering).
       London. monthly, 1959- .
          Trade.

5196. Suburban Relapse. North Miami, Florida. irreg., 1984- .
          New-wave rock.

5197. Superstar. London. monthly, October 1971-April 1972.
          Popular performers.

5198. Superstars of Soul. New York. monthly, 1975- .

5199. Sweet Soul Music. Swindon, Wiltshire. irreg., 1985- .
          Continues, with broadened coverage, item 3388.

5200. Swing: the Guide to Modern Music. Detroit; later New York.
       monthly, April 1938-40.
          Jazz.

5201. Swing 51. Sutton, Surrey. 2 per year, 1980- .
          British traditional and contemporary folk.

5202. Swing Music. London; later Thames Ditton, Surrey. irreg.,
       March 1935-36.
          Jazz.

5203. Swing Shop Mag-List. London. bi-monthly, September 1952-55.
          Listing of jazz releases. Supplements item 4394.

5204. Swinging Newsletter. New York. monthly, 1971-78.
          Jazz. Continued by item 4941.

5205. Take One (later Vox Pop). Bridgeport, Conn. monthly, 1982- .
          Rock.

5206. Talking Blues. London. irreg., 1978- .
          Discographical emphasis.

5207. Talking Machine News and Record Exchange (later Talking
       Machine News and Side Lines; later Talking Machine News and
       Journal of Amusements; later Gramophone, Wireless, and
       Talking Machine News; later London and Provincial Music
       Trades Review). London. monthly, 1903-35.
          Trade. Includes features on current artists.

5208. Talking Machine World (later Radio Music Merchant; later
       Radio Merchant). New York. monthly, 1905-34.
          Trade. Includes features on current artists.

5209. Teen Beat. New York. monthly, 1976- .
          Rock.

5210. Tempo: the Modern Musical Magazine. Los Angeles. monthly,

June 1933-May 1940.
Jazz.

5211. Theatrical and Music Hall Life. London. monthly, 1898.
One issue only published.

5212. Theme. North Hollywood, California. irreg., July 1953-?
Jazz.

5213. Tiger Beat. Hollywood, California. monthly (later bi-
monthly), 1964- .
Rock. Aimed at younger readers.

5214. Time Barrier Express. Yonkers, New York. bi-monthly,
1974- .
Rock. Emphasis on 1950's and 1960's.

5215. Top Pops. Birmingham, England. monthly, 1967-6?

5216. Trail. New York. irreg., 1959-60.
Country. Published by country singer Marvin Rainwater,
and his brother.

5217. Trailing Clouds of Glory. Barnet, Hertfordshire. irreg.,
1974.
West-Coast rock. One issue only published.

5218. Trans-Oceanic Trouser Press (later Trouser Press). New York.
bi-monthly (later monthly), 1974-84.
Rock. Original emphasis on British artists; later with
broader coverage. Subscription copies included free flexi-
disks. Title derived from initials of long-running British
popular music television program, Top of the Pops.

5219. Trax: the London Music Paper. London. weekly, February
1981-?
Rock.

5220. Trick. London. monthly, November 1977-?
New-wave rock.

5221. Trouser Press Collectors' Magazine. New York. bi-monthly,
September 1978-?
For record collectors. Separate publication from item
5218.

5222. Tune-Dex Digest (later Music Business; later Music Vendor;
later Record World). New York. monthly (later weekly),
1944- .
Trade. Emphasis on popular music.

5223. Tunesmith: the Magazine For Songwriters. Concord, New
Hampshire. monthly, 1937-?

5224. Universal Jazz. Reading, Berkshire. monthly, May 1946-46.

North America and Britain (cont.)

5225. Variety. New York. weekly, 1905- .
        Includes coverage of popular music and the musical stage.

5226. Vibrations: the Sound of the Jazz Community. New York.
        monthly, 1967- .

5227. Vintage Jazz Mart. London. monthly, 1953- .
        For record collectors. Absorbed item 4950 (1961).

5228. Vintage Light Music: For the Enthusiast of Light Music On
        78-rpm Records. West Wickham, Kent. quarterly, January
        1975- .

5229. Vintage Record Mart. Rayleigh, Essex. bi-monthly, 1970- .
        For record collectors.

   *   Vox Pop.
        * Cited above as item 5205.

5230. Vox Pop: the Journal of the Workers' Music Association.
        London. monthly, January 1944-September 1945.
        Jazz. Incorporated into item 4990.

5231. Walrus. Narbeth, Pennsylvania. bi-weekly, 197?- .
        Trade. Rock radio stations' playlists and reports.

5232. Washington Folk Strums. Silver Springs, Maryland. irreg.,
        1964-?

5233. Wavelength. New Orleans. monthly, 198?- .
        Rock. Local emphasis.

5234. The Wheel: a Record Collector's Rag. Kannapolis, North
        Carolina. monthly, May-September 1948.
        Jazz emphasis.

5235. Whiskey, Women, and... Haverhill, Massachusetts. irreg.,
        1972-?
        Blues.

   *   Who Put the Bomp.
        * Cited above as item 4793.

5236. The Wire. London. 3 per year, July 1982- .
        Avant-garde jazz.

5237. Words and Music. New York. monthly, 1971- .
        Texts of popular songs.

5238. Yesterday's Memories. New York. bi-monthly, 1975-76.
        Rhythm-and-blues; later rock. Emphasis on 1950's.

5239. Zig Zag. North Marston, Buckinghamshire; later London.
        irreg., 1968- .
        Rock.

B. OTHER COUNTRIES

(i) Australia and New Zealand

5240. Australian Jazz Quarterly: a Magazine For the Connoisseur.
Melbourne, Victoria. quarterly (later irreg.), May 1946-
April 1957.

5241. The Beat. Bondi Beach, New South Wales. monthly, September
1949-?
Jazz.

5242. Blue Rhythm. Melbourne, Victoria. monthly, September-
October 1942.
Jazz. Incorporated into item 5247.

5243. Country and Western Spotlight: Worldwide Coverage of Country
Music News. Otago, New Zealand; later Brisbane, Queensland.
quarterly, 1955- .

5244. Country Music Times. North Quay, Queensland. bi-monthly,
1973- .

5245. Jazz Australia. Sydney, New South Wales. monthly, 1976- .

5246. Jazz Down Under. Camden, New South Wales. bi-monthly,
1974- .

5247. Jazz Notes (later Jazz Notes and Blue Rhythm; later Jazz
Notes). Melbourne, Victoria; later Adelaide, South Australia.
monthly, January 1941- .
Incorporated item 5242.

5248. Juke. Melbourne, Victoria. weekly, 1975- .
Popular.

5249. Jukebox. Auckland, New Zealand. monthly, August 1946-
April 1947.
Jazz.

5250. Music Maker. Sydney, New South Wales. monthly, 1932-73.
Jazz and popular music. Incorporated into item 5252.

5251. R.A.M.: Rock Australia Magazine. Darlinghurst, New South
Wales. bi-weekly, 1975- .

5252. Soundblast. Sydney, New South Wales. monthly, 1973- .
Popular music, and jazz. Incorporates item 5250.

5253. Swing. Lower Hutt, New Zealand. monthly, October 1941-
August 1942.
Jazz.

5254. Swing Session. Wellington, New Zealand. monthly, January
1947-October 1948.
Jazz.

Australia and New Zealand (cont.)

5255. **Tune-In**. Tamworth, New South Wales. monthly, 197?- .
       Country music.

(ii) Austria

5256. **Jazz Forum**. Vienna/Warsaw. bi-monthly, 1967- .
       International coverage. Published jointly by the
       International Jazz Foundation (Vienna), and the Polish Jazz
       Foundation (Warsaw), in simultaneous English, German, and
       Polish editions.

(iii) Belgium

5257. **Soundtrack Collector's Newsletter**. Mechelen. quarterly,
       1975- .
       In English.

(iv) Denmark

5258. **Rock and Roll International**. Tapperoje. bi-monthly, 1979- .
       Vintage rock. In English.

5259. **Western Bulletin**. (Place unknown). quarterly, 1965-?
       Country music. Text in Danish and English.

(v) France

5260. **Afro Music**. Paris. monthly, 1976- .
       African popular music. Edited by Manu Dibango.

5261. **Le Bulletin du Hot Club de France**. Paris. monthly, 1945-45.
       Three issues only published. Continues item 5264.
       Continued by item 5267.

5262. ————. **2nd. series**: Paris. 1948.
       One issue only published. Continued by item 5266.

5263. ————. **3rd. series**: Montauban. 10 per year, 1950- .
       Continues item 5266.

5264. **Jazz Hot: la revue internationale du jazz**. Paris. irreg.,
       May 1935-August 1939.
       Published in French and English editions. Continued by
       item 5261.

5265. Jazz Hot. New series: Paris. monthly, October 1945- .
       Continues item 5267.

5266. La Revue du jazz. Paris. monthly, December 1948-50.
       Continues item 5262. Continued as item 5263.

5267. Revue du jazz hot. Paris. monthly, 1945-45.
       Continues item 5261. Continued by item 5265.

                        (vi) Germany

5268. Format. Tübingen. irreg., 1983- .
       For collectors of rock records. Text in English and
       German.

                        (vii) Holland

5269. Micrography: Jazz and Blues on Microgroove. Alphen aan den
       Rijn. quarterly, 1968- .
       In English. Discographical; lists new releases.

5270. Rockville International. Amsterdam. monthly, 1964-?
       In Dutch and English.

                        (viii) Italy

5271. Modern Jazz. Bologna. irreg., 197?- .
       In English.

                        (ix) Poland

   *   Jazz Forum.
       * Cited above as item 5256.

                        (x) Sri Lanka

5272. S.E.A.C. Jazz News. Colombo. irreg, November 1946-
       July 1947.

                        (xi) Sweden

5273. Jukebox. Halmstad. irreg., 1982- .
       For rock record collectors. In English.

Sweden (cont.)

5274. <u>Rock and Beat Tranquiliser</u>. Sjardhundu. irreg., 1977-?
           British rock of the 1960's. In English.

5275. <u>Surfers Rule</u>. Stockholm. irreg., 1983- .
           Rock; emphasis on surfing music. In English.

(xii) Zaire

5276. <u>Congo Disque: revue de la musique congolaise modèrne</u>.
           Kinshasa. monthly, 1963- .
           Popular African bands and solo performers.

INDEX

Compiled with the assistance of
Catherine A. Iwaschkin.

References are to item numbers.
Excludes general periodicals: see pages 583-616.